Ruth Nielsen

EU Labour Law

DJØF Publishing
Copenhagen 2013

Ruth Nielsen
EU Labour Law

2. edition

Cover: Bo Helsted
Print: Narayana Press, Gylling
Binding: Jysk Bogbind, Holstebro

Printed in Denmark 2013
ISBN 978-87-574-2566-6

Sold and distributed in Scandinavia by:
DJØF Publishing
Copenhagen, Denmark
Email: forlag@djoef.dk
www.djoef-forlag.dk

Sold and distributed in North America by:
International Specialized Book Services (ISBS)
Portland, USA
Email: orders@isbs.com
www.isbs.com

Sold in all other countries by:
The Oxford Publicity Partnership Ltd
Towcester, UK
Email: djof@oppuk.co.uk
www.oppuk.co.uk

Distributed in all other countries by:
Marston Book Services
Abingdon, Oxon, UK
Email: trade.orders@marston.co.uk
www.marston.co.uk

Contents

Preface

This book gives a systematic account of valid EU labour law as it stands in 2013 and of its development over the years from 1958 to 2013. The book describes and analyses the general development of EU labour law, with particular emphasis on two important shifts in contexts and perspectives:

- A shift in focus from an older layer where EU labour law was seen primarily in an Internal Market perspective to a newer layer where EU labour law is seen as part of the legal regulation of both the Internal Market and the fundamental rights the EU guarantees union citizens in the context of Economic and Monetary Union (EMU)
- A shift in focus from seeing labour law as part of many different, separate legal systems (national law, EU law and international law) to a 'one big system model' comprising the mutually interlocked labout law systems at national level in the Member States, at EU-level and in the European part of international labour law.

Ruth Nielsen, Copenhagen, March 2013

CHAPTER ONE

Introduction

1 Main purpose of the book

This book gives a systematic account of valid EU labour law as it stands in 2013 and of its development over the years from 1958 to 2013. The book describes and analyses the general development of EU labour law, with particular emphasis on two important shifts in contexts and perspectives:

- A shift in focus from an older layer where EU labour law was seen primarily in an Internal Market perspective to a newer layer where EU labour law is seen as part of the legal regulation of both the Internal Market and the fundamental rights the EU guarantees union citizens in the context of Economic and Monetary Union (EMU)
- A shift in focus from seeing labour law as part of many different, separate legal systems (national law, EU law and international law) to a 'one big system model' comprising the mutually interlocked labout law systems at national level in the Member States, at EU-level and in the European part of international labour law.

1.1. From internal market law to fundamental rights/EMU law

I use the expression internal market law as referring to the law of free movement (of goods, services, capital and persons (workers and freedom of establishment)) and of competition law. The free movement rules started like EU labour law in an internal market context which still is the most important context for free movement. Since the development of the fundamental rights dimension of the EU, free movement for workers and union citizens must, however, also be seen in a fundamental rights/EMU context. Article 45 of the Charter of Fundamental Rights of the European Union (CFREU) repeats Article 21 TFEU on the free movement rights of union citizens. The original similarities between the four freedoms (goods, services, capital and persons) are probably smaller today than 50-60 years ago, see for the same view the following quotation from Oliver & Roth:[1]

> Surely it is right that the same principles should apply in the absence of any objective reason to make a distinction. Unwarranted divergences should clearly be avoided. But at the end of the day the four freedoms cannot all be treated in the same way. The principal dividing line should be drawn where common sense and humanity suggest: between the movement of human beings, on the one hand, and purely economic transactions on the other.

EU labour law started in the Rome Treaty 1957 with two Treaty articles: Article 45 TFEU on free movement for workers and Articles 157 TFEU on equal pay between men and women. Article 45 TFEU was intended to ensure the principle of free movement for workers. Article 157 TFEU was introduced because France claimed that it had more advanced equal pay provisions than the other initial EU countries. French undertakings, e.g. shoe factories, were therefore at risk of being put at a competitive disadvantage compared to undertakings from other EU countries which could get cheaper female labour than French employers because there was more sex discrimination in wages in the other EU countries. Later, in particular after the creation of the European Union (EU) by the Maastricht Treaty 1992 the fundamental rights dimension of EU law has been developed considerably.

Today (2013), the fundamental rights/EMU context is probably more important for EU labour law than the internal market context.[2] It has a wider scope of application. Free movement rules and EU competition law only apply to cases with cross-border aspects. Many employment or labour conflicts in a Member States take place in situations that are purely internal. In such situations EU free movement law and competition law is not applicable.[3] There are, however, a number of labour law cases which are of a cross-border nature, for example trans-national posting of workers cases. Since the Eastern enlargement of the EU in 2004, the potential 'clash' between EU free movement law and national collective labour law has acquired renewed actuality, see on the *Laval*[4] and *Viking*[5] cases below in Chapter Three.

1. Oliver, Peter & Roth, Wulf-Henning: The Internal Market and the Four Freedoms, Common Market Law Review 2004.
2. The differences between the two approaches – the internal market perspective and the fundamental rights/EMU perspective – are summed up in schematic form in Chapter Ten.
3. See for a brief historical overview below in Chapter Two.
4. Case C-341/05 *Laval* [2007] ECR I-11767.

1.2 From many separate legal systems to a 'one big system model'

One can discuss various possible ways of understanding the character of and relations between legal systems in the European Union, in particular, whether there is one EU legal system distinct from and in addition to the national legal systems (27+1model) [6] and public international law, or whether it is better to conceive of EU law merely as an aspect of the Member States' legal systems (27 model), or whether we should think of there being but one single European legal system of which EU law, the European part of public international law and EU Member States' national legal systems are in some sense subsystems (the one Big system model).[7]

The CJEU has asserted in its early case law that EU law is neither public international law nor national law, but rather a new kind of law (a *sui generis* law) that takes precedence over any national law, whatever it might be.[8] EU law aims to make all legal actors, in particular judicial bodies, in the EU interpret EU law in the same way and avoid or overcome its fragmentation into (27) different legal systems when meeting national law. To facilitate this, a new legal institution – the preliminary reference procedure in Article 267 TFEU – was established.

In my view, it is realistic – at least at the sub-surface level of the legal order – to conceive of the legal order as one big system comprising both sources of law stemming from the EU subsystem, from the national subsystems and from the public international law subsystem. In legal practice – both legislative, judicial and research practice – there is a trend, and has been since the creation of the European Union in the early 1990's, towards increasing interlocking between elements from different subsystems.

5. Case C-438/05 *Viking* [2007] ECR I-10779.
6. I disregard the fact that there are Member States which are multi-legal system states, such as the United Kingdom, which comprises three legal systems (Scotland, Northern Ireland, and England and Wales respectively).
7. See Dickson, Julie: How Many Legal Systems? Some Puzzles Regarding the Identity Conditions of, and Relations Between, Legal Systems in the European Union, http://papers.ssrn.com/sol3/papers.cfm?abstract_id=1279612 (University of Oxford Legal Research Paper Series, Paper No 40/2008). See also Hesselink, Martijn: The Common Frame of Reference as a source of European private law, Tulane Law Review, 2009, p. 919 and Hesselink, Martijn W.: Methodology and Theoretical Disagreement in Ulla Neergaard, Ruth Nielsen and Lynn M. Roseberry (eds): European Legal Method – Paradoxes and Revitalisation, Copenhagen 2011. See also Nielsen, Ruth and Christina D. Tvarnø: Retskilder og Retsteorier, Kbhvn. 2011.
8. Case 6/64 Costa v ENEL [1964] ECR 614.

Older versions of legal positivism and legal realism defined – both in relation to public international law and national law – law and states as different aspects of the same totality. Today, the reality is that both public international law[9] and EU law to a considerable extent have to function without direct support – coercive or otherwise – from a nation state. The question therefore arises whether the EU can do without state(s) to underpin its legal system or whether state support can be found in other ways than those used in the relationship between national law and the nation state. I think a possible answer is that EU law can obtain state support through reliance on The One Big System Model. The Member States' legal systems are today so effectively interlocked with EU law that they do largely enforce it in a manner that is equivalent to the enforcement of national law.

In the first years after the establishment of the EC in the mid-20th century,[10] the CJEU seemed to apply what is above called the '27+1-model' and look at the relationship between elements originating from the EU and elements originating from the Member States as a hierarchical relationship where EU elements have supremacy and direct effect in national law. In the 1960's, the CJEU stated[11] that '... the community constitutes a new legal order of international law ...' and[12] that 'By contrast with ordinary international treaties, the EEC Treaty has created its own legal system ...'. The CJEU in *COSTA/ENEL* from 1964 highlighted the vertical dimension in the interplay between national and EU elements of law in limited fields. It is not clear whether the CJEU as a colloquium sees the EU legal order as one big system comprising elements of both national and EU origin or as a distinct legal system in addition to the national legal systems.[13]

9. See Teubner, Günther: Global Law without a State, Dartmouth 1997.
10. See Maduro, Miguel Poiares and Azoulai, Loïc: The Past and Future of EU Law. The Classics of EU Law Revisited on the 50th Anniversary of the Rome Treaty, London 2010.
11. Case 26/62 Van Gend en Loos [1963] ECR 1.
12. Case 6/64 Costa v ENEL [1964] ECR 585.
13. Individual judges have in articles expressed clear views on that point; see for example in favour of the 'one big system model' Koopmanns, Thijmen: The Theory of Interpretation and the Court of Justice, in O'Keefe, David and Antonio Bavasso (eds): Judicial Review in European Union Law, The Hague 2000, p. 45.

2 Terminology: Labour Law, Welfare Rights and the Constitutionalisation of the European Social Model

2.1 Labour Law

In this book, I use the word 'labour law' as referring to the law relating to 1) employment relations between individual employers and employees, 2) labour relations between employers and collective actors on the labour market (labour market organizations and groups of workers) and 3) working environment issues.

This book deals primarily with labour law and only marginally with other welfare rights. There is, however, a blurred line between labour law and other aspects of social policy law, not least at EU level. In legal acts and a considerable part of the literature, the expression 'the social dimension of the EU' refers both to labour law aspects and other social policy aspects.

Most employment and labour specific provisions in the Treaties are placed in Title X TFEU with the heading 'Social Policy' (Article 151 TFEU – Article 161 TFEU). The objectives of EU Social Policy are the promotion of employment, improved living and working conditions, so as to make possible their harmonisation while the improvement is being maintained, proper social protection, dialogue between management and labour, the development of human resources with a view to lasting high employment and the combating of exclusion. Article 153 TFEU which is the main legal basis in the labour and employment field in the EU deals with the following subjects:

(a) improvement in particular of the working environment to protect workers' health and safety;
(b) working conditions;
(c) social security and social protection of workers;
(d) protection of workers where their employment contract is terminated;
(e) the information and consultation of workers;
(f) representation and collective defence of the interests of workers and employers, including co-determination, subject to paragraph 5;
(g) conditions of employment for third-country nationals legally residing in Union territory;
(h) the integration of persons excluded from the labour market, without prejudice to Article 166;
(i) equality between men and women with regard to labour market opportunities and treatment at work;
(j) the combating of social exclusion;

(k) the modernisation of social protection systems without prejudice to point (c).

The so-called Social Policy in the Treaties is thus a mixture of elements which in national law would be called labour law and social security law (welfare law).

2.2 Welfare Rights

I use the term 'welfare rights' as a broad concept[14] cutting across various legal disciplines (labour law, social security law, health law, etc.) and covering both labour rights and a number of other rights, including both non-economic and economic rights.[15] It includes both social security rights, rights of access to welfare services and welfare-related rights against the state and against individual or collective contractual partners (employers, insurance companies, labour market organisations, etc.), primarily the rights on Equality in Chapter III of the Charter of Fundamental Rights of the European Union (CFREU) and on Solidarity[16] in Chapter IV of the CFREU but also, for example, the various rights that are covered by the concept of 'social advantages' in Article 7(2) of the Migrant Workers Regulation.[17]

Before the coming into force of the Lisbon Treaty the word 'welfare' was only used in the EC Treaty in the context of animal welfare. It is not explicitly used in the CFREU. The word 'welfare' is used in Article 3 TEU (post-Lisbon) on the Union's aims in some – but far from all – language versions. In the English version Article 3(1) EU reads (emphasis added): 'The Union's aim is to promote peace, its values and *the well-being* of its peoples.' In the Danish and Swedish versions of the EU Treaty the Danish and Swedish words for welfare (velfærd, välfärd) are used where the English version uses

14. See for a discussion on broad or narrow conceptions of welfare states Esping-Andersen, Gøsta: Three Worlds of Welfare Capitalism. Princeton 1990.
15. See generally Hervey, Tamara and Jeff Kenner (eds): Economic and Social Rights Under the EU Charter of Fundamental Rights: A Legal Perspective, Oxford 2003.
16. Menéndez, Agustín José: The Sinews of Peace: Rights to Solidarity in the Charter of Fundamental Rights of the European Union, Ratio Juris 2003 p. 374 uses the term 'welfare rights' as covering the rights provided for in Title IV of the CFREU.
17. EU/492/2011. 'Social advantages' include *inter alia* aspects of family reunification. See Case 59/85 *Reed* [1986] ECR 1283 and point 3 in the 1989 Community Charter on Fundamental Rights of Workers which reads: 'The right of freedom of movement shall also imply: harmonisation of conditions of residence in all Member States, particularly those concerning family reunification'. See on the CFREU below in Chapter Two and on free movement of workers in Chapter Five.

'well-being'. The German version uses the word 'Wohlergehen' and the French version 'bien-être'. In the Commission's communication from July 2008 on a renewed social agenda[18] there is a similar difference in different language versions. The CJEU has held[19] that the concept of health in the context of working environment must be interpreted broadly. It referred in that context to the preamble to the Constitution of the WHO where *health* is defined (emphasis added) as a state of 'complete physical, mental and social *well-being*'.

2.3 Constitutionalisation of the European Social Model

After the adoption in 2000 of the Charter of Fundamental Rights of the European Union (CFREU), it has become usual in academic literature to talk about constitutionalisation of the EU.[20] In regard to labour law it is conspicuous that there is practically no mention of the employment or labour constitution which normally is dealt with as an aspect of the so-called social constitution which is used as a broad concept which is defined vaguely. In the TFEU, Social Policy is, as mentioned, the heading of Title X (Articles 151-161 TFEU). Since *Internationale Handelsgesellschaft*[21] the general principles and fundamental rights protected by the CJEU have been inspired by the *constitutional traditions* common to the Member States. In 'The many constitutions of Europe',[22] Tuori argues that the European Constitution is a continuously changing outcome of an on-going process.[23] He distinguishes between the

18. COM(2008)412, Renewed social agenda: Opportunities, access and solidarity in 21st century Europe.
19. Case C-84/94, *UK* v *Council* [1996] ECR I-5755, see further below in Chapter Nine.
20. There is an abundant academic literature on constitutionalisation of the EU, see among many Beate Rudolf: European Union, International Journal of Constitutional Law 2003 p. 135, Gráinne de Búrca and Jo Beatrix Aschenbrenner: The Development of European Constitutionalism and the Role of The EU Charter of Fundamental Rights, Columbia Journal of European Law 2003 p. 355, Udo Di Fabio: A European Charter: Towards a Constitution for the Union, Columbia Journal of European Law 2001 p. 159, Koen Lenaerts and Eddy de Smijter: A 'Bill of Rights' for the European Union, Common Market Law Review 2001 p. 273 and Ingolf Pernice: Integrating the Charter of Fundamental Rights into the Constitution of the European Union: Practical and Theoretical Propositions, Columbia Journal of European Law 2003 p. 5.
21. Case 11/70 *Internationale Handelsgesellschaft* [1970] ECR 1125.
22. Tuori, Kaarlo and Suvi Sankari: The Many Constitutions of Europe, Oxford 2010.
23. See Tuori, Kaarlo: The Relationality of European Constitution(s) – Justifying a new research programme for European constitutional scholarship, in Neergaard, Ulla and Ruth Nielsen: European Legal method – towards a new European Legal Realism?, Copenhagen 2013 (forthcoming).

economic constitution, the juridical constitution, the political constitution, the social constitution and the security constitution.

2.3.1 The two layers of the Economic constitution of the EU

In regard to the economic constitution there is a distinction[24] between the first – micro-economic – layer of the economic constitution which focuses on the Internal Market and which has been provided for in the goal provision of the basic treaties of the EC/EU since the Rome Treaty 1957 and the second – macro-economic – layer of the economic constitution which focuses on the Economic and Monetary Union (EMU) with a financial union based (in the long term) on the euro as its currency. The second layer of the economic constitution was first formulated as a goal for the EU in the Maastricht Treaty 1992. The establishment and development of the internal market is still a goal for the EU whose economic constitution thus now has two layers – the establishment of the Internal Market and of the Economic and Monetary Union (EMU), see Article 3 TEU which mentions both these economic goals for the EU.

In the internal market perspective, the main economic problem law is used to help solving is to remove or reduce barriers to *access to the internal market* for economic actors who want to take advantage of the free movement on that market.

In the fundamental rights/EMU perspective the main economic problem law is used to help solving is the need to *coordinate economic and employment policies and to reduce macroeconomic imbalances*, see the Council Recommendation on broad guidelines for the economic policies of the Member States and of the Union.[25] Guideline two of that Recommendation on 'Addressing macroeconomic imbalances' reads (emphasis added):

> Member States should avoid unsustainable macroeconomic imbalances, arising notably from developments in current accounts, asset markets and the balance sheets of the household and corporate sectors. Member States with large current account imbalances rooted in a persistent lack of competitiveness or due to other reasons should address the underlying causes by acting, for example, on fiscal policy, on *wage developments*, on structural reforms relating to product and financial services markets (including the flow of productivity enhancing capital), on *labour markets, in line with the employment guidelines*, or on any other relevant policy area. In this context, Member States should encourage *the right framework conditions for wage bargaining systems and labour cost developments* con-

24. See further Tuori, Kaarlo: The European Financial Crisis – Constitutional Aspects and Implications, EUI Working Paper LAW 2012/28.
25. Recommendation 2010/410/EU, OJ 2010 L 191.

sistent with price stability, productivity trends over the medium-term and the need to reduce macroeconomic imbalances. Where appropriate, *adequate wage setting in the public sector should be regarded as an important signal* to ensure wage moderation in the private sector in line with the need to improve competitiveness. *Wage setting frameworks, including minimum wages*, should allow for wage formation processes that take into account differences in skills and local labour market conditions and respond to large divergences in economic performance across regions, sectors and companies within a country. *The social partners have an important role to play in this context.* Member States with large current account surpluses should pursue measures aimed at implementing structural reforms conducive to strengthening potential growth and thereby also underpinning domestic demand. *Addressing macroeconomic imbalances, including among Member States, would also help in achieving economic cohesion.*

In order for the EU to be able to develop a coordinated economic and employment policy with a view to enable businesses and work-places in the EU to be competitive on the global market it is necessary for EU law and policy to be perceived as legitimate by the people of the EU (the union citizens). In parallel with the development of the EMU, the EU has therefore developed strong fundamental rights for the union citizens. Discrimination and equality law is not only seen as a fundamental right but also increasingly being designed to promote inclusion of groups at risk of discrimination and the collaboration of the social partners (trade unions and employers' organizations) in developing coordinated employment and economic policies is actively sought by different EU actors.

2.3.2 The relationship between labour law and the economic constitution of the EU

Many legal scholars have commented on the relationship between the economic constitution of the EU and the social constitution. Most of them see the social constitution as subordinate to the economic constitution.[26] Dagmar Schiek argues, however, that the CJEU has developed a socially embedded judicial constitution.[27]

26. See for example Bruun, Niklas, Klaus Lörcher and Isabelle Schömann (eds): The Lisbon Treaty and Social Europe, Oxford 2012, Giubboni, Stefano: Social Rights and Market Freedom in the European Constitution: A Labour Law Perspective. Cambridge 2006 and Hervey, Tamara and Jeff Kenner (eds): Economic and Social Rights Under the EU Charter of Fundamental Rights: A Legal Perspective, Oxford 2003.
27. See Schiek, Dagmar: Economic and Social integration. The challenge for EU constitutional law, Cheltenham 2012 and Schiek, Dagmar: Is there a social ideal of the European Court of Justice? In Neergaard, Ulla, Ruth Nielsen and Lynn Roseberry (eds):

The two shifts in perspective I highlight in this book 1) from an internal market perspective on labour law to a fundamental rights perspective and 2) from many separate legal systems to a 'one big system model' are related to a shift from adapting the view on EU labour law mainly or solely to the first layer of the economic constitution (the Internal Market) to also include the second layer of the economic constitution (the EMU and the concern for macroeconomic balance). In the Preamble to the TEU, the Member States confirm their attachment to fundamental social rights as defined *inter alia* in the 1989 Community Charter of the Fundamental Social Rights of Workers and their resolve to achieve the strengthening and the convergence of their economies and to establish an economic and monetary union. The internal market is not mentioned in the Preamble to the TEU but it is still mentioned as one of the economic goals of the EU in Article 3 TEU, see further below in Chapter Two.

3 Theoretical and methodological approach: Critical legal positivism and legal realism

A legal scholar's choice of theoretical approach is decisive for which research questions are relevant and what kind of data material and general methodological approach should be used to answer them. Legal positivism is a school of thought of philosophy of law and jurisprudence, first developed by nineteenth-century legal thinkers such as Jeremy Bentham (1748-1832) and John Austin (1790-1869). Since the 19th century it has been the prevailing legal theory in Europe.

My main theoretical approach is an EU adapted combination of legal positivism and legal realism, in particular Scandinavian legal realism and critical legal positivism. The latin term *Ius positum* means the posited law. In many legal contexts it refers to the law which is laid down in accordance with a norm of competence in the legal system, for example a directive that is adopted in accordance with Article 294 TFEU. The posited law is thus the law that has been created correctly in conformity with the doctrine of the sources of law and their interpretation which is accepted in a given lgal system. The posited law can have – and will typically have – factual, empirical existence. As Tuori[28] expresses it, modern national law is tied to the nation

The Role of Courts in Developing a European Social Model – Theoretical and Methodological Perspectives, Copenhagen 2010.

28. Tuori, Kaarlo: Critical Legal Positivism, Aldershot 2002 p. 250.

state both in its positing and for its enforcement. Legal positivism focuses mainly on the positing of law (the correct creation of law) while legal realism focuses more on its enforcement. Both aspects are important for the law to become a social fact and, at least as seen in Scandinavian legal realism, closely linked to each other.

3.1 Legal realism

The term 'legal realism' is ambiguous. There are two established schools of 'legal realism' in addition to a possible new European legal realism:[29] Scandinavian legal realism and American legal realism. They are in important respects different, not least compared to legal positivism. Scandinavian legal realism is very close to legal positivism. Alf Ross,[30] who was the leading Danish representative of Scandinavian legal realism in the last century, defined statements in legal science about *valid law* (geltendes Recht) in a particular legal system (for example Danish law), as prophecies of the rules the courts (or – in later works on constitutional law – the state apparatus in general) will follow in future decisions in hypothetical cases because they consider themselves under a duty to do that. Ross stated that his theory is based on a synthesis of ideological and behavioural realism and referred to American legal realism as an example of behavioural realism. The main reason for Ross to equate the function of the courts with the law was that enforcement of law under Scandinavian Legal Realism is a touchstone for law. Only law that is enforced is a tangible reality. Ross saw a close link between law and the coercive power of the state. The answers to questions concerning valid law which are the main research questions posed both by legal positivists and Scandinavian legal realists will therefore often be the same regardless of whether the individual scholar builds on legal positivism or on Scandinavian legal realism.[31] The traditional Anglo-American view seems – to the differ-

29. See Neergaard, Ulla and Ruth Nielsen: European Legal method – towards a new European Legal Realism?, Copenhagen 2013 (forthcoming).
30. Alf Ross' (1899-1979) thoughts on legal philosophy. in a final form, are expressed in his main work: Ret og Retfærdighed, København 1953, translated into English and published in 1958 as On Law and Justice, London 1958, reviewed by Hart in Hart, H. L. A.: Scandinavian Realism, The Cambridge Law Journal 1959 p. 233.
31. See on the close relationship between Scandinavian legal realism and legal positivism the following quotation from Alexander, Gregory S.: Comparing the Two Legal Realisms-American and Scandinavian, The American Journal of Comparative Law 2002 p. 131 in his comparison of American and Scandinavian legal realism (emphasis added): *Scandinavian Legal Realism was a version of legal positivism*, seeking a strict separation between law and politics and law and morality. American Legal Realism,

ence from the Scandinavian view – to be that the doctrines of legal positivism and of legal realism are essentially incompatible.[32]

Legal method in Ross' terminology refers to the doctrine of the sources of law and the way the different sources of law are interpreted. Scandinavian Legal Realism subscribes to examining both the ideology of the judges and their external behavior, typically their contribution to enforcing valid law. The most important manifestation of the judges' ideology is supposed to be the doctrine of the sources of law and legal interpretation. The doctrine of the sources of law provides a basis for a probable prediction of the outcome of hypothetical cases before the courts or other law-applying bodies which in Scandinavian legal realism as defined by Ross is the criterion for valid law; see the following citation from On Law and Justice:[33]

> 'prediction is possible ... because the mental process by which the judge decides to base his decision on one rule rather than another, [is] a process determined by attitudes and concepts, a common normative ideology, present and active in the minds of judges when they act in their capacity as judges.
>
> This ideology is the subject of the doctrine of the sources of law. It ... consists of directives which ... indicate the way in which a judge shall proceed to discover the directive(s) decisive for the question at issue.'

The doctrine of the source of laws and their interpretation is thus a normative ideology which is shared by judges (and other legal actors). Transferred to EU level the Scandinavian legal realism's definition of valid law would not be that valid EU labour law is what the CJEU does because it feels obligated to do so, but that valid EU labour law is what the courts in the EU (CJEU, other international courts, for example ECtHR + the national courts of the Member States) do because they think they are obligated to do so under the doctrine of the sources of law and interpretation (the European legal method) which is a normative ideology they all share.

A shared European legal method is in my view developing. It has specific characteristics in different substantive areas as for example labour law, competition law, company law, etc. There are e.g. specific types of sources of law

on the other hand, was an extension of political Progressivism, insisting that law is deeply infused with questions of power. From this perspective, then, *Scandinavian and American Legal Realism seem to have been nearly opposite jurisprudential movements*.

32. See Leiter, Brian: Legal Realism and Legal Positivism Reconsidered, Ethics 2001 p. 278.
33. Ross, Alf: On Law and Justice, London 1958 p. 75.

in EU labour law such as European collective agreements and some soft law statements, as for example the Community Charter of Fundamental Social Rights of Workers 1989 have greater weight than soft law usually has, see below in chapter Two.

3.2 Critical legal positivism

In the Nordic countries, Tuori has developed legal positivism further into critical legal positivism.[34] He presents the normative and practical faces of law as a multi-layered phenomenon within which there is an important role for critical legal dogmatics in furthering law's self-understanding and coherence. Critical legal positivism presents itself as a further development of legal positivism.[35]

Critical legal positivism sees law as having two faces. It can be approached as a symbolic normative phenomenon, as a *legal order*, on the one hand, and as a set of specific social practices, as *legal practices*, on the other hand. The most important legal practices are law-making (legislation), adjudication and legal research practices. Tuori criticizes classical legal positivism for not paying enough attention to the legitimacy problem. Whether a norm can be considered valid law depends according to critical legal positivism on whether it satisfies the criteria of the doctrine of the sources of law and their interpretation and on whether it is accepted as legitimate in the legal discourse between the legislator, the judiciary and the legal scholars, i.e. the actors behind the main legal practices.

According to critical legal positivism, law and its changes should be examined on three levels: the surface level of the law; the legal culture; and the deep structure of law. The surface level of the law comprises various pieces of legislation as well as the text of judgments and standpoints in legal scholarship. The legal culture constitutes the middle or mediating level of law. It consists of legal-cultural elements, such as general legal concepts and principles, legal theories or doctrines, including doctrines of the sources of law, and patterns of argumentation. The legal-cultural layers stand in constitutive relation to events on the law's surface: they make up the normative, conceptual

34. Tuori, Kaarlo: Critical Legal Positivism, Aldershot 2002, further developed in Tuori, Kaarlo: Ratio and Voluntas: The Tension between Reason and Will in Law. Aldershot: Ashgate 2011.
35. See in particular Hart, H.L.A: The Concept of Law, Oxford, 1994 and Kelsen, Hans: Reine Rechtslehre, 2. Neudruck der 1. Auflage Leipzig und Wien 1934, Aalen, 1994. See also Kelsen, Hans: Introduction to the Problems of Legal Theory (A Translation of the First edition of Reine Rechtslehre 1934), Oxford, 1992.

and methodological reservoir without which the legislator could not enact its laws, the judges issue their rulings, or the scholars write their articles and monographs. In legal practices, they mainly function in an unconscious, tacit way: they form an integral part of the hermeneutic *pre-understanding* (Vorverständnis) through which legal actors approach their specific tasks. The cultural, sub-surface elements of law result from a process of sedimentation, starting from what transpires on the surface. Viewed in this way, legal development starts at the surface level and then gradually over a number of years settles down as deeper layers of law. Legal history is thus a process of sedimentation.

The two aspects of law – law as a legal order and law as legal practices – are in constant interaction. Legal practices could not exist without legal norms. The legal order defines certain social practices as legal, as for example law-making or adjudication (constitutive legal norms) and guide the conduct of the agents of these practices. The legal method (understood as the doctrine of the sources of law and the way they are interpreted) is part of the valid law (*geltendes Recht*) in the multi-layered legal order applicable in the territory of the EU Member States. Law as a *legal order* could also not exist without *legal practices*, which are responsible for its production and reproduction. The term *legal system* is used in critical legal positivism to cover both of the law's two aspects (legal order and legal practices). According to critical legal positivism, legal research practice is of a double character. It is at the same time both legal practice and as such part of the legal system, and research practice and as such part of the social or human science research community.

4 European legal Method – Doctrine of the sources of law and their Interpretation

The questions I examine in this book are, as mentioned in section one, concerned with what is valid EU labour law as it stands in 2013 and the development it has undergone in the years from 1958 to 2013. I highlight the changes in contexts from labour law as internal market law to labour law as fundamental rights law and the change in context from labour law as part of many separate legal systems (one for each member state, + EU law, + public international law) to a 'one big system model' comprising European public international law, EU law and national law of the Member States in the scope of EU-law.

The method I use when answering my questions is a legal-dogmatic (doctrinal) analysis, i.e. I identify the relevant sources of law, interpret them and balance them against each other in accordance with the doctrine of the sources of law I consider part of the currently valid EU law, see on the sources of law in EU labour law below in Chapter Two. The expression 'legal dogmatic' (Rechtsdogmatik) is not much used in the Anglo-American legal culture where the words 'doctrinal legal research' are more widely used. In the Nordic and German legal culture it is more usual to talk about legal-dogmatic (Rechtsdogmatisch) analysis.

EU and international legal sources are generally available on the Internet free of charge for the end user. *Finding the law* is therefore not very difficult for these parts of the law. With regard to national law it may be much more difficult to find the law. The national doctrines of the sources of law vary from country to country, in many countries access to legal sources is partly commercialized so that one will have to buy some sources of law. In addition, the many languages in Europe make the sources of law in some countries inaccessible to many users. In EU law there are many different sources of law stemming from different legal actors and sometimes with inconsistent content. Deciding *which sources of law are relevant and balancing different sources of law against each other* will therefore often be necessary – and controversial.

5 Delimitations

5.1 Not Inter-disciplinary

It is obvious that the development of the EU is not only a legal phenomenon even though law has hitherto played a decisive role in the development of the EU which has expanded the role of law compared to many national labour market cultures and turned non-legal questions into legal questions. Kelemen – who is a US-American political scientist – has argued,[36] that the EU is encouraging the spread of 'Eurolegalism' – a mode of governance that relies on detailed rules containing strict transparency and disclosure requirements and providing for judicial control with nearly everything.

The present book gives only a legal analysis and not a cross-disciplinary analysis integrating approaches of other social sciences (economics, political

36. Kelemen, R.D.: Eurolegalism: The Transformation of Law and Regulation in the European Union, Cambridge, MA (Harvard University Press), 2011.

science, sociology, etc.). The two main economic constitutional goals of the EU (the Internal Market and the EMU) are as stated above explicitly mentioned in the goal provision for the EU in Article 3 TEU, see further below in Chapter Two. EU law is usually interpreted in a systematic and teleological (goal-rational) way. The economic goals of the EU (the Internal Market and the EMU) will therefore – in accordance with the doctrine of the sources of law I apply – be taken into account when interpreting EU labour law but I will not apply economic theories on the interrelationship between law and economics or other non-legal theories on the interplay between law and the other social or humanistic sciences.

The present book can be regarded as cross-disciplinary in a more 'internal' legal meaning of the concept. It is not narrowly limited to labour law but draws also on other legal disciplines, not least on general EU law. In national labour law – at least in the civil law systems in continental Europe – it is usual to distinguish between private law and public law and see labour law as private law. EU law doesn't use that distinction but mixes elements from private law and public law. I also do that in this book.

5.2 Not a systematic account of specific National Legal Systems

In this book I only give a systematic account of valid law stemming from EU or international level, not of labour law stemming from national level in the 27 Member States or some of them. The book is thus not comparative in the 'Länderberichte' sense of the word. A number of general questions about the interplay between national labour law, EU labour law and international labour law, including the interlocking mechanisms between those subsystems in the 'one big system' are, however dealt with.

CHAPTER TWO

Sources of EU Labour Law

1 Introduction

In this Chapter I will first give an overview of the phases in the development of EU labour law linked to the constitutional development of the Treaty basis of the EU and then look into the individual types of sources of law one by one. As set out in Chapter One I will treat the law both at the surface level and at sub-surface levels. There is no explicit exposition of the EU doctrine of the source of law at the surface level of EU law. EU law hereby differs from international law. As set out below in section 8 an authoritative catalogue of sources of international law can be found in Article 38 of the Statute of the International Court of Justice. I classify the sources of EU labour law as follows:

- Primary law (Treaty provisions and general principles and fundamental rights)
- Secondary law
- Soft law
- Case law
- Scholarly Legal writing
- Public international law
- National law of the EU Member States.

It is usual to distinguish between positive and negative integration.[1] Positive integration is based on active legislation see below in section 4 on secondary legislation. Negative integration consists in application of the fundamental

1. See further Barnard, Catherine and Simon Deakin: 'Negative' and 'Positive' Harmonization of Labor Law in the European Union, Columbia Journal of European Law 2002 p. 389.

free movement rights for goods, services, capital and persons provided for in the TFEU and striking down 'national obstacles'. Originally EU law on free movement applied solely to direct and indirect nationality discrimination by the Member States. Over the years, CJEU case law has developed EU free movement law into a broad(er) ban on restrictions. In G*ebhard,*[2] the CJEU held that national measures liable to hinder or make less attractive the exercise of fundamental freedoms guaranteed by the Treaty must fulfil four conditions: they must be applied in a non-discriminatory manner; they must be justified by imperative requirements in the general interest; they must be suitable for securing the attainment of the objective which they pursue; and they must not go beyond what is necessary in order to attain it, see below in section 3.2.10 on the double justification test when free movement is balanced against fundamental rights, e.g. the right to strike.

2 Phases in the Development

First, I will mention some characteristics of labour law before the establishment of the EC/EU in 1958. The period from 1958 to 2013 can in regard to the development of the legal sources of EU labour law be divided into two main phases delimited by reference to the formal treaties on the Community and the European Union:

- From the establishment of the Community by the Rome Treaty 1957[3] to the establishment of the European Union by the Maastricht Treaty 1992[4]
  - The 1960s
  - The 1970es
  - The 1980ies
- From the Maastricht Treaty 1992 until today (2013)
  - From the Maastricht Treaty to the Amsterdam Treaty[5] (1993-1999)
  - From the Amsterdam Treaty to the Lisbon Treaty (1999-2009)
  - After the Lisbon Treaty[6] came into force 1 December 2009

2. Case C-55/94 *Gebhard* [1995] ECR I-4165.
3. The Rome Treaty 1957 signed on 25. March 1957 entered into force 1 January 1958.
4. The Maastricht Treaty signed on 7 February 1992 entered into force 1 November 1993.
5. The Amsterdam Treaty signed on 2 October 1997 entered into force 1 May 1999.
6. The Lisbon Treaty signed on 13 December 2007 entered into force 1 December 2009.

In the first period, the oldest layer of the economic constitution of the EC/EU (the internal market) played a dominant role. In the second period there is more – and growing – attention on the second layer of the economic constitution (the economic and monetary union), see about the constitutionalisation of the EU above in Chapter One.

2.1 Before the EC/EU

There were national labour law systems in most EU Member States before they entered the EC/EU, but in most countries labour law became a special legal discipline only after the Second World War. As Hepple points out:[7]

> labour law is of recent origin. In most countries it became recognized as a distinct division of law only after the Second World War. ...
>
> The exceptions were Germany and Denmark. In the latter, Carl Ussing, a Supreme Court judge who presided over the 'August Committee' of 1908-10, combined academic and practical expertise to produce a sharp analysis which helped to lay the foundations of Denmark's collectivist system ..., but mainly due for reasons of language the impact of the Danish innovations was limited to Scandinavia.

Before the establishment of the EC, international labour law consisted primarily in ILO law. The ILO (international Labour Organisation) was established in 1919 as part of the League of Nations. After the Second World War, ILO became a UN organization. In the Philadelphia Declaration of 1944, the International Labour Conference reaffirmed the fundamental principles on which the ILO is based and, in particular, that 'labour is not a commodity'.[8]

2.2 From Rome to Maastricht: the Community before the establishment of the European Union

In the literature[9] the basic rules on free movement on the internal market and competition law are usually regarded as the first – micro-economic – layer of EU's economic constitution. In the internal market logic it is usual to see labour (the workers) as a commodity, i.e. the EC/EU started out with a view on labour that was/is the opposite of that taken by ILO.

7. Hepple, Bob (ed.): The Making of Labour Law in Europe: A Comparative Study of Nine Countries up to 1945, London 1986 p. 7.
8. See on that provision O'Higgins, Paul: Labour is not a Commodity' – an Irish Contribution to International Labour Law, Industrial Law Journal1997, Vol. 26 Issue 3, p. 225 and further below in section 8.4.
9. See See Tuori, Kaarlo: The European Financial Crisis – Constitutional Aspects and Implications, EUI Working Paper LAW 2012/28.

Since the establishment of the European Union by the Maastricht Treaty 1992 which contains rules on economic and monetary union a second more macro-economic phase of the economic constitution is – as mentioned in Chapter One – developing. The Maastricht Treaty also created union citizenship and strengthened the role of fundamental rights. Workers make up the majority of union citizens and are no longer seen by EU legal actors as solely or primarily a commodity on the internal market.

2.2.1 The late 1950's and the 1960's

If one looks back to the first EEC Treaty, the Rome Treaty 1957 which entered into force 1 January 1958, there were only few labour law provisions. There were only two explicitly binding provisions, namely the then Article 48 EEC on free movement of workers [now Article 45 TFEU] and the then Article 119 EEC [now after amendment Article 157 TFEU] on equal pay between men and women.

The Internal market context was clearly the dominating context for EU labour law in the first years. The goal of establishing an internal market has been one of EU's primary objectives from the inception of the EC/EU in 1958 to the present day. During the first ten years or thereabout of the EC the Customs union was established. The social policy in this period focused on labour mobility. The first regulation on migrant workers[10] was adopted in 1968, see further below in Chapter Five on free movement of workers and union citizens.

2.2.2 The 1970's: legal activism

The five years from 1974-1979 was a period of considerable activity in the employment field at EU level. The EC/EU's first Social Action Programme of 1974[11] was issued in response to a mandate by the Heads of States meeting in Paris at the Summit of October 1972. The final communiqué declared that the Member States attached as much importance to vigorous action in the social field as to the achievement of economic union and considered it essential to ensure the increasing involvement of labour and management in the economic and social decisions of the EU. Accordingly, the Commission was instructed to draw up a Social Action Programme. By a Resolution adopted on 21 January 1974, the Council of Ministers approved the Social Action Pro-

10. EC/1612/68, now repealed and replaced with EU/492/2011, see further in Chapter Five.
11. Bulletin of the European Communities Supplement 2/74, http://aei.pitt.edu/1253/1/social_action_program_COM_73_1600.pdf

gramme involving more than 30 measures over an initial period of three to four years. The three main objectives were: the attainment of full and better employment in the EU, the improvement of living and working conditions, and the increased involvement of management and labour in the economic and social decisions of the EU and of workers in companies.

The idea that EU law has a double – both economic and social aim – was thus clearly stated in EU soft law in the early 1970's. In *Defrenne II*,[12] the CJEU expressed the same view.

Six labour law directives were adopted in the 1970's. Three of them on gender equality: the original Equal Pay Directive from 1975,[13] the original Equal Treatment Directive 1976[14] and the Social Security (gender equality) Directive from 1979.[15] The three other directives from the 1970s were the first Collective Redundancies Directive from 1975,[16] the first Transfer of Undertakings Directive from 1977[17] and the first directive on the Employer's Insolvency from 1980.[18]

Most of the other proposals in the 1974 Social Action Programme have later been carried through the EU's legislative process, in some cases after a very long time and with considerable changes from the early proposals to the adopted legal acts, see for example on information, consultation and participation of workers below in Chapter Four.

In the early 1970's, fundamental rights in the EU were introduced through the case-law of the CJEU mainly as a means to make national supreme courts accept the supremacy of EU law over national law, not so much to meet the EU's social objectives, see below in section 2.3.1 on the development of fundamental rights in the EU.

2.2.3 The 1980's

Margaret Thatcher became conservative UK Prime Minister in 1979 and continued in that position until 1991. The UK government remained conservative until 1997 when a labour government took office in the UK. The conservative

12. Case 43/75 *Defrenne II* [1976] ECR 455.
13. 75/117/EEC, now repealed and replaced by the Recast directive 2006/54/EC on gender equality in employment and occupation, see further in Chapter Six.
14. 76/207/EEC, now repealed and replaced by the Recast directive 2006/54/EC on gender equality in employment and occupation, see further in Chapter Six.
15. 79/7/EEC, see further in Chapter Six.
16. 129/1975/EC, now repealed and replaced by 98/59/EC, see further in Chapter Eight.
17. 187/1977/EC, now repealed and replaced by 2001/23/EC, see further in Chapter Eight.
18. 987/1980, now repealed and replaced by 2008/94/EC, see further in Chapter Eight.

UK government from 1979-1997 was very critical towards most legislative initiatives at EU level in the labour law field and made it difficult/impossible for the EU to develop EU labour legislation further in that period on the basis of the 1974 Social Action Programme which at that time required unanimity.

The UK did, however, accept the adoption of the Single European Act 1986 which was a Treaty amending the EEC Treaty. That Treaty introduced majority voting in Article 118a EEC to adopt minimum requirements with a view to 'encouraging improvements, especially in the working environment, as regards the health and safety of workers'. It also provided a provision, Article 118b EEC which authorised the Commission to develop dialogue between management and labour at European level.

In 1989,[19] eleven of the then 12 members of the EC adopted the Community Charter of Fundamental Rights of Workers[20] as a piece of soft law. Under the Community Charter of Fundamental Rights of Workers, the Community is obliged to provide for the fundamental social rights of workers under the following headings:

Freedom of movement (Articles 1 to 3)
Employment and remuneration (Articles 4 to 6)
Improvement of living and working conditions (Articles 7 to 9)
Social protection (Article 10)
Freedom of association and collective bargaining (Articles 11 to 14)
Vocational training (Article 15)
Equal treatment for men and women (Article 16)
Information and consultation and participation for workers (Articles 17 to 18)
Health protection and safety at the workplace (Article 19)
Protection of children and adolescents (Articles 20 to 23)
Elderly persons (Articles 24 to 25)
Disabled persons (Article 26)
Member States' action (implementation) (Articles 27 to 30)

19. Bercusson, Brian: The European Community's Charter of Fundamental Social Rights of Workers, The Modern Law Review, Vol. 53, 1990 p. 624.
20. That Charter is not published in the Official Journal but there are several publications of it, including at the internet. In this book I have used the one found at Eurofound at http://www.aedh.eu/plugins/fckeditor/userfiles/file/Conventions%20internationales /Community_Charter_of_the_Fundamental_Social_Rights_of_Workers.pdf. Eurofound is a tripartite EU agency which provides expertise on living and working conditions, industrial relations and managing change in Europe, see further http://www.eurofound.europa.eu/index.htm.

The Charter represents a commitment by the Member States to a set of social policy and labour law objectives. Article 28 stipulates: 'The European Council invites the Commission to submit as soon as possible initiatives which fall within its powers, as provided for in the Treaties, with a view to the adoption of legal instruments for the effective implementation, as and when the internal market is completed, of those rights, which come within the Community's area of competence.'

The Community Charter of the Fundamental Social Rights of Workers 1989 is soft law but a piece of soft law that has been given greater weight than soft law usually has. Due to the opposition of the then conservative UK government, the Charter could not be integrated into the EC Treaty in 1989. The UK eventually acceded to the Charter, following the election of a labour government in UK in May 1997. Following adoption of the Community Charter of the Fundamental Social Rights of Workers in Strasbourg in December 1989, [21] the Commission drew up an Action Programme[22] aimed at implementing the Charter, containing 47 proposals for initiatives of various kinds, both binding and non-binding. Adoption of the proposals of the Social Action Programme made slow progress, particularly as regards the binding legal acts. This was in part due to the absence in the then EC Treaty of clear provisions for EU competence to adopt measures needed to guarantee the rights laid down in the Charter. Some progress was made when the Council adopted a Directive[23] on the obligation on employers to inform employees of the conditions applicable to their employment relationship but, otherwise, the main success was the adoption of directives concerning health and safety of employees at work, an area where the Single European Act 1986 established EC competence. The relevant competences were only obtained by the amendments introduced by the Maastricht Treaty's Protocol and Agreement on Social Policy. Thereafter, the obstacles to implementation of the fundamental social rights of workers promised by the 1989 Charter of the Fundamental Social Rights of Workers were primarily political.

After the establishment of the European Union in 1992 there are references to the 1989 Charter on Workers both in Article 151 TFEU [ex Article 136 EEC and before that the Social Policy Agreement for 11 countries at-

21. http://www.aedh.eu/plugins/fckeditor/userfiles/file/Conventions%20internationales/Community_Charter_of_the_Fundamental_Social_Rights_of_Workers.pdf.
22. http://aei.pitt.edu/1345/1/Social_charter_COM_89_568.pdf.
23. 91/533/EEC.

tached to the Maastricht Treaty] and in the explanatory remarks to the CFREU.[24]

2.3 From Maastricht until today (2013)

The adoption of the Maastricht Treaty 1992 marks a turning point in the development of EU labour law. It elevated both the establishment of an economic, monetary and financial union (the second layer of the EU economic constitution) and fundamental rights in the EU to primary EU law.

The goal of establishing an internal market has been one of EU's primary objectives from the inception of the EC/EU in 1958 to the present day. The internal market is to a large extent established by means of legal provisions on free movement for goods, services, capital and persons (workers and freedom of establishment) and competition law. Most labour problems arise in national contexts without trans-border elements. In such cases, the internal market law of the EU doesn't apply. As long as the primary goal of the EU was the establishment and functioning of the Internal Market national labour law issues therefore played only a marginal role in the EU. The EU competence to adoption of secondary legislation was limited and the decision-process difficult. As the main rule it required unanimity.

With the adoption of the Maastricht Treaty in 1992 the Internal Market goal was complemented by the second layer of the EU's macro-economic constitution focusing on establishing an economic and monetary union whose currency is the euro. Today both these variants of the economic constitution are mentioned in the general goal provision in Article 3 TEU.[25] The Maastricht Treaty also inserted a provision on fundamental rights in Article 6 TEU. The original Treaty of Rome 1957 did not contain specific provisions on the protection of fundamental rights. Article 6 TEU was first included in the TEU by the Maastricht Treaty, signed in 1992, and was subsequently amended by the Amsterdam Treaty in 1997. Pre-Lisbon it provided that the Union must respect fundamental rights as guaranteed by the ECHR and as they result from the constitutional traditions common to the Member States, as general principles of Community law. In the macro-economic context of the financial union employment and labour law issues are of central importance. Labour law is therefore no longer a marginal aspect of the EU's economic constitution. The focus on fundamental rights are also particularly important for la-

24. See OJ 2007 C 303.
25. Article 3 TEU provides (emphasis added): ... 3. The Union shall *establish an internal market*. ... 4. The Union shall *establish an economic and monetary union* whose currency is the euro. ...

bour law, see further below in section 3.2. Following the adoption of the Maastricht Treaty a number of labour law directives have been adopted. A common trait is that most of them are about flexibility, for example working time regulation, directives on atypical forms of employment contracts (part-time, fixed term, agency work, etc.) or restructuring of businesses (transfer of undertakings, collective redundancies and employer insolvency), see further below in Chapter Seven, Eight and Nine. EU anti-discrimination law which is a core fundamental rights issue in the EU has also been expanded considerably, see further below in Chapter Six.

2.3.1 From Maastricht to Amsterdam. The two tracks: UK and the 11 other EU-countries

EU labour law in the European Union established by the Maastricht 1992 Treaty started on two tracks, one for the UK and another for the then 11 other Member States. The Social Policy Protocol was the legal mechanism adopted to resolve the impasse reached over the labour law and social policy provisions of the Treaty of Maastricht at the summit in December 1991. Eleven of the EU Member States agreed on the provisions of a new Social Chapter of the EC Treaty, based on the Agreement on Social Policy reached by the European social partners on 31 October 1991. The UK disagreed and continued the policy started by Margaret Thatcher in 1979. The result became the Treaty on European Union signed by all the Member States on 7 February 1992, a Protocol on Social Policy and an Agreement, annexed to the Protocol, between 11 Member States, with the exception of the UK. The Protocol noted that 11 Member States 'wish to continue along the path laid down in the 1989 Social Charter of Workers [and] have adopted among themselves an Agreement to this end'.[26] The Social Protocol provided that all 12 Member States:

> 1. Agree to authorise those 11 Member States [excluding the UK] to have recourse to the institutions, procedures and mechanisms of the Treaty for the purposes of taking among themselves and applying as far as they are concerned the acts and decisions required for giving effect to the above-mentioned Agreement.
>
> 2. The [UK] shall not take part in the deliberations and the adoption by the Council of Commission proposals made on the basis of this Protocol and the above-mentioned Agreement...
>
> 3. Acts adopted by the Council... shall not be applicable to the [UK].'

26. See Treaty On European Union, OJ 1992 C 191 http://eur-lex.europa.eu/en/treaties/dat/11992M/htm/11992M.html#0090000015

The election of a Labour government in the UK in May 1997 led the UK to opt-in, and the Treaty of Amsterdam, agreed on 7 June 1997, provided for the provisions of the Agreement on Social Policy to be incorporated into the EC Treaty.

In order to achieve the objectives of the Community Charter of the Fundamental Social Rights of Workers 1989, the European Commission adopted a Social Action Programme to implement it.[27] It resulted in a number of directives during the 1990s. Among these are the 1992 directive regarding pregnancy and maternity,[28] the 1993 Working Time Directive,[29] the 1994 European Works Council Directive[30] and the directives based on the framework agreements on parental leave,[31] part-time work[32] and fixed-term work.[33]

Only little legislation was adopted under the Social Policy Agreement, namely only the two directives on European works councils and parental leave. Other legal bases were used for the other directives. The pregnancy and maternity directive and the 1993 Working Time Directive were thus adopted on the basis of of Article 118 a EC on working environment which allowed majority voting, see further below in Chapter Nine. Directives adopted under Article 118 a EC were binding for all the then 12 Member States. The UK contested the validity of the original Working Time Directive[34] before the CJEU claiming that working time is not a working environment issue. The Directive could therefore not be adopted under Article 118 a EC but could have been adopted under the Social Policy Agreement in which case it would only have been binding for the 11 Member states that were party to the Agreement and not for the UK. The CJEU held that a provision on Sunday work was invalid but that the Directive apart from that was valid.

The Maastricht Treaty of 1992 with its chapters on increased integration was only accepted at a Danish referendum in 1993, after the so-called Edinburgh Agreement had allowed Denmark to ratify with four reservations: 1) on the final phase of the Economic and Monetary Union and the euro, 2) on the defence cooperation, 3) on an extension of the legal cooperation and 4) on union citizenship, see further below in Chapter Five.

27. COM (89) 568 final.
28. 92/85/EEC.
29. 93/104/EC, see now 2003/88/EC.
30. Directive 94/45/EC, see now the recast directive 2009/38/EC.
31. 96/34/EC, amended by 2010/18/EU.
32. 97/81/EC.
33. 1999/70/EC.
34. Case C-84/94 *UK v Council* [1996] ECR I-5755.

2.3.2 *From Amsterdam to Lisbon*

By the Treaty of Amsterdam of June 1997, the Social Policy Protocol was deleted and the Agreement on Social Policy was incorporated into a revised 'Social Chapter' of the EC Treaty. The Social Chapter of the EC Treaty, as amended by the Treaties of Amsterdam and Nice (Articles 136 et seq EC, now Articles 151 et seq TFEU)), incorporated the Agreement on Social Policy. In matters of equality and discrimination the Amsterdam Treaty became a turning point, see further below in Chapter Six.

Since 1 October 2005, there is a special labour court in the EU – the Civil Service Tribunal – which hears staff cases within the Union.

2.3.3 *The current post-Lisbon period*

Today (2013), the EU is according to Article 2 TEU founded on the values of respect for human dignity, freedom, democracy, equality, the rule of law (Rechtsstaatlichkeit) and respect for human rights, including the rights of persons belonging to minorities. These values are common to the Member States in a society in which pluralism, non-discrimination, tolerance, justice, solidarity and equality between women and men prevail.

Article 2 TEU on EU's values is a new provision inserted in the TEU by the Lisbon Treaty 2007. It is the first time that there is an explicit statement of the values of the EU in its primary law. It is conspicuous that neither *the internal market*, nor *the economic and monetary union*, i.e. the two phenomena that are particularly characteristic of *EU's economic constitutions*, are mentioned as forming part of the EU's values. The EU values explicitly provided for in the Treaties are primarily non-economic and focus on fundamental rights and citizenship.

Today (2013) it is one of the general goals of the EU to promote its values, see belov on Article 3 TEU. The value provision in Article 2 TEU has also specific relevance for the interpretation of the substantive content of labour law both at EU level and in the Member States. Dorsemont[35] has argued that the insertion of the value provision in article 2 TEU by the Lisbon Treaty provides a basis for arguing that consideration of employment and labour rights should be given more weight when balancing them against the fundamental free movement provisions of employers, for example the free movement of services and posting of workers.

35. Dorsemont, Philip: Values and Objectives, in Bruun, Niklas, Klaus Lörcher and Isabelle Schömann (eds): The Lisbon Treaty and Social Europe, Oxford 2012.

3 Primary EU law

Primary EU law comprises the basic Treaties (TEU and TFEU), the Charter of Fundamental Rights of the European Union (CFREU) and other fundamental rights and general principles of EU law. EU primary law is – both in the case law of the CJEU and in legal scholarship[36] – considered as the EU's constitutional basis, see for example *les Verts* where the CJEU stated (emphasis added):[37]

> It must first be emphasized in this regard that the European Economic Community is a Community based on the rule of law, inasmuch as neither its Member States nor its institutions can avoid a review of the question whether the measures adopted by them are in conformity with *the basic constitutional charter, the Treaty.*

In favour of this terminology von Bogdandy refers to the fact that the primary law justifies the exercise of public power, it legitimises acts of the EU, it creates a citizenship, it grants fundamental rights, and it regulates the relationship between legal orders, between public power and the economy, and between law and politics. Numerous common elements of EU primary law and national constitutions thus emerge in a functional comparison.[38]

3.1 The Treaties

Originally there was only one basic Treaty: the Rome Treaty (the EEC Treaty). From Maastricht to Lisbon there were two basic Treaties: the EC Treaty[39] as amended by the Maastricht, Amsterdam and Nice Treaties and the EU Treaty, first adopted as the Maastricht Treaty. After the coming into force of the Lisbon Treaty the expression the Treaties refer to the two Treaties: TFEU, the Treaty on the Functioning of the European Union (the name given to the former EC Treaty by the Lisbon Treaty) and TEU, the Treaty on the Europe-

36. See Lenaerts, Koen and Piet van Nuffel: Constitutional Law of the European Union, London 2005 p. 705 and Ulla Neergaard & Ruth Nielsen: Blurring Boundaries: From the Danish Welfare State to the European Social Model?, online at http://papers.ssrn.com/sol3/papers.cfm?abstract_id=1618758.
37. Case 294/83 *les Verts* [1986] ECR 1339 ground 23.
38. See further Von Bogdandy, Armin: Founding Principles of EU Law: A Theoretical and Doctrinal Sketch, European Law Journal, 2010 p. 95.
39. The Maastricht Treaty changed the name EEC (European Economic Community) to EC (European Community). Originally there were three communities: ECSC (The European Coal and Steel Community) 1952, EEC and EAEC (European Atomic Energy Community). ECSC was time-limited to 50 years and expired in 2002.

an Union. Since the Lisbon Treaty entered into force the Charter of Fundamental Rights of the European Union (CFREU) has had the same legal value as the Treaties (TFEU and TEU), see Article 6 TEU.

The Treaties contain provisions on values and objectives, institutions, legislative procedures, the internal market (free movement and competition law provisions), a (financial) economic and monetary union, fundamental rights and other rights and duties.

3.1.1 General Values and Objectives of the EC/EU

As mentioned earlier there was no provision on the values of the EU in the Treaties before the Lisbon Treaty. Today (2013), the EU is founded on the values of respect for human dignity, freedom, democracy, equality, the rule of law (Rechtsstaatlichkeit) and respect for human rights.

At least since the 1970's the CJEU has held that the EC/EU has a double – both economic and social – goal, see *Defrenne II*.[40] In that case what the CJEU called social was the principle of equal pay between men and women, i.e. related to a core employment relations issue.

The goal of establishing an internal market has been one of EU's primary objectives from the inception of the EC/EU in 1958 to the present day. The internal market is to a large extent established by means of legal provisions on free movement for goods, services, capital and persons (workers and freedom of establishment) and competition law.

With the adoption of the Maastricht Treaty in 1992 it was complemented by the second layer of the EU's macro-economic constitution focusing on establishing an economic and monetary union whose currency is the euro. Today both these variants of the economic constitution are mentioned in the general goal provision in Article 3 TEU.[41] Today, Article 3 TEU also pre-

40. Case 43/75 *Defrenne II* [1976] ECR 455.
41. Article 3 TEU provides (emphasis added):1. The Union's aim is to *promote peace, its values and the well-being of its peoples*. 2. The Union shall *offer its citizens an area of freedom, security and justice without internal frontiers*, in which the free movement of persons is ensured in conjunction with appropriate measures with respect to external border controls, asylum, immigration and the prevention and combating of crime. 3. The Union shall *establish an internal market*. It shall work for the sustainable development of Europe based on balanced economic growth and price stability, *a highly competitive social market economy*, aiming at full employment and social progress, and a high level of protection and improvement of the quality of the environment. It shall promote scientific and technological advance. It shall combat social exclusion and discrimination, and shall promote social justice and protection, equality between women and men, solidarity between generations and protection of the rights

scribes it as goals for the EU to promote its values, fundamental rights, equality and other more social goals.

The most important new words in Article 3 TEU on the goals of the EU are *social market economy* and *solidarity*. The Union shall work for the sustainable development of Europe based on a highly competitive social market economy, aiming at full employment and social progress. Solidarity is mentioned three times in Article 3 TEU. The EU shall promote solidarity between generations, promote solidarity among Member States and contribute to solidarity and mutual respect among peoples.

3.1.2 Specific Objectives of EU Labour Law

In the early 1970's, fundamental rights in the EU were introduced through the case-law of the CJEU, see below in section 2.3.1. Later, in particular since the Maastricht Treaty they have gradually been codified, first in Article 6 TEU and after the Lisbon Treaty also in the Charter of Fundamental Rights of the European Union (CFREU) which now has the same legal values as the Treaties. Most employment and Labour specific provisions in the Treaties are placed in Title X TFEU with the heading 'Social Policy' (Article 151 TFEU – Article 161 TFEU). Article 151 TFEU provides with regard to the labour market:

> The Union and the Member States, having in mind fundamental social rights such as those set out in the European Social Charter signed at Turin on 18 October 1961 and in the 1989 Community Charter of the Fundamental Social Rights of Workers, shall have as their objectives the promotion of employment, improved living and working conditions, so as to make possible their harmonisation while the improvement is being maintained, proper social protection, dialogue between management and labour, the development of human resources with a view to lasting high employment and the combating of exclusion.

of the child. It shall promote economic, social and territorial cohesion, and solidarity among Member States. It shall *respect its rich cultural and linguistic diversity*, and shall ensure that Europe's cultural heritage is safeguarded and enhanced. 4. The Union shall *establish an economic and monetary union* whose currency is the euro. 5. In its relations with the wider world, the Union shall *uphold and promote its values and interests* and contribute to the protection of its citizens. It shall contribute to peace, security, the sustainable development of the Earth, solidarity and mutual respect among peoples, free and fair trade, eradication of poverty and the *protection of human rights*, in particular the rights of the child, as well as to the *strict observance and the development of international law*, including respect for the principles of the United Nations Charter. 6. The Union shall pursue its objectives by appropriate means commensurate with the competences which are conferred upon it in the Treaties.

To this end the Union and the Member States shall implement measures which take account of the diverse forms of national practices, in particular in the field of contractual relations, and the need to maintain the competitiveness of the Union economy.

They believe that such a development will ensue not only from the functioning of the internal market, which will favour the harmonisation of social systems, but also from the procedures provided for in the Treaties and from the approximation of provisions laid down by law, regulation or administrative action.

In the Rome Treaty the counterpart to Article 151 TFEU was Article 117 EEC. Article 117(2) EEC was practically identical with Article 151(3)TFEU, while Article 117(1) EEC was much briefer than the current provisions in Article 151 (1 and 2) TFEU. It provided that Member States agree upon the need to promote improved working conditions and an improved standard of living for workers, so as to make possible their harmonization while the improvement is being maintained. There was no reference in the Rome Treaty to fundamental rights or to the European Social Charter 1961, see on the European Social Charter 1961 below in section 7 on public international law.

A reference to fundamental rights and to the European Social Charter 1961 was included in EU primary law in the Social Protocol and Social Policy agreement attached to the Maastricht Treaty 1992 when the European Union was founded. When the Amsterdam Treaty was adopted in 1997 after the change from conservative to labour government in 1997 in the UK, Article 136 EC got almost the same wording as the present Article 151 TFEU.

3.1.3 The Principle of Conferral

As stated in Article 5 TEU, the limits of EU competences are governed by the principle of conferral. Under that principle, the Union shall act only within the limits of the competences conferred upon it by the Member States in the Treaties to attain the objectives set out therein. Competences not conferred upon the EU in the Treaties remain with the Member States. Direct taxation is for example still under Member States' competence, but they must respect EU primary law on free movement on the internal market when they exercise their legislative competence in tax law.

The EU is thus only competent to adopt measures if it has been given competence to do so in the Treaties. EU Competence can be exclusive, joint with national governments, or supporting, with national governments having lead competence. Part One Title I of the TFEU sets out the categories and areas of EU competence. It distinguishes between exclusive competence for the EU (Article 3 TFEU), shared competence between the EU and its Member States (Article 4 TFEU), coordination measures for economic, employment and social policies (Article 5 TFEU) and competence for the EU to support, coordinate or supplement the actions of the Member States (Article 6 TFEU).

Most EU legal acts related to labour law have their legal base in provisions in areas in which the EU and its Member States according to Article 4 TFEU have shared competence or fall within the areas where the EU only ensures coordination or complementation of the actions of the Member States. Shared competence between the EU and the Member States applies in the following areas: internal market; social policy, for the aspects defined in the TFEU; economic, social and territorial cohesion; agriculture and fisheries, excluding the conservation of marine biological resources; environment; consumer protection; transport; trans-European networks; energy; area of freedom, security and justice; and common safety concerns in public health matters, for the aspects defined in the TFEU.

Under Article 5 TFEU, the Council of the EU *shall* adopt measures, in particular broad guidelines for the economic policies of the Member States and *shall* take measures to ensure coordination of the employment policies of the Member States, in particular by defining guidelines for these policies. In addition, the EU *may* take initiatives to ensure coordination of Member States' social policies.

Under Article 6 TFEU, the EU has competence to carry out actions to support, coordinate or supplement the actions of the Member States. The areas of such action, at European level, are: protection and improvement of human health; industry; culture; tourism; education, vocational training, youth and sport; civil protection; and administrative cooperation.

Article 3 TFEU lists the areas where the EU has exclusive competence.[42] The EU does not have exclusive competence in core labour law areas.

The principle of conferral has applied ever since the foundation of the Community/the European Union in 1957. It is a general principle of EU law and applies correspondingly to other substantive areas of law.

42. I.e. (a) customs union; (b) the establishing of the competition rules necessary for the functioning of the internal market; (c) monetary policy for the Member States whose currency is the euro; (d) the conservation of marine biological resources under the common fisheries policy; (e) common commercial policy and the conclusion of an international agreement when its conclusion is provided for in a legislative act of the Union or is necessary to enable the Union to exercise its internal competence, or in so far as its conclusion may affect common rules or alter their scope.

3.1.4 Expansion of EU legislative competence in matters of labour law

Over the years the areas where legislative competence has been conferred upon the EU have been expanded. In the Rome Treaty 1957, there was very limited EU competence to enact secondary legislation in the field of labour law. The only explicit legal basis was Article 100 EEC, according to which the Council, acting unanimously on a proposal from the Commission could issue directives for the approximation of such provisions laid down by law, regulation or administrative action in Member States as directly affect the establishment or functioning of the common market. It was thus clear in the original Treaty that labour law could only be developed further at EU level if it was useful for the establishment or functioning of the internal market (then called the common market).

Under Article 118 EEC the Commission should promote cooperation between the Member States on a number of labour law issues. By the Single European Act 1986, Article 118 EC was amended to provide EU competence to adopt directives with majority voting on working environment issues. There was already in the Rome Treaty a provision[43] corresponding to the current Article 352 TFEU. It was e.g. legal basis for the first Equal Treatment directive between men and women.[44]

3.1.5 Current legal bases for EU Secondary Legislation in matters of employment and labour

Today (2013), the main legal basis for secondary legislation in the labour law field is Article 153 TFEU which provides (emphasis added):

1. With a view to achieving the objectives of Article 151, the Union shall support and complement the activities of the Member States in the following fields:

(a) improvement in particular of the working environment to protect workers' health and safety;
(b) working conditions;
(c) social security and social protection of workers;
(d) protection of workers where their employment contract is terminated;
(e) the information and consultation of workers;
(f) representation and collective defence of the interests of workers and employers, including co-determination, subject to paragraph 5;
(g) conditions of employment for third-country nationals legally residing in Union territory;
(h) the integration of persons excluded from the labour market, without prejudice to Article 166;

43. See Article 235 EEC.
44. 76/207/EEC, now repealed and replaced by 2006/54/EC.

(i) equality between men and women with regard to labour market opportunities and treatment at work;
(j) the combating of social exclusion;
(k) the modernisation of social protection systems without prejudice to point (c).

2. To this end, the European Parliament and the Council:
(a) may adopt measures designed to encourage cooperation between Member States through initiatives aimed at improving knowledge, developing exchanges of information and best practices, promoting innovative approaches and evaluating experiences, excluding any harmonisation of the laws and regulations of the Member States;
(b) may adopt, in the fields referred to in paragraph 1(a) to (i), by means of directives, minimum requirements for gradual implementation, having regard to the conditions and technical rules obtaining in each of the Member States. Such directives shall avoid imposing administrative, financial and legal constraints in a way which would hold back the creation and development of small and medium-sized undertakings.
The European Parliament and the Council shall act in accordance with the ordinary legislative procedure after consulting the Economic and Social Committee and the Committee of the Regions.
In the fields referred to in paragraph 1(c), (d), (f) and (g), the Council shall act unanimously, in accordance with a special legislative procedure, after consulting the European Parliament and the said Committees.
The Council, acting unanimously on a proposal from the Commission, after consulting the European Parliament, may decide to render the ordinary legislative procedure applicable to paragraph 1(d), (f) and (g).

3. A Member State may entrust management and labour, at their joint request, with the implementation of directives adopted pursuant to paragraph 2, or, where appropriate, with the implementation of a Council decision adopted in accordance with Article 155.

In this case, it shall ensure that, no later than the date on which a directive or a decision must be transposed or implemented, management and labour have introduced the necessary measures by agreement, the Member State concerned being required to take any necessary measure enabling it at any time to be in a position to guarantee the results imposed by that directive or that decision.

4. The provisions adopted pursuant to this Article:
- shall not affect the right of Member States to define the fundamental principles of their social security systems and must not significantly affect the financial equilibrium thereof,
- shall not prevent any Member State from maintaining or introducing more stringent protective measures compatible with the Treaties.

5. The provisions of this Article shall not apply to pay, the right of association, the right to strike or the right to impose lock-outs.

Article 153 TFEU deals with core labour law issues such as improvement of the working environment to protect workers' health and safety; working conditions; protection against dismissal; information and consultation of workers; representation and collective defence of the interests of workers and employers, including co-determination and equality between men and women with regard to labour market opportunities and treatment at work. Most existing labour law directives are adopted with legal basis in Article 153 TFEU or its predecessors, see further in chapter Four on information and consultation, chapter Seven on Employment protection of individual workers, chapter Eight on Employment protection in connection with Restructuring of businesses and chapter Nine on working environment.

In regard to gender discrimination there is a directly applicable Treaty provision on equal pay in Article 157 (1 and 2) and a special legal base for further secondary legislation in Article 157(3) TFEU which provides:

> The European Parliament and the Council, acting in accordance with the ordinary legislative procedure, and after consulting the Economic and Social Committee, shall adopt measures to ensure the application of the principle of equal opportunities and equal treatment of men and women in matters of employment and occupation, including the principle of equal pay for equal work or work of equal value.

A number of gender equality directives have been adopted since the 1970's. Most of them are now replaced by the Recast directive on gender equality in the labour market.[45]

For discrimination on grounds of sex, racial or ethnic origin, religion or belief, disability, age or sexual orientation there is a legal base in Article 19 TFEU which provides:

> 1. Without prejudice to the other provisions of the Treaties and within the limits of the powers conferred by them upon the Union, the Council, acting unanimously in accordance with a special legislative procedure and after obtaining the consent of the European Parliament, may take appropriate action to combat discrimination based on sex, racial or ethnic origin, religion or belief, disability, age or sexual orientation.

Article 19 TFEU is the legal base for the Ethnic Equal treatment Directive[46] and the Employment Directive.[47]

45. 2006/54/EC.
46. 2000/43/EC.
47. 2000/78/EC.

3.1.6 Minimum harmonization or full harmonization

As appears from the text in italics in the above quotation from Article 153 TFEU, the EU has only competence to adopt minimum harmonization, not full harmonization and only by directives, not regulations in matters of labour law apart from gender equality where the EU has a more far-reaching competence to full harmonization and adoption of either directives or regulations. So far the EU has only adopted minimum harmonization on gender equality, see further in chapter Six.

In labour law in general, Member States retain competence to maintain or introduce more worker friendly provisions as long as they are compatible with primary law, in particular the free movement provisions in TFEU. If the more stringent measures amount to restrictions on the free movement guaranteed by TFEU they are unlawful. It has been a contentious issue for example in regard to some national working environment provisions how high a level the Member States can establish without restricting the free movement in a way that is incompatible with the Treaties, see further in Chapter Nine on Working environment law. The tension between the fundamental right of workers to take collective action (strike, blockade, etc.) and the free movement rights of employers under the Treaties has also been much debated, see e.g. *Laval*[48] and *Viking*[49] and further below in Chapter Three on Collective Labour Law and Chapter Seven on Posting of Workers.

In matters of *gender equality* in occupation and employment, the EU has – assessed by the wording of the legal base – in principle competence under Article 157(3) TFEU to adopt both minimum and full harmonisation. So far all the gender equality directives have contained clauses that allow the Member States to go further in the direction of equality. Under Article 19 TFEU there is also – assessed by the wording of that provision – competence to adopt both minimum and full harmonisation in order to combat *discrimination based on sex, racial or ethnic origin, religion or belief, disability, age or sexual orientation.* Directives based on this legal base have so far also contained clauses to the effect that the directives only contain minimum requirements.173 In discrimination law, the EU has thus left the Member States free to set a higher standard of equality than the minimum required by EU law even though it, under the present FEU Treaty – assessed by the wording of the text of the Treaty – would be possible for the EU to adopt full harmonisation.

48. Case C-341/05 *Laval* [2007] ECR I-11767.
49. Case C-438/05 *Viking* [2007] ECR I-10779.

In my view, it does, however, follow from the fundamental human rights character of the prohibition against discrimination and the constitutional context that the Member States are free to choose a higher standard of protection than the one chosen in EU law. In favour of this interpretation, the *Deutsche Telekom*-cases[50] on equal pay may be invoked. These cases were about violations by a German employer (Deutsche Telekom) of the equal pay principle by excluding German part-time workers from pension schemes. Because most part-time workers are women, such exclusion is indirect sex discrimination in violation of the equal pay rules in both EU law and national German law. The German rules apply to periods from the coming into force of the German Grundgesetz in 1949. Article 157 TFEU (ext art. 119 EC and 141 EC) is only directly applicable against employers in regard to equal pay in periods after 8 April 1976, i.e. the date of the jurdgment in *Defrenne II*.

The CJEU held that Article 157 TFEU does not preclude provisions of a Member State which lay down a principle of equal treatment by virtue of which part-time workers are entitled to retroactive membership of an occupational pension scheme and to receive a pension under that scheme, notwithstanding the risk of distortions of competition between economic operators of the various Member States to the detriment of employers established in the first Member State. The application of national law cannot be held to be contrary to the principle of non-discrimination on grounds of nationality merely because other Member States allegedly apply less strict rules. Moreover, *the economic aim pursued by Article 157 TFEU, namely the elimination of distortions of competition between undertakings established in different Member States, is secondary to its social aim, which constitutes the expression of a fundamental human right not to be discriminated against on grounds of sex*. A special time limitation at 17 May 1990 was fixed for pension matters.[51] German law was thus more favourable for discriminated women than EU law. The workers in the Deutsche Telekom cases claimed equal pay for periods for which they had such a claim under German law but not under EU law. The employer Deutsche Telekom asserted that EU law on equal pay – Article 157 FEU – should be interpreted as a maximum provision in order to protect German employers from being treated by stricter standards than employers in other EU countries. Deutsche Telekom did therefore not accept that it should respect the equal pay principle in pension matters for periods before 17 May 1990.

50. Case C-50/96 *Schröder* [2000] ECR I-743, case C-270/97 *Sievers* [2000] ECR I-929 and Joined Case C-234/96 and C-235/96 *Vick et al.* [2000] ECR I-799.
51. In Case C-262/88 *Barber* [1990] ECR I-1889.

As is well known, see above in section 2.2, the EU protection of fundamental rights has been developed in dialogue with the highest national courts partly as a means to ensure their acceptance of the supremacy of EU law over national law. The German Bundesverfassungsgericht has only accepted that EU law takes precedence over German law as long as (So-lange) EU law protects fundamental rights as well as German law does. If EU law on equality and discrimination was interpreted as setting a maximum, the pre-conditions for Germany's acceptance of the supremacy of EU law would no longer be fulfilled. It is therefore not likely that the CJEU will interpret EU equality and anti-discrimination provisions as maximum rules.

A few of the directives with particular relevance for employment, e.g. the posting of workers directive,[52] are adopted on the basis of the general legal basis for *internal market directives* in Article 114 TFEU[53] where the EU – to the difference from the rule in Article 153 TFEU on labour law which only provides for minimum directives – has competence to full harmonization. In working environment matters there is an interaction between internal market directives on free movement of goods, chemical substances, etc. that are based on full harmonization and working environment minimum directives protecting the health and safety of the workers on the basis of Article 153 TFEU. There is a residuary legal basis in Article 352 TFEU.[54]

52. 96/71/EC, see further chapter Three.
53. Article 114 TFEU provides in subsection 1-3: 1. Save where otherwise provided in the Treaties, the following provisions shall apply for the achievement of the objectives set out in Article 26. The European Parliament and the Council shall, acting in accordance with the ordinary legislative procedure and after consulting the Economic and Social Committee, adopt the measures for the approximation of the provisions laid down by law, regulation or administrative action in Member States which have as their object the establishment and functioning of the internal market.
2. Paragraph 1 shall not apply to fiscal provisions, to those relating to the free movement of persons nor to those relating to the rights and interests of employed persons.
3. The Commission, in its proposals envisaged in paragraph 1 concerning health, safety, environmental protection and consumer protection, will take as a base a high level of protection, taking account in particular of any new development based on scientific facts. Within their respective powers, the European Parliament and the Council will also seek to achieve this objective.
54. Which provides: If action by the Union should prove necessary, within the framework of the policies defined in the Treaties, to attain one of the objectives set out in the Treaties, and the Treaties have not provided the necessary powers, the Council, acting unanimously on a proposal from the Commission and after obtaining the consent of the European Parliament, shall adopt the appropriate measures. Where the

3.1.7 From Unanimity to Qualified Majority Voting in Council

When the EC/EU was established in 1958, secondary legislation in the labour law field could only be adopted unanimously. Over the years that has been changed. Today, secondary labour legislation can be adopted by majority voting on nearly all issues. [55]

The voting procedure of the Council of the European Union currently (2013) operates on a system laid down by the Treaty of Nice. The Treaty of Lisbon replaces the system, but only from 2014. Under Article 16(3) TEU, the Council shall act by a qualified majority except where the Treaties provide otherwise. When the ordinary legislative procedure defined in Article 294 TFEU is used, legal acts are thus adopted by qualified majority voting in Council. As from 1 November 2014, a qualified majority shall be defined as at least 55 % of the members of the Council, comprising at least fifteen of them and representing Member States comprising at least 65 % of the population of the Union. A blocking minority must include at least four Council members, failing which the qualified majority shall be deemed attained.[56] The Treaty of Lisbon generally extended the areas where decisions can be taken by qualified majority in comparison to the Treaty of Nice. Of relevance to labour law, it may be noticed that that for example is the case in regard to services of general economic interest (Article 14 TFEU) and social security (Article 48 TFEU).

3.2 Fundamental Rights, in particular Fundamental Labour and Employment Rights in the EU

Fundamental rights in EU law appeared first in the case law of the CJEU. It was originally introduced by the CJEU mainly as a means to ensure acceptance by national supreme courts in particular in Germany and Italy of its case law on supremacy and direct effect. With regard to the labour market the case law of the CJEU on fundamental rights mainly covers equality and non-

measures in question are adopted by the Council in accordance with a special legislative procedure, it shall also act unanimously on a proposal from the Commission and after obtaining the consent of the European Parliament.

55. See, however, Article 153(2 in fine) quoted above which provides: In the fields referred to in paragraph 1(c), (d), (f) and (g), the Council shall act unanimously, in accordance with a special legislative procedure, after consulting the European Parliament and the said Committees. The Council, acting unanimously on a proposal from the Commission, after consulting the European Parliament, may decide to render the ordinary legislative procedure applicable to paragraph 1(d), (f) and (g).
56. See Article 16(4) TEU. The other arrangements governing the qualified majority are laid down in Article 238(2) TFEU.

discrimination. The background to the provisions on Solidarity in the CFREU are mainly found in soft loft law, in particular the the Community Charter of Fundamental Rights of Workers from 1989 and in international labour law, in particular the Council of Europe Social Charter 1961 and the revised European Social Charter 1996.

3.2.1 The Case Law of the CJEU on Fundamental Rights

Since 1970, the CEUJ has developed a case law on fundamental rights. Starting in the late nineteen sixties, increasing concern was expressed in the courts of Germany and Italy on the question as to whether the fundamental rights guaranteed in their national constitutions were recognized and protected within EU law. In response to the threat that national courts would opt for the supremacy of their own national constitutional provisions on fundamental rights protection, the CJEU held that the protection of fundamental rights was a general principle of EU law. In 1969 in *Stauder*,[57] the CJEU for the first time stated that fundamental rights were enshrined in the general principles of Community law and protected by the Court. In *Internationale Handelsgesellschaft* the reference to fundamental rights was expanded by the Court stating that respect for fundamental rights forms an integral part of the general principles of law protected by the CJEU and that these principles were inspired by the *constitutional traditions* common to the Member States.[58] In 1974, the CJEU held in *Nold* that, in addition to Member States' constitutional traditions, *international conventions* could also supply guidelines which could be taken into consideration by the Court on matters concerning claims to fundamental rights.[59] In particular, the ECHR has a special significance in this respect.

The first time fundamental rights were specifically referred to in a labour law case was in 1975 in *Rutili*.[60] In *Rutili*, a migrant Italian worker in France was prohibited from residing in four departments in France. It was clear from the file on the case and from information supplied to the CJEU that the reason for the measures taken against him was that his political and trade union activities during 1967 and 1968 were the subject of complaint. His presence in the departments covered by the decision was for this reason regarded as 'likely to disturb public policy'. The CJEU stated that the concept of public policy used in Article 45(3) TFEU must, where it is used as a justification for dero-

57. Case 29/69 *Stauder* v *Ulm* [1969] ECR 419.
58. Case 11/70 *Internationale Handelsgesellschaft* [1970] ECR 1125.
59. Case 4/73 *Nold* [1974] ECR 491.
60. Case 36/75 *Rutili* v *Minister of the Interior* [1975] ECR 1219.

gating from the *fundamental principles of equality of treatment and freedom of movement for workers* (emphasis added), be interpreted strictly. Taken as a whole, the limitations placed on the powers of Member States in respect of control of aliens are in the view of the CJEU a specific manifestation of the more general principle, enshrined in Articles 8, 9, 10 and 11 ECHR. The CJEU thus characterised both the right to free movement and the limitations on free movement rights as expressions of general and fundamental principles.

In *Defrenne III*,[61] the CJEU stated that there can be no doubt that the elimination of discrimination based on sex forms part of the fundamental rights.

In *Prais*,[62] a Jewish plaintiff complained about a test for recruitment as translator with the Council being held on a date on which she could not participate on grounds of her religion. The CEUJ held that if a candidate informs the appointing authority that religious reasons make certain dates impossible for him the appointing authority should take this into account in fixing the date for written tests and endeavor to avoid such dates. On the other hand if the candidate does not inform the appointing authority in good time of his difficulties, the appointing authority would be justified in refusing to afford an alternative date, particularly if there are other candidates who have been convoked for the test. In *Maurissen*,[63] the CJEU held that in staff cases an EU institution must respect the principle of good administration. In *Dunnett*, [64] the CJEU stated that the European Investment Bank in a staff case was bound to consult staff representatives under a general principle of employment law before taking a decision to withdraw a benefit. In *Laval*[65] and *Viking*,[66] the CJEU stated that the right to take collective action must be recognised as a fundamental right which forms an integral part of the general principles of EU law. In *BECTU*,[67] the advocate general argued that the right to paid annual leave is not only guaranteed in the Working Time Directive but also constitutes a fundamental right. In *Mangold*,[68] the CJEU held that the principle of non-discrimination on grounds of age is a general principle of EU law. The

61. Case 149/77 *Defrenne III* [1978] ECR 1365.
62. Case 130/75 *Prais* [1976] ECR 1589.
63. Case 417/85 [1987] ECR 551.
64. Case T-192/99 *Dunnett* [2001] ECR II-813; FP-I-A-65; FP-II-313.
65. Case C-341/05 *Laval* [2007] ECR I-11767.
66. Case C-438/05 *Viking* [2007] ECR I-10779.
67. Case C-173/99 [2001] ECR I-4881.
68. Case C-144/04 *Mangold* [2005] ECR I-9981.

Court held, under the application of the *Simmenthal* rationale,[69] that the national court, must set aside any provision of national law which may conflict with EU law, in the particular case at hand with the general principle of non-discrimination.

The EU protection of general principles and fundamental rights has been developed in dialogue with the highest national courts partly as a means to ensure their acceptance of the supremacy of EU law over national law. The German *Bundesverfassungsgericht* has only accepted that EU law takes precedence over German law as long as (*Solange*) EU law protects fundamental rights as well as German law does. As Weiler stated:[70]

> 'The surface language of the Court in Stauder and its progeny is the language of human rights. The deep structure all about supremacy ... [It was] an attempt to protect the concept of supremacy threatened because of the apparent (largely theoretical) inadequate protection of human rights in the original Treaty.'

In 1967, the German *Bundesverfassungsgericht* held that a constitutional complaint against regulations adopted by the Council and the Commission of the EC/EU was not admissible under German law. It added, however, (emphasis added):[71]

> 'Die Entscheidung beschränkt sich auf den Ausspruch, daß das Bundesverfassungsgericht nicht unmittelbar mit der Verfassungsbeschwerde gegen Verordnungen des Rates und der Kommission der EWG angerufen werden kann.
>
> Nicht entschieden ist damit, ob und in welchem Umfang das Bundesverfassungsgericht im Rahmen eines zulässigerweise bei ihm anhängig gemachten Verfahrens *Gemeinschaftsrecht an den Grundrechtsnormen des Grundgesetzes messen kann.*'

The German *Bundesverfassungsgericht* addressed its relation to the CJEU in 1974 in the *Solange I* decision. The *Bundesverfassungsgericht* reserved the right to review the compatibility of EU law with the German Constitution as long as the integration process had not progressed so far that EU law also receives a catalogue of fundamental rights decided on by a parliament and of settled validity, which is adequate in comparison with the catalogue of fundamental rights contained in the German Constitution.[72] In its *Solange II* de-

69. Case 106/77 *Simmenthal* [1978] ECR 629.
70. Cited from Coppel, Jason and Adrian O'Neill: The European Court of Justice: Taking Rights Seriously?, Common Market Law Review 1992, p. 669.
71. BVerfGE 22, 293.
72. The German original reads: 'Solange der Integrationsprozeß der Gemeinschaft nicht so weit fortgeschritten ist, daß das Gemeinschaftsrecht auch einen von einem Parla-

cision from 1986, the *Bundesverfassungsgericht* modified its *Solange I* decision and noted in its *Solange II* decision that a measure of protection of fundamental rights had been established in the case law of the CJEU concerning fundamental rights, which in its conception, substance and manner of implementation is essentially comparable with the standards of fundamental rights provided for in the *Grundgesetz*. The *Bundesverfassungsgericht* therefore changed its '*Solange I* formula' into the following: the *Bundesverfassungsgericht* would no longer review secondary EU law on the basis of German fundamental rights norms as long as the European Communities, and in particular the case law of the European Court, generally ensure an effective protection of fundamental rights as against the sovereign powers of the Communities which is to be regarded substantially similar to the protection of fundamental rights required unconditionally by the Constitution, and insofar as they generally safeguard the essential content of fundamental rights.[73]

On 30 June 2009, the German *Bundesverfassungsgericht* assessed the compatibility of the Treaty of Lisbon with German law, judging that there are no decisive constitutional objections to the German Act Approving the Treaty of Lisbon.[74]

ment beschlossenen und in Geltung stehenden formulierten Katalog von Grundrechten enthält, der dem Grundrechtskatalog des Grundgesetzes adäquat ist, ist nach Einholung der in Art. 177 EWGV geforderten Entscheidung des Europäischen Gerichtshofes die Vorlage eines Gerichts der Bundesrepublik Deutschland an das Bundesverfassungsgericht im Normenkontrollverfahren zulässig und geboten, wenn das Gericht die für es entscheidungserhebliche Vorschrift des Gemeinschaftsrechts in der vom Europäischen Gerichtshof gegebenen Auslegung für unanwendbar hält, weil und soweit sie mit einem der Grundrechte des Grundgesetzes kollidiert.' See BVerfGE 37, 271 – *Solange I*.

73. The German original reads: 'Solange die Europäischen Gemeinschaften, insbesondere die Rechtsprechung des Gerichtshofs der Gemeinschaften einen wirksamen Schutz der Grundrechte gegenüber der Hoheitsgewalt der Gemeinschaften generell gewährleisten, der dem vom Grundgesetz als unabdingbar gebotenen Grundrechtsschutz im wesentlichen gleichzuachten ist, zumal den Wesensgehalt der Grundrechte generell verbürgt, wird das Bundesverfassungsgericht seine Gerichtsbarkeit über die Anwendbarkeit von abgeleitetem Gemeinschaftsrecht, das als Rechtsgrundlage für ein Verhalten deutscher Gerichte oder Behörden im Hoheitsbereich der Bundesrepublik Deutschland in Anspruch genommen wird, nicht mehr ausüben und dieses Recht mithin nicht mehr am Maßstab der Grundrechte des Grundgesetzes überprüfen; entsprechende Vorlagen nach Art. 100 Abs. 1 GG sind somit unzulässig.' See BVerfGE 73, 339 – *Solange II*, available at http://www.servat.unibe.ch/fallrecht/bv073339.html.
74. Judgment on 30 June 2009, Bundesverfassungsgericht, BVerfG, 2 BvE 2/08.

3.2.2 The 1977 Joint Declaration on Fundamental Rights and the ECHR

5 April 1977, the European Parliament, the Council and the Commission issued a joint declaration[75] in which they stressed the prime importance they attached to the protection of fundamental rights, as derived in particular from the constitutions of the Member States and the ECHR. The CJEU has occasionally referred to this Declaration.[76]

3.2.3 The Community Charter of the Fundamental Social Rights of Workers 1989

In 1989,[77] eleven of the then 12 members of the EC adopted the Community Charter of Fundamental Rights of Workers[78] as a piece of soft law. Under this Charter, the EU is obliged to provide for the fundamental social rights of workers under the following headings:

Freedom of movement (Articles 1 to 3)
Employment and remuneration (Articles 4 to 6)
Improvement of living and working conditions (Articles 7 to 9)
Social protection (Article 10)
Freedom of association and collective bargaining (Articles 11 to 14)
Vocational training (Article 15)
Equal treatment for men and women (Article 16)
Information and consultation and participation for workers (Articles 17 to 18)
Health protection and safety at the workplace (Article 19)
Protection of children and adolescents (Articles 20 to 23)
Elderly persons (Articles 24 to 25)
Disabled persons (Article 26)
Member States' action (implementation) (Articles 27 to 30)

75. OJ 1977 C 103.
76. See for example Case 44/79 *Hauer* [1979] ECR 3727 and Case 222/84 *Johnston* [1986] ECR 1651.
77. Bercusson, Brian: The European Community's Charter of Fundamental Social Rights of Workers, The Modern Law Review, Vol. 53, 1990 p. 624.
78. That Charter is not published in the Official Journal but there are several publications of it, including at the internet. In this book I have used the one found at Eurofound at http://www.aedh.eu/plugins/fckeditor/userfiles/file/Conventions%20internationales/Community_Charter_of_the_Fundamental_Social_Rights_of_Workers.pdf. Eurofound is a tripartite EU agency which provides expertise on living and working conditions, industrial relations and managing change in Europe, see further http://www.eurofound.europa.eu/index.htm.

The Charter represents a commitment by the Member States to a set of social policy and labour law objectives. Article 28 stipulates: 'The European Council invites the Commission to submit as soon as possible initiatives which fall within its powers, as provided for in the Treaties, with a view to the adoption of legal instruments for the effective implementation, as and when the internal market is completed, of those rights, which come within the Community's area of competence.'

The Community Charter of the Fundamental Social Rights of Workers 1989 is soft law, since, due to the opposition of the UK government, the Charter could not be integrated into the EC Treaty in 1989. The UK eventually acceded to the Charter, following the election of a new government in UK in May 1997.

There are references to the 1989 Charter on Workers both in Article 136 EEC and in the explanatory remarks to the CFREU.[79]

3.2.4 Treaty Provisions, in particular Article 6 TEU and Article 151 TFEU

The original Treaty of Rome 1957 did not contain specific provisions on the protection of fundamental rights. Article 6 EU was first included in the EU Treaty (the Treaty of Maastricht), signed in 1992, and was subsequently amended by the Treaty of Amsterdam in 1997 and the Treaty of Lisbon which substantially revised Article 6 EU which now (post Lisbon) reads (foot note added):

1. The Union recognises the rights, freedoms and principles set out in the Charter of Fundamental Rights of the European Union of 7 December 2000, as adapted at Strasbourg, on 12 December 2007, which shall have the same legal value as the Treaties.

The provisions of the Charter shall not extend in any way the competences of the Union as defined in the Treaties.

The rights, freedoms and principles in the Charter shall be interpreted in accordance with the general provisions in Title VII of the Charter governing its interpretation and application and with due regard to the explanations[80] referred to in the Charter, that set out the sources of those provisions.

2. The Union shall accede to the European Convention for the Protection of Human Rights and Fundamental Freedoms. Such accession shall not affect the Union's competences as defined in the Treaties.

79. See OJ 2007 C 303.
80. See OJ 2007 C 303.

3. Fundamental rights, as guaranteed by the European Convention for the Protection of Human Rights and Fundamental Freedoms and as they result from the constitutional traditions common to the Member States, shall constitute general principles of the Union's law.

The original Treaty of Rome 1957 did not contain specific provisions on the protection of fundamental rights. Article 6 EU was first included in the Treaty on European Union (the Maastricht Treaty), signed in 1992, and was subsequently amended by the Amsterdam Treaty in 1997. Pre-Lisbon it provided that the Union must respect fundamental rights as guaranteed by the ECHR and as they result from the constitutional traditions common to the Member States, as general principles of Community law.

3.2.5 The Charter of Fundamental Rights of the European Union (CFREU) 2000/2007

In 1999, when the European Council decided to draw up a Charter of Fundamental Rights of the European Union it adopted some broad guidelines on what the Charter should contain. It declared (emphasis added):[81]

The European Council believes that this Charter should contain the fundamental rights and freedoms as well as basic procedural rights guaranteed by the *European Convention for the Protection of Human Rights* and Fundamental Freedoms and derived from the *constitutional traditions common to the Member States*, as general principles of Community law. The Charter should also include the *fundamental rights that pertain only to the Union's citizens*. In drawing up such a Charter account should furthermore be taken of *economic and social rights as contained in the European Social Charter and the Community Charter of the Fundamental Social Rights of Workers* (Article 136 TEC), insofar as they do not merely establish objectives for action by the Union.

81. Conclusions of the presidency of the European Council of Cologne (3 and 4 June 1999) on the drawing up of a Charter of Fundamental Rights of the European Union, Annex 4 p. 43, available at http://www.consilium.europa.eu/ueDocs/newsWord/en/ec/57886.doc. See on the background to the Charter de Búrca, Gráinne: The drafting of the European Union Charter of fundamental rights, European Law Review 2001 p. 126, Lammy Betten: The EU Charter of Fundamental Rights: a Trojan Horse or a Mouse?, International Journal of Comparative Labour Law and Industrial Relations 2001 p. 151, Deirdre Curtin: The EU Human Rights Charter and the Union Legal Order: the 'Banns' before the Marriage?, in D O' Keeffe and A. Bavasso (eds), Liber Amicorum in honour of Lord Slynn of Hadley: Judicial review in European Union Law, Kluwer 2000, Engel, Christoph: The European Charter of Fundamental Rights: A Changed Political Opportunity Structure and its Normative Consequences, European Law Journal 2001 p. 151 and Fredman, Sandra, Christopher McCrudden and Mark Freedland: An EU Charter of Fundamental Rights, Public Law 2000 p. 178.

According to the Article 6 (1)(3) TEU, the CFREU shall be interpreted in accordance with the general provisions in Title VII of the Charter governing its interpretation and application and with due regard to the explanations referred to in the Charter, that set out the sources of those provisions.[82]

3.2.6 Changes in the Legal Basis of Fundamental Rights after the Lisbon Treaty

As mentioned, the Lisbon Treaty substantially revised Article 6 TEU. The most important change relates to the legal status of the CFREU. Article 51 CFREU stipulates that the provisions of the CFREU are addressed to the institutions, bodies and organs of the EU with due regard for the principle of subsidiarity and to the Member States only when they are implementing Union law.

The question whether the EU can accede to the ECHR was answered in the negative in 1996.[83] The amended Article 6(2) TEU provides that the Union shall accede to the ECHR. The new Article 6(3) EU builds on the existing Article 6(2) which has been used extensively by the CJEU in developing its fundamental rights jurisprudence. Article 6(3) EU provides that Fundamental rights, as guaranteed by the ECHR and as they result from the constitutional traditions common to the Member States, shall constitute general principles of the Union's law.

Article 53 CFREU provides on the level of protection that nothing in the Charter shall be interpreted as restricting or adversely affecting human rights and fundamental freedoms as recognised, in their respective fields of application, by EU law and international law and by the Member States' constitutions. The Charter does thus not lower the already existing level of protection (the *acquis*). In EU labour law there are more extensive rights on a number of issues covered by the solidarity provisions in the Charter.[84]

82. The Explanatory remarks are published in OJ 2007 C 303.
83. Opinion 2/94 [1996] I-1759.
84. See on the CFREU and the gender equality *acquis* Sophia Koukoulis-Spiliotopoulos: The Lisbon Treaty and the Charter of Fundamental Rights: maintaining and developing the *acquis* in gender equality, European Gender Equality Law Review 2008-1, available at http://ec.europa.eu/employment_social/gender_equality/docs/2008/egelr_2008_final_en.pdf.

3.2.7 Substantive Content of the CFREU

There are seven chapters in the CFREU: Title I. Dignity;[85] Title II. Freedoms;[86] Title III. Equality;[87] Title IV. Solidarity;[88] Title V. Citizens' Rights;[89] Title VI. Justice[90] and Title VII. General Provisions. The CFREU contains 50 'rights, freedoms and principles without identifying which of its provisions are rights, which are freedoms and which are principles. The individual Charter provisions from Title III and IV on Equality and Solidarity are dealt with in the following Chapters where they fit in according to their substantive content.

The substantive content of welfare rights listed in the Charter does not go further than the CJEU could potentially have gone on the basis of the established criteria for recognizing fundamental rights in the EU but. The Charter explicitly mentions some rights that have not hitherto been declared fundamental rights in the case law of the CJEU as for example the right to free placement service in Article 29 CFREU.

85. This title includes: human dignity, right to life, right to integrity of the person, prohibition of torture and inhuman or degrading treatment or punishment and prohibition of slavery and forced labour.
86. This title includes: right to liberty and security, respect for private and family life, protection of personal data, right to marry and right to found a family, freedom of thought, conscience and religion, freedom of expression and information, freedom of assembly and of association, freedom of the arts and sciences, right to education, freedom to choose an occupation and right to engage in work, freedom to conduct a business, right to property, right to asylum and protection in the event of removal, expulsion or extradition.
87. This title includes: equality before the law, non-discrimination, cultural, religious and linguistic diversity, equality between men and women, the rights of the child, the rights of the elderly and integration of persons with disabilities.
88. This title includes: workers' right to information and consultation within the undertaking, right of collective bargaining and action, right of access to placement services, protection in the event of unjustified dismissal, fair and just working conditions, prohibition of child labour and protection of young people at work, family and professional life, social security and social assistance, health care, access to services of general economic interest, environmental protection and consumer protection.
89. This title includes: right to vote and to stand as a candidate at elections to the European Parliament, right to vote and to stand as a candidate at municipal elections, right to good administration, right of access to documents, ombudsman, right to petition, freedom of movement and of residence and diplomatic and consular protection.
90. This title includes: right to an effective remedy and to a fair trial, presumption of innocence and right of defence, principles of legality and proportionality of criminal offences and penalties and the right not to be tried or punished twice in criminal proceedings for the same criminal offence.

3.2.8 Legal Effect of Fundamental Rights internally in EU law

Fundamental rights and general principles of EU law are binding on the institutions of the EU in the exercise of their powers, i.e. at EU level. Decisions have been struck down by the CJEU in staff cases for non-compliance with fundamental rights, see the *Dunnett*[91] and *Maurissen* cases.[92] It also happens that provisions in secondary legislation are considered invalid because they violate fundamental rights, see as a example *Test Achats*.[93]

According to most existing EU law literature, the CJEU applies a teleological method of interpretation and often finds support in provisions in preambles. In *Palacios de la Villa* on age discrimination and *Maruko* on sexual orientation discrimination,[94] the CJEU, however, held that provisions in preambles cannot limit the fundamental principle of non□discrimination.

3.2.9 Legal Effect in National Law of CFREU and other Fundamental Rights and General Principles of EU Law

It is generally a condition for direct effect that the provision at issue is sufficiently precise. After the coming into force of the Lisbon Treaty *CFREU* has according to Article 6 TEU the same legal value as the treaties (TEU and TFEU). Some of the provisions in the Charter are reasonably precise. That is, in particular the case with Article 20[95] on Equality before the law, the prohibition against discrimination in Article 21[96] in respect of the specifically enumerated grounds, Article 24, on the rights of the child, Article 29[97] on free placement services and Article 31(2) on paid annual leave. Many of the labour law provisions in the CFREU are, however, vague and for that reason not directly applicable. See for example the open end of Article 21 which

91. Case T-192/99 *Dunnett* [2001] ECR II-813; FP-I-A-65 ; FP-II-313.
92. Joined Cases C-193/87 and C-194/87 *Maurissen and European Public Service Union* [1990] ECR I-95.
93. Case C-236/09 *Test Achats* [2011] I-773.
94. Case C-411/05, *Palacios de la Villa* [2007] ECR I-8531 and Case C-267/06, *Maruko* [2008] ECR I-1757.
95. Article 20 on Equality before the law reads: 'Everyone is equal before the law.'
96. Article 21 on Non-discrimination reads: '1. Any discrimination based on any ground such as sex, race, colour, ethnic or social origin, genetic features, language, religion or belief, political or any other opinion, membership of a national minority, property, birth, disability, age or sexual orientation shall be prohibited.
    2. Within the scope of application of the Treaties and without prejudice to any of their specific provisions, any discrimination on grounds of nationality shall be prohibited.'
97. Article 29 on the Right of access to placement services reads: 'Everyone has the right of access to a free placement service.'

prohibits discrimination on any grounds, Article 25 on the rights of the elderly, Article 34 on social security and social assistance, Article 35 on health care and Article 36 on access to services of general economic interest. If they acquire the same value as the Treaties they can be relied on in the same way as the CJEU has relied on Article 151 TFEU in the interpretation of other provisions. I will discuss the possible horizontal and vertical direct effect of the individual Charter provisions in the following Chapters where they fit in because of their substantive content.

CFREU and other fundamental rights are according to the case law of the CJREU binding in the Member States both vertically and horizontally but only when the Member States act in the scope of Union law. It is, however, not very clear when a Member States can be said to act in the scope of EU law.

According to Article 51 CFREU, the Charter is in addition to the institutions, bodies, offices and agencies of the EU also addressed to the Member States but only when they are *implementing* Union law. In the Explanations to Article 51 CFREU it is stated (emphasis added) that:

> As regards the Member States, it follows unambiguously from the case-law of the Court of Justice that the requirement to respect fundamental rights defined in the context of the Union is only binding on the Member States when they act *in the scope of Union law* (judgment of 13 July 1989, Case C-5/88 Wachauf [1989] ECR 2609; judgment of 18 June 1991, Case C-260/89 ERT [1991] ECR I-2925; judgment of 18 December 1997, Case C-309/96 Annibaldi [1997] ECR I-7493).

The applicability of EU fundamental rights internally in the Member States is very important for EU labour law. The principle laid down in Article 51 CFREU according to which EU fundamental rights are binding on the Member States when they act in the scope of Union law applies both to those fundamental rights that are explicitly laid down in the CFREU and to other fundamental rights that can be derived from the case law of the CJEU or scholarly interpretation. It is not entirely clear when a situation in a Member State can be interpreted as happening in the scope of Union law.

The situation must be linked to EU law by another legal provision than the fundamental right whose direct applicability is at issue. Freedom of expression is for example a fundamental right in CFREU Article 11[98] but that does not mean that all conflicts between employers and employees about the em-

98. Article 11 CFREU provides: 1. Everyone has the right to freedom of expression. This right shall include freedom to hold opinions and to receive and impart information and ideas without interference by public authority and regardless of frontiers. 2. The freedom and pluralism of the media shall be respected.

ployees' exercise of their freedom of expression are happening in the scope of EU law. Only if a conflict about freedom of expression arises in a situation that is governed by EU law will that be the case. Collective redundancies are, e.g. governed by an EU-directive.[99] If an employer when making collective redundancies select employees to be dismissed on grounds of the way they have exercised their freedom of expression will CFREU Article 11 (probably) apply directly because the situation is in the scope of EU law, see further in Chapter Eights on Restructuring of Businesses.

The expression 'Situations that happen in the scope of EU law' covers at least:

1. situations with cross-border elements where the free movement rules apply and
2. situations where a Member State is implementing a directive, including situations where they go further than the requirements laid down in a minimum directive and including national enforcement measures

If there are cross-border elements in the case and the free movement rules apply they must be balanced against the fundamental rights. In its case law, the CJEU has required Member States to respect the fundamental rights not only when they transpose an EU rule into national law but also when they take measures that may hinder the free movement of persons, services and capital. In *Carpenter*,[100] the CJEU thus stated that a Member State may invoke reasons of public interest to justify a national measure which is likely to obstruct the exercise of the freedom to provide services only if that measure is compatible with the fundamental rights whose observance the Court ensures. In support of this interpretation it referred to *ERT*[101] and *Familiapress*.[102] As a result of this case law migrant workers when exercising their right of free movement will be able to invoke the social rights of the CFREU, even though comparable domestic workers would not be able to do this because the situation in relation to them would be purely internal and therefore not happen in the scope of EU law.

99. 98/59/EC.
100. Case C-60/00 *Carpenter* [2002] I-6279, paragraph 40.
101. Case C-260/89 *ERT* [1991] ECR I-2925, paragraph 43.
102. Case C-368/95 *Familiapress* [1997] ECR I-3689, paragraph 24.

It is clear that the Member States have a duty to observe EU fundamental rights when they transpose a directive, see *Wachauf*[103] where the CJEU held (emphasis added):

The Court has consistently held, in particular in its judgment of 13 December 1979 in Case 44/79 Hauer v Land Rheinland-Pfalz [1979] ECR 3727, that fundamental rights form an integral part of the general principles of the law, the observance of which is ensured by the Court. In safeguarding those rights, the Court has to look to the constitutional traditions common to the Member States, so that measures which are incompatible with the fundamental rights recognized by the constitutions of those States may not find acceptance in the Community. International treaties concerning the protection of human rights on which the Member States have collaborated or to which they have acceded can also supply guidelines to which regard should be had in the context of Community law.

The fundamental rights recognized by the Court are not absolute, however, but must be considered in relation to their *social function*. Consequently, restrictions may be imposed on the exercise of those rights, in particular in the context of a common organization of a market, provided that those restrictions in fact correspond to *objectives of general interest pursued by the Community and do not constitute, with regard to the aim pursued, a disproportionate and intolerable interference, impairing the very substance of those rights*.

Having regard to those criteria, it must be observed that Community rules which, upon the expiry of the lease, had the effect of depriving the lessee, without compensation, of the fruits of his labour and of his investments in the tenanted holding would be incompatible with the requirements of the protection of fundamental rights in the Community legal order. Since *those requirements are also binding on the Member States when they implement Community rules*, the Member States must, as far as possible, apply those rules in accordance with those requirements.

As stated above most employment directives are *minimum directives*. When Member States implement a minimum directive they still have competence to go further in the direction prescribed by the directive than they are required to do. As set out above Article 153(4) TFEU provides that the provisions adopted pursuant to this Article shall not prevent any Member State from maintaining or introducing more stringent protective measures compatible with the Treaties. If they chose to do that one can ask if they only have to respect the fundamental rights in the part of the national implementation they are required to do or whether they also have to respect the fundamental rights in the 'voluntary' part where they go further than they have to. Can they for example lay down rules above the minimum requirements of the directive that are more advantageous for the workers than required by the directive and then limit the advantage to some age groups?

103. Case C-5/88 *Wachauf* [ECR] 1989 p. 2609.

The problem can be illustrated by the *Mangold* case.[104] CJEU held already in *Mangold* – before the coming into force of the Lisbon Treaty and the elevation of CFREU in the hierarchy of the sources of law – that the principle of prohibition of age discrimination in employment was a general principle which could be relied upon directly against an individual employer.

The Mangold case was about fixed term contracts. Such contracts are governed by a directive[105] which prohibits too many successive fixed term contracts but does not require the Member States to introduce any specific rules about the first fixed term employment contract, see further below in Chapter Seven on Employment contracts. Germany had adopted a rule prescribing that it was only valid to enter into a fixed term employment contract if the employer had objective reasons to choose a fixed-term contract and not an open-ended employment contract. This rule that was more protective for the workers than the minimum rule required by the directive did, however, only apply to employees under 52. Employers could enter into fixed-term contracts with employees over 52 at will without any objective reason. Mangold was over 52 and claimed in a suit against the employer that he had been unlawfully discriminated against on grounds of age. The facts of *Mangold* took place before the dead-line for implementation of the employment framework directive[106] which prohibits age discrimination in employment. The CJEU held that the prohibition against age discrimination is a general principle of EU law. It is the responsibility of the national court to guarantee the full effectiveness of that general principle, setting aside any provision of national law which may conflict with EU law, see for more detail below in Chapter Six on Equality and Discrimination.

In regard to the problem we are discussing here, whether a Member State which chooses to implement a minimum directive in a way that is more favourable to (some of) the workers than required by the directive thereby brings the situation within the scope of EU law, the answer given by the CJEU is thus yes. That is very important in regard to labour law. Today, most employment and labour relations happen in situations that are either governed by transposed minimum directives or by national law laying down a higher standard than required by the directive. In all those situations the fundamental rights and general principles of EU law are binding in national law.

104. Case C-144/04 *Mangold* [2005] ECR I-9981.
105. Council Directive 99/70/EC of 28 June 1999 concerning the framework agreement on fixed-term work concluded by ETUC, UNICE and CEEP.
106. 2000/78/EC.

If not otherwise stated, the Member States are free to choose the procedures and sanctions they will use to *enforce* a directive. They must, however, observe the EU fundamental rights and general principles in that context. In *Cavallero*,[107] the CJEU stated in regard to the protection of employees in the event of their employer's insolvency that Member States must, as far as possible, apply EU provisions in accordance with the requirements of the fundamental rights. Fundamental rights include the general principle of equality and non-discrimination. That principle precludes comparable situations from being treated in a different manner unless the difference in treatment is objectively justified. It was clear that, under Spanish law, all workers who are unfairly dismissed are in the same situation in the sense that they are entitled to 'salarios de tramitación'. However, in the event of the employer's insolvency, the Workers' Statute treated dismissed workers differently to the extent that the right to payment by the guarantee institution[108] of claims relating to 'salarios de tramitación' is acknowledged only in respect of those determined by judicial decision, not if they are determined by judicially supervised conciliation. Such a difference in treatment can be accepted only if it is objectively justified which it was not considered to be.[109]

It is a matter of discussion whether the fundamental EU rights must be observed in national labour law also in other situations. In situations where a national court has an obligation of consistent interpretation in relation to domestic laws, i.e. a duty to interpret national law in accordance with EU law there is probably also a duty to include EU fundamental rights and general principles of law in that interpretation.

In *Zambrano*,[110] the advocate general discussed whether full recognition of the rights (including the future rights) that flow from Union citizenship mean that an infant EU citizen has a right, based on EU law rather than national law, to reside anywhere within the territory of the Union (including in the Member State of his nationality). If so, ensuring that he can exercise that right effectively may entail granting residence to his third country national parent if there would otherwise be a substantial breach of fundamental rights. At a more conceptual level, she discussed whether the exercise of rights as a Union citizen dependent – like the exercise of the classic economic 'free-

107. Case C-442/00 *Cavallero* [2002] ECR I-11915.
108. See directive 2008/94/EC on protection of the employees in the event of the employer's insolvency. 2008/94/EC codifies 80/987/EEC, amended by 2002/74/EC.
109. In case C-498/06 *Nunez* [2008] I-921, the CJEU regarded exclusion of extra-judicial conciliation from the payment guarantee as justified.
110. Case C-34/09 *Zambrano* [2011] ECR I-1177.

doms' – on some trans-frontier free movement (however accidental, peripheral or remote) having taken place before the claim is advanced. Or does Union citizenship look forward to the future, rather than back to the past, to define the rights and obligations that it confers. Expressed in another way: is Union citizenship merely the non-economic version of the same generic kind of free movement rights as have long existed for the economically active and for persons of independent means. Or does it mean something more radical: true citizenship, carrying with it a uniform set of rights and obligations, in a Union under the rule of law in which respect for fundamental rights must necessarily play an integral part. The CJEU didn't mention fundamental rights in its judgment.

In *Kremzow*,[111] the CJEU held that where national legislation is concerned with a situation which does not fall within the field of application of EU law, the Court cannot give interpretative guidance. The plaintiff who was in jail contended that some rules of criminal procedure violated fundamental human rights. He argued that the case was within the scope of EU law because the fact that he was in a jail prevented him from exercising his free movement rights.

Ii follows from the foregoing that in many employment and labour law cases fundamental rights and general principles of EU law will have to be respected. There are, however, also labour law cases where EU fundamental rights cannot be invoked. In *Polier*[112] the CJEU refused to answer a question about the compatibility of a French dismissal provision with the CFREU (and some international provisions). The question was:

[L]'ordonnance 2005-893 [...], qui autorise le licenciement du salarié pendant la période de consolidation de deux ans, prévue par le [CNE], sans indiquer la légitimité de la rupture et [...] sans information préalable au regard du droit européen, tel que défini dans la charte des droits fondamentaux [de l'Union européenne], qui précise [...] le droit des travailleurs à ne pas être licencié sans motif valable, [est-elle valide?]

[L]'ordonnance n° 2005-893 [est-elle valide] par rapport à [la convention n° 158?]

[L]es dispositions de l'ordonnance 2005-893 [...] [sont-elles] en conformité avec les dispositions de la charte sociale européenne [?]

111. Case C-299/95 *Kremzow* [1997] ECR I-2629.
112. Case C-361/07, *Polier*, not reported in English, available in French at the CJEU website curia.europa.eu.

In *Vajnai*[113] the problem was whether a penal provision in Hungary prohibiting the use of symbols of the international labour movement on pain of criminal prosecution was compatible with the fundamental EU law principle of non-discrimination. The question was put to the CJEU as to whether Article 6 TEU, the Ethnic Equality Directive[114] or Articles 10, 11 and 12 CFREU allow a person who wishes to express his political convictions by means of a symbol representing them to do so in any Member State. The CJEU rejected the question as inadmissible because the case concerned a purely internal situation in Hungary.

3.2.10 Free Movement and Fundamental Rights. The double justification test

The CJEU has been confronted with the interface between free movement on the internal market and fundamental rights on a number of occasions and has held that free movement and fundamental rights must be balanced against each other. The one does not automatically take precedence over the other. In *Omega Spielhallen,*[115] for example, the CJEU held that the freedom to provide services does not preclude an economic activity from being prohibited on grounds of protecting public policy by reason of the fact that that activity is an affront to human dignity.[116] In *Laval*, on the other hand, it held that lawful industrial action under Swedish law was a violation of the then Article 49 EC [now Article 56 FEU] even though the right to take industrial action is a fundamental right under Article 28 CFREU.

In *Carpenter*[117] and *Festersen*[118] the CJEU ruled that in situations where a restriction on the free movement at the same time adversely affects the enjoyment of a fundamental right the restriction is to be considered particularly restrictive.

In identical terms, the CJEU held in *Viking*[119] and *Laval*[120] that the right to take collective industrial action is a fundamental right which forms an integral part of the general principles of EU law, the compliance of which must be ensured by the CJEU. It referred to Article 28 CFREU in support hereof. It

113. Case C-328/04 *Vajnai* [2005] I-8577.
114. 2000/43/2000.
115. Case C-36/02 *Omega* [2004] ECR I-9609.
116. See more generally on human dignity in the interpretation of human rights law McCrudden, Christopher: Human Dignity and Judicial Interpretation of Human Rights, European Journal of International Law 2008 p. 655.
117. Case C-60/00 *Carpenter* [2002] ECR I-6279.
118. Case C-370/05 *Festersen* [2007] ECR I-1129.
119. Case 438-05 *Viking* [2007] I-10779.
120. Case C-341/05 *Laval* [2007] ECR I-11767.

thus dismissed the view that the right to take collective action as a fundamental right is outside the scope of application of the free movement provisions and that the fundamental right for workers to take industrial action always takes precedence over the right of service providers to access to the labour and services markets of other Member States, see further in Chapter Three.

The balancing exercise between free movement rights and fundamental rights is governed by the two usual justification tests for restrictions on free movement and restrictions on fundamental rights.

Restrictions on free movement are according to the practice of the CJEU only lawful if the restriction pursue´s a legitimate aim, and the means applied to achieve the legitimate end (the restriction) must be appropriate and necessary, i.e. the principle of proportionality must be respected. In *Viking*, the CJEU left the balancing exercise to the national court and only gave some general guidelines while it did the balancing itself in *Laval* and held that the trade unions had used industrial action in support of wage demands that were too unclear and non-transparent to be accepted as justified.

Article 52(3) CFREU provides on the relationship between EU fundamental rights and ECHR that in so far as the CFREU contains rights which correspond to rights guaranteed by the ECHR the meaning and scope of those rights shall be the same as those laid down by the ECHR. This provision does not prevent EU law providing more extensive protection. Article 11 ECHR provides on justification of limitation to rights guaranteed by Article 11 ECHR (emphasis added) that no restrictions shall be placed on the exercise of these rights other than *such as are prescribed by law* and are necessary in a democratic society in the interests of national security or public safety, for the prevention of disorder or crime, for the protection of health or morals or for the protection of the rights and freedoms of others. As regards the right to strike and take other collective action there is overlap between ECHR and CFREU, see below in Chapter Three. The fundamental right, the trade unions exercised in Laval could therefore only be limited if that was prescribed by law – which it was not. In Laval, the CJEU didn't do a justification test for restriction on the fundamental right of the trade unions to take collective action guaranteed in Article 28 CFREU, see further on the Laval case below in Chapter Three.

Syrpis[121] has argued that it is an important effect of the Lisbon Treaty that the justification test for restriction when free movement and fundamental

121. Syrpis, Phil: The Treaty of Lisbon: Much Ado ... But About What?, Industrial Law Journal 2008 p. 219.

rights are balanced against each other must be made both in relation to restrictions to free movement and in relation to restrictions to fundamental rights. In Laval, the CJEU didn't follow that view. It only examined whether a restriction on free movement could be justified not whether a restriction on the fundamental right to take collective action could be justified.

3.2.11 Competing Fundamental Rights

Today there are many fundamental rights. As a result, situations can easily arise in which persons with opposite interests can invoke competing fundamental rights, see as an example the cases discussed in Chapter Six where Christian employees who believed that homosexuality is a sin contended that they suffered a violation of their right to freedom of religion under Article 9 ECHR when their employer required them to perform their work in the same way regardless of whether the customer/client was homosexual or not. Both freedom of religion and the right not to be discriminated against on grounds of sexual orientation are fundamental rights in EU labour law. Sometimes they have to be balanced against each other and cannot be respected to the satisfaction of all at the same time. See also *Hennigs*,[122] where the CJEU held that the principle of non-discrimination on grounds of age proclaimed in Article 21 of the CFREU and given specific expression in the Framework Employment Directive,[123] and more particularly Articles 2 and 6(1) of that directive, must be interpreted as precluding a measure laid down by a collective agreement such as that at issue in the main proceedings which provides that, within each salary group, the basic pay step of a public sector contractual employee is determined on appointment by reference to the employee's age. The fact that EU law precludes that measure and that it appears in a collective agreement does not interfere with the right to negotiate and conclude collective agreements recognised in Article 28 CFREU.

3.3. General Principles

3.3.1 General principle of equal treatment in labour law

EU law has – over the years from 1958 to 2013 – been developing a general principle requiring Member States to observe a general doctrine of objectivity (Sachlichkeit) in matters of labour law. The duty subjects (Pflichtsubjekten) of this norm are the nation states, the labour market organizations – both on the employer and the worker side – and the individual employers.

122. Case C-297/10 *Hennigs* [2011] nyr.
123. 2000/78/EC.

3.3.2 Consultation

In *Dunnett* [124] the CJEU stated that the European Investment Bank in a staff case was bound to consult staff representatives under a general principle of employment law before taking a decision to withdraw a benefit.

4 Secondary EU Law

Under Article 288 TFEU, the EU institutions shall in order to exercise the Union's competences adopt regulations, directives, decisions, recommendations and opinions. A regulation has general application. It is binding in its entirety and directly applicable in all Member States. A directive is binding, as to the result to be achieved, upon each Member State to which it is addressed, but leaves to the national authorities the choice of form and methods. A decision is binding in its entirety. A decision which specifies those to whom it is addressed is binding only on them. Recommendations and opinions have no binding force.

4.1 Directives

In EU labour law directives are the most important form of binding secondary EU legislation. The detailed procedure for adopting secondary employment legislation depends on the legal basis used. Normally it will be the normal legislative procedure laid down in Article 295 TFEU. There is, however a dual system. Instead of using the normal legislative procedure in which the decisive legislative competence is exercised by the Council and the Parliament in cooperation, employment directives can be adopted by the Council on the basis of European collective agreements concluded between the social partners at EU level, see just below.

4.2 Social partners and Collective Agreements at EU level

Originally, the *social partners at EU level* had only a limited consultative role in EU labour law. That has gradually changed. The turning point was the Maastricht Treaty and the attached Social Protocol and Social Policy Agreement. The role of the social partners is still gradually being increased, latest by the adoption of the Lisbon Treaty which entered into force 1 December 2009.

124. Case T-192/99 *Dunnett* [2001] ECR II-813; FP-I-A-65; FP-II-313.

Social dialogue is a fairly new term in EU labour law. The first occurrence of the word is found in the Conclusions of the Council concerning the medium-term Social Action programme 1984.[125] In the mid 1980's contacts and talks – now called social dialogue – between the social partners at European level were restarted in *Val Duchesse* near Brussels. This social dialogue produced the draft for the new social provisions for the EC Treaty, which were enacted in the Agreement on Social Policy in the Treaty of Maastricht which came into force 1 November 1993 and inserted in the EC Treaty by the Treaty of Amsterdam which came into force 1 May 1999.

Today, the social partners at EU level (in particular Business Europe, ETUC and CEEP) have a share in the legislative competence in the EU. According to Article 152 TFEU which is a new provision inserted by the Lisbon Treaty, the Union recognises and promotes the role of the social partners at EU level. The Tripartite Social Summit for Growth and Employment[126] shall contribute to social dialogue.

According to Article 154 TFEU, the Commission has the task of promoting the consultation of management and labour at Union level and shall take any relevant measure to facilitate their dialogue by ensuring balanced support for the parties. To this end, before submitting proposals in the social policy field, the Commission shall consult management and labour on the possible direction of Union action. If, after such consultation, the Commission considers Union action advisable, it shall consult management and labour on the content of the envisaged proposal. Management and labour shall forward to the Commission an opinion or, where appropriate, a recommendation. Management and labour may inform the Commission of their wish to initiate the process provided for in Article 155 TFEU. The duration of this process shall not exceed nine months, unless the management and labour concerned and the Commission decide jointly to extend it. Article 155 TFEU provides:

1. Should management and labour so desire, the dialogue between them at Union level may lead to contractual relations, including agreements.

2. Agreements concluded at Union level shall be implemented either in accordance with the procedures and practices specific to management and labour and the Member States or, in matters covered by Article 153, at the joint request of the signatory parties, by a Council decision on a proposal from the Commission. The European Parliament shall be informed. The Council shall act unanimously where the agreement in question contains one or more

125. OJ 1984 C 175.
126. See Council Decision 2003/174/EC establishing a Tripartite Social Summit for Growth and Employment.

provisions relating to one of the areas for which unanimity is required pursuant to Article 153(2).

The social dialogue process has resulted in the conclusion of agreements, which have subsequently been implemented by the Council as Directives, on parental leave in 1996,[127] part-time work 1997[128] and fixed-term employment contracts in 1999,[129] see further below in Chapter Three 6.2.1 and Chapter Seven.

4.3 Recommendations

Recommendations are the primary source of law used to coordinate economic and employment policies in the EMU, see e.g. the Council Recommendation on broad guidelines for the economic policies of the Member States and of the Union cited above in Chapter One.[130]

5 Case law

There is abundant case law from the CJEU, in particular on EU labour law seen in an internal market perspective, which will be included in the following chapters.

The CJEU's judgments are written without openly stating whether there are dissenting views among the participating judges. The CJEU judgments are therefore sometimes rather self-contradictory and inconsistent because all the participating judges have to agree on a joint text even when there are differing views among them.

It would have been possible to keep the views of individual judges secret and at the same time openly state whether there are dissenting views. If there e.g. are three different views in a Grand Chamber of 13 judges held by 7, 4 and 2 judges respectively, it could be stated that 7 judges find ..., 4 judges

127. Council Directive 96/34/EC of 3 June 1996 on the framework agreement on parental leave concluded by UNICE, CEEP and the ETUC. Now repealed and replaced with Council Directive 2010/18/EU of 8 March 2010 implementing the revised Framework Agreement on parental leave concluded by BUSINESSEUROPE, UEAPME, CEEP and ETUC and repealing Directive 96/34/EC.
128. Council Directive 97/81/EC of 15 December 1997 concerning the Framework Agreement on part-time work concluded by UNICE, CEEP and the ETUC.
129. Council Directive 1999/70/EC of 28 June 1999 concerning the framework agreement on fixed-term work concluded by ETUC, UNICE and CEEP.
130. Recommendation 2010/410/EU, OJ 2010 L 191.

find .... and 2 judges find ... without naming the judges. In my view such a practice would be preferable.

The CJEU is not specialized in labour law and probably knows less of collective labour law and international labour law than labour courts in the Member States typically do. O'Higgins has criticized the CJEU for usually not referring to international labour law standards, in particular ILO law, in its judgments. He assumes that the reason why the CJEU only seldom refers to ILO law and doesn't declare that 'labour is not a commodity', as stated in the ILO Constitution, see below in section 8, is that the CJEU judges are so ignorant of ILO law that they don't know that that is the view of the ILO, see the following (emphasis added):[131]

> It is one of the sad deficiencies of the European Court of Justice, *due no doubt to the ignorance both of the judges* who comprise the Court and of the legal practitioners appearing before it, of the principles of international labour law that the Court rarely refers to international labour standards despite having decided many cases in which these principles would have been relevant.

There can be many reasons to choose silence. It is a possibility that many of the judges of CJEU are so much in agreement with the original internal market logic underlying the first layer of the economic constitution of the EU according to which labour was seen as a commodity that they regard the view of the ILO as unrealistic or irrelevant in an EU context.

Even though the ECHR mainly guarantees civil and political rights there are also a considerable number of cases from the European Court of Human Rights (ECtHR) of relevance to EU labour law. In a case on annulment of a Commission decision, the CJEU referred to the case law of the ECtHR and stated:[132]

> 'It must be added that the Court of Justice, in paragraphs 274 to 276 of the judgment in Limburgse Vinyl Maatschappij and Others v Commission, observed that since the judgment in Orkem v Commission there have been further developments in the case law of the European Court of Human Rights which the Community judicature must take into account when interpreting the fundamental rights. The Court of Justice stated however in that regard that those developments were not such as to put in question the statements of principle in Orkem v Commission.'

131. O'Higgins, Paul: Labour is not a Commodity' – an Irish Contribution to International Labour Law, Industrial Law Journal1997, Vol. 26 Issue 3, p. 225.
132. Case C-301/04 P *Commission* v *SGL Carbon AG* [2006] ECR I-5915, Para. 43.

6 Soft law

As a general rule soft law is not binding and is a source of law with lesser weight than binding law (hard law). Soft law may be defined as 'rules of conduct that are laid down in instruments which have not been attributed legally binding force as such, but nevertheless may have certain (indirect) legal effects, and (that) are aimed at and may produce practical effects.'[133] Soft law has played a decisive role in the development of fundamental rights in EU labour law and non-binding recommendations are the major legal instruments used to coordinate economic and employment policies in the Economic and Monetary Union (EMU).

6.1 The Community Charter of the Fundamental Social Rights of Workers 1989

A few soft law texts have, however, had considerable influence on the development of EU labour law. That is particularly true for the Community Charter of the Fundamental Social Rights of Workers 1989 which was adopted in 1989 by 11 of the then 12 Member States. The UK was unwilling to support it and did generally in the period from 1979-1997 prevent nearly all unanimous decisions on EU labour law. Later, a number of higher ranking sources of law has referred to the Community Charter of the Fundamental Social Rights of Workers 1989. That applies to the preamble to the TEU and Article 151 TFEU on the goals of EU labour Law. In the Explanatory remarks to the CFREU[134] there are 15 references to the Community Charter of the Fundamental Social Rights of Workers 1989 as source of the fundamental rights guaranteed in the CFREU. The ECtHR used the Community Charter of the Fundamental Social Rights of Workers 1989 as source of law in the Sørensen and Ramussen case.[135]

6.2 Social Action programmes

In areas in which the EU lacks legislative powers it gets by with policy coordination. This applies to fiscal policy, as well as employment and social policy. The consequences of the economic crisis in the Eurozone have led to calls for more and better coordination processes in Europe. Social Action Pro-

133. See Senden, Linda: Changes in the relative importance of sources of law – The case of EU soft law in Neergaard, Ulla and Ruth Nielsen (eds): European Legal Method – Paradoxes and Revitalisation, Copenhagen 2011.
134. See OJ 2007 C 303.
135. Sørensen & Rasmussen v Denmark (applications nos. 52562/99 and 52620/99).

grammes are launched periodically by the Commission to promote the EU's social objectives. SAPs identify areas for EU initiatives, which may take the form of legislative proposals and, more often, non-legislative activities. Above in the historical overview a few of them – notably the Social Action Programme 1974 and the Social Action Programme 1989 – have been highlighted.

6.3 The Open Method of Coordination (OMC)

The 'open method of coordination' (OMC) is a process of policymaking which does not lead to binding EU legislative measures nor require Member States to change their law. The open method of coordination (OMC) aims to spread best practices and achieve greater convergence towards the main EU goals. Generally, the OMC works in stages. First, the Council of Ministers agrees on policy goals. Member States then translate guidelines into national and regional policies. Thirdly, specific benchmarks and indicators to measure best practice are agreed upon. Finally, results are monitored and evaluated.

The employment title of the TFEU was originally introduced by the 1997 Treaty of Amsterdam. It is perceived as the original model of the open method of coordination, see now Article 148 TFEU. Employment policy is the paradigm case of the OMC: an annual report leads to guidelines, which the Member States 'shall take into account in their employment policies', followed by an annual report on national employment policy, reviewed in a report by the Council and Commission upon which the European Council may make (non-binding) recommendations to Member States.

6.4 The Lisbon Strategy

The Lisbon Strategy was an action and development plan for the European Union. It was originally set out by the Lisbon European Council of 23-24 March 2000 which articulated a new strategic goal for the EU: 'to become the most competitive and dynamic knowledge-based economy in the world capable of sustainable economic growth with more and better jobs and greater social cohesion'. In March 2005, the European Council re-launched the Lisbon Strategy. The re-launched Strategy is implemented through National Reform Programmes at Member State level. As well as a new strategic goal, the Lisbon Council highlighted the open method of coordination as the principal instrument through which this goal was to be achieved. The application of this method to the European Employment Strategy was confirmed. In 2010, the Lisbon Strategy expired.

6.5 The Europe 2020 Strategy

The overriding goals of the Lisbon Strategy are largely continued in the new ten-year strategy 'Europe 2020'.[136] It is intended to promote Europe's competitiveness, productivity, growth potential, social cohesion and economic convergence. Permanent loss of prosperity, sluggish growth and uncoordinated reforms which would result in high unemployment, social tensions and Europe's 'relative insignificance ... on the world stage' should be averted. To that end, strong growth must be generated which will help the EU to exit from the economic crisis and deal with longer term challenges. This growth is not to be based – and this represents something new in comparison to the old Lisbon Agenda – solely on increasing GDP. Instead, three priority goals are to be pursued simultaneously. Growth in the coming decade is to be:

- smart, developing an economy based on knowledge and innovation;
- sustainable, promoting competitive, but environmentally friendly and resource conserving economies and
- inclusive, promoting high employment and social and international cohesion.

Key instruments for the implementation of the European 2020 Strategy are the so-called Integrated Guidelines for Economic and Employment Policies, which contain the five common objectives of the EU. The EU Member States are to coordinate their policy action with regard to:

- promoting employment: by 2020, 75 per cent of the population aged between 20 and 64 should be in employment;
- vimproving the conditions for research and development: by 2020, three per cent of GDP should be allocated to this;
- achieving European climate protection and energy goals: by 2020, greenhouse gas emissions should be reduced by 20 per cent in comparison to 1990 levels, the share of renewable energies in total energy consumption should be increased to 20 per cent and energy efficiency should be raised by 20 per cent;
- improving levels of education: the school dropout rate should fall below ten per cent by 2020 and the share of higher education graduates among those 30–34 years of age should be increased by at least 40 per cent;

136. Europe 2020. A strategy for smart, sustainable and inclusive growth, COM(2010) 2020.

- reducing poverty and social exclusion: by 2020, at least 20 million fewer people should be at risk of poverty.

6.6 The European Semester

All the Member states have committed to achieving Europe 2020 targets and have translated them into national targets and growth-enhancing policies. But only if the individual efforts of all the countries are coordinated and focused, are they likely result in the desired impact on growth. Therefore the European Commission has set up a yearly cycle of economic policy coordination called the European Semester. Each year the European Commission undertakes a detailed analysis of EU Member States' programmes of economic and structural reforms and provides them with recommendations for the next 12-18 months. The European semester starts when the Commission adopts its Annual Growth Survey, usually towards the end of the year, which sets out EU priorities for the coming year to boost growth and job creation. In March, EU Heads of State and Government issue EU guidance for national policies on the basis of the Annual Growth Survey. The Spring meeting of the European Council – based on the annual growth survey, takes stock of: the overall macroeconomic situation, progress towards the five EU-level targets and progress under the flagship initiatives. It provides policy orientations covering fiscal, macroeconomic structural reform and growth enhancing areas, and advises on linkages between them. In April, Member States submit their plans for sound public finances (Stability or Convergence Programmes) and reforms and measures to make progress towards smart, sustainable and inclusive growth, in areas such as employment, research, innovation, energy or social inclusion (National Reform Programmes). In May/June, the Commission assesses these programmes and provides country-specific recommendations as appropriate. The Council discusses and the European Council endorses the recommendations. Policy advice is thus given to Member States before they start to finalise their draft budgets for the following year. Finally, end of June or in early July, the Council formally adopts the country-specific recommendations. Where recommendations are not acted on within the given timeframe, policy warnings can be issued. There is also an option for enforcement through incentives and sanctions in the case of excessive macroeconomic and budgetary imbalances.

7 Scholarly Legal writing

It follows from the theoretical approach I build on that I regard scholarly legal writing as a legal practice of relevance to the development of valid law, in particular at the sub-surface levels of the law, see above Chapter One. A list of the literature used in this book can be found in the Bibliography. In a review article Brian Bercusson[137] has given an overview of a range of books and articles on European labour law which have emerged in recent years.

In the EU's early period, there was considerable personal overlap between EU law as judge-made law and EU law as '*Professorenrecht*'.[138] Today (2013) the two groups tend to focus on different aspects of the law and different questions even though they still know the same doctrine of the sources of law and their interpretation. Van Gestel, Micklitz and Maduro state[139] that they feel that in the end the attention for the 'why questions' to the difference of the 'what questions' in legal research is what really distinguishes legal scholars from practitioners.

In my view many questions posed in legal research can be framed as what- or why- questions at will.[140] That is particularly true when teleological interpretation is relevant to answer the questions. As mentioned in Chapter One, EU law is usually interpreted in a teleological (goal-rational) way. The economic goals (internal market and economic and monetary union) of the EU are therefore taken into account in this book. Practitioners typically deal with concrete cases while academic scholars typically are more interested in the legal system at a general level, greater systematic parts of it, conceptual analysis, general principles and the like. There is also often a difference in the working conditions. Legal scholars have more time at their disposal and a wider scope for free choice of questions to examine and methods to apply.

137. Bercusson, Brian: European Labour Law in Context: A Review of the Literature, European Law Journal 1999, Vol. 5 Issue 2, p. 87.
138. Leading academic writers as for example Lecourt and Pescatore were judges/presidents of the CJEU for a period.
139. Gestel, Rob van Hans-W. Micklitz & Miguel Poiares Maduro: Methodology in the New Legal World, EUI Working Papers, LAW 2012/13.
140. See also Eckes, Christina: New EU Legal Methods – From Integration to Realism?, in Neergaard, Ulla and Ruth Nielsen: European Legal method – towards a new European Legal Realism?, Copenhagen 2013 (forthcoming).

Originality is typically seen as a positive quality in research[141] but is not valued similarly in judicial and other practice.

8 Public international law

All EU-countries are members of the United Nations, ILO and the Council of Europe. All EU Member States are WTO members, as is the EU in its own right.

8.1 International doctrine of sources of law

International law has developed a fairly strict, understanding of the sources of law. An authoritative catalogue of sources of international law can be found in Article 38 of the Statute[142] of the International Court of Justice. It provides that the International Court of Justice shall apply:

a. international conventions, whether general or particular, establishing rules expressly recognized by the contesting states;
b. international custom, as evidence of a general practice accepted as law;
c. the general principles of law recognized by civilized nations;
d. subject to the provisions of Article 59,[143] judicial decisions and the teachings of the most highly qualified publicists of the various nations, as subsidiary means for the determination of rules of law.

The above provision does not prejudice the power of the International Court of Justice to decide a case *ex aequo et bono*, if the parties agree.

A traditional weakness of public international law is that very often there is no or only weak enforcement possibilities. Law that builds solely on international sources of law is therefore not positively existing law to the same degree as law building on national or EU labour law typically are.

141. See Siems, Mathias M.: Legal Originality, Oxford Journal of Legal Studies, 2008 p. 147.
142. Available at http://www.icj-cij.org/documents/index.php?p1=4&p2=2&p3=0.
143. Article 59 of the Statute of the International Court of Justice provides: The decision of the Court has no binding force except between the parties and in respect of that particular case.

8.2 WTO

The General Agreement on Tariffs and Trade (GATT) was negotiated in 1947. GATT 1947 lives on as GATT 1994, which is an integral part of the WTO Agreement currently in force.

In the early period shortly after the end of World War two there were attempts to adopt global public international law provisions which would balance commercial policies and employment considerations – but they failed. The Havana Charter for an International Trade Organisation (ITO) was a draft treaty drawn up in 1947. It was intended to set up an International Trade Organisation (a precursor to the WTO) and to facilitate the solution of problems relating to international trade in the fields of employment, economic development, commercial policy, business practices and commodity policy. It was, however, never adopted. The Havana Charter contained a provision on fair labour standards in Article 7 under which the signatories should recognize that measures relating to employment must take fully into account the rights of workers under intergovernmental declarations, conventions and agreements. They should recognize that all countries have a common interest in the achievement and maintenance of fair labour standards related to productivity, and thus in the improvement of wages and working conditions as productivity may permit. The members should recognize that unfair labour conditions, particularly in production for export, create difficulties in international trade. Members which were also members of the ILO should cooperate with that organization in giving effect to this undertaking.

The attempt in the Havana Charter, 60 years ago, to integrate labour law and trade law failed. Labour law has since played only a marginal role in international trade law and international trade law only a marginal role in international labour law. Public international law operates at global level in separated parts with either an economic (e.g. WTO law) or a social aim (e.g. ILO law). Today (2013) CSR may be seen as a soft law bridge between international trade law and international labour law.

At regional – European – level there is a much closer interplay between the economic and the social including labour law parts of the law. As set out earlier in this Chapter, EU law has – at least since the mid 1970s[144] – had a double, both social and economic, aim. EU legal sources often draw explicit inspiration from public international law. Martin Scheinin argues[145] that EU

144. See Case 43/75 *Defrenne II* [1976] ECR 455.
145. Scheinin, Martin: International Law and Human Rights – Good or Bad for European Union Law? In Neergaard, Ulla & Nielsen, Ruth (eds): European Legal Method – In a Multi-Level EU Legal Order, Copenhagen 2012.

law has benefited from the sources doctrine of international law, as it developed the basis for its legal order in the form of a set of international treaties. This has enabled the adoption of an international doctrine of sources of law at EU level and the avoidance of endless controversies concerning the differences in the national sources doctrines of continental and common law countries, or northern and southern member states. He points out that international human rights law and also EU law can be seen as a major unifier of national doctrines of sources of law. For instance the ECtHR applies the international law doctrine of sources. Through its role as a de facto constitutional court for Europe and because of the incorporation of the ECHR into most national legal systems and also into EU law through the CFREU, the ECHR is in force in the internal legal systems of the member states with the same content, including with the same sources of law, as it has on the level of international law. Hence, also courts in countries that for domestic legislation would apply a continental or Nordic or common law doctrine of sources will need to follow an international sources doctrine in issues involving fundamental rights.

8.3 ILO (International Labour Organisation)

The ILO was set up in 1919.

8.3.1 Tripartite structure

Within the UN system, the ILO has a special tripartite structure with workers' and employers' organisations participating as equal partners with governments in the work of its governing organs. The same actors as are parties to collective agreements at national level thus adopt Treaties and Recommendations within the framework of ILO. Two bodies have been set up to supervise the application of ILO standards, the Committee on Freedom of Association (since 1952) and the Committee of Experts on the Application of Conventions and Recommendations (since 1959).

8.3.2 Constitution: Labour is not a Commodity

In the Philadelphia Declaration of 1944 (10 May 1944), the International Labour Conference reaffirmed the fundamental principles on which the ILO is based and, in particular, that 'labour is not a commodity'.[146] The Declaration of Philadelphia restated the traditional objectives of the ILO and then branched out in two new directions: the centrality of human rights to social

146. See on that provision O'Higgins, Paul: Labour is not a Commodity' – an Irish Contribution to International Labour Law, Industrial Law Journal1997, Vol. 26 Issue 3, p. 225.

policy, and the need for international economic planning. In 1946, when the ILO's constitution was being revised by the General Conference convened in Montreal, the Declaration of Philadelphia was annexed to the constitution and forms an integral part of it by Article 1.[147]

8.3.3 Conventions and recommendations

The ILO formulates international labour standards in the form of conventions and recommendations setting minimum standards of basic labour rights: freedom of association, the right to organize, collective bargaining, abolition of forced labour, equality of opportunity and treatment, and other standards regulating conditions across the entire spectrum of work related issues. The International Labour Conference adopted a Declaration of Fundamental Principles and Rights at Work in 1998. The Declaration called upon all ILO Member States to apply the principles in line with the original intent of the core ILO conventions on which it is based.

8.3.4 Fundamental rights

Eight ILO-Conventions have been identified by the ILO's Governing Body as being fundamental to the rights of people at work, irrespective of levels of development of individual member states. They are grouped into four categories:

1) Freedom of Association,[148]
2) Abolition of Forced Labour[149]
3) Equality[150]
4) Elimination of Child Labour[151]

8.3.5 Reference to ILO law in EU labour law

There is generally only scant reference to ILO conventions in EU law. That has been criticized in the literature.[152] ILO conventions are, for example, not

147. See http://www.ilo.org/ilolex/english/iloconst.htm.
148. Convention no 87, Freedom of Association and Protection of the Right to Organise Convention, 1948 and convention no 98, Right to Organise and Collective Bargaining Convention, 1949.
149. Convention no 29, Forced Labour Convention, 1930 and convention no 105, Abolition of Forced Labour Convention, 1957.
150. Convention no 100, Equal Remuneration Convention, 1951 and convention no 111, Discrimination (employment and Occupation) Convention, 1958.
151. Convention no138, Minimum Age Convention, 1973 and convention no 182, Worst Forms of Child Labour Convention, 1999.

mentioned in the CFREU or the explanatory remarks accompanying it.[153] In *Laval*[154] and *Viking*,[155] the CJEU did, however, refer to ILO-Convention 87 as a basis for considering the right to take collective action as a fundamental right. The *Laval*-judgment has been widely criticized for tipping the balance between market freedoms and the fundamental right to take collective action in favour of market freedoms.

The eight fundamental ILO conventions are, however, all ratified by all 27 EU countries. Consequently they are 'international obligations common to the Member States', see above on the CJEU's case law on fundamental rights and the Preamble to the CFREU. For that reason they have become more binding as a matter of EU law and not only of international law when the Lisbon Treaty came into force (1 December 2009).

It is, as stated in the Philadelphia declaration and the constitution of ILO, a basic view of the ILO that labour (the workers) should not be seen or treated as a commodity. That view fits badly with the internal market logic but reasonably well with the underlying logic of the economic and monetary union with a high level of fundamental rights for union citizens. Workers in the EU make up the majority of the union citizens. The shift from seeing EU labour law as internal market law to seeing it as fundamental rights law fits easily with a shift from seeing 'labour as a commodity' to seeing workers in the EU as not solely or primarily a commodity but rather as European citizens with fundamental rights.

8.4 Council of Europe Conventions

Two Council of Europe Conventions are of particular interest in EU labour law: The ECHR (European Convention on Human Rights 1950) and the Council of Europe Social Charter 1961, amended by the Council of Europe Revised Social Charter 1996.

8.4.1 1ECHR (European Convention on Human Rights 1950)

The relationship between EU law and the ECHR has changed considerably over time and become closer and more intense. As appears from the account of the development of fundamental rights in the EU given above in section

152. O'Higgins, Paul: Some problems of enforcement of rights under the Community Charter of Fundamental Social Rights of Workers in Vogel-Polsky, Eliane (ed): Quel avenir pour l'Europe sociale: 1992 et après?, Bruxelles 1992 p. 73.
153. See OJ 2007 C 303.
154. Case C-341/05 *Laval* [2007] ECR I-11767.
155. Case C-438/05 *Viking* [2007] ECR I-10779.

3.2, the EU didn't take any interest in fundamental rights before around 1970. The EC/EU started as a trading organisation focused on establishing an internal market while the Council of Europe gave priority to human rights from the outset. Since the early 1970's, the CJEU has developed a case law on fundamental rights, originally with a view to obtain acceptance from leading national courts to the principle of supremacy of EU law and direct effect. Since the creation of the EU by the Maastricht Treaty and the introduction of EU-citizenship fundamental rights have acquired central importance for the EU. France ratified the ECHR Convention in 1974. It was not until later on that the ECHR was ratified by all EU Member States. The ECHR was first specifically referred to by the CJEU in 1975 in *Rutili*,[156] which was also the first labour law case before the CJEU where fundamental rights were at issue. The ECHR has since been quoted by the CJEU on numerous occasions, see below in section 9.2.3.[157] In the *Bosphorus*,[158] Advocate General Jacobs stated:

> ... For practical purposes the Convention [i.e. ECHR] can be regarded as Community law and can be invoked as such both in this court [i.e. CJEU] and in national courts where Community laws are in issue.

In a case on annulment of a Commission decision, the CJEU referred to the case law of the ECtHR and stated:[159]

> 'It must be added that the Court of Justice, in paragraphs 274 to 276 of the judgment in Limburgse Vinyl Maatschappij and Others v Commission, observed that since the judgment in Orkem v Commission there have been further developments in the case law of the European Court of Human Rights which the Community judicature must take into account when interpreting the fundamental rights. The Court of Justice stated however in that regard that those developments were not such as to put in question the statements of principle in Orkem v Commission.'

The ECHR offers some protection of economic and social rights. In Airey v Ireland,[160] the ECtHR stated (emphasis added): Whilst the Convention sets forth what are essentially civil and political rights, many of them have implications of a social or economic nature. The Court therefore considers, like the

156. Case 36/75 *Rutili* [1975] ECR p. 1219.
157. See further Coppel, Jason and Adian O'Neill: The European Court of Justice: Taking Rights Seriously?, Common Market Law Review 1992, p. 669.
158. Case C-84/95 *Bosphorus* [1996] ECR I-3953.
159. Case C-301/04 P *Commission* v *SGL Carbon AG* [2006] ECR p. I-5915, Para. 43.
160. Application no. 6289/73.

Commission, that *the mere fact that an interpretation of the Convention may extend into the sphere of social and economic rights should not be a decisive factor against such an interpretation; there is no water-tight division separating that sphere from the field covered by the Convention.*Compared to the ECHR the CFREU goes much further in protecting economic and social rights.

As mentioned earlier, the question whether the EU can accede to the ECHR was answered in the negative in 1996.[161] In Article 6(3) TEU (post-Lisbon) it is stated that the EU shall accede to the ECHR. From the ECHR side, such accession has been made possible by the addition of a Protocol No 14, which has now entered into force following ratification by Russia. A new second paragraph was added to Article 59 of the ECHR, reading 'The European Union may accede to this Convention'. Its explanatory memorandum noted that all necessary modifications to the Convention required by such accession could be brought about either by an amending protocol to the Convention or by means of an accession treaty to be concluded by the EU. The accession of the EU to the ECHR is not yet completed.

8.4.2 Council of Europe Social Charter 1961, amended by the Council of Europe Revised Social Charter 1996

The ECHR primarily protects civil and political rights. The *Council of Europe Social Charter 1961* and the *revised European Social Charter 1996* are of more direct relevance to labour and employment law. The Council of Europe in a report from 2008 presented the Council of Europe Social Charter in the following way (emphasis added):

> The European Social Charter is *the counterpart of the European Convention of Human Rights in the field of economic and social rights*. It covers a broad range of rights related to housing, health, education, *employment,* social protection and *non-discrimination.*

The content of the solidarity provisions in the CFREU draws heavily on the Council of Europe Revised Social Charter from 1996 to which there are many references in the Explanatory remarks. All 27 EU Member States are signatories to the Revised Social Charter but twelve[162] of them have not ratified this convention and have consequently never been bound by it under public international law. Since the coming into force of the Lisbon Treaty

161. Opinion 2/94 [1996] I-1759.
162. Austria, Czech Republic, Denmark, Germany, Greece, Hungary, Latvia, Luxembourg, Poland, Slovakia, Spain and the United Kingdom.

they are in a number of situations bound by the CFREU and because it refers to the Council of Europe Revised Social Charter from 1996 as source of inspiration for many of its provisions get legal effect in the EU Member States as a matter of EU law regardless of whether they have ever been binding as a matter of public international law.

The first part of the Revised Social Charter from 1996 states that the Parties accept as the aim of their policy, to be pursued by all appropriate means both national and international in character, the attainment of conditions in which the following rights and principles may be effectively realised:

1. Everyone shall have the opportunity to earn his living in an occupation freely entered upon.
2. All workers have the right to just conditions of work.
3. All workers have the right to safe and healthy working conditions.
4. All workers have the right to a fair remuneration sufficient for a decent standard of living for themselves and their families.
5. All workers and employers have the right to freedom of association in national or international organisations for the protection of their economic and social interests.
6. All workers and employers have the right to bargain collectively.
7. Children and young persons have the right to a special protection against the physical and moral hazards to which they are exposed.
8. Employed women, in case of maternity, have the right to a special protection.
9. Everyone has the right to appropriate facilities for vocational guidance with a view to helping him choose an occupation suited to his personal aptitude and interests.
10. Everyone has the right to appropriate facilities for vocational training.
11. Everyone has the right to benefit from any measures enabling him to enjoy the highest possible standard of health attainable.
12. All workers and their dependents have the right to social security.
13. Anyone without adequate resources has the right to social and medical assistance.
14. Everyone has the right to benefit from social welfare services.
15. Disabled persons have the right to independence, social integration and participation in the life of the community.
16. The family as a fundamental unit of society has the right to appropriate social, legal and economic protection to ensure its full development.
17. Children and young persons have the right to appropriate social, legal and economic protection.

18. The nationals of any one of the Parties have the right to engage in any gainful occupation in the territory of any one of the others on a footing of equality with the nationals of the latter, subject to restrictions based on cogent economic or social reasons.
19. Migrant workers who are nationals of a Party and their families have the right to protection and assistance in the territory of any other Party.
20. All workers have the right to equal opportunities and equal treatment in matters of employment and occupation without discrimination on the grounds of sex.
21. Workers have the right to be informed and to be consulted within the undertaking.
22. Workers have the right to take part in the determination and improvement of the working conditions and working environment in the undertaking.
23. Every elderly person has the right to social protection.
24. All workers have the right to protection in cases of termination of employment.
25. All workers have the right to protection of their claims in the event of the insolvency of their employer.
26. All workers have the right to dignity at work.
27. All persons with family responsibilities and who are engaged or wish to engage in employment have a right to do so without being subject to discrimination and as far as possible without conflict between their employment and family responsibilities.
28. Workers' representatives in undertakings have the right to protection against acts prejudicial to them and should be afforded appropriate facilities to carry out their functions.
29. All workers have the right to be informed and consulted in collective redundancy procedures.
30. Everyone has the right to protection against poverty and social exclusion.
31. Everyone has the right to housing.

8.5 Customary international law: Labour is not a Commodity

O'Higgins[163] argues that the widespread adoption in many international instruments, in one form or another, of the concept that 'Labour is not a Commodity', has as consequence that the principle may not only be a rule of trea-

163. O'Higgins, Paul: Labour is not a Commodity' – an Irish Contribution to International Labour Law, Industrial Law Journal1997, Vol. 26 Issue 3, p. 225.

ty law but may also by now have become a rule of customary international law and therefore binding on all states regardless of whether they by ratifying an ILO convention have accepted to be bound by it. In my view, the internal market law perspective on EU law clearly builds on the view that labour/workers can be regarded as a commodity. That is an argument against seeing the understanding preferred by the ILO as an expression of customary law. Anyway it is not very relevant in regard to EU labour law whether states are bound by principles in the ILO constitution regardless of whether they are members of ILO or not since alle EU Member –states are also members of ILO.

8.6 International soft law

Historically, the first part of the total legal system where CSR (corporate social responsibility) and BRHR (business responsibilities for human rights) were addressed was public international law. With regard to the labour market, that development started in the 1970s. In June1976 the OECD governments adopted a 'Declaration on International Investment and Multinational Enterprises'. A set of Guidelines for Multinational Enterprises developed by the IME committee was attached to the declaration as an annex. In 2000, the OECD's Guidelines for Multinational Enterprises were revised. In 1977, the International Labour Organisation (ILO) adopted a 'tripartite declaration of principles concerning multinational enterprises and social policy', which addresses a number of labour law questions and was revised in 2006. There is a Multinational Enterprises Programme (MULTI), which is responsible for follow-up to the 'tripartite declaration of principles concerning multinational enterprises and social policy'. *The United Nations Global Compact* serves as a framework for businesses that are committed to aligning their operations and strategies with ten universally accepted principles in the areas of human rights, labour, the environment and anti-corruption. The Global Compact is a voluntary initiative with two objectives: (1) to mainstream the ten principles of the Global Compact in business activities around the world and (2) to catalyse actions in support of broader UN goals, such as the Millennium Development Goals (MDGs). Four labour law principles are included in the Global Compact, namely: Principle Three: businesses should uphold the freedom of association and the effective recognition of the right to collective bargaining; Principle Four: the elimination of all forms of forced and compulsory labour; Principle Five: the effective abolition of child labour; and Principle Six: eliminate discrimination in respect of employment and occupation. The four labour law principles of the UN Global Compact are taken from the ILO's Declaration on Fundamental Principles and Rights at Work.

9 National Law

9.1 National Law as a Source of EU Labour Law

As set out above in the section on Fundamental Rights and General Principles, the CJEU stated in *Internationale Handelsgesellschaft* that these principles were inspired by the constitutional traditions common to the Member States.[164] In Article 6 (4) TEU there is also reference to the constitutional traditions common to the Member States as sources of the general principles of EU law.

9.2 EU requirements to national law

EU law contributes greatly to linking/locking national law, EU law and public international law together. As mentioned in Chapter One, the CJEU has often used labour law cases to introduce new rules or interpretation principles into EU law.

9.2.1 Horisontal Direct Effect

Many labour law conflicts arise between individual employees and private employers or between collective actors in the private sector. It is therefore not surprising that labour law cases have been among the first where the CJEU has held that Treaty provisions have direct horizontal effect as binding for private individuals (typically employers). Article 45 TFEU on free movement of workers and 157 TFEU on equal pay between men and women give rise to direct effects both in the vertical relationship against the Member States[165] and in horizontal relationships against private employers and organisations. In *Defrenne II*,[166] the CJEU for the first time held that a Treaty provision had direct effect against a private individual (an employer). In *Walrave/Koch v AUCI*[167] and *Dona v Mantero*[168] the CJEU ruled that Article 45 TFEU gives

164. Case 11/70 *Internationale Handelsgesellschaft* [1970] ECR 1125.
165. Case 167/73 *Commission v France (the Merchant Seaman's Case)* [1974] ECR 359 and Case 41/74 *Van Duyn v Home Office* [1975] ECR 1337.
166. Case 43/75 *Defrenne II* [1976] ECR 455.
167. Case 36/74 *Walrave* [1974] ECR 1405. The case concerned rules of an international sporting federation. The CJEU held: Prohibition of such discrimination does not only apply to the action of public authorities but extends likewise to rules of any other nature aimed at regulating in a collective manner gainful employment and the provision of services.
168. Case 13/76 *Donà* [*1*976] ECR 1333. The Case concerned rules laid down by a sporting federation which is competent to control football on the territory of a Member State.

rise to horizontal direct effect[169] against associations or bodies with competence of a collective nature which do not come under public law.[170] In *Angonese*,[171] the CJEU held that direct effect of Article 45 TFEU also applies against individual employers.

Directives do not have horizontal direct effect. The first case where this rule was formulated by the CJEU was *Marshall I*,[172] which was a sex discrimination case about dismissal on grounds of sex in a public hospital in the UK. The UK maintained that a directive can never impose obligations directly on individuals and that it can only have direct effect against a Member State qua public authority and not against a Member State qua employer. The CJEU agreed on the first point but held that direct effect against a Member state applies to the Member States in all its functions, whether employer or public authority.

When dealing with national law elements which are incompatible with EU law elements, the CJEU in later years use the terminology that national courts must disapply or leave inapplicable elements of national law that conflict with EU law, see for example the Melki and Abdeli cases.[173] National courts – regardless of their place in the national judicial hierarchy – are thus – in accordance with the 'one big system model' – required to collaborate on making the combined national and EU law system effective by treating national elements of law which are incompatible with EU elements of law as *inapplicable*.

When dealing with EU law elements, for example directives which are incompatible with higher ranking EU law elements, for example fundamental rights, the CJEU uses the terminology that the lower ranking provision is invalid, see for example *Test Achats*[174] where the CJEU held that Article 5(2)

169. See also Case 222/86 *Heylens* [1987] ECR 4097.
170. See Case 36/74 *Walrave* [1974] ECR 1405, paragraphs 17, 18, 23 and 24; Case 13/76 *Donà* [1976] ECR 1333, paragraphs 17 and 18; Joined Cases C-51/96 and C-191/97 *Deliège* [2000] ECR I-2549, paragraph 47; Case C-176/96 *Lehtonen and Castors Braine* [2000] ECR I-2681, paragraph 35; Case C-309/99 *Wouters and Others* [2002] ECR I-1577, paragraph 120; and Case C-519/04 P *Meca-Medina and Majcen v Commission* [2006] ECR I-6991, paragraph 24.
171. Case C-281/98 *Angonese* [2000] ECR I-4139.
172. Case 152/84 *Marshall I* [1986] ECR p. 723.
173. Joined Cases C-188/10 and C-189/10, *Melki and Abdeli* [ECR] 2010 I-5667.
174. Case C-236/09 *Test Achats* [ECR] 2011 I-00000, nyr.

of Directive 2004/113[175] is *invalid*. The CJEU found that it was incompatible with the general principle of equal treatment of men and women which is a fundamental right in EU law.

9.2.2 Duty to interpret national law in conformity with EU law

The principle of consistent interpretation, i.e. the duty for national authorities to interpret national law in conformity with EU law was launched by CJEU in 1984 in *von Colson and Kamann* in a case on equal treatment in employment between men and women, where the following was stated: [176]

> However, the Member States' obligation arising from a directive to achieve the result envisaged by the directive and their duty under Article 5 of the Treaty to take all appropriate measures, whether general or particular [see now Article 4(3) TEU], to ensure the fulfilment of that obligation, is binding on all the authorities of Member States including, for matters within their jurisdiction, the courts. It follows that, in applying the national law and in particular the provisions of a national law specifically introduced in order to implement directive no 76/207, national courts are required to interpret their national law in the light of the wording and the purpose of the directive in order to achieve the result referred to in the third paragraph of Article 189.

Article 4 TEU plays the role of leverage for the hereby launched obligation to interpret national law in the light and the purpose of the directive in question. Since *von Colson and Kamann*, several cases have followed up on it in various substantive areas of law other than labour law.

Generally, the Member States must interpret national law in accordance with a directive from the expiry of the time-limit for its transposition. In *Adeneler*,[177] in which the CJEU answered preliminary questions on fixed term employment contracts, it held that already from the date upon which a directive has entered into force,[178] the courts of the Member States must refrain as far as possible from interpreting domestic law in a manner which might seriously compromise, after the period for transposition has expired, attainment of the objective pursued by that directive.

175. Council Directive 2004/113/EC of 13 December 2004 implementing the principle of equal treatment between men and women in the access to and supply of goods and services.
176. Case 14/83 *von Colson* [1984] ECR p. 1891, Para. 26.
177. Case C-212/04 *Adeneler* [2006] ECR I-6057.
178. Directives are either (i) published in the Official Journal of the EU, in that case, they enter into force on the date specified in them or, in the absence thereof, on the 20 th day following that of their publication, or (ii) notified to those to whom they are addressed, in that case they take effect upon such notification.

9.2.3 Reference to ECHR as a Source of law

Today, the European Convention on Human Rights (ECHR) is regarded as an integral part of EU law, see above in section 8, and an important source of EU fundamental rights, see *ERT*[179] where the CJEU stated (emphasis added):

> With regard to Article 10 of the European Convention on Human Rights, referred to in the ninth and tenth questions, it must first be pointed out that, as the Court has consistently held, fundamental rights form an integral part of the general principles of law, the observance of which it ensures. For that purpose the Court draws inspiration from the constitutional traditions common to the Member States and from the guidelines supplied by international treaties for the protection of human rights on which the Member States have collaborated or of which they are signatories (see, in particular, the judgment in Case C-4/73 Nold v Commission [1974] ECR 491, paragraph 13). *The European Convention on Human Rights has special significance in that respect (see in particular Case C-222/84 Johnston v Chief Constable of the Royal Ulster Constabulary [1986] ECR 1651, paragraph 18).*

France ratified the ECHR in 1975. It was first after that that all the then six Member States of the EC/EU had ratified the ECHR. The first time fundamental rights were specifically referred to in a labour law case was in 1975 in *Rutili*,[180] which also is the first case where the CJEU referred to the ECHR. In *Rutili*, a migrant Italian worker in France was prohibited from residing in four departments in France. The limitations placed on the powers of Member States in respect of control of aliens are in the view of the CJEU a specific manifestation of the more general principle, enshrined in Articles 8, 9, 10 and 11 ECHR.

9.2.4 Generalisation of labour law in the field of Equality and Non-discrimination

EU Discrimination law started as gender discrimination law in employment in the 1970´s. After the adoption of the Amsterdam Treaty which came into force 1 May 1999, the principle of non-discrimination and the way it was tackled in gender discrimination law in relation to the labour market has been generalized to other discrimination grounds (ethnicity, religion, age, disability, sexual orientation, etc.) and other fields of society than the labour market.

179. Case C-260/89, *ERT* [1991] ECR I-2925.
180. Case 36/75 *Rutili* v *Minister of the Interior* [1975] ECR 1219.

9.2.5 Double aim – both economic and social

Balancing economic and social rights has become a general issue since the Lisbon Treaty according to which it is one of the Union's goals to develop a highly competitive social market economy, see Article 3(3)TEU. At least since the 1970's the CJEU has held that the EC/EU has this double aim, both economic and social, in labour law cases, see *Defrenne II.*[181] In the *Deutsche Telekom*-cases[182] on equal pay, the CJEU held that the the economic aim pursued by Article 157 TFEU, namely the elimination of distortions of competition between undertakings established in different Member States, is secondary to its social aim, which constitutes the expression of a fundamental human right not to be discriminated against on grounds of sex.

9.2.6 Minimum Harmonization

EU Labour law is a major example of an area of law where the Member States by and large only have conferred power to the EU legislator to adopt minimum harmonisation by secondary legislation, see Article 153 TFEU which is the typical legal basis for secondary legislation in EU labour law and above in section 3.

9.2.7 Enforcement

There is no EU labour law enforcement system. In EU law, it is settled case-law that, in the absence of EU rules governing the matter, it is for the domestic legal system of each Member State to designate the courts and tribunals having jurisdiction and to lay down the procedural rules and sanctions, provided, however, that such rules are not less favourable than those governing similar domestic actions and do not render virtually impossible or excessively difficult the exercise of rights conferred by EU law.

Enforcement of the rules adopted at EU level thus takes place in the national legal systems of the Member States in accordance with their normal rules on sanctions and procedures. They must observe the EU fundamental rights and general principles when enforcing EU law, see on *Cavallero* [183] above in section 3.2.9.

181. Case 43/75 *Defrenne II* [1976] ECR 455.
182. Case C-50/96 *Schröder* [2000] ECR I-743, case C-270/97 *Sievers* [2000] ECR I-929 and Joined Case C-234/96 and C-235/96 *Vick et al.* [2000] ECR I-799.
183. Case C-442/00 *Cavallero* [2002] ECR I-11915.

9.3 Changes in National Doctrines of the Sources of Law: Diminishing Role of Collective Agreements and Preparatory Works

National legal orders within the EU have traditionally differed greatly as to the identification and relative primacy/weight of different sources of law. The continental tradition emphasizes the text of the statute as an expression of the will of the sovereign legislature and the same tradition may restrict the use of other, potentially competing sources, such as judicial decisions. In common law traditions, the role of the judiciary is acknowledged as 'finding' the law, judge-made case law therefore becoming an important source of law, often coupled with the legally binding nature of judicial precedents by higher courts. In the Nordic countries, labour law has been a special discipline with collective agreements as a particularly important and special source of law. According to Article 288 TFEU a directive shall be binding, as to the result to be achieved, upon each Member State to which it is addressed, but shall leave to the national authorities the choice of form and methods. One could believe that Article 288 TFEU implies that the Member States are free to choose with what kind of sources of law they will ensure that the objectives of a directive is met. If for example a Member State has a preference for collective agreements over legislation like Denmark had before entering the EC/EU one could believe that it was free to choose to transpose directives into national law by means of collective agreements and avoid statutory legislation. That is, however, not the case.

9.3.1 Collective agreements

In some EU Member States,[184] notably the Nordic countries, collective agreements have traditionally played a very important role as source of national labour law before entry into the EC/EU.[185] The Danish preference for implementation by means of collective agreements must be seen against the historical background of Danish labour law. The traditional preference for collective agreements in the Nordic countries has partly changed. Most issues which were formerly only regulated by collective agreement are today governed by EU law, either primary or secondary legislation or fundamental rights or general principles of EU law. In connection with implementation of directives EU law requires Member States to use some sources of law rather

184. See for a broad overview of collective agreements below in Chapter Three.

185. See further Fahlbeck, Rheinhold: Industrial Relations and Collective Labour Law: Characteristics, Principles and Basic Features', and Hasselbalch, Ole: The Roots – the History of Nordic Labour Law', both in *Scandinavian Studies in Law*, Stockholm, Vol. 43, Stability and Change in Nordic Labour Law, 2002, pp. 87 and 11 respectively.

than others,[186] in particular legislation. Collective agreements as implementing measures are only partly accepted, see further below in Chapter Three.

9.3.2 Preparatory Works

In the Nordic countries, preambles are typically not used when drafting legislation. Many legal actors in these countries regard the preparatory works of legislation as a functional equivalent to preambles. The Nordic legislators' habit of placing some rules or observations about the law in the preparatory works of statutes and the importance attached to preparatory works as a source of law has given rise to two infringement cases brought by the Commission against Denmark and Sweden before the CJEU in connection with implementation of directives, see *Commission* v *Denmark*[187] on the implementation of the Equal Pay Directive from 1975 where the CJEU ruled that Denmark had violated its duties under the EC□Treaty by partly implementing the Equal Pay Directive in the preparatory works of the implementing Act and not in its text and *Commission* v *Sweden*[188] on the implementation of the Directive on unfair terms in consumer contracts[189] where Sweden had implemented part of the Directive in the preparatory works and not in the text of the implementing Act. Denmark and Finland had done the same and intervened in the case in support of Sweden. The Advocate general stated (emphasis added):[190]

> The Commission claims that the importance of the preparatory work has declined as a result of Sweden's accession to the European Union, but the Swedish Government contests that assertion. *It is possible that the preparatory work for a law is still an important source of law in the Nordic countries.*

10 The relationship between International labour law, EU labour law and national labour law

As set out in Chapter One, I think there is a shift in focus from seeing labour law as part of many different, separate legal systems to a 'one big system

186. See further Nielsen, Ruth: Implementation of EC Directives in Denmark, The International Journal of Comparative Labour Law and Industrial Relations, Volume 18 2002.Issue 4, p. 459.
187. Case 143/83 *Commission* v *Denmark* [1985] ECR 427.
188. Case C-478/99 *Commission* v *Sweden* [2002] ECR I-4147.
189. 93/13/EEC.
190. In footnote 32 of his opinion.

model' comprising the mutually interlocked labout law systems of the Member States, the EU and international labour law. It is pretty evident that EU labour and national labour law is very interlocked today both by legal means and through political and economic integration, see further above in section 9.2. How international labour law fits into that model is less clear. Traditionally the national (domestic) systems have retained considerable freedom to choose how much or little weight they would give to their international law obligations.

10.1 National law and international law: The monist and dualist approach in national law

In its pure form, the monist approach to the relationship between international and national law considers the rules of international law to be part of the domestic legal system and requires the domestic courts to apply them directly. Conflicts between international law and rules of domestic origin may in a monist system be solved in various ways, for example by giving priority to international law, to the domestic rules, to the domestic rules of a certain rank, etc. Under EU law, international treaties entered into by the EU form part of EU law without any incorporation being necessary. EU law is thus in principle based on the monist approach.

The Scandinavian countries, on the other hand, have traditionally followed the dualist approach according to which international law is a separate legal system, not directly applicable in national courts.[191] This means that conflicts between international and domestic law can in principle not arise before national courts, which are not allowed to apply international law directly but have a duty to interpret national law in accordance with international law if that is possible. In order for treaties ratified by 'dualist' states to become part of national law, they must be incorporated by national legislation of some kind. In most cases the Scandinavian courts will be able to interpret domestic law so as to comply with the country's international obligations, but on a few occasions the principled dualist approach has been upheld by the courts.

The dualist attitude was for example confirmed by the Swedish Labour Court (Arbetsdomstolen) in the case *Svenska Lokmannaförbundet* v *The State* in 1972.[192] The Labour Court decided a dispute between a small trade union for railway engine drivers and the State as employer, who had refused to ne-

191. See further Scheinin, Martin: International Law and Human Rights – Good or Bad for European Union Law? In Neergaard, Ulla and Ruth Nielsen (eds): European Legal Method – in a Multi-Level EU Legal Order, Copenhagen 2012.

192. Arbetsdomstolens Domar 1972, no. 5.

gotiate a collective agreement. The trade union invoked, *inter alia*, certain international human rights conventions and ILO treaties ratified by Sweden. The Labour Court held that such international instruments could only become 'valid Swedish law' through Swedish legislation, although they could shed light on the meaning of existing Swedish statutes 'which can be assumed to be compatible with our country's international commitments'.[193]

The dualist attitude was also confirmed by a judgment from the Norwegian Supreme Court from May 1997.[194] The Court held that if a particular Norwegian Act prohibiting strikes was inconsistent with ILO Conventions 87 and 98, the Norwegian Act would override international law.

Due to a preference for collective bargaining over statutory regulation,[195] the Nordic (parliamentary) legislators have been somewhat reluctant to fulfil international obligations fully in the field of labour law. Until 1996, it was for example still arguable that Danish private employers under domestic Danish law were legally free to take racist employment decisions, though Denmark ratified the United Nations Convention on the Elimination of All Forms of Racial Discrimination in 1971.

Membership of the EU places the Nordic EU-countries in a new context. The Nordic Member States are now under a duty to follow those parts of international law which the EU has incorporated into EU law in the same way as they must observe other EU law and at the same time 'dualist' as individual nation-states in their individual relation to public international law. It follows from *Kamberaj*,[196] that EU Member States retain their free choice in regard to whether they want to follow the monist or the dualist approach to international law. *Kamberaj* is an Albanian national who has resided and been employed in Italy since 1994. He is the holder of a residence permit for an indefinite period. He complained that he as a third country national with status as long term resident was treated less favourably than EU citizens in regard to housing benefit. The referring Italian court asked *inter alia*:

(2) When there is a conflict between a provision of domestic law and the ECHR, does the reference to the ECHR in Article 6 TEU oblige the national court to apply Articles 14 ECHR and Article 1 of [Protocol No 12] directly, disapplying the incompatible source of

193. See further Bogdan, Michael: Comparative Law Stockholm, 1992.
194. Norsk Rettstidende 1997,580. The Court stated (in Norwegian): 'selv i tilfelle streikeforbudet skulle ha vært i strid med folkerettslige bestemmelser om vern av retten til streik, ville det følge av norsk rett at den provisoriske anordning om tvungen lønnsnemnd var gyldig'.
195. Bruun et al.: The Nordic Labour Relations Model, Dartmouth 1992.
196. Case C-571/10 *Kamberaj* [2012] ECR nyr.

domestic law, without having first to raise the issue of constitutionality before the national constitutional court?

The CJEU stated that Article 6(3) TEU does not govern the relationship between the ECHR and the legal systems of the Member States and nor does it lay down the consequences to be drawn by a national court in case of conflict between the rights guaranteed by that convention and a provision of national law. The EU Member States can thus still choose at their own discretion whether they want to follow the monist or dualist approach in relation to their interntional law commitments.

10.2 Pre-EC/EU international law obligations which are inconsistent with EU law

According to Article 351 TFEU, the rights and obligations arising from agreements concluded before 1 January 1958 or, for acceding Member States, before the date of their accession, between one or more Member States on the one hand, and one or more third countries on the other, are not affected by the provisions of the Treaties. To the extent that such agreements are not compatible with the Treaties, the Member State or States concerned shall take all appropriate steps to eliminate the incompatibilities. This provision has been used in two cases on old (outdated) ILO-conventions prohibiting night work for women.[197] The CJEU held in *Stoeckel*[198] that it is inconsistent with current sex discrimination law to prohibit night work for women on other conditions than for men. It ruled:

> Article 5 of Council Directive 76/207/EEC of 9 February 1976 on the implementation of the principle of equal treatment for men and women as regards access to employment, vocational training and promotion, and working conditions is sufficiently precise to impose on the Member States the obligation not to lay down by legislation the principle that nightwork by women is prohibited, even if that is subject to exceptions, where nightwork by men is not prohibited.

197. ILO Convention NO 4, Night Work (Women) 1919, ILO Convention (Revised) (No. 41), the Night Work (Women), 1934 (No. 41), and Convention No. 89 the Night Work (Women) Convention (Revised), 1948.
198. Case C-345/89 *Stoeckel* [1991] ECR I-4047.

In *Levy*,[199] the CJEU held:

> The national court is under an obligation to ensure that Article 5 of Directive 76/207/EEC of 9 February 1976 on the implementation of the principle of equal treatment for men and women as regards access to employment, vocational training and promotion, and working conditions is fully complied with by refraining from applying any conflicting provision of national legislation, unless the application of such a provision is necessary in order to ensure the performance by the Member State concerned of obligations arising under an agreement concluded with non-member countries prior to the entry into force of the EEC Treaty.

As appears from the text of Article 351 TFEU, the Member States shall take all appropriate steps to eliminate the incompatibilities between their international law obligations and EU law, e.g. by denouncing the international treaties they have ratified which are incompatible with EU law. A number of EU Member States, which had ratified some old ILO night work conventions for women, have denounced them. The incompatibility between ILO law and EU law on this point has thus disappeared.

It has been argued that the limited right to take collective action accepted by the CJEU in *Laval*[200] falls short of the level of protection of the right to strike provided by ILO Convention 87. It has been suggested that the Swedish government in *Laval* should have invoked Article 351 TFEU and contended that the Swedish rules on strikes are necessary to comply with duties undertaken under public international law before membership of the EU and therefore according to Article 351 TFEU take precedence over EU law.[201] As appears from Article 351 TFEU, the Member State must do what it can to eliminate the incompatibilities. In my view, ILO convention 87, which does not even explicitly mention the right to strike, does not protect that right better than Article 28 CFREU, see further on the right to strike and take other collective action below in Chapter Three. Anyway, it would only be a temporary solution. It would follow from the EU Member States' duty of loyal cooperation under Article 4(3) TEU and Article 351 TFEU that Sweden and other EU Member States would then have a duty to denounce ILO Convention No. 87.

199. Case C-158/91 *Levy* [1993] I-4307. See for a similar judgment Case C-13/93 *Minne* [1994] ECR I-371.
200. Case C-341/05 *Laval* [2007] ECR I-11767.
201. See Ronnie Eklund: A Swedish Perspective on Laval, Comparative Labor Law and Policy Journal 2008 p. 551.

CHAPTER THREE

Collective Labour Law: The Right to Organise, Collective Bargaining and Industrial Action

1 Introduction

In this Chapter I deal with classic collective labour law issues like freedom of association, the positive and negative right to organize, collective bargaining and industrial action, i.e. the workers' right to strike, make blockades and use sympathetic actions (secondary actions) in support of strikes or blockades and the employers' right to impose lockouts or boycotts on workers.

2 Sources of Law

2.1 National law

The oldest layer of European collective labour law on the freedom of association and the right to organize, collective bargaining and industrial action is found in national law. Such rules existed as stated in the EU Social Action Programme 1989[1] in all the EU Member States prior to their membership of the EC/EU.

Trade unions and employers' organisations were established in all European countries in the early period of industrialization. The general pattern was that the law originally repressed these organisations, in particular trade unions. Trade union activities were typically a criminal offence.[2] During the

1. http://aei.pitt.edu/1345/1/Social_charter_COM_89_568.pdf .
2. See further Jacobs, Antoine: Collective Self-Regulation in Hepple, Bob: Making of labour law in Europe. A comparative study of nine countries up to 1945, London, 1986 p. 193 *et seq*.

19th century the legal bans were gradually lifted; in 1824 in England, in 1869 in Germany and in 1884 in France. In the Nazi-period in Germany from 1933-45, trade unions were abolished. After the Second World War the positive aspect of the freedom of association, i.e. the right of individuals to form and join a trade union or an association of employers has been firmly established in all the present EU Member States. From national law Germany may be mentioned as an example. In that country Article 9(3) of the Constitution (Grundgesetz) guarantees the freedom of association (Koalitionsfreiheit).[3]

In some of the Eastern European Member States traditional collective labour law rights may have been less well established.[4] In a few countries, among them Denmark, closed shop agreements, i.e. violations of the negative right to organise were considered lawful until the judgments of the ECtHR in the Sørensen and Rasmussen[5] case in 2003 which struck down the right of Council of Europe Member States to allow closed shop agreements, see further below in section 4.5.

2.2 Public International Law

The next layer in time stems from international labour law, first ILO law then a few years later conventions adopted in the framework of the Council of Europe.

2.2.1 ILO Law

The two basic ILO Conventions on collective labour law are Convention No. 87, Freedom of Association and Protection of the Right to Organise Convention, 1948 and Convention No. 98, Right to Organise and Collective Bargain-

3. BAG 17.2.1998, Aus den Gründen: »... Die Koalitionsfreiheit gilt nach Art. 9 Abs. 3 GG für jedermann und für alle Berufe. Das Grundrecht beschränkt sich nicht auf die Gewährleistung der Freiheit des einzelnen, eine Vereinigung zur Förderung der Arbeits- und Wirtschaftsbedingungen zu gründen, ihr beizutreten oder fernzubleiben oder sie zu verlassen. Es schützt vielmehr ebenso die Koalition selbst in ihrem Bestand, ihrer organisatorischen Ausgestaltung und auch in ihrer Betätigung, soweit diese gerade in der Wahrung und Förderung der Arbeits- und Wirtschaftsbedingungen besteht. Umfaßt sind danach auch der Abschluß von Tarifverträgen als wesentlicher Zweck der Koalitionen sowie der Einsatz hierauf gerichteter Mittel wie Arbeitskampfmaßnahmen.« quoted from http://www.betriebsraete.de/bag-1998/1%20AZR%20364-97.TXT published in 1 AZR 364/97.
4. See further Blanpain, Roger og Lajos Nagy: Labour law and industrial relations in Central and Eastern Europe – from planned to market economy – Bulletin of comparative labour relations, nr.31, The Hague, 1996.
5. Sørensen & Rasmussen v Denmark (applications nos 52562/99 and 52620/99).

ing Convention, 1949. ILO Convention No. 87 is ratified by 130 states including all the EU Member States and ILO Convention No. 98 is ratified by 146 states including all the EU Member States. These ILO conventions thus constitute a common legal framework for both national and EU collective labour law.

Article 2 of ILO Convention No. 87, The Freedom of Association and Protection of the Right to Organise Convention, 1948 provides:

> Workers and employers, without distinction whatsoever, shall have the right to establish and, subject only to the rules of the organisation concerned, to join organisations of their own choosing without previous authorisation.

Article 1 of ILO Convention No. 98, The Right to Organise and Collective Bargaining Convention, 1949 lays down that:

1. (1) Workers shall enjoy adequate protection against acts of anti-union discrimination in respect of their employment.
1. (2) Such protection shall apply more particularly in respect of acts calculated to-
   (a) make the employment of a worker subject to the condition that he shall not join a union or shall relinquish trade union membership;
   (b) cause the dismissal of or otherwise prejudice a worker by reason of union membership or because of participation in union activities outside working hours or, with the consent of the employer, within working hours.

The right to strike and take other collective action is not explicitly mentioned in ILO Conventions Nos 87 and 98, see further below in section 7.

2.2.2 Council of Europe Conventions

Article 11 of the *European Convention on Human Rights 1950 (ECHR)* protects the right to freedom of assembly and association, including the right to form trade unions, subject to certain restrictions that are 'in accordance with law' and 'necessary in a democratic society'. It provides:

> Everyone has the right to freedom of peaceful assembly and to freedom of association with others, including the right to form and to join trade unions for the protection of his interests.
>
> No restrictions shall be placed on the exercise of these rights other than such as are prescribed by law and are necessary in a democratic society in the interests of national security or public safety, for the prevention of disorder or crime, for the protection of health or morals or for the protection of the rights and freedoms of others. This Article shall not prevent the imposition of lawful restrictions on the exercise of these rights by members of the armed forces, of the police or of the administration of the State.

The Council of Europe Social Charter 1961[6] to which there is reference in the Preamble to TEU and in Article 151 TFEU provides in Article 5 on the right to organise.

With a view to ensuring or promoting the freedom of workers and employers to form local, national or international organisations for the protection of their economic and social interests and to join those organisations, the Contracting Parties undertake that national law shall not be such as to impair, nor shall it be so applied as to impair, this freedom. The extent to which the guarantees provided for in this article shall apply to the police shall be determined by national laws or regulations. The principle governing the application to the members of the armed forces of these guarantees and the extent to which they shall apply to persons in this category shall equally be determined by national laws or regulations.

and in Article 6 on the right to bargain collectively:

With a view to ensuring the effective exercise of the right to bargain collectively, the Contracting Parties undertake:

1. to promote joint consultation between workers and employers;
2. to promote, where necessary and appropriate, machinery for voluntary negotiations between employers or employers' organisations and workers' organisations, with a view to the regulation of terms and conditions of employment by means of collective agreements;
3. to promote the establishment and use of appropriate machinery for conciliation and voluntary arbitration for the settlement of labour disputes; and recognise:
4. the right of workers and employers to collective action in cases of conflicts of interest, including the right to strike, subject to obligations that might arise out of collective agreements previously entered into.

2.3 EU law

The EC/EU didn't address core collective labour law issues like the right to organize, collective bargaining and the right to strike until the 1980's. By Article 118 b EEC which was inserted in the EEC Treaty by the Single European Act 1986, the Commission[7] was put under a duty to endeavor to develop

6. See Samuel, Lenia: Fundamental Social Rights. Case Law of the European Social Charter, Strassbourg 1997.
7. On the basis of its comparative study, on Labour Law (SEC(89) 1137) and taking into account the conclusions of the Council (Social Affairs), of 30 October 1989 as well as the then current development of the Social Dialogue, the Commission in the Social Action Programme 1989 declared its intention to prepare a communication on the development of collective bargaining including collective agreements at European level with special reference to the settlement of disputes.

the dialogue between management and labour at European level which could, if the two sides considered it desirable, lead to relations based on agreement. The EU is in the process of integrating the social partners into its decisions-making processes in regard to a wide spectrum of issues, see above in Chapter Two on the so-called 'social dialogue', a term which the European Commission in its report from 2000 on Industrial Relations in Europe[8] defines in the following way:

Social dialogue: Process of continuous interaction between the social partners with the aim of reaching agreements on the control of certain economic and social variables, at both macro and micro levels.

2.3.1 The Community Charter of the Fundamental Social Rights of Workers 1989

The Community Charter of the Fundamental Social Rights of Workers 1989,[9] which as mentioned in Chapter Two is only soft law, originally backed by only eleven of the then twelve Member States, but later accepted as source of binding EU law, see further in Chapter Two, goes rather far in providing for collective labour law rights as part of EU law. It states on freedom of association, collective bargaining and the right to strike and take other collective action (emphasis added):

11. Employers and workers of the European Community shall have the right of association in order to constitute professional organisations or trade unions of their choice for the defence of their economic and social interests.

Every employer and every worker shall have the freedom to join or *not to join* such organisations without any personal or occupational damage being thereby suffered by him.

12. Employers or employers' organisations, on the one hand, and workers' organisations, on the other, shall have the right to negotiate and conclude collective agreements under the conditions laid down by national legislation and practice.

The dialogue between the two sides of industry at European level which must be developed, may, if the parties deem it desirable, result in contractual relations, in particular at inter-occupational and sectoral level.

13. The right to resort to collective action in the event of a conflict of interests shall include the right to strike, subject to the obligations arising under national regulations and collective agreements. ...

8. COM(2000)113 p 8.
9. http://www.aedh.eu/plugins/fckeditor/userfiles/file/Conventions%20internationales/Community_Charter_of_the_Fundamental_Social_Rights_of_Workers.pdf.

Even though the Community Charter of the Fundamental Social Rights of Workers 1989 is only soft law it is referred to in primary EU law and therefore has greater weight than soft law usually has. The Preamble to the TEU refers to the Charter. Article 151 TFEU which is the current goal provision for EU Social Policy states, as mentioned in Chapter Two (emphasis added), that 'the Union and the Member States, having in mind fundamental social rights such as those set out in the European Social Charter signed at Turin on 18 October 1961 and *in the 1989 Community Charter of the Fundamental Social Rights of Workers*, shall have as their objectives the promotion of employment, improved living and working conditions, so as to make possible their harmonisation while the improvement is being maintained, proper social protection, dialogue between management and labour, the development of human resources with a view to lasting high employment and the combating of exclusion.' There are also many references to the Community Charter of the Fundamental Social Rights of Workers 1989 as source of the provisions in CFREU in the Explanatory Remarks[10] to that Charter.

There is a considerable overlap in substantive content between the CFREU and the Community Charter of the Fundamental Social Rights of Workers 1989. To the degree the Community Charter of the Fundamental Social Rights of Workers 1989 goes further that the CFREU, as for example in regard to the negative right to organize (the right not to join an organization), the legal effect of the Community Charter of the Fundamental Social Rights of Workers 1989 is in principle limited to that of value and goal provisions. This means that the rights declared in the Community Charter of the Fundamental Social Rights of Workers 1989 and not repeated in the CFREU are not on the basis of the Community Charter of the Fundamental Social Rights of Workers as only source of law directly applicable, enforceable fundamental rights. In support of that interpretation *Zaera*[11] can be referred to. In that case, the CJEU stated on the goal provision in Article 151 TFEU [then Article 117 EEC] that it is not directly applicable but added:

> 14. The fact that the objectives of social policy laid down in Article 117 are in the nature of a programme does not mean that they are deprived of any legal effect. They constitute an important aid, in particular for the interpretation of other provisions of the Treaty and of secondary Community legislation in the social field. The attainment of those objectives must nevertheless be the result of a social policy which must be defined by the competent authorities.

10. OJ 2007 C 303.
11. Case 126/86 *Zaera* [1987] 3697.

As described below in section 4.5. the ECtHR referred to the Community Charter of the Fundamental Social Rights of Workers 1989 as one of the sources of law it used in the *Sørensen and Ramussen* case,[12]

As set out in Chapter Two Article 153 TFEU which is the current main provision on EU competence in labour law empowers the EU legislator to adopt secondary EU legislation on most employment issues that can arise at national level. Article 153(5) TFEU provides that as an exception this provision shall not apply to pay, the right of association, the right to strike or the right to impose lock-outs.

2.3.2 Guidelines for the economic policies in th EMU

As mentioned in Chapter One the Council Recommendation on broad guidelines for the economic policies of the Member States and of the Union[13] provides in Guideline two on 'Addressing macroeconomic imbalances' *inter alia* that 'The social partners have an important role to play in this context'.

2.3.3 CFREU

Article 12 of the CFREU provides on freedom of assembly and of association:

> Everyone has the right to freedom of peaceful assembly and to freedom of association at all levels, in particular in political, trade union and civic matters, which implies the right of everyone to form and to join trade unions for the protection of his or her interests.

and in Article 28 on the right to collective bargaining and action

> Workers and employers, or their respective organisations, have, in accordance with Union law and national laws and practices, the right to negotiate and conclude collective agreements at the appropriate levels and, in cases of conflicts of interest, to take collective action to defend their interests, including strike action.

In *Hennigs*,[14] the CJEU held that the principle of non-discrimination on grounds of age proclaimed in Article 21 of the CFREU and given specific expression in the Framework Employment Directive,[15] and more particularly Articles 2 and 6(1) of that directive, must be interpreted as precluding a measure laid down by a collective agreement such as that at issue in the main proceedings which provides that, within each salary group, the basic pay step

12. *Sørensen & Rasmussen* v *Denmark* (applications nos 52562/99 and 52620/99).
13. Recommendation 2010/410/EU, OJ 2010 L 191.
14. Case C-297/10 *Hennigs* [2011] nyr.
15. 2000/78/EC.

of a public sector contractual employee is determined on appointment by reference to the employee's age. The fact that EU law precludes that measure and that it appears in a collective agreement does not interfere with the right to negotiate and conclude collective agreements recognised in Article 28 CFREU. Articles 2 and 6(1) of the Framework Employment Directive and Article 28 CFREU must be interpreted as not precluding a measure in a collective agreement, such as that at issue in the main proceedings in *Hennig*, which replaces a system of pay leading to discrimination on grounds of age by a system of pay based on objective criteria while maintaining, for a transitional period limited in time, some of the discriminatory effects of the earlier system in order to ensure that employees in post are transferred to the new system without suffering a loss of income.

It is conspicuous that there is no mention in the CFREU of the basic ILO conventions. At the plenary session of the European Parliament on 16 March 2000,[16] the Parliament adopted a resolution recommending that the EU Treaty be amended to (emphasis added):

> add ... *relevant instruments* adopted by the International Labour Organisation (ILO) ... to the reference to the Council of Europe's Convention for the protection of Human Rights and Fundamental Freedoms currently found in Article 6 EU.

The Swedish trade unions[17] suggested a reference to some ILO conventions, see the following (emphasis added):

> The EU Member States and the EU's institutions should be obliged to follow ... the fundamental ILO conventions on *the right of association, the right to strike, the right to bargain collectively* and the prohibition of child labour and enforced labour.

The proposals for reference to ILO Conventions were not followed. In the Explanatory remarks[18] to the CFREU there is reference to the Community Charter on the Fundamental Social Rights of Workers 1989 and the European Social Charter 1961 amended in 1996 as sources of Article 12 and 28 CFREU but no reference to ILO Conventions.

16. A5-0064/2000 European Parliament resolution on the drafting of a European Union Charter of Fundamental Rights (C5-0058/1999 – 1999/2064(COS)).
17. LO's, TCO's and SACO's demands for changes to the EU Treaty, Brussels 13.6.2000, Charte 4355/00, Contrib 219. Available at the Internet at the EU Council's web-site.
18. OJ 2007 C 303.

2.3.4 Free movement of workers

The then Regulation on free movement of workers[19] was amended in 1976 to clarify migrant workers' right to engage in trade union activity.

2.3.5 Case law

In *Kortner*[20] the CJEU stated:

Under the general principles of labour law the freedom of trade union activity recognised under Article 24a of the Staff Regulations means not only that officials and servants have the right without hindrance to form associations of their own choosing, but also that these associations are free to do anything lawful to protect the interests of their members as employees.

The right of action is one of the means available for use by these associations.

16. Under the Community legal system, however, the exercise of this right is subject to the conditions determined by the system of forms of action provided for under the treaties establishing the communities.

17. Thus a staff association which fulfils these conditions is entitled, by virtue of the second paragraph of article 173 of the EEC Treaty [now Article 263 TFEU], to institute proceedings for annulment against a decision addressed to it within the meaning of that provision.

In *Maurissen*[21] the CJEU held that:

Community institutions, and the bodies treated as such for the application of the Staff Regulations by virtue of Article 1 thereof, must refrain from doing anything which might impede the freedom of trade union activity. The freedom of trade union activity thus recognized means not only that officials and servants have the right without hindrance to form associations of their own choosing but also that such associations are free to do anything lawful to protect the interests of their members as employees. It thus follows, in the first place, that the Community institutions and bodies may not prohibit their officials and servants from joining a trade union or staff association or from participating in trade union activities, or impose any penalty whatsoever on them by reason of such membership or activities. It also follows that the Community institutions and bodies must allow trade unions and staff associations to fulfil their proper role, *inter alia* by keeping officials and servants informed, representing them vis-à-vis the institutions and bodies and participating in con-

19. Council Regulation (EEC) No 312/76 of 9 February 1976 amending the provisions relating to the trade union rights of workers contained in Regulation (EEC) No 1612/68 on freedom of movement for workers within the Community. That Regulation is now repealed and replaced with Regulation EU/492/2011, see further below in Chapter Five.
20. 1973175Case 175/73 *Kortner* [1974] ECR 917.
21. Joined 1987193Joined Cases C-193/87 and C-194/87 *Maurissen* [1990] ECR I-95.

sultations with those institutions and bodies on all matters affecting staff, and may not treat them differently without justification

Although freedom to engage in trade union activity constitutes a general principle of labour law, it cannot be extended so as to require EU institutions and bodies to make their messenger services available to trade unions for the distribution to staff of the communications issued by those organizations.

In the *ASTI* case[22] the CJEU held that:

Article 8(1) of Regulation No 1612/68[23] constitutes a particular expression of the principle of non-discrimination in the specific field of workers' participation in trade-union organizations and activities and its scope cannot be limited on the basis of considerations relating to the legal form of the body in question. On the contrary, the exercise of the trade-union rights referred to in that provision extends beyond the bounds of trade-union organizations in the strict sense and includes, in particular, the participation of workers in bodies which, while not being, in law, trade-union organizations, perform similar functions as regards the defence and representation of workers' interests.

That provision must therefore be interpreted as meaning that it precludes legislation refusing workers the right to vote in elections of members of an occupational guild to which they are compulsorily affiliated, to which they must pay contributions, which is responsible for defending the interests of affiliated workers and which performs a consultative function in the legislative field. Neither the legal nature of the guild in question under national law nor the fact that certain of its functions could involve participation in the exercise of powers conferred by public law can justify the exclusion of workers from other Member States from participation in the election of members of that guild.

3 Positive right of Association

The positive right of association is – as regards workers' rights to join trade unions – their right to be a member of a particular trade union according to their own choice and similarly as regards employers' right to join employers' organisations their freedom to choose for themselves which organisation they will join.

The Positive Freedom of Association is guaranteed in a number of provisions at national level, international level and at EU level, see in particular Article 2 of ILO Convention No. 87, Article 1 of ILO Convention No. 98, Aritcle 11 ECHR, Article 5 and 6 of the European Council Social Charter and

22. 1990213Case C-213/90 *Association de Soutien aux Travailleurs Immigrés* [1991] ECR I-74.
23. I.e. the then Regulation on free movement of workers, now replaced with Regulation 492/2011, see further in Chapter Five.

Article 12 and 28 of the CFREU, all cited above in section 2 on the sources of law. The positive right to organize has been dealt wioth in a number of cases.

3.1 Rutili

In *Rutili*[24] the CJEU gave a ruling on the interpretation of Article 45 TFEU on free movement of workers in regard to limitations to that freedom imposed by a Member State who regarded the restriction necessary out of concern for public policy because of the trade union activity of a migrant worker. The CJEU held that an appraisal as to whether measures designed to safeguard public policy are justified must have regard to all rules of Community law. These limitations and safeguards arise, in particular, from the duty imposed on Member States to base the measures adopted exclusively on the personal conduct of the individuals concerned, to refrain from adopting any measures in this respect which service ends unrelated to the requirements of public policy or which adversely affect the exercise of trade union rights. The Court concluded that there is a duty upon the member States:

> to refrain from adopting any measures in this respect which service ends unrelated to the requirements of public policy or which adversely affect the exercise of trade union rights

3.2 Vogt

In Vogt v Germany,[25] the ECtHR held by 10 votes to 9, that Articles 10 and 11 of the ECHR were violated by a dismissal of a German sector employee in accordance with the German *Berufsverbot*. On January 28, 1972, a so-called Radikalenerlass (Anti-Radical Decree) was issued in Germany. Under this law, people who were considered to have radical views, especially if they were members of such parties, could be forbidden to work as civil servants (Beamte), which includes a variety of public sector occupations such as teaching. The decree was a response to terrorism by the Red Army Faction (Rote Armee Fraktion) which was active in Europe in the 1970's nad early 1980's.

Vogt joined the German Communist Party (GCP) in 1972. In 1977, she became a language teacher at a public secondary school and. In 1986, Vogt was suspended based on the *Berufsverbot*. The German courts considered her dismissal legal, considering GCP's aims anti-constitutional and active membership in GCP incompatible with a civil servant's duty of loyalty. In Vogt v

24. Case 36/75 *Rutili* [1975] ECR 1219.
25. Application no. 17851/91.

Germany, the ECtHR considered the dismissal disproportionate to the legitimate aim pursued by the *Berufsverbot*. The court underlined that Vogt was a teacher of German and French in a secondary school, a post which did not intrinsically involve any security risks. There was no evidence that Vogt herself, even outside her work at school, actually made anti-constitutional statements or personally adopted an anti-constitutional stance.

3.3 Moser

In *Moser*[26] a German national who had passed the first teaching examination and sought to become a teacher Moser, applied to the Land Baden-Württemberg authoriteis to be allowed to undertake postgraduate training with the status of probationary official or, alternatively, as an employee under contract. The Land refused to allow Moser to undertake postgraduate training on the ground that he was a member of the German Communist party. He brought an action before a German court whch sent preliminary questions to the CJEU as to whether a person like Moser was a worker within the meaning of Article 45 TFEU. Germany protested against the admissibility of the case because everything in the case was German. The EU free movement rules therefore did not apply. The Commission suggested that the Court should draw the attention of the national court to the limitations to which the principle of the free movement of persons is subject. The CJEU replied that Article 45 TFEU does not apply to situations which are wholly internal to a Member State, such as that of a national of a Member State who has never resided or worked in another Member.

The different results in *Vogt* and *Moser* illustrate the different scope of application of the ECHR and EU fundamental rights in employment matters of a purely internal character. ECHR is applicable in purely national cases while EU fundamental rights are only binding in national law within the scope of EU law. If a case – like for instance *Moser*'s – has no link at all to EU law EU fundamental rights cannot be invoked at national level. As set out in Chapter Two, the CJEU has interpreted the requirement of a link to EU law broadly so that there will often be sufficient connection to EU law for EU fundamental rights to be applicable in national law, but as *Moser* shows there are limits, see also the cases cited above in Chpter Two section 3.2.9.

26. Case 180/83 *Moser* [1984] ECR 2539.

3.4 Wilson

In the *Wilson* case,[27] Wilson was employed as a journalist at the Daily Mail. The local branch, or 'Chapel' of the National Union of Journalists had been recognised since at least 1912 for the purpose of collective bargaining as regards all aspects of the terms and conditions of employment of its members. On 10 November 1989 Wilson in common with other journalists received the following letter from the editor of the Daily Mail:

'Dear Dave,

You probably know that the collective bargaining agreement between the Chapel and the Management is due to end on 1 April 1990. The Company has given notice that it does not intend to negotiate a new agreement with the Chapel and that, from that date, the NUJ will not be recognised as a negotiating body.

Instead, salaries will be reviewed annually each 1 October as they are already for the senior editors. Departmental heads will make recommendations to me for each individual member of their staff. I will, of course, discuss these with my editors in detail and add my own assessment, as I do now, for merit rises. I shall then implement salary increases.

A handbook has been drawn up which contains the benefits and conditions which exist under the current agreement.

Each member of staff will be given a new contract which embodies these conditions together with the Handbook. I think it is worth pointing out that the Handbook includes a grievance procedure.

All journalists who sign their new contracts before 1 January 1990 will be awarded a 4.5% wage increase backdated to 1 October 1989. As I have said, the next review of salaries will be on 1 October 1990.

I would like to point out that, contrary to what is happening on other national newspapers, our new arrangement does not involve any redundancies. Nor any radical changes in the way we produce our papers.

I think you should know that the initiative to end collective bargaining has come from the editors, not the management.

It is the skill of journalists as individuals that makes our papers. We appoint journalists as individuals and we want to continue to treat them as individuals throughout their whole career here, in order that they and our papers shall prosper.

The success of the Daily Mail is based on its team of highly qualified and highly paid journalists. We intend to develop that success and, with it, the careers of our journalists.

Yours sincerely,

...'

Wilson refused to sign a new contract, because he objected to its provisions prohibiting trade union activity during working hours and removing his right

27. Wilson, National Union of Journalists and others v The UK, Applications nos. 30668/96, 30671/96 and 30678/96.

to be represented by the union and the rights of the union to negotiate with management and be consulted on and agree changes to terms and conditions of employment. In subsequent years Wilson's salary increased, but was never raised to the same level as that of employees who had accepted personal contracts.

The ECtHR observed at the outset that although the essential object of Article 11 is to protect the individual against arbitrary interference by public authorities with the exercise of the rights protected, there may in addition be positive obligations to secure the effective enjoyment of these rights. In the present case, the matters about which the applicants complain – principally, the employers' de-recognition of the unions for collective-bargaining purposes and offers of more favourable conditions of employment to employees agreeing not to be represented by the unions – did not involve direct intervention by the State. The responsibility of the UK would, however, be engaged if these matters resulted from a failure on its part to secure to the applicants under domestic law the rights set forth in Article 11 ECHR.

In the Wilson case, it was under UK law open to the employers to seek to pre-empt any protest on the part of the unions or their members against the imposition of limits on voluntary collective bargaining, by offering those employees who acquiesced in the termination of collective bargaining substantial pay rises, which were not provided to those who refused to sign contracts accepting the end of union representation. The corollary of this was that United Kingdom law permitted employers to treat less favourably employees who were not prepared to renounce a freedom that was an essential feature of union membership. Such conduct constituted a disincentive or restraint on the use by employees of union membership to protect their interests. Under UK law at the relevant time it was, therefore, possible for an employer effectively to undermine or frustrate a trade union's ability to strive for the protection of its members' interests. The ECtHR noted that this aspect of domestic law has been the subject of criticism by the Council of Europe Social Charter's Committee of Independent Experts and the ILO's Committee on Freedom of Association. It considered that, by permitting employers to use financial incentives to induce employees to surrender important union rights, the respondent State had failed in its positive obligation to secure the enjoyment of the rights under Article 11 of the ECHR. This failure amounted to a violation of Article 11, as regards both the applicant trade unions and the individual applicants.

4 The Negative Freedom to organise. Closed Shop Agreements

The negative freedom of association, i.e. the right not to join a particular association is protected at national level in most EU Member States. When that right is accepted closed shop agreements, i.e. provisions in collective agreements putting an obligation upon the employer only to employ workers who are members of a particular trade union, are invalid because they infringe the negative freedom of association. As mentioned above, Article 11 of the Community Social Charter 1989, which is a non binding recommendation, protects the negative freedom to organise. It provides (emphasis added):

> Every employer and every worker shall have the freedom to join *or not to join* such organisations without any personal or occupational damage being thereby suffered by him.

At international level there is a non binding provision in Article 20 of the UN Human Rights Declaration which states that 'No one may be compelled to belong to an association'. It was for a number of years a contentious issue whether the binding provision in Article 11 ECHR should be interpreted as covering both the positive and the negative aspects of freedom of association. It clearly covers the positive aspect of this freedom. In Denmark, the prevailing opinion was until the judgments in the Sørensen and Rasmussen case in 2003 that it did not cover the negative aspect of the freedom of association. The ECtHR delivered four judgment touching upon the question before the judgments in the Sørensen and Rasmussen case in 2003. In two[28] of the judgments restrictions in the negative freedom of association were held to be infringements of the ECHR, in the two other judgments such restrictions were accepted as compatible with the ECHR.[29]

4.1 British Rail

In *British Rail*[30] the ECtHR held:

> Assuming that Article 11 does not guarantee the negative aspect of that freedom on the same footing as the positive aspect, compulsion to join a particular trade union may not always be contrary to the Convention.

28. Young/Webster (*British Rail*) and *Sigurjonsson*. Available at the web site of the ECtHR in Strassbourg, http://www.echr.coe.int/eng/Judgments.htm.
29. *Sibson* and *Gustafsson*.
30. *Young, James and Webster* v *the United Kingdom*, judgment of 13 August 1981, 2/1980/33/49-50.

However, a threat of dismissal involving loss of livelihood is a most serious form of compulsion and, in the present instance, it was directed against persons engaged by British Rail before the introduction of any obligation to join a particular trade union.

In the Court's opinion, such a form of compulsion, in the circumstances of the case, strikes at the very substance of the freedom guaranteed by Article 11. For this reason alone, there has been an interference with that freedom as regards each of the three applicants.

4.2 Sibson

The *Sibson* case[31] was about a driver at a depot in Greengate who had been a branch secretary of the Transport and General Workers Union ('TGWU'). A fellow worker accused him of 'milking the funds' of the union whilst he was branch secretary. Sibson subsequently lodged with the local TGWU branch a complaint to the effect that the fellow worker had 'disseminated false statements tending to depreciate' him as one of its officers, but it was dismissed by the branch adjudication panel. Sibson was so dissatisfied with that decision that he resigned from TGWU and joined the United Road Transport Union instead. Some of his fellow workers immediately ostracised him and others obstructed him in the performance of his work.

Between July and October 1985 the employer which operated plants at various places attempted in vain to resolve the dispute. After a period of 'uneasy peace', a substantial majority of the TGWU members at Greengate voted in favour of (a) a closed shop agreement with the employer and (b) industrial action if Sibson continued in employment at that depot after 25 October 1985. At a meeting on 21 October 1985 between the personnel manager of the employer, and the branch committee of the union it was agreed that the strike threat would be lifted if the applicant either rejoined TGWU or was employed on driving work not based at Greengate. On 22 October the applicant told the personnel manager that he would rejoin the union only if he received an apology and that he would not accept the alternative proposed by the personnel manager, namely a move to Chadderton, a depot about 1½ miles away from Greengate. Further meetings were held. At a final meeting on 8 November 1985 Sibson declined to accept either of the alternatives put before him – working at Greengate after rejoining TGWU or moving to Chadderton – and suggested that the management should dismiss him. The personnel manager refused to do that, and added that if Sibson reported to Greengate for work, he would be sent home without pay. Sibson, citing his solicitor's advice that that would constitute constructive dismissal, then said

31. *Sibson* v *the United Kingdom*, judgment of 20 April 1993, 4/1992/349/422.

that he would resign with immediate effect, which he did by letter of the same date. Sibson alleged that, since United Kingdom law provided no meaningful remedy for a person, such as himself, who had suffered a detriment as a result of his not belonging to a particular trade union, he had been the victim of a violation of Article 11 ECHR.

In the opinion of the ECtHR, the facts of the *Sibson* case were such that it could be distinguished from that of *Young, James and Webster*. Having regard to these various factors, the Court came to the conclusion that Mr Sibson was not subjected to a form of treatment striking at the very substance of the freedom of association guaranteed by Article 11 ECHR. There had accordingly been no violation of that provision.

4.3 Sigurjónsson

The *Sigurjónsson* case[32] was about a self-employed Icelandic taxi driver. He was granted a licence to operate a taxicab by the public Committee for Taxicab Supervision on the condition that he was to apply for membership of Frami. After joining Frami, the applicant paid membership fees for a period and then stopped doing so. As a result the public Committee for Taxicab Supervision upheld a request by Frami for the revocation of the applicant's licence. Sigurjónsson instituted proceedings before the Icelandic courts. The Supreme Court annulled the revocation of the applicant's licence. It found that the provision imposing trade-union membership as a prerequisite for granting a licence lacked a statutory basis. Following that ruling, the Althing (the Icelandic Parliament) enacted new legislation which made operating licences for taxi cabs conditional upon trade-union membership.

Sigurjónsson pursued the matter before the ECtHR which underlined that Sigurjónsson objected to being a member of the association in question partly because he disagreed with its policy in favour of limiting the number of taxicabs and, thus, access to the occupation; in his opinion the interests of his country were better served by extensive personal freedoms, including freedom of occupation, than State regulation. Therefore, the Court is of the view that Article 11 can, in the circumstances, be considered in the light of Articles 9 and 10. The pressure exerted on the applicant in order to compel him to remain a member of Frami contrary to his wishes was a further aspect going to the very essence of an Article 11 right. The Court further held::

> The Government submitted that should the Court find that the applicant was protected by Article 11 (art. 11) it would mean a step further than the Young, James and Webster judg-

32. *Sigurdur A. Sigurjónsson* v *Iceland*, judgment of 30 June 1993, 24/1992/369/443.

ment and the above-mentioned passage in the travaux préparatoires would be rendered nugatory.

...

In this connection, it should be recalled that the Convention is a living instrument which must be interpreted in the light of present-day conditions.... Accordingly, *Article 11 must be viewed as encompassing a negative right of association.* It is not necessary for the Court to determine in this instance whether this right is to be considered on an equal footing with the positive right.

4.4 Gustafsson

The *Gustafsson* v *Sweden* case[33] was about a small or medium-sized Swedish employer who owned a summer restaurant. He was not a member of any employers' association and he was not bound by a collective agreement. In late June or early July 1987 he refused to sign a collective agreement with the Hotel and Restaurant Workers' Union (HRF). He referred to his objections of principle regarding the system of collective bargaining. Following Gustafsson's refusal to sign a collective agreement, HRF, in July 1987, placed his restaurant under a 'blockade' and declared a boycott against it. Sympathy industrial action was taken the same month by a number of other Swedish trade unions in accordance with Swedish law of industrial action. As a result deliveries to the restaurant were stopped. In August 1988 the applicant, invoking the ECHR, requested the Government to prohibit HRF from continuing the blockade and the other trade unions from continuing their sympathy action and to order the unions to pay compensation for damages. In the alternative, he requested that compensation be paid by the State. By a decision of 12 January 1989 the Swedish Government (Ministry of Justice) dismissed the applicant's request. Gustafsson complained before the ECtHR that the union action had infringed his right to freedom of association and that the failure of Sweden to protect him against this action constituted a violation of Article 11 ECHR. No unlawful action assessed by Swedish standards of collective labour law had been undertaken and the Swedish government contended that:

In the Government's opinion, the applicant was in effect challenging the system that had been applied in Sweden for sixty years and which could be said to have formed one of the most important elements in what had become known as the Swedish model of industrial relations, believed by many to have contributed significantly to the Swedish welfare state.

...

In these circumstances, the Government considered that Sweden was not under an obligation under Article 11 of the Convention to take positive measures to protect the applicant against the union action.

33. *Gustafsson* v *Sweden*, judgment 25 April 1996, 18/1995/524/610.

The ECtHR concluded:

In sum, the Court reaches the conclusion that the facts of the present case did not give rise to a violation of Article 11 of the Convention.

4.5 Sørensen and Ramussen

In the Sørensen and Ramussen case,[34] Sørensen was a student about to start at university, applied for a job as a holiday-relief worker for the company FDB Distributionen (FDB). He was offered the job from 3 June until 10 August 1996 and informed that his terms of employment included mandatory membership of a trade union called SID, which was affiliated to the Danish Confederation of Trade Unions (LO). Sørensen joined the Danish Free Trade Union, which is not affiliated to the LO. On 23 June 1996 he informed his employer that he did not want to pay the subscription to SID because he had been told that, as a holiday-relief employee, he would not be given full membership of SID. He was dismissed the next day for not satisfying the requirements of his job as he was not a member of a trade union affiliated to the LO. Sørensen brought proceedings in the High Court of Western Denmark against FDB on the ground that Danish law did not comply with Article 11 ECHR as it allowed an employer to require an employee to be member of a specific association in order to obtain employment. On 18 November 1998 the High Court did not find it established that there had been a violation of Article 11 and the judgment was upheld on appeal by the Supreme Court on 8 June 1999. As regards Article 11 ECHR, the Danish Supreme Court stated:

"According to the Young, James and Webster v the United Kingdom judgment of 13 August 1981, Series A no. 44 (the British Rail judgment) it is in breach of Article 11 of the European Convention on Human Rights concerning freedom of association to dismiss an employee who refuses to join a trade union with whom the employer has entered into a closed-shop agreement at a time after the employment of the employee, in so far as membership was not a condition for the employment. The Court emphasised that it did not decide on closed-shop agreements as such, but only on its effect on the three applicants.

In the Sigurður A. Sigurjónsson v Iceland judgment of 30 June 1993, the European Court of Human Rights found a violation of Article 11 in a situation where a holder of a taxi licence had his licence revoked because he resigned from a specific association of taxicab owners. The Court found it of importance that obligatory membership of the association was imposed on him by law and that there was no duty to join the association when Sigurður A. Sigurjónsson obtained his taxi licence as the original requirement to do so lacked a legal basis. As in the British Rail judgment, the Court emphasised that it did not

34. *Sørensen & Rasmussen* v *Denmark* (applications nos 52562/99 and 52620/99).

decide on the scope of Article 11 of the Convention in relation to the negative freedom of association.

Against this background, the Supreme Court finds no reasons in the Sigurður A. Sigurjónsson judgment to assess the lawfulness of closed-shop agreements and their consequences any differently than what appears from the British Rail judgment. The same goes for the remainder of the judgments that the parties have referred to (Sibson v the United Kingdom, judgment of 20 April 1993, Series A no. 258, and Gustafsson v Sweden, judgment of 25 April 1996, Reports of Judgments and Decisions 1996-II)

Rasmussen was a gardener. He became a member of SID in the mid-1980s, but resigned his membership after a few years as he felt unable to support its political affiliations, joining instead the Christian Trade Union (Kristelig Fagforening). Following a period of unemployment, he was offered a job at a nursery (Gartneriet i Regnmark I/S), on condition that he became a member of SID, as the employer had entered into a closed-shop agreement with that trade union. The applicant started the job on 17 May 1999 and rejoined SID, although he still did not agree with its political views.

The Court examined whether the applicants were in fact compelled to join a particular trade union and, in the affirmative, whether such compulsion struck at the very substance of the negative right to freedom of association guaranteed by Article 11 of the Convention. The Court concluded that both applicants were compelled to join SID and that this compulsion struck at the very substance of the freedom of association guaranteed by Article 11 of the Convention. It remains to be determined whether the Danish Government, in authorising the use of closed-shop agreements, failed to secure the applicants' effective enjoyment of their negative right to freedom of association and thereby violated Article 11 ECHR. That depends on whether a fair balance has been struck between the applicants' interests and the need to ensure that trade unions are able to strive for the protection of their members' interest.

The ECtHR noted the special features of the Danish labour market, in particular the fact that the relationship between employers and employees is governed by a combination of agreements (collective and individual), labour-law principles, general statutes and statutory rules. The institution of closed-shop agreements was a long-standing practice in Denmark, although they were unlawful in the public-sector labour market and were not concluded in the part of the private-sector labour market covered by the general agreement between DA and LO. Closed-shop agreements thus at the time of the judgment affected only approximately 220,000 wage earners, which was equivalent to less than 10% of all Danish employees on the labour market.

Before reaching its conclusion the ECtHR referred rather intensely to Article 11 in the Community Charter of the Fundamental Social Rights of

Workers 1989 which as mentioned earlier provides that every employer and every worker has the freedom to join or not to join professional organisations or trade unions without any personal or occupational damage being thereby suffered by them. It also referred to Article 12 CFREU which as mentioned does not explicitly mention the negative right to organize, see the following:

73. Reference should also be made to the Community Charter of the Fundamental Social Rights of Workers, adopted by the heads of State or government of eleven member States of the European Communities on 9 December 1989. This text provides that every employer and every worker shall have the freedom to join or not to join professional organisations or trade unions without any personal or occupational damage being thereby suffered by them (see paragraph 37 above).

74. Article 12 of the Charter of Fundamental Rights of the European Union, proclaimed in Nice on 7 December 2000 (2000/C 364/01) (see paragraph 37 above), is devoted to freedom of assembly and association. The above-mentioned provisions of the Community Charter of the Fundamental Social Rights of Workers are of obvious relevance for the interpretation of the scope of Article 12. It should be noted in this connection that Article 53 of the Nice Charter states that nothing therein shall be interpreted as restricting or adversely affecting human rights and fundamental freedoms as recognised, in their respective fields of application, by European Union law and international law and by international agreements to which the European Union, the Community, or all the member States are party, including the Convention for the Protection of Human Rights and Fundamental Freedoms, and by the member States' constitutions.

75. In view of the above, it appears that there is little support in the Contracting States for the maintenance of closed-shop agreements and that the European instruments referred to above clearly indicate that their use in the labour market is not an indispensable tool for the effective enjoyment of trade union freedoms.

76. In conclusion, taking all the circumstances of the case into account and balancing the competing interests in issue, the Court finds that the respondent State has failed to protect the applicants' negative right to trade union freedom.

77. Accordingly, there has been a violation of Article 11 of the Convention in respect of both applicants.

Since the ECHR is considered an integral part of EU law the result is that closed shop agreements are not only unlawful as a matter of public international law but also as a matter of EU law. CFREU Article 12 must now be interpreted as outlawing closed-shop agreements. Denmark changed its national law after the judgments in the Sørensen and Rasmussen cases and prohibited closed shop agreements by Danish legislation. The case illustrates what the ECtHR has stated many times that the ECHR is a living instrument and that the ECtHR uses a dynamic style of interpretation which has gradually changed the content of the ECHR. When Denmark ratified that Convention in 1953 no one expected that closed shop agreements would be struck down 50 years later. The development of the case law of the ECtHR on closed shop agreements set out above also seems to confirm that there has been a gradual change in the content of the ECHR. It was only after the ECtHR could find support for outlawing closed shop agreements in EU sources of law that it did it fully. The case also illustrates the comparatively great weight the Community Charter of Fundamental Rights of Workers 1989 which as set out in Chapter Two is only soft law has been given.

5 Collective bargaining

5.1 General Characteristic

The most unique aspect of national labour law compared to other legal disciplines is that labour law has developed a specific source of law, namely the collective agreement.[35] In contradistinction to the situation at national level, collective agreements are not autonomous sources of international labour law or EU labour law.

Continental European collective agreements have legal effects comparable to legislation but they are generally a more flexible kind of regulation than statutory legislation while at the same time ensuring a certain minimum level of worker protection. As flexibility is high on the EU employment agenda, especially after the adoption of the Maastricht Treaty 1992, see above in Chapter Two, the EU institutions, in particular the Commission, endeavours to achieve an interaction between EU law and collective agreements at national level which enables EU labour law to benefit from the traditional advantages of collective agreements, see further below. Article 4 of ILO Convention No. 98 provides (emphasis added):

> Measures appropriate to national conditions shall be taken, where necessary, to encourage and promote the full development and utilisation of machinery for voluntary negotiation between employers or employers' organisations and workers' organisations, with a view to the regulation of terms and conditions of employment by means of *collective agreements.*

35. See generally Linden, Marcel van der and Richard Price (eds).: The Rise and Development of Collective Labour Law, Bern 2000.

In *Albany*, *Brentjens* and *Drijvende Bokken*[36] it was discussed, in particular by the Advocate General whether there is a fundamental right to bargain collectively. The CJEU accepted mandatory collective agreements requiring employers to be members of particular pension funds and gave a restrictive interpretation of Article 81 EC, see further below on the interaction of collective agreements and competition law.

5.2 Main Differences at National Level

At the national level there are major variations[37] between EU Member States as regards the legal regulation of collective agreements in respect of negotiating rights and duties, levels of collective bargaining, the binding effect of the collective agreements, the right of workers to strike when a collective agreement is in force (the peace obligation), extension of the normative effect of the agreement and its duration and coverage.

The key difference between continental European collective agreements, on the one side, and English collective agreements, on the other, concerns the *mandatory normative effect of collective agreements.* The general pattern in continental collective labour law is that collective agreements have a mandatory normative effect, ie they cannot be derogated from to the detriment of the worker by individual employment contracts or unilateral employer decisions.

An English collective agreement is largely an extra-legal custom or practice which enters into the individual employment contract as an implied term in the absence of agreement to the contrary in the individual contract of employment. An English collective agreement can be derogated from to the detriment of the worker by express terms in the individual employment contract and thus has no mandatory normative effect.

Collective agreements are now in the process of being developed as an EU source of law and directives allow to some extent for derogations to the detriment of the workers by national collective agreements. It is only agreements in accordance with the continental tradition with mandatory normative effects that are being elevated to EU level and allowed to derogate from directives,

36. See Case C-67/96 *Albany* [1999] ECR I-5751, Joined Cases C-115/97 to C-117/97 *Brentjens* [1999] ECR I-6025 and Case C-219/97 *Drijvende Bokken* [1999] ECR I-6121.
37. See for details European Commission: The Regulation of Working Conditions in the Member States of the European Community, Volume I, Social Europe, Supplement 4/92 p 87 *et seq*.

see below on the interpretation of the concept of a collective agreement in semi-mandatory directives

In the report on Industrial Relations in Europe from 2000,[38] the Commission defines a collective agreement in the following way:

> Collective agreement: An agreement reached through collective bargaining[39] between an employer and one or more trade unions, or between employers' associations and trade union confederations. This agreement regulates the relationships between the parties and the treatment of individual workers, and covers the wages and conditions of the workers affected.

In most continental European Member States of the EU collective agreements are defined by legislation as formal, written agreements which do not qualify as collective agreements unless certain formal or structural requirements are met.[40] As an example the German Tarifvertragsgesetz may be mentioned. It provides:

> § 1 Inhalt und Form des Tarifvertrags
> (1) Der Tarifvertrag regelt die Rechte und Pflichten der Tarifvertragsparteien und enthält Rechtsnormen, die den Inhalt, den Abschluß und die Beendigung von Arbeitsverhältnissen sowie betriebliche und betriebsverfassungsrechtliche Fragen ordnen können.
> (2) Tarifverträge bedürfen der Schriftform.

5.3 Parties to a Collective Agreement

5.3.1 On the Employer Side

The parties to a collective agreement are, generally, individual employers or employers' associations on the one side and trade unions on the other. On the employer side any employer can conclude a collective agreement individually. The employer can also choose to join an employers' organisation whereby it becomes bound by collective agreements concluded by that organisation.

38. COM(2000)113 p 8.
39. Collective bargaining is said to be the process of negotiation by which collective agreements are reached. Such agreements are compromises which reflect the relative bargaining power of the parties, COM(2000)113 p 8.
40. See also the Swedish Co-determination Act (1976:580, sections 23-31), and Finnish Act on collective agreements (436/1946). Denmark lacks a statutory definition of a collective agreement. In Danish law it is not required that a collective agreement be in writing, but in practice most collective agreements are written also in Denmark.

5.3.2 Capacity of Trade Unions to Conclude Collective Agreements

On the worker side the collective agreement must be concluded by a collectivity, typically a trade union.[41] The general pattern in the EU Member States is that trade unions need to satisfy certain formal and structural requirements in order to have capacity to conclude collective agreements.[42] The German Tarifvertragsgesetz provides on the capacity to conclude collective agreements:

§ 2. Tarifvertragsparteien
(1) Tarifvertragsparteien sind Gewerkschaften, einzelne Arbeitgeber sowie Vereinigungen von Arbeitgebern.

The German Federal Labour Court (Bundesarbeitsgericht) has established a range of criteria which must be met in order for an association to be able to be party to a collective agreement (to be 'tariffähig').[43] The association must be created for an indefinite time, must have a corporate structure, have a certain strength in order to be taken seriously by the employers' side and be independent from employer and State influence and from political parties. Finally members should be able to influence the associations' activities.[44]

Similarly in France, the trade union must be a representative organisation. The legal requirement for a trade union to possess representative status was

41. In Denmark any collectivity of workers (not only trade unions) has capacity to conclude a collective agreement but that is an unusual solution in a European perspective.
42. See for further detail European Commission: The Regulation of Working Conditions in the Member States of the European Community, Volume I, Social Europe Supplement 4/92 p. 87 *et seq.*
43. See further Gamillscheg, Franz: Trade Union Representativity in German Law in Bellace, J R and Max Rood (eds): Labour law at the Crossroads: Changing Employment Relationships: Studies in Honour of Benjamin Aaron, The Hague 1997 p. 75.
44. BAG 16.11.1982. Aus den Gründen:
»An die Tariffähigkeit einer Arbeitnehmervereinigung sind bestimmte Mindestanforderungen zu stellen. Die Arbeitnehmervereinigung muß sich als satzungsgemäße Aufgabe die Wahrnehmung der Interessen ihrer Mitglieder in ihrer Eigenschaft als Arbeitnehmer gesetzt haben und willens sein, Tarifverträge abzuschließen. Sie muß frei gebildet, gegnerfrei, unabhängig und auf überbetriebl. Grundlage organisiert sein und das geltende Tarifrecht als verbindl. anerkennen. Die Tariffähigkeit setzt insbesondere voraus, daß die Arbeitnehmervereinigung ihre Aufgabe als Tarifpartner auch sinnvoll erfüllen kann. Dazu gehört eine Durchsetzungskraft gegenüber dem sozialen Gegenspieler, die sicherstellt, daß dieser wenigstens Verhandlungsangebote nicht übersehen kann.«
Quoted from Zusammenstellung grundlegender neuerer Entscheidungen zum kollektiven Arbeitsrecht (http://www.uni-koeln.de/jur-fak/instsozr).

first introduced in France in 1936 as a criterion for the capacity to conclude collective agreements that may be extended (see on *erga omnes* effect below) and subsequently widened to include large areas of union activity. The legal concept of union representativeness implies a process of selection within the trade union movement. Only certain unions that meet certain criteria are deemed capable of representation. French labour law establishes two routes for attributing representative status: a representativeness which, if contested, can be proven principally on the basis of historical criteria (independence from employers, length of existence, experience, patriotic attitude during the Occupation) and secondarily trade union organisations with nationally representative status enjoy certain privileges. The individual unions affiliated to the five confederations with this status[45] are exempt from having to prove their representativeness at sector and company level. These organisations thus enjoy a presumption of representativeness at all levels, which enables them to negotiate sector-level or company agreements which are binding on all the employees covered by such agreements.

The revival of collective bargaining following the adoption of the 35-hour week legislation in 1998 has highlighted the issue of collective agreements signed by unions with only minor support among the workers concerned.[46]

5.4 Obligatory and Normative Effect of Collective Agreements

There are profound differences between the UK, on the one hand, and the continental European countries, on the other, with regard to the legal effects of collective agreements. The distinction between the obligatory and normative function of collective agreements was first developed in legal writing, in

45. CFDT, CFE-CGC, CFTC, CGT and CGT-FO.
46. See further the European Industrial Relations Observatory EIROnline available at http://www.eiro.eurofound.ie/2000/06/features/FR0006170F.html. CFDT has suggested to the other union confederations that they discuss four proposals:
1) for a collective agreement to be valid in the future, it must be signed by one or more unions with a score of at least 50% of employee votes at company-level workforce elections of employee representatives;
2) a 'representative status ballot' should be organised simultaneously in all companies in each sector. This ballot would elect union delegates with the authority to negotiate company-level agreements (they are currently appointed by unions) and would enable support for each union at both company and sector level to be measured;
3) those unions not currently covered by the assumption of representative status should be able to field candidates in the first round of works council and workforce delegate elections;
4) collective agreements should cease to apply indefinitely, so as to encourage renegotiation.

particular in Germany and Denmark. In 'The Making of Labour Law in Europe'[47] Hepple describes the early years of collective labour law in the following way:

> ... 'labour law' is of recent origin. In most countries it became recognised as a distinct division of law only after the Second World War.
>
> ...
>
> The exceptions were Germany and Denmark. In the latter, Carl Ussing, a Supreme Court judge who presided over the 'August Committe' of 1908-10, combined academic and practical expertise to produce a sharp analysis which helped to lay the foundations of Denmark's collectivist system. ..., but mainly due for reasons of language the impact of the Danish innovations was limited to Scandinavia.

The German scholars, however, had a profound influence throughout Europe and can be regarded as the founding fathers of the modern subject. English collective agreements have no obligatory (contractual) and no mandatory normative effect but only acquires legal effect as an implied term in the individual contract of employment. In the continental European countries the general pattern today is that a collective agreement is binding as a contract (its obligatory effect which entails a peace obligation, see below) and has mandatory normative effect. There are many differences between the continental countries in the detailed application of these principles.[48] In an overall assessment of the relative importance of the obligatory (contractual) and mandatory effect of collective agreements Kahn-Freund argued:[49]

> It is not a gross exaggeration to say that the contractual function of collective agreements is mainly for the benefit of management, and its normative function mainly for the benefit of labour.

5.5 Obligatory (or Contractual) Effect

A collective agreement is in some countries a contract by which the trade union sells peace in return for wages and working conditions at a certain level. An English collective agreement is *not* binding as a contract. From a legal point of view it thus has no obligatory or contractual effect. French collective agreements do have an obligatory function but this function is particularly

47. Hepple, Bob: The Making of labour law in Europe. A comparative study of nine countries up to 1945, London, 1986 p. 7.
48. See for details European Commission: The Regulation of Working Conditions in the Member States of the European Community, Volume I, Social Europe Supplement 4/92.
49. Kahn-Freund, Otto: Labour and the Law. London 1977 p. 129.

important in the collective labour law systems in the Northern part of Europe. As Kahn-Freund points out:

> 'the obligatory effect of collective agreements is a German (and also Scandinavian) phenomenon.'[50]

The contractual effect of a collective agreement entails a peace obligation on the worker side, see further below under industrial action.

5.6 The Normative Effect of Collective Agreements

5.6.1 Mandatory Normative Effect

In the continental European countries the general pattern is that collective agreements have a mandatory normative effect which implies that they cannot be derogated from to the detriment of the worker by individual contract.

If an individual contract of employment stipulates terms and conditions which are inconsistent with the collective agreement the individual contract is partially invalid and will have to be amended so as to comply with the collective agreement.

Due to the mandatory normative function of a collective agreement in the continental legal tradition it serves as a parallel to or an alternative to protective employment legislation. This effect establishes a hierarchy between collective agreements and individual employment contracts as sources of law with collective agreements as the higher ranking '*lex superior*'.

5.6.2 Residual Normative Effect

Very often individual employment contracts refer to a collective agreement which will then become part of the individual contract. If the individual contract of employment does not state the exact terms and conditions of the employment relationship the terms of the relevant collective agreement will as an implied term in the individual contract. English collective agreements also have this effect of becoming implied terms in individual employment contracts as long as nothing to the contrary is agreed by the individual parties to the contract. As Kahn-Freund points out the most important legal aspect of collective bargaining in England is what may be called the theory of the implied term. This means that where an employer in whose industry and district a collective agreement is in force enters into a contract of employment with a

50. Kahn-Freund, Otto: Labour Law and Industrial Relations in Great Britain and West Germany in Wedderburn, Kenneth William, Roy Lewis and Jon Clark: Labour Law and Industrial Relations. Building on Kahn-Freund, Oxford 1983 p. 5.

worker whose conditions of employment are governed by that agreement, the terms of the agreement are tacitly incorporated in the contract of employment as implied terms.[51]

Under UK law the parties to the individual employment contract are, however, from a legal point of view free to agree other terms, including terms which are more unfavourable to the employee, than those laid down in the collective agreement which thus has no mandatory normative effect. Contrary to the legal position in the continental countries, individual contracts of employment take precedence over collective agreements under English law. The terms of collective agreements function more or less like customs.

5.7 Personal Scope of the Mandatory Effect

5.7.1 Which Employers are Bound? Erga Omnes Effect

The starting point is that only parties to collective agreements are bound by them. On the employer side this means that an individual employer who has signed a collective agreement is bound by it. An employer who is member of an employer's organisation who has signed a collective agreement is also bound by the collective agreement. In order for a collective agreement to bind other employers than those who are parties to it legislation or administrative intervention is required.

Most EU Member States have a system for extending collective agreements so as to make them binding *erga omnes*, i.e. also on employers who are not parties to them. That possibility does not exist in Italy and the UK and only to a very limited extent in the Nordic countries..[52] In Sweden and Denmark,[53] collective agreements can *not* be extended to cover employers who are not parties to them. In Norway there is a limited possibility of extension of the coverage of collective agreements but it has so far never been used. In Finland there is wider access to give *erga omnes* effect to collective agreements.[54]

51. Kahn-Freund, Otto (ed.): Labour Relations and the Law. A Comparative Study, London 1965 p. 28.
52. See the overview in the Commission's report on Industrial relations in Europe COM(2000)113 p. 41.
53. In Denmark a recent sociological study shows that the coverage of collective agreements in the public sector is close to 100% but in the private sector only around 50%.
54. See for details Ahlberg, Kerstin and Niklas Bruun: Kollektivavtal i EU. Om almängiltiga avtal och social dumping, Stockholm 1996.

5.7.2 Towards which Employees is the Employer Bound

The mandatory normative function of the collective agreement ensures some employees wages and working conditions which are not inferior to those laid down in the collective agreement.

In some countries, for example Denmark, an employer who is bound by a collective agreement must respect it *vis a vis* any employee doing work covered by the substantive scope of the collective agreement irrespective of whether the employee is a union member or not, and if so which union the worker is a member of.

In other countries, for example Germany, an employer who is bound by a collective agreement only has a duty to respect *vis a vis* employees who are members of the trade union with which the employer has concluded the agreement. In principle, the employer and a non-unionised worker have freedom of contract to conclude individual contracts which afford less favourable conditions to non unionised workers than those prescribed by the collective agreement for unionised workers. In practice most German employers tend to choose to not treat non unionised workers less favourable than unionised workers, maybe because such treatment would give the non unionised workers an incitement to join the unions.[55]

5.8 Negotiating Competence and Obligations

The general starting point in European contract law is that the principle of freedom of contract confers a power to conclude contracts on all categories of physical and legal persons, including employers, trade unions and other associations and individual employees. In a European setting it is therefore rather obvious that the employers, employers' associations and trade unions have power (ie legal competence) to negotiate and conclude contracts. It is a different question whether they have a duty to do so.[56]

In most EU Member States the main rule is that there is neither a right nor an obligation for either side to enter into negotiation of or to conclude collec-

55. See further Weiss, Manfred: Germany in Gold, Michael and Manfred Weiss (ed.): Employment and Industrial Relations in Europe, Volume I, The Hagues, London, Boston 1999 p. 65.
56. See above in Chapter II on the distinction between power-conferring norms and duty-imposing norms.

tive agreements. Sweden is the exception. The Swedish Co-Determination Act (Medbestäm-mandelagen) section 10[57] provides:

> An employees' organisation shall have the right to negotiate with an employer regarding any matter relating to the relationship between the employer and any member of the organisation who is or has been employed by that employer. An employer shall have a corresponding right to negotiate with an employees' organisation.
>
> A right of negotiation ... shall also be enjoyed by the employees' organisation in relation to any organisation to which an employer belongs, and by the employers' organisation in relation to the employees' organisation.

There is thus a legal obligation upon the Swedish employer to negotiate with the trade unions. In the rest of Europe the question whether or not an employer should enter into collective bargaining is not decided by law but depends largely either on his own choice or on the relative strength of the trade unions and their ensuing capacity to force the employer to do so by initiating industrial action or threaten to so. The lawful means, in particular threats and other compelling measures which can be applied in the contracting process leading up to a collective agreement are somewhat different from the lawful means in contracting at individual level, see below on industrial action (strikes, etc). In general, more force, both physical and otherwise, is lawful in collective bargaining than in individual contracting. As mentioned above, a trade union's ability to use sufficient force (Durchsetzungskraft) is a precondition for its capacity to conclude collective agreements. As the German Federal Labour Court (Bundesarbeitsgericht) has stated (emphasis added):[58]

> An die Tariffähigkeit einer Arbeitnehmervereinigung sind bestimmte Mindestanforderungen zu stellen ... Dazu gehört eine *Durchsetzungskraft* gegenüber dem sozialen Gegenspieler, die sicherstellt, daß dieser wenigstens Verhandlungsangebote nicht übersehen kann.

57. The Swedish original reads: 10 § 'Arbetstagarorganisation har rätt till förhandling med arbetsgivare i fråga rörande förhållande mellan arbetsgivaren och sådan medlem i organisationen, som är eller har varit arbetstagare hos arbetsgivaren. Arbetsgivare har motsvarande rätt att förhandla med arbetstagarorganisation. Förhandlingsrätt enligt första stycket tillkommer arbetstagarorganisationen även i förhållande till organisation som arbetsgivaren tillhör och arbetsgivarens organisation i förhållande till arbetstagarorganisationen.'
58. BAG 16.11.1982. Quoted from Zusammenstellung grundlegender neuerer Entscheidungen zum kollektiven Arbeitsrecht (http://www.uni-koeln.de/jur-fak/instsozr).

5.9 Collective Agreements and Competition Law

In *Albany*,[59] the CJEU addressed a national system in which under collective agreements which were extended affiliation to a sectoral pension fund was compulsory for all undertakings in that sector. The question referred to the CJEU was whether such a system infringes either Article 4(3) TEU in conjunction with Article 101 TFEU or Article 106(1) TFEU in conjunction with Article 102 TFEU. The cases also raised the issue, in the context of Articles 4(3) TEU and 101 TFEU, whether a collective agreement between employers and employees within a particular sector setting up a sectoral pension scheme falls under Article 101(1) TFEU. The CJEU was thus called upon for the first time to give a ruling on the relationship between the competition rules of the Treaty and agreements reached by collective bargaining between the two sides of industry.

The CJEU first noted that Article 101(1) TFEU prohibits all agreements between undertakings, decisions by associations of undertakings and concerted practices which may affect trade between Member States and which have as their object or effect the prevention, restriction or distortion of competition within the common market. Next, the CJEU underline that the activities of the EU are to include not only a 'system ensuring that competition in the internal market is not distorted' but also 'a policy in the social sphere'. Article 3 TEU provides that a particular task of the Community is 'to promote throughout the Community a harmonious and balanced development of economic activities' and 'a high level of employment and of social protection'.

The CJEU found that it is beyond question that certain restrictions of competition are inherent in collective agreements between organisations representing employers and workers. However, the social policy objectives pursued by such agreements would be seriously undermined if management and labour were subject to Article 101(1) TFEU when seeking jointly to adopt measures to improve conditions of work and employment. In the view of the CJEU, it therefore follows from an interpretation of the provisions of the Treaty as a whole which is both effective and consistent that agreements concluded in the context of collective negotiations between management and labour in pursuit of such objectives must, by virtue of their nature and purpose, be regarded as falling outside the scope of Article 81(1) EC. The CJEU concluded in *Albany* that:

59. See Case C-67/96 *Albany* [1999] ECR I-5751, Joined Cases C-115/97 to C-117/97 *Brentjens* [1999] ECR I-6025 and Case C-219/97 *Drijvende Bokken* [1999] ECR I-6121.

1. Article 3(g) of the EC Treaty [now, after amendment, Article 3(1)(g) EC], Articles 5 and 85 of the EC Treaty [now Articles 10 EC and 81 EC] do not prohibit a decision by the public authorities to make affiliation to a sectoral pension fund compulsory at the request of organisations representing employers and workers in a given sector.

Above in Chapter II, the statement that labour is not a commodity, which is found in the basic ILO texts, was mentioned. As pointed out by Fahlbeck[60] that statement was found already in the US federal anti-trust statute known as the Clayton Act 1914 where its purpose was to fend off collective labour law from anti trust law.

5.10 Collective Agreements in the Hierarchy of the Sources of Law

In the continental European countries, there is generally a hierarchy in labour law between statutory legislation, collective agreements and individual contracts of employment. Statutory legislation is usually mandatory as a consequence of which collective agreements and individual employment contracts which are inconsistent with it are invalid.

In the Nordic countries it has been a contested issue as to whether the labour market organisations have discretion (power/competence) to decide by collective agreement what is to be regarded as equal pay. The ECJ has clearly stated, in *Royal Copenhagen*,[61] that the EU law equal pay principle applies also where the elements of the pay are determined by collective bargaining or by negotiation at local level. The national court may, however, take that fact into account in its assessment of whether differences between the average pay of two groups of workers are due to objective factors unrelated to any discrimination on grounds of sex. In *Jämställdhetsombudsmannen*,[62] the Advocate General noted about the relevance of the collective bargaining framework (emphasis added):

21. At the hearing, the Ombudsman suggested that in Sweden collective bargaining agreements are regarded as immune from Community law, in the sense, presumably, that it is considered to be a defence to a claim of unequal pay that the salary was agreed by collective bargaining. *Such a view is manifestly not in conformity with Community law...*

60. Fahlbeck, Reinhold: Flexibility. Potentials and Pitfalls for Labour Law. An International Analysis, Lund 1998 p. 22.
61. Case C-400/93 Royal Copenhagen [1995] ECR I-1275.
62. Case C-236/98 Jämställdhetsombudsmannen [2000] ECR I-2189. The quotation is from the Opinion of Advocate General Jacobs of 16 december 1999, paragraph 21.

Continental European collective agreements have as set out above a mandatory normative function which means that individual contracts of employment which are inconsistent with an applicable collective agreement are invalid.

In England, collective agreements do not have this mandatory normative function but only constitutes a practice or custom which will form an implied term in the contract in the absence of stipulations to the contrary by the parties to the individual contract. An English collective agreement is thus not *lex superior* in conflict with an individual employment contract. On the contrary, it is secondary to what the parties agree on in the individual contract and, due to the unequal bargaining power of the parties to the individual employment contract, the employer can typically decide that unilaterally.

5.11 Semi-Mandatory Statutory Legislation

In a number of continental countries statutory protective employment legislation is only fully mandatory in respect of derogations by means of individual employment contracts while derogations to the detriment of the workers are allowed in specified situations by means of collective agreements. Sweden is probably the single country where this kind of interaction between statutory legislation and legislation by means of collective bargaining is most developed.[63]

In recent directives at EU level there is likewise some acceptance of derogations by collective agreement. As an example Article 18 of the Working time Directive[64] may be mentioned. It allows, on a number of detailed conditions, derogations from a number of provisions in the working Time directive *by means of collective agreements or agreements between the two sides of industry*. The general purpose of the Working Time Directive is to protect the employees and the directive cannot be derogated from by an individual contract of employment, see on working time regulation below in Chapter Nine.

There is no case law on the interpretation of the term 'collective agreement' when used in semi-mandatory EU directives. In my view, collective agreements within the meaning of a semi-mandatory directive must be interpreted as referring only to collective agreements of the continental European type with mandatory normative effect. If a directive could be derogated from by an ordinary English collective agreement it would be open to derogations by individual contracts of employment and, in practice, due to the unequal

63. In Sweden statutory legislation which can be derogated from by collective agreement is usually termed semi-dispositive legislation (semi-dispositiv lagstiftning in Swedish).
64. 2003/88/EC.

bargaining power of employers and individual employees, derogations by unilateral employer decision.

6 Collective Agreements at European Level

Collective bargaining at the European level exists in different forms. The first being European wide framework agreements laying down basic principles which are then to be incorporated into national collective agreements. Only a limited number of these collective agreements exist probably because of the low degree of internationalization of the trade union organizations.

6.1 Enterprise level cross-border collective agreements

The second type of European collective agreement is enterprise level cross-border collective agreements in multinational firms. A growing number of these agreements exist.[65] The European Works Council Directive[66]and the current proposal for the European Company will (the latter if adopted) develop this kind of European collective agreement.

6.2 EU wide collective agreements

As set out in Chapter Two Article 155 TFEU provides that if management and labour so desire, the dialogue between them at Union level may lead to contractual relations, including agreements. Such agreements concluded at Union level shall be implemented either in accordance with the procedures and practices specific to management and labour and the Member States or, in matters covered by Article 153 TFEU, at the joint request of the signatory parties, by a Council decision on a proposal from the Commission. The European Parliament shall be informed. The Council shall act unanimously where the agreement in question contains one or more provisions relating to one of the areas for which unanimity is required pursuant to Article 153(2) TFEU.

65. A survey of 31 multinational groups of undertakings operating in the Nordic countries and their cross border collective agreement arrangements has been carried out at the request of the Nordic Foundation for Industrial Development, see further Myrvang (1991). See also Gold and Hall (1990); Hall (1992) and the overview article in *European Industrial Relations Review* 228 and 229 (1993).
66. 94/45/EC. Proposal put forward in January 1991 in COM(90) 581, amended proposal of 16. September 1991 in COM(91) 345.

6.2.1 Framework agreements as first steps to directives

The social dialogue process has resulted in the conclusion of agreements, which have subsequently been implemented by the Council as Directives, on parental leave in 1996,[67] part-time work 1997[68] and fixed-term employment contracts in 1999.[69]

The role of the European Parliament in the legislative process is restricted in cases where directives are adopted on the basis of a European collective agreement. Generally the most usual decision-making process when adopting directives is joint decision-making by the Council and European Parliament under Article 295 TFEU. When directives are adopted on the basis of a European collective agreement the decision is under Article 155 TFEU taken by the EU Council without the Parliament participating in the decision process. Questions as to the democratic legitimacy of the European social dialogue may therefore be raised, see just below on the *UEAPME* case.

When the directive on fixed term work was under discussion, the European Parliament expressed at its own initiative an opinion by adopting a Resolution on the framework agreement on the issue concluded between the social partners. The final directive refers to that resolution.[70]

6.2.2 Autonomous framework agreements

The European Framework Agreement on telework concluded between ETUC, UNICE/UEAPME and CEEP on 16 July 2002, the European Framework Agreement on work-related stress concluded between ETUC, UNICE, UEAPME and CEEP on 8 October 2004, the European Framework Agreement on harassment and violence at work concluded by ETUC, Business Europe, UEAPME and CEEP on 26 April 2007 and the European Framework Agreement on inclusive labour markets concluded by ETUC, Business Eu-

67. Council Directive 96/34/EC of 3 June 1996 on the framework agreement on parental leave concluded by UNICE, CEEP and the ETUC. Now repealed and replaced with Council Directive 2010/18/EU of 8 March 2010 implementing the revised Framework Agreement on parental leave concluded by BUSINESSEUROPE, UEAPME, CEEP and ETUC and repealing Directive 96/34/EC.
68. Council Directive 97/81/EC of 15 December 1997 concerning the Framework Agreement on part-time work concluded by UNICE, CEEP and the ETUC.
69. Council Directive 1999/70/EC of 28 June 1999 concerning the framework agreement on fixed-term work concluded by ETUC, UNICE and CEEP.
70. Recital 20 in Council Directive 1999/70/EC of 28 June 1999 concerning the framework agreement on fixed-term work concluded by ETUC, UNICE and CEEP. See also Vigneau, Christophe, Kerstin Ahlberg, Brian Bercusson and Niklas Bruun: Fixed-Term Work in the EU, Stockholm 1999 p. 56.

rope, UEAPME and CEEP on 25 March 2010 have not been transformed into directives, but should be transposed in accordance with procedures and practices specific to management and labour and the Member States.

6.3 The UEAPME Case

The *UEAPME*[71] case concerned an action for annulment of the then parental leave Directive[72] on the framework agreement on parental leave concluded by the UNICE, CEEP and ETUC. This Directive was the first Directive based on a collective agreement at European level concluded between the social partners. The action was brought before the General Court (then the Court of First instance) by a European employers' association (UEAPME) which represents and defends at European level the interests of employers in small and medium-sized undertakings. UEAPME did not participate in the negotiation and conclusion of the collective agreement and sought annulment of the Directive because UEAPME was not included in the procedure resulting in the underlying collective agreement. The application for annulment was dismissed as inadmissible.

In 1983 the Commission had drafted a proposal for a directive on parental leave and leave for family reasons, which the Council never adopted. On 21 January 1995 the Commission decided to consult management and labour on the possible direction of Community action with regard to reconciling working and family life. On 6 April 1995 the applicant (UEAPME) and some other organisations addressed to the Commission a document stating a common position. The signatories to that document urged the Commission to do everything in its power to ensure that certain important issues and certain representatives of management and labour were not excluded from the negotiations. In June 1995, considering Community action to be advisable, the Commission once again consulted management and labour on the content of the envisaged proposal. On 5 July 1995 the applicant and the other associations mentioned above once again submitted a statement of a common position.

On the same day, UNICE, CEEP and the ETUC informed the Commission of their desire to exercise the option available under Article 4(1) of the Social Policy Agreement attached to the Maastricht Treaty [now Article 154

71. Case T-135/96 *UEAPME* [1998] ECR II-2335.
72. 96/34/EC. Now repealed and replaced with Council Directive 2010/18/EU of 8 March 2010 implementing the revised Framework Agreement on parental leave concluded by BUSINESSEUROPE, UEAPME, CEEP and ETUC and repealing Directive 96/34/EC.

TFEU] of opening negotiations on parental leave. On 6 November 1995 UNICE, CEEP and the ETUC agreed on a proposal for a framework agreement. On 14 December 1995 they concluded the framework agreement on parental leave which they submitted to the Commission with the request that it be implemented in accordance with the Social Policy Agreement [now Article 155 TFEU]. That later happened through the adoption of the parental leave Directive.

Meanwhile, by communications of 30 November and 13 December 1995, UEAPME informed the Commission of its regret at having been unable to take part in the dialogue between management and labour, and submitted its criticisms of the proposed framework agreement. On 20 December 1995 the Commission forwarded a copy of the framework agreement to those organisations which, like the applicant, it had consulted or informed beforehand but which were not signatories, inviting them to a meeting on 5 January 1996 for information and discussion. The applicant attended that meeting. It was in those circumstances that the Parental Leave Directive, giving effect to the framework agreement, was adopted by the Council on 3 June 1996.

The applicant (UEAPME) brought an action before the General Court (then the Court of First Instance) for annulment of Directive 96/34/EC under Article 263 TFEU.[73] The General held that the mere fact that the contested measure was a directive was not sufficient to render the action inadmissible. The Community institutions cannot, merely through their choice of legal instrument, deprive individuals of the judicial protection offered by that provision of the Treaty. It is necessary to determine whether, notwithstanding the legislative character of the Parental Leave Directive, the applicant may be regarded as directly and individually concerned by it. In the Court's view, natural or legal persons can claim to be individually concerned by a measure only if it affects them by reason of certain attributes peculiar to them or by reason of circumstances which differentiate them from all other persons.

6.3.1 Right or Duty to Negotiate

The Court found that the applicant could not claim to possess neither a general right to participate in the negotiation stage of the social dialogue procedure provided for in the EC Treaty, nor, in the context of the case before the Court, an individual right to participate in negotiation of the framework

73. That Article provides: Any natural or legal person may, under the same conditions, institute proceedings against a decision addressed to that person or against a decision which, although in the form of a regulation or a decision addressed to another person, is of direct and individual concern to the former.

agreement on parental leave. Article 154 TFEU does not confer on any representative of management and labour, whatever the interests purportedly represented, a general right to take part in any negotiations entered into in accordance with Article 138 EC, even though it is open to any representative of management and labour which has been consulted pursuant to Article 154 TFEU to initiate such negotiations. The mere fact that the applicant contacted the Commission on several occasions asking to participate in the negotiations between other representatives of management and labour did not affect that position, since it is the representatives of management and labour concerned, and not the Commission, which have charge of the negotiation stage.

6.3.2 Representativity

Representativity is generally a requirement for 'Tariffähigkeit' at national level in most continental European countries. This requirement seems to be transferred to EU level. In *UEAPME* the General Court held that Council and the Commission are obliged to ascertain whether, having regard to the content of the collective agreement in question, the signatories, taken together, are sufficiently representative. Where that degree of representativity is lacking, the Commission and the Council must refuse to implement the agreement at Community level. In such a case, the representatives of management and labour which were not parties to the agreement, and whose particular representation – again in relation to the content of the collective agreement – is necessary in order to raise the collective representativity of the signatories to the required level, have the right to prevent the Commission and the Council from implementing the agreement at Community level by means of a legislative instrument. The judicial protection to which the existence of such a right gives rise implies that, where non-signatory representatives with those characteristics bring an action for annulment of the Council measure giving effect to the collective agreement at Community level they must be regarded as directly and individually concerned by that measure.

In *UEAPME*, the Court found that the Council and the Commission had examined both the degree of representativity of the signatories and their representativity with respect to the substantive scope of the framework agreement. The 13th recital in the preamble to the parental leave Directive also indicates that in drawing up the proposal submitted to the Council, the Commission took into account the representative status of the signatories to the framework agreement. The Commission and the Council, acting in conformity with their obligations, in particular those derived from a fundamental democratic principle, properly took the view that the collective representativity of the signatories to the framework agreement was sufficient in relation to that agreement's content for its implementation at Community level by means of a Council legislative measure.

6.3.3 The Principle of Democracy

Under Article 6 TEU the EU is based on the principle of democracy. The participation of the European Commission and the EU Council in the process of social dialogue at EU level has the effect of endowing an agreement concluded between management and labour with a Community foundation of a legislative character, without recourse to the classic procedures provided for under the EC Treaty for the preparation of legislation, which entail the participation of the European Parliament. However, since the procedure referred to in Article 254 TFEU does not provide for the participation of the European Parliament, the principle of democracy on which the Union is founded requires – in the absence of the participation of the European Parliament in the legislative process – that the participation of the people be otherwise assured, in this instance through the parties representative of management and labour who concluded the agreement which is endowed by the Council, acting on a qualified majority, on a proposal from the Commission, with a legislative foundation at Community level.

6.4 Use of collective agreements as means to transpose directives into national law

Collective agreements as implementing measures are, as set out in Chapter Two, only partly accepted. In *Commission* v *Denmark*[74] the Commission brought an infringement action against Denmark for failure to implement the Equal Pay Directive correctly. The CJEU stated that:

> It is true that Member States may leave the implementation of the principle of equal pay in the first instance to representatives of management and labour. That possibility does not, however, discharge them from the obligation of ensuring, by appropriate legislative and administrative provisions, that all workers in the Community are afforded the full protection provided for in the directive. That State guarantee must cover all cases where effective protection is not ensured by other means, for whatever reason, and in particular cases where the workers in question are not union members, where the sector in question is not covered by a collective agreement or where such an agreement does not fully guarantee the principle of equal pay.

74. Case 143/83 *Commission v Denmark* [1985] ECR 427. See for a similar judgment Case 235/84 *Commission* v *Italy* [1986] ECR 2291.

Danish collective agreements are not binding for employers who are not parties to them. It is therefore clear that Danish collective agreements cannot grant rights to all workers and are therefore not sufficient as the sole means of implementing an employment directive which usually provides for rights to all workers/employees. The typical solution in the Nordic countries is the combination model where legislation is adopted but only applies to workers/employees who are not covered by collective agreements ensuring the required protection. Article 153(3) TFEU provides:

> A Member State may entrust management and labour, at their joint request, with the implementation of directives adopted pursuant to paragraph 2, or, where appropriate, with the implementation of a Council decision adopted in accordance with Article 155.
>
> In this case, it shall ensure that, no later than the date on which a directive or a decision must be transposed or implemented, management and labour have introduced the necessary measures by agreement, the Member State concerned being required to take any necessary measure enabling it at any time to be in a position to guarantee the results imposed by that directive or that decision.

Four models of interaction between EU law and domestic law have been used until now in the implementation of directives:[75]

1) ordinary statutory legislation as the sole instrument of implementation
2) a combination of statutory legislation and collective agreement
3) collective agreements with mandatory normative effect which have been extended so as to have *erga omnes* effect as the sole instrument of implementation
4) collective agreements with mandatory normative effect which have not been extended as the sole instrument of implementation.

No one seems to have suggested that an English collective agreement with no mandatory normative effect could be sufficient. It seems obvious that such an agreement would be inadequate as a means of implementing mandatory directives. The EU Council has adopted various resolutions calling for effective implementation of Community law.[76] In Council Resolution of 27 March

75. See Nielsen, Ruth: Implementation of EC Directives in Denmark, The International Journal of Comparative Labour Law and Industrial Relations, Volume 18 2002.Issue 4, p. 459.
76. Notably Council conclusions of 21 December 1992 on the effective implementation and enforcement of community legislation in the area of social affairs and Council

1995 on the transposition and application of Community social legislation the Council calls upon the Commission

4. To maintain and strengthen its system of consultation, notably as regards management and labour:
   (a) consultation of management and labour at Community level provides a firmer foundation for Community social legislation and must therefore be stepped up;
   (b) moreover, wherever possible, Directives should allow management and labour, in accordance with national legislation and/or practices, to be involved in the transposition of Community social legislation through collective bargaining agreements or agreements concluded at national level; however, it is for the Member States to take whatever steps are necessary to ensure that at all times the outcome required by the relevant Directive can be guaranteed;

It further invites the Member States to

(b) to encourage management and labour to play a full and active part in the implementation of Community legislation at national level, in accordance with the procedures proper to each Member State;

The typical solution in the Nordic countries is the combination model where legislation is adopted but only applies to workers not covered by collective agreements ensuring the required protection. Such legislation is in the Nordic vocabulary said to be subsidiary to collective agreements providing the same or better protection for the workers. As an example the Danish Equal Pay Act may be mentioned.

It has been a much debated issue whether Collective Agreements can serve as the sole instrument of implementation. Prior to the Danish referendum in 1993 and the Swedish referendum in 1994 on the Treaty on the European Union Commissioner Flynn provided a letter on the implementation in the Nordic countries. The letter to the Swedish minister of Labour contained the following statement:[77]

The Maastricht Treaty opens the way for a flexible, decentralized approach, as it gives the social partners the possibility of replacing Community legislation by negotiated agreements ...

Resolution of 16 June 1994 on the development of administrative cooperation in the implementation and enforcement of community legislation in the internal market.

77. The Danish LO received a similar letter in 1993.

... it is important to note that the Maastricht Protocol is closely modelled on the existing Swedish practice in that it opens the possibility for agreements between the Social Partners at European level to take the place of legislation ...

... it goes without saying that, if directives nevertheless are adopted, then duly notified collective agreements at national level would be one way in which to implement them. And Sweden would most probably chose this way of implementation as allowed for in Article 2(4) [now Article 137(4) EC]. Non-compliance by firms or individuals could in this case be solved notably by recourse to the normal procedures in effect on the Swedish labour market. Only in the last resort, and as a safety valve might national legislation have to be envisaged.

The Nordic labour market organisations interpret this letter as an expression of a positive attitude to implementation by Nordic collective agreements. The CJEU has been more restrictive in its treatment of collective agreement implementation, see below.

In its report from 2000 on Industrial Relations in Europe[78] the Commission states on the practise of implementing directives by means of collective agreements that (emphasis added):

This practice, validated over the years by the Court of Justice of the European Communities and enshrined in Article 137(4) of the EC Treaty, is more frequent in those countries with a strong tradition of agreement-based regulation such as Belgium, Denmark or Italy. *Nevertheless, it raises the question of general coverage, continuity and appropriate publicity for agreement-based transposal measures.*

The CJEU has dealt with the lawfulness or otherwise of the implementation models outlined above in a number of cases. Model 1 (legislation as sole implementation) and model 3 (collective agreements with *erga omnes* effect as sole implementation) are in compliance with EU law.

In *Commission* v *Belgium*[79] the CJEU accepted that Belgium incorporated the then directive on collective redundancies[80] into national law by a collective agreement with *erga omnes* effect.

In *Commission* v *Kingdom of Denmark*[81] the Commission brought an infringement action against Denmark for failure to implement the Equal Pay Directive. That directive lays down detailed rules regarding certain aspects of the scope of article 141 EC and enacts various provisions whose essential

78. COM(2000)113 p. 37.
79. Case 215/83 *EC Commission* v *Belgium* [1985] ECR 1039.
80. Directive 75/129/EEC, amended by directive 92/56/EEC Now consolidated by 98/59/EC, see further in Chapter Eight.
81. Case 143/83 *EC Commission* v *Denmark* [1985] ECR 427.

purpose is to improve the legal protection of workers who may be wronged by failure to apply the principle of equal pay. Article 2 of the directive requires member states to introduce into their national legal systems:

> such measures as are necessary to enable all employees who consider themselves wronged by failure to apply the principle of equal pay to pursue their claims by judicial process after possible recourse to other competent authorities.

Denmark adopted a law on equal pay for men and women which provided in Article 1 that:

> every person who employs men and women to work at the same place of work must pay them the same salary for the same work ('samme arbejde') under this law if he is not already required to do so pursuant to a collective agreement.

The Commission considered that the Danish legislation did not fulfil all the obligations resulting from the Equal Pay Directive in as much as on the one hand it required employers to pay men and women the same salary exclusively for the same work but not for work to which equal value was attributed, and on the other hand it did not provide for any means of redress enabling workers wronged by the failure to apply the principle of equal pay for work of equal value to pursue their claims. The CJEU held that it is true that Member States may leave the implementation of the principle of equal pay in the first instance to representatives of management and labour. That possibility does not, however, discharge them from the obligation of ensuring, by appropriate legislative and administrative provisions, that all workers in the community are afforded the full protection provided for in the directive. That state guarantee must cover all cases where effective protection is not ensured by other means, for whatever reason, and in particular cases where the workers in question are not union members, where the sector in question is not covered by a collective agreement or where such an agreement does not fully guarantee the principle of equal pay.

In *Commission* v *Italy*[82] the issue was the alleged failure of Italy to implement the directive on collective redundancies.[83] The Italian government observed that, having regard to the whole of the Italian system of protection in the case of dismissals which is provided both by the wide scope given by

82. In Case 91/81 *EC Commission* v *Italy* [1982] ECR 2133.
83. Directive 75/129/EEC, amended by directive 92/56/EEC Now consolidated by 98/59/EC, see further in Chapter Eight.

Italian legislation to the concept of individual redundancy, which is heavily weighted in favour of workers, to the specific provisions laid down by regulation relating to collective redundancies and by the provisions of collective agreements, that system created conditions and established procedures making it possible to attain the objectives of the directive and, in various respects, exceeding its requirements. The Italian government did not dispute that in certain sectors, especially in agriculture and commerce, Italian legislation was not as comprehensive as the provisions of the directive. The CJEU held

10. It is clear from the foregoing that the provisions in this field which are in force in Italy do not suffice to meet the totality of the requirements of the directive.

In *Commission* v *Italy*[84] the CJEU ruled that a Member State may not plead provisions, practices or circumstances existing in its internal legal system in order to justify failure to comply with obligations and time-limits laid down in community directives.

In another infringement case against Italy[85] concerning the transfer of undertakings directive the CJEU held similarly that although the member states may leave the implementation of the social policy objectives pursued by the in the first instance to management and labour, that does not discharge them from the obligation of ensuring, by the appropriate laws, regulations and administrative measures, that all workers in the community are afforded the full protection provided for in the directive. The state guarantee must cover all cases where effective protection is not ensured by other means, in particular where collective agreements cover only specific economic sectors and create obligations only between members of the trade union in question and employers or undertakings bound by the agreements.

The CJEU's case law is now codified in Article 153(4) TFEU. In countries where collective agreements have no *erga omnes* effect, collective agreements are therefore not sufficient as the sole means of implementing directives establishing rights for all individual workers.

84. Case 131/84 *EC Commission* v *Italy* (No 2) [1985] ECR 3531.
85. Case 235/84 *Commission* v *Italy* [1986] ECR 2291.

7 Industrial action

7.1 Sources of law

7.1.1 ILO Conventions

The right to strike or take other industrial action is as mentioned above not set out explicitly in ILO Conventions and Recommendations. ILO Convention No 87, The Freedom of Association and Protection of the Right to Organise Convention establishes the right of workers' and employers' organizations to 'organize their administration and activities and to formulate their programmes', and the aims of such organizations as 'furthering and defending the interests of workers or of employers'. On the basis of these provisions, the two bodies set up to supervise the application of ILO standards, the Committee on Freedom of Association (since 1952) and the Committee of Experts on the Application of Conventions and Recommendations (since 1959), have frequently stated that the right to strike is a fundamental right of workers and of their organizations, and have defined the limits within which it may be exercised, laying down a body of principles in connection with the right to strike. Gernigon et al. summarises these principles in the following way:[86]

A. Consideration of the right to strike as a fundamental right to be enjoyed by workers and their organizations (trade unions, federations and confederations), which is protected at international level, provided that the right is exercised in a peaceful manner.

B. General recognition of the right to strike for workers in the public and the private sectors, with the sole possible exceptions being members of the armed and police forces, public servants who exercise authority in the name of the State and workers employed in essential services in the strict sense of the term (the interruption of which could endanger the life, safety or health of the whole or part of the population), or in situations of acute national crisis.

C. The principles of freedom of association do not cover strikes of a purely political nature, although they do cover those which seek a solution to major issues in economic and social policy. D. A blanket ban on sympathy strikes could lead to abuse. Workers should be able to enjoy the right to take such action when the initial strike they are supporting is itself lawful.

E. A minimum safety service may be imposed in all cases of strike action when such minimum services are intended to ensure the safety of persons, the prevention of accidents and the safety of machinery and equipment.

F. A minimum operational service may be established (in the undertaking or institution in question) in the case of strikes in public utility services and in public services of

86. Gernigon, Bernard, Alberto Odero and Horacio Guido: ILO Principles Concerning The Right To Strike, ILO 1998, International Labour Review, Vol. 137 (1998) No. 4, http://www.ilo.org/wcmsp5/groups/public/@ed_norm/@normes/documents/publication/wcms_087987.pdf.

fundamental importance; employers' and workers' organizations and the public authorities should be able to participate in determining this minimum service.

G. The obligation to give prior notice, the obligation to engage in conciliation, have recourse to voluntary arbitration, comply with a given quorum and obtain the agreement of a given majority where this does not cause the strike to become very difficult or even impossible in practice and the secret ballot method to decide strike action are all acceptable conditions for the exercise of the right to strike.

H. Restrictions on picketing should be confined to cases in which such action ceases to be peaceful, and picketing should not interfere with the freedom to work of non-strikers.

I. Requisitioning of the workers of an undertaking or institution in the event of a strike is admissible only in the case of a strike in an essential service or under circumstances of utmost gravity and in situations of acute national crisis.

J. The hiring of workers to replace strikers seriously impairs the right to strike and is acceptable only in strikes in an essential service or in situations of acute national crisis.

K. Legal provisions regarding wage deductions for days of strike give rise to no objection.

L. Appropriate protection should be afforded to trade union officials and workers against dismissal and other detrimental acts at work for organizing or participating in a legitimate strike, in particular through prompt, efficient and impartial procedures, accompanied by sufficiently dissuasive remedies and sanctions.

M. The protection of freedom of association does not cover abuses in the exercise of the right to strike involving failure to comply with reasonable requirements regarding lawfulness, or consisting of acts of a criminal nature; any sanctions imposed in the event of abuse should not be disproportionate to the seriousness of the violations.

The right to strike has been affirmed in the case law developed by the ILO's Freedom of Association Committee, interpreting Convention No. 87.[87]

7.1.2 Council of Europe Conventions

Article 11 ECHR does not explicitly mention strikes. Today (2013) there is, however, some protection of the right to strike in Article 11 ECHR but it has not always been like that. In older practice, in 1976, in Schmidt and Dahlström versus Sweden,[88] the ECtHR stated:

87. ILO, *Digest of Decisions,* para. 495: 'Freedom of association implies not only the right of workers and employers to form freely organizations of their own choosing, but also the right for the organizations themselves to pursue lawful activities for the defence of their occupational interests.'

88. *Schmidt and Dahlström* v *Sweden* (Application no. 5589/72).

> Article 11 ... leaves each State a free choice of the means to be used [to make collective action possible]. The grant of a right to strike represents without any doubt one of the most important of these means, but there are others

As set out above in section 4.4., the ECtHR in *Gustafsson* v *Sweden*[89] held that Article 11 ECHR does not protect employers against blockades and sympathetic actions from the workers. Over the years, the ECtHR has become more positive towards the right to strike – not least after that right has been guaranteed as a fundamental right in EU law. The right to collective bargaining has been read into art.11 ECHR, as a result of the rulings by the ECtHR in *Demir*[90] and extended to cover the right to strike in *Enerji-Yapi Yol.*[91]

In Demir and Baykara, the ECtHR held that there had been a violation of Article 11 ECHR on account of the failure of Turkey to recognise the right of the applicants, as municipal civil servants, to form a trade union. The Court further held that the annulment of a collective agreement was also a violation of Article 11 ECHR.

In Enerji-Yapi Yol, the ECtHR found a strike ban in the Turkish public sector too restrictive on the rights guaranteed by Article 11 ECHR. The case concerned a state prohibition on public sector trade unions from taking industrial action. Members of the trade union Enerji Yapi-Yol Sen who ignored the prohibition were disciplined and the union brought the case to the ECtHR, alleging that the ban on strikes interfered with their right to form and join trade unions as guaranteed under Article 11 ECHR. While the court acknowledged that the right to strike was not absolute and could be subject to certain conditions and restrictions, it held that a ban applied to all public servants was too wide a restriction. The ECHR held that the disciplinary action was 'capable of discouraging trade union members and others from exercising their legitimate right to take part in such one-day strikes or other actions aimed at defending their members' interests' and amounted to a threat to rights guaranteed under Article 11 ECHR. The strike ban was not in response to a 'pressing social need' and the Turkish government had thus failed to justify the need for the impugned restriction in a democratic society.[92]

As stated above in section 2.2.2 Article 6(4) of the European Social Charter 1961 (revised in 1996) provides explicitly for the right to strike. It states

89. *Gustafsson* v *Sweden*, judgment 25 April 1996, 18/1995/524/610.
90. *Demir and Baykara v Turkey,* Application No.34503/97.
91. *Enerji Yapi-Yol Sen* v *Turkey* Application No. 68959/01.
92. See further Ewing, K.D. and John Hendy: The Dramatic Implications of Demir and Baykara, Industrial Law Journal 2010 p. 2.

that with a view to ensuring the effective exercise of the right to bargain collectively, the Contracting Parties undertake to recognise the right of workers and employers to collective action in cases of conflicts of interest, including the right to strike, subject to obligations that might arise out of collective agreements previously entered into.

7.1.3 EU law

The Community Charter of the Fundamental Social Rights of Workers 1989[93] states as mentioned above on the right to collective action:

13. The right to resort to collective action in the event of a conflict of interests shall include the right to strike, subject to the obligations arising under national regulations and collective agreements. ...

Article 28 CFREU protects the rights of workers and employers, or their respective organisations, in accordance with Union law and national laws and practices, to negotiate and conclude collective agreements at the appropriate levels and, in cases of conflicts of interest, to take collective action to defend their interests, including strike action. That provision was used in Viking and Laval, see below.

7.2 Conflicts of Interest and Conflicts of Right

A fundamental distinction is – in many national labour law systems – drawn between conflicts of interest and conflicts of right. A conflict of interest arises in areas where no valid collective agreement applies. This may be because the matter in dispute has never been covered by a collective agreement, eg due to the employer being non-affiliated to an employers' organisation; or it may be because a previously existing collective agreement has been terminated. In conflicts of interest the parties are free to take industrial action: strike, lock-out, blacking and boycott. A conflict of right arises where the matter in dispute is already covered by a collective agreement. Conflicts of rights must be solved by judicial means and, as the main rule, not by industrial action. In the event of a conflict of right, there is only in few cases a right to resort to industrial action (strikes, etc). The exceptions from the peace obligation are mainly:

93. http://www.aedh.eu/plugins/fckeditor/userfiles/file/Conventions%20internationales/Community_Charter_of_the_Fundamental_Social_Rights_of_Workers.pdf.

- cases where the employer does not pay the wages
- cases where it is necessary to stop working in order to protect the health and welfare of the worker
- cases where the employer requires the workers to do work that is not covered by the collective agreement in force
- cases of lawful sympathetic action.

7.3 Peace Obligation

Particularly in Germany and Scandinavia, a collective agreement entails a peace obligation, ie a duty on the parties to the collective agreement and their members not to take industrial action over a matter covered by the agreement. The peace obligation is the major element of the contractual or obligatory effect of the collective agreement.

The continental EU Member States differ in the detailed rules on the scope *ratione personae* of the peace obligation.[94] In some countries it is only the trade union who has concluded the collective agreement which is legally bound not to organise industrial action. That is the case in France where the individual worker's right to strike is guaranteed in the constitution. In other countries, eg in Scandinavia, the individual workers working under a collective agreement are bound by the peace obligation.

7.4 The Right to Strike as a Fundamental Right. Monti I Regulation

The French farmers case[95] concerned French farmers who launched a campaign to restrict the supply of agricultural products from other Member States, which took the form of threats to wholesalers and retailers in order to induce them to stock exclusively French products.

The European Commission contended before the CJEU that the hindrance to the free movement of goods was a violation of Article 34 TFEU and that Member States (*in casu* France) under Article 4(3) TEU had a duty to take all appropriate measures to ensure fulfilment of the principle of free movement of goods. The CJEU agreed and declared that the French Republic had failed to fulfil its obligations under Article 34 TFEU, in conjunction with Article 4(3) TEU. Following that judgment, the Commission proposed a regulation – usually called the Monti I regualtion – to ensure rapid exchange of information between the Member States and the Commission on obstacles to the free movement of goods. After considerable debate it was enacted in an

94. See for detail Giugni, Gino: The peace obligation in Aaron, Benjamin and K. W. Wedderburn: Industrial Conflict. A comparative legal survey, London 1972 p. 128.
95. Case C-265/95 *Commission* v *France* [1997] ECR I-6959.

amended form as Council Regulation[96] of 7 December 1998 on the functioning of the internal market in relation to the free movement of goods among the Member States was adopted on the base of Article 352 TFEU.

One of the most contentious issues was the relationship between the right to strike and the free movement provisions. It is easy to imagine that the exercise of the right to strike or take other industrial action may operate as a hindrance to the free movement of goods, services or persons. That is, for example, the point in strikes by transport workers. On that issue Article 2 of the Regulation provides:

> This Regulation may not be interpreted as affecting in any way the exercise of fundamental rights as recognised in Member States, including the right or freedom to strike. These rights may also include the right or freedom to take other actions covered by the specific industrial relations systems in Member States.

It follows from the above provision that the Monti I Regulation as such does not restrict the freedom to take industrial action. That does, however, not answer the question as to whether, due to the EU principle of effectiveness, the EU Member States have an obligation to suppress industrial action which hinders the free movement of goods etc. more than they have traditionally done under domestic law, see below in section 8.2 on *Laval*[97] and Monti II.

8 Interplay between national collective labour law and free movement

In this section, I will discuss to what extent use of collective agreements in accordance with what is usual in (national) labour law is compatible with the principles of freedom of establishment and the freedom to provide services as understood by the CJEU *inter alia* in the context of public procurement law . In that regard the principles deriving from the general free movement principles, such as the principle of equal treatment, the principle of non-discrimination, the principle of mutual recognition, the principle of proportionality and the principle of transparency are of particular importance. The interface between free movement law and collective labour law has been at issue in a number of recent cases including the Laval case. National labour law on collective bargaining and the right to take industrial action in order to

96. EC/2679/98. See below in section 8.2.6 on the Monti II Regulation.
97. Case C-341/05 *Laval* [2007] ECR I-11767.

obtain a good bargain vary considerable within the EU.[98] It follows from the case law that both the internal market freedoms and the right of collective bargaining and to take collective action in support thereof must be respected. The opposing rights must be balanced against each other on a case by case basis. It will, however, often be unclear what the outcome of this balancing process will be.

8.1 Viking

In *Viking*,[99] the main issue was whether the Finnish Seamen's Union by threatening to take collective action and the International Transport Worker's Federation by conducting a campaign concerning flag of convenience made it pointless for Viking, a Finnish employer, to establish itself in Estonia and reflag a ferry, which had previously sailed under Finnish flag, to Estonia and whether that was a violation of the freedom of establishment as guaranteed by Article 49 TFEU. In *Viking*, in accordance with existing case law, the CJEU held that the restrictions that were the subject of the case could in principle be justified by reference to an overriding requirement in the general interest, such as the protection of workers, on the condition that it is shown that they are suited to ensure the completion of the goal in question and that they do not take measures beyond what is necessary in order to achieve it. In *Viking*, the CJEU left this assessment to the national court.[100]

In the Viking Line case, the CJEU was asked whether collective action initiated by a trade union against a private company in order to force the latter to join a collective agreement whereby the re-flagging of a ship to another Member State becomes pointless for the company falls outside of the scope of Article 49 TFEU as a consequence of the EU social policy competence under Article 153 TFEU, and in analogy with the argumentation of the CJEU in the Albany case.[101] Article 49 TFEU was regarded as applicable and analogy from the Albany case was rejected in the Viking case.

98. See Andrzej M. Swiatkowski (ed.): The Laval and Viking Cases Freedom of Services and Establishment v. Industrial Conflict in the European Union, Bulletin of Comparative Labour Relations – 69 The volume includes country reports dealing with how the CJEU rulings in the Laval and the Viking Line cases affect European labour law issues (in both individual and collective matters) as well as how they affect national labour law systems in 12 EU countries and Norway and Russia.
99. Case C-438/05 *Viking* [2007] ECR I-10779.
100. See paragraph 85 of the Viking case.
101. Case C-67/96 *Albany* [1999] ECR I-5751.

8.2 Laval

8.2.1 Laval in its historical context – the Law before Lisbon

The judgment in Laval was delivered in December 2007, i.e. a little less than two years before the coming into force of the Lisbon Treaty 1 December 2009. The law at issue in Laval – the balancing of the free movement rights for service providers in Article 56 TFEU and the fundamental rights of the trade unions to collective bargaining about wage levels (including wage levels above the minimum wage in a given country) and collective action in support of its wage claims under Article 28 CFREU – was, as set out in Chapter Two, changed substantially by the Lisbon Treaty. The Lisbon Treaty elevated CFREU, which from 2000 to the coming into force of the Lisbon Treaty was soft law, to Treaty rank.

As set out in Chapter Two as a result of the Lisbon Treaty a double justification test must now be performed when free movement and fundamental rights are balanced against each other.[102] The CJEU did not do that in *Laval*. It did the traditional justification test concerning restrictions on free movement and found that the restrictions on Laval's free movement caused by the trade union activity were too intransparent to be justified. But, the CJEU did not do any test of whether restrictions on the trade unions' fundamental rights to collective bargaining and collective action could be justified. Arguably, it was not required to do that under the law as it stood before the coming into force of the Lisbon Treaty, but today, in so far as the CFREU contains rights which correspond to rights guaranteed by the ECHR the meaning and scope of those rights shall be the same as those laid down by the ECHR, see Article 53 CFREU. Article 11(2) ECHR provides on justification of limitations to fundamental rights guaranteed by Article 11 ECHR that no restrictions shall be placed on the exercise of these rights other than *such as are prescribed by law* and are necessary in a democratic society in the interests of national security or public safety, for the prevention of disorder or crime, for the protection of health or morals or for the protection of the rights and freedoms of others. It is not entirely clear what exactly the justification test for limitations of fundamental rights requires and the Laval judgment does not contribute to clarifying it. There are some formulations in *Laval* which seems to suggest that the CJEU interpreted the Posting of workers directive,[103] see on that below in Chapter Seven, as providing full harmonization and capable of limiting the fundamental right sof trade unions to collective bargaining and collective ac-

102. Syrpis, Phil: The Treaty of Lisbon: Much Ado ... But About What?, Industrial Law Journal 2008 p. 219.
103. 96/71/EC.

tion. Today, under the current law such an interpretation cannot justify a limitation of a fundamental right of Treaty rank which is *lex superior* in relation to directives. If a directive, e.g. the Posting of Workers Directive is inconsistent with a fundamental right, the directive is partly invalid. The fundamental right is not limited just because a directive may say something that is inconsistent with the fundamental right.

It is, in my view, when discussing *Laval*, important to be aware that it was not about the law currently in force but about the law as it stood in the soft law period of the CFREU before the coming into force of the Lisbon Treaty. At the time of *Laval* there was only support for the rights of trade unions to collective bargaining and collective action in public international law (ILO Conventions 87 and 98 and the European Socail Charter 1961, amended in 1996) and in EU soft law (the 1989 Social Charter of the fundament al rights of workers and CFREU Article 28 (pre-Lisbon)). It was not guaranteed in EU primary law – not in the text of the EC Treaty and it had never been recognized by CJEU as a general principle of EU law. It was therefore arguably not – at the time of the judgment – *lex superior* in relation to the Posting of workers Directive. Since the coming into force of the Lisbon Treaty, the fundamental right of trade unions to collective bargaining and collective action is clearly part of primary EU law with the same legal value as other provisions in the Treaties, as for example the free movement provisions and higher value than directive provisions, including those that were adopted to facilitate the functioning of the internal market.

8.2.2 Facts of the Laval case

The *Laval*[104] case was about a Latvian company (Laval) which had won a contract for construction work at a school in the municipality of Vaxholm (Sweden) in an EU tender. In spring 2004, Laval posted Latvian building workers to a Swedish subsidiary of Laval to carry out the work. The Swedish trade union for building workers (byggnadsarbetarförbundet and one of its departments) demanded that Laval should accede to that trade union's general collective agreement with Swedish employers. According to that agreement, wages should be negotiated locally with a fall-back wage of 109 Swedish crowns. In autumn 2004, Laval entered into a collective agreement with the Latvian trade union for building workers. The level of pay in that agreement was much lower than the ordinary level of pay in Sweden. Between June and

104. Case C-341/05 *Laval* [2007] ECR I-11767.

October 2004, some negotiations took place between Laval and the Swedish building workers union, but this did not lead to any result.

8.2.3 The progress of the Laval case

On 19 October 2004, the Swedish building workers union sent a warning to Laval of industrial action in the form of blockade against all work on Laval work-places in Sweden. The blockade took effect 2 November. On 23 November 2004, the Swedish electrical workers union sent a warning of secondary (sympathetic) action against Laval.

Laval claimed that the industrial action (blockade + secondary action) was an unlawful restriction in violation of Article 49 EC [now 56 FEU] on free movement of services and the Posting of Workers Directive[105] and brought a case against the Swedish trade unions for building workers and electrical workers before the Swedish Labour Court 7 December 2004 demanding an *interim injunction* against the Swedish trade unions preventing them from taking industrial action + *damages*. The Labour Court turned down the demand for an *interim injunction* on 22 December 2004. At Christmas 2004, the posted Latvian workers went back to Latvia and did not return to the site in question. Laval went bankrupt in March 2005.

On 29 April 2005, the Swedish Labour Court before delivering judgment on the damages claim decided to stay proceedings and refer preliminary questions to the CJEU under Article 267 TFEU on the interpretation of Article 56 TFEU. The CJEU handed down its judgment on 18 December 2007.

On 2 December 2009, the Swedish Labour Court handed down its judgment.[106] The Labour Court awarded Laval damages from the trade unions with 4 votes to 3. The Swedish Labour Court held that trade unions are liable in damages under EU law on the same conditions as apply to state liability under EU law, i.e. three conditions must be met:[107]

- The EU law breached must have been intended to confer rights on individuals;
- The breach must be sufficiently serious;

105. 96/71/EC.
106. http://www.arbetsdomstolen.se/upload/pdf/2009/89-09.pdf. An unofficial translation by Erik Sjödin of the Swedish Labour Court's judgment in *Laval* into English may be found at the labour law portal http://arbetsratt.juridicum.su.se/
107. Joined Cases C-46 and C-48/93 *Brasserie du Pêcheur v Federal Republic of Germany* and *R v Secretary of State for Transport ex parte Factortame Ltd* [1996] ECR I-1029.

- There must be a direct causal link between the state's breach and the loss suffered.

A judgment from the Swedish Labour Court is normally final and cannot be appealed. Under the Swedish Administration of Justice Act there is, however, on strict conditions, a possibility of nullification of a judgment and of re-opening a case which cannot be appealed if serious errors have been committed. On 6 May 2010, the Swedish LO on behalf of the trade unions that lost in the Laval case, asked the Swedish Supreme Court to re-open the case. It argued that the Labour Court applied EU law in a fundamentally wrong way and that it was a serious procedural error that the Swedish Labour Court did not refer questions to the CJEU under Article 267 FEU on whether there, as held by the Swedish Labour Court, in cases where Article 56 FEU has been violated, is a general principle in EU law under which trade unions are liable in damages as a result of Article 56 FEU's direct, horizontal effect. The Swedish Supreme Court rejected the trade unions' claims both of nullification and of putting further questions to the CJEU.

8.2.4 The industrial action: Blockade and sympathetic action

In Swedish collective labour law (and similarly in the other Nordic countries), a blockade against an employer is an order from a trade union to its own members not to do work for that particular employer. This means that all unionised building workers in Sweden got an order from their trade union not to work for Laval. The blockade was a lawful main action. It had probably no coercive effect on Laval, because he had his own Latvian building workers and could do without work performed by Swedish building workers. The coercive effect in the industrial action was obtained through the next step: the secondary action or sympathetic action instigated by the electrical workers union. That measure had the effect of preventing Swedish electrical workers who were members of the electrical workers union and undertakings which were bound by collective agreements with the electrical workers union from providing work or services for Laval. That probably had the decisive coercive effect. The contracting authority (Vaxholm municipality) would probably not accept a renovated school without electricity as correct performance of the contract Laval had won.

8.2.5 Legal Problem

In *Laval,*[108] the CJEU answered preliminary questions under Article 267 TFEU regarding Article 56 TFEU on the free movement of services and the Posting of Workers Directive.[109] The legal problem was whether Swedish trade unions could take collective action (blockade and secondary action) as a means to obtain a Swedish collective agreement with Laval concerning wages and working conditions or whether it was sufficient that the Latvian employer followed Latvian law, hereunder a collective agreement that had been concluded with a Latvian trade union.

8.2.5.1 Is collective action covered by EU law or a purely national issue?

In *Laval*, the Danish and Swedish governments argued that the right for Swedish workers to take collective action to force a Latvian employer to follow Swedish collective agreements towards posted Latvian workers working in Sweden constitutes a fundamental right and for that reason falls outside the scope of Article 56 TFEU and the Posting of Workers Directive. The CJEU accepted that the right to take collective action is a fundamental right but held that it has to be balanced against the freedom of movement (in the Laval case the free movement of services). This balancing must be undertaken on a case by case basis. [110] It cited Article 28 CFREU in support of this interpretation. The CJEU held the same in *Viking.*[111]

8.2.5.2 Transparency

In *Laval* the Swedish collective action was considered a violation of the free movement provisions, because it was found to be intransparent. Unlike in *Viking*, the CJEU made the assessment itself in *Laval* of whether the collective action could be justified and held that it was not the case. There is no established practice for whether the CJEU makes the proportionality assessment itself or leaves it to the national court.

8.2.5.3 Legitimate goal

A relevant legitimate consideration in *Laval* would be the protection of workers. The CJEU referred both to the protection of the seconded (Latvian) workers[112] and to the right to initiate collective action with the purpose of

108. Case C-341/05 *Laval* [2007] ECR I-11767.
109. 97/71 EC.
110. See paragraph 90 in the Laval case.
111. See paragraph 43 in Case C-438/05 *Viking* [2007] ECR I-10779.
112. See e.g. paragraph 107.

protecting workers in the host Member State (Sweden) from social dumping as legitimate aims that could constitute an imperative requirement in the general interest.[113] Consideration for the Latvian and the Swedish workers in the Laval case presumably pulls in opposite directions. As a consequence of the Swedish actions, the Latvian employer went bankrupt and the Latvian workers lost their jobs. The CJEU also mentions the consideration for ensuring loyal competition between companies in the host country and companies from other EU Member States as a legitimate consideration.[114]

8.2.5.4 EU competence

The question as to whether the EU has competence to govern collective action was also relevant in the Laval case even though it was not explicitly posed in the case. In the Laval case, the Danish Government submitted a plea[115] and claimed that the EU is neither directly nor indirectly competent to govern trade unions' right to strike in order to obtain collective agreement. Reference was hereby made especially to Article 153(5) TFEU and the right to dispute as being a fundamental right. It follows from Article 153(5) TFEU that the EU does not have authority to adopt secondary law under the authority of Article 153 TFEU concerning collective action; however, it cannot be concluded in view of this that collective action falls outside the scope of the EU or the Posting of Workers Directive, which is adopted under the authority of the Treaty rules on the free movement. Accordingly, in the Laval case, the CJEU held that Article 56 TFEU and the Posting of Workers Directive are applicable to collective action.

8.2.5.5 Discrimination

Under Swedish law, *Medbestämmandelagen*[116] (law on workers' participation in decisions) prohibits strikes against an employer already covered by an agreement, who falls directly within the scope of *Medbestämmandelagen*, which typically applies to employers established in Sweden. The Swedish

113. See paragraph 103.
114. See paragraph 75 of the Laval case and from previous practice case C-60/03, Wolff & Müller, E.C.R. 2004 I-9553.
115. The plea can be seen at the web portal *Forum for forskning om arbetsratt*, http://arbetsratt.juridicum.su.se/. The opinion of the Danish government had no support in Danish legal practice, see A 2005.839, where the Danish Labour Court assessed the right to dispute in relation to Article 56 TFEU EC, or in the literature.
116. See Section 42 of *Medbestämmandelagen*, the so-called Les Britannia; see in this regard Nystrom, Birgitta: EU och arbetsratten, Stockholm 2002 p. 129.

ban on strikes against employers that have concluded agreements with other labour unions does not apply to employers such as Laval who do not fall directly within the scope of *Medbestämmandelagen*. This rule in *Medbestämmandelagen* can therefore be reasonably viewed as directly or indirectly discriminatory on grounds of nationality. Accordingly, it was set aside by the CJEU as being contrary to Articles 49 and 50 EC in the Laval case.

8.2.5.6 Free movement in a private law context. Direct, horizontal effect

One of the central questions in *Laval* and *Viking* was whether Articles 49 TFEU and 56 TFEU can be relied upon against industrial action by trade unions. In *Laval* and *Viking*, the CJEU held hat Articles 49 TFEU and 56 TFEU have direct, horizontal effect as binding for trade unions. Hereby the Court developed its previous case law on sports organisations[117] further applying it to trade union federations. Both the Advocate General and the CJEU relied to some extent on *Defrenne II*[118] in which the CJEU pointed out that all agreements intended to regulate paid labour collectively must observe mandatory provisions laid down in the Treaties.

8.2.6 Debate about Laval

The *Laval*-judgment has been widely criticized for tipping the balance between market freedoms and the fundamental right to take collective action in favour of market freedoms.[119] It has also attracted criticism for superficial treatment of the relationship between ILO law and EU law in regard to industrial action, lack of knowledge of basic collective labour law and linguistic carelessness by delivering two materially different judgment in the English language version on the one side and the continental language version (French, German, (Swedish) on the other. Others, for instance Business Europe and a number of Member States, have welcomed the rulings as a clarification of the state of law. The case has also given rise to much activity among EU institutions.

117. See e.g. Case 36/74 *B.N.O. Walrave, L.J.N. Koch* v *Association Union Cycliste Internationale, Koninklijke Nederlandsche Wielren Unie and Federacion Española Ciclismo* [1974] ECR p. 1405.
118. Case 43/75 *Defrenne* [1976] ECR 455.
119. See a number of the contributions in Andrzej M. Swiatkowski (ed.): The Laval and Viking Cases Freedom of Services and Establishment v Industrial Conflict in the European Union, Bulletin of Comparative Labour Relations – 69. See generally on the balancing of markets freedoms and fundamental rights Morijn, John: Balancing Fundamental Rights and Common Market Freedoms in Union Law: Schmidberger and Omega in the Light of the European Constitution, European Law Journal 2006 p. 15.

The most influential political analysis of the consequences of the Laval judgment was made in May 2010 by Mario Monti, in the report 'A new Strategy for the Single Market'.[120] According to Monti, the case law of the CJEU has 'exposed the fault lines that run between the Single Market and the social dimension at national level' and 'revived an old split that had never been healed: the divide between advocates of greater market integration and those who feel that the call for economic freedoms and for breaking up regulatory barriers is code for dismantling social rights protected at national level'. Further, 'the revival of this divide has the potential to alienate from the Single Market and the EU a segment of public opinion, workers' movements and trade unions, which has been over time a key supporter of economic integration'.

In my view, Monti's report is an example of EU law thinking where both the macro-perspective of the second layer of the economic constitution (the economic and monetary union), including the advantages for the EU of fundamental rights protection, including both individual and collective fundamental rights, and the care for the internal market are taken into consideration whereas the Laval judgment of the CJEU is more unilaterally focused on supporting the internal market. It is difficult to see the macro-perspective in the CJEU's reasoning and the care for the fundamental rights of the trade unions.

8.2.6.1 Relevance of ILO law

It may be argued that the limited right to take collective action accepted by the CJEU in *Laval* falls short of the level of protection of the right to strike provided by ILO Convention 87. It has been suggested that the Swedish government in *Laval* should have invoked Article 351 TFEU and contended that the Swedish (and Danish) rules on strikes are necessary to comply with duties undertaken under public international law before membership of the EU and therefore according to Article 351 TFEU take precedence over EU law.[121]

120. Monti, Mario: A New Strategy for the Single Market at the Service of Europe's Economy and Society: Report to the President of the European Commission José Manuel Barroso, Bruxelles 2010.
121. See Eklund, Ronnie: A Swedish Perspective on Laval, Comparative Labor Law and Policy Journal 2008 p. 551, compare Case C-158/91 *Levy* [1993] ECR I-4287 and Case C-13/93 *Minne* [1994] ECR I-371 where France and Belgium defended, with the help of Article 351 TFEU, their commitments under ILO Convention 89 on Night Work for Women Employed in Industry, which the CJEU later found to be contrary to the provisions of the Equal Treatment Directive (76/207EEC).

The CJEU didn't discuss the relationship to ILO law but only briefly mentioned that the right to take collective action was guaranteed by ILO Convention no 87. As mentioned in Chapter Two, Article 351 TFEU only allows Member States to rely on 'old' international law which is inconsistent with their EU law commitments until the incompatibility with EU law can be brought to an end. It is therefore not a very relevant criticism. In my view, it is also not realistic to interpret ILO Convention No. 87 which doesn't even mention the right to strike explicitly as providing better protection than Article 28 CFREU.

8.2.6.2 Ignorance of collective labour law

The CJEU apparently doesn't know what a collective labour law blockade is under Nordic law. There are no EU law concepts on industrial action, the concepts are still defined by national law. The CJEU states in point 34: 'Blockading ('blockad') of the Vaxholm building site began on 2 November 2004. The blockading consisted, inter alia, of preventing the delivery of goods onto the site, placing pickets and prohibiting Latvian workers and vehicles from entering the site. Laval asked the police for assistance but they explained that since the collective action was lawful under national law they were not allowed to intervene or to remove physical obstacles blocking access to the site.' The action described in point 34 of the judgment is not a collective labour law blockade but rather a demonstration maybe in the form of what some would call a physical blockade. A physical blockade is not a labour law action under Nordic law and is not what the main Laval case (the case dealt with by the Swedish Labour Court) was about. The Swedish Labour Court case was a traditional Nordic collective labour law case about industrial action as described above. There is nothing in the Swedish Labour Court's description of the case in its judgment from December 2009 that resembles the above description in point 34 of the CJEU judgments. Readers who are able to read the Swedish Labour Court's judgment should use that Court's description of the dispute rather than the one given by CJEU. In point 37 of the Laval judgment a more realistic description of the sympathetic action is given.

8.2.6.3 Linguistic carelessness

It may be questioned whether the CJEU judgment in *Laval* in different languages can be regarded as expressing a uniform answer to the questions referred to the Court. In the national (Swedish) part of the *Laval* Case, it was argued that the CJEU judgment in that case does not lay down the same rule in the English language version and the continental language versions of the judgment. In brief, the English language version states that what the trade unions did in *Laval* is contrary to EU law, but the continental language versions rather state that a legal system that allows the trade unions to do what they did is contrary to EU law. The English language version states: „

> Article 49 EC and ... are to be interpreted as precluding a trade union, in a Member State ... from attempting, by means of collective action ... to force a provider of services ...

The French (and similarly the German and Swedish versions) states:

> Les articles 49 CE et ... doivent être interprétés en ce sens qu'ils s'opposent à ce que, dans un État member ..., une organisation syndicale puisse tenter de contraindre ...

The main proceeding in the *Laval* Case was as set out earlier a suit by a Latvian contractor who had won a contract for re-building a Swedish school against two (small) Swedish trade unions, which in accordance with Swedish law had taken – under Swedish law lawful – collective actions against him with a view to raising the wages from Latvian to Swedish level. Laval claimed damages from the trade unions (not from the Swedish state which was not a party to the main case before the Swedish Labour Court). The trade unions argued that it was the Swedish state's responsibility not the trade unions' if Swedish law was contrary to EU law. The Swedish Labour Court cited the English language version of the CJEU's *Laval* judgment in support of its ruling against the trade unions. The trade unions argued that it should have used the continental (including the Swedish) versions of the judgment.[122]

8.2.7 The withdrawn Proposal for a Monti II Regulation

In 2012, the Commission presented two proposals as a follow-up to the debate created by *Laval* and *Viking*:[123] a proposal for a Council Regulation[124] – usually called the Monti II Regulation[125] – 'on the exercise of the right to take collective action within the context of the freedom of establishment and the

122. Swedish was the procedural language of the Laval case.
123. See further Malmberg, Jonas and Caroline Johansson: The Commission's Posting Package, European Policy Analysis, July Issue 2012.
124. COM (2012) 130. Proposal for a Council Regulation on the exercise of the right to take collective action within the context of the freedom of establishment and the freedom to provide services.
125. The original 'Monti Regulation' is Regulation (EC) 2679/98 'on the functioning of the internal market in relation to the free movement of goods among the Member States', see above in section 7.4.

freedom to provide services' and a directive on the enforcement of the Posting of Workers Directive.[126] If adopted, the Regulation would have laid down 'the general principles and rules applicable at Union level with respect to the exercise of the fundamental right to take collective action within the context of the freedom of establishment and the freedom to provide services.' It should not affect 'the right or freedom to strike or to take other action covered by the specific industrial relations systems in Member States'. The proposal aimed to clarify EU-level principles and rules concerning the right to take collective action. Its scope included the temporary posting of workers to another Member State, and restructuring and/or relocation involving more than one Member State. The Monti II proposal received objections from 19 national parliaments. After that the Commission withdrew the proposal. The withdrawal of the Monti II proposal is the first application of the new provisions on subsidiarity introduced by the Lisbon Treaty.[127] The wide-spread opposition the Monti II proposal was met with is an illustration of the fact that the rejection of the Laval judgment is not limited to the trade unions and their traditional political friends in socialist and social-democratic parties.

8.3 Rüffert

Rüffert,[128] focuses on the right of public authorities, when awarding contracts for work, to demand that tendering companies commit themselves to pay wages that are in line with rates already agreed through collective bargaining in the place where the work is performed, or whether this amounts to a restriction on the freedom to provide services in violation of Article 56 TFEU.

In practice the most important working condition in relation to posted workers is probably wages. According to ILO there is legislation regarding minimum wages in more than 90% of countries.[129] In twenty Member States

126. COM (2012) 131. Proposal for a Directive of the European Parliament and of the Council on the enforcement of Directive 96/71/EC concerning the posting of workers in the framework of the provision of services, seefurther below in Chspter Seven.
127. In connection with the adoption of the Lisbon Treaty the subsidiarity principle was strengthened by a New Protocol which gave national parliaments significant new power over the adoption of EU secondary legislation. Under Article 4 of the Protocol draft legislative acts must be notified to all national parliaments. Article 6 provides that any National Parliament can raise objections –Yellow card for 1/3 of votes: legislation reviewed – Orange card for 50% of the votes: proposal blocked if > 55% in Council or European Parliament object.
128. Case C-346/06 [2008] ECR I-1989.
129. See http://www.ilo.org/public/english/protection/condtrav/pdf/infosheets/w-1.pdf.

of the EU[130] and in one candidate country (Turkey), collective bargaining is subject to a statutory national minimum wage. The other EU Member States[131] do not have statutory national minimum wage, but rely on employers and trade unions to set minimum earnings through collective bargaining.[132] In most of the EU Member States collective agreements can be extended so as to become generally applicable, see below. Most EU Member States have a system for extending collective agreements so as to make them binding on employers who are not parties to them. That possibility does not exist in Italy and the UK and only to a limited extent in the Nordic countries. In Sweden and Denmark, collective agreements can *not* be extended to cover employers who are not parties to them. In Norway and Finland there is a possibility to give *erga omnes* effect to collective agreements.[133]

In *Rüffert*, the CJEU like in *Laval* had to strike a balance between the freedom to provide services, on the one hand, and the overriding requirements of the protection of workers and the prevention of social dumping, on the other. The German court asked the CJEU whether EU law must be interpreted as precluding national legislation on the award of public contracts that requires contractors and, indirectly, their subcontractors to pay workers posted in the framework of the performance of a public contract at least the remuneration prescribed by the collective agreement in force at the place where those services are performed, on pain of penalties that may go as far as the termination of the works contract, where the collective agreement to which the legislation in question refers is not declared to be of universal application.

The winning company undertook to pay employees employed on the Göttingen-Rosdorf prison building site the wages laid down in the 'Buildings and public works' collective agreement, which applied to this case. It emerged that a Polish subcontractor was paying its workers engaged on the building site only 46.57% of the prescribed wages. The works contract was terminated and proceedings commenced between the contracting authority and the com-

130. Belgium, Spain, Estonia, Greece, France, Hungary, Ireland, Latvia, Lithuania, Luxembourg, Malta, the Netherlands, Poland, Portugal, Slovakia, Slovenia, Czech Republic and the United Kingdom,Bulgaria and Romania.
131. I.e. countries like Norway, Sweden, Finland, Denmark, Switzerland, Germany, Austria, Italy, and Cyprus.
132. See http://epp.eurostat.ec.europa.eu/cache/ITY_OFFPUB/KS-NK-06-009/EN/KS-NK-06-009-EN.PDF.
133. See for details Ahlberg, Kerstin and Niklas Bruun: Kollektivavtal i EU. Om almängiltiga avtal och social dumping, Stockholm 1996.

pany that had won the company to determine whether it was required to pay a contractual penalty for breach of its undertaking concerning rates of pay.

In Germany, labour law is a federal matter whereas procurement law mainly is a matter for the 'Länder'. Germany has a system for declaring collective agreements universally applicable for all undertakings performing services in Germany. The collective agreement at issue in *Rüffert* had not been declared universally applicable in Germany. The procurement Act for Land Niedersachsen (the contracting authority) required contracting authorities to see to it that tenderers for public contracts complied with a 'local' collective agreement for Niedersachsen which laid down a higher level of pay than the universally applicable collective agreement for the construction industry in Germany.

The Advocate General proposed that the CJEU should rule that the Posting of Workers Directive and Article 56 TFEU must be interpreted as not precluding national legislation, such as that of Land Niedersachsen, on the award of public contracts which requires contractors and, indirectly, their subcontractors to pay workers posted in the framework of the performance of a public contract at least the remuneration prescribed by the collective agreement in force at the place where those services are performed. The CJEU did not follow the Advocate General but held that the Posting of Workers Directive, interpreted in the light of Article 49 EC, precludes an authority of a Member State, in a situation such as that at issue in the main proceedings, from adopting a measure of a legislative nature requiring the contracting authority to designate as contractors for public works contracts only those undertakings which, when submitting their tenders, agree in writing to pay their employees, in return for performance of the services concerned, at least as minimum wage the remuneration prescribed by the collective agreement in force at the place where those services are performed.

The CJEU did not consider the relationship between ILO Convention 94 and EU law in *Rüffert*. As Germany has not ratified that convention it was not directly relevant in that case. One may, however, ask if it is a consequence of the ruling in *Rüffert* that there is a contradiction between EU law on free movement and ILO Convention 94, see on Article 351 TFEU above in Chapter Two.

8.4 Commission v Luxembourg

In *Commission* v *Luxembourg*,[134] the CJEU answered questions of interpretation of the Posting of Workers Directive, in particular with regard to the issue of public policy provision contained in Article 3.10 of the Directive. The Commission argued that the Luxembourg legislation transposing the Posting of Workers Directive exceeded what was allowed under Community law *inter alia* on the requirement that Luxembourg collective agreements are complied with The Court considered that it is the actual content of collective agreements that may be defined as public policy, by opposition to collective agreements per se. In any case, the CJEU clarified that classification as public policy provisions can only apply to collective agreements which have been declared universally applicable.

8.5 Commission v Germany

In *Commission* v *Germany*,[135] the Commission obtained a judgment that declared that Germany has infringed the procurement rules because local authorities and local authority undertakings as employers awarded public service contracts concerning occupational pension schemes by stipulating in a collective agreement which servicce provider should provide the pension service without a European call for tender. In *Albany*,[136] the CJEU held that EU competion rules do not prohibit a decision by public authorities to make affiliation to a sectoral pension fund compulsory at the request of organisations representing employers and workers in a given sector, but in *Commission* v *Germany* it took the opposite view on the consequences of free movement rules for collective agreement autonomy.

134. Case C-319/06 *Commission* v *Luxembourg* [2008] ECR I-4323.
135. Case C-271/08 *Commission* v *Germany* [2010] ECR I-7091.
136. Case C-67/96 *Albany* [1999] I-5751.

CHAPTER FOUR

Information, Consultation and Participation

1 Introduction

The general understanding in EU is that information, consultation and participation of workers in relation to their employers' decision processes are useful means to increase the ability of business to adapt to structural changes. Completion of the internal market in which national economies are closely associated, while strengthening the competitiveness of the undertakings, is expected to accelerate mutations and restructurations of a large number of European industries. Timely information and consultation are seen as key to meeting the globalisation challenge through the development of new forms of work organisation. Social dialogue is expected to improve risk anticipation and make work organisation more flexible.

In the 2002 Report on Industrial Relations in Europe[1] the Commission stated that industrial relations will play an increasingly important role at European macroeconomic level. National systems of industrial relations have made an important contribution to macro-economic stability linked to the introduction of the single currency. Industrial relations will have to find a new role within the EMU given the shift of economic and monetary responsibility to the European level. Increasing disparities should be prevented and wage convergence should be based on catching up efforts and a sound process of convergence on productivity levels. The Commission thus sees a link between information, consultation and participation and the second macro-

1. Commission: Industrial Relations in Europe, 2002.

economic layer of the European, economic constitution, see above in Chapter One.[2]

Under EU law there are rights for employees and their representatives to be informed, consulted and in some cases participate in their employers' decision-making processes at plant level in CFREU Article 27 and a number of directives that provide for the information, consultation and sometimes participation of the workers, at both national and transnational levels. See in particular the directive on collective redundancies[3] and the directive on transfer of undertakings,[4] see further in Chapter Eight, the framework directive on working environment,[5] see further in Chapter Nine, the directive on a general framework for informing and consulting employees,[6] see below in section 3, the recast directive on a European Works Council or a procedure in Community-scale undertakings and Community-scale groups of undertakings for the purposes of informing and consulting employees,[7] see below in section 4 and the directive supplementing the Statute for a European company with regard to the involvement of employees,[8] see further below in section 5.

2 Sources of Law

2.1 Public international law and national law

Public international law has not contributed much to rules on information, consultation and participation at plant level. At national level, many countries have such rules but there is great diversity between the Member states. In its reports on Industrial Relations in Europe,[9] the Commission writes that legal

2. See Tuori, Kaarlo: The European Financial Crisis – Constitutional Aspects and Implications, EUI Working Paper LAW 2012/28.
3. 98/59/EC.
4. 2001/23/EC.
5. 89/391/EEC.
6. 2002/14/EC.
7. 2009/38/EC.
8. 2001/86/EC.
9. Commission: Industrial Relations in Europe, 2000, Commission: Industrial Relations in Europe, 2001, Commission: Industrial Relations in Europe, 2002, Commission: Industrial Relations in Europe, 2004, Commission: Industrial Relations in Europe, 2004, Commission: Industrial Relations in Europe, 2006, Commission: Industrial Relations in Europe, 2007, Commission: Industrial Relations in Europe, 2008, Commission: Industrial Relations in Europe, 2010, see http://ec.europa.eu/social/keyDocuments.jsp?type=0&policyArea=0&subCategory=0&country=0&year=0&advSearchKey=IRIE&mode=advancedSubmit&langId=en

provisions for employee representation exist in all countries and are required by EU law by the directive on a general framework for informing and consulting employees.[10]

2.2 EU Law

2.2.1 General

The Community Charter of the Fundamental Social Rights of Workers 1989 stated that[11] information, consultation and participation for workers must be developed along appropriate lines, taking account of the practices in force in the various Member States. This shall apply especially in companies or groups of companies having establishments or companies in several Member States of the European Community. Such information, consultation and participation must be implemented in due time, particularly in the following cases:

- when technological changes which, from the point of view of working conditions and work organisation, have major implications for the work force are introduced into undertakings;
- in connection with restructuring operations in undertakings or in cases of mergers having an impact on the employment of workers;
- in cases of collective redundancy procedures;
- when trans-frontier workers in particular are affected by employment policies pursued by the undertaking where they are employed.

In this perspective, there seems to be a general consensus that these mutations should take place in a context which is socially accepted. To this effect, the interest of promoting and encouraging the development of information, consultation and participation practices is widely shared. While taking account of the existing diversity between Member States in this area, the Commission considers it necessary to propose appropriate instruments with the view of ensuring the generalization of such principles at EU level. Article 27 CFREU provides:

Workers' right to information and consultation within the undertaking
Workers or their representatives must, at the appropriate levels, be guaranteed information and consultation in good time in the cases and under the conditions provided for by Union law and national laws and practices.

10. 2002/14/EC.
11. http://www.aedh.eu/plugins/fckeditor/userfiles/file/Conventions%20internationales/Community_Charter_of_the_Fundamental_Social_Rights_of_Workers.pdf

On the sources of Article 27 CFREU, it is stated in the explanatory remarks[12] that this Article appears in the revised European Social Charter[13] and in the 1989 Community Charter on the fundamental rights of workers.[14] It applies under the conditions laid down by Union law and by national laws. The reference to appropriate levels refers to the levels laid down by Union law or by national laws and practices, which might include the European level when Union legislation so provides. There is a considerable Union *acquis* in this field: Articles 154 and 155 TFEU, the Directives on a general framework for informing and consulting employees in the European Community,[15] collective redundancies,[16] transfer of undertakings,[17] the framework directive on working environment,[18] the recast directive on a European Works Council or a procedure in Community-scale undertakings and Community-scale groups of undertakings for the purposes of informing and consulting employees,[19] see below in section 4 and the directive supplementing the Statute for a European company with regard to the involvement of employees,[20] see further below in section 5.

2.2.2 EU-rules on Information and consultation at national level

The first layer of EU provisions on information and consultation of workers was adopted in connection with the adoption of directives in the 1970's and 1980's on the issues of collective redundancies, transfer of Undertaking and working environment. The Directive from 1975 on collective redundancies[21] laid down a procedure for the consultation of workers' representatives after the employer had provided them with all the relevant information enabling them to make constructive proposals. Likewise, the Directive from 1977 on the safeguarding of workers' rights in the event of transfers of undertakings,

12. See OJ 2007 C 303.
13. Article 21.
14. Points 17 and 18.
15. 2002/14/EC, see below in section 3.
16. 98/59/EC.
17. 2001/23/EC.
18. 89/391/EEC.
19. 2009/38/EC.
20. 2001/86/EC.
21. 75/129/EEC, amended by 92/56/EEC, later repealed and consolidated with Directive 98/59/EC on the approximation of the laws of the Member States relating to collective redundancies.

businesses or parts of businesses[22] provided for the information and consultation of workers' representatives, specifying that such information and consultation must be timely. See on information and consultation in connection with collective redundancies and transfers of undertakings below in Chapter Eight. The Directive on the Implementation of measures to promote the improvement of worker health and safety at the workplace adds the obligation of participation to those of information and consultation.[23]

A general framework for informing and consulting employees in the EU at national level was established in 2002.[24] The general directive on informing and consulting employees in the EU seeks to strengthen dialogue at national level within enterprises and ensure employee involvement in decision-making, with a view to better anticipation of problems and the prevention of crises.

2.2.3 Information, consultation and participation at transnational level

In 1970, the Commission had presented to the Council a draft Regulation concerning the European Company Statute and a draft Directive on the question of worker participation under this Statute. In 1972, The Commission presented a proposal for a draft Fifth Directive on Company Law. It was later amended[25] but never adopted and it is now withdrawn.

It took, however, more than 30 years before the Council Regulation on SE Companies[26] established a Statute for a European company (SE) with a view to creating a uniform legal framework enabling companies from different Member States to plan and carry out the re-organisation of their business on an EU scale. In the autumn 2001, the Directive supplementing the Statute for a European company with regard to the involvement of employees was adopted.[27] There are now (2013) three Directives providing for the involvement of employees (i.e. information, consultation and participation) in enter-

22. 77/187/EE, amended by 98/50/EC, later repealed and replaced with the recast Directive 2001/23/EC.
23. 89/391/EEC.
24. 2002/14/EC.
25. Amended Proposal for a Fifth Directive concerning the structure of public limited companies and the powers and obligations of their organs, O.J. No. C240 of 9.9.83, p. 2; Bull: Supp. E.C. 61.83.
26. Council Regulation (EC) No 2157/2001 of 8 October 2001 on the Statute for a European company (SE).
27. Directive supplementing the Statute for a European company with regard to the involvement of employees 2001/86/EC.

prises adopting either the European Company Statute, the European Cooperative Society Statute[28] or deriving from a cross-border merger.[29]

The European Works Council Directive was originally adopted in 1994 and replaced by a recast directive in 2009.[30] An earlier draft – the so-called Vredeling proposal[31] – had been presented in 1983 and was later withdrawn.

2.2.4 *Traditional directives, no framework agreements between the social partners*

That Commission has attempted to make the Social Partners at European level adopt framework agreements which could later be transposed via a directive, see on that road to labour law directives above in Chapter Two and Three, but the social partners have not been willing or able to agree on any agreement concerning information, consultation and participation of employees. The EU *acquis* on the subject is therefore based on ordinary directives adopted by the Council and the European Parliament.

3 General Framework on Information and Consultation at national level

The EU Directive[32] establishing a general framework for informing and consulting employees plays a key role in promoting social dialogue. It sets minimum principles, definitions and arrangements for information and consultation of employees at the enterprise level within each country. Given the diverse range of industrial relations practices across the Member States, they enjoy substantial flexibility in applying the Directive's key concepts (employees' representatives, employer, employees etc.) and implementing the arrangements for information and consultation. Management and labour play a

28. Directive 2003/72/EC supplementing the Statute for a European Cooperative Society with regard to the involvement of employees.
29. Directive 2005/56/EC on cross-border mergers of limited liability companies.
30. Directive 94/45/EC on the establishment of a European Works Council or a procedure in Community-scale undertakings and Community-scale groups of undertakings for the purposes of informing and consulting employees, now repealed and replaced by Directive 2009/38 on the establishment of a European Works Council or a procedure in Community-scale undertakings and Community-scale groups of undertakings for the purposes of informing and consulting employees (Recast).
31. See Docksey, Christopher: Information and Consultation of Employees: The United Kingdom and the Vredeling Directive, The Modern Law Review 1986 p. 281.
32. 2002/14/EC.

key role in deciding those arrangements. Information and consultation are required on:

- the recent and probable development of the undertaking's or the establishment's activities and economic situation
- the situation, structure and probable development of employment within the undertaking or establishment and any anticipatory measures envisaged, in particular where there is a threat to employment
- decisions likely to lead to substantial changes in work organisation or in contractual relations.

To avoid undue burdens on small and medium-sized enterprises, the Directive applies only to undertakings employing at least 50 employees, or to establishments employing at least 20 employees, according to the choice made by the Member State.

3.1 Background to the directive

On 11 November 1998, the European Commission issued a proposal for a Directive 'establishing a general framework for informing and consulting employees in the European Community'. The initiative followed the refusal of UNICE [now BusinessEurope], the European-level employers' organisation, to enter into negotiations over a European agreement on the subject. The draft Directive provided for rules on the information and consultation of workers at national level – based on agreement or legislation – applying to undertakings with 50 or more employees. The European Trade Union Confederation (ETUC) welcomed the draft Directive, but considered that it did not go far enough on a number of issues. UNICE rejected European legislation in this area as unnecessary.

The possibility of the introduction of an EU-level framework for employee information and consultation was first raised in the European Commission's 1995 medium-term Social Action Programme.[33] In November 1997, the Commission opened a second round of consultations with the European level social partners on the content of possible EU legislation on information and consultation. At the second stage of consultations, the Commission expressed a clear preference for a social partner initiative to reach a European agreement on this topic. However, while ETUC and CEEP indicated their willingness to negotiate on this basis, UNICE [now BusinessEurope] re-

33. COM(95) 134.

mained opposed and in March 1998 rejected joining such talks. In response to UNICE's decision, ETUC called upon the Commission to begin drafting legislation.

The Commission presented its proposal in 1998.[34]

3.2 The Preamble to the directive

In the Preamble to the directive there is reference to the EU's employment strategy based on the concepts of 'anticipation', 'prevention' and 'employability', which are to be incorporated as key elements into all public policies likely to benefit employment, including the policies of individual undertakings, by strengthening the social dialogue with a view to promoting change compatible with preserving the priority objective of employment. It is stated in the Preamble[35] that entry into the third stage of economic and monetary union has extended and accelerated the competitive pressures at European level. This means that more supportive measures are needed at national level. The existing legal frameworks for employee information and consultation at EU and national level tend to adopt an excessively a posteriori approach to the process of change, neglect the economic aspects of decisions taken and do not contribute either to genuine anticipation of employment developments within the undertaking or to risk prevention. All of these political, economic, social and legal developments call for changes to the existing legal framework providing for the legal and practical instruments enabling the right to be informed and consulted to be exercised.

3.3 Object and principles

The purpose of the Directive is according to Article 1 to establish a general framework setting out minimum requirements for the right to information and consultation of employees in undertakings or establishments in the EU. The practical arrangements for information and consultation shall be defined and implemented in accordance with national law and industrial relations at national level.

When defining or implementing practical arrangements for information and consultation, the employer and the employees' representatives shall work in a *spirit of cooperation* and with due regard for their reciprocal rights and obligations, taking into account the interests both of the undertaking or establishment and of the employees.

34. Com 98/612.
35. See poin 12 14 in the Preamble.

3.4 Definitions

Article 2 of the Directive defines a number of central concepts.

3.4.1 Undertaking

According to Article 2(a) 'undertaking' means a public or private undertaking carrying out an economic activity, whether or not operating for gain, which is located within the territory of the Member States.

3.4.2 Establishment

According to Article 2(b) 'establishment' means a unit of business defined in accordance with national law and practice, and located within the territory of a Member State, where an economic activity is carried out on an ongoing basis with human and material resources.

3.4.3 Employer

According to Article 2(c) 'employer' means the natural or legal person party to employment contracts or employment relationships with employees, in accordance with national law and practice.

3.4.4 Employee

According to Article 2(d) 'employee' means any person who, in the Member State concerned, is protected as an employee under national employment law and in accordance with national practice. See on the CGT case[36] below in section 3.5.

3.4.5 Employees' representatives

According to Article 2 (e) 'employees' representatives' means the employees' representatives provided for by national laws and/or practices.

3.4.6 Information and consultation

According to Article 2(f) 'information' means transmission by the employer to the employees' representatives of data in order to enable them to acquaint themselves with the subject matter and to examine it. According to Article 2(g) 'consultation' means the exchange of views and establishment of dialogue between the employees' representatives and the employer.

36. Case C-385/05 *CGT and others* [2007] I-611.

As set out below in section 4 on European Works Councils, the recast Works Councils Directive[37] provided new definitions of information and consulktation. Information' means according to Article 2(f) of the recast directive on Works Councils the transmission of data by the employer to the employees' representatives in order to enable them to acquaint themselves with the subject matter and to examine it; information shall be given at such a time, in such a fashion and with such content as are appropriate to enable employees' representatives to undertake an in-depth assessment of the possible impact and, where appropriate, prepare for consultations with the competent organ of the Community-scale undertaking or Community-scale group of undertakings. Consultation means according to Article 2(g) of the recast EWC-directive the establishment of dialogue and exchange of views between employees' representatives and central management or any more appropriate level of management, at such a time, in such a fashion and with such content as enables employees' representatives to express an opinion on the basis of the information provided about the proposed measures to which the consultation is related, without prejudice to the responsibilities of the management, and within a reasonable time, which may be taken into account within the Community-scale undertaking or Community-scale group of undertakings. As appears the definitions in the recast EWC-directive are considerably more elaborate and detailed than the definitions in the directive[38] establishing a general framework for informing and consulting employees

3.5 Scope

Under Article 3(1) of the Directive it applies, according to the choice made by the Member States, either to undertakings employing at least 50 employees in any one Member State, or to establishments employing at least 20 employees in any one Member State. It is for the Member States to determine the method for calculating the thresholds of employees employed.

In 2005, France adopted a rule providing that an employee engaged after 22 June 2005 who was under 26 years of age should not be taken into account in calculating the size of the workforce of the undertaking by which he was employed until he reached the age of 26, whatever the nature of his contract with the undertaking. A number of French trade unions took proceedings against the French Government claiming that this was contrary to both the collective redundancies directive,[39] see on that directive below in Chapter

37. 2009/38/EC.
38. 2002/14/EC.
39. 98/59/EC.

Eight, and the directive establishing a general framework for informing and consulting employees. In *CGT and others*,[40] the CJEU ruled that Article 3(1) of the general framework directive for informing and consulting employees is to be interpreted as precluding national legislation which excludes, even temporarily, a specific category of workers from the calculation of staff numbers within the meaning of that provision.

The CJEU noted that, pursuant to Article 2(d) of the general framework directive for informing and consulting employees 'employee' means any person who, in the Member State concerned, is protected as an employee under national employment law and in accordance with national practice. It follows that, since it is not disputed that the workers aged less than 26 are protected by French employment legislation, they are employees within the meaning of the general framework directive for informing and consulting employees. The CJEU mentioned that it is true that the second subparagraph of Article 3(1) of the general framework directive for informing and consulting employees provides that Member States are to determine the method for calculating the thresholds of employees employed. That provision concerns determination of the method of calculation of the thresholds of employees employed and not the actual definition of the concept of an employee. Since the Directive defined the group of persons to be taken into account at the time of that calculation, Member States cannot exclude from that calculation a specific category of persons initially included in that group. Thus, although the general framework directive for informing and consulting employees does not prescribe the manner in which the Member States are to take account of employees falling within its scope when calculating the thresholds of workers employed, it does nevertheless require that they be taken into account. The system put into place by the general framework directive for informing and consulting employees is intended to apply to all employees referred to in Article 2(d) of the directive.

The CGT case took place before the expiry of the time limit for implementing the framework employment directive[41] which *inter alia* prohibits age discrimination. Today (2013) legislation as that at issue in the CGT case would be incompatible with the framework employment directive, see further on age discrimination below in Chapter Six.

40. Case C-385/05 *CGT and others* [2007] I-611.
41. 2000/78/EC.

3.6 Practical arrangements for information and consultation

Article 4 of the framework directive for informing and consulting employees provides that in accordance with the principles set out in Article 1 of the directive and without prejudice to any provisions and/or practices in force which is more favourable to employees, the Member States shall determine the practical arrangements for exercising the right to information and consultation at the appropriate level in accordance with this Article. Information and consultation shall at least cover:

(a) information on the recent and probable development of the undertaking's or the establishment's activities and economic situation;
(b) information and consultation on the situation, structure and probable development of employment within the undertaking or establishment and on any anticipatory measures envisaged, in particular where there is a threat to employment;
(c) information and consultation on decisions likely to lead to substantial changes in work organisation or in contractual relations, including those covered by the Community provisions referred to in Article 9(1).

3. Information shall be given at such time, in such fashion and with such content as are appropriate to enable, in particular, employees' representatives to conduct an adequate study and, where necessary, prepare for consultation.

Consultation shall take place:

(a) while ensuring that the timing, method and content thereof are appropriate;
(b) at the relevant level of management and representation, depending on the subject under discussion;
(c) on the basis of information supplied by the employer in accordance with Article 2(f) and of the opinion which the employees' representatives are entitled to formulate;
(d) in such a way as to enable employees' representatives to meet the employer and obtain a response, and the reasons for that response, to any opinion they might formulate;
(e) with a view to reaching an agreement on decisions within the scope of the employer's powers referred to in paragraph 2(c).

3.7 Agreement

According to Article 5 of the framework directive for informing and consulting employees Member States may entrust management and labour at the appropriate level, including at undertaking or establishment level, with defining freely and at any time through negotiated agreement the practical arrangements for informing and consulting employees. These agreements, and agreements existing on the date laid down in Article 11, as well as any subsequent renewals of such agreements, may establish, while respecting the principles set out in Article 1 and subject to conditions and limitations laid down by the Member States, provisions which are different from those referred to in Article 4.

As set out above it follows from Article 1 that when defining or implementing practical arrangements for information and consultation, the employer and the employees' representatives shall work in a *spirit of cooperation* and with due regard for their reciprocal rights and obligations, taking into account the interests both of the undertaking or establishment and of the employees. That is the only minimum provision that cannot be derogated from. All other minimum requirements including those laid down in Article 4 can be derogated from by agreement if the Member States empower management and labour to enter into such agreements. See as an example of the wide scope of discretion left to the national level the *Holst* case,[42] cited below in section 3.9.

3.8 Confidential information

Member States shall provide that, within the conditions and limits laid down by national legislation, the employees' representatives, and any experts who assist them, are not authorised to reveal to employees or to third parties, any information which, in the legitimate interest of the undertaking or establishment, has expressly been provided to them in confidence. This obligation shall continue to apply, wherever the said representatives or experts are, even after expiry of their terms of office. However, a Member State may authorise the employees' representatives and anyone assisting them to pass on confidential information to employees and to third parties bound by an obligation of confidentiality. Member States shall provide, in specific cases and within the conditions and limits laid down by national legislation, that the employer is not obliged to communicate information or undertake consultation when the nature of that information or consultation is such that, according to objective criteria, it would seriously harm the functioning of the undertaking or establishment or would be prejudicial to it. *Grøngaard and Bang*[43] is cited below in section 4.8 on confidential information I relation to European Works Councils.

42. C-405/08 *Holst* [2010] ECR I-985.
43. Case C-384/02 *Grøngaard and Bang* [2005] ECR I-9939.

3.9 Protection of employees' representatives

Member States shall ensure that employees' representatives, when carrying out their functions, enjoy adequate protection and guarantees to enable them to perform properly the duties which have been assigned to them.

In *Holst*,[44] Holst was engaged on 1 July 1984 by BWV under an individual contract of employment as a project engineer. In 2001 Holst was elected as the employees' representative for engineers on BWV's cooperation committee. That committee, which was established pursuant to the Cooperation Agreement,[45] is made up of representatives of management and employees. Within that committee, the employees' representatives included representatives of employees who were members of LO and representatives of other employee groups. The Cooperation Agreement (Samarbejdsaftalen) is a cooperation agreement concluded between the two principal labour and employer organisations in Denmark, namely the Danish Confederation of Trade Unions (Landsorganisationen i Danmark) ('LO') and DA. It deals with the organisation and functioning of cooperation committees within undertakings. The Cooperation Agreement applies to undertakings which have more than 35 employees and contains provisions providing for the establishment of a cooperation committee consisting of representatives of management and employees, referred to respectively as group A and group B. Group B is made up of representatives of unionised LO-affiliated employees and representatives of other categories of employees. Clause 4 of the Cooperation Agreement provides as follows:

> Any member of the cooperation committee group B who does not already enjoy protection as a union representative and who is discharged from the company must be given six weeks' notice of termination over and above the period of notice provided for by the collective agreement. The total period of notice shall not exceed the period of notice applicable to a union representative for the same trade group or similar trade groups. ...

On 24 January 2006, together with other employees, Holst was given six months' notice of termination of his employment on grounds of downsizing by BWV. He challenged the grounds for his dismissal. Holst is a member of IDA, which has acted on his behalf before the national court. On 8 November 2006, IDA, acting on behalf of Holst, brought an action before a Danish court, seeking to have BWV ordered to pay Holst damages in respect of his

44. C-405/08 *Holst* [2010] ECR I-985.
45. In Danish Samarbejdsaftalen mellem LO og DA.

dismissal, pursuant to the Salaried Employees Act.[46] IDA took the view that the dismissal was not based on objective grounds. It further submitted that, as an employees' representative on the cooperation committee, Holst was entitled to more extensive protection against dismissal, pursuant to Article 7 of the framework directive for informing and consulting employees. The Danish court referred preliminary questions to the CJEU on the interpretation of the framework directive for informing and consulting employees. The CJEU concluded:

1. Directive 2002/14/EC of the European Parliament and of the Council of 11 March 2002 establishing a general framework for informing and consulting employees in the European Community must be interpreted as not precluding its transposition by way of a collective agreement which results in a group of employees being covered by the agreement in question, even though the employees in that group are not members of the union which is a party to that agreement and their field of activity is not represented by that union, provided that the collective agreement is such as to guarantee to the employees coming within its scope effective protection of the rights conferred on them by Directive 2002/14.

2. Article 7 of Directive 2002/14 must be interpreted as not requiring that more extensive protection against dismissal be granted to employees' representatives. However, any measure adopted to transpose that directive, whether provided for by legislation or by collective agreement, must comply with the minimum protection threshold laid down in that Article 7.

3.10 Relation to other information and consultation provisions

The framework directive for informing and consulting employees is without prejudice to the specific information and consultation procedures set out in the directives on collective redundancies[47] and transfer og undertakings.[48] The Directive is also without prejudice to provisions adopted in accordance with the directive on European Works Council, see below in section 4, and other rights to information, consultation and participation under national law. Implementation of the framework directive for informing and consulting employees is not sufficient grounds for any regression in relation to the situation which already prevailed in each Member State prior to the adoption of the directive and in relation to the general level of protection of workers in the areas to which the directive applies.

46. In Danish Funktionærloven.
47. Article 2 of Directive 98/59/EC.
48. Article 7 of Directive 2001/23/EC.

4 European Work's Councils

4.1 Backgound

The current Directive for the establishment of an European Works Council (EWC) or a procedure for informing and consulting employees[49] applies to EU-scale undertakings or groups with at least 1000 employees and at least 150 employees in each of two Member States. There are around 970 EWC's represent over 15 million employees.[50] The Directive is a recast directive building on the previous directives on EWC's.[51]

In the proposal for the Directive,[52] the Commission stated that there are some problems with the practical application of the previous Directive.[53] The right to transnational information and consultation lacks effectiveness, as the EWC is not sufficiently informed and consulted in the case of restructuring. European Works Councils have been set up in only 36% of undertakings falling within the scope of the Directive. There are legal uncertainties, particularly with regard to the relationship between the national and transnational levels of consultation, and in cases of mergers and acquisitions. Lastly, the consistency and linkage of the various directives on the information and consultation of employees are insufficient.

In April 2004, the Commission began consultations with the EU-level social partners on measures to enhance the effectiveness of EWC's, including a possible revision of the 1994-Directive.[54] At the time, the positions of the social partners on this matter were divided: the European Trade Union Confederation (ETUC) was pressing the Commission for numerous revisions, while BusinessEurope (previously UNICE) contested the case for overhauling the 1994-Directive. In April 2005, the EU-level employer and trade union bodies – UNICE (now BusinessEurope), UEAPME, CEEP and ETUC – published a joint text, 'Lessons learned on European Works Councils', which assessed

49. 2009/38/EC on the establishment of a European Works Council or a procedure in Community-scale undertakings and Community-scale groups of undertakings for the purposes of informing and consulting employees (Recast).
50. See European Commission: New rules for European works councils – Update 2011.
51. Directive 94/45/EC on the establishment of an EWC or a procedure in Community-scale undertakings and Community-scale groups of undertakings for the purposes of informing and consulting employees, directive 97/74/EC extending it to the UK and Northern Ireland and directive 2006/109/EC adapting Directive 94/45/EC by reason of the accession of Bulgaria and Romania.
52. COM(2008) 419.
53. 94/45/EC.
54. 94/45/EC.

the operation of EWC's and highlighted lessons for the future. Overall, the joint text reported the positive role that EWC's can play in improving the information flow between workers and management, allowing for consultation of workers on relevant cross-border issues affecting the group, developing a corporate culture in transnational groups and gaining acceptance for necessary change.

In July 2005, ETUC and BusinessEurope responded formally to the European Commission's April 2005 Communication on restructuring and employment.[55] The Communication outlines measures aimed at improving the EU's capacity for anticipating and managing restructuring. The Communication was also intended to initiate the second phase of consultation on the revision of the EWC Directive. However, the reaction of the social partners was generally critical. While the ETUC executive committee criticised the Commission for launching a joint consultation on two separate issues: company restructuring and the Directive on EWC's, BusinessEurope affirmed its opposition to the beginning of a second-phase consultation on the revision of the EWC-Directive. The Commission declared the revision of the EWC-Directive to be one of its legislative priorities for 2008. In February of that year, a Commission document formally launched the second-phase consultation. This time, the employer side agreed to negotiate about a revision. ETUC, however, rejected negotiations on the grounds that they feared that these could not be finished early enough to complete the revision process before the next European elections. On 2 July 2008, the Commission published the proposal for a recast Directive.[56]

The main objectives of the Commission's proposal were to enhance the effectiveness of EWC's, particularly by improving the definition of 'information' and 'consultation', to resolve legal uncertainties and problems (e.g. in cases of restructuring) and to harmonise the EWC-Directive with more recent Directives on employee representation as for example the framework directive for informing and consulting employees,[57] see further above in section 3.

The first reaction of the European social partners to the Commission's proposal for a recast of the European Works Council directive opposite positions. While the European Trade Union Confederation (ETUC) welcomed the revision of the 1994 EWC directive, the Confederation of European Business

55. COM(2005) 120.
56. COM(2008) 419.
57. 2002/14/EC.

(BusinessEurope) criticised the proposal as 'over-prescriptive and ill-suited for individual companies'.

During the summer of 2008, however, both parties settled their disagreements and developed a joint advice in a letter to the French Minister for Labour, Social Affairs and Solidarity, on the recast directive. The most important part of the letter concerns the fact that the social partners accept the Commission's proposal for a 'recast' directive as a 'basis for the revision' of the then current EWC directive.[58] In addition, the joint advice proposes the following changes to the Commission's proposal:

- clarifications to the wording of the following articles: 2 (f) (definition of 'information'), 2 (g) (definition of 'consultation'), 5.4 (role of trade union representatives in the special negotiation body), 10.1 (rights of the EWC), 10.4 (training) and 12.3 (fall-back clause regarding the link between EWC's and national bodies);
- revision of Article 13, introducing a new period for voluntary agreements following the adoption of the recast directive. Furthermore, the joint advice demands the deletion of the obligation to dissolve existing EWC's when a new EWC is set up following a major restructuring process.

On 2 October 2008, the General Secretary of ETUC and the General Secretary of BusinessEurope published a second joint letter clarifying the objective of their initial joint advice and arguing for a rapid adoption of the recast directive before the end of 2008. The clarifications related to two points:

- extending the definition of 'information' by an explicit statement that the in-depth information should not slow down decision-making in companies;
- regarding Article 13, the proposal of a new formulation to make clear that Article 13 agreements concluded before September 1996 can be renewed or revised if the parties agree to do so.

Based on the social partners' common position, the political institutions reached an informal agreement on the recast Directive in a meeting on 4 December 2008. On 16 December 2008, the European Parliament adopted the compromise text. The new, recast Directive strengthens the role and rights of EWC's in a number of areas. Notably, it:

58. 94/45/EC.

- reinforces and more clearly defines the information and consultation rights of EWC's;
- links and more clearly differentiates the information and consultation of EWC's and of national bodies, providing a new definition of 'transnational matters' covered by EWC's;
- gives a greater role to trade unions;
- entitles EWC members to training without loss of pay; and
- contains rules on adapting EWC's to structural change in the multinational concerned.

According to figures from the European Trade Union Institute (ETUI)[59] around 2,400 multinationals are potentially covered by the EWC Directive. The data from the ETUI database show that, as at 2012, a total of 1,214 EWCs had been created. However, it should be noted that some multinational companies have installed EWC's at a division level. Therefore, the total number of EWC's is larger than the number of Multinationals that have a EWC. Currently, 931 multinational companies have an active EWC. However, not all eligible Multinationals have established EWCs. This is due to the fact that the introduction of EWCs is not automatic but requires either the initiative of central management or 'the written request of at least 100 employees or their representatives in at least two undertakings or establishments in at least two different Member States'.[60]

4.2 Objective

The purpose of the Work's Councils Directive is according to Article 1 of the Directive to improve the right to information and to consultation of employees in Community-scale undertakings and Community-scale groups of undertakings. To that end, an EWC or a procedure for informing and consulting employees shall be established in every Community-scale undertaking and every Community-scale group of undertakings, where requested in the manner laid down in Article 5(1) on the Special Negotiation Body, see below, with the purpose of informing and consulting employees. The arrangements for informing and consulting employees shall be defined and implemented in such a way as to ensure their effectiveness and to enable the undertaking or group of undertakings to take decisions effectively. Information and consultation of employees must occur at the relevant level of management and repre-

59. See http://www.eurofound.europa.eu/about/index.htm.
60. See Article Article 5(1) of the Directive.

sentation, according to the subject under discussion. To achieve that, the competence of the EWC and the scope of the information and consultation procedure for employees governed by the Directive shall be limited to transnational issues. Matters shall be considered to be transnational where they concern the Community-scale undertaking or Community-scale group of undertakings as a whole, or at least two undertakings or establishments of the undertaking or group situated in two different Member States.

4.3 Definitions

Article 2 and 3 of the Works Council Directive contain definitions. As set out above the definitions of information and consultation are new and meant to clarify the legal position.

4.3.1 European Works Council (EWC)

'European Works Council' means a council established in accordance with Article 1(2) of the EWC directive or the provisions of Annex I, with the purpose of informing and consulting employees. EWC's are bodies representing the European employees of a company. Through them, workers are informed and consulted by management on the progress of the business and any significant decision at European level that could affect their employment or working conditions.

4.3.2 Controlling Undertaking

For the purposes of the EWC-Directive, 'controlling undertaking' means, according to Article 3, an undertaking which can exercise a dominant influence over another undertaking (the controlled undertaking) by virtue, for example, of ownership, financial participation or the rules which govern it. The ability to exercise a dominant influence shall be presumed, without prejudice to proof to the contrary, when an undertaking, in relation to another undertaking directly or indirectly:

(a) holds a majority of that undertaking's subscribed capital;
(b) controls a majority of the votes attached to that undertaking's issued share capital; or
(c) can appoint more than half of the members of that undertaking's administrative, management or supervisory body.

4.3.3 Information

'Information' means according to Article 2(f) of the recast directive the transmission of data by the employer to the employees' representatives in order to enable them to acquaint themselves with the subject matter and to examine it; information shall be given at such a time, in such a fashion and with such content as are appropriate to enable employees' representatives to undertake an in-depth assessment of the possible impact and, where appropriate, prepare for consultations with the competent organ of the Community-scale undertaking or Community-scale group of undertakings. As set out above, the European social partners called for clarification of the definition of information which has now been done with the above definition in Article 2(f) of the recast directive which aligns the definition in regard to EWC with the definition of information in the SE-Directive.[61] In the previous Works Council directive from 1994[62] there was no explicit definition of information.

4.3.4 Consultation

'Consultation' means according to Article 2(g) of the recast directive the establishment of dialogue and exchange of views between employees' representatives and central management or any more appropriate level of management, at such a time, in such a fashion and with such content as enables employees' representatives to express an opinion on the basis of the information provided about the proposed measures to which the consultation is related, without prejudice to the responsibilities of the management, and within a reasonable time, which may be taken into account within the Community-scale undertaking or Community-scale group of undertakings. In the previous directive from 1994 consultation was defined in the following way:

> (f) 'consultation' means the exchange of views and establishment of dialogue between employees' representatives and central management or any more appropriate level of management;

As appears the new definition of consultation is more elaborate and precise in that it requires the consultation to take place at such a time, in such a fashion and with such content as enables employees' representatives to express an opinion on the basis of the information provided about the proposed measures to which the consultation is related, without prejudice to the responsibilities of the management, and within a reasonable time, which may be taken into account within the Community-scale undertaking or Community-scale group of undertakings.

61. Directive supplementing the Statute for a European company with regard to the involvement of employees 2001/86/EC.
62. 94/45/EC.

4.4 Responsibility for the establishment of a European Works Council

The Directive applies to Community-scale undertakings and groups of undertakings with at least 1 000 employees and at least two establishments or undertakings employing at least 150 people in two or more Member States. The Directive does not cover small businesses and does not affect the provision made for information and consultation in the legislation and practices of individual Member States. Community-scale undertakings and groups of undertakings where the central management is not situated in a Member State are covered by the Directive. In this case, responsibility is invested in the central management's representative agent in a Member State or the undertaking employing the greatest number of employees in any one Member State.

4.4.1 Initiative

The establishment of an EWC must be at the instigation either of the central management of the undertaking or group of undertakings, or of the employees or their representatives.

A request by 100 employees from two countries or an initiative by the employer triggers the process of creating a new EWV.

4.4.2 Groups of companies

The CJEU has delivered a few rulings on who in a group of undertakings is responsible for delivering the information which is necessary for the special negotiation body in order to enable it to assess whether the conditions for setting up an EWC are met. In *Anker*[63] the CJEU ruled:

> Article 4(1) and Article 11 of Council Directive 94/45/EC of 22 September 1994 on the establishment of a European Works Council or a procedure in Community-scale undertakings and Community-scale groups of undertakings for the purposes of informing and consulting employees must be interpreted as meaning that Member States are required to impose on undertakings established within their territory and constituting the central management of a Community-scale group of undertakings for the purposes of Article 2(1)(e) and Article 3(1) of the Directive, or the deemed central management under the second subparagraph of Article 4(2), the obligation to supply to another undertaking in the same group established in another Member State the information requested from it by its employees' representatives, where that information is not in the possession of that other undertaking and it is essential for opening negotiations for the setting up of a European Works Council.

63. Case C-349/01 *Anker* [2004] ECR I-6803.

In *Kühne & Nagel*[64] the CJEU ruled that where the central management of a Community-scale group of undertakings is not located in a Member State, central management's responsibility for providing the employees' representatives with the information essential to the opening of negotiations for the establishment of a European Works Council lies with the deemed central management under the second subparagraph of Article 4(2) of the directive. Where central management does not, for the purpose of establishing an EWC make certain information available to the deemed central management, the latter, in order to be able to fulfil its obligation to provide information to the employees' representatives, must request the information essential to the opening of negotiations for the establishment of such a council from the other undertakings belonging to the group which are located in the Member States, and has a right to receive that information from them. The management of each of the other undertakings belonging to the group which are located in the Member States is under an obligation to supply the deemed central management with the information concerned where it is in possession of the information or is in a position to obtain it.

In *Bofrost*[65] the CJEU ruled:

1. On a proper construction of Article 11(1) and (2) of Council Directive 94/45/EC of 22 September 1994 on the establishment of a European Works Council or a procedure in Community-scale undertakings and Community-scale groups of undertakings for the purposes of informing and consulting employees, an undertaking which is part of a group of undertakings is required to supply information to the internal workers' representative bodies, even where it has not yet been established that the management to which the workers' request is addressed is the management of a controlling undertaking within a group of undertakings.

2. Where information relating to the structure or organisation of a group of undertakings forms part of the information which is essential to the opening of negotiations for the setting-up of a European Works Council or for the transnational information and consultation of employees, an undertaking within the group is required to supply the information which it possesses or is able to obtain to the internal workers' representative bodies requesting it. Communication of documents clarifying and explaining the information which is indispensable for that purpose may also be required, in so far as that communication is necessary in order that the employees concerned or their representatives may gain access to information enabling them to determine whether or not they are entitled to request the opening of negotiations.

64. Case C-440/00 *Kühne & Nagel* [2004] I-787.
65. Case C-62/99 *Bofrost* [2001] I-2579.

4.5 Special Negotiating Body

The special negotiating body (SNB), which represents the employees in the negotiations aiming at concluding an agreement on an EWC, is composed of one representative per 10 % portion of the employees in a Member State. It has the right to meet alone before and after any meeting with the central management.

Article 5 of the EWC directive provides that in order to achieve the objective set out in Article 1(1), the central management shall initiate negotiations for the establishment of a European Works Council or an information and consultation procedure on its own initiative or at the written request of at least 100 employees or their representatives in at least two undertakings or establishments in at least two different Member States. For this purpose, a *special negotiating body* shall be established in accordance with the following guidelines:

(a) The Member States shall determine the method to be used for the election or appointment of the members of the special negotiating body who are to be elected or appointed in their territories.
Member States shall provide that employees in undertakings and/or establishments in which there are no employees' representatives through no fault of their own, have the right to elect or appoint members of the special negotiating body.
The second subparagraph shall be without prejudice to national legislation and/or practice laying down thresholds for the establishment of employee representation bodies.
(b) The members of the special negotiating body shall be elected or appointed in proportion to the number of employees employed in each Member State by the Community-scale undertaking or Community-scale group of undertakings, by allocating in respect of each Member State one seat per portion of employees employed in that Member State amounting to 10 %, or a fraction thereof, of the number of employees employed in all the Member States taken together;
(c) The central management and local management and the competent European workers' and employers' organisations shall be informed of the composition of the special negotiating body and of the start of the negotiations.

The special negotiating body shall have the task of determining, with the central management, by written agreement, the scope, composition, functions, and term of office of the European Works Council(s) or the arrangements for implementing a procedure for the information and consultation of employees. With a view to the conclusion of an agreement in accordance with Article 6, the central management shall convene a meeting with the special negotiating body. It shall inform the local managements accordingly. Before and after any meeting with the central management, the special negotiating body shall be entitled to meet without representatives of the central management being present, using any necessary means for communication. For the purpose of the negotiations, the special negotiating body may request assistance from experts of its choice which can include representatives of competent recognised Community-level trade union organisations. Such experts and such trade union representatives may be present at negotiation meetings in an advisory capacity at the request of the special negotiating body. The special negotiating body may decide, by at least two-thirds of the votes, not to open negotiations, or to terminate the negotiations already opened. Such a decision shall stop the procedure to conclude the agreement referred to in Article 6, see below. Where such a decision has been taken, the provisions in Annex I shall not apply. A new request to convene the special negotiating body may be made at the earliest two years after the abovementioned decision unless the parties concerned lay down a shorter period. Any expenses relating to the negotiations shall be borne by the central management so as to enable the special negotiating body to carry out its task in an appropriate manner. In compliance with this principle, Member States may lay down budgetary rules regarding the operation of the special negotiating body. They may in particular limit the funding to cover one expert only.

4.6 Agreement

Article 6 of the recast directive on European Works councils provides a number of minimum requirements for the content of a possible agreement. The central management and the special negotiating body must negotiate in *a spirit of cooperation* with a view to reaching an agreement on the detailed arrangements for implementing the information and consultation of employees. Without prejudice to the autonomy of the parties, the agreement which must be in writing between the central management and the special negotiating body shall determine:

(a) the undertakings of the Community-scale group of undertakings or the establishments of the Community-scale undertaking which are covered by the agreement;
(b) the composition of the European Works Council, the number of members, the allocation of seats, taking into account where possible the need for balanced representation of employees with regard to their activities, category and gender, and the term of office;
(c) the functions and the procedure for information and consultation of the European Works Council and the arrangements for linking information and consultation of the European Works Council and national employee representation bodies, in accordance with the principles set out in Article 1(3);
(d) the venue, frequency and duration of meetings of the European Works Council;
(e) where necessary, the composition, the appointment procedure, the functions and the procedural rules of the select committee set up within the European Works Council;
(f) the financial and material resources to be allocated to the European Works Council;

(g) the date of entry into force of the agreement and its duration, the arrangements for amending or terminating the agreement and the cases in which the agreement shall be renegotiated and the procedure for its renegotiation, including, where necessary, where the structure of the Community-scale undertaking or Community-scale group of undertakings changes.

The central management and the special negotiating body may decide, in writing, to establish one or more information and consultation procedures instead of a European Works Council. The agreement must stipulate by what method the employees' representatives shall have the right to meet to discuss the information conveyed to them. This information shall relate in particular to transnational questions which significantly affect workers' interests. The agreements shall not, unless provision is made otherwise therein, be subject to the subsidiary requirements of Annex I to the recast directive on EWC's. For the purposes of concluding the agreements referred to in paragraphs 2 and 3, the special negotiating body shall act by a majority of its members.

4.7 Subsidiary Requirements

In the event of no agreement being reached, the Directive stipulates that certain subsidiary requirements set out in the Annex to the Directive must be applied. Article 7 of the recast directive provides that in order to achieve the objective set out in Article 1(1), the subsidiary requirements laid down by the legislation of the Member State in which the central management is situated shall apply:

- where the central management and the special negotiating body so decide,
- where the central management refuses to commence negotiations within six months of the request referred to in Article 5(1),

or

- where, after three years from the date of this request, they are unable to conclude an agreement as laid down in Article 6 and the special negotiating body has not taken the decision provided for in Article 5(5).[66]

66. Article 5(5) of the directive provides: The special negotiating body may decide, by at least two-thirds of the votes, not to open negotiations in accordance with paragraph 4, or to terminate the negotiations already opened. Such a decision shall stop the procedure to conclude the agreement referred to in Article 6. Where such a decision has been taken, the provisions in Annex I shall not apply. A new request to convene the special negotiating body may be made at the earliest two years after the abovementioned decision unless the parties concerned lay down a shorter period.

The subsidiary requirements referred to above as adopted in the legislation of the Member States must satisfy the provisions set out in Annex I to the recast directive.

The subsidiary requirements provide that the competence of the European Works Council shall be determined in accordance with Article 1(3) of the recast directive. The information of the European Works Council shall relate in particular to the structure, economic and financial situation, probable development and production and sales of the Community-scale undertaking or group of undertakings. The information and consultation of the European Works Council shall relate in particular to the situation and probable trend of employment, investments, and substantial changes concerning organisation, introduction of new working methods or production processes, transfers of production, mergers, cut-backs or closures of undertakings, establishments or important parts thereof, and collective redundancies. The consultation shall be conducted in such a way that the employees' representatives can meet with the central management and obtain a response, and the reasons for that response, to any opinion they might express. The European Works Council shall be composed of employees of the Community-scale undertaking or Community-scale group of undertakings elected or appointed from their number by the employees' representatives or, in the absence thereof, by the entire body of employees. The election or appointment of members of the European Works Council shall be carried out in accordance with national legislation and/or practice. The members of the European Works Council shall be elected or appointed in proportion to the number of employees employed in each Member State by the Community-scale undertaking or Community-scale group of undertakings, by allocating in respect of each Member State one seat per portion of employees employed in that Member State amounting to 10%, or a fraction thereof, of the number of employees employed in all the Member States taken together. To ensure that it can coordinate its activities, the European Works Council shall elect a select committee from among its members, comprising at most five members, which must benefit from conditions enabling it to exercise its activities on a regular basis. It shall adopt its own rules of procedure.

Four years after the European Works Council is established it shall examine whether to open negotiations for the conclusion of the agreement referred to in Article 6 or to continue to apply the subsidiary requirements adopted in accordance with Annex I.

The European Works Council shall have the right to meet with the central management once a year, to be informed and consulted, on the basis of a report drawn up by the central management, on the progress of the business of the Community-scale undertaking or Community-scale group of undertakings and its prospects. The local managements shall be informed accordingly.

Where there are exceptional circumstances or decisions affecting the employees' interests to a considerable extent, particularly in the event of relocations, the closure of establishments or undertakings or collective redundancies, the select committee or, where no such committee exists, the European Works Council shall have the right to be informed. It shall have the right to meet, at its request, the central management, or any other more appropriate level of management within the Community-scale undertaking or group of undertakings having its own powers of decision, so as to be informed and consulted.

Before any meeting with the central management, the European Works Council or the select committee, shall be entitled to meet without the management concerned being present.

The European Works Council or the select committee may be assisted by experts of its choice, in so far as this is necessary for it to carry out its tasks.

The operating expenses of the European Works Council shall be borne by the central management. The central management concerned shall provide the members of the European Works Council with such financial and material resources as enable them to perform their duties in an appropriate manner. In particular, the cost of organising meetings and arranging for interpretation facilities and the accommodation and travelling expenses of members of the European Works Council and its select committee shall be met by the central management unless otherwise agreed.

In compliance with these principles, the Member States may lay down budgetary rules regarding the operation of the European Works Council. They may in particular limit funding to cover one expert only.

4.8 Confidential information

According to Article 8 of the EWC-directive Member States shall provide that members of special negotiating bodies or of European Works Councils and any experts who assist them are not authorised to reveal any information which has expressly been provided to them in confidence. The same shall apply to employees' representatives in the framework of an information and consultation procedure. That obligation shall continue to apply, wherever the persons referred to in the first and second subparagraphs are, even after the expiry of their terms of office.

Each Member State shall provide, in specific cases and under the conditions and limits laid down by national legislation, that the central management situated in its territory is not obliged to transmit information when its nature is such that, according to objective criteria, it would seriously harm the functioning of the undertakings concerned or would be prejudicial to them.

Each Member State may lay down particular provisions for the central management of undertakings in its territory which pursue directly and essentially the aim of ideological guidance with respect to information and the expression of opinions, on condition that, at the date of adoption of this Directive such particular provisions already exist in the national legislation.

Grøngaard and Bang[67] concerned the interpretation of the insider directive.[68] The issues were whether an employee-elected board member can disclose inside information to a general secretary of his trade union, the relationship between a member of an undertaking's corporate liaison committee and the general secretary of the union he is representing, whether a general secretary of a trade union may disclose information to certain members of that trade union and whether the type of inside information that has been disclosed is a relevant factor when interpreting Article 3(a) of the insider Directive. The CJEU held:

1. Article 3(a) of Council Directive 89/592/EEC of 13 November 1989 coordinating regulations on insider dealing precludes a person, who receives inside information in his capacity as an employees' representative on a company's board of directors or in his capacity as a member of the liaison committee of a group of undertakings, from disclosing such information to the general secretary of the professional organisation which organises those employees and which appointed that person as a member of the liaison committee, unless:

- there is a close link between the disclosure and the exercise of his employment, profession or duties, and
- that disclosure is strictly necessary for the exercise of that employment, profession or duties.

As part of its examination, the national court must, in the light of the applicable national rules, take particular account of:

- the fact that that exception to the prohibition of disclosure of inside information must be interpreted strictly;
- the fact that each additional disclosure is liable to increase the risk of that information being exploited for a purpose contrary to Directive 89/592, and
- the sensitivity of the inside information.

67. Case C-384/02 *Grøngaard and Bang* [2005] ECR I-9939.
68. 89/592/EEC.

4.9 Spirit of cooperation

According to Article 9 of the EWC-directive the central management and the European Works Council shall work in a spirit of cooperation with due regard to their reciprocal rights and obligations. The same shall apply to cooperation between the central management and employees' representatives in the framework of an information and consultation procedure for workers.

4.10 Role and capacity of employee representatives

Article 10 of the recast directive on European Works councils contains provisions on the role and capacity of employee representatives.

4.10.1 Resources

Without prejudice to the competence of other bodies or organisations in this respect, the members of the European Works Council shall have the means required to apply the rights arising from the Directive, to represent collectively the interests of the employees of the Community-scale undertaking or Community-scale group of undertakings.

They shall inform employees of the content and outcome of the information and consultation procedure carried out within the EWC.

4.10.2 Training

Employees' representatives shall be provided with training without loss of wages. Article 10(4) of the directive provides: In so far as this is necessary for the exercise of their representative duties in an international environment, the members of the special negotiating body and of the European Works Council shall be provided with training without loss of wages.

4.10.3 Spread of information

Without prejudice to Article 8 on confidential information, see above, the members of the European Works Council shall inform the representatives of the employees of the establishments or of the undertakings of a Community-scale group of undertakings or, in the absence of representatives, the workforce as a whole, of the content and outcome of the information and consultation procedure carried out in accordance with this Directive.

4.10.4 Protection

Members of special negotiating bodies, members of European Works Councils and employees' representatives exercising their functions under the procedure referred to in Article 6(3) shall, in the exercise of their functions, enjoy protection and guarantees similar to those provided for employees' representatives by the national legislation and/or practice in force in their country of employment. This shall apply in particular to attendance at meetings of special negotiating bodies or European Works Councils or any other meetings within the framework of the agreement referred to in Article 6(3), and the payment of wages for members who are on the staff of the Community-scale undertaking or the Community-scale group of undertakings for the period of absence necessary for the performance of their duties.

4.10.5 Balanced representation

In accordance with the principle of subsidiarity, it is for the Member States to determine who the employees' representatives are and in particular to provide, if they consider appropriate, for a balanced representation of different categories of employees.[69] The special negotiating body must represent employees from the various Member States in a balanced fashion. Employees' representatives must be able to cooperate to define their positions in relation to negotiations with the central management.[70] In Article 6(2)b) of the directive it is provided that the agreement the agreement the special negotiating body and central management shall determine the composition of the EWC, taking into account where possible the need for balanced representation of employees with regard to their activities, category and gender.

4.11 Transnational competence of EWC

Issues fall within the competence of the EWC when they are transnational. Matters shall be considered to be transnational where they concern the Community-scale undertaking or Community-scale group of undertakings as a whole, or at least two undertakings or establishments of the undertaking or group situated in two different Member States. Elements that can be considered in the determination of whether a matter is 'transnational' are the number of Member States concerned, the level of management involved or the importance of the issues for the European workforce given the scope of their potential effects.

4.12 Links with national bodies

Information and consultation of the EWC shall be linked to those of the national employee representation bodies. Arrangements for meeting that aim are

69. See point 20 in the Preamble to Directive 2009/38/EC.
70. See poin 26 in the Preamble to Directive 2009/38/EC.

to be defined by agreement. Failing that, consultations at both European and national levels have to be ensured in case of restructuring.

4.13 Adaptation Clause

Where the structure of the undertaking or group of undertakings changes significantly, for example due to a merger, the EWC(s) needs to be adapted. This adaptation is carried out pursuant to the provisions of the applicable agreement(s) or, by default and where employees so request, in accordance with the negotiation procedure for a new agreement in which the members of the existing EWCs are to be associated. These EWCs will continue to operate, possibly with adaptations, until a new agreement is reached. This clause applies to all situations.[71]

5 Employee information, consultation and participation in a European company (SE)

5.1. Establishment of SE's

The Council Regulation on SE Companies[72] establishes a Statute for a European company (SE) with a view to creating a uniform legal framework enabling companies from different Member States to plan and carry out the reorganisation of their business on an EU scale. An SE can be established in four ways:

- by formation of a subsidiary by two or more companies,
- by transformation (conversion) of an existing public limited-liability company by merger of two or more existing public limited-liability companies,
- by formation of a holding company
- by two or more public or private limited-liability companies,

All types of formation must have a cross-border element: they must always involve companies from at least two different EU Member States. In the case of a transformation, the company must have had a subsidiary in another Member State for at least two years. The SE must be registered in the same Member State in which the administrative head office is located. An SE cannot be created *ex novo*. There is therefore always a situation before the crea-

71. Article 13 of Directive 2009/38/EC.
72. Council Regulation (EC) No 2157/2001 of 8 October 2001 on the Statute for a European company (SE).

tion of the SE and after that, see on the 'before and after principle' below in section 5.4.

By June 2010, about 588 SEs had been established.[73] Only around one quarter (145) were carrying out 'real' economic activities with employees ('normal SEs'). This implies that the vast majority of SEs created to date are not actively doing business employing staff. Many of the SEs (78) are so-called 'shelf' companies that are for sale, or 'empty' SEs (82) that do not yet have any employees. For many SEs (around 283), no information is available at all. The distribution of 'normal' SEs is also very unequal; Germany has by far the most 'normal' SEs (73). Around 45% of normal SEs were established by the conversion of an existing company, while about 25% resulted from mergers. Only a comparatively small number were established as holding companies or as subsidiaries. Half of all normal SEs have fewer than 500 employees.

5.2 Employee involvement in SE Companies

In the autumn 2001, the Directive supplementing the Statute for a European company with regard to the involvement of employees was adopted.[74] As required by Article 15 of the Directive, the Commission reviewed the application of the Directive with a view to proposing any necessary amendments in 2008.[75] Only a comparatively small number were established as holding companies or as subsidiaries. Half of all normal SEs have fewer than 500 employees.[76]

5.3 Aim of the Directive on employee involvement

To complete Europe's internal market, companies must – in the opinion of the Commission – have the option of planning and reorganising their business on an EU scale. A 'European company' (SE) status, with its own legislative framework, is the aim of the SE-Regulation. It allows companies incorpo-

73. See European Foundation for the Improvement of Living and Working Conditions: Employee involvement in companies under the European Company Statute, Luxembourg 2011.
74. Directive supplementing the Statute for a European company with regard to the involvement of employees 2001/86/EC.
75. COM(2008)591 Communication from the Commission on the review of Council Directive 2001/86/EC of 8 October 2001 supplementing the Statute for a European company with regard to the involvement of employees.
76. See European Foundation for the Improvement of Living and Working Conditions: Employee involvement in companies under the European Company Statute, Luxembourg 2011.

rated in different Member States to merge or form a holding company or joint subsidiary, while avoiding the legal and practical constraints arising from the existence of different national legal systems.

The aim of the directive on employee involvement is according to Article 1 of the SE-directive to ensure that the establishment of an SE does not entail the reduction of practices of employee involvement[77] existing within the companies participating in the creation of the SE. The directive calls for a set of rules in this field, preferably through agreement between the employer and the representatives of employees. In the absence of agreement, subsidiary rules apply. Procedures for the information and consultation, as well as, if applicable, participation of employees at transnational level must be ensured whenever an SE is created.

5.4 The 'before and after' principle

In the Preamble to the SE-employee involvement directive[78] it is stated that in order to promote the social objectives of the EU, special provisions have to be set, notably in the field of employee involvement, aimed at ensuring that the establishment of an SE does not entail the disappearance or reduction of practices of employee involvement existing within the companies participating in the establishment of an SE. This objective should be pursued through the establishment of a set of rules in this field, supplementing the provisions of the SE-Regulation. It is also stated (emphasis added):[79]

> (18) It is a fundamental principle and stated aim of this Directive to secure employees' acquired rights as regards involvement in company decisions. Employee rights in force before the establishment of SEs should provide the basis for employee rights of involvement in the SE (the *'before and after' principle*). Consequently, that approach should apply not only to the initial establishment of an SE but also to structural changes in an existing SE and to the companies affected by structural change processes.

5.5 Definitions

Article 2 of the SE-directive defines a number of central concepts. For the purposes of the SE-Directive:

77. Involvement of employees means any mechanism, including information, consultation and participation, through which employees' representatives may exercise an influence on decisions taken within the company (Article 2(h) of the Directive).
78. See point 3 in the Preamble to directive 2001/86/EC.
79. See point 18 in the Preamble to directive 2001/86/EC.

5.5.1 SE

SE means any company established in accordance with the SE-Regulation.[80]

5.5.2 Participating companies

Participating companies means the companies directly participating in the establishing of an SE.

5.5.3 Subsidiary

Subsidiary of a company means an undertaking over which that company exercises a dominant influence defined in accordance the Works Councils directive.[81]

5.5.4 Concerned subsidiary or establishment

Concerned subsidiary or establishment means a subsidiary or establishment of a participating company which is proposed to become a subsidiary or establishment of the SE upon its formation.

5.5.5 Employees' representatives

Employees' representatives means the employees' representatives provided for by national law and/or practice.

5.5.6 Representative body

Representative body means the body representative of the employees set up by the agreements referred to in Article 4 of the SE-directive or in accordance with the provisions of the Annex to that directive, with the purpose of informing and consulting the employees of an SE and its subsidiaries and establishments situated in the Community and, where applicable, of exercising participation rights in relation to the SE.

5.5.7 Special negotiating body

Special negotiating body means the body established in accordance with Article 3 of the SE-directive to negotiate with the competent body of the participating companies regarding the establishment of arrangements for the involvement of employees within the SE.

80. (EC) No 2157/2001.
81. Article 3(2) to (7) of Directive 94/45/EC. Now replaced by directive 2009/38/EC, see above in section 4.

5.5.8 Involvement of employees
Involvement of employees means any mechanism, including information, consultation and participation, through which employees' representatives may exercise an influence on decisions to be taken within the company.

5.5.9 Information
Information means the informing of the body representative of the employees and/or employees' representatives by the competent organ of the SE on questions which concern the SE itself and any of its subsidiaries or establishments situated in another Member State or which exceed the powers of the decision-making organs in a single Member State at a time, in a manner and with a content which allows the employees' representatives to undertake an in-depth assessment of the possible impact and, where appropriate, prepare consultations with the competent organ of the SE.

As appears, this is the same as the definition provided in the recast Works Council directive, see above in section 4.

5.5.10 Consultation
Consultation means the establishment of dialogue and exchange of views between the body representative of the employees and/or the employees' representatives and the competent organ of the SE, at a time, in a manner and with a content which allows the employees' representatives, on the basis of information provided, to express an opinion on measures envisaged by the competent organ which may be taken into account in the decision-making process within the SE.

As appears, this is the same as the definition provided in the recast Works Council directive, see above in section 4.

5.5.11 Participation
Participation means the influence of the body representative of the employees and/or the employees' representatives in the affairs of a company by way of:

- the right to elect or appoint some of the members of the company's supervisory or administrative organ, or
- the right to recommend and/or oppose the appointment of some or all of the members of the company's supervisory or administrative organ.

5.6 Special Negotiation Body
Article 3 of the SE-directive provides that where the management or administrative organs of the participating companies draw up a plan for the estab-

lishment of an SE, they shall as soon as possible after publishing the draft terms of merger or creating a holding company or after agreeing a plan to form a subsidiary or to transform into an SE, take the necessary steps, including providing information about the identity of the participating companies, concerned subsidiaries or establishments, and the number of their employees, to start negotiations with the representatives of the companies' employees on arrangements for the involvement of employees in the SE. For this purpose, a special negotiating body representative of the employees of the participating companies and concerned subsidiaries or establishments shall be created in accordance with the following provisions:

(a) in electing or appointing members of the special negotiating body, it must be ensured:
  (i) that these members are elected or appointed in proportion to the number of employees employed in each Member State by the participating companies and concerned subsidiaries or establishments, by allocating in respect of a Member State one seat per portion of employees employed in that Member State which equals 10 %, or a fraction thereof, of the number of employees employed by the participating companies and concerned subsidiaries or establishments in all the Member States taken together;
  (ii) that in the case of an SE formed by way of merger, there are such further additional members from each Member State as may be necessary in order to ensure that the special negotiating body includes at least one member representing each participating company which is registered and has employees in that Member State and which it is proposed will cease to exist as a separate legal entity following the registration of the SE, in so far as:
    – the number of such additional members does not exceed 20 % of the number of members designated by virtue of point (i), and
    – the composition of the special negotiating body does not entail a double representation of the employees concerned.

  If the number of such companies is higher than the number of additional seats available pursuant to the first subparagraph, these additional seats shall be allocated to companies in different Member States by decreasing order of the number of employees they employ;
(b) Member States shall determine the method to be used for the election or appointment of the members of the special negotiating body who are to be elected or appointed in their territories. They shall take the necessary measures to ensure that, as far as possible, such members shall include at least one member representing each participating company which has employees in the Member State concerned. Such measures must not increase the overall number of members.

Member States may provide that such members may include representatives of trade unions whether or not they are employees of a participating company or concerned subsidiary or establishment. Without prejudice to national legislation and/or practice laying down thresholds for the establishing of a representative body, Member States shall provide that employees in undertakings or establishments in which there are no employees' representatives through no fault of their own have the right to elect or appoint members of the special negotiating body.

The special negotiating body and the competent organs of the participating companies shall determine, by written agreement, arrangements for the involvement of employees within the SE. To this end, the competent organs of the participating companies shall inform the special negotiating body of the plan and the actual process of establishing the SE, up to its registration. Subject to paragraph 6, the special negotiating body shall take decisions by an absolute majority of its members, provided that such a majority also represents an absolute majority of the employees. Each member shall have one vote. However, should the result of the negotiations lead to a reduction of participation rights, the majority required for a decision to approve such an agreement shall be the votes of two thirds of the members of the special negotiating body representing at least two thirds of the employees, including the votes of members representing employees employed in at least two Member States,

- in the case of an SE to be established by way of merger, if participation covers at least 25 % of the overall number of employees of the participating companies, or
- in the case of an SE to be established by way of creating a holding company or forming a subsidiary, if participation covers at least 50 % of the overall number of employees of the participating companies.

Reduction of participation rights means a proportion of members of the organs of the SE within the meaning of Article 2(k), which is lower than the highest proportion existing within the participating companies. For the purpose of the negotiations, the special negotiating body may request experts of its choice, for example representatives of appropriate Community level trade union organisations, to assist it with its work. Such experts may be present at negotiation meetings in an advisory capacity at the request of the special negotiating body, where appropriate to promote coherence and consistency at Community level. The special negotiating body may decide to inform the representatives of appropriate external organisations, including trade unions, of the start of the negotiations. The special negotiating body may decide by the majority set out below not to open negotiations or to terminate negotiations already opened, and to rely on the rules on information and consultation of employees in force in the Member States where the SE has employees.

Such a decision shall stop the procedure to conclude the agreement referred to in Article 4. Where such a decision has been taken, none of the provisions of the Annex shall apply. The majority required to decide not to open or to terminate negotiations shall be the votes of two thirds of the members representing at least two thirds of the employees, including the votes of members representing employees employed in at least two Member States.

The special negotiating body shall be reconvened on the written request of at least 10 % of the employees of the SE, its subsidiaries and establishments, or their representatives, at the earliest two years after the abovementioned decision, unless the parties agree to negotiations being reopened sooner. If the special negotiating body decides to reopen negotiations with the management but no agreement is reached as a result of those negotiations, none of the provisions of the Annex shall apply.

Any expenses relating to the functioning of the special negotiating body and, in general, to negotiations shall be borne by the participating companies so as to enable the special negotiating body to carry out its task in an appropriate manner. In compliance with this principle, Member States may lay down budgetary rules regarding the operation of the special negotiating body. They may in particular limit the funding to cover one expert only.

5.7 Agreement

The competent organs of the participating companies and the special negotiating body shall negotiate in a *spirit of cooperation* with a view to reaching an agreement on arrangements for the involvement of the employees within the SE. Without prejudice to the autonomy of the parties, and subject to paragraph 4, the agreement referred to above between the competent organs of the participating companies and the special negotiating body shall specify:

(a) the scope of the agreement;
(b) the composition, number of members and allocation of seats on the representative body which will be the discussion partner of the competent organ of the SE in connection with arrangements for the information and consultation of the employees of the SE and its subsidiaries and establishments;
(c) the functions and the procedure for the information and consultation of the representative body;
(d) the frequency of meetings of the representative body;
(e) the financial and material resources to be allocated to the representative body;
(f) if, during negotiations, the parties decide to establish one or more information and consultation procedures instead of a representative body, the arrangements for implementing those procedures;
(g) if, during negotiations, the parties decide to establish arrangements for participation, the substance of those arrangements including (if applicable) the number of members

in the SE's administrative or supervisory body which the employees will be entitled to elect, appoint, recommend or oppose, the procedures as to how these members may be elected, appointed, recommended or opposed by the employees, and their rights;
(h) the date of entry into force of the agreement and its duration, cases where the agreement should be renegotiated and the procedure for its renegotiation.

The agreement is not, unless provision is made otherwise therein, subject to the standard rules referred to in the Annex to the SE-directive. Without prejudice to Article 13(3)(a) in the SE-directive, in the case of an SE established by means of transformation, the agreement shall provide for at least the same level of all elements of employee involvement as the ones existing within the company to be transformed into an SE.

5.8 Duration of negotiations

Negotiations shall commence as soon as the special negotiating body is established and may continue for six months thereafter.

5.9 Standard rules

Article 7 of the SE-directive refers to the standard rules in the Annex. In order to achieve the objective described in Article 1 of the SE-Directive, Member States shall lay down standard rules on employee involvement which must satisfy the provisions set out in the Annex to the directive. The standard rules as laid down by the legislation of the Member State in which the registered office of the SE is to be situated shall apply from the date of the registration of the SE where either:

(a) the parties so agree; or
(b) by the deadline laid down in Article 5, no agreement has been concluded, and:
   - the competent organ of each of the participating companies decides to accept the application of the standard rules in relation to the SE and so to continue with its registration of the SE, and
   - the special negotiating body has not taken the decision provided in Article 3(6).

The standard rules fixed by the national legislation of the Member State of registration in accordance with part 3 of the Annex applies only:

(a) in the case of an SE established by transformation, if the rules of a Member State relating to employee participation in the administrative or supervisory body applied to a company transformed into an SE;
(b) in the case of an SE established by merger:
   - if, before registration of the SE, one or more forms of participation applied in one or more of the participating companies covering at least 25 % of the total number of employees in all the participating companies, or

- if, before registration of the SE, one or more forms of participation applied in one or more of the participating companies covering less than 25 % of the total number of employees in all the participating companies and if the special negotiating body so decides,

(c) in the case of an SE established by setting up a holding company or establishing a subsidiary:
- if, before registration of the SE, one or more forms of participation applied in one or more of the participating companies covering at least 50 % of the total number of employees in all the participating companies; or
- if, before registration of the SE, one or more forms of participation applied in one or more of the participating companies covering less than 50 % of the total number of employees in all the participating companies and if the special negotiating body so decides.

If there was more than one form of participation within the various participating companies, the special negotiating body shall decide which of those forms must be established in the SE. Member States may fix the rules which are applicable in the absence of any decision on the matter for an SE registered in their territory. The special negotiating body shall inform the competent organs of the participating companies of any decisions taken pursuant to this paragraph.

The standard rules in the Annex consist of 3 parts. Part 1 deals with the omposition of the body representative of the employees. In order to achieve the objective described in Article 1, and in the cases referred to in Article 7, a representative body shall be set up in accordance with the rules laid down in the first part of the standard rules.[82]

82. Part 1 of the Standard rules provides:
(a) The representative body shall be composed of employees of the SE and its subsidiaries and establishments elected or appointed from their number by the employees' representatives or, in the absence thereof, by the entire body of employees.
(b) The election or appointment of members of the representative body shall be carried out in accordance with national legislation and/or practice. Member States shall lay down rules to ensure that the number of members of, and allocation of seats on, the representative body shall be adapted to take account of changes occurring within the SE and its subsidiaries and establishments.
(c) Where its size so warrants, the representative body shall elect a select committee from among its members, comprising at most three members.
(d) The representative body shall adopt its rules of procedure.
(e) The members of the representative body are elected or appointed in proportion to the number of employees employed in each Member State by the participating companies and concerned subsidiaries or establishments, by allocating in respect of a Member State one seat per portion of employees employed in that Member State which equals 10 %, or a fraction thereof, of the number of employees employed by

Part 2 of the Standard rules lays down provision on information and consultation. The competence and powers of the representative body set up in an SE shall be governed by the rules laid down in the second part of the Standard Rules.[83]

the participating companies and concerned subsidiaries or establishments in all the Member States taken together.
(f) The competent organ of the SE shall be informed of the composition of the representative body.
(g) Four years after the representative body is established, it shall examine whether to open negotiations for the conclusion of the agreement referred to in Articles 4 and 7 or to continue to apply the standard rules adopted in accordance with this Annex.
Articles 3(4) to (7) and 4 to 6 shall apply, mutatis mutandis, if a decision has been taken to negotiate an agreement according to Article 4, in which case the term 'special negotiating body' shall be replaced by 'representative body'. Where, by the deadline by which the negotiations come to an end, no agreement has been concluded, the arrangements initially adopted in accordance with the standard rules shall continue to apply.

83. Those rules provide: (a) The competence of the representative body shall be limited to questions which concern the SE itself and any of its subsidiaries or establishments situated in another Member State or which exceed the powers of the decision-making organs in a single Member State.
(b) Without prejudice to meetings held pursuant to point (c), the representative body shall have the right to be informed and consulted and, for that purpose, to meet with the competent organ of the SE at least once a year, on the basis of regular reports drawn up by the competent organ, on the progress of the business of the SE and its prospects. The local managements shall be informed accordingly.
The competent organ of the SE shall provide the representative body with the agenda for meetings of the administrative, or, where appropriate, the management and supervisory organ, and with copies of all documents submitted to the general meeting of its shareholders.
The meeting shall relate in particular to the structure, economic and financial situation, the probable development of the business and of production and sales, the situation and probable trend of employment, investments, and substantial changes concerning organisation, introduction of new working methods or production processes, transfers of production, mergers, cut-backs or closures of undertakings, establishments or important parts thereof, and collective redundancies.
(c) Where there are exceptional circumstances affecting the employees' interests to a considerable extent, particularly in the event of relocations, transfers, the closure of establishments or undertakings or collective redundancies, the representative body shall have the right to be informed. The representative body or, where it so decides, in particular for reasons of urgency, the select committee, shall have the right to meet at its request the competent organ of the SE or any more appropriate level of management within the SE having its own powers of decision, so as to be informed and consulted on measures significantly affecting employees' interests.

Part 3 of the Standard rules deals with participation.[84]

Where the competent organ decides not to act in accordance with the opinion expressed by the representative body, this body shall have the right to a further meeting with the competent organ of the SE with a view to seeking agreement.
In the case of a meeting organised with the select committee, those members of the representative body who represent employees who are directly concerned by the measures in question shall also have the right to participate.
The meetings referred to above shall not affect the prerogatives of the competent organ.
(d) Member States may lay down rules on the chairing of information and consultation meetings.
Before any meeting with the competent organ of the SE, the representative body or the select committee, where necessary enlarged in accordance with the third subparagraph of paragraph (c), shall be entitled to meet without the representatives of the competent organ being present.
(e) Without prejudice to Article 8, the members of the representative body shall inform the representatives of the employees of the SE and of its subsidiaries and establishments of the content and outcome of the information and consultation procedures.
(f) The representative body or the select committee may be assisted by experts of its choice.
(g) In so far as this is necessary for the fulfilment of their tasks, the members of the representative body shall be entitled to time off for training without loss of wages.
(h) The costs of the representative body shall be borne by the SE, which shall provide the body's members with the financial and material resources needed to enable them to perform their duties in an appropriate manner.
In particular, the SE shall, unless otherwise agreed, bear the cost of organising meetings and providing interpretation facilities and the accommodation and travelling expenses of members of the representative body and the select committee.
In compliance with these principles, the Member States may lay down budgetary rules regarding the operation of the representative body. They may in particular limit funding to cover one expert only.

84. Part 3provides: (a) In the case of an SE established by transformation, if the rules of a Member State relating to employee participation in the administrative or supervisory body applied before registration, all aspects of employee participation shall continue to apply to the SE. Point (b) shall apply mutatis mutandis to that end.
(b) In other cases of the establishing of an SE, the employees of the SE, its subsidiaries and establishments and/or their representative body shall have the right to elect, appoint, recommend or oppose the appointment of a number of members of the administrative or supervisory body of the SE equal to the highest proportion in force in the participating companies concerned before registration of the SE.
If none of the participating companies was governed by participation rules before registration of the SE, the latter shall not be required to establish provisions for employee participation.

5.10 Confidential information

Article 8 of the SE-directive requires Member States to provide that members of the special negotiating body or the representative body, and experts who assist them, are not authorised to reveal any information which has been given to them in confidence. The same shall apply to employees' representatives in the context of an information and consultation procedure. This obligation shall continue to apply, wherever the persons referred to may be, even after the expiry of their terms of office.

Each Member State shall provide, in specific cases and under the conditions and limits laid down by national legislation, that the supervisory or administrative organ of an SE or of a participating company established in its territory is not obliged to transmit information where its nature is such that, according to objective criteria, to do so would seriously harm the functioning of the SE (or, as the case may be, the participating company) or its subsidiaries and establishments or would be prejudicial to them.

6 European Cooperative Society (SCE)

Cooperatives wishing to engage in cross-border business may make use of the Statute of European Cooperative Society (SCE) established by an EU Regulation.[85] The information, consultation and participation rights of em-

The representative body shall decide on the allocation of seats within the administrative or supervisory body among the members representing the employees from the various Member States or on the way in which the SE's employees may recommend or oppose the appointment of the members of these bodies according to the proportion of the SE's employees in each Member State. If the employees of one or more Member States are not covered by this proportional criterion, the representative body shall appoint a member from one of those Member States, in particular the Member State of the SE's registered office where that is appropriate. Each Member State may determine the allocation of the seats it is given within the administrative or supervisory body.

Every member of the administrative body or, where appropriate, the supervisory body of the SE who has been elected, appointed or recommended by the representative body or, depending on the circumstances, by the employees shall be a full member with the same rights and obligations as the members representing the shareholders, including the right to vote.

85. Regulation EU/1435/2003.

ployees in an SCE are safeguarded and promoted by a supplementary Directive.[86] A European Cooperative Society may be created:

- By five or more natural persons resident in at least two Member States
- By five or more natural persons and companies and firms and other legal bodies governed by public or private law, formed under the law of a Member State, resident in, or governed by law of at least two different Member States
- By companies and firms and other legal bodies governed by public or private law, formed under the law of a Member State which are governed by the law of at least two different Member States
- By a merger between cooperatives formed under the law of a Member State with registered office and head offices within the Community if for at least two years it has had an establishment or subsidiary governed by the law of another member state
- By conversion of a cooperative formed under the law of a Member State, which has its registered office and head offices within the Community if for at least two years it has had an establishment or subsidiary governed by the law of another member state.

Information, consultation and in some cases, participation procedures at transnational level are to be used whenever a European Cooperative is created. These procedures are established as a priority through an agreement. The texts of the Regulation and the Directive are available, together with implementation reports. In 2010, the Commission published a report on the review of the Directive.[87] they note certain difficulties, omissions, deficiencies, variations or supplements[88] which require further examination by the Commission.

The Commission concludes that the Directive has been transposed in all Member States only since March 2009. There is therefore a lack of experience in the practical application of the Directive. Furthermore, the Directive is not a stand-alone piece of legislation. It complements the SCE Regulation and shows striking similarities with other directives governing the involve-

86. 2003/72/EC.
87. COM(2010)481.
88. BusinessEurope member organisation CIP considered that the obligations established in national legislation go beyond the Directive in several areas.

ment of employees, such as the SE Directive.[89] The Commission considers that the outcome of the evaluation of these directives and of the Regulation needs to be taken into account before launching any future revision process. These conclusions are shared by all Member States and social partners[90] who have expressed their views in the consultation process to draw up this report. It is, in the view of the Commission, necessary to inquire into the reasons for the very low take-up of the EU legal framework for cooperatives, before considering any moves towards a revision of the Directive.

6.1 Priority to negotiation and alternative route for some 'ex novo' SCEs

The fundamental principle and stated aim of the Directive is to secure employees' rights as regards involvement in the decisions that may affect them. Employee rights that were in force before its establishment should provide the basis for employee rights of involvement in the SCE (the 'before and after' principle). The primary means of seeking to achieve this aim is through an agreement negotiated between the management of the legal entities concerned and the employees' representatives.

This priority given to negotiation replicates the system established in the context of the European Company (SE). However, the Directive establishes an alternative mechanism related to the possibility of creating SCEs 'ex novo'. Article 8 of the Directive provides for specific provisions in the case of SCEs established exclusively by natural persons or by a single legal entity and natural persons, which together employ fewer than 50 employees, or employ 50 or more employees in only one Member State. In such a case, the national provisions on the involvement of employees that are applicable to other entities of the same type situated in the same Member States are to be applied to the SCE, its subsidiaries and establishments (see 3.5).

6.2 Transnational negotiation procedure

The legislation applicable to the negotiation procedure is that of the Member State in which the registered office of the SCE is to be situated. As for the start of negotiations, it is the responsibility of the management or administra-

89. Directive supplementing the Statute for a European company with regard to the involvement of employees 2001/86/EC.
90. ETUC considers that there is no need to simplify the Directive and that, in the event of a revision of the Regulation, there would be a need to consult the social partners. Business Europe member organisation CIP considers that any revision of the legislation should avoid creating additional burdens for business.

tive bodies of the legal entities participating in setting up an SCE to take the necessary steps as soon as they have drawn up a plan to establish the SCE. In their implementing measures, many Member States go beyond the general terms of the Directive in this regard.[91]

For the purpose of the negotiations, a special negotiating body (hereinafter 'SNB') representing the employees has to be created. The SNB's members are to be elected or appointed in proportion to the number of employees employed in each Member State by the participating legal entities and their subsidiaries and establishments[92]. The method to be used for electing or appointing the members to be elected or appointed in their territory is left up to the Member States. Some Member States have not complied with the requirement of the Directive that the methods used should seek to achieve gender balance in the SNB. The Directive addresses the situation at the time when the negotiations start, but does not provide for cases in which this initial situation changes before the end of the negotiations. However, several Member States have adopted provisions to deal with such changes.

The role of the SNB is to negotiate the arrangements for employee involvement within the SCE with the competent organs of the participating entities. However, it may also decide not to open negotiations or to terminate negotiations that are already ongoing. While the principle governing the adoption of decisions by the SNB is a double absolute majority (absolute majority of its members representing an absolute majority of the employees), in the latter case a triple qualified majority is needed (i.e. two thirds of the members representing at least two thirds of the employees, including the votes of members representing employees employed in at least two Member States). This triple majority is also needed (with certain additional conditions) when the outcome of the negotiations is a reduction of participation rights.

The expenses relating to the negotiations are borne by the participating legal entities. Several Member States implemented this provision by limiting these expenses to those which were reasonable, essential or necessary in relation to the economic burden imposed on participating entities. In others, an indicative or open list of expenses has been drawn up. Some transposition laws include both models.

91. Extent of prior information to provide: CZ, IE, LT, PL, SI; Information to employees where no representation exists CZ, DE, IE, LT, NL, PT, SI, UK; Maximum period to start negotiations: ES, LT; but no reference to 'as soon as possible' in PT.
92. Additional seats for representation of employees in case of mergers are also provided for by the Directive. This element has not been implemented in RO.

The SNB may request the assistance of experts of its choice for the purposes of the negotiations. With a few exceptions[93], national laws have limited the number of experts to be funded by the participating companies to one, as allowed by the Directive.

6.3 Autonomy of the parties as to the content of the agreement

One of the main principles of the Directive consists in allowing the parties to define freely the rules which will bind them as far as employees' involvement is concerned. The Directive makes it clear that the agreement is not subject to the standard rules unless it provides otherwise. In order to assist the negotiating parties, the Directive contains a list of items to be addressed in the agreement. This list includes the procedures for the renegotiation of the agreement, where appropriate, in the event of structural changes occurring after the creation of the SCE. This is an addition to similar lists included in the SE Directive and in the then Directive on European Works Councils (EWCs).[94]

There are, however, two important limitations to the autonomy of the parties. Where an SCE is established by means of transformation, the agreement has to provide for at least the same level of all elements of employee involvement as those which existed within the cooperative to be transformed into an SCE. In addition, the possibility to provide for employees to be entitled to participate fully in general meetings, which has been added by the Directive to the items which may be agreed upon, is limited by Article 9 of the Directive.

6.4 Standard rules to be applied in the absence of an agreement

The standard rules apply only in a subsidiary manner, i.e. (a) if the negotiating parties so agree, or (b) if no agreement has been concluded by the deadline of six months (under certain circumstances one year) and if, on the part of the participating entities, their competent bodies decide to continue with the registration of the SCE and, on the part of the employees, the SNB has not decided either not to open negotiations or to terminate negotiations already opened.

As far as employee participation is concerned, and in cases other than transformation, the Directive establishes a minimum percentage of workers covered by participation (25% in the case of a merger and 50% in all other cases) for the standard rules to apply. However, even if those percentages are

93. DE, SE; in BE, a more favorable agreement may provide otherwise; in LV, expenses of 'at least' one expert to be covered.

94. 94/45/EC.

not reached, a decision by the SNB to apply the standard rules is sufficient. Almost all Member States followed these rules and none made use of the option offered by the Directive not to apply standard rules on participation in case of merger.

In the standard rules, employees exercise their rights to be involved in the SCE through a Representative Body. As far as information and consultation are concerned, the competence of the Representative Body is confined to questions of a transnational nature. In order to exercise this competence, the RB has the right to hold a meeting with the competent body of the SCE at least once a year on the basis of regular reports drawn up by the competent body on the development of the business, employment and organisation of the SCE. In addition, the RB is entitled to receive information when there are exceptional circumstances that affect employees' interests to a considerable extent; to request the holding of an extraordinary meeting in order to be informed and consulted; and to express an opinion. A further meeting can be requested if this opinion is not followed by the SCE. National implementing measures do not reveal any specific features in this regard.

As for employee participation, the standard rules provide in the main that the level of participation in the SCE is determined by the level of participation in the participating entities before the SCE was established. Therefore, if none of the participating entities was governed by participation rules before the SCE was registered, the latter does not have to lay down provisions for employee participation. When there are several forms of participation, the SNB shall decide which of those forms will apply to the SCE.

Unlike SEs, SCEs can be established 'ex novo', by natural persons or by a single legal entity and natural persons. Article 8 of the Directive lays down specific provisions in such a case. When a single SCE employs fewer than 50 employees, or employs 50 or more employees in only one Member State, there is no compulsory negotiation process and the national provisions on the involvement of employees that apply to other entities of the same type situated in the same Member States are to be applied to the SCE, its subsidiaries and establishments. However, a negotiation procedure will be launched if it were to be required by one third of the employees or if the threshold of 50 employees were to be reached after the registration of the SCE. There is a specific provision to maintain participation where the seat of the SCE is transferred to another Member State. In general, Member States have transposed these new provisions verbatim.

Article 9 of the Directive provides for a new method of involvement of employees compared to the other directives in this field: namely the entitlement of employees or their representatives to participate in the general meeting, or in the section or sectoral meeting if it exists, with a right to vote. This occurs in the case of transformation, by applying standard rules where such participation was present in the participating cooperative(s), or by agreement. However, the entitlement to participate in general meetings is subject to the limitation laid down in Article 59(4) of the Regulation: namely that the possibility of such participation was acknowledged by national provisions prior to August 2003.[95] The provisions of the Directive do not differ much from those of the other directives dealing with involvement of employees as regards definitions, reservation and confidentiality, the spirit of cooperation governing the relationship between the employees' representatives and the competent body of the SCE, and also the protection and guarantees provided for employees' representatives. The Commission has reviewed the directive.[96] Some issues are common to the various directives[97] dealing with transnational involvement of employees and in particular to the SE-Directive.

The protection of participation rights where a European company or Cooperative Society converts into a company or cooperative of national statute has been raised in the context of the review of the SE Directive.[98] To address this issue, the directive on cross-border mergers, see on that directive below in section 7, obliges the company to adopt a legal form that allows for the exercise of participation rights.

7 Cross-border mergers

The Cross-border Merger Directive[99] facilitates the cross-border mergers of limited-liability companies. It sets up a simple framework in which, as a general rule, each merging company is governed by the provisions of its national law applicable to domestic mergers. The directive was the first measure

95. Only Three Member States are in that situation: Denmark, for which such participation is common practice, Hungary and Luxembourg.
96. COM(2010) 481, Report from the Commission on the review of Council Directive 2003/72/EC of 22 July 2003 supplementing the Statute for a European cooperative society with regard to the involvement of employees.
97. Directives 94/45/EC recast by Directive 2009/38/EC on European works Councils, SE Directive 2001/86/EC – see above), Directive 2005/56/EC of the European Parliament and of the Council of 26 October 2005 on cross-border mergers of limited liability companies, OJ L 310, 25.11.2005, p. 1.
98. See point 4.4 of report COM(2008)591.
99. 2005/56/EC on cross-border mergers of limited liability companies.

adopted under the Commission's 2003 Action Plan on company law and corporate governance in the European Union.

7.1 Only rules on worker participation

The only aspect of information, consultation and participation of employees that is covered by the Cross-border mergers directive is worker participation. Rules on information and consultation of employees in regard to cross-border mergers must be found in other sources of law than the Cross-Border Mergers directive. In the preamble to the Cros-Border Mergers directive it is stated[100] that employees' rights other than rights of participation should remain subject to the national provisions referred to in tge collective redundancies directive,[101] the transfer of undertakings directive,[102] the Directive[103] on a general framework for informing and consulting employees and the directive[104] on European Works Council.

If employees have participation rights in one of the merging companies under the circumstances set out in this Directive and, if the national law of the Member State in which the company resulting from the crossborder merger has its registered office does not provide for the same level of participation as operated in the relevant merging companies, including in committees of the supervisory board that have decision-making powers, or does not provide for the same entitlement to exercise rights for employees of establishments resulting from the cross-border merger, the participation of employees in the company resulting from the cross-border merger and their involvement in the definition of such rights are to be regulated. To that end, the principles and procedures provided for in the Regulation[105] on the Statute for a European company (SE) and in the SE-directive[106] are to be taken as a basis, subject, however, to modifications that are deemed necessary because the resulting company will be subject to the national laws of the Member State where it has its registered office. A prompt start to negotiations under Article 16 of the Directive, with a view to not unnecessarily delaying mergers, may be ensured by Member States in accordance with Article 3(2)(b) of the SE-directive. For

100. In point 12.
101. 98/59/EC.
102. 2001/23/EC.
103. 2002/14/EC.
104. Then 94/45/EC, now recast by 2009/38/EC.
105. (EC) No 2157/2001.
106. 2001/86/EC supplementing the Statute for a European company with regard to the involvement of employees.

the purpose of determining the level of employee participation operated in the relevant merging companies, account should also be taken of the proportion of employee representatives amongst the members of the management group, which covers the profit units of the companies, subject to employee participation. The central provision in the Directive is Article 16. It provides on employee participation:

Without prejudice to paragraph 2, the company resulting from the cross-border merger shall be subject to the rules in force concerning employee participation, if any, in the Member State where it has its registered office.

However, the rules in force concerning employee participation, if any, in the Member State where the company resulting from the cross-border merger has its registered office shall not apply, where at least one of the merging companies has, in the six months before the publication of the draft terms of the cross-border merger, an average number of employees that exceeds 500 and is operating under an employee participation system as defined in the SE-Directive, or where the national law applicable to the company resulting from the cross-border merger does not

(a) provide for at least the same level of employee participation as operated in the relevant merging companies, measured by reference to the proportion of employee representatives amongst the members of the administrative or supervisory organ or their committees or of the management group which covers the profit units of the company, subject to employee representation, or
(b) provide for employees of establishments of the company resulting from the cross-border merger that are situated in other Member States the same entitlement to exercise participation rights as is enjoyed by those employees employed in the Member State where the company resulting from the cross-border merger has its registered office.

In the cases referred to in paragraph 2, the participation of employees in the company resulting from the cross-border merger and their involvement in the definition of such rights shall be regulated by the Member States, *mutatis mutandis* and subject to paragraphs 4 to 7 below, in accordance with the principles and procedures laid down in the Regulation[107] (EC) No 2157/2001 and the following provisions of Directive 2001/86/EC:

(a) Article 3(1), (2) and (3), (4) first subparagraph, first indent, and second subparagraph, (5) and (7);
(b) Article 4(1), (2), points (a), (g) and (h), and (3);
(c) Article 5;
(d) Article 6;
(e) Article 7(1), (2) first subparagraph, point (b), and second subparagraph, and (3). However, for the purposes of this Directive, the percentages required by Article 7(2), first subparagraph, point (b) of Directive 2001/86/EC for the application of the standard rules contained in part 3 of the Annex to that Directive shall be raised from 25 to 33 1/3 %;
(f) Articles 8, 10 and 12;
(g) Article 13(4);
(h) part 3 of the Annex, point (b).

When regulating the principles and procedures referred to in paragraph 3, Member States:

(a) shall confer on the relevant organs of the merging companies the right to choose without any prior negotiation to be directly subject to the standard rules for participation referred to in paragraph 3(h), as laid down by the legislation of the Member State in which the company resulting from the cross-border merger is to have its registered office, and to abide by those rules from the date of registration.
(b) shall confer on the special negotiating body the right to decide, by a majority of two thirds of its members representing at least two thirds of the employees, including the votes of members representing employees in at least two different Member States, not to open negotiations or to terminate negotiations already opened and to rely on the rules on participation in force in the Member State where the registered office of the company resulting from the cross-border merger will be situated.
(c) may, in the case where, following prior negotiations, standard rules for participation apply and notwithstanding these rules, determine to limit the proportion of employee representatives in the administrative organ of the company resulting from the cross-border merger. However, if in one of the merging companies employee representatives constituted at least one third of the administrative or supervisory board, the limitation may never result in a lower proportion of employee representatives in the administrative organ than one third.

The extension of participation rights to employees of the company resulting from the cross-border merger employed in other Member States, referred to in paragraph 2(b), shall not entail any obligation for Member States which

107. Article 12(2), (3) and (4).

choose to do so to take those employees into account when calculating the size of workforce thresholds giving rise to participation rights under national law. When at least one of the merging companies is operating under an employee participation system and the company resulting from the cross-border merger is to be governed by such a system, that company shall be obliged to take a legal form allowing for the exercise of participation rights. When the company resulting from the cross-border merger is operating under an employee participation system, that company shall be obliged to take measures to ensure that employees' participation rights are protected in the event of subsequent domestic mergers for a period of three years after the cross-border merger has taken effect, by applying mutatis mutandis the rules laid down in this Article.

8 The European Economic Interest Grouping (EEIG)

In 1985 the Council adopted Regulation 85/2137/EEC on the European Economic Interest Grouping (EEIG).[108] The Regulation does not contain any worker participation provisions. In the Preamble it is stated that in matters not covered by the Regulation the laws of the Member States and Community law are applicable, for example, with regard to social and labour law, competition law, and intellectual property law. This means that worker participation is governed by the law of the Member State in which the grouping is registered. According to Article 3(2)(c) a grouping may not employ more than 500 employees. This threshold which corresponds to the threshold in the German Betriebsverfassungsgesetz 1952 was inserted at the demand of Germany to avoid circumvention of the German employee participation provisions by German companies forming or joining an EEIG registered in another Member State with more lax worker participation rules.

108. OJ 1985 L 199/1.

CHAPTER FIVE

Free Movement of Workers and Union Citizens

1 Introduction

In this Chaper I give an account of the rules on the status and protection of migrant workers and of union citizenship in European labour law. The existing EU rules on migrant workers comprise different rights and duties in different relationships: there is a ban on discrimination on grounds of nationality, rights to move and reside freely within the territory of other EU-countries and a prohibition against restrictions both by other Member States, by one's own Member State and by employers on the free movement of workers and union citizens.

The EU rules on free movement are directed both to the Member States who are precluded from preventing persons enjoying rights of free movement from moving and residing freely within their territory, and to employers, both private and public, and labour market organisations who must respect the prohibition against discrimination on grounds of nationality and abstain from creating hindrances to the free movement of persons, e.g. by collective bargaining. Generally, the free movement rules limit the freedom of an employer to exercise his managerial discretion at will by rendering it unlawful to take nationality of a Member State of the European Union or the EEA into consideration.

The CJEU has provided a broad interpretation of the law in this area and has elevated the principle of free movement of persons into one of the fundamental rights of EU law and a number of general principles of EU law, for example, the doctrine of proportionality and the principle of non-discrimination, have been used to expand the remedies available to people who have taken advantage of the free movement provisions.[1]

Free movement for workers means that every EU national has the right to work, and at the same time live, in any other EU country. Free movement of Workers within the EU/EEA entitles a worker to look for a job in another EU country, work there without needing a work permit, live there for that purpose, stay there after the employment has finished, enjoy equal treatment with nationals in access to employment, working conditions and all other social and tax advantages that may help her/him to integrate into the host country. The right to free movement of workers is complemented by a system for the co-ordination of social security schemes and by a system to ensure the mutual recognition of diplomas.

The basic rules on free movement for workers date back to the Rome Treaty 1957. In the early internal market perspective workers/Labour was, as set out in Chapter One and Two, primarily seen as a commodity.[2] With the adoption of the Maastricht Treaty in 1992 the Internal Market goal was complemented by the second layer of the EU's macro-economic constitution focusing on establishing an economic and monetary union (EMU). The Maastricht Treaty also inserted a provision on fundamental rights in Article 6 TEU and created union citizenship. Since then, workers constitute the majority of the union citizens. They have both individual and collective fundamental rights, e.g. the right to strike, see above in Chapter Three. Workers' status as union citizens has been used by the CJEU to put an expansive interpretation on the principle of free movement of workers.

2 The sources of law

Article 18 TFEU,[3] Article 21 TFEU and Articles 45 – 48 TFEU have for years guaranteed the free *movement* of persons as a basic principle of EU law.

1. Cf. Arnull, Anthony: The General Principles of EEC Law and the Individual, London 1990.
2. As mentioned in the previous chapters this is the opposite view of that expressed in the Constitution of ILO, see Chapter Two and O'Higgins, Paul: Labour is not a Commodity' – an Irish Contribution to International Labour Law, Industrial Law Journal1997, Vol. 26 Issue 3, p. 225.
3. Article 18 TFEU proivides: Within the scope of application of the Treaties, and without prejudice to any special provisions contained therein, any discrimination on grounds of nationality shall be prohibited.

The CJEU has provided a broad interpretation of the law in this area. Article 45 of the CFREU guarantees every citizen of the Union the right to move and reside freely within the territory of the Member States.

There have been provisions on the free movement for workers and self-employed in the TFEU since the beginning of the EC/EU. They were supplemented by Regulations on the free movement of workers[4] and social security for migrant workers and self-employed persons[5] at an early stage of the Community's development. The basic Treaty-provision on free movement for workers in Article 45 TFEU (previously Article 48 EC) was re-numbered by the Amsterdam Treaty but the text of the provision has only been slightly amended since the original Rome Treaty of 1957. After the coming into force of the Lisbon Treaty 1 December 2009, Article 45 TFEU reads:

1. Freedom of movement for workers shall be secured within the Union.

2. Such freedom of movement shall entail the abolition of any discrimination based on nationality between workers of the Member States as regards employment, remuneration and other conditions of work and employment.

3. It shall entail the right, subject to limitations justified on grounds of public policy, public security or public health:
(a) to accept offers of employment actually made;
(b) to move freely within the territory of Member States for this purpose;
(c) to stay in a Member State for the purpose of employment in accordance with the provisions governing the employment of nationals of that State laid down by law, regulation or administrative action;
(d) to remain in the territory of a Member State after having been employed in that State, subject to conditions which shall be embodied in implementing regulations to be drawn up by the Commission.

4. The provisions of this Article shall not apply to employment in the public service.

The principle of non-discrimination on grounds of Member State nationality lies at the foundation of the EU and has long applied to Member States' treatment of migrant workers with regard not just to employment, but also

4. EEC/1612/68 with many amendments. Now repealed and replaced with Regulation EU/492/2011.
5. EEC/1971/1408. Repealed after a new regulation, EC/883/2004 became applicable 1 May 2010, i.e. from the date of entry into force of an Implementing Regulation EC/987/2009.

with regard to national social policy.[6] Through the CJEU's interpretation of 'social advantages' in Article 7(2) of the Regulation on free movement of workers, a wide range of national welfare functions have been made subject to the requirements of the principle of non-discrimination as regards nationality.

Union citizenship was, as mentioned earlier, established by the Maastricht Treaty that came into force 1 November 1993. Every citizen of the Union has under Article 21 TFEU the right to move and reside freely within the territory of the EU-Member States, subject to the limitations and conditions laid down in the TFEU and by the measures adopted to give it effect, see for more detail the Free Movement and Residence Directive[7] and below in section 4 on union citizenship. Under the residence Directive, workers are entitled to entry and residence in other EU Member States than their home state. Union citizens who are not economically active, e.g. as workers (or students) are only entitled to reside in another EU Member State for more than three months if they have sufficient resources for themselves and their family members not to become a burden on the social assistance system of the host Member State and have comprehensive sickness insurance cover in that state. Workers who belong to the core of the workforce will typically thereby earn an income which will give them sufficient resources to be self-supporting. Job-seekers and a-typical workers may not have such resources. Notwithstanding this, they will in most cases be within the scope of the free movement for workers provisions.

The question of whether there is horizontal, direct effect concerns interrelations between the citizens or the companies, e.g. the relation between a private employer and private trade unions.

According to general theory and practice, Treaty provisions, if they are clear and precise, have direct effect, at least in the vertical relation and to a certain extent also in the horizontal relation. Article 45 TFEU gives rise to direct effects both in the vertical relationship against the Member States[8] and in

6. See Article 7 of Regulation EU/492/2011 (previously 1612/68/EEC) on free movement of workers. Articles 7(2) provides that migrant workers shall enjoy the same social and tax advantages as national workers.
7. 2004/38/EC.
8. There is a vertical, direct effect when an EU rule, e.g. a Treaty provision or a directive, is directly binding on authorities or the like in the vertical relation between the latter and the citizens/undertakings, see on Article 46 TFEU 1973167Case 167/73 *Commission v France (the Merchant Seaman's Case)* [1974] ECR 359 and 1974041Case 41/74 *Van Duyn v Home Office* [1974] ECR 1337.

horizontal relationships against private employers and organisations. In *Walrave/Koch v AUCI*[9] and *Dona v Mantero*[10] the CJEU ruled that Article 45 TFEU gives rise to horizontal direct effects.[11]

In *Angonese*,[12] an Italian national whose mother tongue was German and who was resident in the province of Bolzano, Italy, went to study in Austria between 1993 and 1997. In August 1997, in response to a notice published in a local Italian daily, he applied to take part in a competition for a post with a private banking undertaking in Bolzano, the Cassa di Risparmio. One of the conditions for entry to the competition was possession of a type-B certificate of bilingualism (in Italian and German) ('the Certificate'), which used to be required in the province of Bolzano for access to the former 'carriera di concetto' (managerial career) in the public service. The Certificate is issued by the public authorities of the province of Bolzano after an examination which is held only in that province. It is usual for residents of the province of Bolzano to obtain the Certificate as a matter of course for employment purposes. Obtaining the Certificate is viewed as an almost compulsory step as part of normal training. The national court has found as a fact that, although Angonese was not in possession of the Certificate, he was perfectly bilingual. With a view to gaining admission to the competition, he had submitted a certificate showing completion of his studies as a draughtsman and certificates attesting to his studies of languages (English, Slovene and Polish) at the Faculty of Philosophy at Vienna University and had stated that his professional experience included practising as a draughtsman and translating from Polish into Italian. On 4 September 1997, the Cassa de Risparmio informed Angonese that he could not be admitted to the competition because he had not produced the Certificate. Although he acknowledged the Cassa di Risparmio's right to select its future staff from persons who are perfectly bilingual, Angonese complained that the requirement to have and produce the Certificate was unlawful and contrary to the principle of freedom of movement for workers laid down in Article 45 TFEU. Angonese claimed that the requirement should be declared void and that the Cassa di Risparmio should be ordered to compensate him for his loss of opportunity and to reimburse him the costs he has in-

9. Case 36/74 *Walrave/Koch v AUCI* [1974] ECR 1405. The case concerned rules of an international sporting federation.
10. Case 13/76 *Dona v Mantero* [1976] ECR 1333. The Case concerned rules laid down by a sporting federation which is competent to control football on the territory of a Member State.
11. See also Case 222/86 *Heylens* [1987] ECR 4097.
12. Case C-281/98 *Angonese* [2000] ECR I-4139.

curred in the proceedings. The national court found that non-residents of Bolzano may have difficulty obtaining the Certificate in good time. The requirement for the Certificate imposed by the Cassa de Risparmio was founded on an article of the National Collective Agreement for Savings Banks. It referred the following question to the CJEU::

Is it compatible with Article 39(1), (2) and (3) EC and Articles 3(1) and 7(1) and (4) of Regulation (EEC) No 1612/68 to make the admission of candidates for a competition organised to fill posts in a company governed by private law conditional on possession of the official certificate attesting to knowledge of local languages issued exclusively by a public authority of a Member State at a single examination centre (namely, Bolzano), on completion of a procedure of considerable duration (to be precise, of not less than 30 days, on account of the minimum lapse of time envisaged between the written test and the oral test)?

The national court thus asked essentially whether Article 45 TFEU and Articles 3 and 7 of the Regulation on Free Movement of Workers preclude an employer from requiring persons applying to take part in a recruitment competition to provide evidence of their linguistic knowledge solely by means of one particular diploma, such as the Certificate, issued in a single province of a Member State. As far as the effect of the Regulation was concerned, the CJEU held that the question submitted falls to be examined solely in relation to Article 45 TFEU.

Under that provision, freedom of movement for workers within the EU entails the abolition of any discrimination based on nationality between workers of the Member States as regards employment, remuneration and other conditions of work and employment. The CJEU noted that the principle of non-discrimination set out in Article 39 is drafted in general terms and is not specifically addressed to the Member States. Thus, the Court has held that the prohibition of discrimination based on nationality applies not only to the actions of public authorities but also to rules of any other nature aimed at regulating in a collective manner gainful employment and the provision of services.[13] The Court has held that the abolition, as between Member States, of obstacles to freedom of movement for persons would be compromised if the abolition of State barriers could be neutralised by obstacles resulting from the exercise of their legal autonomy by associations or organisations not governed by public law.[14] Since working conditions in the different Member States are governed sometimes by provisions laid down by law or regulation

13. See Case 36/74 Walrave [1974] ECR 1405, paragraph 17.
14. See Case 36/74 Walrave [1974] ECR 1405, paragraph 18, Case C-415/93 Bosman [1995] ECR I-4921, paragraph 83.

and sometimes by agreements and other acts concluded or adopted by private persons, limiting application of the prohibition of discrimination based on nationality to acts of a public authority risks creating inequality in its application. The Court has also ruled that the fact that certain provisions of the Treaty are formally addressed to the Member States does not prevent rights from being conferred at the same time on any individual who has an interest in compliance with the obligations thus laid down.[15] The CjEU accordingly held, in relation to a provision of the Treaty which was mandatory in nature, that the prohibition of discrimination applied equally to all agreements intended to regulate paid labour collectively, as well as to contracts between individuals. The CJEU found that such considerations must, *a fortiori*, be applicable to Article 45 TFEU, which lays down a fundamental freedom and which constitutes a specific application of the general prohibition of discrimination contained in Article 18 TFEU. In that respect, like Article 157 TFEU, it is designed to ensure that there is no discrimination on the labour market. Consequently, the prohibition of discrimination on grounds of nationality laid down in Article 45 TFEU must be regarded as applying to private persons as well.

As set out in Chapter Three, the main issue in *Viking* [16] was whether the Finnish Seamen's Union by threatening collective action and the International Transport Worker's Federation by leading a campaign concerning flag of convenience made it pointless for Viking, a Finnish employer, to establish itself in Estonia and reflag a ferry, which had previously sailed under Finnish flag, to Estonia. In *Laval*,[17] a Latvian company (Laval) had won a contract for construction work at a school in the municipality of Vaxholm (Sweden) in an EU tender. Laval posted Latvian workers in Sweden to carry out the job. The problem in this case is to what extent the Latvian employer could be forced to comply with a Swedish collective agreement concerning wages and working conditions by collective action (blockade and secondary action) or whether it was sufficient that the Latvian employer followed Latvian law, hereunder a collective agreement that had been concluded with a Latvian trade union. In *Viking* and *Laval*, the CJEU ruled that Articles 49 TFEU and 56 TFEU have direct, horizontal effect as binding on trade union federations. Hereby the

15. See Case 43/75 *Defrenne II* [1976] ECR 455, paragraph 31.
16. Case C-438/05 *Viking* [2007] ECR I-10779.
17. Case C-341/05 *Laval* [2007] ECR I-11767.

CJEU continued its previous practice concerning sports organisations,[18] applying it to trade union federations.

3 Migrant workers within the EU

3.1 The Concept of Worker in regard to Article 45 TFEU

Already in 1964 in *Unger*,[19] the CJEU stated that the term 'worker' must have an EU meaning. The CJEU has developed a broad concept of worker. Any person who pursues activities which are effective and genuine, to the exclusion of activities on such a small scale as to be regarded as purely marginal and ancillary, is regarded as a 'worker'.

According to the CJEU the test for being a worker within the meaning of Article 45 TFEU is that an individual performs services for and under the direction of another, for remuneration. In addition, the work performed must be 'effective and genuine' as opposed to purely 'marginal and ancillary'. The application of these tests has led to an extension of the categories of workers entitled to claim the rights of free movement. Accordingly it has been firmly established that the concept applies to, amongst others, part-time, temporary, seasonal and trainee workers.

Part of the ban on discrimination on grounds of nationality applies to all work done by a worker who is a citizen of a Member State in another Member State. It is for example unlawful to pay a migrant worker less than a domestic worker no matter how marginal and ancillary the work may be. In relation to the right to reside on the basis of status as migrant worker and the social advantages that depend on residence the above test of whether the work is 'effective and genuine' as opposed to purely 'marginal and ancillary' applies.

In *Levin*,[20] the CJEU stated that part-time workers were covered by the Community provisions as long as the work was an 'effective and genuine economic activity'. In *Lawrie Blum v Land Baden Würtemberg*[21] the CJEU ruled that the essential feature of an employment relationship under EU law is that for a certain period of time a person performs services for, and under the direction of, another person in return for which he or she receives remuneration. The CJEU held that it was irrelevant that trainee teachers were not clas-

18. See e.g. Case 36/74 *B.N.O. Walrave* [1974] ECR 1405.
19. Case 75/63 *Unger* [1964] ECR 1977.
20. Case 53/81 *Levin* [1982] ECR 1035.
21. Case 66/85 *Lawrie-Blum* [1986] ECR 2121.

sified as employees in German law and that once the general test had been satisfied it was irrelevant that the contract was primarily for the purposes of training. In *Kempf*,[22] a German national was working part-time in the Netherlands as a music teacher. His earnings were so low that they were topped up to the Dutch minimum subsistence level by sickness and social security benefits. The CJEU reiterated its view that provided the person was carrying out a genuine economic activity it was irrelevant that he or she received other supplemental means of support.

Steymann[23] concerned a German national who became a member of a religious community in the Netherlands. He carried out certain domestic tasks and helped out in the running of the community's commercial activities which involved *inter alia* the running of a discotheque, a drinks shop and a laundry. For this he was given a small amount of 'pocket money' and free board. The CJEU found that his work constituted a genuine and effective activity where the commercial activities were an inherent part of membership of the Bhagwan community.

Raulin[24] concerned the problem whether a worker on an on-call contract was a worker within the meaning of the EU provisions of free movement for workers. The CJEU observed that it was apparent from the reference for a preliminary ruling that under Netherlands law an on-call contract is a means of recruiting workers in sectors, such as the hotel trade, where the volume of work is subject to seasonal variations. Under such a contract, no guarantee is given as to the hours to be worked and, often, the person involved works only a very few days per week or hours per day. The employer is liable to pay wages and grant social advantages only in so far as the worker has actually performed work. The CJEU stated that it has consistently held that the concept of worker has a Community meaning and must not be interpreted in a restrictive manner. Nevertheless, in order to be regarded as a worker, a person must perform effective and genuine activities to the exclusion of activities on such a small scale as to be purely marginal and ancillary. The essential characteristic of an employment relationship is that for a certain period a person performs services for and under the direction of another person in return for which he receives remuneration.

The second question in the case was whether the fact that a person has exercised an economic activity for only a short period means that such activity is purely marginal and ancillary, with the result that the person exercising that

22. Case 139/85 *Kempf* [1986] ECR 1741.
23. Case 196/87 *Steymann* [1988] ECR 6159.
24. Case C-357/89 *Raulin* [1992] ECR I-357.

activity cannot be regarded as a worker. The CJEU held that whilst part-time work is not excluded from the field of application of the rules on freedom of movement for workers, those cover only the pursuit of effective and genuine activities, to the exclusion of activities on such a small scale as to be regarded as purely marginal and ancillary. It is up to the national courts to make the necessary findings of fact in order to establish whether the person concerned can be considered to be a worker within the meaning of that case-law. The national court may, when assessing the effective and genuine nature of the activity in question, take account of the irregular nature and limited duration of the services actually performed under a contract for occasional employment. The fact that the person concerned worked only a very limited number of hours in a labour relationship may be an indication that the activities exercised are purely marginal and ancillary.

By the third question in *Raulin* the national court wished to know whether it must take account, when assessing whether the person concerned is a worker, of activities other than those most recently pursued in the host Member State. The CJEU answered that the aim of Regulation 1612/68 is to facilitate freedom of movement for workers and, to this end, to ensure integration of workers in the host country. The status of migrant worker and, consequently, the right to equality of treatment with national workers, is acquired only through the occupational activities exercised in the host country.

In contrast to the above cases, where the concept of a worker was interpreted fairly broadly, the CJEU refused to accept sheltered employment as falling under the concept of a worker in *Bettray*.[25] The question was whether a person who had undergone treatment for drug addiction and who worked within a scheme established under the Dutch Social Employment Law which aimed at the rehabilitation and reintegration of persons with personal or social problems into society could be classified as a worker under Article 45 TFEU. Referring to its ruling in *Levin*, the CJEU stressed that Article 45 TFEU covers only persons pursuing an effective and genuine economic activity and which had had a rehabilitation function rather than a market activity was not accepted as a 'real and genuine economic activity'.

Similarly the CJEU has held that where work is ancillary to educational studies a person is not classified as worker within the meaning of Article 45 TFEU.[26] In *Merci Convenzionali*,[27] the CJEU held that:

25. Case 344/87 *Bettray* [1989] ECR 1621.
26. Case 197/86 *Brown* [1988] ECR 3205. Cf. Case 39/86 *Lair* [1988] ECR 3161.
27. Case C-179/90 *Merci Convenzionali Porto di Genova* [1991] ECR I-5889.

1. The concept of worker within the meaning of article 48 [now Article 45 TFEU] of the Treaty pre_supposes that for a certain period of time a person performs services for and under the direction of another person in return for which he receives remuneration.

Under Article 45 TFEU the free movement of workers is to be secured within the EU. Article 45 TFEU circumscribes Article 18 TFEU in that it has been interpreted to apply only to workers who are *nationals of one of the Member States.* Article 28 of the EEA Agreement extends the protection under Article 45 TFEU to nationals of the EEA states (Norway, Iceland and Lichtenstein).

In *Lehtonen*,[28] the CJEU examined whether a basketball player carries on an economic activity, and whether he should be regarded as a worker within the meaning of Article 45 TFEU. As to the concept of worker, according to settled case law, it may not be interpreted differently according to each national law but has a Community meaning. It must be defined in accordance with objective criteria which distinguish the employment relationship by reference to the rights and duties of the persons concerned. The essential feature of an employment relationship is that for a certain period of time a person performs services for and under the direction of another person, in return for which he receives remuneration.[29]

The CJEU observed that these concepts define the scope of one of the fundamental freedoms guaranteed by the Treaty and, as such, may not be interpreted restrictively. With respect more specifically to the former concept, it is settled case law that work as a paid employee or the provision of services for remuneration must be regarded as an economic activity within the meaning of the Treaties. However, those activities must be effective and genuine activities and not such as to be regarded as purely marginal and ancillary. As to the concept of worker, according to settled case-law, it may not be interpreted differently according to each national law but has an EU meaning. It must be defined in accordance with objective criteria which distinguish the employment relationship by reference to the rights and duties of the persons concerned. The essential feature of an employment relationship is that for a certain period of time a person performs services for and under the direction of another person, in return for which he receives remuneration. It appeared from the findings of fact made by the national court and from the documents produced to the CJEU that Lehtonen had entered into a contract of employment with a club in another Member State with a view to exercising gainful employment in that State. He thereby accepted an offer of employment actu-

28. Case C-176/96 *Lehtonen* [2000] ECR I-2681.
29. See, in particular, Case 66/85 *Lawrie-Blum* [1986] ECR 2121, paragraphs 16 and 17.

ally made, within the meaning of Article 45(3) (a) TFEU. The CJEU concluded:

> Article 48 of the EC Treaty (now, after amendment, Article 45 TFEU) precludes the application of rules laid down in a Member State by sporting associations which prohibit a basketball club from fielding players from other Member States in matches in the national championship, where they have been transferred after a specified date, if that date is earlier than the date which applies to transfers of players from certain non-member countries, unless objective reasons concerning only sport as such or relating to differences between the position of players from a federation in the European zone and that of players from a federation not in that zone justify such different treatment.

3.1.1 Job seekers

Any national of a Member State, i.e. union citizens, see below in section 4, has the right to look for a job in another Member State. He or she must receive from the national employment offices the same assistance as nationals of the host Member State. According to the CJEU case law, the jobseeker may stay in the host Member State for a period sufficient to enable him to appraise himself of offers of employment and to take the necessary steps to be engaged, normally 6 months. After expiry of such period, he cannot be expelled if he proves that he is continuing to seek employment and that he has genuine chances of being engaged. In *Antonissen*,[30] the referring national court sought to establish whether it is contrary to the provisions of EUlaw governing the free movement of workers for the legislation of a Member State to provide that a national of another Member State who entered the first State in order to seek employment may be required to leave the territory of that State if he has not found employment there after six months. The CJEU stated that Article 45(3) TFEU must be interpreted as enumerating, in a non-exhaustive way, certain rights benefiting nationals of Member States in the context of the free movement of workers and that that freedom also entails the right for nationals of Member States to move freely within the territory of the other Member States and to stay there for the purposes of seeking employment. The CJEU concluded:

> It is not contrary to the provisions of Community law governing the free movement of workers for the legislation of a Member State to provide that a national of another Member State who entered the first State in order to seek employment may be required to leave the territory of that State (subject to appeal) if he has not found employment there after six

30. Case C-292/89 *Antonissen* [1991] ECR I-745.

months, unless the person concerned provides evidence that he is continuing to seek employment and that he has genuine chances of being engaged.

It is now settled case-law that the concept of 'worker' in the context of free movement of workers must not be interpreted narrowly.

In order to be eligible for welfare rights it is, however, not always enough to be a worker. There may be additional requirements of residence,[31] real link[32] and the like. In *Lebon*,[33] the CJEU stated that Article 45 TFEU and the Regulation on Migrans Workers[34] did not entitle those looking for work to the same social benefits as a Member State's own nationals. In *Collins*,[35] it (partly) similarly stated that the right to equal treatment laid down in Article 45(2) TFEU, read in conjunction with Articles 18 TFEU, does not preclude national legislation which makes entitlement to a jobseeker's allowance conditional on a residence requirement.[36] While Member State nationals who move in search for work benefit from the principle of equal treatment only as regards access to employment, those who have already entered the employment market may, on the basis of Article 7(2) of the Regulation on Migrant Workers, claim the same social and tax advantages as national workers, see below in section 3.3.4. on social and tax advantages and section 3.3.5 on first time job seekers' entitlements to social security.

3.1.2 A-typical Workers

In a number of cases, the CJEU has given a broad interpretation to the concept of worker in relation to a-typical work. In *Levin*,[37] the CJEU stated that part-time workers were covered by the EU provisions as long as the work was an 'effective and genuine economic activity'. In *Lawrie Blum*,[38] the CJEU held that a trainee teacher was a worker within the meaning of Article

31. In C-127/08 *Metock* [2008] I-6241, the CJEU stated that there is only a right of family reunification for family members of a Union citizen who has exercised his right of freedom of movement by becoming *established* [emphasis added] in another Member State than his own.
32. Dougan, Michael: The Spatial Restructuring of National Welfare States within the European Union: the Contribution of Union Citizenship and the Relevance of the Treaty of Lisbon in Ulla Neergaard, Ruth Nielsen and Lynn Roseberry (eds): Integrating Welfare Functions into EU Law – From Rome to Lisbon, Copenhagen 2009.
33. Case 316/85 *Lebon* [1987] ECR 2811.
34. Then 1612/68/EEC, now EU/492/2011.
35. Case C-138/02 *Collins* [2004] ECR I-2703.
36. See also case C-224/98 *D'Hoop* [2002] I-6191.
37. Case 53/81 *Levin* [1982] ECR 1035.
38. Case 66/85 *Lawrie-Blum* [1986] ECR 2121.

45 TFEU. *Raulin*[39] concerned the problem whether a worker on an on-call contract was a worker. The CJEU held that whilst part-time work is not excluded from the field of application of the rules on freedom of movement for workers, those cover only the pursuit of effective and genuine activities, to the exclusion of activities on such a small scale as to be regarded as purely marginal and ancillary. It is up to the national courts to make the necessary findings of fact in order to establish whether the person concerned can be considered to be a worker within the meaning of that case-law. The CJEU regards professional sportsmen and sportswomen as workers within the meaning of Article 45 TFEU.[40]

In *Raccanelli*,[41] the CJEU held that a researcher preparing a doctoral thesis on the basis of a grant contract concluded with the Max-Planck-Gesellschaft zur Förderung der Wissenschaften eV, must be regarded as a worker within the meaning of Article 45 TFEU only if his activities are performed for a certain period of time under the direction of an institute forming part of that association and if, in return for those activities, he receives remuneration. It is for the referring court to undertake the necessary verification of the facts in order to establish whether such is the case in the dispute before it.

A private-law association, such as the Max-Planck-Gesellschaft zur Förderung der Wissenschaften eV, must observe the principle of non-discrimination in relation to workers within the meaning of Article 45 TFEU. It is for the referring court to establish whether, in circumstances such as those of the case in the main proceedings, there has been inequality in the treatment of domestic and foreign doctoral students.

In the event that the applicant in the main proceedings is justified in relying on damage caused by the discrimination to which he has been subject, it is for the referring court to assess, in the light of the national legislation applicable in relation to non-contractual liability, the nature of the compensation which he would be entitled to claim.

3.1.3 Social Clients

In *Kempf*,[42] a German national was working part-time in the Netherlands as a music teacher. His earnings were so low that they were topped up to the Dutch minimum subsistence level by sickness and social security benefits.

39. Case C-357/89 *Raulin* [1992] ECR I-357.
40. See case C-415/93 *Bosman* [1995] ECR I-4921, case C-176/96 *Lehtonen* [2000] ECR I-2681 and case C-438/00 *Kolpak* [2003] ECR I-4135.
41. Case C-94/07 *Raccanelli* [2008] ECR I-5939.
42. Case 139/85 *Kempf* [1986] ECR 1741.

The CJEU held that provided the person was carrying out a genuine economic activity it was irrelevant that he or she received other supplemental means of support. *Steymann*[43] concerned a German national who became a member of a religious community in the Netherlands. He carried out certain domestic tasks and helped out in the running of the community's commercial activities. For this he was given a small amount of 'pocket money' and free board. The CJEU found that his work constituted a genuine and effective activity.

In contrast to the above cases, where the concept of a worker was interpreted fairly broadly, the CJEU refused to accept sheltered employment as falling under the concept of a worker in *Bettray.*[44] Similarly the CJEU has held that where work is ancillary to educational studies a person is not classified as worker within the meaning of Article 45 TFEU.[45] In *Trojani,*[46] Trojani performed, for the Salvation Army and under its direction, various jobs for approximately 30 hours a week, as part of a personal reintegration programme, in return for which he received benefits in kind and some pocket money. The CJEU held:

> A person in a situation such as that of the claimant in the main proceedings, first, does not come under Articles 43 EC and 49 EC and, second, can claim a right of residence as a worker within the meaning of Article 39 EC [now Article 45 TFEU}only if the paid activity he carries out is real and genuine. It is for the national court to carry out the examinations of fact necessary to determine whether that is so in the case pending before it.

3.1.4 Family Members of Migrant Workers

The CJEU and the EU legislator have extended the principles concerning free movement of workers to members of the migrant worker's family.[47] Today there are explicit provisions on family members in the Residence Directive.[48]

National rules on *family reunification* with family members who are third country nationals vary from Member State to Member. According to the case law of the CJEU restrictive national rules on family reunification may constitute an unlawful restriction on the freedom of movement for workers.

43. Case 196/87 *Steymann* [1988] ECR 6159.
44. Case 344/87 *Bettray* [1989] ECR 1621.
45. Case 197/86 *Brown* [1988] ECR 3205. Cf. Case 39/86 *Lair* [1988] ECR 3161.
46. Case C-456/02 *Trojani* [2004] I-7573.
47. Case 32/75 *Fiorini* [1975] ECR 1085, Case 261/83 *Castelli* v *ONPTS* [1984] ECR 3199 and Case 249/83 *Hoeckx* [1985] ECR 973 and Article 7(1)d of Directive 2004/38/EC which replaces the now repealed Articles 10 and 11 of Regulation EEC/1612/68.
48. 2004/38/EC.

In *Carpenter*,[49] the CJEU found that Article 49 EC on freedom to provide services, read in the light of the fundamental right to respect for family life, is to be interpreted as precluding, in circumstances such as those in the main proceedings, a refusal, by the Member State of origin of a provider of services established in that Member State who provides services to recipients established in other Member States, of the right to reside in its territory to that provider's spouse, who is a national of a third country.

In *Eind*,[50] the CJEU took a similar view to freedom of movement for workers. The CJEUt held that in the event of a Community worker returning to the Member State of which he is a national, EU law does not require the authorities of that State to grant a right of entry and residence to a third-country national who is a member of that worker's family because of the mere fact that, in the host Member State where that worker was gainfully employed, that third-country national held a valid residence permit issued on the basis of Article 10 of the Regulation on free movement for workers. When a worker returns to the Member State of which he is a national, after being gainfully employed in another Member State, a third-country national who is a member of his family has a right to reside in the Member State of which the worker is a national, even where that worker does not carry on any effective and genuine economic activities.

The EU has also adopted legislation on the right to family reunification.[51]

3.2 The Right to Move to and Reside in another EU-country

The right to enter and reside in another EU Member State goes hand in hand with the right to work in another Member State.

3.2.1 Article 45(3) TFEU

Under Article 45(3) TFEU freedom of movement for workers entails *inter alia* the right, subject to limitations justified on grounds of public policy, public security or public health to move freely within the territory of Member States for this purpose; to stay in a Member State for the purpose of employment in accordance with the provisions governing the employment of nationals of that State laid down by law, regulation or administrative action and to remain in the territory of a Member State after having been employed in that State, subject to conditions which shall be embodied in implementing regulations to be drawn up by the Commission.

49. Case C-60/00 *Carpenter* [2002] ECR I-6279.

3.3 The Ban on Discrimination on Grounds of Nationality

Articles 18 TFEU and 45(2) TFEU provide for the elimination of all discrimination based on nationality. In most cases concerning workers Article 45 TFEU and not Article 18 TFEU will be the appropriate provisions.

In *Merci Convenzionali Porto di Genova spa* [52] the CJEU was asked whether Article 106(1) TFEU, in conjunction with Articles 18 TFEU, 34 TFEU and 102 TFEUEC, preclude rules of a Member State which confer on an undertaking established in that state the exclusive right to organize dock work and require it, for the performance of such work, to have recourse to a dock-work company formed exclusively of nationals, and whether those articles give rise to rights for individuals which the national courts must protect. The CJEU held, as regards the nationality condition imposed on the workers of the dock-work company, that it should be recalled that according to the case-law of the CJEU, the general prohibition of discrimination on grounds of nationality laid down in Article 18 TFEU applies independently only to situations governed by EU law in regard to which the TFEU lays down no specific prohibition of discrimination.[53] As regards workers, that principle has been specifically applied by Article 45 TFEU. More detailed provisions are laid down by Regulation.

According to Article 3 of the Regulation on free movement of workers[54] provisions laid down by law, regulation or administrative practices of the Member States shall not apply where they limit application for and offers of employment, or the right of foreign nationals to take up and pursue employment or subject these offers to conditions not applicable in respect of their own nationals. Article 7 of the Regulation on migrant workers provides that:

> 1. A worker who is a national of a Member State may not, in the territory of another Member State, be treated differently from national workers by reason of his nationality in respect of any conditions of employment and work, in particular as regards remuneration, dismissal, and should he become unemployed, reinstatement or re-employment;
> 2. He shall enjoy the same social and tax advantages as national workers.
> 3. He shall also, by virtue of the same right and under the same conditions as national workers, have access to training in vocational schools and retraining centres.

50. Case C-291/05 *Eind* [2007] ECR I-10719.
51. Directive 2003/86/EC on the right to family reunification.
52. Case C-179/90 *Merci Convenzionali Porto di Genova spa* [1991] ECR I-5889.
53. See for example Case 305/87 *Commission* v *Greece* [1989] ECR 1461, paragraphs 12 and 13; Case C-10/90 *Masgio* [1991] ECR I-1119, paragraph 12).
54. Previously EEC/1612/68, now EC/492/2011.

4. Any clause of a collective or individual agreement or of any other collective regulation concerning eligibility for employment, employment, remuneration and other conditions of work or dismissal shall be null and void in so far as it lays down or authorises discriminatory conditions in respect of workers who are nationals of the other Member States.

The above provisions are directly applicable in the Member States. Article 24 of the Residence Directive[55] provides on Equal treatment:

1. Subject to such specific provisions as are expressly provided for in the Treaty and secondary law, all Union citizens residing on the basis of this Directive in the territory of the host Member State shall enjoy equal treatment with the nationals of that Member State within the scope of the Treaty. The benefit of this right shall be extended to family members who are not nationals of a Member State and who have the right of residence or permanent residence.

Member States are according to Article 24(2) of the Residence directive not obliged to confer entitlement to social assistance during the first three months of residence or, the longer period applying to job seekers, see below in section 3.5.5 on first time job-seekers and the relationship between Article 45(2) TFEU and Article 24 of the Residence Directive, as interpreted in *Collins*[56] and *Vatsouras*[57] nor are they obliged, prior to acquisition of the right of permanent residence, to grant maintenance aid for studies, including vocational training, consisting in student grants or student loans to persons other than workers, self-employed persons, persons who retain such status and members of their families, see below in section 3.5.6. on vocational training and education and the case law cited there.

3.3.1 Direct Discrimination

The CJEU has addressed direct discrimination on grounds of nationality in a few cases.

In *Merci Convenzionali Porto di Genova*[58] the CJEU held that Italian legislation which reserved dock work to Italian nationals was contrary to Article 45(2) TFEU and could not be justified on the basis of the public service exception in Article 45(4) TFEU. Similarly in *Commission* v *Belgium*[59] the CJEU held that Belgian legislation which imposed a Belgian nationality re-

55. 2004/38/EC.
56. Case C-138/02 *Collins* [2004] ECR I-2703.
57. Joined Cases C-22/08 and C-23/08 *Vatsouras* [2009] ECR I-4585.
58. Case C-179/90 *Merci Convenzionali Porto di Genova* [1991] ECR I-5889.
59. Case C-37/93 *Commission v Belgium* [1993] ECR I-6295.

quirement for certain seamen's jobs on board sea vessels, other than those of master and second master, was contrary to Article 45(2) TFEU. In the infringement case against Denmark concerning the *Great Belt bridge*, Denmark was found in violation of Articles 34 TFEU, 45 TFEU and 56 TFEU by putting out an invitation to tender for the building of a bridge over the Great Belt on the basis of a condition requiring the use to the greatest possible extent of Danish materials, goods, labour and equipment.[60]

3.3.2 Indirect Discrimination

The CJEU has held that the ban on discrimination covers both overt and covert (indirect) discrimination.[61] So far, the CJEU has failed to be as specific in prohibiting indirect discrimination in respect of free movement of workers (Article 45 TFEU) as it has ín the areas of free movement of goods (article 34 TFEU) where it has developed the Dassonville-formula, freedom to provide services (Article 56 TFEU) and equal treatment of men and women. In *Dassonville*,[62] the CJEU ruled that all trading rules enacted by Member States which are capable of hindering, directly or indirectly, actually or potentially, intra-Community trade are to be considered as measures having an effect equivalent to quantitative restrictions.

In applying the prohibition on indirect or covert discrimination the CJEU has tended to apply a three stage test.[63] Firstly, it requires proof that the national measure is within the scope of application of the Treaty. Next, the condition must be shown to be discriminatory – that is, the condition applied must be shown to work to the particular disadvantage of non- nationals. Then the Court will consider whether any objective reasons exist to justify the use of the measure (these reasons also being subject to the principle of proportionality).

A comprehensive summary given by the CJEU itself of its case law on indirect discrimination in the context of Article 45 TFEU can be found in the case of *O'Flynn*[64] where the Court stated that it has consistently held that the equal treatment rule laid down in Article 45 TFEU and in Article 7 of the

60. 1989243Case C-243/89 *Commission* v *Denmark* [1993] ECR I-3353.
61. Case 152/73 *Sotgiu* [1974] ECR 153; Case C-33/88 *Allué and Coonan* [1989] ECR 1591.
62. Case 8/74 *Dassonville* [1974] ECR 837.
63. Johnson, E and O'Keeffe, David: From Discrimination to Obstacles to Free Movement: Recent Developments Concerning the Free Movement of Workers 1989-1994 in Common Market Law Review 1994 p 1313.
64. Case C-237/94 *O'Flynn* [1996] ECR I-2617.

Migrans Workers Regulation prohibits not only overt discrimination by reason of nationality but also all covert forms of discrimination which, by the application of other distinguishing criteria, leading in fact to the same result.[65] The Court held[66] that conditions imposed by national law must be regarded as indirectly discriminatory where, although applicable irrespective of nationality, they affect essentially migrant workers[67] or the great majority of those affected are migrant workers,[68] where they are indistinctly applicable but can more easily be satisfied by national workers than by migrant workers[69] or where there is a risk that they may operate to the particular detriment of migrant workers.[70]

It is otherwise only if those provisions are justified by objective considerations independent of the nationality of the workers concerned, and if they are proportionate to the legitimate aim pursued by the national law.[71]

The interpretation of the concept of indirect nationality discrimination laid down by the CJEU in *O'Flynn* has later been codified in the definitions of indirect discrimination in the Ethnic Equal treatment Directive,[72] the Framework Employment Directive[73] and the recast directive on Gender Equality in Employment and Occupation,[74] see further below in Chapter Six.

In the majority of the Member States there are no formal language requirements for employment in the private sector. However, employers in the private sector are usually free to set up language requirements if necessary for performing the job and as long as these requirements do not interfere with antidiscrimination law. The starting point for judging the legitimacy of language

65. Case 152/73, *Sotgiu* [1974] ECR 153, paragraph 11; Case C-27/91 *URSSAF* [1991] ECR I-5531, paragraph 10; Case C-111/91 *Commission* v *Luxembourg* [1993] ECR I-817, paragraph 9; and Case C-419/92 *Scholz* [1994] ECR I-505, paragraph 7.
66. Paragraphs 18 and 19 of the judgment in Case C-237/94 *O'Flynn* [1996] ECR I-2617.
67. Case 41/84 *Pinna* [1986] ECR 1, paragraph 24; Case C-33/88 *Allué* [1989] ECR 1591, paragraph 12; and Case C-27/91 *URSSAF* [1991] ECR I-5531, paragraph 11.
68. Case C-279/89 *Commission* v *United Kingdom* [1992] ECR I-5785 and Case C-272/92 *Spotti* 1993] ECR I-5185, paragraph 18.
69. Case C-111/91 *Commission* v *Luxembourg*, paragraph 10, and Case C-349/87 *Paraschi* [1991] ECR I-4501, paragraph 23.
70. Case C-175/88 *Biehl* [1990] ECR I-1779, paragraph 14, and Case C-204/90 *Bachmann* [1992] ECR I-249, paragraph 9.
71. Case C-204/90 *Bachmann* [1992] ECR I-249, paragraph 27; Case C-111/91 *Commission* v *Luxembourg*, paragraph 12; and Joined Cases C-259/91, C-221/91 and C-332/91 *Allué* [1993] ECR I-4309, paragraph 15.
72. 2000/43/EC.
73. 2000/78/EC.
74. 2006/54/EC.

requirements is what qualifications are needed for the performance of the work concerned.

3.3.3 Reverse Discrimination

Reverse discrimination is discrimination a Member State exercises *vis à vis* its own nationals by treating them less favourably than it treats nationals of other member states. The CJEU has delivered a number of rulings on this issue where it has consistently held that purely internal matters fall outside the scope of Article 39EC etc. The starting point is thus that a member state is free under EU law to discriminate against its own nationals be they workers, self-employed or service providers. In *Moser*[75] the Court did for example accept that (West) Germany operated a Berufsverbot (discrimination against communists) against its own nationals. Migrant workers are (probably) protected against political discrimination under Article 45 TFEU combined with the fundamental rights protected by EU law.

In *Commission* v *France*,[76] the CJEU seemed to suggest that the prohibition against discrimination contained in Article 18 TFEU may have a wider application:

> '... guaranteeing to the State's own nationals that they shall not suffer the unfavourable consequences which could result from the offer or acceptance by nationals of other Member States of conditions of employment or remuneration less advantageous than those obtaining under national law.'

Steen v *Deutsche Bundespost(1)*[77] concerned a German national who wished to continue being employed under a contract of employment once he had finished his training in the German post office. German nationals were normally engaged as civil servants whereas non-nationals were ineligible to become civil servants and were engaged as employees. The CJEU considered that the situation was purely internal to Germany and that Article 45 TFEU did not apply. In the Second *Steen* case[78] the CJEU was asked:

> Is the judgment of the Court of Justice of the European Communities of 28 January 1992 in Case C-332/90 to be interpreted as meaning that the national court is precluded from applying EU law in regard to a purely domestic situation, or does it, as the legally appointed court within the meaning of the second sentence of article 101(1) of the Federal Republic

75. Case 180/83 *Moser* [1984] ECR 2539.
76. Case 167/73 *Commission* v *France* [1974] ECR 359.
77. Case C-332/90 *Volker Steen (1)* [1992] ECR I-341.
78. Case C-132/93 *Volker Steen* (2) [1994] ECR I-2715.

of Germany' s Grundgesetz (basic law), remain entitled, where the Court of Justice lacks jurisdiction, to examine as a preliminary question, in connection with a claim that Article 3(1) of the basic law has been infringed, whether there is discrimination against a German national because the effect of EU law in the event is to place German nationals in a worse position as compared with nationals of other member states?

The Court interpreted the question as meaning that in substance, the national court asked whether, despite the fact that according to the *Steen(1)* judgment EU law is not applicable to the present case, it may consider the discrimination pleaded by *Steen* in the light of national law and decide the case accordingly. In the view of the Court, he only effect of the *Steen(1)* judgment is to preclude EU law from being relied on with respect to a purely internal situation. The CJEU held:

10. It is for the national court, faced with a question of national law, to determine whether there is any discrimination under that law and whether that discrimination must be eliminated and, if so, how.

11. Consequently, the reply to be given to the question put by the national court is that EU law does not preclude a national court from examining the compatibility with its constitution of a national rule which, in a situation unconnected with any of the situations contemplated by EU law, treats national workers less favourably than nationals from other member states.

The CJEU's case law in the area of reverse discrimination has come under increasing criticism. Johnson and O'Keeffe argues that there is a trend towards a new policy on reverse discrimination and comments on the CJEU's ruling in the Second *Steen* judgment:

Implicitly this could mean that Germany is now forced to ensure that national standards meet those set by the Community for migrant workers. If that were the case, and the principle of equality before the law were strictly applied, the *Steen (No 2)* ruling may prov to be of very considerable importance.

A duty to remove inconsistencies between EU law and national law may be based on Article 4 TEU on loyal cooperation. Where there is a Community element to a person's conduct it is possible to use EU law against the home state. In *Scholz*,[79] the CJEU stated:

79. Case C-419/92 *Scholz* [1994] ECR I-505.

8. In this case, it should be noted first of all that the fact that the plaintiff in the main proceedings has acquired Italian nationality has no bearing on the application of the principle of non-discrimination.

9. Any Community national who, irrespective of his place of residence and his nationality, has exercised the right to freedom of movement for workers and who has been employed in another member state, falls within the scope of the aforesaid provisions.

Similar decisions are found in *Knoors*[80] and *Singh.*[81] In *Bouchoucha*[82] and *Nino, Prandina, Goti and Pierini*[83] there was no EU element. In *Hansen og Søn,*[84] a Danish employer whose drivers infringed the Regulation on the harmonization of certain social legislation relating to road transport[85] was punished for an infringement in Holland. Foreign employers could not be punished in Denmark in such a situation but only if the infringement occurred in Denmark. Furthermore foreign employers were in practice never procecuted by Danish authorities. The prosecutor told the Danish court that for practical reasons foreign employers were never prosecuted for their drivers' infringements. Instead a higher fine was imposed upon foreign drivers with non-Danish employers in the belief that their employers would reimburse it when they returned home.[86]

The discrimination against foreign drivers is a clear violation of Article 45 TFEU. It is more doubtful whether the reverse discrimination against Danish employers is an infringement of EU law.

In *Hansen og Søn* questions concerning reverse discrimination was not put before the CJEU which was only asked about the lawfulness of applying penal sanctions on the basis of strict liability. The CJEU held that where EU legislation does not specifically provide any penalty for an infringement or refers for that purpose to national laws, regulations and administrative provisions, Article 4 TEU requires the member states to take all measures necessary to guarantee the application and effectiveness of EU law. For that purpose, whilst the choice of penalties remains within their discretion, they must ensure in particular that infringements of EU law are penalized under condi-

80. Case 115/78 *Knoors* [1979] ECR 399.
81. Case C-370/90 *Singh* [1992] ECR I-4265.
82. Case C-61/89 *Bouchoucha* [1990] ECR I-3551.
83. Joined Cases C-54/88, C-91/88, and C-14/89 *Nino, Prandina, Goti and Pierini* [1990] ECR I-3537.
84. Case C-326/88 *Hansen & Søn* [1990] ECR I-2911.
85. 543/69/EEC.
86. Ugeskrift for Retsvæsen 1995,9.

tions, both procedural and substantive, which are analogous to those applicable to infringements of national law of a similar nature and importance and which, in any event, make the penalty effective, proportionate and dissuasive. Neither Regulation No 543/69 on the harmonization of certain social legislation relating to road transport nor the general principles of EU law preclude the application of national provisions under which an employer whose drivers infringe articles 7(2) and 11 of the Regulation on road transport may be the subject of a criminal penalty notwithstanding the fact that the infringement cannot be imputed to an intentional wrongful act or to negligence on the employer' s part, on condition that the penalty provided for is similar to those imposed in the event of infringement of provisions of national law of similar nature and importance and is proportionate to the seriousness of the infringement committed.

Before the Danish courts it was argued by the employer in *Hansen og Søn* that the reverse discrimination he suffered was an infringement of Article 18 TFEU. This argument was dismissed by the Danish courts. The issue of reverse discrimination has also arisen in relation to freedom to supply services and freedom of establishment. In *Auer*,[87] the French authorities refused to recognise an Italian vetinary qualification obtained by one of its own nationals. The CJEU ruled that Article 49 TFEU could only be applied to nationals of another Member State wishing to exercise the freedom of establishment in France.[88]

3.3.4 Social and tax advantages

The principle of equal treatment of a migrant worker is defined broadly in Article 7(2) of the Migrant Workers Regulation which provides that the migrant worker shall enjoy the same social and tax advantages as national workers. The term 'social advantage' has been given a wide interpretation by the CJEU and covers social advantages given to workers and their families outside the contract of employment,[89] including advantages granted on a discretionary basis.[90]

In *Christini*,[91] the CJEU held that discrimination on grounds of nationality in respect of cheap rail tickets for large families was a violation of Article 7(2) of the Migrant Workers Regulation.

87. Case 136/78 *Auer* [1979] ECR 437.
88. Case C-61/89 *Bouchoucha* [1990] ECR I-3551.
89. Case 32/75 *Fiorini* [1975] ECR 1085.
90. Case 65/81 *Reina* [1982] ECR 33.
91. Case 32/75 *Christini* [1975] ECR 1085.

In *Even*,[92] the CJEU defined social advantages as benefits which, whether or not linked to a contract of employment, are generally granted to national workers primarily because of their objective status as workers.

In *Florence Reed*,[93] the CJEU held that Article 18 TFEU, in conjunction with Article 45 TFEU and Article 7(2) of Migrant Workers Regulation, must be interpreted as meaning that a Member State which permits the unmarried companions of its nationals, who are not themselves nationals of that member state, to reside in its territory cannot refuse to grant the same advantage to migrant workers who are nationals of other member states.

In *Commission* v *Luxembourg*,[94] the CJEU held that a Member State discriminates against nationals of other Member States if it makes the payment of childbirth and maternity allowances conditional upon requirements of prior residence on its territory, because such requirements are more easily met by its own nationals.

In *Commission* v *Denmark*,[95] the CJEU declared that, by introducing and maintaining in force a system for life assurance and pensions under which tax deductions and tax exemptions for payments are granted only for payments under contracts entered into with pension institutions established in Denmark, whereas no such tax relief is granted for payments made under contracts entered into with pension institutions established in other Member States, Denmark had failed to fulfil its obligations under Articles 45 TFEU, 49 TFEU and 56 TFEU.

3.3.5 First time job-seekers

As mentioned earlier, first-time job-seekers are not workers within the meaning of Article 7 of the Migrant Workers Regulation. They are, however, workers within the meaning of Article 45 TFEU and protected by the discrimination ban in that provision and the general ban on nationality discrimination in Article 18 TFEU. In *Collins*,[96] the CJEU stated on that issue:

> 30. In this connection, it is to be remembered that the Court's case-law draws a distinction between Member State nationals who have not yet entered into an employment relationship in the host Member State where they are looking for work and those who are already working in that State or who, having worked there but no longer being in an employment

92. Case 207/78 *Even* [1979] ECR 2019.
93. Case 59/85 *Reed* [1986] ECR 1283.
94. Case C-111/91 *Commission* v *Luxembourg* [1993] ECR I-817.
95. Case C-150/04 [2007] ECR I-1163.
96. Case C-138/02 *Collins* [2004] ECR I-2703, paragraphs 30-33.

relationship, are nevertheless considered to be workers (see Case 39/86 Lair [1988] ECR 3161, paragraphs 32 and 33).

31. While Member State nationals who move in search for work benefit from the principle of equal treatment only as regards access to employment, those who have already entered the employment market may, on the basis of Article 7(2) of Regulation No 1612/68, claim the same social and tax advantages as national workers (see in particular, Lebon, cited above, paragraph 26, and Case C-278/94 Commission v Belgium [1996] ECR I-4307, paragraphs 39 and 40).

32. The concept of 'worker' is thus not used in Regulation No 1612/68 in a uniform manner. While in Title II of Part I of the regulation this term covers only persons who have already entered the employment market, in other parts of the same regulation the concept of 'worker' must be understood in a broader sense.

33. Accordingly, the answer to the first question must be that a person in the circumstances of the appellant in the main proceedings is not a worker for the purposes of Title II of Part I of Regulation No 1612/68. It is, however, for the national court or tribunal to establish whether the term 'worker' as referred to by the national legislation at issue is to be understood in that sense.

The question may be raised as to whether the consequence of the above difference between different categories of workers is that first-time job-seekers have no social rights or whether they do have some entitlements to benefits that facilitate access to the labour market. Article 24(2) of the Residence Directive[97] provides as mentioned earlier that Member States are not obliged to confer entitlement to social assistance on union citizens during the first three months of residence or, the longer period applying to job seekers (normally 6 months, see *Antonissen*[98] cited above). This question was addressed by the CJEU in *Collins*[99] and *Vatsouras.*[100]

Collins was born in the United States and possessed dual Irish and American nationality. As part of his college studies, he spent one semester in the United Kingdom in 1978. In 1980 and 1981 he returned there for a stay of approximately 10 months, during which he did part-time and casual work in pubs and bars and in sales. He went back to the United States in 1981. He subsequently worked in the United States and in Africa. Collins returned to the United Kingdom on 31 May 1998 in order to find work there in the social

97. 2004/38/EC.
98. Case C-292/89 *Antonissen* [1991] ECR I-745.
99. Case C-138/02 *Collins* [2004] ECR I-2703.
100. Joined Cases C-22/08 and C-23/08 *Vatsouras* [2009] ECR I-4585.

services sector. On 8 June 1998 he claimed jobseeker's allowance, which was refused on the ground that he was not habitually resident in the United Kingdom. Collins contended that he was entitled to the jobseeker's allowance as a matter of EU law. Preliminary questions on that issue were put to the CJEU which held that nationals of a Member State seeking employment in another Member State fall within the scope of Article 45 TFEU and, therefore, enjoy the right laid down in Article 45(2) TFEU to equal treatment. As regards the question whether the right to equal treatment enjoyed by nationals of a Member State seeking employment in another Member State also encompasses benefits of a financial nature such as the job-seekers allowance. The CJEU has held that Member State nationals who move in search of employment qualify for equal treatment only as regards access to employment in accordance with Article 45 TFEU and Articles 2 and 5 of the migrant Workers Regulation, but not with regard to social and tax advantages within the meaning of Article 7(2) of that regulation.[101] Article 2 of the Migrans Workers Regulation concerns the exchange of applications for and offers of employment and the conclusion and performance of contracts of employment, while Article 5 of the regulation relates to the assistance afforded by employment offices. Those articles do not expressly refer to benefits of a financial nature. However, in order to determine the scope of the right to equal treatment for persons seeking employment, this principle should be interpreted in the light of other provisions of Community law, in particular Article 18 TFEU. The CJEU concluded:

> 3. The right to equal treatment laid down in Article 48(2) of the EC Treaty (now, after amendment, Article 39(2) EC), read in conjunction with Articles 6 and 8 of the EC Treaty (now, after amendment, Articles 12 EC and 17 EC), does not preclude national legislation which makes entitlement to a jobseeker's allowance conditional on a residence requirement, in so far as that requirement may be justified on the basis of objective considerations that are independent of the nationality of the persons concerned and proportionate to the legitimate aim of the national provisions.

In *Vatsouras*[102] the first question was

> 1. Is Article 24(2) of Directive 2004/38 ... compatible with Article 12 EC [now Article 18 TFEU], read in conjunction with Article 39 EC [now Article 45 TFEU]?

101. Case 316/85 *Lebon* [1987] ECR 2811 *and* Case C-278/94 Commission v Belgium [1996] ECR I-4307.
102. Joined Cases C-22/08 and C-23/08 *Vatsouras* [2009] ECR I-4585.

The CJEU stated in response to the first question that Article 24(2) of the Residence Directive[103] establishes a derogation from the principle of equal treatment enjoyed by Union citizens other than workers, self-employed persons, persons who retain such status and members of their families, who reside within the territory of the host Member State. Under that provision, the host Member State is not obliged to confer entitlement to social assistance on, among others, job-seekers for the longer period during which they have the right to reside there. Nationals of a Member State seeking employment in another Member State fall within the scope of Article 45 TFEU and therefore enjoy the right to equal treatment laid down in paragraph 2 of that provision.[104] In view of the establishment of citizenship of the Union and the right to equal treatment enjoyed by citizens of the Union, it is no longer possible to exclude from the scope of Article 45(2) TFEU a benefit of a financial nature intended to facilitate access to employment in the labour market of a Member State.[105] It is, however, legitimate for a Member State to grant such an allowance only after it has been possible to establish *a real link*[106] between the job-seeker and the labour market of that State. The existence of such a link can be determined, in particular, by establishing that the person concerned has, for a reasonable period, in fact genuinely sought work in the Member State in question.

The CJEU concluded that it follows that nationals of the Member States seeking employment in another Member State who have established real links with the labour market of that State can rely on Article 45(2) TFEU in order to receive a benefit of a financial nature intended to facilitate access to the labour market. It is for the national authorities to establish the existence of a real link with the labour market.

3.3.6 Vocational training and education

Vocational training has been an area of Community action since the Treaty of Rome 1957, education was not formally recognised as an area of EU compe-

103. *2004/38/EC.*
104. Case C-258/04 *Ioannidis* [2005] ECR I-8275, paragraph 21.
105. Here the CJEU referred to Case C-138/02 *Collins* [2004] ECR I-2703, paragraph 63, and *Ioannidis*, paragraph 22.
106. Emphasis added. See on the CJEU's real link practice Case C-224/98 *D'Hoop* [2002] ECR I-6191 and Dougan, Michael: The Spatial Restructuring of National Welfare States within the European Union: the Contribution of Union Citizenship and the Relevance of the Treaty of Lisbon in Ulla Neergaard, Ruth Nielsen and Lynn Roseberry (eds): Integrating Welfare Functions into EU Law – From Rome to Lisbon, Copenhagen 2009.

tency until the adoption of the Maastricht Treaty 1992 which established the European Union, see now Article 165 and 166 TFEU.

Under Article 7(1)-(3) of the Regulation on free movement for workers[107] a worker who is a national of a Member State may not, in the territory of another Member State, be treated differently from national workers by reason of his nationality in respect of any conditions of employment and work, in particular as regards remuneration, dismissal, and, should he become unemployed, reinstatement or re-employment. He shall enjoy the same social and tax advantages as national workers. He shall also, by virtue of the same right and under the same conditions as national workers, have access to training in vocational schools and retraining centres.

The CJEU has interpreted vocational training broadly so that migrant workers must be treated equally with nationals of the host state with regard to many aspects of education and training. Problems relating to migrant workers' vocational training are covered by the Regulation on migrant workers Article 7 (2) and (3) and the CJEU uses the general ban on nationality discrimination in Article 18 TFEU to broaden the rules.

Article 7(3) of the Regulation confers entitlements to access to training in vocational schools and retraining centres on migrant workers on the same conditions as nationals of the host state. Under the Regulation there is full equal treatment.

When Article 18 TFEU is used intermediate solutions where certain aspects are considered within the scope of Article 18 TFEU while othersare regarded as outside of EU competency can be found. With regard to higher education a distinction is made between fees for participating in the education which should be the same regardless of nationality and maintenance during the study which can be differentiated according to nationality. The CJEU considers right to participate in vocational training as a social advantage within the meaning of Article 7(2) of the Regulation on migrant workers. The Council adopted in 1993 a directive[108] on free movement and rsidence rights for students. The directive was repealed and replaced with the recidence directive.[109]

The CJEU had already before the adoption of the 1993-sirective on free movement for students developed a comprehensive case law, see *Forcheri*,[110]

107. Previously EC/1612/68, now repealed and codified by EC/492/2011.
108. 93/96/EEC.
109. 2004/38/EC.
110. Case 152/82 *Forcheri* [1983] ECR 2323.

Gravier,[111] *Barra*en,[112] *Blaizot,*[113] *Lair,*[114] *Malcolm-Brown,*[115] *Bidar,*[116] *Grzelczyk*[117] and *Förster.*[118]

L.N.[119] concerned a Union citizen who at the same time was a worker within the meaning of Article 45 TFEU and a student. entered Denmark on 6 June 2009. On 10 June 2009 N. was offered full-time employment in an international wholesale firm. On 10 August 2009, N. filed an application for education assistance from September 2009 onwards. On 10 September 2009, N. began his studies at the CBS (Copenhagen Business School). N. then resigned from his employment with the international wholesale firm, but then carried on other part-time employment. On 27 October 2009, N was informed that his application for education assistance had been rejected. On 30 October 2009, Mr N. filed a complaint against that decision with the Ankenævnet for Statens Uddannelsesstøtte (Appeals Tribunal, the Danish Students' Grants and Loans Scheme), arguing that he had the status of 'worker' within the meaning of Article 45 TFEU and was entitled to education assistance. The CJEU held:

> Articles 7(1)(c) and 24(2) of Directive 2004/38/EC of the European Parliament and of the Council of 29 April 2004 on the right of citizens of the Union and their family members to move and reside freely within the territory of the Member States amending Regulation (EEC) No 1612/68 and repealing Directives 64/221/EEC, 68/360/EEC, 72/194/EEC, 73/148/EEC, 75/34/EEC, 75/35/EEC, 90/364/EEC, 90/365/EEC and 93/96/EEC must be interpreted as meaning that a European Union citizen who pursues a course of studies in a host Member State whilst at the same time pursuing effective and genuine employment activities such as to confer on him the status of 'worker' within the meaning of Article 45 TFEU may not be refused maintenance aid for studies which is granted to the nationals of that Member State. It is for the national court to make the necessary findings of fact in order to ascertain whether the employment activities of the applicant in the main proceedings are sufficient to confer that status on him. The fact that the person entered the territory of the host Member State with the principal intention of pursuing a course of study is not relevant for determining whether he is a 'worker' within the meaning of Article 45 TFEU and, accordingly, whether he is entitled to that aid under the same terms as a national of the

111. Case 293/83 *Gravier* [1985] ECR 593.
112. Case 309/85 *Barra* [1988] ECR 355.
113. Case 24/86 *Blaizot* [1988] ECR 379.
114. Case 39/86 *Lair* [1988] ECR 3161.
115. Case197/86 *Malcolm Brown* [1988] ECR 3205.
116. Case C-209/03 *Bidar* [2005] ECR I-2119.
117. Case C-184/99 *Grzelczyk* [2001] ECR I-6193.
118. Case C-158/07 *Förster* [2008] ECR I-8507.
119. Case C-46/12 *L.N.* [2013] ECR nyr. (judgment of 21 February 2013).

host Member State under Article 7(2) of Regulation (EEC) No 1612/68 of the Council of 15 October 1968 on freedom of movement for workers within the Community

3.4 The public sector

Civil servants and employees in the public sector are workers in the sense of Article 45 TFEU, The rules on free movement of workers in principle apply to them. There is, however, one exception. Member States are allowed to restrict to their own nationals those posts in which the exercise of public authority and the responsibility for safeguarding the general interest of the State is involved. Article 45(4) TFEU states that

4. The provisions of this Treaty shall not apply to employment in the public service.

The wording of this provision seems to suggest a fairly broad understanding of what constitutes the exercise of public authority but the CJEU has put a narrow interpretation on Article 39(4). Each Member State has its own conception of the public service and, in varying degrees, restricts public service occupations to its own nationals. The CJEU has stated that the concept must have a EU law meaning and the criterion applied must be functional and not institutional, taking into account the nature of the tasks and responsibilities inherent in the post. The CJEU has provided criteria to be applied on a case by case basis.

In *Sotgiu*,[120] the CJEU ruled that taking into account the fundamental nature of the principles of freedom of movement and equality of treatment of workers in the scheme EC the exceptions made by Article 39(4) EC cannot have a scope going beyond the aim in view of which this derogation was included. The CJEU held that the interests which the exception in Article 39(4) EC allows member states to protect are satisfied by the opportunity of restricting admission of foreign nationals to certain activities in the public service. This provision cannot justify discriminatory measures with regard to remuneration or other conditions of employment against workers once they have been admitted to the public service. The nature of the legal relationship between the employee and the employing administration is of no consequence in this respect.

In *Commission* v *Belgium*,[121] the CJEU ruled that the derogation contained in Article 39(4) EC merely permits workers from other member states to be debarred from certain activities which involve participation in the exercise of

120. Case 152/73 *Sotgiu* [1974] ECR 153.
121. Case 149/79 *Commission* v *Belgium* [1980] ECR 3881.

powers conferred by public law. The CJEU provided two criteria to be applied. The first was direct or indirect participation in the exercise of powers conferred by public law and the second was that the duties were designed to safeguard the interests of the State or other public authorities. These criteria are cumulative.

Commission v *Belgium* concerned public functions in the municipal sector. It may be asked whether the public service derogation in respect of the municipalities has been changed (removed?) as a result of the establishment of Union Citizenship. Article 17 EC inserted by the Maastricht Treaty on the European Union declares that 'Citizenship of the Union is hereby established'. Article 19 EC confers the right to vote and to stand as a candidate in municipal elections on every citizen of the Union residing in a Member State of which he is not a national. This implies that the top political posts in the municipalities which are based on elections cannot be reserved for a Member State's own nationals. It can therefore be argued that when the political leaders of a municipality can be of any nationality within the European Union there is no reason why the same should not apply to top civil servants in the municipalities.

In *Commission v France*,[122] the CJEU found a French law restricting the appointment of nurses in public hospitals to French nationals to be incompatible with Article 39(4) EC. In *Lawrie-Blum*[123] a practical training scheme for teachers within the framework of the German civil service was not covered by the Article 39(4) EC. In *Allué and Coonan v Universita delgi Studi di Venezia*[124] the CJEU held that teachers in state universities were not covered by the public service exception and neither were posts in French secondary schools in *Bleis*[125] Here, a German national sought registration for the external competition to gain a certificate of competence as a secondary school teacher in France. The defence that the post fell within Article 45(4) TFEU was dismissed by the CJEU since the issue had already been settled in *Lawrie-Blum*. In *Commission v Italy*[126] there was discrimination as regards job security, promotion prospects, pay and pensions in the case of foreign workers employed by the National Research Council. The CJEU held that such posts which were not involved in sensitive research work did not fall within the public service derogation.

122. Case 307/84 *Commission v France* [1986] ECR 1725.
123. Case 66/85 [1986] ECR 2121.
124. Case C-33/88 [1989] ECR 1591.
125. Case C-4/91 *Bleis* [1991] ECR-I 5627.
126. Case 225/85 *Commission* v *Italy* [1987] ECR 2625.

In *Reyners v Belgian State*[127] the Belgian government argued that the profession of 'avocat' fell within Article 55 EC. The CJEU rejected this argument, holding that Article 45 EC only applied to activities connected with the exercise of official authority which involved the exercise of prerogative power. This definition would cover the judiciary but not the legal professions as such.

The Italian Government invoked the public authority exception in an infringement action[128] where Italy had provided that only companies in which all or a majority of the shares were either directly or indirectly in public or state ownership could conclude agreements for the development of data-processing systems for the public authorities. Italy failed in its argument and the Court held that the exception must be restricted to activities which in themselves involve a direct and specific connection with the exercise of official authority. That was not the case in respect of activities concerning the design, programming and operation of data-processing systems for the public authorities, since they are of a technical nature and thus unrelated to the exercise of official authority. In *Lottomattica,*[129] Italy repeated this argument but failed again.

3.5 Restrictions to the Free Movement of Workers

The ban on discrimination prohibits not only discrimatory measures but all measures having an equivalent effect upon the free movement of goods, workers, self-employed persons and service providers. In respect of individual persons it is in some cases doubtful whether they are workers (Article 45 TFEU), self-employed or service providers (Article 56 TFEU). In *Royer*[130] the CJEU argued that the different provisions were based upon the same principles in so far as they concerned the entry into and residence in the territory of Member States of persons covered by EU law and the prohibition of discrimination based on nationality.

In *Vlassopoulou*[131] the CJEU broadened the scope of the ban on discrimination not by applying an extensive interpretation to the prohibition against indirect discrimination but by the use of Article 4 TEU to strike down a national non-discriminatory practice which hindered the free movement. The CJEU held:

127. Case 2/74 *Reyners* [1974] ECR 631.
128. Case C-3/88 *Commission* v *Italy* [1989] ECR 4035.
129. Case C-272/91 *Commission* v *Italy* [1994] ECR I-1409.
130. Case 48/75 *Royer* [1976] ECR 497.
131. Case C-340/89 *Vlassopoulou* [1991] ECR I-235.

14. Moreover, it is also clear from the judgment in Case 71/76 Thieffry v Conseil de l' ordre des avocats à la cour de Paris [1977] ECR 765, at paragraph 16, that, in so far as EU law makes no special provision, the objectives of the Treaty, and in particular freedom of establishment, may be achieved by measures enacted by the member states, which, under Article 5 [now 10] of the Treaty, must take 'all appropriate measures, whether general or particular, to ensure fulfilment of the obligations arising out of this treaty or resulting from action taken by the institutions of the community' and abstain from 'any measure which could jeopardize the attainment of the objectives of this treaty'.

15. It must be stated in this regard that, even if applied without any discrimination on the basis of nationality, national requirements concerning qualifications may have the effect of hindering nationals of the other member states in the exercise of their right of establishment guaranteed to them by Article 52 of the EEC Treaty. That could be the case if the national rules in question took no account of the knowledge and qualifications already acquired by the person concerned in another member state.

The trend in the evolution has been that the ban on discrimination goes beyond outlawing discrimination to also eliminate other obstacles to the free movement of persons.[132] The scope of Article 45 TFEU is thereby being brought in line with that of Article 34 TFEU on free movement of goods. It is now (2013) settled case-law that any national measure which, although applicable without discrimination on grounds of nationality, is liable to hamper or to render less attractive the exercise by a national of a Member State of the freedom of movement of workers, is an obstacle to that fundamental freedom guaranteed by the TFEU.[133] In *Gebhard*,[134] the CJEU held

37 It follows, however, from the Court's case-law that national measures liable to hinder or make less attractive the exercise of fundamental freedoms guaranteed by the Treaty must fulfil four conditions: they must be applied in a non-discriminatory manner; they must be justified by imperative requirements in the general interest; they must be suitable for securing the attainment of the objective which they pursue; and they must not go beyond what is necessary in order to attain it (see Case C-19/92 Kraus v Land Baden-Württemberg [1993] ECR I-1663, paragraph 32).

132. Johnson, E and O'Keeffe, David: From Discrimination to Obstacles to Free Movement: Recent Developments Concerning the Free Movement of Workers 1989-1994 in Common Market Law Review 1994 p 1313.
133. See, to that effect, Case C-19/92 Kraus [1993] ECR I-1663, paragraph 32.
134. Case C-55/94 *Gebhard* [1995] ECR I-4165.

In *Bosman*,[135] the CJEU confirmed this interpretation which arguably implies that there is no difference between the protection of the free movement of goods and persons.

3.6 Ordre public (public policy, public security and public health)

Under Articles 45(3) TFEU the Member States are allowed to restrict the free movement of persons on the grounds of public policy, public health and public security.

3.6.1 Secondary Legislation

The restrictions on the right of entry and residence which Member States may impose on grounds of public policy, security or health are governed by secondary EU-legislation. Today (2013) the most important piece of legislation is Chapter VI of the Free Movement and Residence Directive.[136] The Directive updates and consolidates previous EU rules, including CJEU case law, relating to the entry, residence and departure of EU citizens and members of their families.[137]

Council Directive 64/221/EEC[138]contained some general rules on the application of the derogations to the right to free movement and these rules have been subject to further interpretation and clarification by the CJEU. Article 2 of the Directive applied the Directive to all measures concerning entry, issue or renewal of residence permits or expulsion from a Member State taken on the grounds of public policy, public security or public health. These grounds cannot be invoked to serve economic ends. The expiry of the identity card or passport used by the person to enter the host state and obtain a residence permit could not be used to justify expulsion from the host state (Article 3(3)). In *Van Duyn*[139] the CJEU ruled that certain provisions of Council Directive 64/221/EEC could create vertical direct effect. The CJEU ruled that the concept of public policy is an EU law concept which must be interpreted strictly but accepted that it may vary from Member State to Member State. In a later case, *Rutili*,[140] the CJEU added that a Member State cannot restrict the

135. Case C-415/93 *Bosman* [1995] ECR I-4921.
136. Directive 2004/38/EC on the right of citizens of the Union and their family members to move and reside freely within the territory of the Member States.
137. Until 2004, they were defined in Council Directive 64/221/EEC and Directives 90/364/EEC, 90/365/EEC and 93/96/EC.
138. OJ 1964 L 56/850.
139. Case 41/74 *Van Duyn* [1974] ECR 1337.
140. Case 36/75 *Rutili* [1975] ECR 1219.

right to free movement of the individual unless the presence of the individual constitutes 'a genuine and sufficiently serious threat to public policy'. Any restrictions on the right to free movement must be interpreted in accordance with the principle of proportionality. The CJEU referred to the rights guaranteed under Articles 8 to 11 of the ECHR 1950 and the fact that the only legitimate limitations which could be placed on such rights were those which were necessary for the protection of interests in a democratic society. In *Rutili* the Court was also asked whether Article 45 TFEU applied only to legislative decisions or whether it also applied to administrative decisions applying the national legislation. The Court ruled that Article 45 TFEU applied to both forms of decision-making. The court also addressed the right of *internal* free movement, stating that restrictions cannot be imposed on the right of residence or internal free movement of migrant workers except where similar measures are imposed upon the nationals of the host state.

The public policy concept was drawn even more narrowly in *Bouchereau*[141] when the Court added that the concept of public policy must always presuppose a genuine and serious threat 'affecting one of the fundamental interests of society'. In this case the UK government tried to argue that the word 'measures' in Articles 2 and 3 of the Directive did not include judicial decisions. The Court ruled that the different language versions of the Directive must be given a uniform interpretation by reference to the general scheme and wording of the Directive. The Court ruled that a judicial decision recommending deportation is a 'measure' within the meaning of Article 3 of the Directive.

Any measures taken on the grounds of public policy or public security must be based exclusively on the personal conduct of the individual concerned (Article 3(1)). Article 3(2) provides that previous criminal convictions do not in themselves constitute grounds for invoking the proviso. In order for a Member State to justify the exclusion of an individual the Court has ruled that the 'personal conduct' under consideration does not have to be illegal but the host state must have taken steps to register its disapproval of the conduct by considering it to be socially harmful.[142] In *Van Duyn* the Court was asked to consider whether membership of an organisation can be regarded as 'personal conduct' within the meaning of Article 3(1). The Court distinguished between past and present conduct. Past association cannot count as personal conduct whereas present association, being a voluntary act, can. The *Van*

141. Case 30/77 *Bouchereau* [1977] ECR 1999.
142. Case 41/74 *Van Duyn* v *Home Office* [1974] ECR 1337.

Duyn case must now be read in the light of the later cases of *Rutili*,[143]*Bouchereau*[144] and *Adoui and Cornuaille*.[145] The later case concerned the expulsion of French prostitutes from Belgium. Prostitution was not prohibited by Belgian legislation and the Court ruled that a Member State could not deny residence to non-nationals for committing acts which were not subject to repressive or other genuine or effective measures against the host states' nationals. The national court also asked for clarification of general preventative measures under Article 3 of the Directive. In the earlier case of *Bonsignore v Oberstadtdirektor of the City of Cologne*[146] the Court had ruled that a Member State could only use the public policy proviso for breaches of the peace and public security by the individual concerned. In *Adoui* the measures were taken by Belgium because it was anxious to remove foreign prostitutes from its territory because they could promote criminal activities. It was declared that the measures were of a general nature and Belgium had not looked at each case individually to discover if an individual prostitute was indeed a threat to public policy.

The issue of whether a previous criminal conviction can be used by a Member State to show that the individual has a propensity to act in the same way again in the future was raised in *R v Bouchereau*.[147] The Court ruled that the existence of previous convictions could only be taken into account and used as evidence of personal conduct which constituted a *present* threat to public policy by showing a propensity to act in the same way again. Past conduct alone could constitute a threat to public policy; it was a matter of fact and degree to be decided on an individual basis.

The public health derogation is the most tightly defined of the derogations. It may only be used to justify a refusal of entry or the issue of a first residence permit in the host state. Disease and disabilities occurring after a first residence permit has been issued cannot be used to justify a refusal to renew a residence permit or expel a person claiming under the free movement provisions (Article 4(2)). Only the diseases listed in the Annex, List A, to the Directive may be used to justify the application of the public health derogation. These diseases are tuberculosis, syphilis, diseases subject to quarantine as listed in the International Health Regulation No 2 of WHO of 25 May 1951 and other infectious contagious parasitic diseases if they are the subject of

143. Case 36/75 [1975] ECR 1219..
144. Case 30/77 *Rutili* [1977] ECR 1999.
145. Joined Cases 115/81 and 116/81 *Adoui and Cornuaille* [1982] ECR 1665.
146. Case 6/74 *Bonsignore* [1975] ECR 297.
147. Case 30/77 *Bouchereau* [1977] ECR 1999.

provisions for the protection of nationals of the host state. The issue of how to control the spread of AIDS has posed a particular problem for the Member States since any routine testing would be contrary to the free movement provisions.

It should be noted that in List B of the Annex to Council Directive 64/221/EEC the health risks of drug addiction, profound mental disturbance, manifest conditions of psychotic disturbance with agitation, delirium, hallucinations or confusion may threaten public policy or public security.

3.6.2 The Ordre Public Provisions in the Free Movement and Residence Directive

Article 27 and 28 of the Residence Directive[148] codify the above case law of the CJEU concerning public policy and public security.

Article 27 of the Directive lays down general principles. Member States may restrict the freedom of movement and residence of Union citizens and their family members, irrespective of nationality, on grounds of public policy, public security or public health. These grounds cannot be invoked to serve economic ends. Measures taken on grounds of public policy or public security shall comply with the principle of proportionality and shall be based exclusively on the personal conduct of the individual concerned. Previous criminal convictions shall not in themselves constitute grounds for taking such measures. The personal conduct of the individual concerned must represent a genuine, present and sufficiently serious threat affecting one of the fundamental interests of society. Justifications that are isolated from the particulars of the case or that rely on considerations of general prevention shall not be accepted.

Article 28 of the Directive provides for protection against expulsion. Before taking an expulsion decision on grounds of public policy or public security, the host Member State shall take account of considerations such as how long the individual concerned has resided on its territory, his/her age, state of health, family and economic situation, social and cultural integration into the host Member State and the extent of his/her links with the country of origin. The host Member State may not take an expulsion decision against Union citizens or their family members, irrespective of nationality, who have the right of permanent residence on its territory, except on serious grounds of public policy or public security. An expulsion decision may not be taken against Un-

148. 2004/38/EC.

ion citizens, except if the decision is based on imperative grounds of public security, as defined by Member States, if they:

(a) have resided in the host Member State for the previous ten years; or
(b) are a minor, except if the expulsion is necessary for the best interests of the child, as provided for in the United Nations Convention on the Rights of the Child of 20 November 1989.

3.6.3 Justification of restrictions

The CJEU's practice of justification of restrictions on the free movement is extensive. In the Gebhard case, the Court held[149] that national measures national measures liable to hinder or make less attractive the exercise of fundamental freedoms guaranteed by the Treaty:

1. must be applied in a non-discriminatory manner;
2. must be justified by imperative requirements in the general interest;
3. must be suitable for securing the attainment of the objective which they pursue; and
4. must not go beyond what is necessary in order to attain it.

In *Viking*,[150] in consistence with existing case law, the CJEU held that the restrictions that were the subject of the case could in principle be justified by reference to an imperative requirement in the general interest, such as the protection of workers, on the condition that it is shown that they are suited to ensure the completion of the goal in question and that they do not take measures beyond what is necessary in order to achieve it. In the Viking case, the CJEU left this assessment to the national court.[151]

Unlike in the Viking case, the CJEU made the assessment itself in the Laval case of whether the collective action could be justified and held that it was not the case. There is no established practice for whether the CJEU makes the proportionality assessment itself or leaves it to the national court.

3.6.4 Overriding Reasons of General Interest

A relevant legitimate consideration in the Laval case would be the protection of workers. The CJEU referred to that the protection of the seconded (Latvi-

149. Case C-55/94 *Gebhard* [1995] ECR I-4165, paragraph 37.
150. Case C-438/05 *Viking* [2007] ECR I-10779.
151. See paragraph 85 of the Viking case.

an) workers[152] and the right to initiate collective action with the purpose of protecting workers in the host Member State (Sweden) from social dumping can both constitute an imperative requirement in the general interest.[153] The consideration for the Latvian and the Swedish workers in the Laval case presumably pulls in the opposite direction. As a consequence of the Swedish actions, the Latvian employer went bankrupt and the Latvian workers lost their jobs. The CJEU also mentions the consideration for ensuring loyal competition between companies in the host country and companies from other EU Member States as a legitimate consideration.[154]

Syndesmos may be mentioned as an example of a labour market-related case where the CJEU regarded the pursued considerations as illegitimate.[155] In this case, the problem was whether requirements under Greek law that tourist guides had to be employed on a contract of employment and that the job could not be assigned to a self-employed tourist guide were contrary to Article 49 EC. Greece claimed that the requirements were reasoned on the consideration for good labour relations within the tourism field. The CJEU rejected that good labour relations as a means to stop a collective strike and avoid negative implications for the economy of a country could justify a restriction on Article 49 EC.[156]

3.6.5 The principle of transparency

Laval[157] set aside the Swedish collective action, as it was found to be obscure. As mentioned, *Laval* concerned posting of workers in connection with the completion of a public contract that had been in an EU tendering procedure. In Whereas-clause 2 in the Preamble of the Procurement Directive[158], it is provided that public contracts are governed by the principle of free movement and the principles derived hereof, for instance the principle of transpar-

152. See e.g. paragraph 107.
153. See paragraph 103.
154. See paragraph 75 of the Laval case and from previous practice case C-60/03 *Wolff & Müller* [2004] ECR I-9553.
155. Case C-398/95 *Syndesmos* [1997] ECR I-3091.
156. The Court hereby referred to Case C-288/89 *Gouda* [1992] ECR I-4007. The CJEU's interpretation in the Syndesmos case is now codified in Article 16(2), (d) of the Service Directive, see further Nielsen, Ruth: The Services Directive, Rights of Recipients of Services and the Welfare State(s), in Neergaard, Ulla, Ruth Nielsen and Lynn Roseberry (eds): The Services Directive – Consequences for the Welfare State and the European Social Model, DJØF Publishing 2008.
157. Case C-341/05 Laval [2007] ECR I-11767.
158. 2004/18/EC.

ency. In continuation hereof, Article 2 of the Directive provides that contracting authorities shall act in a transparent way. Thus there is no doubt that the contracting entity in the Laval case (the municipality of Vaxholm) is governed by the principle of transparency.

In *Laval*, the principle of transparency was extended to also being binding upon trade unions seeking to enter into a collective agreement governing the working conditions for seconded labour in connection with a tender. In procurement contexts the principle of transparency is regarded as following from the principle of free movement of services in Article 56 TFEU,[159] suggesting that transparency in relation to secondment of labour must be respected irrespective of whether the contract to be performed by the seconded labour is awarded by tender or by a private contract.

The Posting of Workers Directive[160] also aims at making working conditions transparent for employers in countries other than the host country; cf. Article 4(3), according to which the Member States shall take appropriate measures to make the information on the terms and conditions of employment generally available. It may be questioned whether Sweden (and Denmark) satisfies this obligation, but this state responsibility cannot be imposed on private trade unions.

3.7 Migrant workers and fundamental rights

If Member States put restrictions on the free movement rights of migrant workers they must respect the EU fundamental rights, see above in section Two. In *Konstandinidis* [161] advocate general Jacobs stated:

> 46. In my opinion, a Community national who goes to another Member State as a worker or self-employed person under Articles 48, 52 or 59 of the Treaty is entitled not just to pursue his trade or profession and to enjoy the same living and working conditions as nationals of the host State; he is in addition entitled to assume that, wherever he goes to earn his living in the European Community, he will be treated in accordance with a common code of fundamental values, in particular those laid down in the European Convention on Human Rights. In other words, he is entitled to say 'civis europeus sum' and to invoke that status in order to oppose any violation of his fundamental rights.

Gulmann as advocate general in *Bostock*[162] commented after referring Jacobs' view on it in the following way:

159. See the Preamble to the Procurement Directive, 2004/18/EC.
160. 96/71/EC.
161. Case C-168/91 *Konstandinidis* [1993] ECR I-1191.

In its judgment in that case on 30 March 1993 the Court did not adopt a view on that suggestion which, in my opinion, is too far-reaching.

4 EU Citizenship

EU citizenship was introduced by the Maastricht Treaty 1992. It expanded the scope of the obligation of non-discrimination and other fundamental rights on grounds of nationality to include all EU citizens in areas covered by EU law, regardless of whether they are engaged in any cross-border economic activity. Although no secondary legislation8 requires the Member States to grant the same social advantages to all Union citizens – as opposed to 'workers' – on the same basis as they are granted to their nationals, the CJEU has held in several cases that Articles 18 TFEU and Article 21 TFEU preclude nationality discrimination against Union citizens, who are lawfully resident in the host state, and that the right to equal treatment with the host state's nationals extends to non-contributory social benefits.[163] Although in some of the cases the CJEU appears to rely on the fact that the social benefit falls within the scope of secondary EU legislation,[164] in others the CJEU has clear-

162. Case C-2/92 *Bostock* [1994] I-955.
163. C-85/96 *Martinez Sala* [1998] ECR I-2691 (child-raising allowance intended to meet family expenses and automatically granted to persons fulfilling certain objective criteria, without any individual and discretionary assessment of personal needs; Article 12 EC precludes requirement that non-German nationals produce an additional document to qualify for the allowance); Case C-184/99 *Grzelczyk* [2001] ECR I-6193 (Article 12 EC precludes denial of Belgian minimex to foreign students who do not fall within the scope of Regulation No. 1612/68); Case C-224/98 *D'Hoop* [2002] ECR I-6191 (Requirement that secondary education be completed in Belgium to qualify for national tideover allowance, which is granted to assist students in the transition from education to employment, indirectly discriminatory too general and exclusive); Case C-456/02 *Trojani* [2004] ECR I-7573 (Union citizen, who does not satisfy the legal requirements to claim a right of residence under Article 21 TFEU and the Residence Directive, but nevertheless has legal residence under national law could claim the right to equal treatment under Article 18 TFEU with regards to entitlement to social assistance benefit that falls within the material scope of the Treaty); Case C-138/02 *Collins* [2004] ECR [2004] ECR I-2703.
164. See Case C-85/96 *Martinez Sala* [1998] ECR I-2691, para 45 (the type of benefit at issue falls within the material scope of EU law because it is a family benefit within the meaning of Article 4(1)(h) of Regulation 1408/71/EEC) and Case C-456/02 *Trojani* [2004] ECR I-7573, para 42 (Article 12 EC could be found to apply because the Court had previously held, in *Grzelczyk*, that a social assistance benefit such as the minimex falls within the scope of the Treaty).

ly indicated that it is the exercise of the free movement rights granted by Article 21(2) EC that affords the Union citizen the protection of the Treaty's prohibition against nationality discrimination.[165]

While this case law has clearly expanded the scope of Member States' social obligations to include not just workers and other economic migrants, but all EU citizens making use of their right to move freely and reside in any Member State, it is also clear from the case law that EU citizens' entitlement to social benefits is not absolute and that the Member States may subject eligibility to these benefits to certain objective, i.e. non-discriminatory, conditions in order to protect their legitimate interests. In two cases involving benefits aimed at assisting the beneficiary to gain access to the employment market, *D'Hoop* and *Collins*, the Court has affirmed Member States' right to impose requirements to ensure that the applicant has a real link with the relevant geographical employment market. These requirements must be applied in such a way that they comply with the basic Community principle of proportionality.

Furthermore, while recognising that Article 21 TFEU clearly does not give EU citizens an absolute right to reside in another Member State than their home state, the CJEU asserts in *Trojani*, that that does not mean that such a person cannot, during his lawful residence in the host Member State, benefit from the fundamental principle of equal treatment as laid down in Article 18 TFEU.[166] Thus, given that Directive 2004/58/EC conditions legal residence of economically inactive EU citizens on being financially self-sufficient,[167] the CJEU accepts that 'it remains open to the host Member State to take the view that a national of another Member State who has recourse to social assistance no longer fulfils the conditions of his right of residence.'[168] However, an application for social assistance may not automatically lead to deportation proceedings. Such a response is subject to the general principles of EU law, in particular the principle of proportionality.

This body of case law makes it clear that EU citizenship is not merely a symbolic concept, but rather constitutes the basic status of all nationals of EU Member States, and that this status gives rise to certain rights and privileges,

165. Case C-224/98 *D'Hoop* [2002] ECR I-6191, para 29.
166. Case C-456/02 *Trojani* [2004] ECR I-7573, para 40.
167. Directive 2004/53/EC, Art. 1(1).
168. Case C-456/02 *Trojani* [2004] ECR I-7573, para 45.

including entitlement to a range of social benefits, in the Member States where they are lawfully resident.[169]

4.1 Sources of law

The most important rules on union citizenship are found in Article 20-25 TEUF and in the Residence Directive.[170] Article 20 TFEU provides:

1. Citizenship of the Union is hereby established. Every person holding the nationality of a Member State shall be a citizen of the Union. Citizenship of the Union shall be additional to and not replace national citizenship.

2. Citizens of the Union shall enjoy the rights and be subject to the duties provided for in the Treaties. They shall have, inter alia:
(a) the right to move and reside freely within the territory of the Member States;
(b) the right to vote and to stand as candidates in elections to the European Parliament and in municipal elections in their Member State of residence, under the same conditions as nationals of that State;EN C 326/56 Official Journal of the European Union 26.10.2012
(c) the right to enjoy, in the territory of a third country in which the Member State of which they are nationals is not represented, the protection of the diplomatic and consular authorities of any Member State on the same conditions as the nationals of that State;
(d) the right to petition the European Parliament, to apply to the European Ombudsman, and to address the institutions and advisory bodies of the Union in any of the Treaty languages and to obtain a reply in the same language.

These rights shall be exercised in accordance with the conditions and limits defined by the Treaties and by the measures adopted thereunder.

Article 21 TFEU provides that every citizen of the Union shall have the right to move and reside freely within the territory of the Member States, subject to the limitations and conditions laid down in the Treaties and by the measures adopted to give them effect. The CJEU ruled in *Baumbast*[171] that Article 21 TEUF has direct effect.

Under Article 22 TFEU every citizen of the Union residing in a Member State of which he is not a national shall have the right to vote and to stand as a candidate at municipal elections in the Member State in which he resides, under the same conditions as nationals of that State. Every citizen shall ac-

169. See Opinion of Advocate General Geelhoed delivered on 11 November 2004 in Case C-209/03 *Bidar* [2005] ECR I-2119 [2005], para 28.
170. 2004/38/EC.
171. Case C-413/99 *Baumbast* [2002] ECR I-7091.

cording to Article 23 TFEU, in the territory of a third country in which the Member State of which he is a national is not represented, be entitled to protection by the diplomatic or consular authorities of any Member State, on the same conditions as the nationals of that State.

The Free Movement and Residence Directive[172] codified and reviewed the then existing EU instruments dealing separately with workers, self-employed persons, as well as students and other inactive persons in order to simplify and strengthen the right of free movement and residence of all Union citizens. Under the Directive Union citizenship is the fundamental status of nationals of the Member States when they exercise their right of free movement and residence.

With a view to remedying the previous sector-by-sector, piecemeal approach to the right of free movement and residence and facilitating the exercise of this right, the Directive is a single legislative act which amended the provisions on family reunification in the Regulation from 1968 on freedom of movement for workers within the EU,[173] and repealed a number of older legal acts.[174] The Directive streamlined the arrangements for exercising freedom of movement, which, depending on the level of integration in the host Member State, range from the right of residence without formalities up to three months, to removing any conditions or differential treatment and to putting non-nationals on an equal footing with nationals after five years of residence in the host Member State; finally, it tightened up the definitions of restrictions on the right of residence. Furthermore the Directive facilitated the right to free movement and residence of family members of a Union citizen, irrespective of nationality.

CFREU contains fundamental rights enjoyed by union citizens, see on fundamental rights above in Chapter Two.

172. Directive 2004/38/EC on the right of citizens of the Union and their family members to move and reside freely within the territory of the Member States.
173. (EEC) No 1612/68, later repealed and replaced with EU/492/2011.
174. Council Directive 68/360/EEC of 15 October 1968 on the abolition of restrictions on movement and residence within the Community for workers of Member States and their families, Council Directive 73/148/EEC of 21 May 1973 on the abolition of restrictions on movement and residence within the Community for nationals of Member States with regard to establishment and the provision of services, Council Directive 90/364/EEC of 28 June 1990 on the right of residence, Council Directive 90/365/EEC of 28 June 1990 on the right of residence for employees and self-employed persons who have ceased their occupational activity and Council Directive 93/96/EEC of 29 October 1993 on the right of residence for students.

4.2 The Right to Entry and Residence in other EU Countries

This Residence Directive lays down:

(a) the conditions governing the exercise of the right of free movement and residence within the territory of the Member States by Union citizens and their family members;
(b) the right of permanent residence in the territory of the Member States for Union citizens and their family members;
(c) the limits placed on the rights set out in (a) and (b) on grounds of public policy, public security or public health.

The Residence Directive divides the periods a union citizen can reside in another EU Member State into three periods: an initial period, an intermediate period and a period of right to permanent residence

4.2.1 The initial period, 3-6 months

According to Article 6 of the Residence Directive all Union citizens have the right of residence on the territory of another Member State for a period of up to three months without any conditions or any formalities other than the requirement to hold a valid identity card or passport. The above provision also applies to family members in possession of a valid passport who are not nationals of a Member State, accompanying or joining the Union citizen. According to the Preamble to the Directive[175] the above provision is without prejudice to a more favourable treatment applicable to job-seekers as recognised by the case-law of the Court of Justice. According to the CJEU case law, a jobseeker may as set out above in section 3.1.1 stay in the host Member State for a period sufficient to enable him to appraise himself of offers of employment and to take the necessary steps to be engaged, normally 6 months. After expiry of such period, he cannot be expelled if he proves that he is continuing to seek employment and that he has genuine chances of being engaged, see further *Antonissen.*[176]

4.2.2 The intermediate period

According to Article 7 all Union citizens have the right of residence on the territory of another Member State for a period of longer than three months if they are workers or self-employed persons in the host Member State. In no case should an expulsion measure be adopted against workers, self-employed persons or job-seekers as defined by the CJEU practice, see above, save on grounds of public policy or public security. A Union citizen who is no longer

175. See point 9.
176. Case C-292/89 *Antonissen* [1991] ECR I-745.

a worker or self-employed person retains the status of worker or self-employed person in the following circumstances:

(a) he/she is temporarily unable to work as the result of an illness or accident;
(b) he/she is in duly recorded involuntary unemployment after having been employed for more than one year and has registered as a job-seeker with the relevant employment office;
(c) he/she is in duly recorded involuntary unemployment after completing a fixed-term employment contract of less than a year or after having become involuntarily unemployed during the first twelve months and has registered as a job-seeker with the relevant employment office. In this case, the status of worker shall be retained for no less than six months;
(d) he/she embarks on vocational training. Unless he/she is involuntarily unemployed, the retention of the status of worker shall require the training to be related to the previous employment.

4.2.3 Permanent residence after 5 years

Under Article 16 of the Residence Directive Union citizens who have resided legally for a continuous period of five years in the host Member State have the right of permanent residence there. Under Article 17 of the Directive the right of permanent residence in the host Member State is enjoyed before completion of a continuous period of five years of residence by:

(a) workers or self-employed persons who, at the time they stop working, have reached the age laid down by the law of that Member State for entitlement to an old age pension or workers who cease paid employment to take early retirement, provided that they have been working in that Member State for at least the preceding twelve months and have resided there continuously for more than three years.
If the law of the host Member State does not grant the right to an old age pension to certain categories of self-employed persons, the age condition shall be deemed to have been met once the person concerned has reached the age of 60;
(b) workers or self-employed persons who have resided continuously in the host Member State for more than two years and stop working there as a result of permanent incapacity to work. If such incapacity is the result of an accident at work or an occupational disease entitling the person concerned to a benefit payable in full or in part by an institution in the host Member State, no condition shall be imposed as to length of residence;
(c) workers or self-employed persons who, after three years of continuous employment and residence in the host Member State, work in an employed or self-employed capacity in another Member State, while retaining their place of residence in the host Member State, to which they return, as a rule, each day or at least once a week.

For the purposes of entitlement to the rights referred to in points (a) and (b), periods of employment spent in the Member State in which the person concerned is working shall be regarded as having been spent in the host Member State.

Periods of involuntary unemployment duly recorded by the relevant employment office, periods not worked for reasons not of the person's own making and absences from work or cessation of work due to illness or accident shall be regarded as periods of employment.

4.3 Equal Treatment

Article 24(1) of the Residence Directive on Equal treatment provides:

1. Subject to such specific provisions as are expressly provided for in the Treaty and secondary law, all Union citizens residing on the basis of this Directive in the territory of the host Member State shall enjoy equal treatment with the nationals of that Member State within the scope of the Treaty. The benefit of this right shall be extended to family members who are not nationals of a Member State and who have the right of residence or permanent residence.

4.4 Social security rights of union citizens

Article 24(2) of the Residence Directive on Equal treatment provides:

2. By way of derogation from paragraph 1, the host Member State shall not be obliged to confer entitlement to social assistance during the first three months of residence or, where appropriate, the longer period provided for in Article 14(4)(b), nor shall it be obliged, prior to acquisition of the right of permanent residence, to grant maintenance aid for studies, including vocational training, consisting in student grants or student loans to persons other than workers, self-employed persons, persons who retain such status and members of their families.

It is thus up to the host Member State to decide whether it will grant social assistance during the first three months of residence, or for a longer period in the case of job-seekers, to Union citizens other than those who are workers or self-employed persons or who retain that status or their family members, or maintenance assistance for studies, including vocational training, prior to acquisition of the right of permanent residence, to these same persons.

Before acquiring the right of permanent residence, the right of residence of the persons concerned shall remain subject to the requirement that they are able to show that they are workers or self-employed persons or that they have sufficient resources for themselves and their family members not to become a burden on the social assistance system of the host Member State. According to Article 8(4) of the Residence Directive 4. Member States may not lay down a fixed amount which they regard as 'sufficient resources', but they must take into account the personal situation of the person concerned. In all cases this amount shall not be higher than the threshold below which nationals of the host Member State become eligible for social assistance, or, where this criterion is not applicable, higher than the minimum social security pension paid by the host Member State.

As set out above in section 3.3.5 the question may be raised as to whether the difference between different categories of workers means that first-time job-seekers have no social rights. This question was addressed by the CJEU in *Collins*[177] and *Vatsouras.*[178] The answer given by the CJEU is that one must distinguish between social assistance within the meaning of Article 24(2) and financial benefits that facilitate access to the labour market which are covered by Article 45(2) TFEU and in regard to which first time job-seekers must be accorded equal treatment with nationals of the host state.

5 Third country nationals

The Amsterdam Treaty introduced EU competence regarding immigration and asylum. Article 79 TFEU provides that the Union shall develop a common immigration policy aimed at ensuring, at all stages, the efficient management of migration flows, fair treatment of third-country nationals[179] residing legally in Member States, and the prevention of, and enhanced measures to combat, illegal immigration and trafficking in human beings. For the purposes of the above provision, the European Parliament and the Council, acting in accordance with the ordinary legislative procedure, shall adopt measures in the following areas:

(a) the conditions of entry and residence, and standards on the issue by Member States of long-term visas and residence permits, including those for the purpose of family reunification;
(b) the definition of the rights of third-country nationals residing legally in a Member State, including the conditions governing freedom of movement and of residence in other Member States;
(c) illegal immigration and unauthorised residence, including removal and repatriation of persons residing without authorisation;
(d) combating trafficking in persons, in particular women and children.

177. Case C-138/02 *Collins* [2004] ECR I-2703.
178. Joined Cases C-22/08 and C-23/08 *Vatsouras* [2009] ECR I-4585.
179. See Roseberry, Lynn: The Integration of Welfare Functions into EU Law through the Principle of Non-discrimination and the Consequences for Third Country Nationals in Ulla Neergaard, Ruth Nielsen and Lynn M. Roseberry (eds): Integrating Welfare Functions into EU Law, Copenhagen 2009.

The Union may conclude agreements with third countries for the readmission to their countries of origin or provenance of third-country nationals who do not or who no longer fulfil the conditions for entry, presence or residence in the territory of one of the Member States. The European Parliament and the Council, acting in accordance with the ordinary legislative procedure, may establish measures to provide incentives and support for the action of Member States with a view to promoting the integration of third-country nationals residing legally in their territories, excluding any harmonisation of the laws and regulations of the Member States. This Article shall not affect the right of Member States to determine volumes of admission of third-country nationals coming from third countries to their territory in order to seek work, whether employed or self-employed.

There is a special Protocol on the position of Denmark annexed to the Treaty on European Union. Denmark is not taking part in the adoption of directives on immigration and asylum and is not bound by the directive described in this section.

5.1 Discrimination on grounds of nationality with regard to third country nationals

There is no general rule in EU law prohibiting discrimination on grounds of third-country nationality. The TFEU only directly prohibits discrimination on grounds of Member States nationality.[180] Third-country nationality discrimination is specifically excepted from the scope of the Directive on racial discrimination.[181] That Directive is based on Article 19 TFEU which provides the legal base for EU legislation to combat discrimination based on racial or ethnic origin, and other factors, see further in Chapter Six. Article 3(2) of the Directive expressly provides that the Directive

> does not cover difference of treatment based on nationality.

Third country workers who are long-term resident enjoy to a considerable extent a right to equal treatment with workers in the host state but have only limited freedom of movement to other Member States. Article 11(1) and (2) of the Long Term Residents Directive on equal treatment provide:

180. Article 18 TFEU.
181. 2000/43/EC, see further in Chapter Six.

1. Long-term residents shall enjoy equal treatment with nationals as regards:
   (a) access to employment and self-employed activity, provided such activities do not entail even occasional involvement in the exercise of public authority, and conditions of employment and working conditions, including conditions regarding dismissal and remuneration;
   (b) education and vocational training, including study grants in accordance with national law;
   (c) recognition of professional diplomas, certificates and other qualifications, in accordance with the relevant national procedures;
   (d) social security, social assistance and social protection as defined by national law;
   (e) tax benefits;
   (f) access to goods and services and the supply of goods and services made available to the public and to procedures for obtaining housing;
   (g) freedom of association and affiliation and membership of an organisation representing workers or employers or of any organisation whose members are engaged in a specific occupation, including the benefits conferred by such organisations, without prejudice to the national provisions on public policy and public security;
   (h) free access to the entire territory of the Member State concerned, within the limits provided for by the national legislation for reasons of security.

2. With respect to the provisions of paragraph 1, points (b), (d), (e), (f) and (g), the Member State concerned may restrict equal treatment to cases where the registered or usual place of residence of the long-term resident, or that of family members for whom he/she claims benefits, lies within the territory of the Member State concerned.

As appears long-term residents only enjoy equal treatment with nationals as regards access to employment and self-employed activity, provided such activities do not entail even *occasional* involvement in the exercise of public authority. This is a much broader exception from the equal treatment principle than allowed by Article 45(4) TFEU for EU citizens, see above in section 3.4.

The equal treatment obligation in the Long Term Residents Directive is subject to 'may clauses' in Article 11(3) and Article 11(4) which provide:

3. Member States may restrict equal treatment with nationals in the following cases:
(a) Member States may retain restrictions to access to employment or self-employed activities in cases where, in accordance with existing national or Community legislation, these activities are reserved to nationals, EU or EEA citizens;
(b) Member States may require proof of appropriate language proficiency for access to education and training. Access to university may be subject to the fulfilment of specific educational prerequisites.

4. Member States may limit equal treatment in respect of social assistance and social protection to core benefits.

5. Member States may decide to grant access to additional benefits in the areas referred to in paragraph 1. Member States may also decide to grant equal treatment with regard to areas not covered in paragraph 1.

5.2 Agreements between EU and Third Countries

The EU has concluded agreements with several third countries which contain clauses on equal treatment as regards conditions of work. This means that nationals of those third countries must be treated the same way as nationals of the EU Member States. The most important of the agreements are the following:

5.2.1 Iceland, Liechtenstein and Norway

One of the most important of the agreements between the EU and third countries is the EEA agreement, which equates the status of EEA nationals with those of EU nationals.[182] Although Iceland, Liechtenstein and Norway are not members of the EU, their nationals can work in the EU on the same footing as EU nationals, since they belong to the European Economic Area.

5.2.2 Switzerland

Under the EU-Switzerland agreement on the free movement of persons, Swiss nationals are free to live and work in the EU and likewise EU nationals in Switzerland. Workers from some EU countries (the Czech Republic, Estonia, Latvia, Lithuania, Hungary, Poland, Slovenia and Slovakia) may, however, face temporary restrictions on working in Switzerland. Bulgarian and Romanian nationals are not yet covered by the agreement, so their right to work in Switzerland is simply governed by Swiss national law.

5.2.3 Turkey

The right of Turkish nationals to move to an EU country to work depends on the laws of that country. But in accordance with the EEC-Turkey Association Agreement of 1963, its 1970 Protocol and subsidiary legislation, Turkish workers who are legally employed in an EU country and who are duly registered as belonging to the labour force there have the following rights:

after one year legal employment they are entitled to a renewal of the work permit for the same employer if a job is available

182. The Agreement establishing the European Economic Area, 1992, O.J. 1994 L 1/3 extends to nationals of Norway, Iceland and Liechtenstein and their family members the benefit of all the EU law rules on free movement of persons.

after three years legal employment they may change employers and respond to any other offer of employment for the same occupation
after four years legal employment they enjoy free access to any paid employment in that EU country

The aim of the EEC-Turkey Association Agreement is 'to promote ... the strengthening of trade and economic relations between the Parties'.[183] Turkish nationals working legally in an EU country are entitled to the same working conditions as the nationals of that country. These rights have been the subject of numerous preliminary rulings by the CJEU, which has applied Community concepts to interpretation of the agreement. The CJEU has 'considered it essential to transpose, so far as possible, the principles enshrined in those Treaty articles [Article 48, 49, and 50 EEC, now, after amendment, Articles 39, 40, and 41] to Turkish workers who enjoy the rights conferred by Decision No 1/80'.[184] Yet, Turkish workers do not have the same rights as EU citizens, as they do not have any right to permanent resident status under this body of law. Their right to employment and residence is contingent on having the status of 'worker' or on being a dependent family member, as defined by the CJEU's case law.[185] Turkish workers do not have a right to freedom of movement to other EU countries.

5.2.4 Countries with no agreement

For nationals of these countries, the right to work in an EU country mainly depends on the laws of that country except as regards people who are the spouse or children of an EU migrant worker. EU rules do cover the following areas for workers from all nonEU countries:

non-EU nationals who are long-term residents in the EU
the right to family reunification
admission for non-EU researchers
admission for students, exchange pupils, unpaid training or voluntary service
And new EU rules have been proposed on:
the rights of highly-skilled workers from outside the EU (EU blue card scheme)
simplified entry procedures and rights for all non-EU migrant workers.

183. Article 2(1), EEC-Turkey Association Agreement.
184. See Case C-434/93 *Bozkurt* [1995] ECR I-1475, paragraph 20.
185. See, e.g., Case C-1/97 *Birden* [1998] ECR I-7747.

5.3 Council of Europe Convention no 93 on the legal Status of Migrant Workers

The Convention aims to eliminate the discrimination that exists in national legislations and to guarantee that migrant workers and members of their families are treated no less favourably than the nationals of the receiving State.

The Convention covers the principal aspects of the legal situation of the migrant workers, in particular recruitment, medical examinations and occupational tests, travel, residence and work permits, family reunion, conditions of work and transfer of savings. It also covers the issues of social security, medical and social assistance, expiry of work contracts, licensing, re-employment and the right to appeal to the judiciary or administrative authority of the receiving State.

The Convention is only ratified by 11 Council of Europe states of which six (Italy, France, Netherlands, Spain, Portugal and Sweden) are EU Member States.

5.4 Long-term Residents

The European Council, at its special meeting in Tampere on 15 and 16 October 1999, stated that the legal status of third-country nationals should be approximated to that of Member States' nationals and that a person who has resided legally in a Member State for a period of time to be determined and who holds a long-term residence permit should be granted *in that Member State* (emphasis added) a set of uniform rights which are as near as possible to those enjoyed by citizens of the European Union. In November 2003 the Long-Term Residents Directive[186] was adopted.

5.4.1 Conditions for Acquiring Status as Long-term Residents

To acquire long-term resident status, third-country nationals must fulfill the following conditions:

1. Legal residence for an uninterrupted period of five years (Article 4)
2. Possession of a minimum level of resources, (Article 5)
3. Absence of any threat to public order (Article 6)
4. Member States may require third-country nationals to comply with integration conditions, in accordance with national law.

186. Directive 2003/109/EC concerning the status of third-country nationals who are long-term residents.

They should prove that they have adequate resources and sickness insurance, to avoid becoming a burden for the Member State. Member States, when making an assessment of the possession of stable and regular resources may take into account factors such as contributions to the pension system and fulfilment of tax obligations and third-country nationals who wish to acquire and maintain long-term resident status should not constitute a threat to public policy or public security. The notion of public policy may cover a conviction for committing a serious crime.

5.4.2 Exclusion of A-typical Workers

Article 3(2) of the Long Term Residents Directive provides for the exclusion of certain categories of third country nationals from long term residents status. Third country nationals who reside in a Member State on temporary grounds, such as, au pair or seasonal worker, or as workers posted by a service provider for the purposes of cross-border provision of services, or as cross-border providers of services or in cases where their residence permit has been formally limited.

5.4.3 Equal Treatment

Article 11(1) of Long-Term Residents Directive is worded as follows:

1. Long-term residents shall enjoy equal treatment with nationals as regards:

(a) access to employment and self-employed activity, provided such activities do not entail even occasional involvement in the exercise of public authority, and conditions of employment and working conditions, including conditions regarding dismissal and remuneration;
(b) education and vocational training, including study grants in accordance with national law;
(c) recognition of professional diplomas, certificates and other qualifications, in accordance with the relevant national procedures;
(d) social security, social assistance and social protection as defined by national law;
(e) tax benefits;
(f) access to goods and services and the supply of goods and services made available to the public and to procedures for obtaining housing;
(g) freedom of association and affiliation and membership of an organisation representing workers or employers or of any organisation whose members are engaged in a specific occupation, including the benefits conferred by such organisations, without prejudice to the national provisions on public policy and public security;
(h) free access to the entire territory of the Member State concerned, within the limits provided for by the national legislation for reasons of security.

In *Kamberaj*,[187] the CJEU held that

> Article 11(1)(d) of Council Directive 2003/109/EC of 25 November 2003 concerning the status of third-country nationals who are long-term residents must be interpreted as precluding a national or regional law, such as that at issue in the main proceedings, which provides, with regard to the grant of housing benefit, for different treatment for third-country nationals enjoying the status of long-term resident conferred pursuant to the provisions of that directive compared to that accorded to nationals residing in the same province or region when the funds for the benefit are allocated, in so far as such a benefit falls within one of the three categories referred to in that provision and Article 11(4) of that directive does not apply.

Member States may restrict equal treatment with nationals in the following cases:

(a) Member States may retain restrictions to access to employment or self-employed activities in cases where, in accordance with existing national or Community legislation, these activities are reserved to nationals, EU or EEA citizens;
(b) Member States may require proof of appropriate language proficiency for access to education and training. Access to university may be subject to the fulfilment of specific educational prerequisites.

Article 12(1) of Directive 2003/109 provides that Member States may take a decision to expel a long-term resident solely where he/she constitutes an actual and sufficiently serious threat to public policy or public security. Article 12(2) lays down that the expulsion decision may not be founded on economic considerations.

5.5 Illegal immigration

There is a directive[188] of 18 June 2009 providing for minimum standards on sanctions and measures against employers of illegally staying third-country nationals.

187. Case C-571/10 *Kamberaj* [2012] ECR nyr.
188. 009/52/EC.

CHAPTER SIX

Equality and Non-Discrimination

1 Introduction

In this Chapter I will first highlight the main sources of law. Equality and non-discrimination law is a substantive area where the change in context from an internal market perspective to a fundamental rights/EMU perspective is very visible and recognized in legal practice both by the EU legislator, judiciary and legal scholars. Originally – when the EC was founded in the 1950's – EC anti-discrimination law was mainly seen as an appendix to the internal market. The EU only later developed into a more legal, political and macroeconomic union. In the proposal for the directive on Equal treatment between women and men in the access to and supply of goods and services the Commission thus stated (emphasis added):[1]

> Equal treatment between women and men and non-discrimination on grounds of sex are fundamental principles of Community law. The European Union's approach to equality has developed considerably over time, so that the original emphasis on equal pay and on avoiding distortions of competition between Member States has been replaced by *a concern for equality as a fundamental right.*

In the Council Recommendation on broad guidelines for the economic policies of the Member States and of the Union[2] the aim of promoting Inclusive growth is underlined. It is stated:

> (10) The policies of the Union, and Member States' reform programmes should finally also aim at *'inclusive growth'*. Inclusive growth means building a cohesive society in which people are empowered to anticipate and manage change, thus to actively participate in society and the economy. Member States' reforms should therefore ensure access and oppor-

1. COM(2003)657 p. 2.
2. Recommendation 2010/410/EU.

tunities for all throughout the lifecycle, thus *reducing poverty and social exclusion, through removing barriers to labour market participation especially for women, older workers, young people, the disabled and legal migrants.*

Equality and non-discrimination is an issue both in national law, EU law and public international law and has served as an area where – in particular national law and EU law – is increasingly being locked together. It can therefore also be seen as an exemplification of the change towards 'the one big system model', see above in Chapter One.

After having highlighted the main sources of law in section 2 I will discuss equality and non-discrimination in relation to the individual discrimination grounds (gender, ethnicity, etc.) in section 3-8, a general ban on discrimination in employment and occupation in section 9, exceptions in section 10 and enforcement in section 11.

EuroBarometer has recently examined the views of the Europeans on whether discrimination is widespread.[3] Discrimination is regarded as rather widespread. Ethnicity, disability, sexual orientation and gender are considered the most often used discrimination grounds.

2 Sources of Law

Equality and non-discrimination was regulated in national law in most EU Member States before their entry into the EC/EU. The topic was also regulated in public international law before it was taken up in EU law.

2.1 Public International Law

2.1.1 ILO

As set out in Chapter Two, two of the fundamental rights ILO conventions are about equality and non-discrimination in employment:

Convention no 100, Equal Remuneration Convention, 1951 and
Convention no 111, Discrimination (employment and Occupation) Convention, 1958

ILO Equal Remuneration Convention No. 100 was adopted in 1951. Article 1 of the convention provides that

3. See http://ec.europa.eu/public_opinion/archives/ebs/ebs_393_fact_dk_en.pdf

(a) the term remuneration includes the ordinary, basic or minimum wage or salary and any additional emoluments whatsoever payable directly or indirectly, whether in cash or in kind, by the employer to the worker and arising out of the worker's employment;
(b) the term equal remuneration for men and women workers for work of equal value refers to rates of remuneration established without discrimination based on sex.

Article 2 of the convention provides that each Member shall, by means appropriate to the methods in operation for determining rates of remuneration, promote and, in so far as is consistent with such methods, ensure the application to all workers of the principle of equal remuneration for *men and women* workers for work of equal value. 2. This principle may be applied by means of:

(a) national laws or regulations;
(b) legally established or recognised machinery for wage determination;
(c) collective agreements between employers and workers; or
(d) a combination of these various means.

Article 3 of the convention provides that where such action will assist in giving effect to the provisions of the Convention measures shall be taken to promote objective appraisal of jobs on the basis of the work to be performed. According to Article 4 of the Convention each Member shall co-operate as appropriate with the employers' and workers' organisations concerned for the purpose of giving effect to the provisions of the Convention.

ILO Discrimination (Employment and Occupation) Convention No. 111 was adopted in 1958. Article 1 provides that the term discrimination includes

(a) any distinction, exclusion or preference made on the basis of race, colour, sex, religion, political opinion, national extraction or social origin, which has the effect of nullifying or impairing equality of opportunity or treatment in employment or occupation;
(b) such other distinction, exclusion or preference which has the effect of nullifying or impairing equality of opportunity or treatment in employment or occupation as may be determined by the Member concerned after consultation with representative employers' and workers' organisations, where such exist, and with other appropriate bodies.

2.1.2 Council of Europe Conventions

There are three non-discrimination norms under the ECHR and its protocols: Article 14 of the ECHR,[4] which is a subsidiary provision prohibiting discrim-

4. Article 14 ECHR provides: The enjoyment of the rights and freedoms set forth in this Convention shall be secured without discrimination on any ground such as sex,

ination in the enjoyment of Convention rights. Article 1 of Protocol No. 12,[5] which is a general non-discrimination norm prohibiting discrimination in the enjoyment of any right set forth by law or discrimination by any public authority. Art. 9 ECHR[6] on freedom of religion goes further than the ban on discrimination on grounds of religion in the employment framework directive in protecting employees.[7]

The ECHR which is ratified by all EU Member States and has, since *ERT,*[8] been regarded as an integral part of EU law,[9] see above in Chapter Two, thus does not contain a self-standing prohibition against gender or ethnic discrimination or other discrimination grounds apart from religion, only the ban in Article 14 on discrimination in the exercise of the substantive rights which are protected in the ECHR. Protocol No. 12 to ECHR, which in Article 1 contains a general norm prohibiting discrimination in the enjoyment of any right set forth by law or discrimination by any public authority is not ratified by all EU Member States, e.g. not by Denmark.

None of the ECHR provisions prescribes a test of discrimination and the grounds of discrimination in Article 14 are open-ended. The ECtHR's jurisprudence has clarified that the provision prohibits different treatment of individuals in analogous situations, and equal treatment of individuals in signifi-

race, colour, language, religion, political or other opinion, national or social origin, association with a national minority, property, birth or other status.

5. Article 1 of Protocol 12 provides: General prohibition of discrimination.
1 The enjoyment of any right set forth by law shall be secured without discrimination on any ground such as sex, race, colour, language, religion, political or other opinion, national or social origin, association with a national minority, property, birth or other status.
2 No one shall be discriminated against by any public authority on any ground such as those mentioned in paragraph 1.
6. Article 9 ECHR provides: Article 9 – Freedom of thought, conscience and religion
1. Everyone has the right to freedom of thought, conscience and religion; this right includes freedom to change his religion or belief and freedom, either alone or in community with others and in public or private, and to manifest his religion or belief, in worship, teaching, practice and observance.
2. Freedom to manifest one's religion or beliefs shall be subject only to such limitations as are prescribed by law and are necessary in a democratic society in the interests of public safety, for the protection of public order, health or morals, or for the protection of the rights and freedoms of others.
7. 2000/78/EEC.
8. Case C-260/89 *ERT* [1991] ECR I-2925, paragraph 43.
9. See on gender discrimination Besson, Samantha: Gender Discrimination under EU and ECHR Law: Never Shall the TwainMeet?, Human Rights Law Review 2008 p. 647.

cantly different situations, unless there is a reasonable and objective justification. The test of objective and reasonable justification is applicable to both direct and indirect discrimination claims, unlike under EU sex equality law. It requires that there is a legitimate aim and a 'reasonable relationship of proportionality' between the means employed and the goals aimed at realising. While, so far, there has been no case challenging affirmative action, it seems that it could be justified under the test of reasonable and objective justification.[10]

In the Council of Europe Social Charter 1961 and the Revised Social Charter 1996 it is stated in the Preamble: 'Considering that the enjoyment of social rights should be secured without discrimination on grounds of race, colour, sex, religion, political opinion, national extraction or social origin.' Apart from that, discrimination is not mentioned in the Convention.

2.1.3 United Nation Conventions

CCPR (Covenant on Civil and Political Rights) was adopted in 1966 and entered into force in 1976. Article 26 of the convention provides:

> All persons are equal before the law and are entitled without any discrimination to the equal protection of the law. In this respect, the law shall prohibit any discrimination and guarantee to all persons equal and effective protection against discrimination on any ground such as race, colour, sex, language, religion, political or other opinion, national or social origin, property, birth or other status.

CESCR (Covenant on Economic, Social and Cultural Rights) was adopted in 1966 and entered into force in 1976. Article 2 of the convention provides:

> 2. The States Parties to the present Covenant undertake to guarantee that the rights enunciated in the present Covenant will be exercised without discrimination of any kind as to race, colour, sex, language, religion, political or other opinion, national or social origin, property, birth or other status.

CEDAW[11] the Convention on the Elimination of All Forms of Discrimination against Women was adopted on 18 December 1979 by the United Na-

10. See further Arnardóttir, Oddny Mjöll: Equality and Non-discrimination under the European Convention on Human Rights, The Hague, London, New York, 2003.
11. http://www.un.org/womenwatch/daw/cedaw/

tions General Assembly. It entered into force on 3 September 1981.[12] Article 11 of the Convention provides:

1. States Parties shall take all appropriate measures to eliminate discrimination against women in the field of employment in order to ensure, on a basis of equality of men and women, the same rights, in particular:
(a) The right to work as an inalienable right of all human beings;
(b) The right to the same employment opportunities, including the application of the same criteria for selection in matters of employment;
(c) The right to free choice of profession and employment, the right to promotion, job security and all benefits and conditions of service and the right to receive vocational training and retraining, including apprenticeships, advanced vocational training and recurrent training;
(d) The right to equal remuneration, including benefits, and to equal treatment in respect of work of equal value, as well as equality of treatment in the evaluation of the quality of work;
(e) The right to social security, particularly in cases of retirement, unemployment, sickness, invalidity and old age and other incapacity to work, as well as the right to paid leave;
(f) The right to protection of health and to safety in working conditions, including the safeguarding of the function of reproduction.

2. In order to prevent discrimination against women on the grounds of marriage or maternity and to ensure their effective right to work, States Parties shall take appropriate measures:
(a) To prohibit, subject to the imposition of sanctions, dismissal on the grounds of pregnancy or of maternity leave and discrimination in dismissals on the basis of marital status;
(b) To introduce maternity leave with pay or with comparable social benefits without loss of former employment, seniority or social allowances;
(c) To encourage the provision of the necessary supporting social services to enable parents to combine family obligations with work responsibilities and participation in public life, in particular through promoting the establishment and development of a network of child-care facilities;
(d) To provide special protection to women during pregnancy in types of work proved to be harmful to them.

12. See Hellum, Anne: CEDAW and the Discipline of Women s Law: Continuity and Change in the Understanding of Gender and Law in Nielsen, Ruth and Christina Tvarnø (eds): Scandinavian Women's Law in the 21st Century, Copenhagen 2012.

CERD (Convention on the Elimination of Racial Discrimination) 1965 Article 2 provides:

1. States Parties condemn racial discrimination and undertake to pursue by all appropriate means and without delay a policy of eliminating racial discrimination in all its forms and promoting understanding among all races, and, to this end:
(a) Each State Party undertakes to engage in no act or practice of racial discrimination against persons, groups of persons or institutions and to en sure that all public authorities and public institutions, national and local, shall act in conformity with this obligation;
(b) Each State Party undertakes not to sponsor, defend or support racial discrimination by any persons or organizations;
(c) Each State Party shall take effective measures to review governmental, national and local policies, and to amend, rescind or nullify any laws and regulations which have the effect of creating or perpetuating racial discrimination wherever it exists;
(d) Each State Party shall prohibit and bring to an end, by all appropriate means, including legislation as required by circumstances, racial discrimination by any persons, group or organization;
(e) Each State Party undertakes to encourage, where appropriate, integrationist multiracial organizations and movements and other means of eliminating barriers between races, and to discourage anything which tends to strengthen racial division.

2. States Parties shall, when the circumstances so warrant, take, in the social, economic, cultural and other fields, special and concrete measures to ensure the adequate development and protection of certain racial groups or individuals belonging to them, for the purpose of guaranteeing them the full and equal enjoyment of human rights and fundamental freedoms. These measures shall in no case en tail as a con sequence the maintenance of unequal or separate rights for different racial groups after the objectives for which they were taken have been achieved.

The UN Disability Convention and its Optional Protocol was adopted on 13 December 2006. It is the first comprehensive human rights treaty of the 21st century and is the first human rights convention to be open for signature by regional integration organizations such as e.g. the EU. The Convention entered into force on 3 May 2008. It is ratified both by the EU and all its Member States. It is the first human rights convention the EU as such has ratified. As set out in Chapter Two, EU is in the process of ratifying ECHR. The EU's ratification of international conventions on human rights which are also ratified by the Member States of the EU at national level can be seen as a step towards linking EU labour law, international labour law and national labour law closer together into 'one big system', see above in Chapter One.

The Disability Convention is intended as a human rights instrument with an explicit, social development dimension. It adopts a broad categorization of persons with disabilities. It clarifies and qualifies how all categories of rights apply to persons with disabilities and identifies areas where adaptations have to be made for persons with disabilities to effectively exercise their rights and areas where their rights have been violated, and where protection of rights must be reinforced. Article 2 of the Convention defines that following concepts for the purposes of the Convention:

'Communication' includes languages, display of text, Braille, tactile communication, large print, accessible multimedia as well as written, audio, plain-language, human-reader and augmentative and alternative modes, means and formats of communication, including accessible information and communication technology;

'Language' includes spoken and signed languages and other forms of non spoken languages;

'Discrimination on the basis of disability' means any distinction, exclusion or restriction on the basis of disability which has the purpose or effect of impairing or nullifying the recognition, enjoyment or exercise, on an equal basis with others, of all human rights and fundamental freedoms in the political, economic, social, cultural, civil or any other field. It includes all forms of discrimination, including denial of reasonable accommodation;

'Reasonable accommodation' means necessary and appropriate modification and adjustments not imposing a disproportionate or undue burden, where needed in a particular case, to ensure to persons with disabilities the enjoyment or exercise on an equal basis with others of all human rights and fundamental freedoms;

'Universal design' means the design of products, environments, programmes and services to be usable by all people, to the greatest extent possible, without the need for adaptation or specialized design. 'Universal design' shall not exclude assistive devices for particular groups of persons with disabilities where this is needed.

The principles of the Convention are according to Article 3

a. Respect for inherent dignity, individual autonomy including the freedom to make one's own choices, and independence of persons;
b. Non-discrimination;
c. Full and effective participation and inclusion in society;
d. Respect for difference and acceptance of persons with disabilities as part of human diversity and humanity;
e. Equality of opportunity;
f. Accessibility;
g. Equality between men and women;
h. Respect for the evolving capacities of children with disabilities and respect for the right of children with disabilities to preserve their identities.

Article 27 on Work and employment provides

1. States Parties recognize the right of persons with disabilities to work, on an equal basis with others; this includes the right to the opportunity to gain a living by work freely chosen or accepted in a labour market and work environment that is open, inclusive and accessible to persons with disabilities. States Parties shall safeguard and promote the realization of the right to work, including for those who acquire a disability during the course of employment, by taking appropriate steps, including through legislation, to, inter alia:

a) Prohibit discrimination on the basis of disability with regard to all matters concerning all forms of employment, including conditions of recruitment, hiring and employment, continuance of employment, career advancement and safe and healthy working conditions;
b) Protect the rights of persons with disabilities, on an equal basis with others, to just and favourable conditions of work, including equal opportunities and equal remuneration for work of equal value, safe and healthy working conditions, including protection from harassment, and the redress of grievances;
c) Ensure that persons with disabilities are able to exercise their labour and trade union rights on an equal basis with others;
d) Enable persons with disabilities to have effective access to general technical and vocational guidance programmes, placement services and vocational and continuing training;
e) Promote employment opportunities and career advancement for persons with disabilities in the labour market, as well as assistance in finding, obtaining, maintaining and returning to employment;
f) Promote opportunities for self-employment, entrepreneurship, the development of cooperatives and starting one's own business;
g) Employ persons with disabilities in the public sector;
h) Promote the employment of persons with disabilities in the private sector through appropriate policies and measures, which may include affirmative action programmes, incentives and other measures;
i) Ensure that reasonable accommodation is provided to persons with disabilities in the workplace;
j) Promote the acquisition by persons with disabilities of work experience in the open labour market;
k) Promote vocational and professional rehabilitation, job retention and return-to-work programmes for persons with disabilities.

2. States Parties shall ensure that persons with disabilities are not held in slavery or in servitude, and are protected, on an equal basis with others, from forced or compulsory labour.

2.2 EU Law from Rome to Amsterdam

Discrimination law is one of the oldest and most developed parts of EU labour law.[13] Until 1 May 1999 when the Amsterdam Treaty came into force, there were only explicit EU legislation on non-discrimination on grounds of nationality and sex, and as far as gender was concerned, mainly in employment and occupation. Anti-discrimination law thus started as an appendix to the internal market regulation and the prevention of competition. In the 35 years from the adoption of the EC Treaty in 1957 to the Maastricht Treaty in 1992, there was virtually no change in the EU's formal goals as formulated in the former Article 2 EC, see above n Chapter Two. By the Maastricht Treaty, which entered into force 1.11.1993, the European Union (EU) was created and the purpose as defined in the former Article 2 EC changed significantly. In the following years, the constitutional and fundamental rights dimension of gender equality has been developed intensively.

EU gender anti-discrimination law originated in one provision on equal pay (now Article 157 TFEU) between men and women, which was included in the original EEC Treaty from 1957. It has been complemented by secondary EU legislation since the 1970's. The CJEU has interpreted the equal treatment legislation reasonably expansively. During the first 40 years or thereabout of the EC/EU's existence, i.e. from the Rome Treaty 1957 to the Amsterdam Treaty 1997 EU equality law was mainly developed throught the CJEU's expansive approach to interpreting EU legislation (Article 157 TFEU and the equality directives from the 1970's). The adoption of the Amsterdam Treaty 1997 which entered into force 1.5.1999 marks a turning point in the development.

In 1957, the then EC Treaty contained only one single provision (Article 119 EEC, now Article 157 TFEU) on gender discrimination, namely the principle of equal pay between men and women for work of equal value. The equal pay provision in Article 119 EEC was inserted in the Treaty on the demand of France, which believed that there were stricter rules on equal pay in France than in some of the other original Member States of the EU and wanted a uniform level of equal pay protection in order to protect businesses established in France against distortion of competition.

13. See Haar, Beryl Philine ter and Paul Copeland: What are the Future Prospects for the European Social Model? An Analysis of EU Equal Opportunities and Employment Policy, European Law Journal 2010 p. 273. See on EU labour law generally Barnard, Catherine: EC Employment Law, Oxford 2012 and Riesenhuber, Karl: European Employment Law, Intersentia 2012.

In the first years nothing happened, but the EU has pursued a strong non-discrimination agenda since the mid-1970s and has, at EU level, given high priority to anti-discrimination. Since the mid 1970s, a number of directives prohibiting sex discrimination have been adopted.[14] Most of them were repealed and replaced by the recast directive on gender equality in employment and occupation in 2006,[15] see on that directive below in section 2.3.1.

The CJEU has played an important role in the field of equal treatment between men and women, in particular in the period from the 1970s to the 1990s.[16] The three *Defrenne* Cases[17] dealt with various aspects of the original equal pay provision in the Treaty. In *Defrenne I* the Court held that a retirement pension established within the framework of a social security scheme laid down by legislation falls outside the scope of the equal pay provision in the Treaty.

In *Defrenne II*, the CJEU held that Art. 119 EEC (now Article 157 TFEU) had direct effect as binding for private employers and that the equal pay provision in the Treaty not only had the original economic aim of securing equal competition between employers established in different Member States, but had a double aim, both economic and social.

In *Defrenne III*, Defrenne – a female air hostess – tried to rely on the equal pay provision in the Treaty against a sex discriminatory dismissal practice of her employer, the referring court asked whether the principle of equal pay laid down by article 119 EEC may be interpreted as requiring general equality of working conditions for men and women, so that the insertion into the contract of employment of an air hostess of a clause bringing the contract to an end when she reaches the age of 40 years, it being established that no such limit is attached to the contract of male cabin attendants who carry out the same work, constitutes discrimination prohibited by the said provision. The CJEU held that the equal pay provision should not be applied to dismissal on grounds of sex.

The referring court also asked whether, apart from the specific provisions of Article 119 EEC [now Article 157 TFEU], EU law contained any general

14. See in particular the Equal Pay Directive (75/117/EEC) and the Equal Treatment Directive (76/207/EEC), now repealed and replaced by the recast directive 2006/54/EC.
15. 2006/54/EC.
16. See Kilpatrick, Claire: Gender Equality: A Fundamental Dialogue in Sciarra, Silvana (ed.), Labour law in the courts – National judges and the European Court of Justice, Oxford, 2001.
17. Case 80/70 *Defrenne I* [1971] ECR p. 445; Case 43/75 *Defrenne II* [1976] ECR p. 455; and Case 149/77 *Defrenne III* [1978] ECR p. 1365.

principle prohibiting discrimination based on sex as regards the conditions of employment and working conditions of men and women. The CJEU replied that the principle of non-discrimination on grounds of sex was a fundamental right, but since the *Defrenne III* Case was about a problem (dismissal) that at the material time of the case was outside the scope of EU law, EU law on fundamental rights could not be relied upon; see the following citation from the CJEU's answer:[18]

> The court has repeatedly stated that respect for fundamental personal human rights is one of the general principles of community law, the observance of which it has a duty to ensure.
>
> 27. There can be no doubt that the elimination of discrimination based on sex forms part of those fundamental rights ...
>
> 30. On the other hand, as regards the relationships of employer and employee which are subject to national law, the community had not, at the time of the events now before the Belgian courts, assumed any responsibility for supervising and guaranteeing the observance of the principle of equality between men and women in working conditions other than remuneration.

In the infringement case against Denmark on ground of the first Danish Equal pay Act,[19] see further above in Chapter Two and Three, the CJEU struck down traditional elements in the Nordic legislative practice, namely the reliance on preparatory works of statutory law and collective agreements, as insufficient in connection with implementation of the Equal pay Directive. The CJEU held that Denmark had failed to fulfill its obligations under the EEC Treaty by placing part of the Directive's provisions in the preparatory works of the Danish Equal pay Act. It argued that the principles of legal certainty and the protection of individuals require an unequivocal wording which would give the persons concerned a clear and precise understanding of their rights and obligations and would enable the courts to ensure that those rights and obligations are observed.

The *Deutsche Telekom* Cases on equal pay were about violations by a German employer (Deutsche Telekom) of the equal pay principle by excluding German part-time workers from pension schemes.[20] Because most part-

18. Para. 26.
19. Case 143/83 *Commission* v *Denmark*, [1985] ECR p. 427.
20. Case C-50/96 *Schröder* [2000] ECR p. I-743; Case C-270/97 *Sievers* [2000] ECR p. I-929; and Joined Cases C-234/96 and C-235/96 *Vick et al.* [2000] ECR p. I-799.

time workers in Germany are women, such exclusion is indirect sex discrimination in violation of the equal pay rules in both EU law and national German law. The German rules apply to periods from the coming into force of the German *Grundgesetz* in 1949. Article 157 TFEU (ext art. 119 EC and 141 EC) is only directly applicable against employers in regard to equal pay in periods after 8 April 1976; see *Defrenne II*.[21] In *Barber*, a special time limitation at 17 May 1990 was fixed for pension matters.[22] The workers in the *Deutsche Telekom* Cases claimed equal pay for periods for which they had such a claim under German law but not under EU law. The employer Deutsche Telekom asserted that EU law on equal pay – Article 157 TFEU – should be interpreted as a maximum provision in order to protect German employers from distortion of competition by being treated by stricter equal pay standards than employers which were established in other EU countries. Deutsche Telekom did therefore not accept that it should respect the equal pay principle in pension matters for periods before 17 May 1990. As appears from the above, German law was more favorable for discriminated women than EU law, *i.e.* their fundamental right not to be discriminated against waus better protected by German law than by EU law.

The CJEU held that the equal pay provision in Article 157 TFEU [then Article 119 EC] does not preclude provisions of a Member State which lay down a principle of equal treatment by virtue of which part-time workers are entitled to retroactive membership of an occupational pension scheme and to receive a pension under that scheme, notwithstanding the risk of distortions of competition between economic operators of the various Member States to the detriment of employers established in the first Member State. The application of national law cannot be held to be contrary to the principle of non-discrimination on grounds of nationality merely because other Member States allegedly apply less strict rules. Moreover, the economic aim pursued by Article 157 TFEU [then Article 119 EC], namely the elimination of distortions of competition between undertakings established in different Member States, is secondary to its social aim, which constitutes the expression of a fundamental human right not to be discriminated against on grounds of sex.

2.3 After the adoption of the Amsterdam Treaty

The Amsterdam Treaty introduced some important formal innovations. It incorporated the requirement of mainstreaming gender equality in the EC Trea-

21. Case 43/75 *Defrenne II* [1976] ECR p. 455.
22. Case C-262/88 *Barber* [1990] ECR p. I-1889.

ty, first Article 3(3) EC, now Article 8 TFEU. It also introduced Article 13 of the EC Treaty [now Article 19 TFEU], which subsequently became the legal basis for an expanded anti-discrimination regime prohibiting discrimination not only on grounds of gender but also on grounds of ethnic origin, religion, age, handicap and sexual orientation. The new anti-discrimination regime assigns a variety of roles to a range of non-state actors. It creates, finances and operates a set of transnational networks of public and private actors. It puts emphasis on alternative remedial or dispute resolution processes in addition to judicial enforcement. It broadens the central norm of non-discrimination to include a wider conception of indirect discrimination and a range of 'second-generation' equality issues such as harassment and victimization. Finally it shifts the emphasis from a narrow negative prohibition to a set of positive obligations including the requirement of reasonable accommodation in respect of persons with handicap and a general policy of gender mainstreaming.

The adoption of the Treaty of Amsterdam 1997, [which entered into force on 1 May 1999], marked a turning point in the development of EU anti-discrimination law. The Treaty of Amsterdam introduced important innovations. In the (Amsterdam) Treaty, there were five provisions that explicitly focused on gender equality: Article 2 EC on gender equality as an objective for the EU, see now Article 3 TEU, Art. 3(2) EC on gender mainstreaming, see now Article 8 and 10 TFEU, Article 13 EC [now Article 19 TFEU], which gave the EU a legal basis to unanimously adopt legislation prohibiting discrimination because of sex, race and ethnic origin, religion, sexual orientation, age and disability in all areas covered by EU competence, Article 137 EC [now Article 153 TFEU], which gave the EU a legal basis for a qualified majority to adopt minimum directives on gender equality in occupation and Article 141 EC [Article 157 TFEU] on equal pay and equal treatment, which contains a directly enforceable right to equal pay and provides a legal basis for a qualified majority to adopt legislation (regulations, directives, etc.) on gender equality in employment.

2.3.1 Gender Equality

The 1976 Equal Treatment Directive[23] was amended in 2002.[24] The Recast directive on gender equality in employment and occupation[25] was proposed

23. 76/207/EEC.
24. 2002/73/EC.
25. Directive 2006/54/EC of the European Parliament and of the Council of 5 July 2006 on the implementation of the principle of equal opportunities and equal treatment of men and women in matters of employment and occupation (recast).

by the Commission in 2004.[26] The recast directive on gender equality in employment and occupation incorporates and updates several existing Directives: the Equal Pay Directive,[27] the Equal Treatment Directive as amended in 2002,[28] the Occupational Social Security Directive as amended[29] and the Burden of Proof Directive.[30]

Article 1 of the recast directive on gender equality in employment and occupation provides on the purpose of the directive that it is to ensure the implementation of the principle of equal opportunities and equal treatment of men and women in matters of employment and occupation. To that end, it contains provisions to implement the principle of equal treatment in relation to:

(a) access to employment, including promotion, and to vocational training;
(b) working conditions, including pay;
(c) occupational social security schemes.

It also contains provisions to ensure that such implementation is made more effective by the establishment of appropriate procedures.

Article 2 of the recast directive defines the different variants of the concept of discrimination in the same way as the other discrimination directives, see below in section 3.

2.3.2 Ethnic discrimination

On the basis of Article 13 EC [now Article 19 TFEU] a number of directives[31] prohibiting discrimination because of sex, race and ethnic origin, reli-

26. Com (2004)279.
27. Council Directive 75/117/EEC of 10 February 1975 on the approximation of the laws of the Member States relating to the application of the principle of equal pay for men and women.
28. Directive 2002/73/EC of the European Parliament and of the Council of 23 September 2002 amending Council Directive 76/207/EEC on the implementation of the principle of equal treatment for men and women as regards access to employment, vocational training and promotion, and working conditions.
29. Council Directive 96/97/EC of 20 December 1996 amending Directive 86/378/EEC on the implementation of the principle of equal treatment for men and women in occupational social security scheme.
30. Council Directive 97/80/EC of 15 December 1997 on the burden of proof in cases of discrimination based on sex.
31. See the Ethnic Equality Directive (2000/43/EC), the Employment Framework Directive (2000/78) and the Gender Equality (Goods and Service) Directive (2004/113EC). On 2.7.2008 the Commission put forward proposals for a new (hori-

gion, sexual orientation, age and disability in all areas covered by EU competence were adopted. Gender equality in employment is still – also after the adoption of the Amsterdam Treaty – governed by directives adopted on the legal bases found in the employment parts of the Treaties. The Ethnic Equality Directive[32] implementing the principle of equal treatment between persons irrespective of racial or ethnic origin was proposed by the Commission in 1999[33] as part of a series of measures aiming to combat discrimination. The Commission published a report[34] on the directive in 2006.

The purpose of the Directive is to lay down a framework for combating discrimination on the grounds of racial or ethnic origin, with a view to putting into effect in the Member States the principle of equal treatment.

Article 2(1) of the Ethnic Equal Treatment Directive provides that the principle of equal treatment shall mean that there shall be no direct or indirect discrimination based on racial or ethnic origin. Article 2(2) defines the basic concepts (direct and indirect discrimination and harassment) in the same way as in the other discrimination directives, see below in section 3. Article 3 provides on the Scope of the Directive that within the limits of the powers conferred upon the EU, the Directive applies to all persons, as regards both the public and private sectors, including public bodies, in relation to:

(a) conditions for access to employment, to self-employment and to occupation, including selection criteria and recruitment conditions, whatever the branch of activity and at all levels of the professional hierarchy, including promotion;
(b) access to all types and to all levels of vocational guidance, vocational training, advanced vocational training and retraining, including practical work experience;
(c) employment and working conditions, including dismissals and pay;
(d) membership of and involvement in an organisation of workers or employers, or any organisation whose members carry on a particular profession, including the benefits provided for by such organisations;
(e) social protection, including social security and healthcare;
(f) social advantages;
(g) education;

zontal) directive on equal treatment irrespective of religion or belief, disability, age or sexual orientation outside the workplace.

32. Council Directive 2000/43/EC of 29 June 2000 implementing the principle of equal treatment between persons irrespective of racial or ethnic origin.
33. Com 99/566.
34. COM(2006) 643. The application of Directive 2000/43/EC of 29 June 2000 implementing the principle of equal treatment between persons irrespective of racial or ethnic origin.

(h) access to and supply of goods and services which are available to the public, including housing.

The Directive does not cover difference of treatment based on nationality and is without prejudice to provisions and conditions relating to the entry into and residence of third-country nationals and stateless persons on the territory of Member States, and to any treatment which arises from the legal status of the third-country nationals and stateless persons concerned.

In *Runevič-Vardyn*,[35] the CJEU held that national rules which provide that a person's surnames and forenames may be entered on the certificates of civil status of that State only in a form which complies with the rules governing the spelling of the official national language relate to a situation which does not come within the scope of Ethnic Equal Treatment Directive. It must follow from this judgment that employers

2.3.3 Framework for equal treatment in employment and occupation regardless of religion or belief, age, disability and sexual orientation

The Framework Employment Directive[36] was proposed by the Commission in 1999.[37] According to Article 1 of the Framework Employment Directive the purpose of the Directive is to lay down a general framework for combating discrimination on the grounds of religion or belief, disability, age or sexual orientation as regards employment and occupation, with a view to putting into effect in the Member States the principle of equal treatment.

Article 2(1) of the Framework Employment Directive provides that the principle of equal treatment shall mean that there shall be no direct or indirect discrimination whatsoever on any of the grounds referred to in Article 1, i.e. religion or belief, disability, age or sexual orientation. Article 2(2) defines the basic concepts (direct and indirect discrimination and harassment) in the same way as in the other discrimination directives, see below in section 3.

Article 3 of the Framework Employment Directive provides that within the limits of the areas of competence conferred on the EU, the Directive shall apply to all persons, as regards both the public and private sectors, including public bodies, in relation to:

35. Case C-391/09 *Runevič-Vardyn* [2011] ECR I-3787.
36. Council Directive 2000/78/EC of 27 November 2000 establishing a general framework for equal treatment in employment and occupation.
37. Com (99)565.

(a) conditions for access to employment, to self-employment or to occupation, including selection criteria and recruitment conditions, whatever the branch of activity and at all levels of the professional hierarchy, including promotion;
(b) access to all types and to all levels of vocational guidance, vocational training, advanced vocational training and retraining, including practical work experience;
(c) employment and working conditions, including dismissals and pay;
(d) membership of, and involvement in, an organisation of workers or employers, or any organisation whose members carry on a particular profession, including the benefits provided for by such organisations.

The Directive does not cover differences of treatment based on nationality and is without prejudice to provisions and conditions relating to the entry into and residence of third-country nationals and stateless persons in the territory of Member States, and to any treatment which arises from the legal status of the third-country nationals and stateless persons concerned. The Directive does – according to Article 3(5) – not apply to payments of any kind made by state schemes or similar, including state social security or social protection schemes.

It applies both to the public sector and the private sector including public bodies as well as for paid and unpaid work. Member States may provide that the Directive, in so far as it relates to discrimination on the grounds of disability and age, shall not apply to the armed forces.

In *Dittrich*,[38] the CJEU ruled that Article 3(1)(c) and 3(3) of the Framework Employment Directive must be interpreted as meaning that assistance granted to public servants in the event of illness, such as that granted to public servants of the Bundesrepublik Deutschland under the Law on federal public servants (Bundesbeamtengesetz), falls within the scope of that directive if it is the responsibility of the State, as a public employer, to finance it, this being a matter for the national court to determine.

2.3.4 CFREU

The Lisbon Treaty strengthened the rules on equality and anti-discrimination. It also elevated the EU Charter of Fundamental Rights to Treaty rank. This means that the question of whether equality directives have direct horizontal effect as binding for private employers and other private entities (trade unions, etc.) now is less important since the ban on discrimination in Article 21 of the CFREU – at least in relation to the protection criteria; sex, ethnicity, religion, age, disability, sexual orientation, is likely to have direct horizontal effect, see below in section 9.

38. Joined Cases C-124/11, C-125/11 and C-143/11 *Dittrich* [2012] ECR nyr.

3 Basic discrimination concepts

One of the innovations in discrimination law delivered by the CJEU is the evolution of the concept of indirect discrimination.[39] Since 2000, the central discrimination concepts are laid down in the respective directives and are often the subject of further interpretation by the CJEU. The following concepts are used in all the currently valid equality directives:[40]

- Direct discrimination occurs '(...) where one person is treated less favourably on grounds of sex or one of the other protected grounds than another is, has been or would be treated in a comparable situation.'
- Indirect discrimination occurs '(...) where an apparently neutral provision, criterion or practice would put persons of one sex or a person affected by one of the other protected grounds at a particular disadvantage compared with persons of other groups, unless that provision, criterion or practice is objectively justified by a legitimate aim, and the means of achieving that aim are appropriate and necessary.'
- Instruction to discriminate on grounds of a person's sex or one of the other protected grounds is in EU law equated with discrimination.
- Harassment occurs '(...) where unwanted conduct related to the sex, ethnic origin, age, etc. of a person occurs with the purpose or effect of violating the dignity of a person, and of creating an intimidating, hostile, degrading, humiliating or offensive environment.'
- Sexual harassment occurs '(...) where any form of unwanted verbal, non-verbal or physical conduct of a sexual nature occurs, with the purpose or effect of violating the dignity of a person, in particular when creating an intimidating, hostile, degrading, humiliating or offensive environment.'

CEDAW Article I provides:

For the purposes of the present Convention, the term 'discrimination against women' shall mean any distinction, exclusion or restriction made on the basis of sex which has the effect or purpose of impairing or nullifying the recognition, enjoyment or exercise by women, irrespective of their marital status, on a basis of equality of men and women, of human

39. See in particular Case 170/84 Bi*lka* [1986] ECR p. 1607.
40. See the Ethnic Equality Directive (2000/43/EC) Article 2, the Employment Framework Directive (2000/78/EC) Article 2, the Recast Gender Equality (Employment and Occupation) Directive (2006/54/EC) Article 2, and the Gender Equality (Goods and Service) Directive (2004/113EC) Article 2.

rights and fundamental freedoms in the political, economic, social, cultural, civil or any other field.

3.1 Direct Discrimination

As a rule, direct discrimination is prohibited unless a specific exception applies, such as that the sex of the person concerned is a determining factor for the job, for example a male character in a film has to be a man. The definition of direct sex discrimination, as defined in Article 2 (1) of the Recast Directive[41] reads as follows:

> For the purpose of this Directive, the following definitions shall apply: direct discrimination: where one person is treated less favourably on grounds of sex than another is, has been or would be treated in a comparable situation.

There needs to be (1) a treatment based on or related to the ground of sex, which is (2) unfavourable (3) in comparison with the other sex. Women are – according to this definition – not only being treated differently as compared with men, but are also being treated badly.

Several EU rulings on direct discrimination states that the protected criterion need not be the sole reason for the employer's action to make the action directly discriminatory. It is sufficient that the protected criterion plays a role in the employer's action or decision. This understanding of the concept of direct discrimination was first established in *Dekker*[42] where an employer refused to hire a woman who had indicated that she was pregnant when she applied for the position. The employer justified the decision not to hire her with reference to the costs of hiring a pregnant woman because he would not be reimbursed by the social services for her salary during maternity leave. The CJEU held that the economic considerations in such a situation were associated with pregnancy. Therefore, there was direct discrimination because of sex. The CJEU has subsequently repeated the view that pregnancy discrimination is direct sex discrimination in several cases.[43]

In *Feryn*,[44] an employer in connection with recruitment of new employees publicly declared that he would reject applications from persons of a particular ethnic origin. Such an opinion can lead to no one from the unwanted group seeking a position with the employer. A Belgian anti-racism body ap-

41. 2006/54/EC.
42. Case C-177/88 *Dekker* [1990] ECR I-3941.
43. See e.g. Case 109/00 *Tele Danmark* [2004] ECR I-6993.
44. Case C-54/07 *Feryn* [2008] ECR I-5187.

pealed to a Belgian court, which asked a series of questions to the CJEU. One of the questions was whether there may be direct discrimination without (individual) victims. The CJEU answered that question in the affirmative.

The traditional view is that direct discrimination cannot be justified in any other way than to demonstrate that the discriminatory act is covered by an exception laid down in the Directive. The fact that an employer will incur much trouble and costs if he doesn't discriminate against a pregnant employee cannot justify such discrimination.

3.2 Indirect Discrimination

Compared to the case of direct discrimination, the possibilities for justification of indirect discrimination are much broader. The current definition of indirect discrimination was first laid down in the Ethnic Equality Directive. In the proposal for that directive,[45] the Commission refers to the definition developed by the CJEU in *Flynn*,[46] see above in Chapter Five.

In the anti-discrimination directives adopted after 2000, indirect discrimination is defined as occurring where an apparently neutral provision, criterion or practice would put persons of one sex or a person affected by one of the other protected grounds (ethnicity, age, religion, sexual orientation or disability) at a particular disadvantage compared with persons of other groups, unless that provision, criterion or practice is objectively justified by a legitimate aim, and the means of achieving that aim are appropriate and necessary. Indirect discrimination is concerned with the effects of a certain treatment and takes into account everyday social realities.

The current definition differs from the definition the CJEU had originally developed in its case law on gender equality. The Court's 'old' definition was codified in the burden of proof directive from 1997.[47] Article 2 of the burden of proof directive from 1997 read (emphasis added):

Definitions
1. For the purposes of this Directive, the principle of equal treatment shall mean that there shall be no discrimination whatsoever based on sex, either directly or indirectly.

2. For purposes of the principle of equal treatment referred to in paragraph 1, indirect discrimination shall exist where an apparently neutral provision, criterion or practice *disadvantages a substantially higher proportion of the members of one sex* unless that provision,

45. COM (99)566.
46. Case C-237/94 *O'Flynn* [1996] ECR p. I-2617.
47. 97/80/EC.

criterion or practice is appropriate and necessary and can be justified by objective factors unrelated to sex.

This definition emphasizes a quantitative criterion ('disadvantages a substantially higher proportion of one sex') and that there actually is an effect. It is not enough that it is an obvious possibility.

Compared to the newer definitions in the directive adopted after 2000, the main difference is that in the 'old' definition in the burden of proof Directive the emphasis was on the quantitative criterion, i.e. the decisive criterion was that a substantially higher proportion of one sex were treated worse than people of the opposite sex, and that there actually was an effect.

The definition of the new directives (i.e. the ethnic equal treatment directive from 2000,[48] the Employment Framework Directive from 2000[49] and the recast gender equal treatment directive from 2006[50]) has abolished the quantitative criterion. If significantly more persons from the protected group are hit, it will typically indicate that they suffer special disadvantage compared to persons of the opposite group, but it may also be the case when it cannot be shown statistically. It is no longer necessary that the negative effect is realized, only that the 'suspect' criterion is likely to have negative effect on a protected group. This interpretation is supported by the other language versions. The English version reads: 'would put at a disadvantage', the French: 'est susceptible d'entraîner désavantage' and the German: 'können benachteiligen'.

However, the new directives preserved the core of the former definition of indirect discrimination. The design of the concept of indirect discrimination is built in such a way that it matches or can be seen as a manifestation of the principle of proportionality. The leading case is *Bilka*,[51] Sag 170/84, Saml. 1986 s. 1607, where CJEU adopted a three-pronged test for indirect discrimination, which it has referred to in many later cases. It means that an employer who uses an apparently neutral criterion, which *de facto* has an uneven effect on a gender or a certain age group, ethnic group, persons with disabilities, sexual orientation, etc., must prove

1) that the chosen criterion pursue a legitimate aim,
2) that it is necessary to use it in order to achieve this goal, and that

48. 2000/43/EC.
49. 2000/78/EC.
50. 2006/54/EC.
51. Case 170/84 *Bilka* [1986] ECR 1607.

3) there is a reasonable proportion between goals and means.

Less favourable treatment of part-time workers will often amount to indirect sex discrimination against women because most part-time employees in EU countries are women. Compared to the case of direct discrimination, the possibilities for justification of indirect discrimination are much broader. The justification possibilities are designed in the same way as the principle of proportionality and like that principle provides a scope for taking diversity between the Member States into account.

Moreno[52] concerned a 66 year old woman who applied for a (Spanish) public law retirement pension. Previously, she had worked exclusively as a cleaner for a Residents' Association part-time for four hours a week for 18 years. Her application for a pension was refused on the ground that she had not completed the minimum contribution period of 15 years, required for entitlement to a retirement pension, as provided under the relevant Spanish legislation. Moreno brought an action before a Spanish court in which she submitted that the provision under which her application for a pension had been refused, entailed a breach of the principle of equality. She also submitted that she had suffered *indirect sex discrimination*, since it is an indisputable statistical fact that women workers are the principal users of this type of contract (approximately 80%). The CJEU considered Article 157 TFEU on equal pay, Directive 79/7/EEC on equal treatment in social security, Directive 97/81/EC on the Framework Agreement on part-time work and the Recast Directive 2006/54/EC on gender equality in employment. The CJEU held:

> Article 4 of Council Directive 79/7/EEC of 19 December 1978 on the progressive implementation of the principle of equal treatment for men and women in matters of social security must be interpreted as precluding, in circumstances such as those of the case before the referring court, legislation of a Member State which requires a proportionally greater contribution period from part-time workers, the vast majority of whom are women, than from full-time workers for the former to qualify, if appropriate, for a contributory retirement pension in an amount reduced in proportion to the part-time nature of their work.

In *Tyrolean Airways*,[53] the CJEU ruled that Article 2(2)(b) of the Framework Employment Directive[54] on indirect discrimination must be interpreted as not precluding a provision of a collective agreement which takes into account, for the purposes of grading in the employment categories provided for in that

52. Case C-385/11 *Moreno* [2012] ECR nyr.
53. Case C-132/11 *Tyrolean Airways* [2012] ECR nyr.
54. 2000/78/EC.

agreement and, therefore, determination of the level of pay, only the professional experience acquired as a cabin crew member of a specific airline, while excluding substantively identical experience acquired in the service of another airline belonging to the same group of companies.

3.3 Harassment and Sexual Harassment

Harassment and sexual harassment include the violation of a person's dignity and the creation of an intimidating, hostile, degrading, humiliating or offensive environment.

Harassment on the ground of inter alia race, religion, disability and sexual orientation was first included in Ethnic Equality Directive[55] and in the Framework Employment Equality Directive.[56] After that, a similar provision concerning harassment on the ground of sex was included in the Amended Equal Treatment Directive,[57] where it is stated that harassment is discrimination within the meaning of the Directive, and where this is defined as unwanted conduct related to the sex of a person occurs with the purpose or effect of violating the dignity of a person, and of creating an intimidating, hostile, degrading, humiliating or offensive environment.

The main difference between harassment on grounds of sex and sexual harassment is that in case of harassment on grounds of a person's sex, the person is ill-treated because he or she is a woman or a man. The prohibition against harassment on grounds of sex has an equivalent in prohibitions against harassment on grounds of racial or ethnic origin, religion or belief, disability, age or sexual orientation.

In the case of sexual harassment, it rather involves a person being subject to unwelcome sexual advances or, for instance, that the behaviour of the perpetrator aims at obtaining sexual favours.

3.4 Instruction to Discriminate

Instruction to discriminate may occur not only within the framework of an employment relationship, but also beyond it, for instance where an employer instructs a recruitment bureau to advertise a certain position for only men (e.g. a security officer), whereas gender is not in fact a determining requirement for the position. As examples of discriminatory examples the following

55. 2000/43/EC.
56. 2000/78/EC.
57. 2002/73/EC.

may be mentioned:[58] the Temporary work agency or Employment service bureau that accepts the condition of the principal that the temporary worker should be available for a period of six months, in which period maternity leave would not be acceptable; a cleaning company that follows the instruction that in certain homes no cleaners wearing headscarves are to be used; a hospital that knows that certain patients do not want to be treated by men and respects that wish; an employer who instructs a nightclub's security staff to keep a critical eye on dark-skinned visitors and to ask them for their membership card; an employer who knows that his employee intimidates customers of a certain ethnic origin and tolerates that behaviour; a political party that commissions a graphic artist to design a poster with texts that amount to xenophobia.

4 Gender Equality

4.1 The concept of worker and pregnant worker in regard to gender equality

In the area of Free Movement of persons, the CJEU considers[59] that 'the concept of worker has an EU law meaning and must not be interpreted in a restrictive manner,' see further above in Chapter Five. The CJEU has also interpreted the concept of worker broadly for the purpose of applying EU gender equality law and pregnancy and maternity rights. In *Mayr*, [60] the CJEU ruled that women undergoing in vitro fertility treatment (IVF) must be protected against dismissal from the start of the transplantation of the fertilized ova. When the dismissal occurs before the ova are technically implanted, the worker cannot be protected by the Pregnancy Directive, but the CJEU pointed out that to dismiss a woman because she is undergoing IVF was contrary to the Equal Treatment Directive. In *Danosa*, [61] the CJEU held that women in executive positions are workers within the meaning of the Pregnancy Directive, see further below in Chapter Nine.

4.2 Equal Pay

ILO-Convention no. 100 on equal pay provides in Article 1 b) that

58. Asscher-Vonk, Irene: Instruction to Discriminate, EGELR (European Gender Equality Law Review) 2012/1.
59. See Case C-357/89 *Raulin* [1992] ECR I-1027 and above in Chapter Five.
60. Case C-506/06 *Mayr OHG* [2008] ECR I-1017.
61. Case C-232/09 *Danosa* [2010] ECR I-11405.

(b) the term equal remuneration for men and women workers for work of equal value refers to rates of remuneration established without discrimination based on sex.

And in Article 2(1)

1. Each Member shall, by means appropriate to the methods in operation for determining rates of remuneration, promote and, in so far as is consistent with such methods, ensure the application to all workers of the principle of equal remuneration for men and women workers for work of equal value.

Article 157 TFEU provides (emphasis added):

1. Each Member State shall ensure that the principle of equal pay for male and female workers for equal work or *work of equal value* is applied.

2. For the purpose of this Article, 'pay' means the ordinary basic or minimum wage or salary and any other consideration, whether in cash or in kind, which the worker receives directly or indirectly, in respect of his employment, from his employer. Equal pay without discrimination based on sex means:
(a) that pay for the same work at piece rates shall be calculated on the basis of the same unit of measurement;
(b) that pay for work at time rates shall be the same for the same job.

In the preamble to the recast directive[62] it is stated that in accordance with settled case-law of the CJEU, in order to assess whether workers are performing the same work or work of equal value, it should be determined whether, having regard to a range of factors including the nature of the work and training and working conditions, those workers may be considered to be in a comparable situation. The CJEU has established that, in certain circumstances, the principle of equal pay is not limited to situations in which men and women work for the same employer.[63] The Member States, in collaboration with the social partners, should continue to address the problem of the continuing gender-based wage differentials and marked gender segregation on the labour market by means such as flexible working time arrangements which enable both men and women to combine family and work commitments more successfully. This could also include appropriate parental leave arrangements which could be taken up by either parent as well as the provision of accessible and affordable child-care facilities and care for dependent persons.

62. See point 9-11 in the Preamble to 2006/54/EC.
63. See Case C-320/00 *Lawrence* [2002] ECR I-7325.

Article 157 TFEU is complemented by the equal pay provision in Article 4 of the recast directive.[64] That Article reads:

For the same work or for work to which equal value is attributed, direct and indirect discrimination on grounds of sex with regard to all aspects and conditions of remuneration shall be eliminated. In particular, where a job classification system is used for determining pay, it shall be based on the same criteria for both men and women and so drawn up as to exclude any discrimination on grounds of sex.

The CJEU has decided many cases on equal pay.

4.2.1 The definition of pay

Article 157 TFEU on equal pay for men and women equal work or work of equal value, states in its second paragraph that:

'For the purpose of this Article, 'pay' means the ordinary basic or minimum wage or salary and any other consideration, whether in cash or in kind, which the worker receives directly or indirectly, in respect of his employment, from his employer.'

According to the case law of the CJEU[65] on this provision, pay includes not only basic pay, but also, for example, overtime supplements, special bonuses paid by the employer, travel facilities, compensation for attending training courses and training facilities, termination payments in case of dismissal and occupational pensions.

4.2.2 Pay, pensions and social security

Old age pensions are in most countries based on a three pillars scheme: i.e. there are statutory social security schemes,[66] occupational pension schemes which at EU level are governed by Article 157 TFEU and Article 4 of the recast directive on gender equality in employment and occupation[67] – in some countries based on collective agreements – and on private insurances.[68]

64. 2006/54/EC.
65. See for example Case C-300/06 *Voß* [2007] ECR I-10573, Case C-333/97 *Lewen* [1999] ECR I-7243, Case 12/81 *Garland* [1982] ECR 359, Case C-360/90 *Bötel* [1992] ECR I-3589, Case C-33/89 *Kowalska* [1990] ECR I-2591, Case 170/84 *Bilka* [1986] ECR 1607, Case C-262/88 *Barber* [1990] ECR I-1889.
66. At EU level governed by 79/7/EEC on gender equality in statutory social security schemes.
67. 2006/54/EC.
68. At EU level governed by 2004/113/EC.

In *Moreno*,[69] a woman applied for a retirement pension. Previously, she had worked as a cleaner part-time for four hours a week for 18 years. Her application for a pension was refused on the ground that she had not completed the minimum contribution period of 15 years, required for entitlement to a retirement pension. The preliminary issue raised by the questions referred by the national court is whether a pension such as that at issue in the main proceedings falls within the scope of Clause 4 of the Framework Agreement on part-time,[70] Article 157 TFEU on equal pay for men and women, Article 4 of the recast directive on gender equality in employment and occupation[71] and/or of Article 4 of the gender equality directive on social security.[72]

The CJEU stated that it should be noted that 'pay' within the meaning of Article 157(2) TFEU covers pensions which depend on the employment relationship between worker and employer, excluding those deriving from a statutory scheme, to the financing of which workers, employers and possibly the public authorities contribute in a measure determined less by the employment relationship than by considerations of social policy.[73] Accordingly, that concept cannot be extended to encompass social security schemes or benefits – such as retirement pensions – which are directly governed by statute to the exclusion of any element of negotiation within the undertaking or occupational sector concerned and which are obligatorily applicable to general categories of employee.[74] Similarly, 'employment conditions' for the purposes of Clause 4(1) of the Framework Agreement covers pensions which depend on an employment relationship between worker and employer, excluding statutory social security pensions, which are determined less by that relationship than by considerations of social policy. A pension such as that at issue in the main proceedings – which is the most general of the pensions regulated by Spanish law – appears to be determined less by an employment relationship between worker and employer than by considerations of social policy, in accordance with the case-law cited in paragraphs 20 and 21 above, and to which

69. Case C-385/11 *Moreno* [2012] ECR nyr.
70. See Directive 97/81/EC of 15 December 1997 concerning the Framework Agreement on part-time work concluded by UNICE, CEEP and the ETUC.
71. 2006/54/EC.
72. 79/7/EEC.
73. See Joined Cases C-395/08 and C-396/08 *Bruno and Others* [2010] ECR I-5119, paragraph 41 and the case-law cited.
74. See Case C-366/99 *Griesmar* [2001] ECR I-9383, paragraph 27 and the case-law cited.

Article 157 TFEU and Clause 4 of the Framework Agreement therefore do not apply. The CJEU held:

Article 4 of Council Directive 79/7/EEC of 19 December 1978 on the progressive implementation of the principle of equal treatment for men and women in matters of social security must be interpreted as precluding, in circumstances such as those of the case before the referring court, legislation of a Member State which requires a proportionally greater contribution period from part-time workers, the vast majority of whom are women, than from full-time workers for the former to qualify, if appropriate, for a contributory retirement pension in an amount reduced in proportion to the part-time nature of their work.

4.2.3 Job classification systems

Rummler[75] was about an employer's freedom to reward muscle strength on the basis of a pay system that was based on men's muscle power as the norm and only assessed the work as strenuous if it was strenuous for a person with average male muscles. Gisela Rummler was employed as a skilled worker in a printing plant. She was paid according to a pay system that graded salary after the heavy loads the work entailed. The national court asked whether the Equal Pay Directive of 1975[76] entailed that the professional classification systems should not differentiate the wages in accordance with a) the extent to which a job requires/strains muscles and b) whether a job is hard or not. The CJEU held that

(1) Council Directive 75/117 of 10 February 1975 on the approximation of the laws of the Member States relating to the application of the principle of equal pay for men and women does not prohibit the use, in a job classification system for the purpose of determining rates of pay, of the criterion of muscle demand or muscular effort or that of the heaviness of the work if, in view of the nature of the tasks involved, the work to be performed does require the use of a certain degree of physical strength, so long as the system as a whole, by taking into account other criteria, precludes any discrimination on grounds of sex.

(2) It follows from Directive 75/117 that:
(a) the criteria governing pay rate classification must ensure that the work which is objectively the same attracts the same rate of pay whether it is performed by a man or a woman;
(b) the use of values reflecting the average performance of workers of one sex as a basis for determining the extent to which work makes demands or requires effort or whether it is heavy constitutes a form of discrimination on grounds of sex, contrary to the directive;

75. Case 237/85 *Rummler* [1986] ECR 2101.
76. 75/117/EEC, now repealed and replaced by the recast directive 2006/54/EC.

(c) in order for a job classification system not to be discriminatory as a whole, it must, in so far as the nature of the tasks carried out in the undertaking permits, take into account criteria for which workers of each sex may show particular aptitude.

There is no duty to use job classification systems. If the employer does that – possibly in accordance with a collective agreement – it must be based on an overall assessment. It follows from the equal pay provisions that the system as a whole must take into account criteria for which workers of each sex may show particular aptitude. If dexterity is job relevant it should also be rewarded.

In *Brunnhofer*,[77] the CJEU ruled that the principle of equal pay for men and women laid down in Article 157 TFEU and elaborated in the recast directive must be interpreted as follows:

- a monthly salary supplement to which the employees concerned are entitled under their individual employment contracts, paid by the employer in respect of their employment, constitutes pay within the scope of Article 157 TFEU and the Directive; equal pay must be ensured not only on the basis of an overall assessment of all the consideration granted to employees but also in the light of each aspect of pay taken in isolation;
- the fact that a female employee who claims to be the victim of discriminationon grounds of sex and the male comparator are classified in the same job category under the collective agreement governing their employment is not in itself sufficient for concluding that the two employees concerned are performing the same work or work to which equal value is attributed within the meaning of Article 119 of the Treaty and Article 1 of the Directive, since this fact is only one indication amongst others that this criterion is met;
- as a general rule, it is for employees who consider themselves to be the victims of discrimination to prove that they are receiving lower pay than that paid by the employer to a colleague of the other sex and that they are in fact performing the same work or work of equal value, comparable to that performed by the chosen comparator; the employer may then not only dispute the fact that the conditions for the application of the principle of equal pay for men and women are met in the case but also put forward objective grounds, unrelated to any discrimination based on sex, to justify the difference in pay;

77. Case C-381/99 *Brunnhofer* [2001] ECR I-4961.

- a difference in pay is capable of being justified by circumstances not taken into consideration under the collective agreement applicable to the employees concerned, provided that they constitute objective reasons unrelated to any discrimination based on sex and in conformity with the principle of proportionality;
- in the case of work paid at time rates, a difference in pay awarded, at the time of their appointment, to two employees of different sex for the same job or work of equal value cannot be justified by factors which become known only after the employees concerned take up their duties and which can be assessed only once the employment contract is being performed, such as a difference in the individual work capacity of the persons concerned or in the effectiveness of the work of a specific employee compared with that of a colleague.

4.2.4 Education and vocational training

Differences in education/vocational training will often justify differences in wages. In *Danfoss*,[78] which was about equal work and work of equal value, the CJEU held that the employer can only reward a special training if it is shown that such training is relevant for the performance of the employee's specific tasks. This applies regardless of whether female employees generally have a lower academic level of education than men, and the criterion therefore have gender-biased effect. In *Wiener Gebietskrankenkasse*[79] where apparently the same work was done by workers with different skills – in the case of doctors and psychologists – the CJEU held that there was no question of equal work. The psychologists were placed on the same level as office workers, nurses and dental technicians, while doctors authorized to act as specialists were classified as other doctors and dentists. The CJEU held that there is no question of equal work when the same employment is exercised over a longer period of workers with different skills. The reason was that the two groups of workers were not in a comparable situation, because the two groups had different training and as a result, different skills, which had been the basis of their employment, to perform various tasks or functions.

4.2.5 Seniority/Experience

It has, after the CJEU judgment in *Danfoss*, been assumed that seniority can be used as justification for pay differences, without the employer having to

78. Case C-109/88 *Danfoss* [1989] 3199.
79. Case C-309/97 *Wiener Gebietskrankenkasse* [1999] ECR I-2865.

establish the importance of seniority for the fulfillment of the particular job. The CJEU modified this interpretation in *Nimz*[80] The CJEU stated as follows:

> Although experience goes hand in hand with length of service, and experience enables the worker in principle to improve performance of the tasks allotted to him, the objectivity of such a criterion depends on all the circumstances in a particular case, and in particular on the relationship between the nature of the work performed and the experience gained from the performance of that work upon completion of a certain number of working hours. However, it is a matter for the national court, which alone is competent to evaluate the facts, to determine in the light of all the circumstances whether and to what extent a provision in a collective agreement such as that here at issue is based on objectively justified factors unrelated to any discrimination on grounds of sex.

The CJEU thus indicated that seniority must not always be accepted as an objective criterion, as this depends on all the circumstances of the case, particularly how long experience has been achieved. In some cases, it is considered so obvious that a criterion is likely to fulfill a legitimate objective that the employer does not have to prove that the concrete criterion is suitable and lawful, unless there are specific reasons which militate against it. In *Cadman*,[81] the CJEU held that in situations where the use of seniority in determining pay leads to wage differentials between men and women for equal work or work of equal value, the employer shall not establish specifically that recourse to the criterion of seniority is suitable to achieve this purpose, unless the worker provides evidence that can give rise to serious doubts in that regard. This is because seniority is usually suitable to attain the legitimate objective of rewarding experience acquired which enables the worker to perform his duties better.

4.2.6 Part time discrimination as indirect sex discrimination

The CJEU has developed a comprehensive case law on discrimination of full-time and part-time employees as indirect sex discrimination.[82] There is also

80. Case C-184/89 *Nimz* [1991] I-297.
81. Case C-17/05 *Cadman* [2006] ECR I-9583.
82. See in particular Case 170/84 *Bilka* [1986] ECR 1607, Case C-171/88 *Rinner-Kühn* [1989] ECR 2743, Case C-167/97 *Seymour-Smith* [1999] ECR I-623, Case C-278/93 *Freers and Speckmann* [1996] ECR I-1165, Case C-243/95 *Hill and Stapleton* [1998] ECR I-3739, and Joined Cases C-279/96 to C-281/96 *Ansaldo Energia and Others* [1998] ECR I-5025.

case law on discrimination against part-time employees in violation of the part-time directive,[83] see on that directive further below in Chapter Seven.

4.2.7 Part time and overtime payment

In *Helmig*,[84] the CJEU held held that there is no difference in treatment between part-time workers and full-time workers where the relevant national provisions provide for overtime supplements only in respect of hours worked in addition to normal working hours as fixed by collective agreement, and not in respect of those worked in addition to the normal working hours fixed for an individual. The CJEU found that, in those circumstances, part-time employees do, in fact, receive the same overall pay as full-time employees for the same number of hours worked, and that is so both where the hours worked by the part-time employee do not exceed the normal working hours as fixed by collective agreement and where they do, since the overtime supplements provided for in the latter situation are payable to both categories of worker.

By contrast, in *Elsner-Lakeberg*,[85] the CJEU held that there is a difference in treatment between part-time and full-time workers where the applicable national provisions provide that all workers are required to work a minimum of three hours per month over and above their own normal working hours in order to be able to claim an overtime supplement. In that case, Elsner-Lakeberg, who was a teacher, taught for 15 hours per week, while full-time teachers taught for 24.5 hours per week. Ms Elsner-Lakeberg had worked 2.5 hours overtime during one month. Accordingly, she was not entitled to remuneration for that overtime. As a result, she was paid on the basis of 15 teaching hours even though she had worked 17.5 hours. By contrast, a full-time teacher who had worked 17.5 teaching hours was paid for 17.5 teaching hours, given that he had not exceeded his normal weekly working hours. The Court held that there was a difference in treatment as regards remuneration since, for an equal number of teaching hours worked, part-time workers were less well paid than full-time workers.

In *Voß*,[86] the national provision at issue provided A civil servant is obliged to work without remuneration beyond his normal weekly working hours if mandatory job-related circumstances require him to do so and the overtime is limited to exceptional cases. If he is obliged to work for more than five hours

83. 97/81/EC.
84. C-78/93 *Helmig and Others* [1994] ECR I-5727.
85. Case C-285/02 *Elsner-Lakeberg* [2004] ECR I-5861.
86. Case C-300/06 *Voß* [2007] ECR I-10573.

per month outside of normal working hours on account of additional work which is required or sanctioned for job purposes, then he shall be granted, within three months, extra leave corresponding to the overtime worked. If extra leave is not possible for mandatory job-related reasons, civil servants in grades in which remuneration is proportional to seniority may instead receive pay for a period of up to 480 hours per year.

Thus, a part-time teacher whose normal weekly working hours are 23 teaching hours per week and who works 3.5 hours over and above those normal working hours receives less pay than that received by a full-time teacher for 26.5 teaching hours. The CJEU held:

> Article 141 EC [now Article 157 TFEU] is to be interpreted as precluding national legislation on the remuneration of civil servants, such as that at issue in the main proceedings – which defines overtime, for both full-time civil servants and part-time civil servants, as hours worked over and above their normal working hours, and which remunerates those additional hours at a rate lower than the hourly rate applied to their normal working hours, so that part-time civil servants are less well paid than full-time civil servants in respect of hours which are worked over and above their normal working hours, but which are not sufficient to bring the number of hours worked overall above the level of normal working hours for full-time civil servants – where:
> – in the group of workers subject to that legislation, a considerably higher percentage of women is affected as compared with the percentage of men so affected; and
> – the difference in treatment is not justified by objective factors wholly unrelated to discrimination based on sex.

4.3 Equal treatment as regards access to employment, vocational training and promotion and working conditions

The Recast Directive on gender equality in employment and occupation provides for the principle of equal treatment between women and men which means that there should be no discrimination whatsoever – direct or indirect – on grounds of sex.

4.3.1 Prohibition of discrimination

Article 14 of the recast directive provides that there shall be no direct or indirect discrimination on grounds of sex in the public or private sectors, including public bodies, in relation to:

> (a) conditions for access to employment, to self-employment or to occupation, including selection criteria and recruitment conditions, whatever the branch of activity and at all levels of the professional hierarchy, including promotion;
> (b) access to all types and to all levels of vocational guidance, vocational training, advanced vocational training and retraining, including practical work experience;

(c) employment and working conditions, including dismissals, as well as pay as provided for in Article 141 of the Treaty;
(d) membership of, and involvement in, an organisation of workers or employers, or any organisation whose members carry on a particular profession, including the benefits provided for by such organisations.

Member States may provide, as regards access to employment including the training leading thereto, that a difference of treatment which is based on a characteristic related to sex shall not constitute discrimination where, by reason of the nature of the particular occupational activities concerned or of the context in which they are carried out, such a characteristic constitutes a genuine and determining occupational requirement, provided that its objective is legitimate and the requirement is proportionate.

4.3.2 Return from maternity leave

Article 15 of the recast directive provides that a woman on maternity leave shall be entitled, after the end of her period of maternity leave, to return to her job or to an equivalent post on terms and conditions which are no less favourable to her and to benefit from any improvement in working conditions to which she would have been entitled during her absence.

4.3.3 Different Dismissal ages for men and women

In *Marshall*,[87] the CJEU held that a general policy concerning dismissal involving the dismissal of a woman solely because she has attained the qualifying age for a state pension, which age is different under national legislation for men and for women, constitutes discrimination on grounds of sex, contrary to the recast directive on gender equality in employment and occupation.

4.4 Pregnancy and maternity/paternity related issues

Since the early 1990s, protection of pregnancy, maternity and parenthood has been one of the aims of EU law.[88] For this purpose a complex array of primary (Treaty provisions) and secondary (mostly directives) legislation has been gradually developed. Article 2(2)(c) of the Recast Directive provides that the definition of discrimination includes 'any less favourable treatment of a woman related to pregnancy or maternity leave'. In addition, there are several

87. Case 152/84 *Marshall* [1986] ECR 723.
88. See in particular Council Directive 92/85/EEC of 19 October 1992 on the introduction of measures to encourage improvements in the safety and health at work of pregnant workers and workers who have recently given birth or are breastfeeding, OJ [1992] L348/1.

soft law and political initiatives. The case law of the CJEU, has also largely contributed to the development of this area of law.

The Pregnancy Directive[89] is primarily aimed at improving health and safety at work for pregnant workers, workers who have recently given birth and workers who are breastfeeding. It provides for two sorts of measures, namely health and safety and protection against unfavourable treatment on grounds of pregnancy. See on the health and safety measures below in Chapter Nine. The discrimination issues including dismissal, harassment, refusal to renew fixed-term contracts of employment or to recruit and detrimental changes in the terms of the contract of employment upon return from maternity leave. Amendments to the Pregnant Workers Directive[90] have been proposed by the European Commission as part of the 2008 Work-Life Balance Packet,[91] which includes a number of proposed measures concerning the reconciliation of work and family life designed to modernise and rationalise reconciliation policies and ultimately to bring them in line with the existing equality legislation and case law. The amendments include, *inter alia*, a longer period of paid maternity leave and a new period of paternity leave. There is, however, considerable disagreement among the Member States about the proposal. At the time of writing it is uncertain what will happen to it.

4.4.1 Discrimination in the access to employment – recruitment process and monitoring

Since the decision in *Dekker*,[92] the CJEU has established two principles. First, as only women can become pregnant, the refusal to engage a pregnant woman because of pregnancy or maternity amounts to direct discrimination. To qualify dismissal on grounds of pregnancy as direct discrimination means, in principle, that it cannot be justified in any way, in particular by economic considerations,[93] except with explicit exemptions.[94] Second, in certain cir-

89. Council Directive 92/85/EEC on the introduction of measures to encourage improvements in the safety and health at work of pregnant workers and workers who have recently given birth or are breastfeeding.
90. Proposal for a Directive of the European Parliament and of the Council amending Council Directive 92/85/EEC on the introduction of measures to encourage improvements in the safety and health at work of pregnant workers and workers who have recently given birth or are breastfeeding, COM(2008) 637.
91. EU Commission, COM(2008) 635.
92. Case C-177/88 *Dekker* [1990] ECR I-3941.
93. See for example Case C-343/92 *M.A. De Weerd* [1994] ECR I-571.
94. Case 248/83 *Commission* v *Germany* [1985] ECR 1459; Case 222/84 *Johnston* [1986] ECR 1651.

cumstances, such as pregnancy, a male comparator is not necessary. This is reflected also in Article 15 of the Recast Directive, which provides that at the end of her maternity leave a woman is entitled 'to return to her job or to an equivalent post on terms and conditions which are no less favourable to her and to benefit from any improvement in working conditions to which she would have been entitled during her absence'. By now these principles appear to have been embedded in the relevant domestic legislation of the Member states.

The CJEU has developed the framework of legislative rights relating to pregnancy, maternity, parental and paternity leaves by providing a broad interpretation of these rights. In the early cases of *Dekker*[95] and *Hertz*,[96] the CJEU established that as only women can become pregnant, a refusal to employ or the dismissal of a pregnant woman based on her pregnancy or her maternity amounts to direct discrimination on the grounds of sex, contrary to Article 2(2) of the Recast Directive).[97] On the basis of this principle, the CJEU has further held that any unfavourable treatment directly[98] or indirectly[99] connected to pregnancy or maternity constitutes direct sex discrimination. In addition, the CJEU has held that the protection of pregnancy and maternity rights is aimed at promoting substantive gender equality,[100] the health of mother directly following the birth of a child and the relationship between the new mother and her new-borns[101] as well as between a father and his child.[102] The CJEU has also made it clear on several instances, most notably in the decision in *Hill*[103] that the principle of reconciliation between work and family life is a corollary of the principle of equality. The specific protection against dismissal of pregnant and new mothers, start from the moment the employer is informed of the pregnancy until the return of the worker to work following

95. Cases C-177/88 *Dekker* [1990] ECR I-3941.
96. C-179/88 *Hertz* ECR I-3979.
97. See C-320/01 *Busch* [2003] ECR I-2041 and C-394/96 *Brown [*1998] ECR I-4185.
98. Case C-32/93 *Webb* [1994] ECR I-3567.
99. Case C-421/92 *Habermann-Beltermann* [1994] ECR I-1657.
100. Cases C-207/98 *Mahlburg* [2000] ECR I-549 and C-136/95 *Thibault* [1998] ECR I-2011.
101. Cases 184/83 *Ulrich Hofman kasse* [1984] ECR 3047, C-207/98 *Mahlburg* [2000] ECR I-549; C-136/95 *Thibault* [1998] ECR I-2011; C-421/92 *Habermann-Beltermann* [1994] ECR I-1657; C-32/93 *Webb* [1994] ECR I-3567 and C-394/96 *Brown* v *Rentokil* [1998] ECR I-4185 at § 18.
102. Case C-104/09 *Álvarez* [2010] ECR I-8661.
103. Case C-243/95 *Hill and Stapleton* [1998] ECR I-3739. See also C-1/95 *Gerster* [1997] ECR I-5253.

her period of maternity leave. If the worker is absent following her period of maternity leave for reasons of illness, even if the illness is pregnancy related, the special protection does not apply anymore but she can claim equal treatment with a sick male worker.

In *Mahlburg*, [104] the CJEU has held that no other interest, not even economic interest can prevail over the protection of pregnancy and maternity leave. Thus, refusing to employ a woman because she is pregnant cannot be justified on grounds of the financial loss the employer would suffer for the duration of the maternity leave.[105] Similarly, if the woman appointed cannot be employed in the post concerned for the duration of her pregnancy, the employer cannot raise the excuse of financial loss.

Pregnancy and maternity rights cannot be dependent on whether the woman's presence at work during the period corresponding to maternity leave is essential to the proper functioning of the undertaking in which she is employed,[106] even if the contract of employment was concluded for a fixed term.[107] The CJEU has also made clear that health and safety obligations cannot be taken into consideration in such a way as to be detrimental to pregnant workers.[108] A worker does not have an obligation to disclose her pregnancy either during recruitment[109] or at any other stage of her employment.[110]

4.4.2 The remuneration of pregnant workers and workers on maternity leave

The question of pay in relation to pregnancy and maternity rights has been a difficult issue. The CJEU held that the position of workers on maternity leave is not comparable to that of a worker actually at work. Although male and female workers are entitled to equal pay for work of equal value under Article 157 TFEU, when a worker is on maternity leave, her right to remuneration

104. Case C-207/98 *Mahlburg* [2000] ECR I-549.
105. Cases C-177/88 *Dekker* [1990] ECR I-3941 and C-207/98 *Mahlburg* [2000] ECR I-549.
106. Case C-32/93 *Webb* [1994] ECR I-3567 at § 26.
107. Cases C-109/00 *Tele Danmark A/S* [2001] ECR I-2785 and C-438/99 *Melgar* [2001] ECR I-6915 at §§ 43-47.
108. Cases C-66/96 *Høj Pedersen* and others [1998] ECR I-7327 and C-207/98 *Mahlburg* [2000] ECR I-549.
109. Case C-32/93 *Webb* [1994] ECR I-3567.
110. Case C-320/01 *Busch* [2003] ECR I-2041.

(and to equal pay) falls under the regime of Article 11 of the pregnancy Directive,[111] see below in Chapter Nine.

4.4.3 Dismissals during maternity and parental leave

Under Article 2(2) of the Recast Directive and Article 10 of the Pregnancy Directive, pregnant workers and workers on maternity leave are protected from dismissal during the period from the beginning of their pregnancy to the end of the maternity leave. Article 33 of the CFREU provides:

1. The family shall enjoy legal, economic and social protection.

2. To reconcile family and professional life, everyone shall have the right to protection from dismissal for a reason connected with maternity and the right to paid maternity leave and to parental leave following the birth or adoption of a child.

In the Explanations to the Charter it is stated that Article 33(1) is based on Article 16 of the European Social Charter. Paragraph 2 draws on the Pregnancy Directive[112] and the Parental Leave Directive.[113] It is also based on Article 8 (protection of maternity) of the European Social Charter and draws on Article 27 (right of workers with family responsibilities to equal opportunities and equal treatment) of the revised Social Charter 1996. It is further stated that 'Maternity' covers the period from conception to weaning. There is thus under Article 33 of the CFREU a right to protection from dismissal for a reason connected with maternity from conception to weaning, no matter whether weaning takes place before or after the end of the maternity and parental leave period.

ILO Maternity Protection Convention No 183 from 2000 has been ratified by nine EU Member States (Denmark not included). The ILO Maternity Protection Recommendation No 191 provides that where practicable, provision should be made for the establishment of facilities for nursing under adequate hygienic conditions at or near the workplace.

In *Paquay*,[114] the CJEU ruled that the prohibition to dismissal of pregnant women or women who are on maternity leave as determined in the Pregnancy Directive is not limited to the notification of a decision to dismiss but it also includes the steps leading up to such a decision during that protected period.

111. 92/85/EEC.
112. 92/85/EEC.
113. 96/34/EC.
114. Case C-460/06 *Paquay* [2007] ECR I-8511.

Therefore the dismissal of a woman, which takes place almost immediately after returning from maternity leave is considered to fall within the protected period. The CJEU has also clarified the conditions for the calculation of compensation for dismissal when this occurs during part-time parental leave.[115] The CJEU held that the concept of 'rights acquired or in the process of being acquired' in the agreement must cover all the rights and benefits, whether in cash or in kind, derived directly or indirectly from the employment relationship. Accordingly, national legislation which would result in the rights flowing from the employment relationship being reduced in the event of parental leave could discourage workers from taking such leave and could encourage employers to dismiss workers who are on parental leave rather than other workers. The Court therefore concludes that the framework agreement on parental leave precludes, where an employer unilaterally terminates a worker's full-time employment contract of indefinite duration, without urgent cause or without observing the statutory period of notice, and while the worker is on part-time parental leave, the compensation to be paid to the worker from being determined on the basis of the reduced salary being received when the dismissal takes place. In other words, the European Court of Justice decided that the indemnity in lieu of notice of an employee benefiting from parental leave should be calculated as if the employee had not reduced his working hours, thus on the basis of his full-time salary.

4.4.4 Effective judicial protection

The CJEU has established that a pregnant woman must be entitled to effective judicial protection.[116] Thus, if national law lays down a time-limit for a pregnant woman dismissed from employment during pregnancy which is too short and also bars pregnant women from obtaining damages when other employees can get them, the law in question discriminates against female employees.

Whilst the decision in *Pontin* represents a clear case of direct discrimination, the Court has also addressed cases of indirect discrimination such as the requirement of flexibility and mobility and the length of service. In *Danfoss*[117] the Court held that adaptability to variable hours, place of work or training was justifiable only if these criteria were 'of importance for the performance of specific tasks entrusted to the employee'. However, it also added that, 'length of service goes hand in hand with experience and since experi-

115. Case C-116/08 *Meerts* [2009] ECR I-10063.
116. Case C-63/08 *Pontin* [2009] ECR I-10467.
117. Case C-109/88 *Danfoss* [1989] ECR I-3199.

ence generally enables the employee to perform his duties better, the employer is free to reward it without having to establish the importance it has in the performance of specific tasks entrusted to the employee'.

4.4.5 The Parental Leave Directive

The measures contained in the Pregnant Workers Directive are supplemented by the Parental Leave Directive,[118] which sets minimum standards designed to facilitate the reconciliation of work with family life. This Directive implements the Framework Agreement of the European social partners on parental leave and time off on grounds of *force majeure* and repeals Directive 96/34[119] It provides that Member States shall grant all employees a, in principle, non-transferable and unpaid right to four months parental leave which can be used until the child has reached the age of 8, although the precise age is to be determined by the Member States (clause 2). The two most important changes introduced by the 2010 amendments to the Directive, are the extension to the period that parents can take off (from three to four months) and most of all the fact that, in order to encourage a more equal take-up of leave by both parents, at least one month shall be provided on a non-transferable basis. However, the modalities of application of the non-transferable period are left to the Member States. A fundamental problem is that the right to take parental leave remains unpaid and this has proven to be a considerable deterrent, in particular amongst fathers.

The Parental Leave Directive further provides protection from discrimination for workers on the grounds of applying for or taking parental leave and, at the end of the leave, workers have the right to return to the same job or, if that is not possible, to an equivalent or similar job consistent with their employment contract or employment relationship (clause 5). Workers also have the right to request changes to their working hours for a limited period; in considering such requests, employers must balance the needs of the workers and the company (clause 6). The Directive also provides a right to leave on grounds of *force majeure* for urgent family reasons (clause 7). Finally the Directive also grants these rights in the case of adoption.

In *Chatzi*,[120] the CJEU interpreted the provisions of the parental leave Directive. The CJEU was asked whether Directive 96/34/EC, interpreted in con-

118. Council Directive 2010/18/EU of 8 March 2010 implementing the revised Framework Agreement on parental leave concluded by BUSINESSEUROPE, UEAPME, CEEP and ETUC.
119. Directive 96/34/EC, OJ [2010] L68/13.
120. Case C-149/10 *Zoi Chatzi* [2010] ECR I-8489.

junction with Article 24 CFREU, can be regarded as also creating in parallel a right to parental leave for the child. If twins are born, does the grant of one period of parental leave constitutes unfair discrimination on the basis of birth and a restriction on the right of twins? The European Court replied that the Parental Leave Directive does not award to the child a personal right of parental leave. In addition, the provisions of the Directive do not mean that the birth of twins establishes a right to a number of parental leaves equal to the number of children born. The Court clarified that under the light of the principle of equal treatment, the Directive imposes on the national legislators the establishment of a parental leave system, where, depending on the situation in the relevant member state, it ensures to the parents of twins a treatment that takes into account their special needs as appropriate. It is for each Member State to ascertain whether national legislation meets this requirement and to interpret – to the extent possible – this national legislation in line with EU law.

In *Kiiski*,[121] the CJEU held that an employee who had been granted parental leave, and then discovered that she was pregnant and due to give birth part-way through her parental leave, should be allowed to end her parental leave early and return to work in order to benefit from paid maternity leave.

Similarly, in *Busch*,[122] the Court examined the case of a nurse wishing to return to work before the end of a period of parental leave and in order to do so she informed her employer that she was pregnant again. Although, her new pregnancy was likely to prevent her from carrying out all of her normal duties, the Court held that the employer was not permitted to prevent her from returning early.

Over the years, the Court of Justice has interpreted the prohibition of pregnancy discrimination generously and proactively. Article 28(1) also provides that the Directive shall be without prejudice to provisions concerning the protection of women, particularly as regards pregnancy and maternity. This is further reinforced by the dictum in recitals 23 to 25 of the preamble to the Recast Directive, which provide a safeguard in the form of an acknowledgment of the Court of Justice's case law in this area. Article 15 grants a woman on maternity leave or a man on paternity leave in the Member States that recognise such a right (Article 16), the right to return to her or his job or to an equivalent post on terms that are no less favourable to her/him and to benefit from any improvement in working conditions to which s/he would be

121. Case C-116/06 *Sari Kiiski* v *Tampereen Kaupunki* [2007] ECR I-7643.
122. Case C-320/01 *Wiebke Busch* v *Klinikum Neustadt GmbH & Co. Betriebs-KG* [2003] ECR I-2041.

entitled during her/his absence. Article 16 moreover includes protection against dismissal for fathers who exercise those rights. The same rights are granted to either parent on adoption leave (in the Member States that recognise this right). In these cases, the rights are tied to the event of the adoption itself.

4.4.6 Fixed-term contracts

The non-renewal of fixed term contract because of pregnancy and maternity constitutes direct sex discrimination contrary to EU gender equality law. The Court has addressed this issue in a string of cases.[123] In *Melgar*,[124] the CJEU stated that 'where non renewal of a fixed term contract is motivated by the worker's state of pregnancy, it constitutes direct discrimination on grounds of sex' Contrary to EU law.

4.4.7 Breastfeeding etc.

In *Alvarez*,[125] the national law granted women who had given birth within the last 9 months a right to breaks or reduction of working hours. In practice she had that right regardless of whether she actually breastfed the child. Female workers had that right regardless of whether the father was a worker. Male workers who had become fathers had the same right if the mother was also a worker but not if the mother was not a worker. The CJEU held:[126]

> Article 2(1), (3) and (4) and Article 5 of Council Directive 76/207/EEC of 9 February 1976 on the implementation of the principle of equal treatment for men and women as regards access to employment, vocational training and promotion, and working conditions, must be interpreted as precluding a national measure such as the one at issue in the main proceedings, which provides that female workers who are mothers and whose status is that of an employed person are entitled, in various ways, to take leave during the first nine months following the child's birth, whereas male workers who are fathers with that same status are not entitled to the same leave unless the child's mother is also an employed person.

4.5 Mainstreaming

Art. 8 TFEU provides that 'in all its activities, the Union shall aim to eliminate inequalities, and to promote equality, between men and women.' Article

123. Case C-32/93 *Webb* [1994] ECR I-3567; Case C-109/00 *Tele Danmark* [2001] ECR I-2785.
124. Case C-438/99 *Melgar* [2001] ECR I-6915.
125. Case C-104/09 *Álvarez* [2010] ECR I-8661.
126. See also Case C-366/99 Griesmar [2001] ECR I-9383 and Case C-476/99 *Lommers* [2002] ECR I 2891.

10 TFEU requires that 'In defining and implementing its policies and activities, the Union shall aim to combat discrimination based on sex, racial or ethnic origin, religion or belief, disability, age or sexual orientation.'

Article 23 CFREU with the heading 'Equality between women and men' provides that

> Equality between women and men must be ensured in all areas, including employment, work and pay.
>
> The principle of equality shall not prevent the maintenance or adoption of measures providing for specific advantages in favour of the under-represented sex.

Article 29 of the recast directive provides on Gender mainstreaming:

> Member States shall actively take into account the objective of equality between men and women when formulating and implementing laws, regulations, administrative provisions, policies and activities in the areas referred to in this Directive.

5 Discrimination on Grounds of Religion or Belief

As appears from section 2.3.3, discrimination on grounds of religion or belief is prohibited in employment and occupation. Under Article 4(2) of the Framework Employment Directive, Member States may, however, maintain national legislation in force at the date of adoption of the Directive or provide for future legislation incorporating national practices existing at the date of adoption of this Directive pursuant to which, in the case of occupational activities within churches and other public or private organisations the ethos of which is based on religion or belief, a difference of treatment based on a person's religion or belief shall not constitute discrimination where, by reason of the nature of these activities or of the context in which they are carried out, a person's religion or belief constitute a genuine, legitimate and justified occupational requirement, having regard to the organisation's ethos. This difference of treatment shall be implemented taking account of Member States' constitutional provisions and principles, as well as the general principles of EU law, and should not justify discrimination on another ground. Provided that its provisions are otherwise complied with, the Directive shall thus not prejudice the right of churches and other public or private organisations, the ethos of which is based on religion or belief, acting in conformity with national constitutions and laws, to require individuals working for them to act in good faith and with loyalty to the organisation's ethos.

In *Prais*,[127] a Jewish plaintiff complained about a test for recruitment as translator with the Council being held on a date on which she could not participate on grounds of her religion. The CEUJ held that if a candidate informs the appointing authority that religious reasons make certain dates impossible for him the appointing authority should take this into account in fixing the date for written tests and endeavor to avoid such dates. On the other hand if the candidate does not inform the appointing authority in good time of his difficulties, the appointing authority would be justified in refusing to afford an alternative date, particularly if there are other candidates who have been convoked for the test.

On 15 January 2013, The European ECtHR issued its judgment in *Eweida* and *others* v *UK*,[128] in which it ruled on the joined cases of four Christians who claimed that the UK had violated their rights under Article 9 ECHR (freedom of religion) and/or Article 14 ECHR (prohibition of discrimination). In all bar one of the cases, which involved employees who had either been disciplined or dismissed as a result of their refusal to carry out a part of their job which they felt would be contrary to their Christian faith, the ECtHR found that the UK had not violated the individuals' rights.

Two of the cases (Eweida and Chaplin) concerned employees who claimed that their employers had discriminated against them on the ground of their religion because the employers enforced a uniform policy which prevented them from wearing a cross visibly around their neck. In the case of *Eweida*, her employer, the private company British Airways (BA), suspended her without pay in 2006 as her refusal to remove her cross breached a uniform policy intended to maintain a strong corporate image. In Chaplin's case, in 2009 her state hospital employer refused to allow her to wear a cross visibly round her neck in her nursing role, due to the health and safety risk it posed to her and her patients.

The other two cases, those of MacFarlane and Ladele, involved employees who would not carry out a part of their job (provide services to homosexual couples) due to their conviction that to do so would be contrary to the requirements of their Christian faith, which they believed meant that they could not condone homosexual acts or union. In the case of Ladele, from 2005, her public authority employer required her, as a registrar, to conduct civil partnership registrations for same-sex couples. Ladele's refusal to carry out such registrations and complaints from other staff members ultimately led to her

127. Case 130/75 *Prais* [1976] ECR 1589.

128. Case of Eweida *and others* v *UK* (Applications nos 48420/10, 59842/10, 51671/10 and 36516/10).

dismissal for failing to comply with the authority's 'Dignity for All' policy which required no discrimination against staff and service users. In the case of MacFarlane, his private employer Relate dismissed him knowing that he believed that 'homosexual activities' were a sin and considering that this was impacting on his willingness to carry out his job in line with its equal opportunities policy, by providing psycho-sexual counselling to same-sex couples.

The ECtHR found that the three Article 9 ECHR claims related to a 'manifestation' by the applicant of a religious belief and so fell within the scope of Article 9(1) protection. The ECtHR's decision turned on whether the restriction by the state of this manifestation (either directly as a public employer or through the positive obligation owed by the state courts to uphold Convention rights when making their judgments) was justified as a proportionate means of achieving a legitimate aim. In the case of Eweida, the ECtHR held, by a five to two majority, that the UK had violated Eweida's rights as a fair balance had not been struck between the various competing interests. They stated that the UK's Court of Appeal had accorded too much weight to British Airways's maintenance of a corporate image when balancing it with Eweida's right to freedom of religion.

The ECtHR unanimously agreed that the right balance had been struck in Chaplin and MacFarlane's cases and the interference with their Article 9 rights was proportionate. Considering that the test of proportionality would be similar under Article 14 ECHR, the ECtHR did not consider it separately in any detail. In the case of Ladele, whose claim was a breach of Article 14 ECHR (taken with Article 9), the ECtHR found by a five to two majority that there had been no violation of her right. Specifically it found that, although the authority's policy puts Ladele at a disadvantage because of her religious beliefs, it could nevertheless be justified as proportionate in its aim to protect the rights of others to be free from discrimination.

6 Discrimination on Grounds of Age

In *Mangold*,[129] the CJEU ruled that the principle of non-discrimination on grounds of age is a general principle of EU law. The CJEU held that the national court must set aside any provision of national law which may conflict with EU law, in the particular case at hand with the general principle of non-discrimination. The facts in *Mangold* took place before the expiry of the

129. Case C-144/04 *Mangold* [2005] ECR I-9981.

dead-line for implementation of the Framework Employment Directive had expired in Germany. There was a link to EU law because Germany had implemented the fixed-term work directive[130] in an age discriminatory way. That was considered a violation of primary EU law, i.e. the general EU law principle of non-discrimination on grounds of age.

6.1 Permissible Differences under Article 6 of Directive 2000/78

Differences in treatment on grounds of age are permissible when they are objectively and reasonably justified by a legitimate labour market aim and are appropriate and necessary to the achievement of that aim (protection of young people and older workers, requirements as to the extent of job experience, etc.). Article 6 in the employment framework directive[131] provides:

Justification of differences of treatment on grounds of age
1. Notwithstanding Article 2(2), Member States may provide that differences of treatment on grounds of age shall not constitute discrimination, if, within the context of national law, they are objectively and reasonably justified by a legitimate aim, including legitimate employment policy, labour market and vocational training objectives, and if the means of achieving that aim are appropriate and necessary.

Such differences of treatment may include, among others:

(a) the setting of special conditions on access to employment and vocational training, employment and occupation, including dismissal and remuneration conditions, for young people, older workers and persons with caring responsibilities in order to promote their vocational integration or ensure their protection;
(b) the fixing of minimum conditions of age, professional experience or seniority in service for access to employment or to certain advantages linked to employment;
(c) the fixing of a maximum age for recruitment which is based on the training requirements of the post in question or the need for a reasonable period of employment before retirement.

A very considerable part of the case law from the CJEU on age discrimination concerns the interpretation of this provision.

6.2 Retirement Ages

In *Rosenbladt*,[132] the CJEU held that Articles 1 and 2 of the Framework Employment Directive must be interpreted as meaning that they do not preclude a Member State from declaring a collective agreement containing a clause on the automatic termination of employment contracts, like that at issue in the

130. 1999/70/EC.
131. 2000/78/EC.
132. Case C-45/09 *Rosenbladt* [2010] I-9391.

main proceedings, to be of general application, provided that it does not deprive employees who have reached retirement age of the protection from discrimination on grounds of age conferred on them by those provisions.

In an infringement case against *Hungary*,[133] the CJEU declared that by adopting a national scheme requiring compulsory retirement of judges, prosecutors and notaries when they reach the age of 62 – which gives rise to a difference in treatment on grounds of age which is not proportionate as regards the objectives pursued – Hungary has failed to fulfil its obligations under Articles 2 and 6(1) of the Framework Employment Directive.

In *ODAR*,[134] the CJEU held:

1. Articles 2(2) and 6(1) of Council Directive 2000/78/EC of 27 November 2000 establishing a general framework for equal treatment in employment and occupation must be interpreted as not precluding rules of an occupational social security scheme under which, in the case of workers older than 54 years of age who are made redundant on operational grounds, a calculation is to be made of the compensation on the basis of the earliest possible date on which their pension will begin – unlike the standard method of calculation, which takes account in particular of the length of service – with the result that the compensation paid to those workers is lower than the compensation resulting from the application of that standard method, though still at least one half of the standard amount.

2. Article 2(2) of Directive 2000/78 must be interpreted as precluding rules of an occupational social security scheme under which, in the case of workers older than 54 years of age who are made redundant on operational grounds, the compensation to which they are entitled is calculated on the basis of the earliest possible date on which their pension will begin – unlike the standard formula, under which account is taken inter alia of the length of service – with the result that the compensation paid is lower than the standard formula compensation, although still at least one half thereof, and that alternative calculation method takes account of the possibility of receiving an early retirement pension on the ground of disability.

Hörnfeldt[135] concerned Swedish legislation conferring on employees an unconditional right to work until the age of 67 and providing for automatic termination of the employment relationship at the end of the month in which the employee reaches that age. Account was not taken of the amount of the retirement pension. The CJEU held:

The second subparagraph of Article 6(1) of Council Directive 2000/78/EC of 27 November 2000 establishing a general framework for equal treatment in employment and occupa-

133. C-286/12 *Commission* v *Hungary* [2012] ECR nyr.
134. Case C-152/11 *Odar* [2012] ECR nyr.
135. Case C-141/11 *Hörnfeldt* [2012] ECR nyr.

tion must be interpreted as not precluding a national measure, such as that at issue in the main proceedings, which allows an employer to terminate an employee's employment contract on the sole ground that the employee has reached the age of 67 and which does not take account of the level of the retirement pension which the person concerned will receive, as that measure is objectively and reasonably justified by a legitimate aim relating to employment policy and labour-market policy and constitutes an appropriate and necessary means by which to achieve that aim.

In *Hennigs*,[136] the CJEU held that the principle of non-discrimination on grounds of age proclaimed in Article 21 of the CFREU and given specific expression in the Framework Employment Directive, and more particularly Articles 2 and 6(1) of that directive, must be interpreted as precluding a measure laid down by a collective agreement such as that at issue in the main proceedings which provides that, within each salary group, the basic pay step of a public sector contractual employee is determined on appointment by reference to the employee's age. The fact that EU law precludes that measure and that it appears in a collective agreement does not interfere with the right to negotiate and conclude collective agreements recognised in Article 28 CFREU. Articles 2 and 6(1) of the Framework Employment Directive and Article 28 CFREU must be interpreted as not precluding a measure in a collective agreement, such as that at issue in the main proceedings in *Hennig*, which replaces a system of pay leading to discrimination on grounds of age by a system of pay based on objective criteria while maintaining, for a transitional period limited in time, some of the discriminatory effects of the earlier system in order to ensure that employees in post are transferred to the new system without suffering a loss of income.

In *Fuchs*,[137] the CJEU ruled that the Framework Employment Directive does not preclude a law, such as the Law on the civil service of the Land Hessen (Hessisches Beamtengesetz which provides for the compulsory retirement of permanent civil servants – in this instance prosecutors – at the age of 65, while allowing them to continue to work, if it is in the interests of the service that they should do so, until the maximum age of 68, provided that that law has the aim of establishing a balanced age structure in order to encourage the recruitment and promotion of young people, to improve personnel management and thereby to prevent possible disputes concerning employees' fitness to work beyond a certain age, and that it allows that aim to be achieved by appropriate and necessary means. In order for it to be demon-

136. Case C-297/10 *Hennigs* [2011] nyr.
137. Joined Cases C-159/10 and C-160/10 *Fuchs* [2011] ECR nyr.

strated that the measure concerned is appropriate and necessary, the measure must not appear unreasonable in the light of the aim pursued and must be supported by evidence the probative value of which it is for the national court to assess. A law such as the Law on the civil service of the Land Hessen, as amended by the Law of 14 December 2009, which provides for the compulsory retirement of prosecutors when they reach the age of 65, does not lack coherence merely because it allows them to work until the age of 68 in certain cases or also contains provisions intended to restrict retirement before the age of 65, and other legislation of the Member State concerned provides for certain – particularly elected – civil servants to remain in post beyond that age and also the gradual raising of the retirement age from 65 to 67 years.

In *Prigge*,[138] the CJEU held that Article 2(5)[139] of the Framework Employment Directive must be interpreted as meaning that the Member States may authorise, through rules to that effect, the social partners to adopt measures within the meaning of Article 2(5) in the areas referred to in that provision that fall within collective agreements on condition that those rules of authorisation are sufficiently precise so as to ensure that those measures fulfil the requirements set out in Article 2(5). A measure such as that at issue in the main proceedings, which fixes the age limit from which pilots may no longer carry out their professional activities at 60 whereas national and international legislation fixes that age at 65, is not a measure that is necessary for public security and protection of health, within the meaning of Article 2(5). Article 4(1)[140] of Directive 2000/78 must be interpreted as precluding a

138. Case C-447/09 *Prigge* [2011] ECR nyr.

139. Article 2(5) reads: 'This Directive shall be without prejudice to measures laid down by national law which, in a democratic society, are necessary for public security, for the maintenance of public order and the prevention of criminal offences, for the protection of health and for the protection of the rights and freedoms of others.'

140. Article 4(1) on Occupational requirements reads: 1. Notwithstanding Article 2(1) and (2), Member States may provide that a difference of treatment which is based on a characteristic related to any of the grounds referred to in Article 1 shall not constitute discrimination where, by reason of the nature of the particular occupational activities concerned or of the context in which they are carried out, such a characteristic constitutes a genuine and determining occupational requirement, provided that the objective is legitimate and the requirement is proportionate.

2. Member States may maintain national legislation in force at the date of adoption of this Directive or provide for future legislation incorporating national practices existing at the date of adoption of this Directive pursuant to which, in the case of occupational activities within churches and other public or private organisations the ethos of which is based on religion or belief, a difference of treatment based on a person's religion or belief shall not constitute discrimination where, by reason of the nature of

clause in a collective agreement, such as that at issue in the main proceedings, that fixes at 60 the age limit from which pilots are considered as no longer possessing the physical capabilities to carry out their professional activity while national and international legislation fix that age at 65. The first paragraph of Article 6(1) of Directive 2000/78 must be interpreted to the effect that air traffic safety does not constitute a legitimate aim within the meaning of that provision.

In *Kleist*,[141] the CJEU held that the prohibition against sex discrimination must be interpreted as meaning that national rules which, in order to promote access of younger persons to employment, permit an employer to dismiss employees who have acquired the right to draw their retirement pension, when that right is acquired by women at an age five years younger than the age at which it is acquired by men, constitute prohibited direct discrimination on the grounds of sex.

In *Georgiev*,[142] the CJEU ruled:

> Council Directive 2000/78/EC of 27 November 2000 establishing a general framework for equal treatment in employment and occupation, in particular Article 6(1), must be interpreted as meaning that it does not preclude national legislation, such as that at issue in the main proceedings, under which university professors are compulsorily retired when they reach the age of 68 and may continue working beyond the age of 65 only by means of fixed-term one-year contracts renewable at most twice, provided that that legislation pursues a legitimate aim linked inter alia to employment and labour market policy, such as the delivery of quality teaching and the best possible allocation of posts for professors between the generations, and that it makes it possible to achieve that aim by appropriate and necessary means. It is for the national court to determine whether those conditions are satisfied.
>
> Since this is a dispute between a public institution and an individual, if national legislation such as that at issue in the main proceedings does not satisfy the conditions set out in Article 6(1) of Directive 2000/78, the national court must decline to apply that legislation.

these activities or of the context in which they are carried out, a person's religion or belief constitute a genuine, legitimate and justified occupational requirement, having regard to the organisation's ethos. This difference of treatment shall be implemented taking account of Member States' constitutional provisions and principles, as well as the general principles of Community law, and should not justify discrimination on another ground.
Provided that its provisions are otherwise complied with, this Directive shall thus not prejudice the right of churches and other public or private organisations, the ethos of which is based on religion or belief, acting in conformity with national constitutions and laws, to require individuals working for them to act in good faith and with loyalty to the organisation's ethos.

141. Case C-356/09 *Kleist* [2010] ECR I-11939.
142. C-250/09 and C-268/09 *Georgiev* [2010] I-11869.

In *Rosenbladt*,[143] the CJEU ruled that:

1. Article 6(1) of Council Directive 2000/78/EC of 27 November 2000 establishing a general framework for equal treatment in employment and occupation must be interpreted as meaning that it does not preclude a national provision such as Paragraph 10(5) of the General Law on equal treatment (Allgemeines Gleichbehandlungsgesetz), under which clauses on automatic termination of employment contracts on the ground that the employee has reached the age of retirement are considered to be valid, in so far as, first, that provision is objectively and reasonably justified by a legitimate aim relating to employment policy and the labour market and, second, the means of achieving that aim are appropriate and necessary. The implementation of that authorisation by means of a collective agreement is not, as such, exempt from any review by the courts but, in accordance with the requirements of Article 6(1) of that directive, must itself pursue a legitimate aim in an appropriate and necessary manner.

2. Article 6(1) of Directive 2000/78 must be interpreted as meaning that it does not preclude a measure such as the automatic termination of employment contracts of employees who have reached retirement age, set at 65, provided for by Paragraph 19(8) of the framework collective agreement for employees in the commercial cleaning sector (Allgemeingültiger Rahmentarifvertrag für die gewerblichen Beschäftigten in der Gebäudereinigung).

In *Domnica Petersen*,[144] the CJEU held that Article 2(5) of the Framework Employment directive must be interpreted as precluding a national measure, such as that at issue in the main proceedings, setting a maximum age for practising as a panel dentist, in this case 68 years, where the sole aim of that measure is to protect the health of patients against the decline in performance of those dentists after that age, since that age limit does not apply to non-panel dentists. Article 6(1) of Directive 2000/78 must be interpreted as not precluding such a measure where its aim is to share out employment opportunities among the generations in the profession of panel dentist, if, taking into account the situation in the labour market concerned, the measure is appropriate and necessary for achieving that aim. It is for the national court to identify the aim pursued by the measure laying down that age limit, by ascertaining the reason for maintaining the measure. If legislation such as that at issue in the main proceedings, having regard to its objective, were contrary to Directive 2000/78, it would be for the national court hearing a dispute between an individual and an administrative body to decline to apply that legislation, even if it were prior to that directive and national law made no provision for disapplying it.

143. Case C-45/09 *Rosenbladt* [2010] I-9391.
144. Case C-341/08 *Domnica Petersen* [2010] I-47.

In *Palacios de la Villa*,[145] the CJEU ruled:

The prohibition on any discrimination on grounds of age, as implemented by Council Directive 2000/78/EC of 27 November 2000 establishing a general framework for equal treatment in employment and occupation, must be interpreted as not precluding national legislation such as that at issue in the main proceedings, pursuant to which compulsory retirement clauses contained in collective agreements are lawful where such clauses provide as sole requirements that workers must have reached retirement age, set at 65 by national law, and must have fulfilled the conditions set out in the social security legislation for entitlement to a retirement pension under their contribution regime, where

- the measure, although based on age, is objectively and reasonably justified in the context of national law by a legitimate aim relating to employment policy and the labour market, and
- the means put in place to achieve that aim of public interest do not appear to be inappropriate and unnecessary for the purpose.

6.3 Other Questions

In *Ingeniørforeningen i Danmark*,[146] the CJEU held that Articles 2 and 6(1) of the Framework employment directive must be interpreted as precluding national legislation pursuant to which workers who are eligible for an old-age pension from their employer under a pension scheme which they have joined before attaining the age of 50 years cannot, on that ground alone, claim a *severance allowance* aimed at assisting workers with more than 12 years of service in the undertaking in finding new employment.

Wolf[147] concerned the compatibility with EU law of a national provision setting a maximum age of 30 years for the recruitment of officials to posts in the fire service. The CJEU held that Article 4(1)[148] of Directive 2000/78/EC must be interpreted as not precluding national legislation, such as that at issue in the main proceedings, which sets the maximum age for recruitment to intermediate career posts in the fire service at 30 years.

145. Case C-411/05 *Palacios de la Villa* [2007] I-8531.
146. Case C-499/08 *Ingeniørforeningen i Danmark* (acting on behalf of Ole Andersen) [2010] I-9343.
147. Case C-229/08 *Wolf* [2010] I-1.
148. Article 4(1) reads: 1. Notwithstanding Article 2(1) and (2), Member States may provide that a difference of treatment which is based on a characteristic related to any of the grounds referred to in Article 1 shall not constitute discrimination where, by reason of the nature of the particular occupational activities concerned or of the context in which they are carried out, such a characteristic constitutes a genuine and determining occupational requirement, provided that the objective is legitimate and the requirement is proportionate.

In *Hütter.*[149] the CJEU ruled that Articles 1, 2 and 6 of the Framework Employment Directive must be interpreted as precluding national legislation which, in order not to treat general education less favourably than vocational education and to promote the integration of young apprentices into the labour market, excludes periods of employment completed before the age of 18 from being taken into account for the purpose of determining the incremental step at which contractual public servants of a Member State are graded.

Kücükdeveci[150] concerned national legislation on dismissal which didn't take the period of employment completed before the employee reaches the age of 25 into account in calculating the notice period. The CJEU held that EU law, more particularly the principle of non-discrimination on grounds of age as given expression by Directive 2000/78/EC must be interpreted as precluding national legislation, such as that at issue in the main proceedings, which provides that periods of employment completed by an employee before reaching the age of 25 are not taken into account in calculating the notice period for dismissal. It is for the national court, hearing proceedings between individuals, to ensure that the principle of non-discrimination on grounds of age, as given expression in Directive 2000/78, is complied with, disapplying if need be any contrary provision of national legislation, independently of whether it makes use of its entitlement, in the cases referred to in the second paragraph of Article 267 TFEU, to ask the CJEU for a preliminary ruling on the interpretation of that principle.

In *Age Concern,*[151] the CJEU held that Article 6(1) of the Framework Employment Directive must be interpreted as meaning that it does not preclude a national measure which does not contain a precise list of the aims justifying derogation from the principle prohibiting discrimination on grounds of age. However, Article 6(1) offers the option to derogate from that principle only in respect of measures justified by legitimate social policy objectives, such as those related to employment policy, the labour market or vocational training. It is for the national court to ascertain whether the legislation at issue in the main proceedings is consonant with such a legitimate aim and whether the national legislative or regulatory authority could legitimately consider, taking account of the Member States' discretion in matters of social policy, that the means chosen were appropriate and necessary to achieve that aim. Article 6(1) of the Framework Employment Directive gives Member States the option to provide, within the context of national law, for certain kinds of differ-

149. Case C-88/08 *Hütter* [2009] I-5325.
150. Case C-555/07 *Kücükdeveci* [2010] I-365.
151. Case C-388/07 *Age Concern* [2009] I-1569.

ences in treatment on grounds of age if they are 'objectively and reasonably' justified by a legitimate aim, such as employment policy, or labour market or vocational training objectives, and if the means of achieving that aim are appropriate and necessary. It imposes on Member States the burden of establishing to a high standard of proof the legitimacy of the aim relied on as a justification. No particular significance should be attached to the fact that the word 'reasonably' used in Article 6(1) of the directive does not appear in Article 2(2)(b) thereof.

Bartsch[152] concerned an occupational pension scheme which excluded the right to a pension of a spouse which was more than 15 years younger than the deceased former employee. The case took place before the time-limit allowed to the Member State for transposition of the Framework Employment Directive had expired. The case therefore had no link with EU law and the general EU law principle of prohibition against age discrimination could not be invokes, see above in Chapter Two on the effect of EU fundamental rights in national law.

7 Discrimination on Grounds of Disability

In *Coleman*,[153] the CJEU held that the Framework Employment Directive and, in particular, Articles 1 and 2(1) and (2)(a) thereof, must be interpreted as meaning that the prohibition of direct discrimination laid down by those provisions is not limited only to people who are themselves disabled. Where an employer treats an employee who is not himself disabled less favourably than another employee is, has been or would be treated in a comparable situation, and it is established that the less favourable treatment of that employee is based on the disability of his child, whose care is provided primarily by that employee, such treatment is contrary to the prohibition of direct discrimination laid down by Article 2(2)(a).

Directive 2000/78, and, in particular, Articles 1 and 2(1) and (3) thereof, must be interpreted as meaning that the prohibition of harassment laid down by those provisions is not limited only to people who are themselves disabled. Where it is established that the unwanted conduct amounting to harassment which is suffered by an employee who is not himself disabled is related to the disability of his child, whose care is provided primarily by that em-

152. Case C-427/06 *Bartsch* [2008] I-7245.
153. Case C 303/06 *Coleman* [2008] I-5603.

ployee, such conduct is contrary to the prohibition of harassment laid down by Article 2(3).

7.1 Concept of disability

The UN Disability Convention contains no specific definition of disability, but some indications of what to focus on. The UN concept of disability is environmentally related. Disability is not a characteristic of people with impairments, but something that occurs in the interaction between people with certain impairments and barriers in their environment, see point e) in the Preamble to the Convention, which reads:

> Recognizing that disability is an evolving concept and that disability results from the interaction between persons with impairments and attitudinal and environmental barriers that hinders their full and effective participation in society on an equal basis with others,

The disability-concept is the UN Convention is thus an interactive concept where an impairment of physical, mental, intellectual or sensory nature in interaction with the surrounding society leads to a greater or lesser disability. The purpose of the UN Convention is to promote, protect and ensure that all people with impairments can fully enjoy all human rights and fundamental freedoms on an equal basis with others, and to promote respect for their inherent dignity. In societies with a high level of inclusion an impairment which in a society with a lower level of inclusion would lead to disability need not become a disability that hinders participation in the work-force. If one compares fairly similar countries like Denmark and Sweden, the Swedish labour market includes a higher proportion of persons with impairments than the Danish labour market.[154] EU law requires employers to provide reasonable accommodation for persons with disabilities, see Article 5 of the Framework Employment directive and below in section 7.2. The use of the term 'reasonable' in the Directive leaves the Member States a wide margin of appreciation as to how much adaptation of the workplace to the person with an impairment shall be required of the employer.

In *Chacón Navas*,[155]the CJEU stated on the concept of disability that the concept is not defined by the Framework Employment directive itself. Nor does the directive refer to the laws of the Member States for the definition of

154. See Liisberg, Maria Ventegodt: Disability and Employment – A Contemporary Disability Human Rights Approach Applied to Danish, Swedish and EU Law and Policy, Intersentia, 2011.

155. Case C-13/05 *Chacón Navas* [2006] ECR I-6467.

that concept. It follows from the need for uniform application of EU law and the principle of equality that the terms of a provision of EU law which makes no express reference to the law of the Member States for the purpose of determining its meaning and scope must normally be given an autonomous and uniform interpretation throughout the EU, having regard to the context of the provision and the objective pursued by the legislation in question.

As is apparent from Article 1, the purpose of the Framework Employment directive is to lay down a general framework for combating discrimination based on any of the grounds referred to in that article, which include disability, as regards employment and occupation. In the light of that objective, the concept of 'disability' for the purpose of the Framework Employment directive must, in accordance with the rule set out in paragraph 40 of this judgment, be given an autonomous and uniform interpretation. The Framework Employment directive aims to combat certain types of discrimination as regards employment and occupation. In that context, the concept of 'disability' must be understood as referring to a limitation which results in particular from physical, mental or psychological impairments and which hinders the participation of the person concerned in professional life. By using the concept of 'disability' in Article 1 of that directive, the legislature deliberately chose a term which differs from 'sickness'. The two concepts cannot therefore simply be treated as being the same.

There is nothing in the Framework Employment directive to suggest that workers are protected by the prohibition of discrimination on grounds of disability as soon as they develop any type of sickness. It follows from the above considerations that a person who has been dismissed by his employer solely on account of sickness does not fall within the general framework laid down for combating discrimination on grounds of disability by the Framework Employment directive.

7.2 Employer's duty to Reasonable accommodation for disabled persons

In order to guarantee compliance with the principle of equal treatment in relation to persons with disabilities, the employer shall according to Article 5 of the Framework Employment directive provide reasonable accommodation. This means that employers shall take appropriate measures, where needed in a particular case, to enable a person with a disability to have access to, participate in, or advance in employment, or to undergo training, unless such measures would impose a disproportionate burden on the employer. This burden shall not be disproportionate when it is sufficiently remedied by measures existing within the framework of the disability policy of the Member State concerned.

8 Discrimination on Grounds of Sexual Orientation

In *Römer*,[156] the CJEU held that the Framework Employment Directive is to be interpreted as meaning that supplementary retirement pensions which constitute pay within the meaning of Article 157 TFEU, do not fall outside the material scope of the Directive either on account of Article 3(3) thereof or on account of recital 22 in the preamble thereto. Article 1 in conjunction with Articles 2 and 3(1)(c) of Directive 2000/78 preclude a provision of national law under which a pensioner who has entered into a registered life partnership receives a supplementary retirement pension lower than that granted to a married, not permanently separated, pensioner, if

- in the Member State concerned, marriage is reserved to persons of different gender and exists alongside a registered life partnership such as that provided for by the Law on registered life partnerships (Gesetz über die Eingetragene Lebenspartnerschaft) of 16 February 2001, which is reserved to persons of the same gender, and
- there is direct discrimination on the ground of sexual orientation because, under national law, that life partner is in a legal and factual situation comparable to that of a married person as regards that pension. It is for the referring court to assess the comparability, focusing on the respective rights and obligations of spouses and persons in a registered life partnership, as governed within the corresponding institutions, which are relevant taking account of the purpose of and the conditions for the grant of the benefit in question.

Should the national law on supplementary retirement and survivors' pensions for employees constitute discrimination within the meaning of Article 2 of Directive 2000/78, the right to equal treatment could be claimed by an individual such as the applicant in the main proceedings at the earliest after the expiry of the period for transposing the Directive, namely from 3 December 2003, and it would not be necessary to wait for that provision to be made

156. Case C-147/08 *Römer* [2011] ECR I-3591.

consistent with EU law by the national legislature. In *Maruko*,[157] the ECJ delivered a similar judgment. It ruled:

1. A survivor's benefit granted under an occupational pension scheme such as that managed by the Versorgungsanstalt der deutschen Bühnen falls within the scope of Council Directive 2000/78/EC of 27 November 2000 establishing a general framework for equal treatment in employment and occupation.

2. The combined provisions of Articles 1 and 2 of Directive 2000/78 preclude legislation such as that at issue in the main proceedings under which, after the death of his life partner, the surviving partner does not receive a survivor's benefit equivalent to that granted to a surviving spouse, even though, under national law, life partnership places persons of the same sex in a situation comparable to that of spouses so far as concerns that survivor's benefit. It is for the referring court to determine whether a surviving life partner is in a situation comparable to that of a spouse who is entitled to the survivor's benefit provided for under the occupational pension scheme managed by the Versorgungsanstalt der deutschen Bühnen.

9 General ban on discrimination in Employment and Occupation

9.1 General principle of equal application of EU law. Article 20 CFREU

The general principle of equal application of the law is old in the European culture. The equal treatment rule is a fundamental principle of, and part of the foundation of the EU, as the CJEU has pointed out in many cases, see for example *Brunnhofer*:[158]

... the general principle of equality which prohibits comparable situations from being treated differently unless the difference is objectively justified, forms part of the foundations of the Community.

That principle is now codified in Article 20 CFREU on Equality before the law. It reads: 'Everyone is equal before the law'. In the Explanatory remarks[159] the following sources are mentioned as background to Article 20 CFREU:

157. Case C-267/06 *Maruko* [2008] ECR I-1757.
158. Case C-381/99 *Brunnhofer* [2001] ECR I-4961.
159. See OJ 2007 C 303.

This Article corresponds to a general principle of law which is included in all European constitutions and has also been recognised by the Court of Justice as a basic principle of Community law (judgment of 13 November 1984, Case 283/83 Racke [1984] ECR 3791, judgment of 17 April 1997, Case C-15/95 EARL [1997] ECR I-1961, and judgment of 13 April 2000, Case C-292/97 Karlsson [2000] ECR 2737).

9.2 Article 21 CFREU

Article 21 on Non-discrimination reads:

1. Any discrimination based on any ground such as sex, race, colour, ethnic or social origin, genetic features, language, religion or belief, political or any other opinion, membership of a national minority, property, birth, disability, age or sexual orientation shall be prohibited.

2. Within the scope of application of the Treaties and without prejudice to any of their specific provisions, any discrimination on grounds of nationality shall be prohibited.

In the Explanatory remarks the following sources of law are referred to as explanation to Article 21 CFREU: It is stated that paragraph 1 draws on Article 19 TFEU, Article 14 ECHR and Article 11 of the Convention on Human Rights and Biomedicine as regards genetic heritage. In so far as this corresponds to Article 14 of the ECHR, it applies in compliance with it. There is no contradiction or incompatibility between paragraph 1 and Article 19 TFEU which has a different scope and purpose: Article 19 confers power on the Union to adopt legislative acts, including harmonisation of the Member States' laws and regulations, to combat certain forms of discrimination, listed exhaustively in that Article. Such legislation may cover action of Member State authorities (as well as relations between private individuals) in any area within the limits of the Union's powers. In contrast, the provision in Article 21(1) CFREU does not create any power to enact anti-discrimination laws in these areas of Member State or private action, nor does it lay down a sweeping ban of discrimination in such wide-ranging areas. Instead, it only addresses discriminations by the institutions and bodies of the Union themselves, when exercising powers conferred under the Treaties, and by Member States when they are implementing Union law, see above in Chapter Two on when the CFREU and other fundamental rights must be respected in national law. Paragraph 1 therefore does not alter the extent of powers granted under Article 19 TFEU nor the interpretation given to that Article.

Paragraph 2 corresponds to the first paragraph of Article 18 TFEU which as mentioned earlier contains a general ban on discrimination on grounds of nationality and must be applied in compliance with that Article.

10 Exceptions from the Ban on Discrimination

10.1 Maternity Protection

Article 28 of the recast directive provides that the Directive shall be without prejudice to provisions concerning the protection of women, particularly as regards pregnancy and maternity. The Directive is also without prejudice to the provisions of the Parental Leave Directive[160] and the Pregnancy Directive.[161] Recital 24 of the Preamble to the recast directive provides that:

(24) The Court of Justice has consistently recognised the legitimacy, as regards the principle of equal treatment, of protecting a woman's biological condition during pregnancy and maternity and of introducing maternity protection measures as a means to achieve substantive equality. This Directive should therefore be without prejudice to Council Directive 92/85/EEC of 19 October 1992 on the introduction of measures to encourage improvements in the safety and health at work of pregnant workers and workers who have recently given birth or are breastfeeding [12]. This Directive should further be without prejudice to Council Directive 96/34/EC of 3 June 1996 on the framework agreement on parental leave concluded by UNICE, CEEP and the ETUC.

10.2 Paternity and adoption leave

Article 16 of the recast directive on gender equality in employment and occupation provides that the Directive is without prejudice to the right of Member States to recognise distinct rights to paternity and/or adoption leave. Those Member States which recognise such rights shall take the necessary measures to protect working men and women against dismissal due to exercising those rights and ensure that, at the end of such leave, they are entitled to return to their jobs or to equivalent posts on terms and conditions which are no less favourable to them, and to benefit from any improvement in working conditions to which they would have been entitled during their absence.

10.3 Positive Action

Member States have the right to maintain and adopt measures intended to prevent or compensate for existing inequalities (measures to promote the integration of young people, the transition from work to retirement, etc.). Article 3 of the recast directive on gender equality[162] in employment and occupation on positive action provides that Member States may maintain or adopt measures within the meaning of Article 157(4) TFEU with a view to ensuring

160. 96/34/EC.
161. 92/85/EEC.
162. 2006/54/EC.

full equality in practice between men and women in working life. The measures permitted as positive action provisions aim at eliminating or counteracting the detrimental effects on an underrepresented sex, often women/ethnic groups etc. which arise from existing attitudes, behaviour and structures based on the idea of a traditional division of roles in society.

Article 157(4) TFEU provides:

> 4. With a view to ensuring full equality in practice between men and women in working life, the principle of equal treatment shall not prevent any Member State from maintaining or adopting measures providing for specific advantages in order to make it easier for the underrepresented sex to pursue a vocational activity or to prevent or compensate for disadvantages in professional careers.

The CJEU has accepted positive action in some cases.[163]

10.4 Genuine Occupational Qualifications

In certain cases differences in treatment may be justified by the nature of the post or the conditions in which the job is performed. Recital 19 of the Preamble to the recast directive provides that:

> (19) Ensuring equal access to employment and the vocational training leading thereto is fundamental to the application of the principle of equal treatment of men and women in matters of employment and occupation. Any exception to this principle should therefore be limited to those occupational activities which necessitate the employment of a person of a particular sex by reason of their nature or the context in which they are carried out, provided that the objective sought is legitimate and complies with the principle of proportionality.

Article 4 of the Ethnic Equal Treatment Directive provides that Notwithstanding Article 2(1) and (2), Member States may provide that a difference of treatment which is based on a characteristic related to racial or ethnic origin shall not constitute discrimination where, by reason of the nature of the particular occupational activities concerned or of the context in which they are carried out, such a characteristic constitutes a genuine and determining occupational requirement, provided that the objective is legitimate and the requirement is proportionate.

Article 4(1) of the Framework Employment Directive provides that notwithstanding Article 2(1) and (2) which prohibit discrimination on grounds of religion or belief, disability, age or sexual orientation, Member States may

163. See case C-407/98 *Abrahamsson* [2000] ECR I-5539, case C-79/99 *Schnorbus* [2000] ECR I-10997 and case C-476/99 *Lommers* [2002] ECR I-2891.

provide that a difference of treatment which is based on a characteristic related to any of the grounds referred to in Article 1 shall not constitute discrimination where, by reason of the nature of the particular occupational activities concerned or of the context in which they are carried out, such a characteristic constitutes a genuine and determining occupational requirement, provided that the objective is legitimate and the requirement is proportionate.

11 Enforcement and Monitoring

11.1 Minimum Requirements

Article 27 of the recast directive provides that Member States may introduce or maintain provisions which are more favourable to the protection of the principle of equal treatment than those laid down in this Directive. Implementation of the recast Directive shall under no circumstances be sufficient grounds for a reduction in the level of protection of workers in the areas to which it applies, without prejudice to the Member States' right to respond to changes in the situation by introducing laws, regulations and administrative provisions which differ from those in force on the notification of this Directive, provided that the provisions of this Directive are complied with.

Article 8 of the Framework Employment Directive on Minimum requirements provides that Member States may introduce or maintain provisions which are more favourable to the protection of the principle of equal treatment than those laid down in this Directive. The implementation of this Directive shall under no circumstances constitute grounds for a reduction in the level of protection against discrimination already afforded by Member States in the fields covered by the Directive. In *Bullicke*,[164] the CJEU ruled that:

> 2. Article 8 of the Directive must be interpreted as not precluding a national procedural rule, adopted in order to implement the Directive, which has the effect of amending earlier legislation which provided for a time-limit for claiming compensation for discrimination on grounds of sex.

Article 6 of the Ethnic Equal Treatment Directive contains a similar provision.

164. Case C-246/09 *Bulicke* [2010] I-7003.

11.2 Defence of Rights

Article 17 of the Recast directive provides that Member States shall ensure that, after possible recourse to other competent authorities including where they deem it appropriate conciliation procedures, judicial procedures for the enforcement of obligations under this Directive are available to all persons who consider themselves wronged by failure to apply the principle of equal treatment to them, even after the relationship in which the discrimination is alleged to have occurred has ended. Member States shall ensure that associations, organisations or other legal entities which have, in accordance with the criteria laid down by their national law, a legitimate interest in ensuring that the provisions of this Directive are complied with, may engage, either on behalf or in support of the complainant, with his/her approval, in any judicial and/or administrative procedure provided for the enforcement of obligations under this Directive. The above provisions are without prejudice to national rules relating to time limits for bringing actions as regards the principle of equal treatment.

Chapter II of the Ethnic Equal Treatment Directive contains provisions on defence of rights in Article 7 which requires Member States to ensure that judicial and/or administrative procedures, including where they deem it appropriate conciliation procedures, for the enforcement of obligations under this Directive are available to all persons who consider themselves wronged by failure to apply the principle of equal treatment to them, even after the relationship in which the discrimination is alleged to have occurred has ended. Member States shall ensure that associations, organisations or other legal entities which have, in accordance with the criteria laid down by their national law, a legitimate interest in ensuring that the provisions of this Directive are complied with, may engage, either on behalf or in support of the complainant, with his or her approval, in any judicial and/or administrative procedure provided for the enforcement of obligations under the Directive.

Chapter II of the Framework Employment Directive contains provisions on defence of rights. Article 9 requires Member States to ensure that judicial and/or administrative procedures, including where they deem it appropriate conciliation procedures, for the enforcement of obligations under this Directive are available to all persons who consider themselves wronged by failure to apply the principle of equal treatment to them, even after the relationship in which the discrimination is alleged to have occurred has ended. Member States shall ensure that associations, organisations or other legal entities which have, in accordance with the criteria laid down by their national law, a legitimate interest in ensuring that the provisions of this Directive are complied with, may engage, either on behalf or in support of the complainant, with his or her approval, in any judicial and/or administrative procedure provided for the enforcement of obligations under this Directive. In *Bullicke*,[165] the CJEU ruled that:

1. The primary law of the European Union and Article 9 of Council Directive 2000/78/EC of 27 November 2000 establishing a general framework for equal treatment in employment and occupation must be interpreted as not precluding a national procedural rule under which a victim of discrimination in recruitment on grounds of age must make a claim against the perpetrator of that discrimination within two months in order to obtain compensation for pecuniary or non-pecuniary damage, provided:

- firstly, that that time-limit is not less favourable than that applicable to similar domestic actions in employment law,
- secondly, that the fixing of the point from which that time-limit starts to run does not render practically impossible or excessively difficult the exercise of rights conferred by the Directive.

It is for the national court to ascertain whether those two conditions are met.

11.3 Burden of Proof

In *Danfoss*,[166] the CJEU ruled that (1) where an undertaking applies a system of pay which is totally lacking in transparency, it is for the employer to prove that his practice in the matter of wages is not discriminatory, if a female worker establishes, in relation to a relatively large number of employees, that the average pay for women is less than that for men. The case law of the CJEU was codified in the Burden of Proof Directive in 1997.[167] The rule on shared burden of proof is now in regard to gender found in Article 19 in the recast directive. The rule has been generalized to also cover the other unlawful grounds of discrimination, see Article 8 of the Ethnic Equal Treatment Directive and Article 10 of the Framework Employment Directive on burden of proof.

Article 19 of the recast directive on gender equality in employment and occupation provides that Member States shall take such measures as are necessary, in accordance with their national judicial systems, to ensure that, when persons who consider themselves wronged because the principle of equal treatment has not been applied to them establish, before a court or other competent authority, facts from which it may be presumed that there has been

165. Case C-246/09 *Bulicke* [2010] I-7003.
166. Case C-109/88 *Danfoss* [1989] 3199.
167. Council Directive 97/80/EC of 15 December 1997 on the burden of proof in cases of discrimination based on sex.

direct or indirect discrimination, it shall be for the respondent to prove that there has been no breach of the principle of equal treatment. The above provision shall not prevent Member States from introducing rules of evidence which are more favourable to plaintiffs.

The above shall also apply to the situations covered by Article 157 TFEU and, insofar as discrimination based on sex is concerned, by the Pregnancy Directive[168] and the Parental Leave Directive.[169]

Article 8 of the Ethnic Equal Treatment Directive on burden of proof provides that Member States shall take such measures as are necessary, in accordance with their national judicial systems, to ensure that, when persons who consider themselves wronged because the principle of equal treatment has not been applied to them establish, before a court or other competent authority, facts from which it may be presumed that there has been direct or indirect discrimination, it shall be for the respondent to prove that there has been no breach of the principle of equal treatment. The above provision does not prevent Member States from introducing rules of evidence which are more favourable to plaintiffs.

Article 10 of the Framework Employment Directive on burden of proof provides that Member States shall take such measures as are necessary, in accordance with their national judicial systems, to ensure that, when persons who consider themselves wronged because the principle of equal treatment has not been applied to them establish, before a court or other competent authority, facts from which it may be presumed that there has been direct or indirect discrimination, it shall be for the respondent to prove that there has been no breach of the principle of equal treatment. The above provision does not prevent Member States from introducing rules of evidence which are more favourable to plaintiffs.

In *Meister*,[170] the CJEU ruled that:

> Article 8(1) of Council Directive 2000/43/EC of 29 June 2000 implementing the principle of equal treatment between persons irrespective of racial or ethnic origin, Article 10(1) of Council Directive 2000/78/EC of 27 November 2000 establishing a general framework for equal treatment in employment and occupation and Article 19(1) of Directive 2006/54/EC of the European Parliament and of the Council of 5 July 2006 on the implementation of the principle of equal opportunities and equal treatment of men and women in matters of employment and occupation must be interpreted as not entitling a worker who claims plausibly that he meets the requirements listed in a job advertisement and whose application was

168. 92/85/EEC.
169. 96/34/EC.
170. Case C-415/10 *Meister* [2012] ECR nyr.

rejected to have access to information indicating whether the employer engaged another applicant at the end of the recruitment process.

Nevertheless, it cannot be ruled out that a defendant's refusal to grant any access to information may be one of the factors to take into account in the context of establishing facts from which it may be presumed that there has been direct or indirect discrimination. It is for the referring court to determine whether that is the case in the main proceedings, taking into account all the circumstances of the case before it.

In *Feryn,*[171] the CJEU ruled that:

2. Public statements by which an employer lets it be known that under its recruitment policy it will not recruit any employees of a certain ethnic or racial origin are sufficient for a presumption of the existence of a recruitment policy which is directly discriminatory within the meaning of Article 8(1) of Directive 2000/43. It is then for that employer to prove that there was no breach of the principle of equal treatment. It can do so by showing that the undertaking's actual recruitment practice does not correspond to those statements. It is for the national court to verify that the facts alleged are established and to assess the sufficiency of the evidence submitted in support of the employer's contentions that it has not breached the principle of equal treatment.

In *Age Concern,*[172] the CJEU held that Article 6(1) of the Framework Employment Directive must be interpreted as imposing on Member States the burden of establishing to a high standard of proof the legitimacy of the aim relied on as a justification.

11.4 Victimisation

Article 24 of the recast directive provides on victimisation that Member States shall introduce into their national legal systems such measures as are necessary to protect employees, including those who are employees' representatives provided for by national laws and/or practices, against dismissal or other adverse treatment by the employer as a reaction to a complaint within the undertaking or to any legal proceedings aimed at enforcing compliance with the principle of equal treatment.

According to Article 9 of the Ethnic Equal Treatment Directive Member States shall introduce into their national legal systems such measures as are necessary to protect employees against dismissal or other adverse treatment by the employer as a reaction to a complaint within the undertaking or to any legal proceedings aimed at enforcing compliance with the principle of equal treatment.

171. Case C-54/07 *Feryn* [2008] ECR I-5187.
172. Case C-388/07 *Age Concern* [2009] I-1569.

According to Article 11 of the Framework Employment Directive, Member States shall introduce into their national legal systems such measures as are necessary to protect employees against dismissal or other adverse treatment by the employer as a reaction to a complaint within the undertaking or to any legal proceedings aimed at enforcing compliance with the principle of equal treatment.

11.5 Dissemination of information

Article 10 of the Ethnic Equal Treatment Directive on dissemination of information provides that Member States shall take care that the provisions adopted pursuant to the Directive, together with the relevant provisions already in force in this field, are brought to the attention of the persons concerned by all appropriate means, for example at the workplace, throughout their territory.

Article 12 of the Framework Employment Directive on dissemination of information provides that Member States shall take care that the provisions adopted pursuant to the Directive, together with the relevant provisions already in force in this field, are brought to the attention of the persons concerned by all appropriate means, for example at the workplace, throughout their territory.

11.6 Social and Civil dialogue

Article 21 of the recast directive on gender equality in employment and occupation provides on Social dialogue that Member States shall, in accordance with national traditions and practice, take adequate measures to promote social dialogue between the social partners with a view to fostering equal treatment, including, for example, through the monitoring of practices in the workplace, in access to employment, vocational training and promotion, as well as through the monitoring of collective agreements, codes of conduct, research or exchange of experience and good practice. Where consistent with national traditions and practice, Member States shall encourage the social partners, without prejudice to their autonomy, to promote equality between men and women, and flexible working arrangements, with the aim of facilitating the reconciliation of work and private life, and to conclude, at the appropriate level, agreements laying down anti-discrimination rules in the fields referred to in Article 1 which fall within the scope of collective bargaining. These agreements shall respect the provisions of this Directive and the relevant national implementing measures. Member States shall, in accordance with national law, collective agreements or practice, encourage employers to promote equal treatment for men and women in a planned and systematic way in the workplace, in access to employment, vocational training and promotion. To this end, employers shall be encouraged to provide at appropriate regular intervals employees and/or their representatives with appropriate information on equal treatment for men and women in the undertaking. Such information may include an overview of the proportions of men and women at different levels of the organisation; their pay and pay differentials; and possible measures to improve the situation in cooperation with employees' representatives.

Article 22 of the recast directive on dialogue with non-governmental organisations requires Member States to encourage dialogue with appropriate non-governmental organisations which have, in accordance with their national law and practice, a legitimate interest in contributing to the fight against discrimination on grounds of sex with a view to promoting the principle of equal treatment.

Under Article 11 of the Ethnic Equal Treatment Directive on Social dialogue Member States shall, in accordance with their national traditions and practice, take adequate measures to promote dialogue between the social partners with a view to fostering equal treatment, including through the monitoring of workplace practices, collective agreements, codes of conduct and through research or exchange of experiences and good practices. Where consistent with their national traditions and practice, Member States shall encourage the social partners, without prejudice to their autonomy, to conclude at the appropriate level agreements laying down anti-discrimination rules in the fields referred to in Article 3 which fall within the scope of collective bargaining. These agreements shall respect the minimum requirements laid down by the Directive and by the relevant national implementing measures. Article 12 on civil dialogue with non-governmental organisations requires Member States to encourage dialogue with appropriate non-governmental organisations which have, in accordance with their national law and practice, a legitimate interest in contributing to the fight against discrimination on any of the grounds referred to in Article 1 with a view to promoting the principle of equal treatment.

Under Article 13 of the the Framework Employment Directive on Social dialogue Member States shall, in accordance with their national traditions and practice, take adequate measures to promote dialogue between the social partners with a view to fostering equal treatment, including through the monitoring of workplace practices, collective agreements, codes of conduct and through research or exchange of experiences and good practices. Where consistent with their national traditions and practice, Member States shall encourage the social partners, without prejudice to their autonomy, to conclude at the appropriate level agreements laying down anti-discrimination rules in the fields referred to in Article 3 which fall within the scope of collective bargaining. These agreements shall respect the minimum requirements laid down by the Directive and by the relevant national implementing measures. Article 14 on civil dialogue with non-governmental organisations requires Member States to encourage dialogue with appropriate non-governmental organisations which have, in accordance with their national law and practice, a legitimate interest in contributing to the fight against discrimination on any of the grounds referred to in Article 1 with a view to promoting the principle of equal treatment.

11.7 Bodies for the promotion of equal treatment

Article 20 of the recast directive on gender equality in employment and occupation provides on the setting up of Equality bodies for the promotion, analysis, monitoring and support of equal treatment without discrimination on grounds of sex that:

1. Member States shall designate and make the necessary arrangements for a body or bodies for the promotion, analysis, monitoring and support of equal treatment of all persons without discrimination on grounds of sex. These bodies may form part of agencies with responsibility at national level for the defence of human rights or the safeguard of individuals' rights.

2. Member States shall ensure that the competences of these bodies include:
(a) without prejudice to the right of victims and of associations, organisations or other legal entities referred to in Article 17(2), providing independent assistance to victims of discrimination in pursuing their complaints about discrimination;
(b) conducting independent surveys concerning discrimination;
(c) publishing independent reports and making recommendations on any issue relating to such discrimination;
(d) at the appropriate level exchanging available information with corresponding European bodies such as any future European Institute for Gender Equality.

Chapter III of the Ethnic Equal Treatment Directive on bodies for the promotion of equal treatment provides in Article 13 of the Directive similarly that Member States shall designate a body or bodies for the promotion of equal treatment of all persons without discrimination on the grounds of racial or ethnic origin. These bodies may form part of agencies charged at national level with the defence of human rights or the safeguard of individuals' rights. Member States shall ensure that the competences of these bodies include:

- without prejudice to the right of victims and of associations, organisations or other legal entities referred to in Article 7(2), providing independent assistance to victims of discrimination in pursuing their complaints about discrimination,
- onducting independent surveys concerning discrimination,
- publishing independent reports and making recommendations on any issue relating to such discrimination.

To the difference of the rules on gender and ethnic discrimination the Framework Employment Directive does not require that Member States designate special bodies for the promotion of equal treatment without discrimination on grounds of religion or belief, disability, age or sexual orientation.

11.8 Compensation or reparation

Article 18 of the recast directive on gender equality in employment and occupation provides that Member States shall introduce into their national legal systems such measures as are necessary to ensure real and effective compensation or reparation as the Member States so determine for the loss and damage sustained by a person injured as a result of discrimination on grounds of sex, in a way which is dissuasive and proportionate to the damage suffered. Such compensation or reparation may not be restricted by the fixing of a prior upper limit, except in cases where the employer can prove that the only damage suffered by an applicant as a result of discrimination within the meaning of this Directive is the refusal to take his/her job application into consideration. In *Draehmpaehl*,[173] the CJEU held:

1. When a Member State chooses to penalize, under rules overning civil liability, breach of the prohibition of discrimination, Council Directive 76/207/EEC of 9 February 1976 on the implementation of the principle of equal treatment for men and women as regards access to employment, vocational training and promotion, and working conditions, and, in particular, Articles 2(1) and 3(1) thereof, preclude provisions of domestic law which make reparation of damage suffered as a result of discrimination on grounds of sex in the making of an appointment subject to the requirement of fault.

2. Directive 76/207 does not preclude provisions of domestic law which prescribe an upper limit of three months' salary for the amount of compensation which may be claimed by an applicant where the employer can prove that, because the applicant engaged had superior qualifications, the unsuccessful applicant would not have obtained the vacant position even if there had been no discrimination in the selection process. In contrast, the Directive pre-

173. Case C-180/95 *Draehmpaehl* [1997] ECR I-2195.

cludes provisions of domestic law which, unlike other provisions of domestic civil and labour law, prescribe an upper limit of three months' salary for the amount of compensation which may be claimed by an applicant discriminated against on grounds of sex in the making of an appointment where that applicant would have obtained the vacant position if the selection process had been carried out without discrimination.

3. Directive 76/207 precludes provisions of domestic law which, unlike other provisions of domestic civil and labour law, impose a ceiling of six months' salary on the aggregate amount of compensation which, where several applicants claim compensation, may be claimed by applicants who have been discriminated against on grounds of their sex in the making of an appointment.

The CJEU referred to *Dekker*[174] in support of the result that reparation of damage suffered as a result of discrimination on grounds of sex in the making of an appointment cannot be made subject to the requirement of fault (culpa).

11.9 Sanctions/penalties

Article 25 of the recast directive on gender equality in employment and occupation provides that Member States shall lay down the rules on penalties applicable to infringements of the national provisions adopted pursuant to this Directive, and shall take all measures necessary to ensure that they are applied. The penalties, which may comprise the payment of compensation to the victim, must be effective, proportionate and dissuasive. The Member States shall notify those provisions to the Commission by 5 October 2005 at the latest and shall notify it without delay of any subsequent amendment affecting them. In *von Colson and Kamann*,[175] the CJEU held that:

1. Directive No 76/207/EEC does not require discrimination on grounds of sex regarding access to employment to be made the subject of a sanction by way of an obligation imposed on the employer who is the author of the discrimination to conclude a contract of employment with the candidate discriminated against.

2. As regards sanctions for any discrimination which may occur, the directive does not include any unconditional and sufficiently precise obligation which, in the absence of implementing measures adopted within the prescribed time-limits,, may be relied on by an individual in order to obtain specific compensation under the directive, where that is not provided for or permitted under national law.

3. Although Directive No 76/207/EEC, for the purpose of imposing a sanction for the breach of the prohibition of discrimination, leaves the Member States free to choose be-

174. Case C-177/88 *Dekker* [1990] ECR I-3941.
175. Case 14/83 *von Colson* [1984] ECR p. 1891.

tween the different solutions suitable for achieving its objective, it nevertheless requires that if a Member State chooses to penalize breaches of that prohibition by the award of compensation, then in order to ensure that it is effective and that it has a deterrent effect, that compensation must in any event be adequate in relation to the damage sustained and must therefore amount to more than purely nominal compensation such as, for example, the reimbursement only of the expenses incurred in connection with the application. It is for the national court to interpret and apply the legislation adopted for the implementation of the directive in conformity with the requirements of Community law, in so far as it is given discretion to do so under national law.

Article 15 of the Directive on Ethnic Equal Treatment provides that Member States shall lay down the rules on sanctions applicable to infringements of the national provisions adopted pursuant to this Directive and shall take all measures necessary to ensure that they are applied. The sanctions, which may comprise the payment of compensation to the victim, must be effective, proportionate and dissuasive. In *Feryn*,[176] the CJEU ruled that:

3. Article 15 of Directive 2000/43 requires that rules on sanctions applicable to breaches of national provisions adopted in order to transpose that directive must be effective, proportionate and dissuasive, even where there is no identifiable victim.

Article 17 of the Framework Employment Directive provides that Member States shall lay down the rules on sanctions applicable to infringements of the national provisions adopted pursuant to this Directive and shall take all measures necessary to ensure that they are applied. The sanctions, which may comprise the payment of compensation to the victim, must be effective, proportionate and dissuasive. As appears the provision is identical with Article 15 of the Directive on Ethnic Equal Treatment, see above.

176. Case C-54/07 *Feryn* [2008] ECR I-5187.

CHAPTER SEVEN

Employment Contracts and Employment Relationships

1 Introduction

This chapter deals with the EU regulation of employment contracts and employment relationships, in particular posting of workers, the employer's obligation to inform employees of the conditions applicable to the contract or employment relationship, part-time work, fixed term contracts and temporary agency work.

Employment contracts of indefinite duration are the general form of employment relationship. Since the 1990's, the EU has, however, focused on regulating various forms of atypical employment contracts or employment relationships with a view to promoting the fundamental rights/EMU perspective on law described in Chapter One and – as stated e.g. in the Preamble to the Temporary Works Agency directive – flexicurity, which strikes a balance between *flexibility* and *security* in the labour market and helps both workers and employers to seize the opportunities offered by globalisation.

2 Sources of law

2.1 National law

In the national law of most of the EU Member States, labour or employment law as a special discipline is of recent origin. As stated by Hepple[1] it became recognised as a distinct division of law only after the Second World War. Be-

1. Hepple, Bob: The Making of labour law in Europe. A comparative study of nine countries up to 1945, London, 1986 p. 7.

fore that is was just seen as part of general contract law. In most countries employment or labour law contains many rules which protect the worker/employee as the presumed weak party to the contract.

2.2 Public International law

In public international law there has not been the same focus on atypical forms of employment as in EU law. Placement services have, however, been the object of ILO conventions since the 1930's. The most up to date Convention on the subject is the Private Employment Agencies Convention, 1997,[2] see further below in section 8. There is an ILO Convention on protection against dismissal,[3] see further below in section 10.

2.3 EU law

2.3.1 Directives

The EU has adopted directives on posting of workers,[4] the employer's obligation to inform employees of the conditions applicable to the contract or employment relationship,[5] part-time work,[6] fixed term contracts[7] and temporary agency work.[8]

2.3.2 Fundamental rights

Article 29 CFREU on the right of access to placement services provides that 'everyone has the right of access to a free placement service.' Article 30 CFREU on protection in the event of unjustified dismissal provides that 'Every worker has the right to protection against unjustified dismissal, in accordance with Union law and national laws and practices.'

In the Preamble to the directive on Temporary Agency Work there is reference both to the CFREU and the Community Charter of the Fundamental

2. ILO Convention no 181.
3. ILO Convention No. 158 and Recommendation No. 166 concerning termination of employment.
4. See Directive 96/71/EC of the European Parliament and of the Council of 16 December 1996 concerning the posting of workers in the framework of the provision of services.
5. See Directive 91/533/EEC of 14 October 1991 on an employer's obligation to inform employees of the conditions applicable to the contract or employment relationship.
6. See Directive 97/81/EC of 15 December 1997 concerning the Framework Agreement on part-time work concluded by UNICE, CEEP and the ETUC.
7. See Directive 99/70/EC of 28 June 1999 concerning the framework agreement on fixed-term work concluded by ETUC, UNICE and CEEP.
8. Directive 2008/104/EC on temporary agency work.

Social Rights of Workers from 1989.[9] It is declared that the directive respects the fundamental rights and complies with the principles recognised by the CFREU. In particular, it is designed to ensure full compliance with Article 31 of the CFREU, which provides that every worker has the right to working conditions which respect his or her health, safety and dignity, and to limitation of maximum working hours, to daily and weekly rest periods and to an annual period of paid leave. The reference to the Community Charter of the Fundamental Social Rights of Workers 1989 is to point 7 which provides *inter alia*, that the completion of the internal market must lead to an improvement in the living and working conditions of workers in the EU. This process will be achieved by harmonising progress on these conditions, mainly in respect of forms of work such as fixed-term contract work, part-time work, temporary agency work and seasonal work.

As set out in Chapter Two, the CJEU held in *Polier*[10] that a French law which permitted dismissals without a valid reason was outside the scope of EU law with the consequence that EU fundamental rights could not be invoked in national law. The CJEU therefore refused to answer a question about the compatibility of a French dismissal provision with the CFREU and some international Conventions (ILO Convention no. 158 on termination of employment and the Council of Europe Social Charter).

3 Choice of Law and international jurisdiction

3.1 The Rome I Regulation

In recital 34-37 of the Rome I Regulation[11] it is stated that the rule on individual employment contracts (in Article 8 of the Regulation) should not prejudice the application of the overriding mandatory provisions of the country to which a worker is posted in accordance with the Posting of Workers Directive, see below. It is further stated that employees should not be deprived of the protection afforded to them by provisions which cannot be derogated from by agreement or which can only be derogated from to their benefit. As

9. http://www.aedh.eu/plugins/fckeditor/userfiles/file/Conventions%20internationales/ Community_Charter_of_the_Fundamental_Social_Rights_of_Workers.pdf.
10. Case C 361/07, *Polier*, not reported in English, available in French at the CJEU website curia.europa.eu.
11. Regulation EC/593/2008 of the European Parliament and of the Council on the law applicable to contractual obligations (Rome I). The Rome I Regulation does not apply in Denmark due to the Danish reservation concerning justice and home affairs.

regards individual employment contracts, work carried out in another country should be regarded as temporary if the employee is expected to resume working in the country of origin after carrying out his tasks abroad. The conclusion of a new contract of employment with the original employer or an employer belonging to the same group of companies as the original employer should not preclude the employee from being regarded as carrying out his work in another country temporarily.

The parties can choose the applicable law according to Article 3 of the Regulation. The application of the chosen law cannot have the result of depriving the employee of the protection afforded to him by the mandatory rules of the law applicable by default, i.e. in the absence of choice.

The law applicable by default is the *lex loci laboris*, namely, the law of the country 'in which' or, 'from which' the employee habitually carries out his work in performance of the contract. The expression 'from which' was not contained in the Convention. It has been introduced – following the case-law of the CJEU[12] on Article 19 of the Brussels I Regulation[13] – to cope with those employees who do not carry out their job in the territory of only one country, but where there is a country which constitutes a sort of 'base of operations'. The new text clarifies that the country where the employee habitually works is not deemed to have changed just because he is temporarily posted to another country or countries. Recital 36 Rome I points out that the concept of temporarily posted has to be interpreted in a subjective ex ante way ('if the employee is expected to resume working in the country of origin after carrying out his task abroad').

Where it appears from the circumstances as a whole that the contract is most closely connected with a country other than that indicated according to the abovementioned rules, the law of that country shall apply.

Article 8 of the Rome I Regulation provides on individual employment contracts:

> 1. An individual employment contract shall be governed by the law chosen by the parties in accordance with Article 3. Such a choice of law may not, however, have the result of depriving the employee of the protection afforded to him by provisions that cannot be derogated from by agreement under the law that, in the absence of choice, would have been applicable pursuant to paragraphs 2, 3 and 4 of this Article.

12. Case C-125/92 *Geels* [1993] ECR I-4075, Case C-383/95 *Rutten* [1997] ECR I-57 and Case C-37/00 *Weber* [2002] ECR I-2013.
13. Repealed and replaced by Regulation (EU) No 1215/2012 of the European Parliament and of the Council of 12 December 2012 on jurisdiction and the recognition and enforcement of judgments in civil and commercial matters.

2. To the extent that the law applicable to the individual employment contract has not been chosen by the parties, the contract shall be governed by the law of the country in which or, failing that, from which the employee abitually carries out his work in performance of the contract. The country where the work is habitually carried out shall not be deemed to have changed if he is temporarily employed in another country.

3. Where the law applicable cannot be determined pursuant to paragraph 2, the contract shall be governed by the law of the country where the place of business through which the employee was engaged is situated.

4. Where it appears from the circumstances as a whole that the contract is more closely connected with a country other than that indicated in paragraphs 2 or 3, the law of that other country shall apply.

Under the Rome I Regulation, the legal relations between an employer who temporarily posts labour to another country fall under the law of the home country and not the host country; thus in *Laval*,[14] Latvian, not Swedish law.

3.2 The Rome Convention

The Rome Convention[15] which in regard to other EU Member States than Denmark has been replaced by the Rome I Regulation on the law applicable to contractual obligations is in respect of employment contracts very similar to the Rome I Regulation. Article 3 of the Convention provides that, as a general rule, the parties are free to choose the applicable law. In the absence of choice, the contract of employment is governed, under Article 6(2) of the Convention, by the law of the country in which the employee habitually carries out his work, even if he is temporarily employed in another country.

4 Posting of workers in the framework of the provision of services

4.1 Scope

According to the posting of workers directive[16] a worker is 'a posted worker' when he is employed in one EU Member State but sent by his employer on a temporary basis to carry out his work in another Member State. For example, a service provider may win a contract in another country and send his em-

14. Case C-341/05 *Laval* [2007] ECR I-11767.
15. OJ 1980 L 266.
16. 96/71/EC.

ployees there to carry out the contract. This trans-national provision of services, where employees are sent to work in a Member State other than the one they usually work in, gives rise to a distinctive category, namely that of 'posted workers'. This category does not include migrant workers who go to another Member State to seek work and are employed there. The Posting of Workers Directive covers employees being sent to another Member State in three situations:

1. When an employer posts a worker to another Member States on his own account and under his direction, under a contract which the employer has concluded with the party in the State for whom the services are intended;
2. When an employer posts a worker to an establishment or to an undertaking owned by the group in the territory of a Member State;
3. When the employer, being a temporary employment undertaking or placement agency, hires out a worker to a user undertaking established or operating in another Member States.

The employment relationship between the employer and the posted worker must be maintained during the period of posting. See further on temporary agency work below in section 8.

4.2 Aim and legal basis of the posting of workers directive

By guaranteeing fair competition and respect for the rights of posted works, the EU legislation provides a framework so that businesses and workers can use the opportunities offered by the internal market and globalisation. The legal basis of the Posting of Workers directive is Article 114 TFEU (ex Article 95 EC) on the establishment and functioning of the internal market, see above in Chapter Two. It does thus not follow from Article 153 TFEU that the directive – like most employment law directives – is a minimum directive. Internal market directives can be anything from minimum directives to directives providing for full harmonization. To guarantee that the rights and working conditions of a posted worker are protected throughout the European Union, and to avoid 'social dumping' where foreign service providers can undercut local service providers because their labour standards are lower, the EU law has established a core of mandatory rules regarding the terms and conditions of employment to be applied to an employee posted to work in another Member State. These rules will reflect the standards of local workers in the host Member State (that is, where the employee is sent to work).

Generally, the Posting of Workers Directive is somewhat unclear, and its extent has been subject to debate.[17] This is due to the fact that the purposes of the Directive are partially conflicting. On the one side, it is intended to advance the free movement of services across the borders; on the other side, it shall ensure fair competition and measures warranting that the rights of workers are respected.[18] This dual purpose of the Directive became topical in connection with the Eastern enlargement of the EU as of 1 May 2004.[19] This is illustrated by *Laval*[20] and *Viking*.[21]

Furthermore, the Posting of Workers directive lays down the obligation for Member States to cooperate among themselves and to grant public access to information on national employment conditions.

4.3 Posting of workers and choice of law

The Posting of Workers Directive is primarily a choice of law directive,[22] which governs which law shall apply in the relation between an employer posting workers and those workers. Compared to the Rome Convention, the contribution of the Posting of Workers Directive is primarily to designate at EU level a number of mandatory rules in transnational posting situations. If there had been no special rules on posting of workers it would follow from Article 8(2) in the Rome I Regulation that, if the law applicable to the individual employment contract has not been chosen by the parties, the contract shall be governed by the law of the country in which the employee habitually carries out his work in performance of the contract. The country where the work is habitually carried out shall not be deemed to have changed if he is temporarily employed in another country. The employment contracts of posted workers from low wage countries would therefore be governed by the law of their home country.

The posted workers directive changed this rule as regards central employment conditions like minimum wages and some other core working con-

17. See Davies, Paul: Posted Workers: Single Market or Protection of National Labour Law Systems?, Common Market Law Review 1997 p. 571.
18. See e.g. paragraph 5 in the preamble of the Directive.
19. See for an article arguing for the right of companies to use the potential advantage of access to low-cost labour Reich, Norbert: Free Movement v. Social Rights in an Enlarged Union – the Laval and Viking Cases before the ECJ, German Law Journal 2008 p. 125, http://www.germanlawjournal.com/.
20. Case C-341/05 *Laval* [2007] ECR I-11767.
21. Case C-438/05 *Viking* [2007] ECR I-10779.
22. See on the Directive Liukkunen, Ulla: The Role of Mandatory Rules in International Labour Law – A Comparative Study in the Conflict of Laws, Helsinki 2004.

dition. The idea of the directive is that where a Member State has certain minimum terms and conditions of employment, these must also apply to workers posted to that State. However, there is nothing to stop the employer applying working conditions that are more favourable to workers such as, for instance, those of the sending member State (that is, where the employee usually works). The core of mandatory rules on posting covers a wide range of issues such as maximum work periods and minimum rest periods, minimum paid annual leave, minimum rates of pay, equal treatment and the conditions of hiring out workers, in particular the supply of workers by temporary employment undertakings. The legislation also tackles issues such as health and safety at work and includes protective measures in the terms and conditions of employment of pregnant women, of children and of young people.

The Posting of Workers Directive moves certain subjects – first and foremost the core area in Article 3(1), (a) to (g) – from the law of the home country to the law of the host country. In addition, the legislator in the host country may – within a public policy (ordre public) limit – require some additional subjects be dealt with under the law of the host country.

According to the Swedish Labour Court's decision to refer the matter in *Laval*, Laval claimed in the Swedish main case that acceptance of the Swedish collective agreement would impose an extensive choice of law in favour of Swedish labour law in conflict with the international private law rule in the Rome Convention and the Posting of Workers Directive. The company would under the Swedish collective agreement at issue be bound by the Swedish Employment Protection Act, a requirement which according to the Commission is contrary to the Posting of Workers Directive.[23]

In regard to posted workers the Posting of Workers Directive takes precedence over the choice of law rules in the Rome Convention and the Rome I Regulation. Under the Rome Convention, the legal relations between an employer who temporarily posts labour to another country thus fall under the law of the home country and not the host country; thus in the Laval case, Latvian, not Swedish law, i.e. the opposite of the rule under the Posting of Workers Directive.

4.4 Main Content of the Directive

The Directive seeks to guarantee that posted workers will enjoy, whatever the law applicable to the employment relationship the application of certain minimum protective provisions in force in the Member State to which they are

23. See COM(2003) 458 p. 14.

posted. To this end, Article 3(1) of the Directive lays down the mandatory rules to be observed by employers during the period of posting in regard to the following issues:

(a) maximum work periods and minimum rest periods;
(b) minimum paid annual holidays;
(c) the minimum rates of pay, including overtime rates; this point does not apply to supplementary occupational retirement pension schemes;
(d) the conditions of hiring-out of workers, in particular the supply of workers by temporary employment undertakings;
(e) health, safety and hygiene at work;
(f) protective measures with regard to the terms and conditions of employment of pregnant women or women who have recently given birth, of children and of young people;
(g) equality of treatment between men and women and other provisions on non-discrimination

4.5 Statutory minimum standards

The host country may by statute, administrative act, or universally applicable collective agreements fix any level (possibly a high level) of minimum standards that respect the general framework of Article 56TFEU as regards matters within the core area of the Directive.

In *Laval*, the CJEU held that the level of protection which must be guaranteed to workers posted to the territory of the host Member State is limited, in principle, to that provided for in Article 3(1), first subparagraph, (a) to (g) of the Posting of Workers Directive, unless, pursuant to the law or collective agreements in the Member State of origin, those workers already enjoy more favourable terms and conditions of employment as regards the matters referred to in that provision. It did, however, also state:[24]

> It must be noted, in this respect, that since the purpose of Directive 96/71 is not to harmonise systems for establishing terms and conditions of employment in the Member States, the latter are free to choose a system at the national level which is not expressly mentioned among those provided for in that directive, provided that it does not hinder the provision of services between the Member States

In practice the most important working condition in relation to posted workers is probably minimum wages. Pursuant to the Posting of Workers Directive, the term 'minimum wage' is defined in accordance with national law and/or case law in the Member State in whose area the worker is posted; i.e.

24. In paragraph 68.

in *Rüffert*[25] according to German law and in *Laval*, according to Swedish law.[26] Nevertheless, both in *Rüffert* and *Laval*,[27] the ECJ found that the wage claim at issue was not a minimum wage claim.

4.6 Topics within the core area of Article 3(1) of the Posting of Workers Directive

Pursuant to the Posting of Workers Directive, the core area of working conditions listed in Article 3(1), (a) to (g) of the Directive (working hours, holidays, minimum rates of pay, temporary workers, working environment, children and young people/pregnant women, equality of treatment) shall be determined under the rules of the law of the host country and not the law of the home country provided that these are laid down by certain sources of law (legislation, administrative acts, and generally applicable collective agreements) or, in countries (such as Sweden and Denmark) where minimum wage legislation and generally applicable collective agreements do not exist, collective agreements that have been extended under Article 2(8) of the Posting of Workers Directive.

By statutory acts, administrative acts, or generally applicable collective agreements, any level (including a high level) of minimum standards may be fixed within the framework of Article 56 TFEU as regards matters within the core area of the Posting of Workers Directive, see below on minimum wage legislation.

Pursuant to Article 3(7) of the Posting of Workers Directive, the provisions in Article 3(1) to (6) of the Directive do not preclude the application of working conditions and conditions of employment that are more favourable to the workers. The parties to the individual employment contract can thus agree more favourable conditions than those following from statutory minimum standards in the host country. However, according to the Laval Judgment, there is no corresponding contractual freedom for collective agreements.

4.7 Minimum Wages

In practice the most important working condition in relation to posted workers is probably wages. According to ILO there is legislation regarding minimum wage fixing in more than 90% of countries.[28] In twenty Member States

25. Case C-346/06 [2008] ECR I-0000 nyr.
26. See Article 3(1) *in fine* of the Posting of Workers Directive.
27. See paragraph 51 in the Rüffert case and paragraph 70 in the Laval case.
28. See http://www.ilo.org/public/english/protection/condtrav/pdf/infosheets/w-1.pdf.

of the EU (Belgium, Spain, Estonia, Greece, France, Hungary, Ireland, Latvia, Lithuania, Luxembourg, Malta, the Netherlands, Poland, Portugal, Slovakia, Slovenia, Czech Republic and the United Kingdom,Bulgaria and Romania) and in one candidate country (Turkey), collective bargaining is subject to a statutory national minimum wage. The other EU Member States do not have a statutory national minimum wage, i.e. countries like Norway, Sweden, Finland, Denmark, Switzerland, Germany, Austria, Italy, and Cyprus have no minimum wage laws, but rely on employers and trade unions to set minimum earnings through collective bargaining.[29] In most of the EU Member States collective agreements can be extended so as to become generally applicable, see below.

The minimum wage level is between 34% and 50% of average gross monthly earnings in industry and the services sector. In January 2006, the gross minimum wage varied among the EU Member States from 129 euro (Latvia) to 1503 euro (Luxembourg).

Article 4 of the Council of Europe's Social Charter (1961) provides:

> with a view to ensuring the effective exercise of the right to a fair remuneration, the Contracting Parties undertake:
> 1. to recognise the right of workers to a remuneration such as will give them and their families a decent standard of living . . .

The Community Charter of Fundamental Social Rights for Workers 1989 which is soft law provides in Article 5:

> All employment shall be fairly remunerated.
> To this end, in accordance with arrangements applying in each country:
> (i) workers shall be assured of an equitable wage, i.e., a wage sufficient to enable them to have a decent standard of living.

4.8 Universally Applicable Collective Agreements

Most EU Member States have a system for extending collective agreements so as to make them binding on employers who are not parties to them. That possibility does not exist in Italy and the UK and only to a limited extent in the Nordic countries.[30] In Sweden and Denmark,[31] collective agreements

29. See http://epp.eurostat.ec.europa.eu/cache/ITY_OFFPUB/KS-NK-06-009/EN/KS-NK-06-009-EN.PDF.
30. See the overview in the Commission's report on Industrial relations in Europe COM(2000)113 p 41.

can*not* be extended to cover employers who are not parties to them. In Norway there is a limited possibility of extension of the coverage of collective agreements. In Finland there is wider access to give *erga omnes* effect to collective agreements.[32]

In the Rüffert case[33] the CJEU had to strike a balance between the freedom to provide services, on the one hand, and the overriding requirements of the protection of workers and the prevention of social dumping, on the other. The Oberlandesgericht (Higher Regional Court), Celle (Germany), asked the CJEU whether EU law must be interpreted as precluding national legislation on the award of public contracts that requires contractors and, indirectly, their subcontractors to pay workers posted in the framework of the performance of a public contract at least the remuneration prescribed by the collective agreement in force at the place where those services are performed, on pain of penalties that may go as far as the termination of the works contract, where the collective agreement to which the legislation in question refers is not declared to be of universal application. The relevant national legislation (the Law of Land Niedersachsen on the award of public contracts (Landesvergabegesetz) provided under the heading 'Declaration that the collective agreements will be complied with':

> 'Contracts for building services shall be awarded only to undertakings which, when lodging a tender, undertake in writing to pay their employees, when performing those services, at least the remuneration prescribed by the collective agreement at the place where those services are performed and at the time prescribed by the collective agreement. For the purposes of the first sentence, the term 'services' means services provided by the principal contractor and by subcontractors. The first sentence shall also apply to the award of transport services in local public transport.'

Paragraph 4(1) of the Law, headed 'Use of subcontractors', provided:

> 'The contractor may assign to subcontractors services for which his establishment is set up only where the contracting authority has given written consent in a given case. The tenderers are required at the stage they lodge their tenders to state which services are to be devolved to subcontractors. In so far as services are assigned to subcontractors, the contractor must also undertake to impose on the subcontractors the obligations laid down in Para-

31. In Denmark a recent sociological study shows that the coverage of collective agreements in the public sector is close to 100% but in the private sector only around 70%.
32. See for details Ahlberg, Kerstin and Niklas Bruun: Kollektivavtal i EU. Om almängiltiga avtal och social dumping, Stockholm 1996.
33. Case C-346/06 [2008] ECR I-1989.

graphs 3, 4 and 7(2) applicable to contractors and to monitor compliance with these obligations by the subcontractors.'

The company Objekt und Bauregie undertook to pay employees employed on the Göttingen-Rosdorf prison building site the wages laid down in the 'Buildings and public works' collective agreement, which applied to this case. It emerged that a Polish subcontractor of Objekt und Bauregie was paying its 53 workers engaged on the building site only 46.57% of the prescribed minimum wage and a formal finding to that effect was made in a notice issued against the person primarily responsible at the Polish company. The works contract was terminated following a criminal investigation and proceedings commenced between Land Niedersachsen and the liquidator of the assets of Objekt und Bauregie to determine whether Objekt und Bauregie was required to pay a contractual penalty amounting to EUR 84 934.31 (1% of the amount of the contract) for breach of its undertaking concerning rates of pay. The case was appealed to the Oberlandesgericht Celle (Higher Regional Court, Celle). Uncertain as to the lawfulness of the provision laying down a contractual penalty, that court has asked the CJEU to decide whether the freedom to provide services precludes a statutory obligation requiring a contractor in a public works contract to undertake to pay its employees at least the remuneration prescribed by the applicable collective agreement.

In Germany labour law is a federal matter whereas procurement law is a matter for the 'Länder'. Germany has a system for declaring collective agreements universally applicable for all undertakings performing services in Germany.

The collective agreement at issue in the Rüffert case had not been declared universally applicable in Germany. The procurement Act for Land Niedersachsen required contracting authorities to see to it that tenderers for public contracts complied with a 'local' collective agreement for Niedersachsen which laid down a higher level of pay than the universally applicable collective agreement for the construction industry in Germany. In answer to a written question from the CJEU, Land Niedersachsen had confirmed this.

The Advocate General proposed that the CJEU should rule that the Posting of Workers Directive and Article 49 EC must be interpreted as not precluding national legislation, such as the Landesvergabegesetz of Land Niedersachsen, on the award of public contracts which requires contractors and, indirectly, their subcontractors to pay workers posted in the framework of the performance of a public contract at least the remuneration prescribed by the collective agreement in force at the place where those services are performed, on pain of penalties that may go as far as the termination of the works contract, if the collective agreement to which the legislation in question refers is not declared to be universally applicable. The CJEU did not follow the Advocate General but held that the Posting of Workers Directive, interpreted in the light of Article 56 TFEU, precludes an authority of a Member State, in a situation such as that at issue in the main proceedings, from adopting a measure of a legislative nature requiring the contracting authority to designate as contractors for public works contracts only those undertakings which, when submitting their tenders, agree in writing to pay their employees, in return for performance of the services concerned, at least as minimum wage the remuneration prescribed by the collective agreement in force at the place where those services are performed.

Pursuant to the Posting of Workers Directive, the term 'minimum wage' is defined in accordance with national law and/or case law in the Member State in whose area the worker is posted; i.e. in the Rüffert case according to German law and in the Laval case, according to Swedish law.[34] Nevertheless, both in the Rüffert and the Laval case,[35] the CJEU found that the wage claim at issue was not a minimum wage claim.

For the enforcement of demands concerning minimum wage in countries that (like Sweden and Denmark) have not set minimum wage by statute, administrative act, or generally applicable collective agreement, there is freedom to act according to the Laval Judgment[36] within the frame of Article 56 TFEU, i.e. the same statutory rights that have been regarded as existing law by most hitherto. Therefore, what is to be considered minimum wage is of great importance to the practical implications of the Laval Judgment for the right to take collective action to obtain a certain pay level, see below.

4.9 Outside of the Core Area. Public Policy (Ordre Public)

Under Article 3(10) of the Posting of Workers Directive, the Directive does not preclude the Member States from imposing work conditions and conditions of employment in areas other than the core areas mentioned above on national companies and companies from other States in compliance with the EC Treaty, as long as it is a matter of basic principles of law (public policy). In the Commission's communication on the completion of the Posting of Workers Directive, the Commission adopts a very narrow interpretation of the public policy concept in this provision.[37] As an example of something the

34. See Article 3(1) *in fine* of the Posting of Workers Directive.
35. See paragraph 51 in the Rüffert case and paragraph 70 in the Laval case.
36. See paragraph 68 in the Laval case.
37. COM(2003) 458 p. 14.

Member States are not allowed to, the Commission mentions extending of national legislation on job security to apply on seconded labour, which would be the consequence of the Swedish collective agreement in the Laval case. Article 3(10) of the Directive has recently been interpreted by the CJEU in an action against Luxembourg for failure to fulfil obligations under the Treaty.[38] When the Posting of Workers Directive was adopted, Declaration No 10 on Article 3(10) of the Directive was recorded in the minutes of the Council of the European Union as follows: 'The Council and the Commission stated: the expression 'public policy provisions' should be construed as covering those mandatory rules from which there can be no derogation and which, by their nature and objective, meet the imperative requirements of the public interest. These may include, in particular, the prohibition of forced labour or the involvement of public authorities in monitoring compliance with legislation on working conditions.' The contested Luxembourg legislation provided:

(1) All the laws, regulations and administrative provisions and those resulting from collective agreements which have been declared universally applicable or an arbitration decision with a scope similar to that of universally applicable collective agreements which concern the following matters:

1. the written contract of employment or the document established pursuant to [Council] Directive 91/533/EEC of 14 October 1991 on an employer's obligation to inform employees of the conditions applicable to the contract or employment relationship (OJ 1991 L 288, p. 32);
2. the minimum rates of pay and automatic adjustment to reflect changes in the cost of living;
3. working time and weekly rest periods;
4. paid leave;
5. annual closure periods;
6. public holidays;
7. the rules on temporary work and the loan of workers;
8. the rules on part-time and fixed-term work;
9. the protective measures applicable to the terms and conditions of employment of children and of young people and of pregnant women or women who have recently given birth;
10. non-discrimination;
11. collective labour agreements;
12. enforced inactivity in accordance with the legislation on bad weather or technical layoffs;

38. Case C-319/06 [2008] ECR I-4323. Advocate General Trstenjak gave her Opinion on 13 September 2007.

13. clandestine or illegal work, including the provisions on work permits for workers who are not nationals of a Member State of the European Economic Area;
14. the safety and health of workers in the workplace in general and, in particular, the accident prevention rules of the Association d'assurance contre les accidents (Accident Insurance Association) issued in accordance with Article 154 of the Social Security Code and the minimum requirements concerning safety and health laid down by Grand-Ducal Regulation, adopted following the mandatory opinion of the Conseil d'Etat and with the approval of the Conference of the Presidents of the Chamber of Deputies on the basis of Article 14 of the amended Law of 17 June 1994 on the safety and health of workers in the workplace.

shall constitute mandatory provisions falling under national public policy as regards, in particular, collective labour agreements or contracts in accordance with the Law of 27 March 1986 approving the Convention of Rome of 19 June 1980 on the law applicable to contractual obligations and are as such applicable to all workers performing an activity in the territory of the Grand Duchy of Luxembourg, including those temporarily posted to Luxembourg, regardless of the duration or purpose of the posting.

(2) The provisions of paragraph 1 of this article shall apply to all workers irrespective of their nationality in the service of any undertaking, regardless of its nationality or the location of its registered or head office.

The CJEU held that by declaring the provisions of points (1), (2), (8) and (11) of the above law to be mandatory provisions falling under national public policy Luxembourg had failed to fulfil its obligations under the Posting of Workers Directive and Article 56 TFEU.

In *Laval*, the CJEU held that only Member States and not private trade unions can ensure basic principles of law (public policy). Thus according to the Laval Judgment, there is no autonomous freedom to act in respect of the collective agreement regulation of matters outside the scope of the core areas listed in Article 3(1), (a) to (g) of the Posting of Workers Directive. For instance action to obtain collective agreement on job security for posted workers is not possible and perhaps the Member States cannot ensure this result by statute either.

4.10 Posting of Workers and collective action

The collective dimension between a seconding employer (e.g. Laval) and trade unions seeking a collective agreement (e.g. the Swedish unions in the Laval case) is not explicitly governed by the Posting of Workers Directive. In the preamble to the Directive[39] it is stated that 'this Directive is without prejudice to the law of the Member States concerning collective action'. This interpretation of the Directive read with Article 49 EC by the CJEU in the Laval case nevertheless entails certain amendments/restrictions in Nordic law as regards the access to collective action.

As set out above Articles 49 and 56 TFEU prohibit both direct and indirect discrimination due to nationality as well as nationality-neutral restrictions on the free movement. In several cases the CJEU has decided on cross-border contracts in relation to the Treaties, particularly Article 56 TFEU on the free movement of services.[40] *Rush Portuguesa* is still a leasing case. The CJEU among other things held (emphasis added) that:[41]

> EU law does not preclude Member States from extending their legislation, or *collective labour agreements* entered into by both sides of industry, to any person who is employed, even temporarily, within their territory, no matter in which country the employer is established.

This paragraph from *Rush Portuguesa* is repeated in the preamble to the Posting of Workers Directive.[42] According to the wording, this means collective labour agreements of all kinds concerning all kinds of working conditions, not limited to minimum wage or conditions within statutory minimum standards.

4.11 ILO Convention 94 on Labour Clauses in Public Contracts

According to ILO Convention no. 94 from 1949 on labour clauses in public contracts, public works contracts, services contracts etc. must contain clauses ensuring the workers pay, working hours and other working conditions that are no less favourable than the ones applicable by collective agreement, arbi-

39. Paragraph 22 of the preamble. See for an equivalent provision Article 1(7) of the Service Directive, 2006/1 23/EC and Hendrickx: The Services Directive and Social Dumping: National Labour Law Under Strain? in Ulla Neergaard, Ruth Nielsen and Lynn M. Roseberry (eds): The Services Directive – Consequences for the Welfare State and the European Social Model, Copenhagen 2008.
40. See generally on the practice of the CJEU Giesen, Richard: Posting: Social Protection of Workers vs. Fundamental Freedoms?, Common Market Law Review 2003 p. 143. In the Laval case, *Arbetsdomstolen* had asked about Article 12 EC, but when Article 49 EC applies, Article 12 EC cannot be used. Therefore the CJEU did not answer this part of the question.
41. Case C-113/89 *Rush Portuguesa* [1990] ECR 1-1417, paragraph 18.
42. See paragraph 12.

tral award, national legislation or administrative acts to similar work within the same trade or industry in the region where the work is carried out.

ILO convention 94 is ratified by 59[43] countries including 10 EU countries (Austria, Belgium, Bulgaria, Cyprus, Denmark, Finland, France, Italy, Netherlands and Spain). The United Kingdom ratified the convention in 1950 but denounced it in 1982. One EEA country (Norway) has also ratified this convention. ILO Convention 94 applies to contracts which fulfil the following conditions:

(a) that one at least of the parties to the contract is a public authority;
(b) that the execution of the contract involves--
 (i) the expenditure of funds by a public authority; and
 (ii) the employment of workers by the other party to the contract;
(c) that the contract is a contract for--
 (i) the construction, alteration, repair or demolition of public works;
 (ii) the manufacture, assembly, handling or shipment of materials, supplies or equipment; or
 (iii) the performance or supply of services; and
(d) that the contract is awarded by a central authority of a Member of the International Labour Organisation for which the Convention is in force.

The competent authority shall determine the extent to which and the manner in which the Convention shall be applied to contracts awarded by authorities other than central authorities. The Convention applies to work carried out by subcontractors or assignees of contracts; appropriate measures shall be taken by the competent authority to ensure such application.

Under Article 2 contracts to which the Convention applies shall include clauses ensuring to the workers concerned wages (including allowances), hours of work and other conditions of labour which are not less favourable than those established for work of the same character in the trade or industry concerned in the district where the work is carried on --

(a) by collective agreement or other recognised machinery of negotiation between organisations of employers and workers representative respectively of substantial proportions of the employers and workers in the trade or industry concerned; or
(b) by arbitration award; or
(c) by national laws or regulations.

According to Article 5 of the Convention adequate sanctions shall be applied, by the withholding of contracts or otherwise, for failure to observe and apply

43. See http://www.ilo.org/ilolex/cgi-lex/ratifcc.pl?C094.

the provisions of labour clauses in public contracts. Appropriate measures shall be taken, by the withholding of payments under the contract or otherwise, for the purpose of enabling the workers concerned to obtain the wages to which they are entitled.

A Member which has ratified the Convention may denounce it after the expiration of ten years from the date on which the Convention first comes into force, by an act communicated to the Director-General of the International Labour Office for registration. Such denunciation shall not take effect until one year after the date on which it is registered.

The CJEU did not consider the relationship between ILO Convention 94 and EU law in *Rüffert*. As Germany has not ratified that convention it was not directly relevant in that case. One may, however, ask if it is a consequence of the ruling in *Rüffert* that there is a contradiction between EU law on free movement and ILO Convention 94. Under Article 352 TFEU the rights and obligations arising from agreements concluded before 1 January 1958 or, for acceding States, before the date of their accession, between one or more Member States on the one hand, and one or more third countries on the other, shall not be affected by the provisions of the EC Treaty. To the extent that such agreements are not compatible with the EC Treaty, the Member States concerned shall take all appropriate steps to eliminate the incompatibilities. In a short-term perspective those Member States which have ratified ILO Convention 94 on labour clauses before joining the EU must continue to observe their duties under that convention. In a long-term perspective there will be a duty to denounce ILO Convention 94 if it is incompatible with the EC Treaty. If there are problems of compatibility between EU law and ILO law on this point it is, however, rather between the Posting of Workers Directive and the ILO Convention than between the 2 TFEUand the ILO Convention. The Posting of Workers Directive was adopted under circumstances that have changed considerably since the enlargement of the EU with Central and Eastern European countries. The time may therefore be ripe for a revision of the Posting of Workers Directive.

Information requirements

In the *Limosa* case,[44] Belgium imposed a prior declaration requirement on self-employed service providers established in other Member States. The CJEU declared that,

44. Case C-577/10 *Commission* v *Belgium* [2012] ECR nyr.

by adopting Articles 137(8), 138, third indent, 153 and 157(3) of the Programme Law (I) of 27 December 2006, in the version in force since 1 April 2007, namely by imposing a prior declaration requirement on self-employed service providers established in Member States other than the Kingdom of Belgium in respect of their activity in Belgium, the Kingdom of Belgium has failed to fulfil its obligations under Article 56 TFEU;

There is a similar provision in the Danish rules on the RUT-register.

5 Employer's Obligation to inform employees of applicable working conditions

5.1 Background

The directive on an employer's obligation to inform employees of the conditions applicable to the contract or employment relationship[45] was proposed by the Commission in 1990.[46]

5.2 Aim

The aim of the directive on the employer's obligation to inform employees of the conditions applicable to the contract or employment relationship is to protect employees against possible infringements of their rights, in view of the increase in the number of types of employment relationships, by establishing at EU level the obligation for employers to inform employees in writing of their conditions of employment.

5.3 Scope

The Directive applies to all paid employees with a contract or employment relationship defined and/or governed by the law in force in a Member State. Member States may exclude from its scope workers who have a contract or employment relationship:

- with a total duration not exceeding one month or with a working week not exceeding eight hours; or
- of a casual and/or specific nature where there are objective considerations justifying non-application of the Directive.

45. 91/533/EEC.
46. Com 90/0563.

5.4 Obligation to provide information

Employers must according to Article 2(1) of the directive on an employer's obligation to inform employees of the conditions applicable to the contract or employment relationship notify an employee to whom the Directive applies of the essential aspects of the contract or employment relationship.

The information referred to above shall according to Article 2(2) of the directive cover at least the following:

(a) the identities of the parties;
(b) the place of work; where there is no fixed or main place of work, the principle that the employee is employed at various places and the registered place of business or, where appropriate, the domicile of the employer;
(c) (i) the title, grade, nature or category of the work for which the employee is employed; or
(ii) a brief specification or description of the work;
(d) the date of commencement of the contract or employment relationship;
(e) in the case of a temporary contract or employment relationship, the expected duration thereof;
(f) the amount of paid leave to which the employee is entitled or, where this cannot be indicated when the information is given, the procedures for allocating and determining such leave;
(g) the length of the periods of notice to be observed by the employer and the employee should their contract or employment relationship be terminated or, where this cannot be indicated when the information is given, the method for determining such periods of notice;
(h) the initial basic amount, the other component elements and the frequency of payment of the remuneration to which the employee is entitled;
(i) the length of the employee's normal working day or week;
(j) where appropriate;
(i) the collective agreements governing the employee's conditions of work; or
(ii) in the case of collective agreements concluded outside the business by special joint bodies or institutions, the name of the competent body or joint institution within which the agreements were concluded.

In *Lange*,[47] the employee (Lange) was employed as from 1 June 1998 as a lathe operator under a contract of employment. Article 1 of that contract provides inter alia that the length of the working week is to be 40 hours. The contract gives no details concerning overtime. Lange refused to work overtime at the request of his employer in order to fulfil orders within time-limits agreed with a customer, for which reason the employer terminated his contract. Lange brought an action against his dismissal before the Arbeitsgericht

47. Case C-262/88 *Lange* [1990] ECR I-1889.

Bremen, requesting that he keep his job in the event of his action being successful. The employer contended that the action should be dismissed. The German court asked the CJEU whether the provision in Article 2(2)i on normal working hours put an obligation on the part of an employer to bring to the notice of an employee any term whereby the employee is obliged to work overtime whenever requested to do so by the employer. That question was answered in the negative. The CJEU added that it must however be observed that an obligation to inform employees whether, and if so under what conditions, they may be required to work overtime may arise from another provision of the Directive.

Article 2(1) of the Directive lays down the principle that the employer is obliged to notify employees of the essential aspects of the contract or employment relationship. That obligation, which is described in the seventh recital in the preamble to the Directive as a general requirement, concerns all the aspects of the contract or employment relationship which are, by virtue of their nature, essential elements. Article 2(2) of the Directive does not reduce the scope of that general requirement. It is – in the view of the CJEU – clear from the wording of that provision that the elements listed in it do not constitute an exhaustive enumeration of the essential elements referred to in Article 2(1). Accordingly, apart from the elements mentioned in Article 2(2) of the Directive, any element which, in view of its importance, must be considered an essential element of the contract or employment relationship of which it forms part must be notified to the employee. That applies in particular to a term under which an employee is obliged to work overtime whenever requested to do so by his employer.

The referring court also asked whether a failure by the employer to give an employee the requisite information concerning an essential element of the contract or employment relationship rendered that element inapplicable. The CJEU answered that question in the negative.

In *Kampelmann*,[48] the CJEU held that the notification referred to in Article 2(1) of the directive on an employer's obligation to inform employees of the conditions applicable to the contract or employment relationship, in so far as it informs an employee of the essential aspects of the contract or employment relationship and, in particular, of the points listed in Article 2(2)(c), enjoys the same presumption as to its correctness as would attach, in domestic law, to any similar document drawn up by the employer and communicated

48. Joined Cases C-253/96, C-254/96, C-255/96, C-256/96, C-257/96 and C-258/96 *Kampelmann and others* [1997] ECR I-6907.

to the employee. The employer must none the less be allowed to bring any evidence to the contrary, by showing that the information in the notification is either inherently incorrect or has been shown to be so in fact.

The Court further held that individuals may rely on Article 2(2)(c) of the directive directly before the national courts as against the State and any organizations or bodies which are subject to the authority or control of the State or have special powers beyond those which result from the normal rules applicable to relations between individuals, either where the State has failed to transpose the Directive into national law within the prescribed period or where it has not done so correctly. Article 2(2)(c) clearly and unequivocally lists a number of the essential aspects of the contract of which an employer is obliged to notify an employee, namely 'the title, grade, nature or category of the work for which the employee is employed' or 'a brief specification or description of the work'. Furthermore, the fact that that provision allows the Member State to choose between two categories of information to be notified to the employee does not render it impossible to determine with sufficient precision, on the basis of the provisions of the Directive alone, the content of the rights thus conferred on individuals, the scope of which is not in the discretion of the Member State whichever choice it makes.

It is not open to a Member State to transpose Article 2(2)(c)(ii) of the Directive, which requires an employer to give employees a brief specification or description of their work, in such a way as to allow the employer, in every case, to confine the information to be notified to the employee to a mere job designation.

5.5 Means of information

The information may be set out in a written contract of employment, in a letter of engagement or in one or more other written documents. These must be given to the employee within two months of commencement of employment, failing which the employee must be given a written declaration signed by the employer.

5.6 Expatriate employees

Article 4 of the directive provides in employees required to work in another country must be in possession before departure of one of the documents referred to in point 3, which must include the following additional information:

- duration of employment abroad;
- currency to be used for payment of remuneration;

- any benefits attendant on the employment abroad;
- where appropriate, the conditions governing the employee's repatriation.

These provisions do not apply where the duration of employment abroad is one month or less. Any change to the terms of the contract or employment relationship must be recorded in writing.

5.7 Minimum directive

The Directive does not affect the Member States' prerogative to apply or introduce provisions which are more favourable to employees.

5.8 Defence of Rights

Article 8 of the directive provides that Member States shall introduce into their national legal systems such measures as are necessary to enable all employees who consider themselves wronged by failure to comply with the obligations arising from this Directive to pursue their claims by judicial process after possible recourse to other competent authorities.

Member States may provide that access to the means of redress referred to in paragraph 1 are subject to the notification of the employer by the employee and the failure by the employer to reply within 15 days of notification.

However, the formality of prior notification may in no case be required in the cases referred to in Article 4 on expatriate employees, neither for workers with a temporary contract or employment relationship, nor for employees not covered by a collective agreement or by collective agreements relating to the employment relationship.

In *Ruben Andersen*,[49] the CJEU held that Article 8(1) of the directive on an employer's obligation to inform employees of the conditions applicable to the contract or employment relationship must be interpreted as meaning that it does not prohibit national rules which provide that a collective agreement which is intended to transpose the provisions of the directive into national law are to apply to an employee even though he is not a member of an organisation which is a party to that agreement.

The second subparagraph of Article 8(2) of Directive 91/533 on an employer's obligation to inform employees of the conditions applicable to the contract or employment relationship must be interpreted as meaning that it does not prevent an employee who is not a member of a union which is a party to a collective agreement governing his employment relationship being re-

49. Case C-306/07 *Ruben Andersen* [2008] ECR I-10279.

garded as 'covered by' that agreement within the meaning of the abovementioned provision.

The words 'a temporary contract or employment relationship' in the second subparagraph of Article 8(2) of Directive 91/533 on an employer's obligation to inform employees of the conditions applicable to the contract or employment relationship must be interpreted as referring to contracts and employment relationships entered into for a short period. If no norm has been laid down for that purpose in a Member State's rules, it is for the national courts to determine the duration in each case in the light of the specific characteristics of certain sectors or certain occupations or activities. That duration must, however, be fixed so as to provide effective protection of the rights conferred on workers by the directive.

6 Part Time Work

6.1 Background

The directive on part-time work[50] was proposed by the Commission in 1997[51] on the basis of the Framework agreement on part-time work concluded by UNICE [now Business Europe], CEEP and the ETUC.

The purpose of the agreement on part-time work as negotiated by the social partners in 1997 is to provide for the removal of discrimination against part-time workers and to improve the quality of part-time work. It is also intended to facilitate the development of part-time work on a voluntary basis and to contribute to the flexible organisation of working time in a manner which takes into account the needs of employers and workers. The agreement covers all part-time workers as defined by national law and practice.

6.2 Scope

The Framework Agreement applies according to Clause 2 to part-time workers who have an employment contract or employment relationship as defined by the law, collective agreement or practice in force in each Member State.

Member States, after consultation with the social partners in accordance with national law, collective agreements or practice, and/or the social partners at the appropriate level in conformity with national industrial relations practice may, for objective reasons, exclude wholly or partly from the terms of

50. See Directive 97/81/EC of 15 December 1997 concerning the Framework Agreement on part-time work concluded by UNICE, CEEP and the ETUC.
51. Com (97)392.

this Agreement part-time workers who work on a casual basis. Such exclusions should be reviewed periodically to establish if the objective reasons for making them remain valid.

Wippel[52] concerned part-time work in the form of 'work on demand'. On 28 September 1998, a framework contract of employment based on the principle of 'work on demand' was entered into between Wippel and an employer. Under that contract, working hours and organisation of working time were determined on a case-by-case basis by agreement between the parties. The employer sought Wippel's services according to workload. She could refuse the offer of work without having to justify such refusal. The annex to the contract of employment provided that Wippel would not be guaranteed a fixed income since both parties expressly refrained from laying down a specified amount of work. The documents before the CJEU indicate that the employer merely offered the claimant the prospect of being able to work around three days per week and two Saturdays per month. Her pay was EUR 6.54 per hour plus any sales commission.

During the course of her period of employment, from October 1998 to June 2000, Wippel worked irregularly, the amount of her remuneration varying accordingly. In June 2000, Wippel brought proceedings before the Arbeits- und Sozialgericht Wien (Labour and Social Court, Vienna), claiming that the employer should pay to her the amount of EUR 11 929.23, together with costs and ancillary amounts. She maintains that the employer is liable to her for the difference between the amount due in respect of the maximum amount of work that could have been demanded of her and the actual number of hours which she worked. Wippel asserts that the maximum monthly working time should have constituted the basis for calculating her remuneration for each of the months during which she worked for the employer.

Wippel also claimed that the absence in her contract of employment of an agreement as to working hours and the organisation of working time constituted discrimination on the ground of sex. The referring court asked the following preliminary questions to the CJEU:

1. (a) Must Article 141 EC, Article 1 of Council Directive 75/117 and Clause 2 of the Framework Agreement on part-time work concluded by UNICE, CEEP and the ETUC ... and Point 9 of the Community Charter of the Fundamental Social Rights of Workers of 9 December 1989 be construed as meaning (in regard to the concept of 'worker') that full protection is also afforded to persons such as the claimant in the present case who, under a comprehensive framework contract of employment,

52. Case C-313/02 *Wippel* [2004] I-9483.

agree terms on pay, termination of employment and the like but also include a provision for hours of work and working time to depend on workload and to be agreed by the parties on a case-by-case basis?

(b) Does a person come within the concept of 'worker' for the purposes of Question 1(a) where there is a prospect, without any binding commitment, of work amounting to around three days per week and two Saturdays each month?

(c) Does a person come within the concept of 'worker' for the purposes of Question 1(a) where she actually works around three days a week and two Saturdays in each month?

(d) Is the Community Charter of the Fundamental Social Rights of Workers ... legally binding, at least in so far as other provisions of Community law have to be interpreted in light of it?

2. Are Article 141 EC, Article 1 of Directive 75/117, Article 5 of Directive 76/207 ... and Clause 4 of the Framework Agreement on part-time work to be construed as meaning that there is no objectively justified unequal treatment?

The CJEU replied:

1. A worker with a contract of employment, such as that in the main proceedings, under which hours of work and the organisation of working time are dependent upon the quantity of available work and are determined only on a case-by-case basis by agreement between the parties, comes within the scope of Council Directive 76/207/EEC of 9 February 1976 on the implementation of the principle of equal treatment for men and women as regards access to employment, vocational training and promotion, and working conditions.

Such workers also come within the scope of the Framework Agreement annexed to Council Directive 97/81/EC of 15 December 1997 concerning the Framework Agreement on part-time work concluded by UNICE, CEEP and the ETUC where:

- they have a contract or employment relationship as defined by the law, collective agreement or practices in force in the Member State;
- they are employees whose normal working hours, calculated on a weekly basis or on average over an employment period which may be up to a year, are less than those of a comparable full-time worker within the meaning of Clause 3(2) of that framework agreement, and
- in regard part-time workers working on a casual basis, the Member State has not excluded them, wholly or partly, from the benefit of the terms of that agreement.

O'*Brian*[53] concerned the question as to whether part-time judges in the UK are part-time workers within the scope of the part-time directive. The CJEU held that it is a matter for national law to decide who should be considered a part-time worker. If judges are covered by the part-time directive and the an-

53. Case C-393/10 *O'Brian* [2012] ECR nyr.

nexed Framework Agreement on part-time the directive precludes them from being denied access to a retirement pension scheme which is open to full-time judges unless such differentiation is objectively justified. The CJEU stated:

1. European Union law must be interpreted as meaning that it is for the Member States to define the concept of 'workers who have an employment contract or an employment relationship' in Clause 2.1 of the Framework Agreement on part-time work concluded on 6 June 1997 which appears in the Annex to Council Directive 97/81/EC of 15 December 1997 concerning the Framework Agreement on part-time work concluded by UNICE, CEEP and the ETUC, as amended by Council Directive 98/23/EC of 7 April 1998, and, in particular, to determine whether judges fall within that concept, subject to the condition that that does not lead to the arbitrary exclusion of that category of persons from the protection offered by Directive 97/81, as amended by Directive 98/23, and that agreement. An exclusion from that protection may be allowed only if the relationship between judges and the Ministry of Justice is, by its nature, substantially different from that between employers and their employees falling, according to national law, under the category of workers.

2. The Framework Agreement on part-time work concluded on 6 June 1997 which appears in the Annex to Directive 97/81, as amended by Directive 98/23, must be interpreted as meaning that it precludes, for the purpose of access to the retirement pension scheme, national law from establishing a distinction between full-time judges and part-time judges remunerated on a daily fee-paid basis, unless such a difference in treatment is justified by objective reasons, which is a matter for the referring court to determine.

6.3 Definitions

6.3.1 Part time worker

A part-time worker is in clause 3 of the framework agreement on part-time defined as an employee whose normal hours of work, calculated on a weekly basis or on average over a period of employment of up to one year, are less than the normal hours of work of a comparable full-time worker.

6.3.2 Comparable full-time worker

The term 'comparable full-time worker' means a full-time worker in the same establishment having the same type of employment contract or relationship, who is engaged in the same or a similar work/occupation, due regard being given to other considerations which may include seniority and qualification/skills.

Where there is no comparable full-time worker in the same establishment, the comparison shall be made by reference to the applicable collective agreement or, where there is no applicable collective agreement, in accordance with national law, collective agreements or practice.

6.4 The principle of non-discrimination

Clause 4 of the Framework agreement on part-time work lays down the principle of non-discrimination. It provides:

1. In respect of employment conditions, part-time workers shall not be treated in a less favourable manner than comparable full-time workers solely because they work part time unless different treatment is justified on objective grounds.

2. Where appropriate, the principle of pro rata temporis shall apply.

3. The arrangements for the application of this clause shall be defined by the Member States and/or social partners, having regard to European legislation, national law, collective agreements and practice.

4. Where justified by objective reasons, Member States after consultation of the social partners in accordance with national law, collective agreements or practice and/or social partners may, where appropriate, make access to particular conditions of employment subject to a period of service, time worked or earnings qualification. Qualifications relating to access by part-time workers to particular conditions of employment should be reviewed periodically having regard to the principle of non-discrimination as expressed in Clause 4.1.

6.4.1 Prohibition against unjustified discrimination solely on grounds of part time

As appears from the above, Clause 4(1) of the Framework Agreement prohibits discrimination against part time workers solely because they work part-time. As set out in Chapter Six, prohibitions against discrimination on grounds of gender, ethnicity, age, religion, disability and sexual orientation apply not only to discrimination solely on the prohibited ground but apply also to discriminations where the prohibited criteria (sex, ethnicity, age, etc.) only is a contributory reason for the unfavourable treatment but not necessarily the only reason. On this point the prohibition against part-time discrimination is thus weaker than the prohibition against for example direct and indirect sex discrimination. As set out in Chapter Six discrimination on ground of part-time will often be indirect sex discrimination because more women than men work part-time. The CJEU has developed a comprehensive case law on discrimination of full-time and part-time employees in relation to indirect sex discrimination.[54]

54. See in particular Case 170/84 *Bilka* [1986] ECR 1607, Case C-171/88 *Rinner-Kühn* [1989] ECR 2743, case C-167/97 *Seymour-Smith* [1999] ECR I-623, Case C-278/93 *Freers and Speckmann* [1996] ECR I-1165, Case C-243/95 *Hill and Stapleton* [1998]

The discrimination concepts used with regard to gender, ethnic, age, religion, disability and sexual orientation discrimination require less favourable treatment on the forbidden grounds not different treatments, see further above in Chapter Six.

In *Bruno and others*[55] the employees were cabin crew members employed by the airline Alitalia. They work part-time in accordance with what are known as 'vertical – cyclical part – time' arrangements. That system consists in a method of organisation under which the employee works only during certain weeks or certain months of the year, on full or reduced hours. The CJEU ruled:

> With regard to retirement pensions, Clause 4 of the Framework Agreement on part-time work annexed to Council Directive 97/81/EC of 15 December 1997 concerning the Framework Agreement on part-time work concluded by UNICE, CEEP and the ETUC must be interpreted as precluding national legislation which, for vertical-cyclical part-time workers, disregards periods not worked in calculating the period of service required to qualify for such a pension, unless such a difference in treatment is justified on objective grounds.
>
> 2. If the referring court reached the conclusion that the national legislation at issue in the main proceedings is incompatible with Clause 4 of the Framework Agreement, Clauses 1 and 5(1) of the agreement would have to be interpreted as also precluding such legislation.

In *Wippel*,[56] the CJEU ruled that:

> 2. Clause 4 of the Framework Agreement annexed to Directive 97/81 and Articles 2(1) and 5(1) of Directive 76/207 must be interpreted as meaning that:
> – they do not preclude a provision, such as Paragraph 3 of the Arbeitszeitgesetz (Law on working time), which lays down a basic maximum working time of 40 hours per week and eight hours per day, and which thus also regulates maximum working time and the organisation of working time in regard to both full-time and part-time workers.
> – in circumstances where all the contracts of employment of the other employees of an undertaking make provision for the length of weekly working time and for the organisation of working time, they do not preclude a contract of part-time employment of workers of the same undertaking, such as that in the main proceedings, under which the length of weekly working time and the organisation of working time are not fixed but are dependent on quantitative needs in terms of work to be performed determined on a case-by-case basis, such workers being entitled to accept or refuse that work.

ECR I-3739, and Joined Cases C-279/96 to C-281/96 *Ansaldo Energia and Others* [1998] ECR I-5025.

55. Joined Cases C-395/08 and C-396/08 *Bruno and others* [2010] ECR I-5119.
56. Case C-313/02 *Wippel* [2004] I-9483.

6.4.2 Pro rata temporis

The principle of *pro rata temporis* applies, meaning that certain working conditions will apply according to the time worked. In Joined cases *Heimann and Toltschin*,[57] the CJEU held that:

Article 31(2) of the Charter of Fundamental Rights of the European Union and Article 7(1) of Directive 2003/88/EC of the European Parliament and of the Council of 4 November 2003 concerning certain aspects of the organisation of working time must be interpreted as meaning that they do not preclude national legislation or practice, such as a social plan agreed between an undertaking and its works council, under which the paid annual leave of a worker on short-time working is calculated according to the rule of pro rata temporis.

Zentralbetriebsrat der Landeskrankenhäuser Tirols[58] concerned disadvantageous provisions provided for by national legislation for contractual public servants working part-time, on a casual basis, or under a fixed-term contract. The CJEU interpreted the *pro rata temporis* principle as part of the principle of equal treatment. In regard to the *pro rata temporis* principle the referring national court asked the CJEU whether a worker who goes from full time to part time is entitled to holiday calculated on the basis of the time he worked while on full time, see the following:

Is the pro rata temporis principle, as set out in Clause 4. 2 of the framework agreement, to be interpreted as precluding a provision of national law such as Paragraph 55(5) of the L-VBG, under which in the event of a change in the working hours of an employee, the amount of leave not yet taken is adjusted proportionally to the new working hours, with the result that the worker who reduces his working hours from full-time to part-time, has his entitlement to leave accumulated while working full-time reduced or, as a part-time worker, he can only take that leave with a reduced level of payment for leave?

The CJEU held that

Relevant European Union law and, in particular, Clause 4.2 of the framework agreement on part-time work, concluded on 6 June 1997 which is annexed to Council Directive 97/81/EC of 15 December 1997 concerning the framework agreement on part-time work concluded by UNICE, CEEP and the ETUC, as amended by Council Directive 98/23/EC of 7 April 1998, must be interpreted as precluding a national provision such as Paragraph 55(5) of the Law of the Province of Tyrol on contractual public servants (Tiroler Landes-Vertragsbedienstetengesetz) of 8 November 2000, in the version in force up to 1 February 2009, under which, in the event of a change in the working hours of a worker, the amount

57. Joined Cases C 229/11 and C 230/11 *Heimann and Toltschin* [2012] nyr.
58. Case C-486/08 *Zentralbetriebsrat der Landeskrankenhäuser Tirols* [2010] ECR I-3527.

of leave not yet taken is adjusted in such a way that a worker who reduces his working hours from full-time to part-time suffers a reduction in the right to paid annual leave he has accumulated but not been able to exercise while working full-time, or he can only take that leave with a reduced level of holiday pay.

6.4.3 Justification

It follows from the wording of Clause 4(1) that the prohibition against discrimination solely on ground of part-time only applies unless different treatment is justified on objective grounds. It would appear that both direct and indirect discrimination on ground of part-time can be objectively justified. As set out in Chapter Six there is much wider scope for justification of indirect discrimination on the discrimination grounds dealt with in Chapter Six than for justification of direct discrimination.

Where justified by objective reasons, Member States, after consultation with the social partners, may make access to particular conditions of employment subject to a period of service, time worked or earnings qualification.

6.5 Opportunities for part-time work

6.5.1 Duties of Member States and Social Partners

Member States and social partners must identify, review and eliminate obstacles which limit opportunities for part-time workers. Part-time workers have the same active and passive collective rights as full-time workers. Clause 5 of the Framework Agreement on part-time work provides that in the context of Clause 1 of this Agreement and of the principle of non-discrimination between part-time and full-time workers:

(a) Member States, following consultations with the social partners in accordance with national law or practice, should identify and review obstacles of a legal or administrative nature which may limit the opportunities for part-time work and, where appropriate, eliminate them;
(b) the social partners, acting within their sphere of competence and through the procedures set out in collective agreements, should identify and review obstacles which may limit opportunities for part-time work and, where appropriate, eliminate them.

In *Michaeler*,[59] the CJEU held that

Clause 5(1)(a) of the Framework Agreement on part-time work concluded by UNICE, CEEP and the ETUC annexed to Council Directive 97/81/EC of 15 December 1997 con-

59. Joined Cases C-55/07 and C-56/07 *Michaeler* and others [2008] ECR I-3135.

cerning the Framework Agreement on part-time work concluded by UNICE, CEEP and the ETUC must be interpreted as precluding national legislation such as that at issue in the main proceedings which requires that copies of part-time employment contracts be sent to the authorities within 30 days of their signature.

6.5.2 Employers' duties

2. A worker's refusal to transfer from full-time to part-time work or vice-versa does not in itself constitute a valid reason for termination of employment, without prejudice to termination in accordance with national law, collective agreements and practice, for other reasons such as may arise from the operational requirements of the establishment concerned. As far as possible, employers should give consideration to:
(a) requests by workers to transfer from full-time to part-time work that becomes available in the establishment;
(b) requests by workers to transfer from part-time to full-time work or to increase their working time should the opportunity arise;
(c) the provision of timely information on the availability of part-time and full-time positions in the establishment in order to facilitate transfers from full-time to part-time or vice versa;
(d) measures to facilitate access to part-time work at all levels of the enterprise, including skilled and managerial positions, and where appropriate, to facilitate access by part-time workers to vocational training to enhance career opportunities and occupational mobility;
(e) the provision of appropriate information to existing bodies representing workers about part-time working in the enterprise.

7 Fixed Term contracts

The Directive[60] concerning the framework agreement on fixed-term work concluded by ETUC, UNICE and CEEP was adopted 28 June 1999

7.1 Background

7.1.1 The framework agreement on fixed-term work

On 14 January 1999, the central European-level social partners – the Union of Industrial and Employers' Confederations of Europe (UNICE, now Business Europe), the European Centre of Enterprises with Public Participation and of Enterprises of General Economic Interest (CEEP) and the European Trade Union Confederation (ETUC) – reached a draft framework agreement

60. Council Directive 1999/70/EC of 28 June 1999 concerning the framework agreement on fixed-term work concluded by ETUC, UNICE [now BusinessEurope] and CEEP.

on the rights of workers on fixed-term contracts. The text was officially signed on 18 March 1999.

The background to the agreement was that, with non-standard forms of employment becoming more common in the 1980s and 1990s, the European Commission and the European labour movement were increasingly concerned to create a European framework of legislation to protect the rights of workers on 'atypical' contracts. Draft Directives proposed by the Commission sought to provide for minimum employment rights for all workers on such contracts. However, successive proposals failed to gain approval in the Council of Ministers and in September 1995, the Commission initiated consultations with the European-level social partners on the rights of workers in atypical forms of employment. As UNICE was reluctant to debate the issues of part-time and fixed-term employment together, the social partners decided, in 1996, initially to negotiate on part-time work under the mechanisms then set out in the Social policy Agreement annexed to the Maastricht Treaty. These talks led to the signing of the framework agreement on part-time work in June 1997. UNICE then declared its willingness to enter into negotiations on fixed-term contracts, and the talks eventually led to the agreement signed in March 1999.

The social partners asked the Commission to present their agreement to the Council for implementation across the Member States through a Directive under Article 155 TFEU, see further above in Chapter Two and Three. Following assessments, the Commission adopted its Proposal for a Council Directive concerning the framework agreement on fixed-term work concluded by UNICE, CEEP and the ETUC[61] on 1 May 1999. The fixed-term work agreement relates to working conditions, which come under Article 153 TFEU.

7.2 Purpose

Clause 1 of the framework agreement on fixed term contracts provides that the purpose of the framework agreement is to:

(a) improve the quality of fixed-term work by ensuring the application of the principle of non-discrimination;
(b) establish a framework to prevent abuse arising from the use of successive fixed-term employment contracts or relationships.

61. (COM(1999)203.

In *Vassallo*,[62] the CJEU held that the framework agreement on fixed-term work must be interpreted as not in principle precluding national legislation which, where there is abuse arising from the use of successive fixed-term employment contracts or relationships by a public-sector employer, precludes their being converted into contracts of indeterminate duration, even though such conversion is provided for in respect of employment contracts and relationships with a private-sector employer, where that legislation includes another effective measure to prevent and, where relevant, punish the abuse of successive fixed-term contracts by a public-sector employer. A similar result was reached in *Marrosu*.[63]

7.3 Scope

The framework agreement applies – according to Clause 2 – to fixed-term workers who have an employment contract or employment relationship as defined in law, collective agreements or practice in each Member State.

Member States can after consultation with the social partners and/or the social partners may provide that this agreement does not apply to:

(a) initial vocational training relationships and apprenticeship schemes;
(b) employment contracts and relationships which have been concluded within the framework of a specific public or publicly-supported training, integration and vocational retraining programme.

In *Adeneler*,[64] the CJEU held that the directive and the Framework Agreement on fixed-term work can apply also to fixed-term employment contracts and relationships concluded with the public authorities and other public-sector bodies. The provisions of those two instruments contain nothing to permit the inference that their scope is limited to fixed-term contracts concluded by workers with employers in the private sector alone.

7.4 Definitions

Clause 3 of the Framework agreement defines ‘fixed-term worker’ and ‘comparable permanent worker’.

62. Case C-180/04 *Vasallo* [2006] ECR I-7251.
63. Case C-53/04 *Marrosu* [2006] ECR I-7213.
64. Case C-212/04 *Adeneler* [2006] ECR I-6057.

7.4.1 Fixed term worker

For the purpose of the framework agreement the term 'fixed-term worker' means a person having an employment contract or relationship entered into directly between an employer and a worker where the end of the employment contract or relationship is determined by objective conditions such as reaching a specific date, completing a specific task, or the occurrence of a specific event.

7.4.2 Comparable permanent worker

For the purpose of this agreement, the term 'comparable permanent worker' means a worker with an employment contract or relationship of indefinite duration, in the same establishment, engaged in the same or similar work/ occupation, due regard being given to qualifications/skills.

Where there is no comparable permanent worker in the same establishment, the comparison shall be made by reference to the applicable collective agreement, or where there is no applicable collective agreement, in accordance with national law, collective agreements or practice.

7.5 Non-discrimination

Clause 4 provides for the general principle of non-discrimination in employment conditions to be applied to fixed-term contract workers. It reads:

1. In respect of employment conditions, fixed-term workers shall not be treated in a less favourable manner than comparable permanent workers solely because they have a fixed-term contract or relation unless different treatment is justified on objective grounds.
2. Where appropriate, the principle of pro rata temporis shall apply.
3. The arrangements for the application of this clause shall be defined by the Member States after consultation with the social partners and/or the social partners, having regard to Community law and national law, collective agreements and practice.
4. Period-of service qualifications relating to particular conditions of employment shall be the same for fixed-term workers as for permanent workers except where different length-of service qualifications are justified on objective grounds.

Clause 4(1) has direct effect, see *Impact*,[65] cited below in section 7.6. As appears Clause 4 of the fixed-term work directive is very similar to Clause 4 of the part-time framework agreement.

In *Valenza*,[66] the CJEU held that Clause 4 of the framework agreement on fixed-term work must be understood as precluding national legislation which

65. Case C-268/06 *Impact* [2008] ECR I-2483.

completely prohibits periods of service completed by a fixed-term worker for a public authority being taken into account in order to determine the length of service of that worker upon his recruitment on a permanent basis by that same authority as a career civil servant, unless that prohibition is justified on 'objective grounds' for the purposes of clause 4(1) and/or (4). The mere fact that the fixed-term worker completed those periods of service on the basis of a fixed term employment contract or relationship does not constitute such an objective ground.

In *Santana*,[67] the CJEU ruled that the fixed-term work directive must be interpreted, on the one hand, as applying to contracts and relationships concluded with the public authorities and other public-sector bodies and, on the other, as precluding any difference in treatment as between career civil servants and comparable interim civil servants of a Member State, based solely on the ground that the latter are employed for a fixed term, unless different treatment is justified on objective grounds for the purposes of clause 4(1) of the framework agreement.

Clause 4 of the framework agreement on fixed-term work must be interpreted as precluding account not being taken of periods of service completed as an interim civil servant in a public administration for the purposes of permitting such a person, who has subsequently become a career civil servant, to obtain an internal promotion available only to career civil servants, unless that exclusion is justified by objective grounds for the purposes of clause 4(1) of that agreement. The mere fact that the interim civil servant completed those periods of service under a fixed-term employment contract or relationship does not constitute such an objective ground.

The primary law of the EU, the fixed-term work directive and the framework agreement are to be interpreted as not precluding, in principle, national legislation which provides that, where an action brought by a career civil servant challenging a decision rejecting his candidature for a competition is based on the fact that the promotion procedure was contrary to clause 4 of the framework agreement, that action must be brought within two months of the publication of the competition notice. Nevertheless, such a time-limit could not be relied upon against a career civil servant, who has been a candidate in that competition, who has been admitted to the tests and whose name was placed on the definitive list of successful candidates for that competition, if that were liable to render practically impossible or excessively difficult the

66. Joined Cases C-302/11 to C-305/11 *Valenza* [2012] ECR nyr.
67. C-177/10 *Santana* [2011] ECR nyr.

exercise of the rights conferred by the framework agreement. In those circumstances, time for the purposes of the two-month time-limit could run only from notification of the decision annulling the civil servant's admission to that competition and his appointment as a career civil servant in the higher group.

In Joined Cases *Gavieiro and Torres* C-444/09 and C-456/09, the CJEU held that a length-of-service increment is, as an employment condition, covered by clause 4(1) of the framework agreement on fixed-term work. Consequently, fixed-term workers may contest treatment which, with regard to payment of that increment, is less favourable than that which is given to permanent workers in a comparable situation and for which there is no objective justification. The temporary nature of the employment relationship of certain public servants is not, in itself, capable of constituting an objective ground within the meaning of that clause of the framework agreement.

The mere fact that a national provision contains no reference to the fixed-term work directive does not preclude that provision from being regarded as a national measure transposing the directive.

Clause 4(1) of the framework agreement on fixed-term work is unconditional and sufficiently precise for interim civil servants to be able to rely on it as against the State before a national court in order to obtain recognition of their entitlement to length-of-service increments in respect of the period starting with the date by which Member States should have transposed Directive 1999/70 and ending with the date of entry into force of the national law transposing that directive into the domestic law of the Member State concerned, subject to compliance with the relevant provisions of national law concerning limitation.

Even though the national legislation transposing Directive 1999/70 contains a provision which, whilst recognising the right of interim civil servants to be paid the three-yearly length-of-service increments, excludes the retrospective application of that right, the competent authorities of the Member State concerned are obliged, under European Union law and in relation to a provision of the framework agreement on fixed-term work, annexed to Directive 1999/70, having direct effect, to give that right to payment of the increments retrospective effect to the date by which the Member States should have transposed Directive 1999/70.

In *Alonso*, [68] the CJEU held that the concept of 'employment conditions' referred to in clause 4(1) of the framework agreement on fixed-term work

68. Case C-307/05 *Alonso* [2007] ECR I-7109.

must be interpreted as meaning that it can act as a basis for a claim which seeks the grant to a fixed-term worker of a length-of-service allowance which is reserved under national law solely to permanent staff. Clause 4(1) of the framework agreement must be interpreted as meaning that it precludes the introduction of a difference in treatment between fixed-term workers and permanent workers which is justified solely on the basis that it is provided for by a provision of statute or secondary legislation of a Member State or by a collective agreement concluded between the staff union representatives and the relevant employer.

In *BECTU*,[69] the problem was whether a national provision in the UK under which entitlement to paid annual leave did not arise until a worker had been continuously employed for 13 weeks was compatible with the Working time directive. Broadcasting, Entertainment, Cinematographic and Theatre Union (BECTU) was a trade union with about 30 000 members working in the broadcasting, film, theatre, cinema and related sectors in jobs such as sound recordists, cameramen, special effects technicians, projectionists, editors, researchers, hairdressers and make-up artistes. BECTU claimed that most of its members are engaged on short-term contracts – frequently for less than 13 weeks with the same employer – so that many of them do not satisfy the condition laid down for entitlement to paid annual leave. Accordingly, the persons concerned are deprived of any entitlement to paid annual leave and of any right to an allowance in lieu merely because, although they work on a regular basis, they do so for successive employers. The CJEU ruled that such a condition was contrary to the Working time directive,[70] see further in Chapter Nine.

7.6 Measures to prevent abuse

Clause 5(1) of the framework agreement calls upon Member States to introduce – 'where there are no equivalent legal measures to prevent abuse' – one or more of the following measures:

(a) objective reasons justifying the renewal of such contracts or relationships;
(b) a maximum duration of successive fixed-term employment contracts or relationships; or
(c) the number of renewals of such contracts or relationships.

69. Case C-173/99 *BECTU* [2001] ECR I-4881.
70. 2003/88/EC.

The Framework Agreement on fixed-term work proceeds on the premiss that employment contracts of indefinite duration are the general form of employment relationship, while recognising that fixed-term employment contracts are a feature of employment in certain sectors or in respect of certain occupations and activities (see paragraphs 6 and 8 of the general considerations in the Framework Agreement). Consequently, the benefit of stable employment is viewed as a major element in the protection of workers,[71] whereas it is only in certain circumstances that fixed-term employment contracts are liable to respond to the needs of both employers and workers.[72] From this angle, the Framework Agreement seeks to place limits on successive recourse to the latter category of employment relationship, a category regarded as a potential source of abuse to the disadvantage of workers, by laying down as a minimum a number of protective provisions designed to prevent the status of employees from being insecure.

Thus, clause 5(1) of the Framework Agreement is intended specifically to 'prevent abuse arising from the use of successive fixed-term employment contracts or relationships'. To this end, clause 5 imposes on Member States the obligation to introduce into domestic law one or more of the measures listed in clause 5(1)(a) to (c) where equivalent legal provisions intended to prevent effectively the misuse of successive fixed-term employment contracts do not already exist in the Member State concerned.

In *Impact*,[73] the CJEU ruled that Clause 5(1) of the Framework Agreement does not have direct effect, see on Impact below. See also *Deutsche Lufthansa*,[74] where the national law was incompatible with Article 5 of the fixed-term work directive.

In *Adeneler*,[75] the CJEU held that the Framework Agreement is to be interpreted as meaning that, in so far as domestic law of the Member State concerned does not include, in the sector under consideration, any other effective measure to prevent and, where relevant, punish the misuse of successive fixed-term contracts, the Framework Agreement precludes the application of national legislation which, in the public sector alone, prohibits absolutely the conversion into an employment contract of indefinite duration of a succession of fixed-term contracts that, in fact, have been intended to cover 'fixed and

71. See Case C-144/04 *Mangold* [2005] ECR I-9981, paragraph 64.
72. See the second paragraph of the preamble to the Framework Agreement and paragraph 8 of the general considerations.
73. Case C-268/06 *Impact* [2008] ECR I-2483.
74. Case C-109/09 *Deutsche Lufthansa* [2011] I-01309.
75. Case C-212/04 *Adeneler* [2006] ECR I-6057.

permanent needs' of the employer and must therefore be regarded as constituting an abuse.

T he CJEU also held that as the concept of 'objective reasons' is not defined by the Framework Agreement, its meaning and scope must be determined on the basis of the objective pursued by the Framework Agreement and of the context of clause 5(1)(a) thereof.[76] Clause 5(1)(a) envisages Objective reasons justifying the renewal of such contracts or relationships'.

The signatory parties to the Framework Agreement considered that the use of fixed term employment contracts founded on objective reasons is a way to prevent abuse (see paragraph 7 of the general considerations in the Framework Agreement). It is true that the Framework Agreement refers back to the Member States and social partners for the detailed arrangements for application of the principles and requirements which it lays down, in order to ensure that they are consistent with national law and/or practice and that due account is taken of the particular features of specific situations (see paragraph 10 of the general considerations in the Framework Agreement). While the Member States thus have a margin of appreciation in the matter, the fact remains that they are required to guarantee the result imposed by Community law, as follows not only from the third paragraph of Article 249 EC, but also from the first paragraph of Article 2 of Directive 1999/70 read in conjunction with the 17th recital in its preamble. In those circumstances, the concept of Objective reasons', within the meaning of clause 5(1)(a) of the Framework Agreement, must be understood as referring to precise and concrete circumstances characterising a given activity, which are therefore capable in that particular context of justifying the use of successive fixed term employment contracts. Those circumstances may result, in particular, from the specific nature of the tasks for the performance of which such contracts have been concluded and from the inherent characteristics of those tasks or, as the case may be, from pursuit of a legitimate social-policy objective of a Member State.

On the other hand, a national provision which merely authorises recourse to successive fixed-term employment contracts in a general and abstract manner by a rule of statute or secondary legislation does not accord with the requirements as stated in the preceding two paragraphs. Such a provision, which is of a purely formal nature and does not justify specifically the use of successive fixed-term employment contracts by the presence of objective factors relating to the particular features of the activity concerned and to the

76. The CJEU referred to Case C-17/03 *VEMW* and Others [2005] ECR I-4983, paragraph 41, and the case-law cited, and Case C-323/03 *Commission* v *Spai*n [2006] ECR I-2161.

conditions under which it is carried out, carries a real risk that it will result in misuse of that type of contract and, accordingly, is not compatible with the objective of the Framework Agreement and the requirement that it have practical effect. Thus, to admit that a national provision may, automatically and without further precision, justify successive fixed-term employment contracts would effectively have no regard to the aim of the Framework Agreement, which is to protect workers against instability of employment, and render meaningless the principle that contracts of indefinite duration are the general form of employment relationship. More specifically, recourse to fixed-term employment contracts solely on the basis of a general provision of statute or secondary legislation, unlinked to what the activity in question specifically comprises, does not permit objective and transparent criteria to be identified in order to verify whether the renewal of such contracts actually responds to a genuine need, is appropriate for achieving the objective pursued and is necessary for that purpose.

Consequently clause 5(1)(a) of the Framework Agreement is to be interpreted as precluding the use of successive fixed term employment contracts where the justification advanced for their use is solely that it is provided for by a general provision of statute or secondary legislation of a Member State. On the contrary, the concept of 'Objective reasons' within the meaning of that clause requires recourse to this particular type of employment relationship, as provided for by national legislation, to be justified by the presence of specific factors relating in particular to the activity in question and the conditions under which it is carried out.

In *Huet*,[77] the CJEU ruled that Clause 5 of the framework agreement on fixed-term work must be interpreted as meaning that a Member State, which provides in its national legislation for conversion of fixed-term employment contracts into an employment contract of indefinite duration when the fixed-term employment contracts have reached a certain duration, is not obliged to require that the employment contract of indefinite duration reproduces in identical terms the principal clauses set out in the previous contract. However, in order not to undermine the practical effect of, or the objectives pursued by the fixed-term directive, that Member State must ensure that the conversion of fixed-term employment contracts into an employment contract of indefinite duration is not accompanied by material amendments to the clauses of the previous contract in a way that is, overall, unfavourable to the person

77. Case C-251/11 *Huet* [2012] ECR nyr.

concerned when the subject-matter of that person's tasks and the nature of his functions remain unchanged.

In *Kücük*,[78] the CJEU ruled that Clause 5(1)(a) of the Framework Agreement on fixed-term work must be interpreted as meaning that a temporary need for replacement staff, provided for by national legislation may, in principle, constitute an objective reason under that clause. The mere fact that an employer may have to employ temporary replacements on a recurring, or even permanent, basis and that those replacements may also be covered by the hiring of employees under employment contracts of indefinite duration does not mean that there is no objective reason under clause 5(1)(a) of the Framework Agreement or that there is abuse within the meaning of that clause. However, in the assessment of the issue whether the renewal of fixed-term employment contracts or relationships is justified by such an objective reason, the authorities of the Member States must, for matters falling within their sphere of competence, take account of all the circumstances of the case, including the number and cumulative duration of the fixed-term employment contracts or relationships concluded in the past with the same employer.

In *Impact*,[79] the CJEU ruled:

1. Community law, in particular the principle of effectiveness, requires that a specialised court which is called upon, under the, albeit optional, jurisdiction conferred on it by the legislation transposing Council Directive 1999/70/EC of 28 June 1999 concerning the framework agreement on fixed-term work concluded by ETUC, UNICE and CEEP, to hear and determine a claim based on an infringement of that legislation, must also have jurisdiction to hear and determine an applicant's claims arising directly from the directive itself in respect of the period between the deadline for transposing the directive and the date on which the transposing legislation entered into force if it is established that the obligation on that applicant to bring, at the same time, a separate claim based directly on the directive before an ordinary court would involve procedural disadvantages liable to render excessively difficult the exercise of the rights conferred on him by Community law. It is for the national court to undertake the necessary checks in that regard.

2. Clause 4(1) of the framework agreement on fixed-term work concluded on 18 March 1999, which is annexed to Directive 1999/70, is unconditional and sufficiently precise for individuals to be able to rely upon it before a national court; that is not the case, however, as regards Clause 5(1) of the framework agreement.

3. Article 10 EC [now Article 4(3) TEU], the third paragraph of Article 249 EC [now Article 288 TFEU], and Directive 1999/70 must be interpreted as meaning that an authority of

78. Case C-586/10 *Kücük* [2012] ECR nyr.
79. Case C-268/06 *Impact* [2008] ECR I-2483.

a Member State acting in its capacity as a public employer may not adopt measures contrary to the objective pursued by that directive and the framework agreement on fixed-term work as regards prevention of the abusive use of fixed-term contracts, which consist in the renewal of such contracts for an unusually long term in the period between the deadline for transposing Directive 1999/70 and the date on which the transposing legislation entered into force.

4. In so far as the applicable national law contains a rule that precludes the retrospective application of legislation unless there is a clear and unambiguous indication to the contrary, a national court hearing a claim based on an infringement of a provision of national legislation transposing Directive 1999/70 is required, under Community law, to give that provision retrospective effect to the date by which that directive should have been transposed only if that national legislation includes an indication of that nature capable of giving that provision retrospective effect.

5. Clause 4 of the framework agreement on fixed-term work must be interpreted as meaning that employment conditions within the meaning of that clause encompass conditions relating to pay and to pensions which depend on the employment relationship, to the exclusion of conditions relating to pensions arising under a statutory social-security scheme.

7.7 Information and employment opportunities

Clause 6 obliges employers to inform fixed-term workers about vacancies which become available in the undertaking. UNICE rejected ETUC's demand to give fixed-term employees preferential access to such vacancies.

7.8 Information and consultation

Clause 7 of the Framework Agreement provides that fixed-term workers shall be taken into consideration in calculating the threshold above which workers' representative bodies provided for in national and EU law may be constituted in the undertaking as required by national provisions.

The arrangements for the application of clause 7.1 shall be defined by Member States after consultation with the social partners and/or the social partners in accordance with national law, collective agreements or practice and having regard to clause 4.1.

As far as possible, employers should give consideration to the provision of appropriate information to existing workers' representative bodies about fixed-term work in the undertaking.

7.9 Provisions on implementation

According to Clause 8 of the Framework Agreement Member States and/or the social partners can maintain or introduce more favourable provisions for workers than set out in this agreement. The Framework Agreement is without prejudice to any more specific EU provisions, and in particular EU provisions concerning equal treatment or opportunities for men and women. Implementation of the Framework Agreement shall – according to clause 8(3) – not constitute valid grounds for reducing the general level of protection afforded to workers in the field of the agreement. The Framework Agreement does not prejudice the right of the social partners to conclude at the appropriate level, including European level, agreements adapting and/or complementing the provisions of this agreement in a manner which will take note of the specific needs of the social partners concerned. The prevention and settlement of disputes and grievances arising from the application of this agreement shall be dealt with in accordance with national law, collective agreements and practice.

In *Sorge*,[80] the CJEU ruled that Clause 8(3) of the framework agreement on fixed-term work must be interpreted as not precluding domestic legislation which has abolished the requirement for the employer to indicate in fixed-term contracts concluded for the purpose of replacing absent workers the names of those workers and the reasons for their replacement, and which merely provides that such fixed-term contracts must be in writing and must indicate the reasons for the use of those contracts, in so far as those new conditions are offset by the adoption of other safeguards or protective measures or concern only a limited category of workers having entered into a fixed-term employment contract, which it is for the national court to ascertain. Because clause 8(3) of the framework agreement has no direct effect, it is for the national court, if it should be led to conclude that the national legislation at issue in the main proceedings is incompatible with EU law, not to disapply that provision but, so far as possible, to give it an interpretation in conformity with the fixed-term work directive and with the objective pursued by the framework agreement.

7.10 Working Environment

The directive supplementing the measures to encourage improvements in the safety and health at work of workers with a fixed-duration employment relationship or a temporary employment relationship[81] applies according to Article 1 of the directive to:

80. Case C-98/09 *Sorge* [2010] I-5837.
81. Directive 91/383/EEC of 25 June 1991 supplementing the measures to encourage improvements in the safety and health at work of workers with a fixed- duration employment relationship or a temporary employment relationship.

1. employment relationships governed by a fixed-duration contract of employment concluded directly between the employer and the worker, where the end of the contract is established by objective conditions such as: reaching a specific date, completing a specific task or the occurence of a specific event;

2. temporary employment relationships between a temporary employment business which is the employer and the worker, where the latter is assigned to work for and under the control of an undertaking and/or establishment making use of his services.

The purpose of the Directive is to ensure that workers with an employment relationship as referred to in Article 1 of the Directive are afforded, as regards safety and health at work, the same level of protection as that of other workers in the user undertaking and/or establishment. The existence of an employment relationship as referred to in Article 1 shall not justify different treatment with respect to working conditions inasmuch as the protection of safety and health at work are involved, especially as regards access to personal protective equipment. The framework directive on working environment[82] and the individual Directives on working environment within the meaning of that Directive[83] shall apply in full to workers with an employment relationship as referred to in Article 1 of the directive supplementing the measures to encourage improvements in the safety and health at work of workers with a fixed- duration employment relationship or a temporary employment relationship, without prejudice to more binding and/or more specific provisions set out in this Directive.

8 Temporary Agency Work

8.1 Background

8.1.1 Public International Law

As mentioned abpve in section 2 there is a Private Employment Agencies Convention, 1997.[84] For the purpose of that Convention the term private employment agency means any natural or legal person, independent of the public authorities, which provides one or more of the following labour market services:

82. 89/391/EEC, see further in Chapter Nine.
83. See 89/391/EEC Article 16 (1).
84. ILO Convention no 181.

(a) services for matching offers of and applications for employment, without the private employment agency becoming a party to the employment relationships which may arise therefrom;
(b) services consisting of employing workers with a view to making them available to a third party, who may be a natural or legal person (referred to below as a 'user enterprise') which assigns their tasks and supervises the execution of these tasks;
(c) other services relating to jobseeking, determined by the competent authority aft er consulting the most representative employers and workers organizations, such as the provision of information, that do not set out to match specific offers of and applications for employment.

Article 11 of the Convention requires Member States to take the necessary measures to ensure adequate protection for the workers employed by private employment agencies in relation to:

(a) freedom of association;
(b) collective bargaining;
(c) minimum wages;
(d) working time and other working conditions;
(e) statutory social security benefits;
(f) access to training;
(g) occupational safety and health;
(h) compensation in case of occupational accidents or diseases;
(i) compensation in case of insolvency and protection of workers claims;
(j) maternity protection and benefi ts, and parental protection and benefits.

8.1.2 Consultations with social partners

On 27 September 1995, the Commission consulted management and labour at EU level in accordance with Article 155 TFEU on the course of action to be adopted at EU level with regard to flexibility of working hours and job security of workers. After that consultation, the Commission considered that EU action was advisable and on 9 April 1996, further consulted management and labour. In the introduction to the framework agreement on fixed-term work concluded on 18 March 1999, the signatories indicated their intention to consider the need for a similar agreement on temporary agency work and decided not to include temporary agency workers in the Framework Agreement on fixed-term work. The general cross-sector organisations, namely the Union of Industrial and Employers' Confederations of Europe (UNICE [now Business Europe], the European Centre of Enterprises with Public Participation and of Enterprises of General Economic Interest (CEEP) and the European Trade Union Confederation (ETUC), informed the Commission in a joint letter of 29 May 2000 of their wish to initiate the process provided for in

Article 155 TFEU. On 21 May 2001, the social partners acknowledged that their negotiations on temporary agency work had not produced any agreement.

8.1.3 Proposals from the Commission

The Commission presented its Proposal for a Directive on working conditions for Temporary Workers in 2002.[85]

8.1.4 Flexibility and adaptation to a fundamental rights/EMU perspective and globalisation

The Preamble to the Directive begins with a reference to the CFREU and the Community Charter of the Fundamental Social Rights of Workers from 1989. It is declared that the directive respects the fundamental rights and complies with the principles recognised by the CFREU. In particular, it is designed to ensure full compliance with Article 31 of the CFREU, which provides that every worker has the right to working conditions which respect his or her health, safety and dignity, and to limitation of maximum working hours, to daily and weekly rest periods and to an annual period of paid leave. The reference to the Community Charter of the Fundamental Social Rights of Workers 1989 is to point 7 which provides *interalia*, that the completion of the internal market must lead to an improvement in the living and working conditions of workers in the EU. This process will be achieved by harmonising progress on these conditions, mainly in respect of forms of work such as fixed-term contract work, part-time work, temporary agency work and seasonal work.

It is stated in the Preamble that new forms of work organisation and a greater diversity of contractual arrangements for workers and businesses, better combining flexibility with security, would contribute to adaptability. The December 2007 European Council endorsed the agreed common principles of flexicurity, which strike a balance between flexibility and security in the labour market and help both workers and employers to seize the opportunities offered by globalisation.

8.2 Aim of the temporary works agency directive

The Directive on Temporary Agency Work[86] defines a general framework applicable to the working conditions of temporary workers in the EU. The

85. See COM (2002)149 and the amended proposal for a Directive on working conditions for Temporary Workers COM (2002) 701.
86. 2008/104/EC.

Directive aims to guarantee a minimum level of effective protection to temporary workers and to contribute to the development of the temporary work sector as a flexible option for employers and workers. The Directive ensures greater transparency and increases confidence in the temporary work sector. It thus improves protection for the workers concerned while giving greater flexibility to companies. Article 2 in Directive on Temporary Agency Work states on the aim of the Directive:

> The purpose of this Directive is to ensure the protection of temporary agency workers and to improve the quality of temporary agency work by ensuring that the principle of equal treatment, as set out in Article 5, is applied to temporary agency workers, and by recognising temporary work agencies as employers, while taking into account the need to establish a suitable framework for the use of temporary agency work with a view to contributing effectively to the creation of jobs and to the development of flexible forms of working.

8.3 Scope of the directive

According to Article 1 of the Directive it applies to the contracts or to the employment relations which connect a worker with a temporary agency. The Directive applies to workers with a contract of employment or employment relationship with a temporary work agency who are assigned to user undertakings to work temporarily under their supervision and direction. The Directive applies to public and private undertakings which are temporary-work agencies or user undertakings engaged in economic activities whether or not they are operating for gain.

Member States may, after consulting the social partners, provide that the Directive does not apply to employment contracts or relationships concluded under a specific public or publicly supported vocational training, integration or retraining programme.

8.4 Definitions

For the purposes of the temporary agency work directive Article 3 of the directivet defines a number of central concepts:

8.4.1 Worker

(a) 'worker' means any person who, in the Member State concerned, is protected as a worker under national employment law.

8.4.2 Temporary-work agency

(b) 'temporary-work agency' means any natural or legal person who, in compliance with national law, concludes contracts of employment or employment relationships with temporary agency workers in order to assign them to user undertakings to work there temporarily under their supervision and direction.

8.4.3 Temporary agency worker

(c) 'temporary agency worker' means a worker with a contract of employment or an employment relationship with a temporary-work agency with a view to being assigned to a user undertaking to work temporarily under its supervision and direction.

8.4.4 User undertaking

(d) 'user undertaking' means any natural or legal person for whom and under the supervision and direction of whom a temporary agency worker works temporarily.

8.4.5 Assignment

(e) 'assignment' means the period during which the temporary agency worker is placed at the user undertaking to work temporarily under its supervision and direction.

8.4.6 Basic working and employment conditions

(f) 'basic working and employment conditions' means working and employment conditions laid down by legislation, regulations, administrative provisions, collective agreements and/or other binding general provisions in force in the user undertaking relating to:
(i) the duration of working time, overtime, breaks, rest periods, night work, holidays and public holidays;
(ii) pay.

8.4.7 Relationship to national law

This Directive shall be without prejudice to national law as regards the definition of pay, contract of employment, employment relationship or worker. Member States shall not exclude from the scope of the Directive workers, contracts of employment or employment relationships solely because they relate to part-time workers, fixed-term contract workers or persons with a contract of employment or employment relationship with a temporary work agency.

8.5 Restrictions or prohibitions on the use of temporary agency work

Article 4 of the temporary work agency directive provides:

1. Prohibitions or restrictions on the use of temporary agency work shall be justified only on grounds of general interest relating in particular to the protection of temporary agency workers, the requirements of health and safety at work or the need to ensure that the labour market functions properly and abuses are prevented.

2. By 5 December 2011, Member States shall, after consulting the social partners in accordance with national legislation, collective agreements and practices, review any restrictions or prohibitions on the use of temporary agency work in order to verify whether they are justified on the grounds mentioned in paragraph 1.

3. If such restrictions or prohibitions are laid down by collective agreements, the review referred to in paragraph 2 may be carried out by the social partners who have negotiated the relevant agreement.

4. Paragraphs 1, 2 and 3 shall be without prejudice to national requirements with regard to registration, licensing, certification, financial guarantees or monitoring of temporary-work agencies.

5. The Member States shall inform the Commission of the results of the review referred to in paragraphs 2 and 3 by 5 December 2011.

In *Webb*,[87] the CJEU was asked whether the expression 'services' in Article 57 TFEU includes the service of providing manpower. The answer the CJEU gave to that question was in the affirmative. The Court further held:

2. Article 59 [now Article 56 TFEU] does not preclude a Member State which requires agencies for the provision of manpower to hold a licence from requiring a provider of services established in another Member State and pursuing activities on the territory of the first Member State to comply with that condition even if he holds a licence issued by the State in which he is established, provided, however, that in the first place when considering applications for licences and in granting them the Member State in which the service is provided makes no distinction based on the nationality of the provider of the services or his place of establishment, and in the second place that it takes into account the evidence and guarantees already produced by the provider of the services for the pursuit of his activities in the Member State in which he is established.

87. Case 279/80 *Webb* [1981] ECR 3305.

8.6 The principle of equal treatment

Article 5 of the directive on temporary agency work lays down that the basic working and employment conditions of temporary agency workers shall be, for the duration of their assignment at a user undertaking, at least those that would apply if they had been recruited directly by that undertaking to occupy the same job. As mentioned above Article 3(f) of the directive defines 'basic working as employment conditions' as working and employment conditions laid down by legislation, regulations, administrative provisions, collective agreements and/or other binding general provisions in force in the user undertaking relating to:

(i) the duration of working time, overtime, breaks, rest periods, night work, holidays and public holidays;
(ii) pay.

The principle of equal treatment also applies to the protections and rights accorded to permanently employed pregnant workers and permanently employed mothers who are breast-feeding. The same rights are to be accorded to their temporarily employed counterparts.

8.6.1 Working time

As regards the duration of working time, overtime, breaks, rest periods, night work, holidays and public holidays, the Directive provides for the implementation of the principle of equal treatment without any restrictions. However, this is without prejudice to the derogations which may be applied under the conditions laid down in Articles 5(2) to 5(4).

8.6.2 Pay

As set out in Chapter Six, Article 157 TFEU on equal pay for men and women equal work or work of equal value, states in its second paragraph that:

> 'For the purpose of this Article, 'pay' means the ordinary basic or minimum wage or salary and any other consideration, whether in cash or in kind, which the worker receives directly or indirectly, in respect of his employment, from his employer.'

According to the case law of the CJEU[88] on this provision, pay includes not only basic pay, but also, for example, overtime supplements18, special bo-

88. See for example Case C-300/06 *Voß* [2007] ECR I-10573, Case C-333/97 *Lewen* [1999] ECR I-7243, Case 12/81 *Garland* [1982] ECR 359, Case C-360/90 *Bötel*

nuses paid by the employer19, travel facilities20, compensation for attending training courses and training facilities21, termination payments in case of dismissal22 and occupational pensions. In the light of the above-mentioned case law, the Commission pointed out that if a Member State decided to exclude, for instance, occupational pension schemes from the notion of pay when transposing the Directive, it may not be followed by the CJEU. The Commission further underlined that the provision contained in Article 5(4), second subparagraph according to which 'Member States shall specify, in application of Article 3(2), whether occupational social security schemes, including pension, sick pay or financial participation schemes are included in the basic working and employment conditions' was only applicable to those Member States making use of Article 5(4). Nevertheless, it is clear that certain elements, for instance statutory social security schemes, are not considered by the existing case law to be part of pay and, as a consequence, Member States remain free to exclude them from the scope of pay even if they do not make use of Article 5(4).

As explicitly stated in Article 153(5) TFEU the provisions of this article shall not apply to pay. However, this provision of the Treaty does not prevent the European legislator from establishing the principle of equal treatment with respect to pay in favour of temporary agency workers, which, as a consequence, directly determines their pay level by reference to the pay that they would have been entitled to if they had been recruited by the user undertaking to occupy the same job. This has been explicitly confirmed in *Alonso*, where the CJEU stated:[89]

40 More particularly, the exception relating to 'pay' set out in Article 137(5) EC [now Article 153 (5) TFEU] is explained by the fact that fixing the level of wages falls within the contractual freedom of the social partners at a national level and within the relevant competence of Member States. In those circumstances, in the present state of Community law, it was considered appropriate to exclude determination of the level of wages from harmonisation under Article 136 EC et seq [now Article 151 TFEU].

41 The 'pay' exception cannot, however, be extended to any question involving any sort of link with pay; otherwise some of the areas referred to in Article 137(1) EC [now Article 153 (1) would be deprived of much of their substance.

[1992] ECR I-3589, Case C-33/89 *Kowalska* [1990] ECR I-2591, Case 170/84 *Bilka* [1986] ECR 1607, Case C-262/88 *Barber* [1990] ECR 1990 I-1889.

89. Case C-307/05 *Alonso* [2007] ECR I-7109, in particular in points 40 and 41.

Article 5(2) of the directive on temporary agency work provides that as regards pay, Member States may, after consulting the social partners, provide that an exemption be made to the principle of equal treatment where temporary agency workers who have a permanent contract of employment with a temporary-work agency continue to be paid in the time between assignments.

8.7 Duties of the User Company

The user company shall keep temporary workers informed of any permanent vacancies. Member States must ensure that any clauses preventing the conclusion of a contract of employment or an employment relationship between the user undertaking and the temporary worker are null and void or may be declared null and void.

They shall have equal access to amenities and collective services at work. Member States should facilitate training access for temporary workers.

8.8 No recruitment fees. Free of charge placement services as a fundamental right

Temporary workers should not be charged any recruitment fees. Article 29 CFREU provides on the right of access to placement services that 'Everyone has the right of access to a free placement service'.

8.9 Temporary agency work and posting of workers

As set out above in section 4, the posting of workers directive[90] covers employees being sent to another Member State in situation when a temporary employment undertaking or placement agency hires out a worker to a user undertaking established or operating in another Member State.[91]

90. 96/71/EC.

91. See on the interplay between the posting of workers directive and the temporary agency work directive Preisler, Marie: EU directive on temporary agency work could reduce social dumping, Nordic Labour Journal April 07, 2011. Nordic Labour Journal is published by the Norwegian Work Research Institute in Oslo on commission from the Nordic Council of Ministers, see generally on Nordic Labour Journal http://www.nordiclabourjournal.org/om-oss

9 Employment and remuneration

The Community Charter of the Fundamental Social Rights of Workers from 1989 provides in point 4-6 that:

4. Every individual shall be free to choose and engage in an occupation according to the regulations governing each occupation.

5. All employment shall be fairly remunerated. To this effect, in accordance with arrangements applying in each country:
- workers shall be assured of an equitable wage, i.e. a wage sufficient to enable them to have a decent standard of living;
- workers subject to terms of employment other than an open-ended full-time contract shall receive an equitable reference wage;
- wages may be withheld, seized or transferred only in accordance with the provisions of national law; such provisions should entail measures enabling the worker concerned to continue to enjoy the necessary means of subsistence for himself and his family.

6. Every individual must be able to have access to public placement services free of charge.

Article 29 CFREU also provides that 'Everyone has the right of access to a free placement service.'

10 Dismissal

The ILO Convention on Termination of Employment[92] regulates termination of employment at the initiative of the employer. Termination of an employment relationship by an employee is outside the scope of the Convention. The same applies to termination which arises out of a freely negotiated agreement reached by both parties. Similarly, the Convention does not apply to cases where an employee willingly resigns or takes voluntary retirement. The main provision of the Convention is Article 4 according to which the employment of a worker shall not be terminated unless there is a valid reason for such termination connected with the capacity or conduct of the worker or based on the operational requirements of the undertaking, establishment or service. Article 11 of the Convention provides that, unless an employee is guilty of seri-

92. ILO Convention No. 158 concerning termination of employment. See also and Recommendation No. 166.

ous misconduct, a worker whose employment is terminated shall be entitled to a reasonable period of notice.

Article 30 CFREU on protection in the event of unjustified dismissal provides that

> Every worker has the right to protection against unjustified dismissal, in accordance with Union law and national laws and practices.

In the Explanatory remarks to the CFREU,[93] it is stated that the above provision draws on Article 24 of the revised Social Charter.[94] There is also reference to the directives on transfer of undertakings[95] and on the protection of employees in the event of the insolvency of their employer.[96]

As set out in Chapter Two, the CJEU held in *Polier*[97] that a French law which permitted dismissals without a valid reason was outside the scope of EU law with the consequence that EU fundamental rights could not be invoked in national law. The CJEU therefore refused to answer a question about the compatibility of a French dismissal provision with the CFREU and some international Conventions (ILO Convention no. 158 on termination of employment and the Council of Europe Social Charter).

93. OJ 2007 C 303.
94. http://conventions.coe.int/Treaty/en/Treaties/Html/163.htm
95. 2001/23/EC, see further Chapter Eight.
96. 80/987/EEC as amended by Directive 2002/74/EC, now repealed and codified by 2008/94/EC, see further Chapter Eight.
97. Case C-361/07, *Polier*, not reported in English, available in French at the CJEU website curia.europa.eu

CHAPTER EIGHT

Restructuring of Businesses

1 Introduction

In this Chapter restructuring of businesses refer to collective redundancies, transfer of undertakings and insolvency of the employer. The basic rules on these subject date back to the 1970's, i.e. the early period of EU labour law dominated by the internal market perspective on employment law. In *Nolan*,[1] the CJEU explicitly stated that the collective redundancies directive forms part of the legislation concerning the internal market and used that as an argument for interpreting the directive as not covering public sector employees, see further below in section 3.2.3. The rules described in this Chapter has been codified or recast in the years after the adoption of the Maastricht Treaty 1992 and the ensuing development of the fundamental rights/EMU perspective on EU labour law.

2 Sources of Law

2.1 National law and public international law

Some – but not all EU Member States – had rules on collective redundancies, transfer of undertaking and protection of the outstanding wage claims of workers in the case of their employer's insolvency. The subjects discussed in this Chapter were not before the inception of the EC/EU – and are still not – regulated in international labour law.

1. Case C-583/10 *Nolan* [2012] ECR nyr.

2.2 EU Soft law

Already in the Social Action Programme 1974,[2] the Council took note of the Commission's undertaking to submit to it, before 1 April 1974, proposals relating to a directive on the harmonization of laws with regard to the retention of rights and advantages in the event of changes in the ownership of undertakings, in particular in the event mergers.

The Community Charter of the Fundamental Social Rights of Workers 1989 stated:[3]

> The improvement must cover, where necessary, the development of certain aspects of employment regulations such as procedures for collective redundancies and those regarding bankruptcies.

Information, consultation and participation for workers must be developed along appropriate lines, taking account of the practices in force in the various Member States. This shall apply especially in companies or groups of companies having establishments or companies in several Member States of the European Community. Such information, consultation and participation must be implemented in due time, particularly in the following cases:

- when technological changes which, from the point of view of working conditions and work organisation, have major implications for the work force are introduced into undertakings;
- in connection with restructuring operations in undertakings or in cases of mergers having an impact on the employment of workers;
- in cases of collective redundancy procedures;
- when trans-frontier workers in particular are affected by employment policies pursued by the undertaking where they are employed.

The 1989 Charter on fundamental Rights for Workers, see above in Chapter Two, and the Social Action Programme 1989[4] which is closely related to the implementation of that Charter discuss restructuring of businesses in a broad perspective with a view to improving the EU's competiveness in a more global perspective.

2. Bulletin of the European Communities, Supplement 2/74.
3. http://www.aedh.eu/plugins/fckeditor/userfiles/file/Conventions%20internatio nales/Community_Charter_of_the_Fundamental_Social_Rights_of_Workers.pdf
4. http://aei.pitt.edu/1345/1/Social_charter_COM_89_568.pdf

2.3 EU Directives

The first collective redundancies directive from 1975[5] and the first transfer of undertakings directive from 1977[6] were adopted as a result of the first EU Social Action Programme 1974. The first directive on the protection of employees in the event of the insolvency of their employer was adopted in 1980.[7]

2.4 Primary EU law

There are no Treaty provisions on collective redundancies, transfer of undertakings or employer insolvency and no mention of these subjects in the CFREU. In the Explanatory remarks to CFREU[8] there is reference to the directives on collective redundancies[9] and transfer of undertakings[10] in the explanation to Article 27 CFREU on Workers' right to information and consultation within the undertaking.

In *Scattolon*[11] the referring court asked the CJEU the following question (emphasis added):

> 4) Must *the general [EU]-law principles* of legal certainty, the protection of legitimate expectations, procedural equity, effective judicial protection, and the right to an independent tribunal and, more generally, to a fair hearing, guaranteed by [Article 6 TEU] in conjunction with Article 6 of the [ECHR] and with Articles 46, 47 and 52(3) of the Charter of Fundamental Rights of the European Union, proclaimed at Nice on 7 December 2000, as incorporated in the Treaty of Lisbon, be interpreted as precluding the adoption by the Italian State, after a significant period of time (5 years), of a specific interpretative provision which is at variance with the wording to be interpreted and in conflict with the consistent and settled interpretation of the institution responsible for ensuring uniform interpretation of the law, a provision which, moreover, is relevant for the purpose of resolving disputes to which the Italian State is itself a party?

The CJEU did not find it necessary to answer the question after having answered three previous questions about whether a transfer within the meaning of EU law had taken place which was answered in the affirmative and the legal consequences of that transfer.

5. Directive 75/129/EEC, amended by 92/56/EEC, now repealed and consolidated by 98/59/EC.
6. 77/187/EEC, amended by 98/50/EC, now repealed and codified by 2001/23/EC.
7. 80/987/EEC, amended by 2002/74/EC, now repealed and codified by 2008/94/EC..
8. See OJ 2007 C 303.
9. 98/59/EC.
10. 2001/23/EC.
11. Case C-108/10 *Scattolon* [2011] ECR nyr.

2.5 Must EU Fundamental Rights be observed in the context of collective redundancies, transfer of undertakings and insolvency of the employer?

As set out in Chapter Two, CFREU and other fundamental rights are according to the case law of the CJREU binding in the Member States both vertically and horizontally but only when the Member States act in the scope of Union law. One can ask whether the Member States are acting in the scope of EU law when an employer make collective redundancies, transfer of undertaking or when the employer is insolvent with the effect that the EU fundamental rights must be observed. There is no case law to clarify the matter. In my view, the answer is probably in the affirmative.

2.6 Case Law

There is a considerable amount of case law from the CJEU which will be included in the following. There is no case law from ECtHR on the subjects dealt with in this Chapter.

3 Collective Redundancies

The current directive[12] from 1998 on collective redundancies is based on a proposal submitted by the Commission in 1996.[13] The current is a consolidated version of two older directives[14] on the same subject which have been repealed. It is intended to harmonise Member States' laws on the procedure and practical arrangements for collective redundancies, in order to afford greater protection to workers in the event of collective redundancies.

3.1 What is a collective redundancy?

For the purposes of the Directive, 'collective redundancies' means according to Article 1 of the Directive dismissals effected by an employer for one or more reasons not related to the individual workers concerned where, according to the choice of the Member States, the number of redundancies is:

(i) either, over a period of 30 days:

12. Council Directive 98/59/EC of 20 July 1998 on the approximation of the laws of the Member States relating to collective redundancies.
13. Com 96/620.
14. Directive 75/129/EEC and Directive 92/56/EEC.

- at least 10 in establishments normally employing more than 20 and less than 100 workers,
- at least 10% of the number of workers in establishments normally employing at least 100 but less than 300 workers,
- at least 30 in establishments normally employing 300 workers or more,

(ii) or, over a period of 90 days, at least 20, whatever the number of workers normally employed in the establishments in question;

In 2005, France adopted a rule providing that an employee engaged after 22 June 2005 who was under 26 years of age should not be taken into account in calculating the size of the workforce of the undertaking by which he was employed until he reached the age of 26, whatever the nature of his contract with the undertaking. A number of French trade unions took proceedings against the French Government claiming that this was contrary to both the collective redundancies directive and the directive establishing a general framework for informing and consulting employees,[15] see on that directive above in Chapter Four. In *CGT and others*,[16] the CJEU ruled that Article 1(1)(a) of the Directive must be interpreted as precluding national legislation which excludes, even temporarily, a specific category of workers from the calculation of staff numbers set out in that provision. See also above in Chapter Six on age discrimination.

For the purpose of calculating the number of redundancies provided for in the first subparagraph of point (a), terminations of an employment contract which occur on the employer's initiative for one or more reasons not related to the individual workers concerned shall be assimilated to redundancies, provided that there are at least five redundancies.

Terminations of an employment contract which occur on the employer's initiative include not only situations in which the employer dismisses the workers but also situations in which the employer inspires employees to resign voluntarily by offering severance payment, retirement payment, redundancies payments and similar incentives.

In *Mayor*,[17] the CJEU ruled that Article 1(1) of the Redundancies Directive must be interpreted as not precluding national legislation according to which the termination of contracts of employment of a number of workers, whose employer is a natural person, as a result of the *death* of that employer

15. 2002/14/EC.
16. Case C-385/05 *CGT and others* [2007] I-611.
17. Case C-323/08 *Mayor* [2009] ECR I-11621.

is not classified as collective redundancy. The Directive does not preclude national legislation which provides for different compensation depending on whether the workers lost their jobs as a result of the death of the employer or as a result of a collective redundancy.

In *Junk*,[18] a German Arbeitsgericht put the following questions to the CJEU:

> 1. Is [the directive] to be interpreted to the effect that 'redundancy' ['Entlassung'] within the meaning of Article 1(1)(a) thereof is to be construed as meaning the notice of dismissal ['Kündigung'] as the first act in bringing the employment relationship to an end or does 'redundancy' mean the termination of the employment relationship upon expiry of the period of notice?
>
> 2. If 'redundancy' ['Entlassung'] is to be construed as meaning the notice of dismissal, does the directive require that both the consultation procedure under Article 2 of the directive and the notification procedure under Articles 3 and 4 thereof must have been concluded before the notices of dismissal ['Kündigungen'] are announced?'

The CJEU answered that Articles 2 to 4 of the directive on collective redundancies must be construed as meaning that the event constituting redundancy consists in the declaration by an employer of his intention to terminate the contract of employment.

In *Commission* v *Portugal*,[19] the CJEU declared that, by restricting the concept of collective redundancies to redundancies for structural, technological or cyclical reasons, and by failing to extend that concept to dismissals for any reason not related to the individual workers concerned, Portugal had failed to fulfil its obligations under Articles 1 and 6 of the collective redundancies directive.

3.2 Scope of the Directive

3.2.1 Termination as a result of a judicial decision on grounds of insolvency

The scope of the original Collective Redundancies Directive in respect of insolvency situations was at issue in *Nielsen & Søn* in liquidation.[20] In *Lauge*,[21] the CJEU held that the derogations provided for in the Directive on Collective Redundancies do not apply to collective redundancies occurring on the

18. Case C-188/03 *Junk* [2005] ECR I-885.
19. Case C-55/02 *Commission* v *Portugal* [2004] ECR I-9387.
20. Case 284/83 *Nielsen & Søn* [1985] ECR 553.
21. Case C-250/97 *Lauge* [1998] ECR I-8737.

same day as that on which the employer files a winding-up petition and terminates the undertaking's activities, and the competent court subsequently, and without any deferment other than that resulting from the date which it sets for the hearing, issues a winding-up order pursuant to the winding-up petition, that order taking effect for a number of purposes from the date on which the petition was filed. In joined cases *Claes et al.*,[22] the CJEU ruled:

Articles 1 to 3 of Council Directive 98/59/EC of 20 July 1998 on the approximation of the laws of the Member States relating to collective redundancies must be interpreted as applying to a termination of the activities of an employing establishment as a result of a judicial decision ordering its dissolution and winding up on grounds of insolvency, even though, in the event of such a termination, national legislation provides for the termination of employment contracts with immediate effect.

2. Until the legal personality of an establishment whose dissolution and winding up have been ordered has ceased to exist, the obligations under Articles 2 and 3 of Directive 98/59 must be fulfilled. The employer's obligations pursuant to those provisions must be carried out by the management of the establishment in question, where it is still in place, even with limited powers of management over that establishment, or by its liquidator, where that establishment's management has been taken over in its entirety by the liquidator.

3.2.2 Fixed-term work

The Directive does not apply to collective redundancies effected under contracts of employment concluded for limited periods of time or for specific tasks except where such redundancies take place prior to the date of expiry or the completion of such contracts;

3.2.3 Public sector employees

The Directive does not apply to workers employed by public administrative bodies or by establishments governed by public law. In *Nolan*,[23] the CJEU was asked questions under Article 267 TFEU on redundancies as a consequence of the closure of an American military base in the UK. The Court held that redundancies as a result of the closure of a military base was in any way outside the scope of the directive regardless of whether it was a military base of a Member State or a third country. The CJEU stated in Nolan that the collective redundancies Directive forms part of the legislation concerning the internal market. Whilst the size and functioning of the armed forces does have

22. Joined Cases C-235/10 to C-239/10 *Claes, Jeanjean, Rémy, Schneider and Tran* [2011] ECR nyr.
23. Case C-583/10 *Nolan* [2012] ECR nyr.

an influence on the employment situation in a given Member State, considerations concerning the internal market or competition between undertakings do not apply to them. As the CJEU has already held, activities which, like national defence, fall within the exercise of public powers are in principle excluded from classification as economic activity. In support of that view it referred to *Scattalon*,[24] see further below in section 4.4.2 on transfer of undertakings and collective agreements.

3.2.4 Crews of seagoing vessels

The Directive does not apply to the crews of seagoing vessels.

3.3. Groups of companies

In groups of companies the question arises as to who bears the obligations as employer, the parent company or the subsidiary. In *Akavan*,[25] the CJEU held:

3. Article 2(1) of Directive 98/59, read in conjunction with the first subparagraph of Article 2(4) of that directive, must be interpreted to mean that, in the case of a group of undertakings consisting of a parent company and one or more subsidiaries, the obligation to hold consultations with the workers' representatives falls on the subsidiary which has the status of employer only once that subsidiary, within which collective redundancies may be made, has been identified.

4. Article 2(1) of Directive 98/59, read in conjunction with Article 2(4) of that directive, must be interpreted to mean that, in the case of a group of undertakings, the consultation procedure must be concluded by the subsidiary affected by the collective redundancies before that subsidiary, on the direct instructions of its parent company or otherwise, terminates the contracts of employees who are to be affected by those redundancies.

3.4 Enforcement. Individual or collective

In *Mono Car Styling*,[26] the CJEU ruled that:

1. Article 6 of Council Directive 98/59/EC of 20 July 1998 on the approximation of the laws of the Member States relating to collective redundancies, read in conjunction with Article 2 thereof, is to be interpreted as not precluding national rules which introduce procedures intended to permit both workers' representatives and the workers themselves as individuals to ensure compliance with the obligations laid down in that directive, but which limit the individual right of action of workers in regard to the complaints which may be raised and makes that right subject to the requirement that workers' representatives

24. Case C-108/10 *Scattolon* [2011] ECR nyr.
25. Case C-44/08 *Akavan* [2009] ECR I-8163.
26. Case C-12/08 *Mono Car Styling* [2009] ECR I-6653.

should first have raised objections with the employer and that the worker concerned has informed the employer in advance of his intention to query whether the information and consultation procedure has been complied with.

2. The fact that national rules, establishing procedures which permit workers' representatives to ensure that the employer has complied with all the information and consultation obligations set out in Directive 98/59, impose limits and conditions on the individual right of action which it also grants to every worker affected by collective redundancy is not of such a nature as to infringe the principle of effective judicial protection.

3. Article 2 of Directive 98/59 must be interpreted as precluding national rules which reduce the obligations of an employer who intends to proceed with collective redundancies below those laid down in Article 2 of that directive. In applying domestic law, the national court is required, applying the principle of interpreting national law in conformity with Community law, to consider all the rules of national law and to interpret them, so far as possible, in the light of the wording and purpose of Directive 98/59 in order to achieve an outcome consistent with the objective pursued by the directive. Consequently, it must ensure, within the limits of its jurisdiction, that the obligations binding such an employer are not reduced below those laid down in Article 2 of that directive.

3.5 Minimum directive

Member States may apply or introduce provisions which are more favourable to workers.

3.6 Other Questions

In *Rockfon A/S* v *Specialarbejderforbundet i Danmark* the CJEU held that Article 1(1)(a) of the Directive is to be interpreted as meaning that it does not preclude two or more interrelated undertakings in a group, neither or none of which has decisive influence over the other or others, from establishing a joint recruitment and dismissal department so that, in particular, dismissals on grounds of redundancy in one of the undertakings can take place only with that department' s approval. The sole purpose of the Directive is partial harmonization of collective redundancy procedures and its aim is not to restrict the freedom of undertakings to organize their activities and arrange their personnel departments in the way which they think best suits their needs.

3.7 Consultations

Any employer contemplating collective redundancies must hold consultations with the workers' representatives with a view to reaching an agreement. These consultations shall, at least, cover ways and means of avoiding collective redundancies or reducing the number of workers affected, and of mitigating the consequences by recourse to accompanying social measures aimed at redeploying or retraining those workers made redundant.

3.7.1 When should consultations be held?

Article 2 of the Directive provides that where an employer is contemplating collective redundancies, he shall begin consultations with the workers' representatives in good time with a view to reaching an agreement. In *Akavan*,[27] the CJEU held:

1. Article 2(1) of Council Directive 98/59/EC of 20 July 1998 on the approximation of the laws of the Member States relating to collective redundancies must be interpreted to mean that the adoption, within a group of undertakings, of strategic decisions or of changes in activities which compel the employer to contemplate or to plan for collective redundancies gives rise to an obligation on that employer to hold consultations with workers' representatives.

2. Whether the obligation has arisen for the employer to start consultations on the collective redundancies contemplated does not depend on whether the employer is already able to supply to the workers' representatives all the information required in Article 2(3)(b) of Directive 98/59.

In *Junk*,[28] the CJEU held that the employer must finish the consultation process before he decides to give notice of termination of the employment contracts. See on *Junk* above in section 3.1. Likewise, the CJEU in In *Akavan*[29] held:

4. Article 2(1) of Directive 98/59, read in conjunction with Article 2(4) of that directive, must be interpreted to mean that, in the case of a group of undertakings, the consultation procedure must be concluded by the subsidiary affected by the collective redundancies before that subsidiary, on the direct instructions of its parent company or otherwise, terminates the contracts of employees who are to be affected by those redundancies.

3.7.2 What should the consultations cover?

Consultations shall, at least, cover ways and means of avoiding collective redundancies or reducing the number of workers affected, and of mitigating the consequences by recourse to accompanying social measures aimed, inter alia, at aid for redeploying or retraining workers made redundant.

27. Case C-44/08 *Akavan* [2009] ECR I-8163.
28. Case C-188/03 *Junk* [2005] ECR I-885.
29. Case C-44/08 *Akavan* [2009] ECR I-8163.

3.7.3 External Experts

The Directive lays down that Member States may make provision for workers' representatives to call on the services of experts in accordance with measures in force at national level. T

3.7.4 Information to be provided by the employer

The employer is to provide workers' representatives with all relevant information during the course of the consultations and, in any event, is to notify them of the following in writing:

the reasons;
the period during which redundancies are to be effected;
the number and category of workers normally employed;
the number to be made redundant;
the criteria used to select those workers to be made redundant;
the method used to calculate compensation (where applicable).

3.8 Notification of the competent authority

The Directive on collective redundancies lays down the procedure to be followed:

First, the employer notifies the competent public authority in writing of any projected collective redundancies. This notification must contain all the relevant information concerning the projected redundancies and consultations held, except for the method used to calculate compensation. However, where the cessation of activity is the result of a judicial decision, notification is only necessary at the express request of the authority.

Then, the employer forwards a copy of the notification to the workers' representatives, who may send comments to the competent public authority.

Collective redundancies take effect at the earliest 30 days after the notification; the competent public authority uses this period to seek solutions. Member States may grant the public authority the power to reduce this period or to extend it to 60 days following notification in cases where the problems cannot be resolved. This is not compulsory for collective redundancies following a cessation of activity resulting from a judicial decision. Wider powers of extension may be granted. The employer must be informed of any extension and the grounds for it before expiry of the initial period.

3.9 Institutional requirements

In the UK, worker representation has traditionally been channeled through independent and recognized trade unions: the so-called 'single channel' approach.[30] The dual-channel approach of the Continent, where worker representation is conducted through both trade unions and elected worker representatives in the work-place, as for example the German Betriebsrat and the Danish Samarbejdsudvalg, is unfamiliar to the British tradition. When implementing the original directives on collective redundancies[31] and transfer of undertakings[32] the UK required that recognized trade unions be consulted. If the employer had not recognized a trade union he was not required to perform any information and consultation of employees. The Commission considered that a violation of the directives and took proceedings against the UK. In the infringement case against the UK,[33] over the collective redundancies directive, the Commission argued that the UK had failed to fulfil its obligations under the directive on collective redundancies,[34] by not providing for the designation of workers' representatives in an undertaking where the employer refused to recognize such representatives. The Commission made a similar allegation[35] in respect of the Directive[36] on transfers of undertakings. The CJEU held that in the Directives on Collective Redundancies and Acquired Rights, 'the Community legislature intended both to ensure comparable protection for workers' rights in the different Member States and to harmonize the costs which such protective rules entail for Community undertakings.' The CJEU thus took a view that was adapted to the internal market logic of the early layers of EU labour law, see above in Chapter One.

4 Transfer of Undertakings

As mentioned above in section 2.2. the first Transfer of Undertakings Directive[37] was adopted in 1977 as a result of the first EU Social Action Programme 1974. In 1998 the Council adopted a Directive[38] amending the origi-

30. See on that the 2000 Industrial Relations in Europe report from the Commission.
31. 75/129/EEC.
32. 77/187/EEC.
33. Case C-383/92 *Commission* v *UK* [1994] I-2479.
34. Articles 2 and 3 of Directive 75/129/EEC.
35. Case C-382/92 *Commission* v *UK* [1994] I-2435.
36. 77/187/EEC.
37. 77/187/EEC.
38. 98/50/EC.

nal Transfer of Undertakings Directive and in 2001, the Transfer of Undertakings Directive was codified.[39]

4.1 Main problems

Two main problems are regulated in the EU rules on transfer of undertaking:

1) Whether a transfer within the meaning of EU law has taken place and
2) legal consequences of such a transfer.

4.2 National Background

The Transfer of Undertakings directive established the rule that there is automatic and compulsory continuation of the employment relationship between the employee and the transferor-employer with the transferee-employer.. That rule was before the adoption of the directive in 1977 well known law in some EU countries, notably France and Germany who could continue without changing anything. In Denmark, it was the opposite of the preexisting law. Denmark therefore had to adopt legislation which changed the law radically and all actors had to learn new rules. That situation created some uncertainty as to the precise content of the law. That uncertainty was increased by the fact that the different language versions of the directive are not totally identical. *Wendelboe*[40] and *Danmols*[41] concerned problems related to the different language versions. The language problems were aggravated by the way Denmark had chosen to implement the directive. The Danish implementing law deviated in important respects from the text of the Danish version of the directive. In the first years after the adoption of the Directive many of the preliminary questions to the CJEU came from Denmark. The early Danish questions essentially sought clarification of whether the directive meant the same as the Danish implementing legislation.[42]

4.3 Aim of the Directive

Directive 2001/23 is intended only as a means of 'partial harmonization,' extending the protection guaranteed to workers by the laws of the individual

39. 2001/23/EC.
40. Case 19/83 *Wendelboe* [1985] ECR 457.
41. Case 105/84 *Danmols* [1985] ECR 2639.
42. See further Nielsen, Ruth: Europeanization of Nordic Labour Law', Scandinavian Studies in Law, Stockholm, 2002, Vol. 43, Stability and Change in Nordic Labour Law, p. 37, available from http://www.scandinavianlaw.se/index.php?page=index-database.

Member States to cover the case *404 where an undertaking is transferred. It is not, according to the CJEU in *Danmols*, intended to 'establish a uniform level of protection throughout the Community on the basis of common criteria.' For this reason the Court has been prepared to allow national courts a considerable degree of discretion in applying the Directive. For example, it has permitted national traditions to inform the meaning of key terms, such as the definition of 'employee.' National law also prescribes the consequences of a refusal to be transferred, the sanction in the case of the failure to inform and consult worker representatives, and the dismissal of a worker in the event of a transfer.

4.4 Definitions

For the purpose of the Directive the following definitions apply:

4.4.1 'Transferor'

'Transferor' means any natural or legal person who, by reason of a transfer within the meaning of Article 1(1), ceases to be the employer in respect of the undertaking, business or part of the undertaking or business.

4.4.2 'Transferee'

'Transferee' means any natural or legal person who, by reason of a transfer within the meaning of Article 1(1), becomes the employer in respect of the undertaking, business or part of the undertaking or business.

4.4.3 'Representatives of employees'

'Representatives of employees' and related expressions shall mean the representatives of the employees provided for by the laws or practices of the Member States.

4.4.4 'Employee'

'Employee' means any person who, in the Member State concerned, is protected as an employee under national employment law.

4.4.5 Contract of employment or employment relationship

Article 3(1) of the Directive provides that the transferor's rights and obligations arising from a contract of employment or from an employment relationship existing on the date of a transfer shall, by reason of such transfer, be transferred to the transferee, see below in section 4.6 on the legal effects of a transfer.

4.4.5.1 In relation to national law

The Directive is according to Article 2(2) without prejudice to national law as regards the definition of contract of employment or employment relationship. Member States may, however, not exclude from the scope of the Directive contracts of employment or employment relationships solely because: (a) of the number of working hours performed or to be performed, (b) they are employment relationships governed by a fixed duration contract of employment[43] or (c) they are temporary employment relationships.[44]

4.4.5.2 Transfers in groups of companies. Who is the employer?

In *Albron*,[45] the CJEU held that in the event of a transfer, within the meaning of Directive 2001/23 on the approximation of the laws of the Member States relating to the safeguarding of employees' rights in the event of transfers of undertakings, businesses or parts of undertakings or businesses, of an undertaking belonging to a group to an undertaking outside that group, it is also possible to regard as a 'transferor', within the meaning of Article 2(1)(a) of that directive, the group company to which the employees were assigned on a permanent basis without however being linked to the latter by a contract of employment, even though there exists within that group an undertaking with which the employees concerned were linked by such a contract of employment.

The requirement under Article 3(1) of the transfer of undertakings Directive that there be either an employment contract, or, in the alternative and thus as an equivalent, an employment relationship at the date of the transfer suggests that, in the mind of the Union legislature, a contractual link with the transferor is not required in all circumstances for employees to be eligible for the protection conferred by Directive the transfer of undertakings Directive. On the other hand, it is not apparent from the transfer of undertakings Directive that the relationship between the employment contract and the employment relationship is one of subsidiarity and that, therefore, where there is a plurality of employers, the contractual employer must systematically be

43. Within the meaning of Article 1(1) of Council Directive 91/383/EEC supplementing the measures to encourage improvements in the safety and health at work of workers with a fixed-duration employment relationship or a tempory employment relationship.
44. Within the meaning of Article 1(2) of Directive 91/383/EEC, and the undertaking, business or part of the undertaking or business transferred is, or is part of, the temporary employment business which is the employer.
45. Case C-242/09 *Albron* [2010] I-10309.

given greater weight. Since the transfer of an undertaking, within the meaning of the transfer of undertakings Directive, presupposes, in particular, a change in the legal or natural person who is responsible for the economic activity of the entity transferred and who, in that capacity, establishes working relations as employer with the staff of that entity, in some cases despite the absence of contractual relations with those employees, the position of a contractual employer, who is not responsible for the economic activity of the economic entity transferred, cannot systematically take precedence, for the purposes of determining the identity of the transferor, over the position of a non-contractual employer who is responsible for that activity.

The CJEU further stated that in exercising its jurisdiction under Article 267 TFEU, it is only exceptionally that the CJEU may, in application of the general principle of legal certainty inherent in the legal order of the EU, be moved to restrict for any person concerned the opportunity of relying on a provision which it has interpreted with a view to calling in question legal relationships established in good faith. Two criteria must be fulfilled before such a limitation can be imposed, namely, that those concerned should have acted in good faith and that there should be a risk of serious difficulties. In that regard, when no concrete evidence has been submitted to the Court of Justice of a risk of serious difficulties in connection with massive litigation which might be brought, following a judgment of the Court of Justice on the interpretation of Directive 2001/23, against undertakings which have carried out a transfer falling within that directive, there is no cause to limit the temporal effects of such a judgment. Moreover, the fact that the undertaking making such a transfer has already made a severance payment to employees who have entered into the service of the transferee undertaking is in any event irrelevant.

4.5 Scope. When is there a 'transfer' within the meaning of EU law?

4.5.1 Change of employer not of owner is decisive

4.5.1.1 Change og employer without change og ownership

There can be a change of employer without any change in the owner of the business. In Daddy's Dance Hall[46] an employee (Tellerup) was employed as a restaurant manager by Irma Catering A/S, which had taken a non-transferable lease of restaurants and bars belonging to A/S Palads Teatret. The lease was subsequently terminated, and on 28 January 1983 Irma Catering dismissed its staff with the statutory notice. A new lease was concluded

46. Case 324/86 *Daddy's Dance Hall* [1988] ECR 739.

between A/S Palads Teatret and Daddy's Dance Hall A/S. Daddy's Dance Hall immediately re-employed the employees of the former lessee to do the same jobs as before. The new management contract concluded with Tellerup stipulated, however, that his remuneration, which had previously been in the form of commission, would henceforth take the form of a fixed salary. Furthermore, at Tellerup's request the parties agreed on a trial period of three months during which either side could give 14 days' notice. On that basis Tellerup was dismissed on 26 April 1983 with 14 days' notice. The main proceedings concerned in essence the period of notice to which the plaintiff was entitled. Højesteret considered that its decision in the case depended on the interpretation of the provisions of the the transfer of undertakings Directive.[47] It therefore stayed the proceedings and referred the following questions to the CJEU for a preliminary ruling:

'(1) Must Article 1 (1) of Council Directive 77/187/EEC of 14 February 1977 on the approximation of the laws of the Member States relating to the safeguarding of employees' rights in the event of transfers of undertakings, businesses or parts of businesses be interpreted as meaning that the directive applies where a non-transferable lease of a business is terminated and as a result, without there being any interruption in the running of the business, the owner leases the business to a new lessee, who re-employs the staff, who had been given notice but had not left their employment, and buys the former lessee's stock?'

'(2) Can an employee who enters into an agreement with the purchaser of a business waive rights under the directive where by so doing he obtains certain advantages so that his conditions of employment, taken as a whole, are not altered in such a way as to leave him in a worse position?'

The CJEU referred to its ruling in *Ny Mølle Kro*[48] and stated that, that the purpose of Directive 77/187/EEC is to ensure, so far as possible, that the rights of employees are safeguarded in the event of a change of employer by allowing them to remain in employment with the new employer on the terms and conditions agreed with the transferor. The directive is therefore applicable where, following a legal transfer or merger, there is a change in the natural or legal person who is responsible for carrying on the business and who by virtue of that fact incurs the obligations of an employer vis-à-vis employees of the undertaking, regardless of whether or not ownership of the undertaking is transferred.

47. Then 77/187/EEC, now 2003/23/EC.
48. Case 287/86 *Ny Mølle Kro* [1987] ECR 5465.

4.5.1.2 Change of ownership without change of employer. Purchases of shares

The Directive on transfer of undertakings does not apply to transfers of company control through a purchase of shares, which is the most common way to effect a change in the corporate control.

4.5.2 Broad or narrow interpretation

The single most litigated issue before the CJEU concerning transfer of undertakings is the proper interpretation of the concept of a transfer. Before the adoption of the directive there were two different approaches to this concept in national law requiring compulsory transfer. French law took a broad view and regarded a transfer of an activity, e.g. a cleaning activity as covered by the concept. German law, on the other hand, took a more narrow view, and required there to be an organised entity. The directive was adopted with unanimity. Points on which there were different views were not clarified in the text of the directive but left to later developments in case law or by amendment of the Directive. The CJEU has over the years repeatedly been confronted with questions as to whether the concept of a transfer should be construed broadly as covering the mere transfer of an activity or narrowly as requiring an organised entity which has retained its identity. The responses of the Court have been somewhat ambiguous and varying,[49] see below in section 4.3.4 on *Schmidt* and *Süzen*.

When the Transfer of Undertakings Directive was amended in 1998, and codified in 2001, Article 1 got its current wording which seems more in line with the German than the French tradition:

(a) This Directive shall apply to any transfer of an undertaking, business, or part of an undertaking or business to another employer as a result of a legal transfer or merger.
(b) Subject to subparagraph (a) and the following provisions of this Article, there is a transfer within the meaning of this Directive where there is a transfer of an economic entity which retains its identity, meaning an organized grouping of resources which has the objective of pursuing an economic activity, whether or not that activity is central or ancillary.

49. See Laulom Sylvaine: Transfers of Undertakings. Part I. The European Court of Justice in the dialogue on transfers of undertakings: A fallible interlocutor? in Sciarra, Silvana (ed.): Labour Law in the Courts, Oxford 2001.

4.5.3 An economic entity which retains its identity

In *Spijkers*,[50] the questions posed to the CJEU were:

(1) Is there a transfer within the meaning of Article 1 (1) of Council Directive No 77/187 where buildings and stock are taken over and the transferee is thereby enabled to continue the business activities of the transferor and does in fact subsequently carry on business activities of the same kind in the buildings in question?

(2) Does the fact that at the time when the buildings and stock were sold the business activities of the vendor had entirely ceased and that in particular there was no longer any goodwill in the business prevent there being a 'transfer' as defined in Question 1?

(3) Does the fact that the circle of customers is not taken over prevent there being such a transfer?

The CJEU held that a transfer of an undertaking, business or part of a business does not occur merely because its assets are disposed of. Instead it is necessary to consider, in a case such as the present, whether the business was disposed of as a going concern, as would be indicated, inter alia, by the fact that its operation was actually continued or resumed by the new employer, with the same or similar activities. In order to determine whether those conditions are met, it is necessary to consider all the facts characterizing the transaction in question, including the type of undertaking or business, whether or not the business's tangible assets, such as buildings and movable property, are transferred, the value of its intangible assets at the time of the transfer, whether or not the majority of its employees are taken over by the new employer, whether or not its customers are transferred and the degree of similarity between the activities carried on before and after the transfer and the period, if any, for which those activities were suspended. It should be noted, however, that all those circumstances are merely single factors in the overall assessment which must be made and cannot therefore be considered in isolation. It is for the national court to make the necessary factual appraisal, in the light of the criteria for interpretation set out above, in order to establish whether or not there is a transfer in the sense indicated above.

The requirement that the undertaking must have preserved its economic identity was also dealt with in *Ny Mølle Kro*.[51] In that case the CJEU held that the Directive:

50. Case 24/85 *Spijkers* [1986] ECR 1119.
51. Case 287/86 *Ny Mølle Kro* [1987] ECR 5465.

envisages the case in which the business retains its identity inasmuch as it is transferred as a going concern, which may be indicated in particular by the fact that its operation is actually continued or resumed by the new employer, with the same or similar activities.

In *P Bork*,[52] the ECJ held that the fact that the transfer is effected in two stages does not prevent the Directive from applying, provided that the undertaking in question retains its identity. In order to determine whether those conditions are met, it is necessary to consider all the circumstances surrounding the transaction in question, including, in particular, whether or not the undertaking's tangible and intangible assets and the majority of its employees are taken over, the degree of similarity between the activities carried on before and after the transfer and the period, if any, for which those activities ceased in connection with the transfer.

4.5.4 Contracting out

Contracting out situations have been dealt with by the CJEU in *Rask*[53] (canteen services) where the CJEU ruled in favour of there being a transfer within the meaning of the Directive in a contracting out situation. Both the ECJ and the EFTA Court have delivered a number of rulings on this issue.[54]

In *Schmidt*[55] the plaintiff (Schmidt) in the main proceedings, who was employed by a Savings Bank to clean the premises of its branch office in Wacken, was dismissed in February 1992 on account of the refurbishment of that branch office, in which the Savings Bank wished to entrust the cleaning to Spiegelblank, the firm which was already responsible for the cleaning of most of the Savings Bank's other premises. Spiegelblank offered to employ Schmidt for a monthly wage which was higher than that which she had previously been receiving. Schmidt, however, was not prepared to work on those terms, as she calculated that her hourly wage would in fact be lower as a result of the increase in the surface area to be cleaned. The CJEU held that when an undertaking entrusts by contract the responsibility for operating one of its services, such as cleaning, to another undertaking which thereby assumes the obligations of an employer towards employees assigned to those

52. 130 Case 101/87 *Bork* [1988] ECR 3057.
53. Case C-209/91 *Rask* [1992] ECR I-5755.
54. See from the EFTA Court: Case 2/95 Eilert Eidesund v Stavanger Catering A/S advisory opinion of 25.9.1996, Case E-2/96, Jørn Ulstein and Per Otto Røiseng v Asbjørn Møller, advisory opinion of 19 December 1996 and Case E-3/96, Tor Angeir Ask and Others v ABB Offshore Technology AS and Aker Offshore Partner A/S, advisory opinion of 14 March.
55. Case C-392/92 *Schmidt* [1994] I-1311.

duties, that operation may come within the scope of the directive. It referred to its judgment in Rask[56] in support of the view that the fact that the activity transferred is for the transferor merely an ancillary activity not necessarily connected with its objects cannot have the effect of excluding that operation from the scope of the directive. Nor is the fact that the activity in question in Spiegelblank was performed, prior to the transfer, by a single employee sufficient to preclude the application of the directive since its application does not depend on the number of employees assigned to the part of the undertaking which is the subject of the transfer. It should be noted that one of the objectives of the directive, as clearly stated in the second recital in the preamble thereto, is to protect employees in the event of a change of employer, in particular to ensure that their rights are safeguarded. That protection extends to all staff and must therefore be guaranteed even where only one employee is affected by the transfer.

In *Süzen*,[57] the following questions were put to the CJEU:

1. On the basis of the judgments of the Court of Justice of 14 April 1994 in Case C-392/92 Schmidt [1994] ECR I-1311 and of 19 May 1992 in Case C-29/91 Redmond Stichting [1992] ECR I-3189, is Directive 77/187/EEC applicable if an undertaking terminates a contract with an outside undertaking in order then to transfer it to another outside undertaking?

2. Is there a legal transfer within the meaning of the directive in the case of the operation described in Question 1 even if no tangible or intangible business assets are transferred?

The CJEU held that Article 1(1) of Directive 77/187/EEC is to be interpreted as meaning that the directive does not apply to a situation in which a person who had entrusted the cleaning of his premises to a first undertaking terminates his contract with the latter and, for the performance of similar work, enters into a new contract with a second undertaking, if there is no concomitant transfer from one undertaking to the other of significant tangible or intangible assets or taking over by the new employer of a major part of the workforce, in terms of their numbers and skills, assigned by his predecessor to the performance of the contract.

In *Oy Liikenne*,[58] the CJEU held that the taking over by an undertaking of non-maritime public transport activities – such as the operation of scheduled local bus routes – previously operated by another undertaking, following a

56. Case C-209/91 *Rask* [1992] ECR I-5755.
57. Case C-13/95 *Süzen* [1997] ECR I-1259.
58. Case C-172/99 *Oy Liikenne* [2001] ECR I-745.

procedure for the award of a public service contract132 may fall within the material scope of the Transfer of Undertakings Directive. In the case at issue no assets (busses and other material) were transferred, only manpower. The Commission submitted, referring to Süzen, that the absence of a transfer of assets between the old and new holders of the contract for bus transport is of no importance, whereas the fact that the new contractor took on an essential part of the employees of the old contractor is decisive. The CJEU remarked that is has indeed held that an economic entity may, in certain sectors, be able to function without any significant tangible or intangible assets, so that the maintenance of the identity of such an entity cannot, logically, depend on the transfer of such assets. The CJEU ruled, however, in Oy Liikenne, that bus transport cannot be regarded as an activity based essentially on manpower, as it requires substantial plant and equipment. The fact that the tangible assets used for operating the bus routes were not transferred from the old to the new contractor therefore constitutes a circumstance to be taken into account. In a sector such as scheduled public transport by bus, where the tangible assets contribute significantly to the performance of the activity, the absence of a transfer to a significant extent from the old to the new contractor of such assets, which are necessary for the proper functioning of the entity, must lead to the conclusion that the entity does not retain its identity. In the Finnish part of the Oy Liikenne case the Finnish Supreme Court followed the CJEU.

4.5.5 Organisational autonomy

In *Klarenberg*,[59] the CJEU held:

> Article 1(1)(a) and (b) of Council Directive 2001/23/EC of 12 March 2001 on the approximation of the laws of the Member States relating to the safeguarding of employees' rights in the event of transfers of undertakings, businesses or parts of undertakings or businesses must be interpreted as meaning that that directive may also apply in a situation where the part of the undertaking or business transferred does not retain its organisational autonomy, provided that the functional link between the various elements of production transferred is preserved, and that that link enables the transferee to use those elements to pursue an identical or analogous economic activity, a matter which it is for the national court to determine.

4.5.6 All undertakings, public or private, which are engaged in economic activities

The Directive applies to all undertakings, public or private, which are engaged in economic activities whether or not they are operating for gain. In

59. Case C-466/07 *Klarenberg* [2009] ECR I-803.

Henke,[60] there was a transfer of administrative functions from a municipality to an administrative collectivity which was formed by neighbouring municipalities in a rural district by means of a public-law agreement in order to strengthen their administration. The CJEU held that such a transfer was outside of the scope of the the Transfer of Undertakings Directive, see the following conclusion of the Court:

Article 1(1) of Council Directive 77/187/EEC of 14 February 1977 on the approximation of the laws of the Member States relating to the safeguarding of employees' rights in the event of transfers of undertakings, businesses or parts of businesses must be interpreted as meaning that the concept of a 'transfer of an undertaking, business or part of a business' does not apply to the transfer of administrative functions from a municipality to an administrative collectivity such as the one in question in the main proceedings.

In *Collino*,[61] the CJEU held that the transfer of undertakings directive may apply to a situation in which an entity operating telecommunications services for public use and managed by a public body within the State administration is, following decisions of the public authorities, the subject of a transfer for value, in the form of an administrative concession, to a private-law company established by another public body which holds its entire capital. The persons concerned by such a transfer must, however, originally have been protected as employees under national employment law. The CJEU summarized its practice on the requirement that the undertaking must be involved in economic activities in the following way:

30 First, it is settled case-law that the Directive applies to all transfers of entities which are engaged in economic activities, whether or not they operate with a view to profit (see, in particular, Case C-382/92 Commission v United Kingdom [1994] ECR I-2435, paragraphs 44 to 46).

31 On the other hand, the reorganisation of structures of the public administration or the transfer of administrative functions between public administrative authorities does not constitute a transfer of an undertaking within the meaning of the Directive. In those cases the transfer concerns activities involving the exercise of public authority (Case C-298/94 Henke v Gemeinde Schierke and Verwaltungsgemeinschaft 'Brocken' [1996] ECR I-4989, paragraphs 14 and 17).

32 So, the fact that the service transferred was the subject of a concession by a public body such as a municipality cannot exclude application of the Directive if the activity in ques-

60. Case C-298/94 *Henke* [1996] ECR I-4989.
61. Case C-343/98 *Collino* [2000] ECR I-6659.

tion does not involve the exercise of public authority (Joined Cases C-173/96 and C-247/96 Sánchez Hidalgo and Others [1998] ECR I-8237, paragraph 24).

33 The Court has held – in the context of competition law, admittedly, but the ruling may be applied to the present case – that the management of public telecommunications equipment and the placing of such equipment at the disposal of users on payment of a fee amount to a business activity (Case 41/83 Italy v Commission [1985] ECR 873, paragraph 18, and, impliedly, Joined Cases C-271/90, C-281/90 and C-289/90 Spain and Others v Commission [1992] ECR I-5833). Moreover, the circumstance that the operation of the public telecommunications network is entrusted to a body forming part of the public administration cannot prevent that body from being classified as a public undertaking (Case C-69/91 Decoster [1993] ECR I-5335, paragraph 15, and Case C-92/91 Taillandier [1993] ECR I-5383, paragraph 14).

34 Second, the circumstance that the transfer results from unilateral decisions of the public authority rather than from an agreement does not render the directive inapplicable (Case C-29/91 Redmond Stichting v Bartol [1992] ECR I-3189, paragraphs 15 to 17). The Court thus held that the Directive applies in a situation in which a public authority decides to terminate the subsidy paid to one legal person engaged in assisting drug addicts, as a result of which the activities of that legal person are fully and definitively terminated, and to transfer it to another legal person with a similar aim (Redmond Stichting, paragraph 21).

35 In those circumstances, a transfer such as that in the main proceedings falls within the material scope of the Directive.

In *Scattolon*,[62] the CGEU held that the takeover by a public authority of a Member State of staff employed by another public authority and entrusted with the supply to schools of auxiliary services including, in particular, tasks of maintenance and administrative assistance constitutes a transfer of an undertaking falling within the scope of the transfer of undertakings directive, where that staff consists in a structured group of employees who are protected as workers by virtue of the domestic law of that Member State.

4.6 Legal consequences of there being a transfer: Safeguarding of employees' rights

Article 3 of the transfer of undertakings directive provides:

1. The transferor's rights and obligations arising from a contract of employment or from an employment relationship existing on the date of a transfer shall, by reason of such transfer, be transferred to the transferee.

62. Case C-108/10 *Scattolon* [2011] ECR nyr.

Member States may provide that, after the date of transfer, the transferor and the transferee shall be jointly and severally liable in respect of obligations which arose before the date of transfer from a contract of employment or an employment relationship existing on the date of the transfer.

2. Member States may adopt appropriate measures to ensure that the transferor notifies the transferee of all the rights and obligations which will be transferred to the transferee under this Article, so far as those rights and obligations are or ought to have been known to the transferor at the time of the transfer. A failure by the transferor to notify the transferee of any such right or obligation shall not affect the transfer of that right or obligation and the rights of any employees against the transferee and/or transferor in respect of that right or obligation.

3. Following the transfer, the transferee shall continue to observe the terms and conditions agreed in any collective agreement on the same terms applicable to the transferor under that agreement, until the date of termination or expiry of the collective agreement or the entry into force or application of another collective agreement.

Member States may limit the period for observing such terms and conditions with the proviso that it shall not be less than one year.

4. (a) Unless Member States provide otherwise, paragraphs 1 and 3 shall not apply in relation to employees' rights to old-age, invalidity or survivors' benefits under supplementary company or intercompany pension schemes outside the statutory social security schemes in Member States.

(b) Even where they do not provide in accordance with subparagraph (a) that paragraphs 1 and 3 apply in relation to such rights, Member States shall adopt the measures necessary to protect the interests of employees and of persons no longer employed in the transferor's business at the time of the transfer in respect of rights conferring on them immediate or prospective entitlement to old age benefits, including survivors' benefits, under supplementary schemes referred to in subparagraph (a).

4.6.1 Unchanged continuance of the individual contract of employment

In case of a transfer, the rights and duties of the employment contracts of the employees from the transferred undertaking will be recognised. The Directive applies to all types of employment relationships, without distinction in relation to: the number of working hours, performed or to be performed or the type of employment contract (undetermined, fixed-duration, or temporary).

As appears from the above citation of Article 3, Article 3(1) of the Directive states the principle that the transferee is bound to the contractual and employment law obligations of the transferor. The transferor has to state what these are beforehand. Article 3(1) reads:

Transfer of employment relationships The rights and obligations of employees are maintained where an undertaking is the subject of a transfer. These rights and duties are connected with an existing employment contract or relationship.

In *Collino*,[63] the CJEU held that Article 3(1) of the transfer of undertakings directive must be interpreted as meaning that, in calculating the rights of a financial nature attached, in the transferee's business, to employees' length of service, such as a termination payment or salary increases, the transferee must take into account the entire length of service, in both his employment and that of the transferor, of the employees transferred, in so far as his obligation to do so derives from the employment relationship between those employees and the transferor, and in accordance with the terms agreed in that relationship.

In *Katsikas*,[64] the question was:

> Does the grant to an employee of a right of objection by which, in the event of a transfer of the business, he can prevent the transfer of his employment relationship to the transferee of the business, constitute a more favourable legal provision within the meaning of Article 7 of Council Directive 77/187/EEC?

The CJEU held that Article 3(1) is to be interpreted as not precluding an employee of the transferor on the date of the transfer of the undertaking, within the meaning of Article 1(1) of the directive, from objecting to the transfer of his contract of employment or employment relationship to the transferee. The directive does not, however, require Member States to provide that, in the event of the employee deciding of his own accord not to continue with the contract of employment or employment relationship with the transferee, the contract or relationship should be maintained with the transferor. Neither does the directive preclude this. In such a case, it is for the Member States to determine what the fate of the contract of employment or employment relationship with the transferor should be.

4.6.2 Collective agreements

As appears from the above citation of Article 3, Article 3(3) of the Directive on transfer of undertakings states that following the transfer, the transferee shall continue to observe the terms and conditions agreed in any collective agreement on the same terms applicable to the transferor under that agreement, until the date of termination or expiry of the collective agreement or the entry into force or application of another collective agreement. Member States may limit the period for observing such terms and conditions with the proviso that it shall not be less than one year.

63. Case C-343/98 *Collino* [2000] ECR I-6659.
64. Joined Cases C-132/91, 138/91, & 139/9 *Katsikas* [1992] ECR I-6577.

In principle, the working conditions of the employees are maintained for the duration of the collective agreement of the undertaking. However, these conditions may be amended, at least one year after the transfer of the undertaking and if the Member States so authorise. In *Ny Mølle Kro*, [65] the CJEU was asked by the Danish Labour Court:

(4) Must Article 3(2)[66] of the Directive be interpreted as meaning that the transferee must continue to observe the terms of a collective agreement binding the transferor regarding pay and working conditions notwithstanding the fact that at the time of the transfer no employees were employed by the undertaking?

The CJEU reformulated the question as meaning that the Arbejdsretten (the Labour Court) essentially asked whether Article 3(2) of the then Transfer of Undertakings Directive must be interpreted as obliging the transferee to continue to observe the terms and conditions agreed in any collective agreement in respect of workers who were not employed by the undertaking at the time of its transfer.

According the Danish Confederation of Trade Unions that question should be answered in the affirmative. On the other hand, Dansk Arbejdsgiverforening (the Danish Confederation of Employers), the United Kingdom and the Commission emphasized that only persons who are employed by the undertaking at the time of the transfer may take advantage of the Directive, and not persons who are engaged after the transfer. The CJEU held, as it had previously stated, in its judgment in *Danmols*, [67] that the purpose of the Directive is to ensure, as far as possible, that the contract of employment or employment relationship continues unchanged with the transferee, in order to prevent the workers concerned from being placed in a less favourable position solely as a result of the transfer. It is therefore consistent with the scheme of the Directive to interpret it as meaning that unless otherwise expressly provided, it may be relied on solely by workers whose contract of employment or employment relationship is in existence at the time of the transfer subject, however, to compliance with the mandatory provisions of the Directive concerning protection of employees from dismissal as a result of the transfer. It followed that Article 3(2) of the Directive is intended to ensure the continued observance by the transferee of the terms and conditions of employment agreed in a collective agreement only in respect of workers who were already

65. Case 287/86 *Ny Mølle Kro* [1987] ECR 5465.
66. In 2001/23/EC the provision on collective agreements is found in Article 3(3).
67. Case 105/84 *Danmols* [1985] ECR 2639.

employed by the undertaking at the date of the transfer, and not as regards persons who were engaged after that date. For those reasons the reply to the fourth question was that Article 3(2) of the Transfer of Undertakings Directive, properly construed, does not oblige the transferee to continue to observe the terms and conditions agreed in a collective agreement in respect of workers who were not employed by the undertaking at the time of the transfer.

In *Scattolon*,[68] Scattolon was employed by the municipality of Scorzè since 16 May 1980 as a cleaner in State schools. She worked as a local authority ATA employee until 31 December 1999. After 1 January 2000, pursuant to the applicable Italian law, she was transferred onto the list of State ATA employees. In accordance with a Ministerial Decree she was placed on a salary scale corresponding, on that list, to nine years of service. Having thus not obtained recognition of her service of about 20 years with the municipality and considering that she had thus suffered a considerable reduction in her remuneration, Scattolon brought an action before the Tribunale di Venezia seeking recognition of the whole of that length of service and classification, in consequence, in the grade corresponding, for State ATA employees, to length of service of between 15 and 20 years.

The CJEU ruled that where a transfer within the meaning of Directive 77/187 leads to the immediate application to the transferred workers of the collective agreement in force with the transferee, and where the conditions for remuneration are linked in particular to length of service, Article 3 of that directive precludes the transferred workers from suffering, in comparison with their situation immediately before the transfer, a substantial loss of salary by reason of the fact that their length of service with the transferor, equivalent to that completed by workers in the service of the transferee, is not taken into account when determining their starting salary position with the latter. It is for the national court to examine whether, at the time of the transfer at issue in the main proceedings, there was such a loss of salary.

In *Werhof*,[69] the CJEU was asked whether Article 3(1) of the transfer of undertakings directive must be interpreted as meaning that, where an undertaking is transferred and a contract of employment refers to a collective agreement to which the transferor is a party but not the transferee, the transferee is not bound by collective agreements subsequent to the one in force at the time of the transfer. The CJEU answered that Article 3(1) of the Directive

68. Case C-108/10 *Scattolon* [2011] ECR nyr.
69. Case C-499/04 *Werhof* [2006] ECR I-2397.

must be interpreted as not precluding, in a situation where the contract of employment refers to a collective agreement binding the transferor, that the transferee, who is not party to such an agreement, is not bound by collective agreements subsequent to the one which was in force at the time of the transfer of the business.

In *Juuri*,[70] the CJEU held that it is for the referring court to assess the situation at issue in the case before it in the light of the interpretation of Article 3(3) of Directive 2001/23 as meaning that the continued observance of the terms and conditions agreed in a collective agreement which expires on the date of the transfer of the undertaking is not guaranteed after that date.

4.7 Dismissals

The transfer of an undertaking is according to Article 4 of the transfer of undertakings directive not a lawful ground for dismissal. Dismissals may only take place for economic, technical or organisational reasons.

In *Dethier*,[71] the CJEU held that on a proper construction of Article 4(1) of Directive 77/187, both the transferor and the transferee may dismiss employees for economic, technical or organisational reasons. Employees unlawfully dismissed by thetransferor shortly before the undertaking is transferred and not taken onby the transferee may claim, as against the transferee, that their dismissalwas unlawful.

In *Merckx*,[72] the CJEU held that Article 3(1) of the transfer of undertakings Directive does not preclude an employee employed by the transferor at the date of the transfer of an undertaking from objecting to the transfer to the transferee of the contract of employment or the employment relationship. In such a case, it is for the Member States to determine what the fate of the contract of employment or employment relationship with the transferor should be. However, where the contract of employment or the employment relationship is terminated on account of a change in the level of remuneration awarded to the employee, Article 4(2) of the Directive requires the Member States to provide that the employer is to be regarded as having been responsible for the termination.

In *Juuri*,[73] the CJEU ruled that Article 4(2) of Directive 2001/23/EC must be interpreted as meaning that, in cases where the termination of a contract of employment or an employment relationship is brought about because the

70. Case C-396/07 *Juuri* [2008] I-8883.
71. Case C-319/94 *Dethier* [1998] ECR I-1061.
72. Case C-171/94 *Merckx* [1996] I-1253.
73. Case C-396/07 *Juuri* [2008] I-8883.

conditions for the applicability of that provision have been met, independently of any failure on the part of the transferee employer to fulfil its obligations under that directive, the Member States are not required to guarantee the employee a right to financial compensation, for which the transferee employer is liable, in accordance with the same conditions as the right upon which an employee can rely where the contract of employment or the employment relationship is unlawfully terminated by his employer. However, the national court is required, in a case within its jurisdiction, to ensure that, at the very least, the transferee employer in such a case bears the consequences that the applicable national law attaches to termination by an employer of the contract of employment or the employment relationship, such as the payment of the salary and other benefits relating, under that law, to the notice period with which an employer must comply.

4.8 Mandatory

The transfer of undertakings directive is mandatory. In *Daddy's Dance Hall*,[74] the CJEU held – in line with its case law on equal pay, see in Chapter Six – that the Directive is mandatory on each point so that it cannot be derogated from on one point to the disadvantage of the employee even if the contract on other points are more favourable to the employee than required by the directive so that it seen as a whole is advantageous for the employee.

4.9 Derogations

According to Article 5 Member states can derogate from Art. 3 and 4 if the company is insolvent. The rights and obligations of employees are not preserved where the transfer is undertaken as part of insolvency or bankruptcy proceedings. To prevent the misuse of insolvency proceedings in order to deprive employees of their rights in the case of a transfer, Member States may take appropriate measures in order to prevent this type of practice.

4.10 Employee representatives/trade unions

Article 6 of the directive on transfer of undertakings states that employee representatives' positions should not change where the undertaking retains autonomy through the transfer. It is talking mainly about unions. During a transfer, employee representatives shall maintain their function until their reappointment is possible. Employees must continue to be represented, including in the case of bankruptcy or insolvency proceedings. The rights of trade un-

74. Case 324/86 *Daddy's Dance Hall* [1988] ECR 739.

ion representatives are preserved even if their term of office expires as a result of the transfer of the undertaking.

In *Uribe*,[75] the CJEU ruled that a transferred economic entity preserves its autonomy, within the meaning of Article 6(1) of Directive 2001/23/EC provided that the powers granted to those in charge of that entity, within the organisational structures of the transferor, namely the power to organise, relatively freely and independently, the work within that entity in the pursuit of its specific economic activity and, more particularly, the powers to give orders and instructions, to allocate tasks to employees of the entity concerned and to determine the use of assets available to the entity, all without direct intervention from other organisational structures of the employer, remain, within the organisational structures of the transferee, essentially unchanged. The mere change of those ultimately in charge cannot in itself be detrimental to the autonomy of the entity transferred, except where those who have become ultimately in charge have available to them powers which enable them to organise directly the activities of the employees of that entity and therefore to substitute their decision making within that entity for that of those immediately in charge of the employees.

4.11 Information

Article 7(1) of the Directive provides

> 1. The transferor and transferee shall be required to inform the representatives of their respective employees affected by the transfer of the following:
> - the date or proposed date of the transfer,
> - the reasons for the transfer,
> - the legal, economic and social implications of the transfer for the employees,
> - any measures envisaged in relation to the employees.

The transferor must give such information to the representatives of his employees in good time, before the transfer is carried out.

The transferee must give such information to the representatives of his employees in good time, and in any event before his employees are directly affected by the transfer as regards their conditions of work and employment.

Member States whose laws, regulations or administrative provisions provide that represenatives of the employees may have recourse to an arbitration board to obtain a decision on the measures to be taken in relation to employees may limit the obligations laid down in paragraphs 1 and 2 to cases where

75. Case C-151/09 *Uribe* [2010] ECR I-7591.

the transfer carried out gives rise to a change in the business likely to entail serious disadvantages for a considerable number of the employees. The information and consultations shall cover at least the measures envisaged in relation to the employees. The information must be provided and consultations take place in good time before the change in the business as referred to in the first subparagraph is effected.

The obligations laid down in this Article shall apply irrespective of whether the decision resulting in the transfer is taken by the employer or an undertaking controlling the employer. In considering alleged breaches of the information and consultation requirements laid down by this Directive, the argument that such a breach occurred because the information was not provided by an undertaking controlling the employer shall not be accepted as an excuse.

Member States may limit the obligations laid down in paragraphs 1, 2 and 3 to undertakings or businesses which, in terms of the number of employees, meet the conditions for the election or nomination of a collegiate body representing the employees.

Member States shall provide that, where there are no representatives of the employees in an undertaking or business through no fault of their own, the employees concerned must be informed in advance of:

- the date or proposed date of the transfer,
- the reason for the transfer,
- the legal, economic and social implications of the transfer for the employees,
- any measures envisaged in relation to the employees.

Employees are informed of the transfer conditions either directly or through the intermediary of their representatives. In particular, this information concerns the date or proposed date of the transfer, the reasons for the transfer, the legal, economic and social implications, and any measures envisaged in relation to the employees.

Member States may require that the transferor notifies the transferee of all the rights and obligations which will be transferred. However, the employees are still transferred even if this communication is not carried out.

4.12 Consultation

Article 7(2) of the transfer of undertakings directive provides that where the transferor or the transferee envisages measures in relation to his employees, he shall consult the representatives of his employees in good time on such measures with a view to reaching an agreement.

In addition, trade union representatives are consulted before measures concerning employees are adopted.

4.13 Participation

The directive provides for no co-determination rights for the employees or the trade unions or other kinds of worker participation in the decision-process beyond information and consultation.

5 Employer Insolvency

The current directive[76] on the protection of employees in the event of the insolvency of their employer was adopted in 2008.

5.1 Background

The Commission presented its proposal for the current directive in 2006.[77] The current directive [78] on the protection of employees in the event of the insolvency of their employer is a codified version of two older directives on the same issue.[79]

The CJEU has answered a number of preliminary questions about the former directives. In *Francovich*[80] on state liability for for loss and damage resulting from breach of its obligations under EU law to transpose a directive correctly into national law, it held that the Member States are liable in damages to aggrieved individuals for non-implementation or incomplete implementation of the directive on the following three conditions:

1) the result prescribed by the directive should entail the grant of rights to individuals.
2) it should be possible to identify the content of those rights on the basis of the provisions of the directive.
3) the existence of a causal link between the breach of the State's obligation and the loss and damage suffered by the injured parties.

76. 2008/94/EC.
77. See (Com)2006/657.
78. 2008/94/EC.
79. 80/987/EEC and 2002/74/EC.
80. Joined Cases C-6/1990 and C-9/90 *Francovich* [1991] ECR I-5357.

Suffritti[81] concerned the question as to whether direct effect of the directive could be relied upon before the expiry of the time limit for implementation. The answer is that the direct effect of the directive cannot be invoked before the expiry of the time limit for implementation. *Miret*[82] dealt with the right of managing staff to protection of their wage claims. The CJEU held that they cannot be excluded from the scope of the directive if they are considered workers under national law. *Bonifaci,*[83] *Palmisani,*[84] *Maso,*[85] *Gilson*[86] and *Regeling*[87] concerned various restrictions on the payment obligation. In *Mosbæk*[88] and *Everson,*[89] the CJEU addressed some transnational aspects, see below.

The 1980-directive was amended in 2002.[90] The amendments aimed to a wide extent to codify the case law of the CJEU.

The current Directive ensures payment of employees' outstanding claims in the event of employer insolvency. It requires Member States to set up an institution to guarantee the payments. The guarantee institutions must ensure payment of employees' outstanding claims for a period determined by Member States. The Directive lays down an EU minimum guarantee period covering the remuneration for the last three months (within a reference period of at least six months) or eight weeks (within a reference period of at least eighteen months). As regards occupational supplementary pension entitlements, the Directive requires Member States to adopt the necessary measures to protect them. This means that Member States have great flexibility when deciding the content of the measures.

If an insolvent employer had activities in at least two EU Member States, an employee's outstanding claims must be met by the institution in the Member State where the employee worked.

81. Joined Cases C-140/91, C-141/91, C-278 and C-279/91 Suffritti and others [1992] RCR I-6337.
82. Case C-334/92 *Mire*t [1993] ECR I-6911.
83. Joined Cases C-94 and C-95/95 *Bonifaci* [1997] ECR I-3969.
84. Case C-261/95 *Palmisani* [1997] ECR I-4025.
85. Case C-373/95 *Maso* [1997] ECR I-4051.
86. Case C-235/95 *Gilson* [1998] I-4531.
87. Case C-125/97 *Regeling* [1998] ECR I-4493.
88. Case C-117/96 *Mosbæk* [1997] ECR I-5017.
89. Case C-198/98 *Everson* [1999] I-8903.
90. 2002/74/EC.

5.2 Main Problems

The directive aims to provide for the protection of employees in the event of the insolvency of their employer and to ensure a minimum degree of protection, in particular in order to guarantee payment of their outstanding claims. To this end, the Member States must establish a body which guarantees payment of the outstanding claims of the employees concerned. In order to ensure equitable protection for the employees concerned. The state of insolvency is defined in the light of the legislative trends in the Member States. That concept also includes insolvency proceedings other than liquidation. In is ensured that the employees referred to in the part time directive[91] and the directive[92] on fixed-term work are not excluded from the scope of the Directive.

5.3 Scope of the current directive

According to Article 1 of the directive on the protection of employees in the event of the insolvency of their employer the Directive applies to employees' claims arising from contracts of employment or employment relationships and existing against employers who are in a state of insolvency within the meaning of Article 2(1) of the Directive, see below in section 5.3. Member States may, by way of exception, exclude claims by certain categories of employee from the scope of the Directive, by virtue of the existence of other forms of guarantee if it is established that these offer the persons concerned a degree of protection equivalent to that resulting from the Directive. Where such provision already applies in their national legislation, Member States may continue to exclude from the scope of this Directive:

(a) domestic servants employed by a natural person;
(b) share-fishermen.

5.4 Definitions

Insolvency

For the purposes of the directive on the protection of employees in the event of the insolvency of their employer, an employer shall according to Article 2 of the directive be deemed to be in a state of insolvency where a request has been made for the opening of collective proceedings based on insolvency of the employer, as provided for under the laws, regulations and administrative provisions of a Member State, and involving the partial or total divestment of

91. 97/81/EC.
92. 1999/70/EC.

the employer's assets and the appointment of a liquidator or a person performing a similar task, and the authority which is competent pursuant to the said provisions has:

(a) either decided to open the proceedings; or
(b) established that the employer's undertaking or business has been definitively closed down and that the available assets are insufficient to warrant the opening of the proceedings.

Concepts defined by national law
The directive on the protection of employees in the event of the insolvency of their employer is without prejudice to national law as regards the definition of the terms 'employee', 'employer', 'pay', 'right conferring immediate entitlement' and 'right conferring prospective entitlement'.

Minimum requirements
The Member States may not exclude from the scope of the Directive:

(a) part-time employees within the meaning of Directive 97/81/EC;
(b) employees with a fixed-term contract within the meaning of Directive 1999/70/EC;
(c) employees with a temporary employment relationship within the meaning of Article 1(2) of Directive 91/383/EEC.

Member States may not set a minimum duration for the contract of employment or the employment relationship in order for employees to qualify for claims under this Directive.

The directive on the protection of employees in the event of the insolvency of their employer does not prevent Member States from extending employee protection to other situations of insolvency under national law. Such procedures shall not however create a guarantee obligation for the institutions of the other Member States in the cases referred to in Chapter IV of the Directive on transnational situations.

5.5 Guarantee institutions
According to Article 3 of the directive on the protection of employees in the event of the insolvency of their employer Member States shall take the measures necessary to ensure that guarantee institutions guarantee, subject to Article 4 of the Directive, payment of employees' outstanding claims resulting from contracts of employment or employment relationships, including, where provided for by national law, severance pay on termination of employment relationships. The claims taken over by the guarantee institution

shall be the outstanding pay claims relating to a period prior to and/or, as applicable, after a given date determined by the Member States.

Article 4 of the Directive provides that Member States shall have the option to limit the liability of the guarantee institutions referred to in Article 3. If Member States exercise this option, they shall specify the length of the period for which outstanding claims are to be met by the guarantee institution. However, this may not be shorter than a period covering the remuneration of the last three months of the employment relationship prior to and/or after the date referred to in the second paragraph of Article 3. Member States may include this minimum period of three months in a reference period with a duration of not less than six months. Member States having a reference period of not less than 18 months may limit the period for which outstanding claims are met by the guarantee institution to eight weeks. In this case, those periods which are most favourable to the employee shall be used for the calculation of the minimum period.

Member States may set ceilings on the payments made by the guarantee institution. These ceilings must not fall below a level which is socially compatible with the social objective of the Directive. If Member States exercise this option, they shall inform the Commission of the methods used to set the ceiling.

Under Article 5 of the Directive Member States shall lay down detailed rules for the organisation, financing and operation of the guarantee institutions, complying with the following principles in particular:

(a) the assets of the institutions must be independent of the employers' operating capital and be inaccessible to proceedings for insolvency;
(b) employers must contribute to financing, unless it is fully covered by the public authorities;
(c) the institutions' liabilities must not depend on whether or not obligations to contribute to financing have been fulfilled.

5.6 Transnational situations – private international law

If an undertaking with activities in the territories of at least two Member States is in a state of insolvency within the meaning of Article 2(l), the institution responsible for meeting employees' outstanding claims shall according to Article 9 of the directive on the protection of employees in the event of the insolvency of their employer be that in the Member State in whose territory they work or habitually work.

The extent of employees' rights shall be determined by the law governing the competent guarantee institution.

Member States shall take the measures necessary to ensure that, in the cases referred to above decisions taken in the context of insolvency proceedings referred to in Article 2(1), which have been requested in another Member State, are taken into account when determining the employer's state of insolvency within the meaning of the Directive.

Article 10 provides that for the purposes of implementing Article 9, Member States shall make provision for the sharing of relevant information between their competent administrative authorities and/or the guarantee institutions mentioned in the first paragraph of Article 3, making it possible in particular to inform the guarantee institution responsible for meeting the employees' outstanding claims.

In *Mosbæk*,[93] Mosbæk, who lived in Denmark, was employed from 1 June 1993 by the English company Colorgen Ltd ('Colorgen') as commercial manager for Denmark, Norway, Sweden, Finland and, subsequently, Germany. In July 1994, Colorgen was declared insolvent, and its employees, including Mosbæk, were dismissed. Mosbæk declared, both to the Danish Guarantee Fund (Lønmodtagernes Garantifond) and to the company's English receiver, an outstanding claim of DKR 471 996, representing her salary, commissions and expenses. The Danish Guarantee Fund refused to settle the claim on the ground that responsibility lay with the guarantee institution of the State where the employer was established, in this case the UK National Insurance Fund. Mosbæk brought proceedings against the Danish Guarantee Fund before a Danish court which referred the following preliminary question to the CJEU:

In a situation where the employer is not established in the Member State in which the employee is resident and is solely represented in the State of the employee's residence by way of the said employee's work, which inter alia is carried out in office premises rented by the employer for the employee's use, is it the guarantee institution in the country where the employer is established or the guarantee institution in the country where the employee is resident which, on the employer'sinsolvency, according to Article 3 of Directive 80/987/EEC is to guarantee payment of the employee's outstanding claims resulting from the employment relationship in question?

The CJEU held that:

Where the employer is established in a Member State other than that in which the employee resides and was employed, the guarantee institution responsible, under Article 3 of Council Directive 80/987/EEC of 20 October 1980 on the approximation of the laws of the

93. Case C-117/96 *Mosbæk* [1997] ECR I-5017.

> Member States relating to the protection of employees in the event of the insolvency of their employer, for the payment of that employee's claims in the event of the employer's insolvency is the institution of the State in which, in accordance with Article 2(1) of the directive, either it is decided to open the proceedings for the collective satisfaction of creditors' claims or it has been established that the employer's undertaking or business has been closed down.

The factual situation in *Everson*[94] differed from that in *Mosbæk* in that the employer in Everson was established in more than one EU Member State. The CJEU held:

> Where the employees adversely affected by the insolvency of their employer were employed in a Member State by the branch established in that State of a company incorporated under the laws of another Member State, where that company has its registered office and in which it was placed in liquidation, the competent institution, under Article 3 of Council Directive 80/987/EEC of 20 October 1980 on the approximation of the laws of the Member States relating to the protection of employees in the event of the insolvency of their employer, for payment to those employees of outstanding claims is that of the State within whose territory they were employed.

As set out above it now follows from Article 9 of the codified directive[95] on the protection of employees in the event of the insolvency of their employer that if an undertaking with activities in the territories of at least two Member States is in a state of insolvency, the responsible guarantee institution for meeting employees' outstanding claims is that in the Member State where the employees have their place of work.

5.7 Enforcement

As set out in Chapter Two, if not otherwise stated, the Member States are free to choose the procedures and sanctions they will use to *enforce* a directive. They must, however, observe the EU fundamental rights and general principles in that context. In *Cavallero*,[96] the CJEU stated in regard to the protection of employees in the event of their employer's insolvency that Member States must, as far as possible, apply EU provisions in accordance with the requirements of the fundamental rights. Fundamental rights include the general principle of equality and non-discrimination. That principle precludes comparable situations from being treated in a different manner unless the difference in treatment is objectively justified. It was clear that, under Spanish

94. Case C-198/98 *Everson* [1999] I-8903.
95. 2008/94/EC.
96. Case C-442/00 *Cavallero* [2002] ECR I-11915.

law, all workers who are unfairly dismissed are in the same situation in the sense that they are entitled to 'salarios de tramitación'. However, in the event of the employer's insolvency, the Workers' Statute treated dismissed workers differently to the extent that the right to payment by the guarantee institution of claims relating to 'salarios de tramitación' is acknowledged only in respect of those determined by judicial decision, not if they are determined by judicially supervised conciliation. Such a difference in treatment can be accepted only if it is objectively justified which it was not considered to be.[97]

97. In case C-498/06 *Nunez* [2008] I-921, the CJEU considered exclusion of extra-judicial conciliation from the payment guarantee justified.

CHAPTER NINE

Working Environment Law

1 Introduction

At national level working environment regulation dates back to the early period of industrialization in the 19th century. The first layer of regulation was factory legislation.

Free movement on the internal market for dangerous machinery or chemical substances may cause harm to workers' health and safety when they use the machinery or are exposed to the chemicals in their working environment. It is the purpose of working environment provisions to protect workers against physical and psychological risks at work.

This Chapter gives an overview of the basic rules and principles on working environment. There are many very detailed provisions on working environment which are not included in the exposition of the law given in this Chapter.

2 The Sources of law

2.1 International and national Labour law

The ILO which has existed since 1919 has an old tradition of comprehensive and detailed regulation of the working environment. Many EU legal acts on working environment issues draw inspiration from ILO legal acts, often without clear reference to the source of inspiration.[1] The ILO Convention No. 155 concerning Occupational Safety and Health and the Working Environment from 1981 entered into force 11 August 1983. There are many similari-

1. See Murray, Jill: Transnational Labour Regulation: The ILO and EC Compared, The Hague, London, Boston 2001.

ties between this convention and the EU Framework Directive on the Working Environment.[2]

All the EU Member States had national rules on health and safety for workers before they entered the EC/EU.

2.2 EU labour law

Before the adoption of the Single European Act 1986 there was no specific provision on the protection of the safety and health of workers. Nevertheless, a substantial amount of EU legislation of a somewhat technical nature was adopted in this area on the basis of 'multi-purpose' articles, such as Article 100 EEC [now Article 115 TFEU] concerning the approximation of laws. However, use of that provision was subject to two restrictions: it required proof that a proposal for a directive directly affected the establishment or functioning of the internal market and unanimity on the part of the Member States.

The EEC Treaty only contained two express references to 'working conditions' in Articles 117 [now Article 151 TFEU] and 118 EEC concerning social policy. However, Article 117 EEC was deemed not to confer legislative competence in social matters on the EU. Article 118 EEC, which covered matters relating, in particular, to employment, labour law and working conditions, basic and advanced vocational training, social security, prevention of occupational accidents and diseases, occupational hygiene, and the right of association and collective bargaining between employers and workers, restricted the EU's competence in the framework '... of cooperation between Member States, which is to be organized by the Commission'.[3]

The EU has contributed intensely since the late 1980's to the legal regulation of working environment issues. Working Environment Law is, as set out in Chapter Two, the first labour law topic where adopting secondary EU legislation by majority voting in Council became possible.

The Framework Directive on the Working Environment[4] with its wide scope of application as well as individual working environment directives focusing on specific aspects of safety and health at work constitute the fundamentals of EU working environment legislation. These directives set out *minimum requirements* and *fundamental principles*, such as the principle of pre-

2. 89/391/EEC.
3. See Joined Cases 281/85, 283/85 to 285/85 and 287/85 *Germany, France, Netherlands, Denmark and United Kingdom* v *Commission* [1987] ECR 3203, paragraph 14.
4. 89/391/EEC.

vention and risk assessment, as well as the responsibilities of employers and employees. In addition, a series of European guidelines aim to facilitate the implementation of European directives as well as European standards which are adopted by European standards organisations.

As mentioned in Chapter Two, the Single European Act 1986 which was a Treaty amending the EEC Treaty, introduced majority voting in Article 118 a EEC [now Article 153 TFEU] to adopt minimum requirements with a view to 'encouraging improvements, especially in the working environment, as regards the health and safety of workers'. Due to the tension between the then conservative UK government and the governments of the then 11 other Member States the 1992 directive regarding pregnancy and maternity[5] and the 1993 Working Time Directive[6] adopted on the basis of Article 118 a EC [now Article 153(1)a TFEU] on working environment which allowed majority voting. Directives adopted under Article 118 a EC were binding for all the then 12 Member States, see further below in section 3.3 on the concept of working Environment.

The UK contested the validity of the original 1993 Working Time Directive[7] in an annulment action before the CJEU claiming that working time is not a working environment issue. Prior to the UK annulment case on the 1993 Working Time Directive, the CJEU has dealt with health and safety issues in a few cases. In Opinion 2/91,[8] delivered on 19 March 1993, on ILO Convention No 170 concerning safety in the use of chemicals at work, the CJEU stated that 'in order to help achieve this objective [that is, harmonization, referred to in Article 118a(1)], the Council has the power to adopt minimum requirements by means of directives', and proceeded to infer that 'the Community thus enjoys an internal legislative competence in the area of social policy', concluding that ILO Convention No 170 falls within the purview of the EU. In *ASTI,* [9] a request for a preliminary ruling, the reference to Article 118a by the national court proved to be irrelevant, with the result that the Court did not have to deal with the point at issue. Finally, in *Kirsammer-Hack,* [10] the Court simply noted that '... by providing that directives adopted in the fields of health and safety of workers are to avoid imposing administrative, financial and legal constraintsin a way which would hold back the crea-

5. 92/85/EEC.
6. 93/104/EC, see now 2003/88/EC.
7. Case C-84/94 *UK* v *Council* [1996] ECR I-5755.
8. Opinion 2/91 [1993] ECR I-1061, paragraphs 16 and 17.
9. Case C-213/90 *ASTI* [1991] ECR I-3507.
10. Case C-189/91 *Kirsammer-Hack* [1993] ECR I-6185.

tion and development of small and medium-sized undertakings, Article 118 a EEC, which was introduced by the Single European Act into the chapter concerning social provisions, indicates that such undertakings may be the subject of special economic measures'.

Following the adoption of the Single European Act in 1986, the Framework Directive on Working Environment[11] was adopted in 1989. Under Article 16 of the Directive the council can on a proposal from the Commission adopt Individual working Environment Directives *inter alia* on the subjects listed in an annex to the Directive.

With the Treaty of Amsterdam in 1997, the legislative competence in the fields of European social policies was further strengthened by the incorporation of the social agreement into the EC Treaty. The Lisbon Treaty – apart from the renumbering of the Articles on social policy – kept the substance of the provisions of ex Articles 136 ff TEC (now Articles 151 ff of the TFEU).

Article 31 CFREU provides on 'Fair and just working conditions' that every worker has the right to working conditions which respect his or her health, safety and dignity. Every worker has the right to limitation of maximum working hours, to daily and weekly rest periods and to an annual period of paid leave.

The CJEU has a considerable case law on working environment issues, not least working time.

3 Framework Directive on Working Environment[12]

The framework directive is divided into four sections. Section I, entitled 'General Provisions', consists of four articles. Articles 1 and 2 define the object and scope of the directive respectively, while Article 3 defines the terms worker', 'employer', workers' representative' and prevention'. 'Member States shall take the necessary steps to ensure that employers, workers and workers' representatives are subject to the legal provisions necessary for the implementation of this Directive'.

Section II of the framework directive, entitled 'Employers' Obligations', consists of eight articles. Section III of the framework directive consists of a single article which defines workers' responsibility in relation to safety issues (Article 13). Finally, Section IV of the framework directive concerns 'Miscel-

11. 391/89/EEC.
12. Directive 89/391 on the introduction of measures to encourage improvements in the safety and health of workers at work.

laneous Provisions', including Article 16 under which 'daugther directives, can be adopted within the framework of the directive. Article 18(1) provides that 'Member States shall bring into force the laws, regulations and administrative provisions necessary to comply with this Directive by 31 December 1992'. The repercussions of the transposition on national legal systems varied across Member States. In some Member States, the Framework Directive had considerable legal consequences due to inadequate national legislation while in others no major adjustments were necessary.

3.1 Legal Basis

Today (2013) the main legal basis for secondary EU legislation is Article 153(1)a TFEU which provides:

1. With a view to achieving the objectives of Article 151, the Union shall support and complement the activities of the Member States in the following fields:
(a) improvement in particular of the working environment to protect workers' health and safety;

3.2 Objective

The object of the Directive is to introduce measures to encourage improvements in the safety and health of workers at work. To that end it contains general principles concerning the prevention of occupational risks, the protection of safety and health, the elimination of risk and accident factors, the informing, consultation, balanced participation in accordance with national laws and/or practices and training of workers and their representatives, as well as general guidelines for the implementation of the said principles. The Directive shall be without prejudice to existing or future national and EU provisions which are more favourable to protection of the safety and health of workers at work.

3.3 The Concept of Working Environment

The UK contested the validity of the original 1993 Working Time Directive[13] in an annulment action before the CJEU claiming that working time is not part of the concept of working environment. The Directive could therefore not lawfully be adopted under Article 118 a EC but could have been adopted under the Social Policy Agreement[14] in which case it would only have been

13. Case C-84/94 *UK* v *Council* [1996] ECR I-5755.
14. See Treaty On European Union, OJ 1992 C 191 http://eur-lex.europa.eu/en/treaties/dat/11992M/htm/11992M.html#0090000015

binding for the 11 Member states that were parties to that Agreement and not for the UK, see further in Chapter Two, section 2.2.1 on the two tracks in the EU decision-making process from Maastricht to Amsterdam. The CJEU held that a provision in the Directive on Sunday work was invalid but that the 1993 Working Time Directive apart from that was valid, i.e. that working time issues are within the scope of the concept of working environment.

The UK maintained that there is no scientific material justifying the link between safety and health, on the one hand, and several aspects of working time dealt with in the Working Time directive and referred to in general terms, such as average weekly working time, paid annual leave and rest periods, on the other.

The advocate general referred to the fact that the concept of working environment in Article 118 a EEC came from Denmark and therefore should be interpreted broadly like the Danish concept of 'arbejdsmijø,' see the following (footnote omitted):

42. Confirmation of the view favouring a broad interpretation of that concept may be found in the origin of Article 118 a, namely in a proposal made by the Kingdom of Denmark at the Inter-Governmental Conference on the Single Act. The concept of 'working environment' ('arbejdsmiljø') in Danish law is a very broad one, covering the performance of work and conditions at the workplace, as well as technical equipment and the substances and materials used. Accordingly, the relevant Danish legislation is not limited to classic measures relating to safety and health at work in the strict sense, but also includes measures concerning working hours, psychological factors, the way work is performed, training in hygiene and safety, and the protection of young workers and worker representation with regard to security against dismissal or any other attempt to undermine their working conditions. The concept of 'working environment' is not immutable, but reflects the social and technical evolution of society.

It is a little ironical that the Danish origin of the working environment concept was invoked in favour of a broad interpretation of that concept. In the Danish labour law tradition from before EU membership many working time issues were regarded as classic collective bargaining issues and not as something that should be governed by working environment legislation, see below on the Working time directive and its belated implementation in Denmark because Denmark for some years maintained that the provisions in the Directive on working time which corresponded to Danish collective agreement provisions could be transposed into Danish law solely by means of collective agreements without Danish legislation being necessary, see on EU requirements to the national sources of law that can be used to implement EU directive above in Chapter Two. Denmark finally gave in and adopted a Danish statutory Act on Working Time.

3.4 Scope

The framework working environment directive applies to all sectors of activity, both public and private (industrial, agricultural, commercial, administrative, service, educational, cultural, leisure, etc.).

The Directive shall not be applicable where characteristics peculiar to certain specific public service activities, such as the armed forces or the police, or to certain specific activities in the civil protection services inevitably conflict with it. In that event, the safety and health of workers must be ensured as far as possible in the light of the objectives of the Directive.

3.5 Definitions

For the purposes of the framework Directive, the following terms shall have the following meanings:

(a) worker: any person employed by an employer, including trainees and apprentices but excluding domestic servants;
(b) employer: any natural or legal person who has an employment relationship with the worker and has responsibility for the undertaking and/or establishment;
(c) workers' representative with specific responsibility for the safety and health of workers: any person elected, chosen or designated in accordance with national laws and/or practices to represent workers where problems arise relating to the safety and health protection of workers at work;
(d) prevention: all the steps or measures taken or planned at all stages of work in the undertaking to prevent or reduce occupational risks.

3.5.1 Workers

For the purposes of the Directive a worker is any person employed by an employer, including trainees and apprentices but excluding domestic servants. Compared to the concept of a worker in Article 45 TFEU, see Chapter Five on Migrant workers within the meaning of Article 45 TFEU, the concept of worker in the Framework Directive is narrow. It only embraces those actually in employment, not job applicants or retired workers or students. It is also not totally clear how it relates to atypical forms of work, see below in Chapter Seven on the employment contract.

3.5.2 Employers: EU Law and Corporate Enterprise

An employer is defined as any natural or legal person who has an employment relationship with the worker and has responsibility for the undertaking and/or establishment. Worker participation is often a controversial issue because of the complex structure of the employer, where important management decisions are made by central management in a parent company, while the employment contracts are entered into by local management in a subsidiary company. It is therefore an increasingly important question as to who is the employer. Does the Framework Directive provide for direct access of workers to the central management of their parent company, which may be located in another country, in working environment matters or does it only provide for consultation rights viz à viz local management? The answer depends on how the concept of an employer is interpreted by the CJEU. There is no relevant case law. In my view, an employer within the meaning of the Directive, must be the real decision maker. In some groups of companies the parent company makes the policy decisions concerning the working environment. If that is the case, the participation rights of the workers both of the parent company and of subsidiaries must be rights against the parent company.

It could also be argued that the employer within the meaning of the Directive must be an entity which can act as an adequate counterpart to the workers' representatives which are defined by reference to national law and practice (see below). In some countries, for example Germany, a works council at group of undertakings level (Konzernbetriebsraat) exists which has competence in working environment matters. In order for it to have a counterpart on the employer side, the employer must also be able to be the central management of the group of undertakings.

The European Works Councils Directive[15] contains a definition of a controlling undertaking, a definition which might be an appropriate basis for definition of the concept of an employer in regard to other aspects of information, consultation and participation. For the purposes of the European Works Councils Directive, 'controlling undertaking' means an undertaking which can exercise a dominant influence over another undertaking (the controlled undertaking) by virtue, for example, of ownership, financial participation or the rules which govern it. The ability to exercise a dominant influence shall be presumed, without prejudice to proof to the contrary, when an undertaking, in relation to another undertaking directly or indirectly:

(a) holds a majority of that undertaking's subscribed capital;
(b) controls a majority of the votes attached to that undertaking's issued share capital;
or
(c) can appoint more than half of the members of that undertaking's administrative, management or supervisory body.

15. 2009/38/EC on the establishment of a European Works Council or a procedure in Community-scale undertakings and Community-scale groups of undertakings for the purposes of informing and consulting employees, originally the now repealed directive 94/45/EC.

3.5.3 Workers' Representatives

A workers' representative with specific responsibility for the safety and health of workers is, according to the Directive, any person elected, chosen or designated in accordance with national laws and/or practices to represent workers where problems arise relating to the health and safety protection of workers at work.

By referring to national laws and practices as regards the designation of workers' representatives the Directive avoids the difficulties of harmonizing national institutional structures in this field. In some countries, for example Denmark, there are special working environment representatives. In other countries, for example Germany, these matters are dealt with by the works councils.

The requirement that there must be balanced participation may, however, make it necessary to change some national provisions relating to the institutional set up, see further below under information, consultation and balanced participation. See also above in Chapter Four on information, Consultation and Participation.

3.6 General Provisions

Article 5 of the framework directive contains the following General provision

1. The employer shall have a duty to ensure the safety and health of workers in every aspect related to the work.
2. Where, pursuant to Article 7 (3), an employer enlists competent external services or persons, this shall not discharge him from his responsibilities in this area.
3. The workers' obligations in the field of safety and health at work shall not affect the principle of the responsibility of the employer.
4. This Directive shall not restrict the option of Member States to provide for the exclusion or the limitation of employers' responsibility where occurrences are due to unusual and unforeseeable circumstances, beyond the employers' control, or to exceptional events, the consequences of which could not have been avoided despite the exercise of all due care.

Member States need not exercise the option referred to in the first subparagraph.

Article 5 of the Framework Directive has given rise to an infringement action against the UK.[16] In the UK the general obligation of the employer required by Article 5 of the directive was drafted in the following way:

16. Case C-127/05 *Commission* v *UK* [2007] ECR I-4619.

'It shall be the duty of every employer to ensure, so far as is reasonably practicable, the health, safety and welfare at work of all his employees.'

The Commission sought a declaration from the CJEU that, by restricting the duty upon employers to ensure the safety and health of workers in all aspects related to work to a duty to do this only so far as is reasonably practicable', the UK had failed to fulfil its obligations under Article 5(1) and (4) of the framework directive. The CJEU dismissed the case and stated that it must be concluded that the Commission has not established to the requisite legal standard that, in qualifying the duty on employers to ensure the safety and health of workers in every aspect related to the work by limiting that duty to what is reasonably practicable, the United Kingdom has failed to fulfil its obligations under Article 5(1) and (4) of Directive 89/391.

3.7 Obligations of the employer

3.7.1 Employer's Liability

Article 5 of the Working Environment Framework Directive provides that the the employer shall have a duty to ensure the safety and health of workers in every aspect related to the work. Where, pursuant to Article 7 (3), an employer enlists competent external services or persons, this shall not discharge him from his responsibilities in this area. 3. The workers' obligations in the field of safety and health at work shall not affect the principle of the responsibility of the employer. According to Article 5(4) the Directive shall not restrict the option of Member States to provide for the exclusion or the limitation of employers' responsibility where occurrences are due to unusual and unforeseeable circumstances, beyond the employers' control, or to exceptional events, the consequences of which could not have been avoided despite the exercise of all due care. Member States need not exercise the option referred to above.

In the UK Article 5 of the Directive was transposed by a provision which read:

'It shall be the duty of every employer to ensure, so far as is reasonably practicable, the health, safety and welfare at work of all his employees.'

The Commission took the view that the transposition of Directive 89/391, as effected by the United Kingdom, does not lead to the result intended by Article 5(1) of that directive, even if that provision is read in conjunction with the exception provided for in Article 5(4) thereof. According to the Commission, although Article 5(1) of Directive 89/391 does not impose a duty upon employers to ensure an absolutely safe working environment, it implies that the employer remains responsible for the consequences of any event detrimental to the health and safety of workers occurring in his undertaking. The only derogation possible from such a responsibility is in the circumstances expressly laid down in Article 5(4) of Directive 89/391. That provision, which is an exception to the general principle that the employer is responsible, must be interpreted strictly.

In the ensuing infringement case against the UK,[17] the CJEU first examined whether Article 5(1) of Directive 89/391 requires Member States, as the Commission submitted, to impose no-fault liability on employers for all accidents which occur in the workplace. In the view of the CJEU it cannot be asserted that the employer should be subject to no- fault liability by reason merely of Article 5(1) of Directive 89/391. That provision simply embodies the general duty of safety to which the employer is subject, without specifying any form of liability.

Then the CJEU analysed the Commission's complaint inasmuch as it alleges that the UK did not correctly transpose Article 5(1) of Directive 89/391 as regards the extent of the general duty on employers to ensure the safety and health of workers. In that regard, although the Commission submits that the duty on the employer is absolute, it expressly acknowledges that that duty does not imply that the employer is required to ensure a zero-risk working environment. In its reply, the Commission also acknowledges that, as a result of carrying out a risk assessment, the employer may conclude that the risks are so small that no preventive measures are necessary. In those circumstances, the key point, according to the Commission, is that the employer would remain responsible if an accident were to occur. The burden of proof in an infringement case is on the Commission. The CJEU held that the Commission has not established that, in excluding a form of no-fault liability, the disputed clause in UK law limits, in disregard of Article 5(1) and (4) of Directive 89/391, employers' responsibility.

In *Hansen and Son,*[18] the problem was whether Member States were allowed to enforce EU law on health and safety by prescribing liability for employers without culpa. The CJEU held that:

> Neither Regulation (EEC) No 543/69 of the Council of 25 March 1969 on the harmonization of certain social legislation relating to road transport nor the general principles of Community law preclude the application of national provisions under which an employer whose drivers infringe Articles 7(2) and 11 of the regulation may be the subject of a criminal penalty notwithstanding the fact that the infringement cannot be imputed to an inten-

17. Case C-127/05 *Commission* v *UK* [2007] ECR I-4619.
18. Case C-326/88 *Hansen and Son* [1990] ECR 2911.

tional wrongful act or to negligence on the employer's part, on condition that the penalty provided for is similar to those imposed in the event of infringement of provisions of national law of similar nature and importance and is proportionate to the seriousness of the infringement committed.

3.7.2 General obligations of employers

Article 6 of the Working Environment Framework Directive provides on the General obligations of employers:

1. Within the context of his responsibilities, the employer shall take the measures necessary for the safety and health protection of workers, including prevention of occupational risks and provision of information and training, as well as provision of the necessary organization and means.

The employer shall be alert to the need to adjust these measures to take account of changing circumstances and aim to improve existing situations.

2. The employer shall implement the measures referred to in the first subparagraph of paragraph 1 on the basis of the following general principles of prevention:
(a) avoiding risks;
(b) evaluating the risks which cannot be avoided:
(c) combating the risks at source;
(d) adapting the work to the individual, especially as regards the design of work places, the choice of work equipment and the choice of working and production methods, with a view, in particular, to alleviating monotonous work and work at a predetermined work-rate and to reducing their effect on health.
(e) adapting to technical progress;
(f) replacing the dangerous by the non-dangerous or the less dangerous;
(g) developing a coherent overall prevention policy which covers technology, organization of work, working conditions, social relationships and the influence of factors related to the working environment;
(h) giving collective protective measures priority over individual protective measures;
(i) giving appropriate instructions to the workers.

3. Without prejudice to the other provisions of this Directive, the employer shall, taking into account the nature of the activities of the enterprise and/or establishment:
(a) evaluate the risks to the safety and health of workers, inter alia in the choice of work equipment, the chemical substances or preparations used, and the fitting-out of work places.
Subsequent to this evaluation and as necessary, the preventive measures and the working and production methods implemented by the employer must:
  - assure an improvement in the level of protection afforded to workers with regard to safety and health,
  - be integrated into all the activities of the undertaking and/or establishment and at all hierarchical levels;

(b) where he entrusts tasks to a worker, take into consideration the worker's capabilities as regards health and safety;

(c) ensure that the planning and introduction of new technologies are the subject of consultation with the workers and/or their representatives, as regards the consequences of the choice of equipment, the working conditions and the working environment for the safety and health of workers;
(d) take appropriate steps to ensure that only workers who have received adequate instructions may have access to areas where there is serious and specific danger.

4. Without prejudice to the other provisions of this Directive, where several undertakings share a work place, the employers shall cooperate in implementing the safety, health and occupational hygiene provisions and, taking into account the nature of the activities, shall coordinate their actions in matters of the protection and prevention of occupational risks, and shall inform one another and their respective workers and/or workers' representatives of these risks.

5. Measures related to safety, hygiene and health at work may in no circumstances involve the workers in financial cost.

3.7.3 The principle of prevention

The Substitution Principle, i.e. the duty to replacing the dangerous by the non-dangerous or the less dangerous is also of particular importance. The Directive obliges employers to take appropriate preventive measures to make work safer and healthier. The new obligation to put in place prevention measures implicitly stresses the importance of new forms of safety and health management as part of general management processes. Recital 13 of the Preamble to the Directive states:

Whereas the improvement of workers' safety, hygiene and health at work is an objective which should not be subordinated to purely economic considerations;

3.7.4 The principle of risk evaluation

The duty for the employer to make a risk evaluation of the risks which cannot be avoided is an important innovative element in EU labour law. It didn't exist in the national labour law of many EU-countries before membership of the EU. The Directive introduces as a key element the principle of risk assessment and defines its main elements (e.g. hazard identification, worker participation, introduction of adequate measures with the priority of eliminating risk at source, documentation and periodical re-assessment of workplace hazards).

3.8 Serious, imminent and unavoidable danger

Workers who, in the event of serious, imminent and unavoidable danger, leave their workstation and/or a dangerous area may not be placed at any disadvantage because of their action and must be protected against any harmful and unjustified consequences, in accordance with national laws and/or practices.

3.9 Information, Consultation and Participation

The framework Working Environment Directive from 1989[19] added the obligation of participation to those of information and consultation. Today (2013), the most important existing EU provisions on information, consultation and worker participation are probably those found in the Framework Directive on the working environment, see generally on information, consultation and worker participation above in Chapter Four..

3.9.1 Objective

In the Preamble to the Working Environment Framework Directive information and balanced participation of the workers are called for in the following recitals:

> Whereas, in order to ensure an improved degree of protection, workers and/or their representatives must be informed of the risks to their safety and health and of the measures required to reduce or eliminate these risks; whereas they must also be in a position to contribute, by means of balanced participation in accordance with national laws and/or practices, to seeing that the necessary protective measures are taken;
>
> Whereas information, dialogue and balanced participation on safety and health at work must be developed between employers and workers and/or their representatives by means of appropriate procedures and instruments, in accordance with national laws and/or practices;

In general terms the Directive's approach aims at establishing a policy for the industrial relations of the working environment based on participation rather than confrontation between workers and management.[20]

3.9.2 Information

Article 10 of the Working Environment Framework Directive provides that the employer shall take appropriate measures so that workers and/or their representatives in the undertaking and/or establishment receive, in accordance with national laws and/or practices which may take into account inter alia the

19. 89/391/EEC.
20. Biagi, Marco: From Conflict to Participation in Safety: Industrial Relations and the Working Environment in Europe 1992 in The International Journal of Comparative Labour Law and Industrial Relations 1990 p. 67.

size of the undertaking and/or establishment, all necessary information concerning:

(a) the safety and health risks and protective and preventive measures and activities in respect of both the undertaking and/or establishment in general and each type of workstation and/or job;
(b) the measures taken pursuant to Article 8(2).
(c) such information shall also be provided in a suitable form to temporary workers and hired workers present in the establishment or enterprise.

The employer shall take appropriate measures so that workers with specific functions in protecting the safety and health of workers, or workers' representatives with specific responsibility for the safety and health of workers shall have access, in order to perform their duties and in accordance with national laws and/or practices, to:

(a) the risk assessment and protective measures referred to in Article 9(1)(a) and (b);
(b) the list and reports referred to in Article 9(1)(c) and (d);
(c) the information yielded by protective and preventive measures, inspection agencies and bodies responsible for safety and health.

3.9.3 Consultation and Participation

According to Article 11 of the Working Environment Framework Directive employers shall consult workers and/or their representatives and allow them to take part in discussions on all questions relating to safety and health at work. This pre-supposes the consultation of workers, the right of workers and/or their representatives to make proposals, and *balanced* participation in accordance with national laws and/or practices.

3.9.4 Balanced Participation in Advance and in Due Time

Workers with specific functions in protecting the safety and health of workers or workers' representatives with specific responsibility for the safety and health or workers shall participate in a *balanced* way, in accordance with national laws and/or practices, or be consulted in advance and in due time by the employer with regard to:

(a) any measure which may substantially affect safety and health;
(b) the designation of workers referred to in Article 8(2) and the activities referred to in Article 7(1);
(c) the information referred to in Article 9(1) and Article 10;
(d) the enlistment, where appropriate, of the competent services or persons outside the undertaking and/or establishment, as referred to in Article 7 (3);
(e) the planning and organization of the training referred to in Article 12.

Workers with specific functions for the protection of the safety and health of workers at work, and workers' representatives, may call on the employer to take appropriate measures and submit to him/her relevant proposals by means of which all risks to workers may be reduced and/or sources of danger eliminated. The expression 'balanced participation' is not very clear and is likely to give rise to referrals to the CJEU,[21] see also above in Chapter Four on balanced participation.

Workers' representatives must be given the opportunity to submit their observations during inspection visits by the competent authority.

3.9.5 Protection of Workers

Workers' representatives with specific responsibility for the safety and health of workers shall have the right to ask the employer to take appropriate measures and to submit proposals to him to that end to mitigate hazards for workers and/or to remove sources of danger. Employers must allow workers' representatives with specific responsibility for the safety and health of workers adequate time off work, without loss of pay, and provide them with the necessary means to enable such representatives to exercise their rights and functions deriving from this Directive.

The workers and workers' representatives may not be placed at any disadvantage because of their specific responsibility for the safety and health of workers. Employers must allow workers' representatives with specific responsibility for the safety and health of workers adequate time off work, without loss of pay, and provide them with the necessary means to enable such representatives to exercise their rights and functions derived from this Directive.

Workers and/or their representatives are entitled to appeal, in accordance with national law and/or practice, to the authority responsible for safety and health protection at work if they consider that the measures taken and the means employed by the employer are inadequate for the purposes of ensuring safety and health at work. Workers' representatives must be invited to – and be able to submit their observations at – inspection visits by the competent authorities.

21. Cf. Biagi, Marco: From Conflict to Participation in Safety: Industrial Relations and the Working Environment in Europe 1992 in The International Journal of Comparative Labour Law and Industrial Relations 1990 p. 67.

3.9.6 Training

Article 12 of the Working Environment Framework Directive provides that employers shall ensure that each worker receives adequate safety and health training, in particular in the form of information and instructions specific to his/her workstation or job on recruitment, in the event of a transfer or a change of job, in the event of the introduction of new working equipment or a change in equipment, and in the event of the introduction of any new technology.

4 Individual Directives

Within the general frame established by the framework directive a considerable number of – often very detailed – individual directives on various working environment topics have been adopted. The European Agency for Safety and Health at Work (EU-OSHA)[22] divides them into the following groups:

Workplaces, equipment, signs, personal protective equipment [23]
Exposure to chemical agents and chemical safety [24]

22. https://osha.europa.eu/en/about.
23. – Use of work equipment Directive 2009/104/EC concerning the minimum safety and health requirements for the use of work equipment by workers at work (second individual Directive within the meaning of Article 16(1) of Directive 89/391/EEC), risks from explosive atmospheres Directive 99/92/EC on the minimum requirements for improving the safety and health protection of workers potentially at risk from explosive atmospheres (15th individual Directive within the meaning of Article 16(1) of Directive 89/391/EEC), safety and/or health signsDirective 92/58/EEC on the minimum requirements for the provision of safety and/or health signs at work (ninth individual Directive within the meaning of Article 16 (1) of Directive 89/391/EEC), use of personal protective equipment Directive 89/656/EEC on the minimum health and safety requirements for the use by workers of personal protective equipment at the workplace (third individual directive within the meaning of Article 16 (1) of Directive 89/391/EEC), workplace requirements Directive 89/654/EEC of 30 November 1989 concerning the minimum safety and health requirements for the workplace (first individual directive within the meaning of Article 16 (1) of Directive 89/391/EEC).
24. Indicative occupational exposure limit values Directive 2009/161/EU establishing a third list of indicative occupational exposure limit values in implementation of Council Directive 98/24/EC and amending Commission Directive 2000/39/EC (Text with EEA relevance), exposure to asbestos at work Directive 2009/148/EC on the protection of workers from the risks related to exposure to asbestos at work (Text with EEA relevance) indicative occupational exposure limit values Directive 2006/15/EC establishing a second list of indicative occupational exposure limit values in imple-

Exposure to physical hazards[25]
Exposure to biological agents[26]
Provisions on workload, ergonomic and psychosocial risks[27]

mentation of Council Directive 98/24/EC and amending Directives 91/322/EEC and 2000/39/EC, carcinogens or mutagens at work Directive 2004/37/EC on the protection of workers from the risks related to exposure to carcinogens or mutagens at work (Sixth individual Directive within the meaning of Article 16(1) Directive 89/391/EEC), indicative occupational exposure limit values Directive 2000/39/EC – of 8 June 2000 establishing a first list of indicative occupational exposure limit values in implementation of Council Directive 98/24/EC on the protection of the health and safety of workers from the risks related to chemical agents at work, risks related to chemical agents at work Directive 98/24/EC on the protection of the health and safety of workers from the risks related to chemical agents at work (fourteenth individual Directive within the meaning of Article 16(1) of Directive 89/391/EEC), indicative limit values Directive 91/322/EEC on establishing indicative limit values by implementing Council Directive 80/1107/EEC on the protection of workers from the risks related to exposure to chemical, physical and biological agents at work.

25. Artificial optical radiation Directive 2006/25/EC on the minimum health and safety requirements regarding the exposure of the workers to risks arising from physical agents (artificial optical radiation, 19th individual Directive within the meaning of Article 16(1) of Directive 89/391/EEC), electromagnetic fields and waves Directive 2004/40/EC on the minimum health and safety requirements regarding the exposure of the workers to risks arising from electromagnetic fields and waves (18th individual Directive within the meaning of Art. 16(1) of Directive 89/391/EEC) as amended by Directive 2012/11/EU of 19 April 2012 extending the deadline for transposition to 31 October 2013, Noise Directive 2003/10/EC on the minimum health and safety requirements regarding the exposure of workers to the risks arising from physical agents (noise) (Seventeenth individual Directive within the meaning of Article 16(1) of Directive 89/391/EEC). Vibration Directive 2002/44/EC on the minimum health and safety requirements regarding the exposure of workers to the risks arising from physical agents (vibration) (sixteenth individual Directive within the meaning of Article 16(1) of Directive 89/391/EEC), ionizing radiation Directive 96/29/Euratom laying down basic safety standards for the protection of the health of workers and the general public against the dangers arising from ionizing radiation.
26. Biological agents at work Directive 2000/54/EC on the protection of workers from risks related to exposure to biological agents at work (seventh individual directive within the meaning of Article 16(1) of Directive 89/391/EEC).
27. Display screen equipment Directive 90/270/EEC on the minimum safety and health requirements for work with display screen equipment (fifth individual Directive within the meaning of Article 16 (1) of Directive 89/391/EEC), Manual handling of loads Directive 90/269/EEC on the minimum health and safety requirements for the manual handling of loads where there is a risk particularly of back injury to workers (fourth individual Directive within the meaning of Article 16 (1) of Directive 89/391/EEC).

Sector specific and worker related provisions[28]

In 2004, the European Commission issued a Communication[29] on the practical implementation of the provisions of some of the directives.[30] This Communication stated that there was evidence of the positive influence of EU legislation on national standards for occupational safety and health made up of both national implementing legislation and mineral-extracting industries – drilling practical application in enterprises and public sector institutions. In general, the report concluded that EU legislation had contributed to instilling a culture of prevention throughout the European Union as well as to rationalising and simplifying national legislative systems. At the same time, however, the report highlighted various flaws in the application of the legislation

28. Prevention from sharp injuries in the hospital and healthcare sector Directive 2010/32/EU implementing the Framework Agreement on prevention from sharp injuries in the hospital and healthcare sector concluded by HOSPEEM and EPSU (Text with EEA relevance), Young workers Directive 94/33/EC on the protection of young people at work, work on board fishing vessels Directive 93/103/EC concerning the minimum safety and health requirements for work on board fishing vessels (thirteenth individual Directive within the meaning of Article 16 (1) of Directive 89/391/EEC), mineral-extracting industries Directive 92/104/EEC of 3 December 1992 on the minimum requirements for improving the safety and health protection of workers in surface and underground mineral-extracting industries (twelfth individual Directive within the meaning of Article 16 (1) of Directive 89/391/EEC), Mineral-extracting industries – drilling Directive 92/91/EEC concerning the minimum requirements for improving the safety and health protection of workers in the mineral-extracting industries through drilling (eleventh individual Directive within the meaning of Article 16 (1) of Directive 89/391/EEC), Pregnant workers Directive 92/85/EEC of 19 October 1992 on the introduction of measures to encourage improvements in the safety and health at work of pregnant workers and workers who have recently given birth or are breastfeeding (tenth individual Directive within the meaning of Article 16 (1) of Directive 89/391/EEC) temporary or mobile construction sites Directive 92/57/EEC on the implementation of minimum safety and health requirements at temporary or mobile construction sites (eighth individual Directive within the meaning of Article 16 (1) of Directive 89/391/EEC), Medical treatment on board vessels Directive 92/29/EEC on the minimum safety and health requirements for improved medical treatment on board vessels, fixed-duration or temporary employment relationship Directive 91/383/EEC supplementing the measures to encourage improvements in the safety and health at work of workers with a fixed-duration employment relationship or a temporary employment relationship.
29. COM [2004] 62.
30. Namely 89/391 EEC (framework directive), 89/654 EEC (workplaces), 89/655 EEC (work equipment), 89/656 EEC (personal protective equipment), 90/269 EEC (manual handling of loads) and 90/270 EEC (display screen equipment).

that were holding back achievement of its full potential. It also noted cases where infringement proceedings had been opened.

5 Vulnerable groups

Article 15 of the Working Environment Framework Directive[31] that particularly sensitive risk groups must be protected against the dangers which specifically affect them.

5.1 Women as compared to men: night work for women

Today, it is inconsistent with current sex discrimination law to differentiate between men and women in the rules on working environment apart from what is allowed in relation to pregnant women and women who has recently given birth, see on them below. There are, however, some old (outdated) ILO-conventions prohibiting night work for women.[32] The CJEU held in *Stoeckel*[33] that it is inconsistent with current sex discrimination law to prohibit night work for women on other conditions than for men. It ruled:

> Article 5 of Council Directive 76/207/EEC of 9 February 1976 on the implementation of the principle of equal treatment for men and women as regards access to employment, vocational training and promotion, and working conditions is sufficiently precise to impose on the Member States the obligation not to lay down by legislation the principle that nightwork by women is prohibited, even if that is subject to exceptions, where nightwork by men is not prohibited.

In *Levy*,[34] the CJEU held:

> The national court is under an obligation to ensure that Article 5 of Directive 76/207/EEC of 9 February 1976 on the implementation of the principle of equal treatment for men and women as regards access to employment, vocational training and promotion, and working conditions is fully complied with by refraining from applying any conflicting provision of national legislation, unless the application of such a provision is necessary in order to ensure the performance by the Member State concerned of obligations arising under an

31. 89/391/EEC.
32. ILO Convention NO 4, Night Work (Women) 1919, ILO Convention (Revised) (No. 41), the Night Work (Women), 1934 (No. 41), and Convention No. 89 the Night Work (Women) Convention (Revised), 1948.
33. Case C-345/89 *Stoeckel* [1991] ECR I-4047.
34. Case C-158/91 *Levy* [1993] I-4307. See for a similar judgment Case C-13/93 *Minne* [1994] ECR I-371.

agreement concluded with non-member countries prior to the entry into force of the EEC Treaty.

According to Article 351 TFEU, the rights and obligations arising from agreements/treaties under public international law concluded before 1 January 1958 or, for acceding Member States, before the date of their accession, between one or more Member States on the one hand, and one or more third countries on the other, are not affected by the provisions of the Treaties. To the extent that such agreements are not compatible with the Treaties, the Member State or States concerned shall take all appropriate steps to eliminate the incompatibilities. As appears from the text of Article 351 TFEU, the Member States shall take all appropriate steps to eliminate the incompatibilities between their international law obligations and EU law, e.g. by denouncing the international treaties they have ratified which are incompatible with EU law. A number of EU Member States, which had ratified some old ILO night work conventions for women, have denounced them. The incompatibility between ILO law and EU law on this point has therefore disappeared.

5.2 Children and young persons

The EU has adopted minimum requirements for the protection of young workers (under 18 years of age) and their health and safety at work. It also outlaws child labour.

The EU Directive on the protection of young people at work[35] provides that Member States must prohibit the employment of children (i.e. those under the age of 15 or still in full-time compulsory education). Some exceptions are possible for cultural, artistic, sports and advertising activities as well as for certain training contracts and certain kinds of light work by those aged at least 13 or 14. The employment of young people must be strictly controlled and protected under the conditions provided for in the Directive.

The Directive sets out the employer's general obligations to protect and monitor young workers' health and safety. It also specifies types of employment which must not be carried out by young people. This includes work which exceeds their mental or physical capacities and work involving harmful exposure to dangerous substances. There are also provisions on working hours, night work, rest periods, annual leave and rest breaks.

35. 94/33/EC on the Protection of Young People at Work.

5.3 Pregnancy and maternity/paternity

5.3.1 The Pregnancy Directive

As mentioned in Chapter Six, the Pregnancy Directive[36] is primarily aimed at improving health and safety at work for pregnant workers, workers who have recently given birth and workers who are breastfeeding. It provides for two sorts of measures, namely health and safety and protection against unfavourable treatment on grounds of pregnancy. See on the discrimination issues above in Chapter Six. The two obligations should work in harmony.

The Pregnancy Directive was proposed by the Commission in 1990.[37] In the Preamble to the Directive it is stated that the Commission, in its action programme for the implementation of the Community Charter of the fundamental social rights of workers 1989, has included among its aims the adoption by the Council of a Directive on the protection of pregnant women at work. Pregnant workers, workers who have recently given birth or who are breastfeeding must be considered a specific risk group in many respects, and measures must be taken with regard to their safety and health. The protection of the safety and health of pregnant workers, workers who have recently given birth or workers who are breastfeeding should not treat women on the labour market unfavourably nor work to the detriment of directives concerning equal treatment for men and women. The CJEU has also stated that obligations regarding health and safety cannot be taken into consideration in such a way as to be detrimental to pregnant workers.[38]

Some types of activities may pose a specific risk, for pregnant workers, workers who have recently given birth or workers who are breastfeeding, of exposure to dangerous agents, processes or working conditions; such risks must therefore be assessed and the result of such assessment communicated to female workers and/or their representatives; should the result of this assessment reveal the existence of a risk to the safety or health of the female worker, provision must be made for such worker to be protected;

Pregnant workers and workers who are breastfeeding must not engage in activities which have been assessed as revealing a risk of exposure, jeopardizing safety and health, to certain particularly dangerous agents or working conditions. Provision should be made for pregnant workers, workers who

36. Council Directive 92/85/EEC on the introduction of measures to encourage improvements in the safety and health at work of pregnant workers and workers who have recently given birth or are breastfeeding.

37. Com (90)406 and Com (90)692.

38. Cases C-66/96 *Høj Pedersen* and others [1998] ECR I-7327 and C-207/98 *Mahlburg* [2000] ECR I-549.

have recently given birth or workers who are breastfeeding not to be required to work at night where such provision is necessary from the point of view of their safety and health. The vulnerability of pregnant workers, workers who have recently given birth or who are breastfeeding makes it necessary for them to be granted the right to maternity leave of at least 14 continuous weeks, allocated before and/or after confinement, and renders necessary the compulsory nature of maternity leave of at least two weeks, allocated before and/or after confinement. The risk of dismissal for reasons associated with their condition may have harmful effects on the physical and mental state of pregnant workers, workers who have recently given birth or who are breastfeeding. Provision should be made for such dismissal to be prohibited. Measures for the organization of work concerning the protection of the health of pregnant workers, workers who have recently given birth or workers who are breastfeeding would serve no purpose unless accompanied by the maintenance of rights linked to the employment contract, including maintenance of payment and/or entitlement to an adequate allowance. Provision concerning maternity leave would also serve no purpose unless accompanied by the maintenance of rights linked to the employment contract and or entitlement to an adequate allowance. The concept of an adequate allowance in the case of maternity leave must be regarded as a technical point of reference with a view to fixing the minimum level of protection and should in no circumstances be interpreted as suggesting an analogy between pregnancy and illness,

5.3.2 Purpose

According to Article 1 of the Pregnancy Directive it purpose is to implement measures to encourage improvements in the safety and health at work of pregnant workers and workers who have recently given birth or who are breastfeeding. The provisions of Directive 89/391/EEC, except for Article 2(2) thereof,[39] shall apply in full to the whole area covered by the above provision, without prejudice to any more stringent and/or specific provisions contained in the Pregnancy Directive. The Directive may not have the effect of reducing the level of protection afforded to pregnant workers, workers who have recently given birth or who are breastfeeding as compared with the situ-

39. Article 2(2) of directive 89/391/EEC reads: 2. This Directive shall not be applicable where characteristics peculiar to certain specific public service activities, such as the armed forces or the police, or to certain specific activities in the civil protection services inevitably conflict with it. In that event, the safety and health of workers must be ensured as far as possible in the light of the objectives of this Directive.

ation which exists in each Member State on the date on which this Directive is adopted.

5.3.3 Definitions

Article 2 of the Pregnancy Directive defines the following terms:

Pregnant worker shall mean a pregnant worker who informs her employer of her condition, in accordance with national legislation and/or national practice. In *Danosa*, [40] the CJEU held that women in executive positions are workers within the meaning of the Pregnancy Directive, see the following:

A member of a capital company's Board of Directors who provides services to that company and is an integral part of it must be regarded as having the status of worker for the purposes of Council Directive 92/85/EEC of 19 October 1992 on the introduction of measures to encourage improvements in the safety and health at work of pregnant workers and workers who have recently given birth or are breastfeeding (tenth individual Directive within the meaning of Article 16(1) of Directive 89/391/EEC), if that activity is carried out, for some time, under the direction or supervision of another body of that company and if, in return for those activities, the Board Member receives remuneration. It is for the national court to undertake the assessments of fact necessary to determine whether that is so in the case pending before it.

2. Article 10 of Directive 92/85 is to be interpreted as precluding national legislation, such as that at issue in the main proceedings, which permits a member of a capital company's Board of Directors to be removed from that post without restriction, where the person concerned is a 'pregnant worker' within the meaning of that directive and the decision to remove her was taken essentially on account of her pregnancy. Even if the Board Member concerned is not a 'pregnant worker' within the meaning of Directive 92/85, the fact remains that the removal, on account of pregnancy or essentially on account of pregnancy, of a member of a Board of Directors who performs duties such as those described in the main proceedings can affect only women and therefore constitutes direct discrimination on grounds of sex, contrary to Article2(1) and(7) and Article 3(1)(c) of Council Directive 76/207/EEC of 9 February 1976 on the implementation of the principle of equal treatment for men and women as regards access to employment, vocational training and promotion, and working conditions, as amended by Directive 2002/73/EC of the European Parliament and of the Council of 23 September 2002.

Worker who has recently given birth shall mean a worker who has recently given birth within the meaning of national legislation and/or national practice and who informs her employer of her condition, in accordance with that legislation and/or practice.

40. Case C-232/09 *Danosa* [2010] ECR I-11405.

Worker who is breastfeeding shall mean a worker who is breastfeeding within the meaning of national legislation and/or national practice and who informs her employer of her condition, in accordance with that legislation and/or practice.

5.3.4 Guidelines

Article 3 of the Pregnancy Directive provides that in consultation with the Member States and assisted by the Advisory Committee on Safety, Hygiene and Health Protection at Work, the Commission shall draw up guidelines on the assessment of the chemical, physical and biological agents and industrial processes considered hazardous for the safety or health of pregnant workers. These guidelines shall also cover movements and postures, mental and physical fatigue and other types of physical and mental stress connected with the work done by pregnant workers. The purpose of the guidelines is to serve as a basis for the risk assessment referred to in Article 4 (1) of the Pregnancy Directive, see below. To this end, Member States shall bring these guidelines to the attention of all employers and all female workers and/or their representatives in the respective Member State.

5.3.5 Risk assessment and information

Article 4 of the Pregnancy Directive provides that for all activities liable to involve a specific risk of exposure to the agents, processes or working conditions of which a non-exhaustive list is given in Annex I to the Directive, the employer shall assess the nature, degree and duration of exposure, in the undertaking and/or establishment concerned, of pregnant workers, in order to:

- assess any risks to the safety or health and any possible effect on the pregnancys or breastfeeding of workers within the meaning of Article 2,
- decide what measures should be taken.

Without prejudice to Article 10 of Directive 89/391/EEC, workers within the meaning of Article 2 of the Pregnancy Directive and workers likely to be in one of the situations referred to in Article 2 in the undertaking and/or establishment concerned and/or their representatives shall be informed of the results of the assessment referred to in paragraph 1 and of all measures to be taken concerning health and safety at work.

5.3.6 Action further to the results of the assessment

Article 5 of the Pregnancy Directive provides that without prejudice to Article 6 of Directive 89/391/EEC, if the results of the assessment referred to in

Article 4 (1) reveal a risk to the safety or health or an effect on the pregnancy or breastfeeding of a worker, the employer shall take the necessary measures to ensure that, by temporarily adjusting the working conditions and/or the working hours of the worker concerned, the exposure of that worker to such risks is avoided.

If the adjustment of her working conditions and/or working hours is not technically and/or objectively feasible, or cannot reasonably be required on duly substantiated grounds, the employer shall take the necessary measures to move the worker concerned to another job.

If moving her to another job is not technically and/or objectively feasible or cannot reasonably be required on duly substantiated grounds, the worker concerned shall be granted leave in accordance with national legislation and/or national practice for the whole of the period necessary to protect her safety or health.

The provisions of this Article shall apply *mutatis mutandis* to the case where a worker pursuing an activity which is forbidden pursuant to Article 6 becomes pregnant or starts breastfeeding and informs her employer thereof.

5.3.7 Cases in which exposure is prohibited

Article 6 of the Pregnancy Directive provides that in addition to the general provisions concerning the protection of workers, in particular those relating to the limit values for occupational exposure:

1. pregnant workers within the meaning of Article 2 (a) may under no circumstances be obliged to perform duties for which the assessment has revealed a risk of exposure, which would jeopardize safety or health, to the agents and working conditions listed in Annex II, Section A;

2. workers who are breastfeeding, within the meaning of Article 2 (c), may under no circumstances be obliged to perform duties for which the assessment has revealed a risk of exposure, which would jeopardize safety or health, to the agents and working conditions listed in Annex II, Section B.

5.3.8 Night work

Article 7 of the Pregnancy Directive prohibits night work for pregnant women. It reads:

1. Member States shall take the necessary measures to ensure that workers referred to in Article 2 are not obliged to perform night work during their pregnancy and for a period following childbirth which shall be determined by the national authority competent for safety and health, subject to submission, in accordance with the procedures laid down by the

Member States, of a medical certificate stating that this is necessary for the safety or health of the worker concerned.

2. The measures referred to in paragraph 1 must entail the possibility, in accordance with national legislation and/or national practice, of:
(a) transfer to daytime work; or
(b) leave from work or extension of maternity leave where such a transfer is not technically and/or objectively feasible or cannot reasonably by required on duly substantiated grounds.

5.3.9 Maternity leave

Article 8 of the Pregnancy Directive provides that Member States shall take the necessary measures to ensure that workers within the meaning of Article 2 are entitled to a continuous period of maternity leave of a least 14 weeks allocated before and/or after confinement in accordance with national legislation and/or practice. The maternity leave stipulated in paragraph 1 must include compulsory maternity leave of at least two weeks allocated before and/or after confinement in accordance with national legislation and/or practice. See on the CJEU's interpretation of Article 8 of the Pregnancy Directive *Boyle*.[41]

5.3.10 Time off for ante-natal examinations

According to Article 9 of the Pregnancy Directive Member States shall take the necessary measures to ensure that pregnant workers within the meaning of Article 2 (a) are entitled to, in accordance with national legislation and/or practice, time off, without loss of pay, in order to attend ante-natal examinations, if such examinations have to take place during working hours.

5.3.11 Prohibition of dismissal

Article 10 of the Pregnancy Directive provides that in order to guarantee workers, within the meaning of Article 2, the exercise of their health and safety protection rights as recognized under this Article, it shall be provided that:

1. Member States shall take the necessary measures to prohibit the dismissal of workers, within the meaning of Article 2, during the period from the beginning of their pregnancy to the end of the maternity leave referred to in Article 8 (1), save in exceptional cases not connected with their condition which are permitted under national legislation and/or practice and, where applicable, provided that the competent authority has given its consent;

41. Case C-411/96 *Boyle* [1998] ECR I-6401.

2. if a worker, within the meaning of Article 2, is dismissed during the period referred to in point 1, the employer must cite duly substantiated grounds for her dismissal in writing;

3. Member States shall take the necessary measures to protect workers, within the meaning of Article 2, from consequences of dismissal which is unlawful by virtue of point 1.

In *Melgar*,[42] the CJEU held that Article 10 of the Pregnancy Directive, which prohibits the dismissal of pregnant workers, has direct effect and is to be interpreted to the effect that, in the absence of transposition measures taken by a Member State within the period prescribed by that directive, it confers on individuals rights on which they may rely before a national court against the authorities of that State.

In allowing derogations from the prohibition of dismissal of pregnant workers, workers who have recently given birth or workers who are breastfeeding in cases not connected with their condition which are permitted under national legislation and/or practice, Article 10(1) of the Pregnancy Directive does not require the Member States to specify the particular grounds on which such workers may be dismissed.

Whilst the prohibition of dismissal laid down in Article 10 of the Pregnancy Directive applies to both employment contracts for an indefinite period and fixed-term contracts, see *Tele Danmark*, [43] non-renewal of such a contract, when it comes to an end as stipulated, cannot be regarded as a dismissal prohibited by that provision. However, where non-renewal of a fixed-term contract is motivated by the worker's state of pregnancy, it constitutes direct discrimination on grounds of sex contrary to the recast directive on gender equality in employment and occupation,[44] see further in Chapter Six.

In providing that the dismissal of a pregnant worker, of a worker who has recently given birth or of a worker who is breastfeeding may take place, in exceptional cases and, where applicable, provided that the competent authority has given its consent, Article 10(1) of the Pregnancy Directive is not to be interpreted as imposing on Member States any obligation to have a national authority, having found that there is an exceptional case justifying the dismissal of such a worker, give its consent prior to the employer's decision to dismiss the worker.

42. Case C-438/99 *Melgar* ECR [2001] ECR I-6915.
43. Case 109/00 *Tele Danmark* [2004] ECR I-6993.
44. 2006/54/EC.

5.3.12 Employment rights

Article 11 of the Pregnancy Directive provides that in order to guarantee workers within the meaning of Article 2 the exercise of their health and safety protection rights as recognized in this Article, it shall be provided that:

1. in the cases referred to in Articles 5, 6 and 7, the employment rights relating to the employment contract, including the maintenance of a payment to, and/or entitlement to an adequate allowance for, workers within the meaning of Article 2, must be ensured in accordance with national legislation and/or national practice;

2. in the case referred to in Article 8, the following must be ensured:
(a) the rights connected with the employment contract of workers within the meaning of Article 2, other than those referred to in point (b) below;
(b) maintenance of a payment to, and/or entitlement to an adequate allowance for, workers within the meaning of Article 2;

3. the allowance referred to in point 2 (b) shall be deemed adequate if it guarantees income at least equivalent to that which the worker concerned would receive in the event of a break in her activities on grounds connected with her state of health, subject to any ceiling laid down under national legislation;

4. Member States may make entitlement to pay or the allowance referred to in points 1 and 2 (b) conditional upon the worker concerned fulfilling the conditions of eligibilty for such benefits laid down under national legislation. These conditions may under no circumstances provide for periods of previous employment in excess of 12 months immediately prior to the presumed date of confinement.

Women on maternity leave can only rely on the minimum guaranteed allowance set in Article 11(2)(b) of the Pregnancy Directive, which cannot be less than the sick leave pay.[45] Workers on maternity leave are not therefore entitled to continue to receive their full pay or to be paid any allowance that are dependent on the performance of specific functions in particular circumstances and are intended to compensate for the disadvantages related to those functions. However, the pay received during maternity leave must at least in part be determined on the basis of the pay earned before the maternity leave begins, and any pay rise awarded between the beginning of the reference period and the end of the maternity leave must be taken into account in calculating such pay. The CJEU has decided[46] that workers are entitled to have any pay

45. Case C-432/93 *Gillespie* [1995] ECR 1-4705 and Case C-411/96 *Boyle* [1998] ECR I-6401.
46. C-147/02 *Alabaster* [2004] ECR I-3101.

increase received before the start of their maternity leave taken into consideration in the calculation of the earnings-related element of her statutory maternity pay. In addition, the CJEU has held that maternity leave has to be included in the calculation of seniority when determining conditions for access to work.[47]

6 Working time

The EU rules on working time are in many ways similar to older ILO provisions.[48]

6.1 Background and context

The current Working Time Directive,[49] is a codification of the first Working Time directive from 1993[50] as amended in 2000.[51] Article 31 CFREU provides on Fair and just working conditions, that

1. Every worker has the right to working conditions which respect his or her health, safety and dignity.

2. Every worker has the right to limitation of maximum working hours, to daily and weekly rest periods and to an annual period of paid leave.

The Commission proposed the current working time directive in 2002.[52] Attempts have been made to amend the directive, in particular the rules the CJEU interprets as providing that inactive periods in on-call service is working time, see *Jaeger*[53] and *SIMAP*.[54]

6.2 Purpose and scope

The Working Time Directive applies according to Article 1 of the directive to

47. In Cases C-294/04 *Herrero* [2006] ECR I-15.13 and C-284/02 *Sass* [2004] ECR I-11143.
48. See Murray, Jill: Transnational Labour Regulation: The ILO and EC Compared, The Hague, London, Boston 2001.
49. 2003/88/EC.
50. 93/104/EC.
51. By Directive 2000/34/EC.
52. Com (2002)336.
53. Case C-151/02 *Jaeger* [2003] ECR I-8389.
54. Case C-303/98 *SIMAP* [2000] ECR I-7963.

(a) minimum periods of daily rest, weekly rest and annual leave, to breaks and maximum weekly working time; and to
(b) certain aspects of night work, shift work and patterns of work. The Directive applies to all sectors of activity, both public and private, within the meaning of Article 2 of the Framework directive on Working Environment

6.3 Definitions

Article 2 of the Working Time Directive defines that following terms:

6.3.1 Working time

Working time means any period during which the worker is working, at the employer's disposal and carrying out his activity or duties, in accordance with national laws and/or practice.

In *SIMAP*,[55] the CJEU held that time spent on call by doctors in primary health care teams must be regarded in its entirety as working time, and where appropriate as overtime, within the meaning of Directive 93/104 if they are required to be at the health centre. If they must merely be contactable at all times when on call, only time linked to the actual provision of primary health care services must be regarded as working time.

6.3.2 Rest period

Rest period means any period which is not working time.

6.3.3 Night time

Night time means any period of not less than seven hours, as defined by national law, and which must include, in any case, the period between midnight and 5.00.

6.3.4 Night worker

Night worker means:

(a) on the one hand, any worker, who, during night time, works at least three hours of his daily working time as a normal course; and
(b) on the other hand, any worker who is likely during night time to work a certain proportion of his annual working time, as defined at the choice of the Member State concerned:
   (i) by national legislation, following consultation with the two sides of industry; or
   (ii) by collective agreements or agreements concluded between the two sides of industry at national or regional level;

55. Case C-303/98 *SIMAP* [2000] ECR I-7963.

In *SIMAP*,[56] the CJEU held that doctors in primary health care teams who are regularly on call at night may not be regarded as night workers by virtue of Article 2 (4) (b) of the Working Time Directive alone.

6.3.5 *Shift work*

Shift work means any method of organising work in shifts whereby workers succeed each other at the same work stations according to a certain pattern, including a rotating pattern, and which may be continuous or discontinuous, entailing the need for workers to work at different times over a given period of days or weeks.

6.3.6 *Shift worker*

Shift worker means any worker whose work schedule is part of shift work. In *SIMAP*,[57] the CJEU held that work performed by doctors in primary health care teams whilst on call constitutes shift work and such doctors are shift workers within the meaning of Article 2(5) and (6) of Directive 93/104.

6.3.7 *Mobile worker*

Mobile worker means any worker employed as a member of travelling or flying personnel by an undertaking which operates transport services for passengers or goods by road, air or inland waterway.

6.3.8 *Offshore work*

Offshore work means work performed mainly on or from offshore installations (including drilling rigs), directly or indirectly in connection with the exploration, extraction or exploitation of mineral resources, including hydrocarbons, and diving in connection with such activities, whether performed from an offshore installation or a vessel.

6.3.9 *Adequate rest*

Adequate rest means that workers have regular rest periods, the duration of which is expressed in units of time and which are sufficiently long and continuous to ensure that, as a result of fatigue or other irregular working patterns, they do not cause injury to themselves, to fellow workers or to others and that they do not damage their health, either in the short term or in the longer term.

56. Case C-303/98 *SIMAP* [2000] ECR I-7963.
57. Case C-303/98 *SIMAP* [2000] ECR I-7963.

6.4 Main content of the current directive

Under the current Working Time Directive,[58] each Member State must ensure that every worker is entitled to:

- a limit to weekly working time, which must not exceed 48 hours on average, including any overtime
- a minimum daily rest period, of 11 consecutive hours in every 24 hours
- a rest break during working time, if the worker is on duty for longer than six hours
- a minimum weekly rest period of 24 uninterrupted hours for each seven-day period, which is added to the 11 hours' daily rest
- paid annual leave, of at least four weeks per year
- extra protection in the case of night work

The Directive also sets out special rules for working time in a small range of sectors: doctors in training, offshore workers, sea fishing workers, workers in urban passenger transport. There are separate directives on working time for certain workers in specific transport sectors.

6.5 Weekly working time

Article 6 provides on maximum weekly working time that Member States shall take the measures necessary to ensure that, in keeping with the need to protect the safety and health of workers:

(a) the period of weekly working time is limited by means of laws, regulations or administrative provisions or by collective agreements or agreements between the two sides of industry;
(b) the average working time for each seven-day period, including overtime, does not exceed 48 hours.

6.6 Daily rest period

Under Article 3 of the Directive Member States shall take the measures necessary to ensure that every worker is entitled to a minimum daily rest period of 11 consecutive hours per 24-hour period. In *Jaeger*,[59] the CJEU held that that the Working Time Directive precludes legislation of a Member State which classifies as rest periods an employee's periods of inactivity in the context of on-call duty, see further below in section 6.9.

58. 2003/88/EC.
59. Case C-151/02 *Jaeger* [2003] ECR I-8389.

6.7 Rest break during working time

Article 4 of the Directive provides on breaks during working time that Member States shall take the measures necessary to ensure that, where the working day is longer than six hours, every worker is entitled to a rest break, the details of which, including duration and the terms on which it is granted, shall be laid down in collective agreements or agreements between the two sides of industry or, failing that, by national legislation.

6.8 Weekly rest period of 24 uninterrupted hours

Under Article 5 of the Directive Member States shall take the measures necessary to ensure that, per each seven-day period, every worker is entitled to a minimum uninterrupted rest period of 24 hours plus the 11 hours' daily rest referred to in Article 3. If objective, technical or work organisation conditions so justify, a minimum rest period of 24 hours may be applied.

6.9 Paid annual leave

Article 7 of the Directive on annual leave provides that

1. Member States shall take the measures necessary to ensure that every worker is entitled to paid annual leave of at least four weeks in accordance with the conditions for entitlement to, and granting of, such leave laid down by national legislation and/or practice.

2. The minimum period of paid annual leave may not be replaced by an allowance in lieu, except where the employment relationship is terminated.

Article 31(2) CFREU provides that 'Every worker has the right to limitation of maximum working hours, to daily and weekly rest periods and to an annual period of paid leave'. The CJEU has developed a considerable case law on paid annual leave as a fundamental right, see below.

In *Heimann*[60] and other, the CJEU stated that, it should be noted first of all that, according to settled case-law, the entitlement of every worker to paid annual leave must be regarded as a particularly important principle of European Union social law (see Joined Cases C-350/06 and C-520/06 Schultz-Hoff and Others [2009] ECR I-179, paragraph 54, and Case C-337/10 Neidel [2012] ECR I-0000, paragraph 28). The right to paid annual leave is, as a principle of European Union social law, expressly laid down in Article 31(2) of the Charter of Fundamental Rights of the European Union, which Article

60. Case C-229/11 and C-230/11 *Heimann* [2012] ECR nyr.

6(1) TEU recognises as having the same legal value as the Treaties (see Case C-214/10 KHS [2011] ECR I-0000, paragraph 37, and Neidel, paragraph 40).

23 Secondly, it must be recalled that the right to paid annual leave may not be interpreted restrictively (Case C-78/11 ANGED [2012] ECR I nyr.

6.9.1 Qualifying period of employment

In *BECTU*,[61] the problem was whether a national provision in the UK under which entitlement to paid annual leave did not arise until a worker had been continuously employed for 13 weeks was compatible with the Working time directive. Broadcasting, Entertainment, Cinematographic and Theatre Union (BECTU) was a trade union with about 30 000 members working in the broadcasting, film, theatre, cinema and related sectors in jobs such as sound recordists, cameramen, special effects technicians, projectionists, editors, researchers, hairdressers and make-up artistes. BECTU claimed that most of its members are engaged on short-term contracts – frequently for less than 13 weeks with the same employer – so that many of them do not satisfy the condition laid down for entitlement to paid annual leave. Accordingly, the persons concerned are deprived of any entitlement to paid annual leave and of any right to an allowance in lieu merely because, although they work on a regular basis, they do so for successive employers. The advocate general argued that the right to paid annual leave is not only guaranteed in the Working Time Directive but also constitutes a fundamental right. The CJEU ruled:

> Article 7(1) of Council Directive 93/104/EC of 23 November 1993 concerning certain aspects of the organisation of working time does not allow a Member State to adopt national rules under which a worker does not begin to accrue rights to paid annual leave until he has completed a minimum period of 13 weeks' uninterrupted employment with the same employer.

6.9.2 Illness

In *Anged*,[62] the CJEU ruled:

> Article 7(1) of Directive 2003/88/EC of the European Parliament and of the Council of 4 November 2003 concerning certain aspects of the organisation of working time must be interpreted as precluding national provisions under which a worker who becomes unfit for work during a period of paid annual leave is not entitled subsequently to the paid annual leave which coincided with the period of unfitness for work.

61. Case C-173/99 *BECTU* [2001] ECR I-4881.
62. Case 78/11 *ANGED* [2012] nyr.

6.9.3 Pro rata temporis principle

In *Heimann*[63] and other, the CJEU held:

> Article 31(2) of the Charter of Fundamental Rights of the European Union and Article 7(1) of Directive 2003/88/EC of the European Parliament and of the Council of 4 November 2003 concerning certain aspects of the organisation of working time must be interpreted as meaning that they do not preclude national legislation or practice, such as a social plan agreed between an undertaking and its works council, under which the paid annual leave of a worker on short-time working is calculated according to the *pro rata temporis* rule.

The CJEU held in *Zentralbetriebsrat der Landeskrankenhäuser Tirols*[64] that although it is generally appropriate to apply the pro rata temporis principle for holidays when an employee works part-time, this principle cannot be applied retrospectively to annual leave already accrued before the transition from full-time to part-time work.

6.9.4 Annual leave and maternity/parental leave

A growing number of cases are concerned with the clashes between periods of annual leave and periods of maternity leave or parental leave. The CJEU addressed the issue of the interaction between the right to maternity leave as guaranteed by the Pregnancy Directive[65] and the right to paid annual leave under Article 7(1) of the Working Time Directive in *Gomez*.[66] The CJEU held that a worker must be able to take her annual leave during a period that did not overlap with her maternity leave, even where a collective agreement fixed periods of leave for all workers.

The decision in *Zentralbetriebsrat der Landeskrankenhäuser Tirols* will be relevant to workers who return from maternity leave and arrange with their employer to work on a part-time basis. As workers continue to accrue annual leave while on maternity leave, this judgment confirms that they will be entitled to take that accrued holiday upon their return to work as if they had worked on a full-time basis. In addition, the CJEU made clear that holidays accrued before a period of parental leave should not be lost. A worker on parental leave is entitled to keep the annual leave she has accrued and should be permitted to carry it over to following leave years when she returns to work.

63. Case C-229/11 and C-230/11 *Heimann* [2012] ECR nyr.
64. Case C-486/08 *Zentralbetriebsrat der Landeskrankenhäuser Tirols* [2010] ECR I-3527.
65. 92/85/EEC.
66. Case C-342/01 *Gomez* [2004] ECR I-2605.

6.9.5 Different treatment of workers (Arbeiter) and salaried employees (Angestellte)

Under Danish law there is a d Differentiation between workers (arbejdere) and salaried employees (funktionærer). Workers (arbejdere, in German Arbeiter) are treated less favourably than salaried employees (funktionærer, in German Angestellte) on a number of points for example with regard to payment during paid annual leave in the Holiday Act. The question arises as to whether Article 20[67] and 31(2) on paid annual leave in the Charter have direct effect and supremacy over the Danish Holiday Act so that a Danish worker can claim the same as a salaried employee would be entitled to. In my view the answer is yes. Paid annual leave is provided for in the Working Time Directive[68] which Denmark is implementing in a way that treats workers and salaried employees differently. That is in my view a violation of Article 20 of the Charter, see also *Mangold*[69] in which case the CJEU held that there is a general principle in EU law preventing Member States from implementing the fixed-term dontract directive[70] differently for workers of different age. The German constitutional court held in 1990[71] that a provision in BGB (Bürgerliches Gesetzbuch) providing for shorter periods of notice for workers (Arbeiter) than for salaried employees (Angestellte) was inconsistent with the German Constitution § 3(2).[72] An important factor in the development of the CJEU case law on fundamental rights has, as appears from Chapter Two, been its link to the doctrine of the supremacy of EU law over national law and the concern of the CJEU to avoid revolt among national constitutional courts against this doctrine by elevating fundamental rights to general principles of EU law. This context makes it unlikely that the CJEU will give an interpretation to Charter provisions, as for example Article 20 CFREU, that provides for a lower level of protection than the equivalent provision in the German Constitution § 3(2). This is important for the likely spread of German style fundamental rights via the CFREU to countries like Denmark with

67. It reads: 'All persons are equal before the law', in German 'Alle Menschen sind vor dem Gesetz gleich'.
68. Originally 93/104/EC, now 2003/88/EC.
69. Case C-144/04 *Mangold* [2005] ECR I-9981.
70. Council Directive 99/70/EC of 28 June 1999 concerning the framework agreement on fixed-term work concluded by ETUC, UNICE and CEEP.
71. BVerfGE 82, 126, available at http://www.oefre.unibe.ch/law/dfr/bv082126.html. Se Susanne Baer: Constitutional Equality: Equality: The Jurisprudence of the German Constitutional Court, Columbia Journal of European Law 1999 p. 249.
72. It reads: 'Alle Menschen sind vor dem Gesetz gleich'.

a weak tradition for protection of fundamental rights in labour and welfare law.

6.10 On call service

In *SIMAP*,[73] the CJEU held that time spent on call by doctors in primary health care teams must be regarded in its entirety as working time, and where appropriate as overtime, within the meaning of Directive 93/104 if they are required to be at the health centre. If they must merely be contactable at all times when on call, only time linked to the actual provision of primary health care services must be regarded as working time. In *Jaeger*,[74] the CJEU similarly held that:

> 1. Council Directive 93/104/EC of 23 November 1993 concerning certain aspects of the organisation of working time must be interpreted as meaning that on-call duty (Bereitschaftsdienst) performed by a doctor where he is required to be physically present in the hospital must be regarded as constituting in its totality working time for the purposes of that directive even where the person concerned is permitted to rest at his place of work during the periods when his services are not required with the result that that directive precludes legislation of a Member State which classifies as rest periods an employee's periods of inactivity in the context of such on-call duty.

6.11 Reference periods

Article 16 of the Working time directive provides that Member States may lay down:

> (a) for the application of Article 5 (weekly rest period), a reference period not exceeding 14 days;
> (b) for the application of Article 6 (maximum weekly working time), a reference period not exceeding four months.
> The periods of paid annual leave, granted in accordance with Article 7, and the periods of sick leave shall not be included or shall be neutral in the calculation of the average;
> (c) for the application of Article 8 (length of night work), a reference period defined after consultation of the two sides of industry or by collective agreements or agreements concluded between the two sides of industry at national or regional level.
> If the minimum weekly rest period of 24 hours required by Article 5 falls within that reference period, it shall not be included in the calculation of the average.

73. Case C-303/98 *SIMAP* [2000] ECR I-7963.
74. Case C-151/02 *Jaeger* [2003] ECR I-8389.

6.12 Derogations

Article 17 of the Working Time Directive allows Member States to derogate from Articles 3 to 6, 8 and 16 when, on account of the specific characteristics of the activity concerned, the duration of the working time is not measured and/or predetermined or can be determined by the workers themselves.

Derogations provided for in paragraphs 3, 4 and 5 may be adopted by means of laws, regulations or administrative provisions or by means of collective agreements or agreements between the two sides of industry provided that the workers concerned are afforded equivalent periods of compensatory rest or that, in exceptional cases in which it is not possible, for objective reasons, to grant such equivalent periods of compensatory rest, the workers concerned are afforded appropriate protection. Derogations may be made from Articles 3, 4, 5, 8 and 16:

(a) in the case of activities where the worker's place of work and his place of residence are distant from one another, including offshore work, or where the worker's different places of work are distant from one another;
(b) in the case of security and surveillance activities requiring a permanent presence in order to protect property and persons, particularly security guards and caretakers or security firms;
(c) in the case of activities involving the need for continuity of service or production, particularly:
   (i) services relating to the reception, treatment and/or care provided by hospitals or similar establishments, including the activities of doctors in training, residential institutions and prisons;
   (ii) dock or airport workers;
   (iii) press, radio, television, cinematographic production, postal and telecommunications services, ambulance, fire and civil protection services;
   (iv) gas, water and electricity production, transmission and distribution, household refuse collection and incineration plants;
   (v) industries in which work cannot be interrupted on technical grounds;
   (vi) research and development activities;
   (vii) agriculture;
   (viii) workers concerned with the carriage of passengers on regular urban transport services;
(d) where there is a foreseeable surge of activity, particularly in:
   (i) agriculture;
   (ii) tourism;
   (iii) postal services;
(e) in the case of persons working in railway transport:
   (i) whose activities are intermittent;
   (ii) who spend their working time on board trains; or
   (iii) whose activities are linked to transport timetables and to ensuring the continuity and regularity of traffic;
(f) in the circumstances described in Article 5(4) of Directive 89/391/EEC;

(g) in cases of accident or imminent risk of accident.

Derogations may be made from Articles 3 and 5:

(a) in the case of shift work activities, each time the worker changes shift and cannot take daily and/or weekly rest periods between the end of one shift and the start of the next one;
(b) in the case of activities involving periods of work split up over the day, particularly those of cleaning staff.

In *Jaeger*,[75] the CJEU held that the Working Time Directive must be interpreted as meaning that:

- in circumstances such as those in the main proceedings, that directive precludes legislation of a Member State which, in the case of on-call duty where physical presence in the hospital is required, has the effect of enabling, in an appropriate case by means of a collective agreement or a works agreement based on a collective agreement, an offset only in respect of periods of on-call duty during which the worker has actually been engaged in professional activities;
- in order to come within the derogating provisions set out in Article 17(2), subparagraph 2.1(c)(i) of the directive, a reduction in the daily rest period of 11 consecutive hours by a period of on-call duty performed in addition to normal working time is subject to the condition that equivalent compensating rest periods be accorded to the workers concerned at times immediately following the corresponding periods worked;
- furthermore, in no circumstances may such a reduction in the daily rest period lead to the maximum weekly working time laid down in Article 6 of the directive being exceeded.

In *Isère*,[76] the CJEU that persons employed under contracts such as the educational commitment contracts at issue in the main proceedings, carrying out casual and seasonal activities in holiday and leisure centres, and completing a maximum of 80 working days per annum, are within the scope of the Working Time Directive. 2. Persons employed under contracts such as the educational commitment contracts at issue in the main proceedings, carrying out casual and seasonal activities at holiday and leisure centres, fall within the

75. Case C-151/02 *Jaeger* [2003] ECR I-8389.
76. Case C-428/09 *Isère* [2010] ECR I-9961.

scope of the derogation in Article 17(3)(b) and/or 17(3)(c) of the Directive. National legislation which restricts the activity carried out under such contracts to 80 days per annum does not satisfy the conditions set out in Article 17(2) of that directive which govern the application of that derogation, to the effect that the workers concerned are to be afforded equivalent periods of compensatory rest or, in exceptional cases where the granting of such periods is not possible for objective reasons, appropriate protection.

In *SIMAP*,[77] the CJEU held Time spent on call by doctors in primary health care teams must be regarded in its entirety as working time, and where appropriate as overtime, within the meaning of Directive 93/104 if they are required to be at the health centre. If they must merely be contactable at all times when on call, only time linked to the actual provision of primary health care services must be regarded as working time.

5. Work performed by doctors in primary health care teams whilst on call constitutes shift work and such doctors are shift workers within the meaning of Article 2(5) and (6) of Directive 93/104.

6. In the absence of national provisions transposing Article 16(2) of Directive 93/104 or, as the case may be, expressly adopting one of the derogations provided for in Article 17(2), (3) and (4) thereof, those provisions may be interpreted as having direct effect, and therefore they confer on individuals a right whereby the reference period for the implementation of the maximum duration of their weekly working time must not exceed 12 months.

7. The consent given by trade-union representatives in the context of a collective or other agreement is not equivalent to that given by the worker himself, as provided for in the first indent of Article 18(1)(b)(i) of Directive 93/104.

7 Stress, Harassment and Violence at Woek

7.1 Stress

In October 2004, the European social partners signed a Framework agreement on work-related stress[78] as an autonomous agreement. The objective of the agreement is to provide employers and workers with a framework to iden-

77. Case C-303/98 *SIMAP* [2000] ECR I-7963.
78. Implementation of the European Autonomous Framework Agreement on Work-Related Stress, Report by the European Social Partners, 2008:

tify and prevent or manage problems of work-related stress. Stress is defined as:

> a state, which is accompanied by physical, psychological or social complaints or dysfunctions and which results from individuals feeling unable to bridge a gap with the requirements or expectations placed on them. ... Stress is not a disease but prolonged exposure to it may reduce effectiveness at work and may cause ill-health.

The agreement recognises that work-related stress can be caused by different factors such as work content, work organisation, work environment, poor communication, etc. The aim of the agreement is to increase the awareness and understanding of employers, workers and their representatives of work-related stress, and to draw their attention to signs that could indicate problems of work-related stress. It provides employers and workers with a framework to identify and prevent or manage problems of work-related stress. It furthermore provides a non-exhaustive list of potential stress factors which can help identifying eventual problems. If such a problem is identified, action must be taken to prevent, eliminate or reduce it. The agreement therefore highlights a number of both collective and individual measures which can be taken both as specific measures at identified stress factors or as part of an integrated stress policy encompassing both preventive and responsive measures.

The agreement applies to all workplaces and all workers, irrespective of the size of the company, field of activity, or form of employment contract or relationship, although it is recognised that not all work places and not all workers are necessarily affected by work-related stress.

Work-related stress has been recognised as one of the main sources of work-related health problems. In the communication on the Community strategy on health and safety at work 2002-2006, the European Commission adopted a global approach to well-being at work, taking account of changes in the world of work and the emergence of new risks, particularly psychosocial ones. The European Commission began to consult the European social partners on work-related stress in 2002. As there have been no legal provisions specifically aiming at work-related stress, action at Community level was seen as necessary to ensure a minimum level of protection for workers against work-related stress. In the consultation of the social partners on stress and its effects on health and safety at work, the European Commission refers to an estimated cost of at least 20 billion euro each year, based on 1999 figures for the European countries. A first interim assessment took place at the meeting of the Social Dialogue Committee on 28 June 2006.

The agreement gives guidance as regards measures to prevent, eliminate or reduce problems of work-related stress. In the case that a problem with work-related stress is identified or action must be taken to prevent, eliminate or reduce stress, the responsibility for determining the appropriate measures rests with the employer. Workers have a general duty to comply with measures determined by the employer. The framework agreement is due to be implemented within three years. It entails a clause on the monitoring of the implementation of the agreement and providing of annual interim reports in the first three years and a full report in the fourth year.

7.2 Harassment and Violence

In 2007, the European social partners (ETUC, BUSINESSEUROPE, CEEP and UEAPME) signed a framework agreement on harassment and violence at work. The agreement aims to prevent and, where necessary, manage problems of bullying, sexual harassment and physical violence at the workplace. Companies in Europe will have to adopt a policy of zero-tolerance towards such behaviour and draw up procedures to deal with cases of harassment and violence where they occur. Data suggests that one in 20 workers (5%) reports being exposed to bullying and/or harassment each year.

The European agreement condemns all forms of harassment and violence and refers to the employer's duty to protect workers against these situations. Companies will need to set out procedures to follow when cases of harassment or violence arise. These can include an informal stage involving a person trusted by management and the workforce. Complaints should be investigated and dealt with quickly. The principles of dignity, confidentiality, impartiality and fair treatment need to be respected. The agreement underlines that appropriate measures will be taken against the perpetrator, including disciplinary action up to dismissal, while the victim will receive support with reintegration, if needed.

8 Free Movement on the Internal Market and Working Environment Protection

Free movement on the internal market for dangerous machinery or chemical substances may cause harm to workers' health and safety when they use the machinery or are exposed to the chemicals in their working environment. The question therefore arises whether the national working environment authorities can prohibit or otherwise restrict the use of lawfully marketed machinery or chemical substances or whether that would be an unlawful restriction on the free movement of goods. The CJEU has developed a long-standing case law on free movement of goods.[79] According to *Dassonville*[80] all trading rules enacted by Member States which are capable of hindering, directly or indirectly, actually or potentially, trade within the EU are to be considered as measures having an effect equivalent to quantitative restrictions and are, on that basis, prohibited by Article 34 TFEU. In its *Cassis de Dijon* case law,[81] the CJEU has accepted the principle of mutual recognition according to which a product which is lawfully marketed in one EU Member State cannot be denied access to the markets of the other EU Member States. The EU has also endeavored to prevent dangerous machinery and hazardous chemicals from being put lawfully on the market anywhere in the EU, see below on CE marking and Reach. Anyway, cases do arise in which workers' health and safety are put at risk or injured by free moving goods, see some illustrating cases below in section 9.3.

8.1 CE Marking

CE marking is an indicator of a product's compliance with EU legislation. It enables the free movement of products within the Internal Market. By affixing the CE marking on a product, a manufacturer is declaring, on his sole responsibility, conformity with all of the legal requirements to achieve CE marking and therefore ensuring validity for that product to be sold throughout the EU. Only those product categories subject to specific directives that provide for the CE marking are required to be CE marked. CE marking merely states that the product is assessed before being placed on the market and thus satisfies the legislative requirements (e.g. a harmonised level of safety) to be sold there. It means that the manufacturer has verified that the product complies with all relevant essential requirements (e.g. health and safety requirements) of the applicable directive(s) – or, if stipulated in the directive(s), had it examined by a notified conformity assessment body. It is the manufacturer's responsibility to carry out the conformity assessment, to set up the technical file, to issue the declaration of conformity and to affix CE marking on a product.

79. See generally Barnard, Catherine: The Substantive Law of the EU: The Four Freedoms, Oxford 2010.
80. Case 8/74 *Dassonville* [1974] ECR 837.
81. Case 120/78 *Cassis de Dijon* [1979] ECR 649.

8.2 REACH

REACH is the EU Regulation on chemicals and their safe use.[82] It deals with the **R**egistration, **E**valuation, **A**uthorisation and Restriction of **Ch**emical substances. The Regulation entered into force on 1 June 2007. The aim of REACH is to improve the protection of human health and the environment through the better and earlier identification of the intrinsic properties of chemical substances. At the same time, REACH aims to enhance innovation and competitiveness of the EU chemicals industry. The REACH Regulation places greater responsibility on industry to manage the risks from chemicals and to provide safety information on the substances. Manufacturers and importers are required to gather information on the properties of their chemical substances, which will allow their safe handling, and to register the information in a central database run by the European Chemicals Agency (ECHA) in Helsinki. The Agency acts as the central point in the REACH system: it manages the databases necessary to operate the system, co-ordinates the in-depth evaluation of suspicious chemicals and is building up a public database in which consumers and professionals can find hazard information.

The Regulation also calls for the progressive substitution of the most dangerous chemicals when suitable alternatives have been identified. One of the main reasons for developing and adopting the REACH Regulation was that a large number of substances have been manufactured and placed on the market in Europe for many years, sometimes in very high amounts, and yet there is insufficient information on the hazards that they pose to human health and the environment. REACH provisions are being phased-in over 11 years.

8.3 Case Law

8.3.1 Società Italiana Petroli

In *Società Italiana Petroli*[83] the problem was whether the Member States could fis more protective rules on exposure to carcinogens than thos laid down in the Working Environment directives on carcinogens. Italiana Petroli entered into a number of agreements with Borsana for the supply of petrol for motor vehicles. By letter of 3 June 1996 Borsana asked Italiana Petroli, pursuant to the provisions of Legislative Decree No 626/94 read in conjunction with the directives on carcinogens, to supply petrol with the lowest possible benzene content, in order to protect the health of its employees. Italiana Petroli considered that it was not possible to comply with Borsana's request be-

82. EC 1907/2006.
83. Case C-2/97 *Società Italiana Petroli* [1998] ECR I-8597.

cause of the divergences between Legislative Decree No 626/94. Italiana Petroli expressed its doubts as to the compatibility of the carcinogens directive and Legislative Decree No 626/94 with the free movement of goods provisions in the Treaties, inasmuch as they impose an additional duty on employers to reduce, as far as technical progress allows, exposure to carcinogens, and therefore to the benzene present in petrol, below the limit fixed by Directive 85/210[84] and even below the yet lower limits fixed in Decree Law No294/96. In those circumstances, on 25 June 1996, Italiana Petroli brought proceedings against Borsana in the Tribunale di Genova for a declaration that it was not obliged to supply Borsana with petrol with a benzene content lower than the levels fixed by Directive 85/210 and Decree Law No 294/96.

The CJEU held:

> Article 4 of Council Directive 90/394/EEC of 28 June 1990 on the protection of workers from the risks related to exposure to carcinogens at work (Sixth individual directive within the meaning of Article 16(1) of Directive 89/391/EEC) must be interpreted to the effect that the employer's obligationto reduce or replace a carcinogen is not contingent on the outcome of theassessment of risks referred to in Article 3 of that directive.
>
> Article 5 of Directive 90/394 must be interpreted to the effect that the employer's obligation to avoid or reduce exposure to a carcinogen is contingent on the outcome of the assessment of risks referred to in Article3 of that directive.
>
> A national provision which requires the employer to reduce workers' exposure to a carcinogen irrespective of the assessment of risks is not contrary to that directive where it constitutes a more stringent measure for the protection of working conditions authorised by Article 118a(3) of the EC Treaty and Directive 90/394.
>
> Article 4 of Council Directive 89/655/EEC of 30 November 1989 concerning the minimum safety and health requirements for the use of work equipment by workers at work (Second individual Directive within the meaning of Article 16(1) of Directive 89/391/EEC) does not preclude a Member State from setting a time-limit for adapting existing working equipment that expires before 31 December 1996, provided that the time-limit is not so short that it does not enable employers to effect such adaptation or entail a cost that is clearly excessive as compared with what they would have hadto meet if the time-limit had been longer.

The CJEU thus accepted that the Working Environment directives adopted on the basis of Article 153 TFEU within the framework of the Framework on Working Environment Directive are only minimum directives which the Member States can complement with more worker protective rules. They do

84. Council Directive 85/210/EEC of 20 March 1985 on the approximation of the laws of the Member States concerning the lead content of petrol.

not, like the free movement rules of the TFEU and the internal market directives, provide full harmonisation.

8.3.2 Yonemoto

Yonemoto[85] concerned the interpretation of the machinery directive[86] on the occasion of a work accident in which a Finnish worker suffered a serious accident. A machine cut off eight of his fingers. The machine was manufactured in another EU country than Finland and imported to Finland. The machine was equipped with CE-marking in accordance with the machinery directive and the manufacturer of the machine had given a written guarantee of the machine's conformity with the requirements in force. The Finnish working environment authorities held the importer (Yonemoto) responsible for the accident and sentenced him to a fine and liability in damages towards the injured worker. Yonemoto considered that the Finnish authorities or Finnish court may not, without infringing Article 34 TFEU, require the importer to have checks made in Finland of a machine type-approved in another EU Member State and bearing the CE marking. The importer's obligation was in his view limited to making sure that the manufacturer of the machine has had the type of machine in question approved in accordance with EU norms by an approved body, provided the machine with instructions for use and maintenance and the CE marking, and issued a declaration of conformity for the machine. Requiring more of the importer would – in Yonemoto's view – be an unlawful restriction on the free movement of goods under Article 34 TFEU. In *Yonemoto*, the CJEU held that:

> Directive 98/37/EC of the European Parliament and of the Council of 22 June 1998 on the approximation of the laws of the Member States relating to machinery precludes the application of national provisions which require the importer in a Member State of machinery manufactured in another Member State, bearing the CE marking and accompanied by an EC declaration of conformity, to ensure that that machinery meets the essential health and safety requirements laid down by that directive.
>
> 2. That directive does not preclude the application of national provisions which require the importer in a Member State of a machine manufactured in another Member State to:
> – ensure, before the machinery is delivered to the user, that it bears the CE marking and is accompanied by the EC declaration of conformity translated into the language or one of the languages of the Member State into which the machinery is imported, and instructions translated into the language or languages of that State,·

85. C-40/04 *Yonemoto* [2005] ECR I-7755.
86. 98/37/EC.

- provide, after the machinery has been delivered to the user, all appropriate information and cooperation to the national inspection authorities if it transpires that that machinery poses risks to safety or health, provided that such requirements do not amount to making the importer subject to the obligation to verify himself that the machinery complies with the essential health and safety requirements laid down by that directive.

3. Article 10 EC [now Article 4 TEU] and the third paragraph of Article 249 EC [now Article 288 TFEU] must be interpreted as not precluding a Member State from imposing criminal penalties to ensure compliance with the obligations laid down by Directive 98/37, provided that those penalties are analogous to those applicable to infringements of national law of a similar nature and importance and are, in any event, effective, proportionate and deterrent.

8.3.3 AGM-COS.MET

AGM-COS.MET[87] also concerned the interpretation of the machinery directive. The reference was made in the course of proceedings between A.G.M.-COS.MET, a company established under Italian law, and the Finnish State and Lehtinen, an the Ministry of Social Affairs and Health, concerning compensation for the damage AGM claims to have suffered as a result of breaches of the Directive. The Machinery Directive defines the essential health and safety requirements relating to the design and construction of machinery and safety components and the rules for the assessment of conformity, declaration of conformity and marking of machinery. Article 2 of the Directive provides:

1. Member States shall take all appropriate measures to ensure that machinery or safety components covered by this Directive may be placed on the market and put into service only if they do not endanger the health or safety of persons and, where appropriate, domestic animals or property, when properly installed and maintained and used for their intended purpose.

2. This Directive shall not affect Member States' entitlement to lay down, in due observance of the Treaty, such requirements as they may deem necessary to ensure that persons and in particular workers are protected when using the machinery or safety components in question, provided that this does not mean that the machinery or safety components are modified in a way not specified in the Directive.

On 11 May 2000 the Ministry of Social Affairs and Health received a report in a 'market supervision case'. According to the report, an examination of the vehicle lift of type G 35 T/E manufactured by AGM had disclosed certain de-

87. Case C-470/03 *AGM-COS.MET* [2007] ECR I-2749.

fects, in particular bending of the front lifting arms and weak locking of the lifting arms. Following that report, the Ministry of Social Affairs and Health sent the Finnish importer of those lifts, a letter stating that there were grounds for suspecting that the G 35 T/E vehicle lifts manufactured by AGM did not meet the requirements of Law 299/1958 on safety at work. In the course of the procedure thus initiated by the Ministry of Social Affairs and Health, Lehtinen drafted a report in which he stated inter alia that the importer had performed a test of the locking system in order to demonstrate that the structure of the vehicle lifts in question complied with standard SFS-EN 1493. According to the report, the test had disclosed a defect in that system. In a memorandum, Lehtinen repeated his observations, but stated that the new locking system proposed by AGM was better. At a meeting on 20 December 2000 attended by representatives of the importer and by Kanerva, administrator, and Lehtinen, as an expert, on behalf of the Ministry of Social Affairs and Health, it was accepted that the locking system as redesigned complied with the rules. However, the final position taken by the authorities would have to depend on a certification examination by an authorised body, a procedure which AGM said was then under way. It was also decided on that occasion that the decision to be taken by the Ministry of Social Affairs and Health would not be made public, the importer informing users at the appropriate time. On 20 December 2000 Kanerva submitted the case to Hurmalainen, head of the health and safety division of the Ministry of Social Affairs and Health, for a decision. Kanerva proposed that the placing on the market and putting into service of the vehicle lifts in question should be prohibited, subject to certain qualifications. However, Hurmalainen did not adopt the decision proposed to him, but sent the case back for examination, as he considered that he did not have sufficient evidence. On 17 January 2001 Lehtinen, with the permission of his immediate superior, and a representative of the importer were interviewed for the 20.30 news programme on national television channel TV 1. On that occasion the presenter explained that, according to the Finnish health and safety authorities, the lifts in question, although approved in Italy, did not correspond to the applicable European standards. The presenter also said that, according to those authorities, the structure should bear the weight even if the vehicle was presented in the least favourable lifting conditions. The importer's representative, for his part, admitted that the locking system was defective, but denied that there were any other problems with the lifting system, and claimed that the lifting arms would bear any weight provided that the vehicle was driven onto the lift in the correct direction. Lehtinen stated that the vehicle lifts could present an immediate danger, in that workers would be working beneath the load. He also said that the notified body used by AGM had misinterpreted the rules then applicable. On 8 February 2001 Hurmalainen sent a fax to Kuikko, the representative of the Central Association of Industry and Employers, in which he said that he had opposed the ban on sales suggested by Kanerva and Lehtinen, on the ground that it had not seemed reasonable to him to take a measure that could disturb the working of the internal market, since only one accident had occurred in Finland, the cause of which was moreover uncertain. On 16 February 2001 Hurmalainen removed Lehtinen from dealing with cases concerning the vehicle lifts made by AGM, on the ground that in a pending case he had publicly expressed a point of view differing from the official position of the Ministry of Social Affairs and Health and had thus acted contrary to the ministry's instructions and its communication policy. A subsequent report, drawn up on 20 March 2001 by the health and safety division of the Ministry of Social Affairs and Health, criticised Lehtinen for acting in breach of the principle of sound administration and in a manner injurious to the economic interests of AGM by collaborating with AGM's competitors. On 17 February 2001 an article under the headline 'Expert warns against treacherous vehicle lifts' appeared in a regional newspaper. According to the order for reference, the article was written on the basis of an interview with Lehtinen and expressly stated that the products concerned were the AGM vehicle lifts. It was also mentioned that Hurmalainen, head of the ministry's health and safety division, regards what Lehtinen says as his personal views.

On 14 June 2001 the health and safety division of the Ministry of Social Affairs and Health took a decision in which it noted in particular that 'in the present case no factors [had] come to light on the basis of which the ministry should adopt market supervision measures against the manufacturer or importer of the AGM vehicle lifts'. That document pointed out that that 'opinion [did] not, however, prevent the ministry from adopting those measures if there [was] occasion to reassess the matter as a result of additional information or for any other reason'. As grounds for its decision, the Ministry of Social Affairs and Health observed that 'the manufacturer [had] corrected, as regards new equipment, and the importer [was] endeavouring to correct, as regards equipment in service, the technical faults identified'. On 1 October 2001 the Ministry of Social Affairs and Health gave Lehtinen a written warning under the Law on State officials, on the ground that he had breached his obligations as an official by continuing, after the case of the AGM vehicle lifts had been withdrawn from him, to give a misleading picture of the ministry's point of view in a press release and a memorandum addressed to the health and safety district office, and by acting contrary to the ministry's communications policy. By decision of 6 March 2002, the Civil Service Appeals Committee dismissed Lehtinen's complaint seeking to have the warning annulled. On the other hand, the committee considered in that decision that Lehtinen's conduct in the television interview of 17 January 2001 had not been so incorrect that a written warning was justified. On 10 September 2003 the Supreme Administrative Court upheld the committee's decision. AGM brought proceedings before the referring court seeking an order that the Finnish State and Lehtinen jointly compensate it for the damage allegedly suffered, in particular a loss of turnover in Finland and elsewhere in Europe.

The question arises, according to the referring court, of whether in the light of the CJEU's case-law, in particular *Dassonville*,[88] trade within the EU could have been hindered contrary to Article 34 TFEU when Lehtinen, at that time an official of the competent authority, publicly expressed a negative opinion on the compliance with standards of certain vehicle lifts manufactured by AGM, an opinion which may have led to the fall in sales of that company's products on the Finnish market. Since the potential obstacle to cross-border trade does not follow from a decision taken by the competent authority on the basis of national provisions but from the conduct of an official belonging to that authority before the authority took its decision in the case in question, the referring court was uncertain as to whether the criterion defined in *Dassonville* allows the actual acts of an official to be regarded as measures having equivalent effect to quantitative restrictions, in particular where, in practice, the effect of those acts was the same as if the authority concerned had taken a similar decision under provisions of national law. The referring court also wished the CJEU to rule on whether a vehicle lift such as that at issue in the main proceedings complies with the essential safety requirements laid down by the Machinery Directive if it is not designed or constructed to bear a load under the least favorable lifting conditions. The referring court put the following questions to the CJEU:

1. Is there a measure having equivalent effect to quantitative restrictions within the meaning of Article 28 EC [now Article 34 TFEU], or a measure which should be abstained from under the second paragraph of Article 10 EC [now Article 4 TEU], if an expert official belonging to the State's health and safety at work organisation who does not have decision-making power, after a market supervision case has been raised but before the decision in the case, expresses his opinion on the main news programme of a national TV channel and in daily newspapers with wide circulation and also in commercial and labour market associations, in such a way that his statements, direct or repeated by others, on the hazard to health and even to life of the machinery manufactured and marketed by a specified manu-

88. Case 8/74 *Dassonville* [1974] ECR 837.

facturer which is the subject of the market supervision case may give the machinery negative publicity and affect its marketing?

2. Is Directive 98/37/EC on machinery to be interpreted as meaning that a vehicle lift is contrary to the essential safety requirements it lays down if it is not constructed in accordance with standard SFS-EN 1493, in such a way that in designing the structure account is not taken of the placing of the vehicle on the lifting arms in either driving direction and the load calculations of each lifting arm are not done for the least favourable loading situation?

3. (a) If Question 1 is answered in the affirmative, are the official's actions described in that question disproportionate having regard to the legitimate aim based on the protection of human health and life and hence contrary to the EC Treaty, even if Question 2 were also to be answered in the affirmative, having regard to the nature of the actions and in particular the fact that possible hazards could have been made known and the occurrence of hazards prevented by methods other than those described in Question 1, that the actions were taken even before the competent authority had made a decision in the market supervision case, and that the actions were likely in particular by being directed to a specified product to damage the marketing of that product?
   (b) If the question of proportionality in Question 3(a) is for the national court to decide, is the main weight to be attached to the possible non-compliance with the European or national safety requirements or to the circumstances of the publication of the non-compliance with the requirements?

4. May the actions of an official described in Question 1 be justified in the conditions described in Question 3(a) on the basis of freedom of speech within the meaning of Article 10 of the European Convention on Human Rights, even if they are contrary to Articles 28 EC and 30 EC or to Article 10 EC?

5. (a) If the actions of an official described in Question 1 are contrary to Articles 28 EC and 30 EC or to Article 10 EC, is the breach so manifest and serious that, if the other conditions of liability are satisfied, the State is obliged under EC law to compensate the damage which may have been incurred by the undertaking marketing the machinery?
   (b) Is the breach described in Question 5(a) manifest and serious even in a case where the authority/official with decision-making competence cannot be blamed for any fault or omission and the authority/official has not in any connection approved the measures or helped to bring about their actual consequences?
   (c) Can Article 10 EC and in particular its second paragraph create rights for individuals in the circumstances described in Question 1?
   (d) Can an official himself, in addition to the State, be similarly liable under EC law, in the circumstances mentioned in Question 1, for compensation for his actions, if they are contrary to EC law?
   (e) Is the obtaining of compensation based on EC law impossible in practice or excessively difficult if in accordance with national provisions compensation for economic damage other than damage to persons and things may be obtained only if the damage has been caused by a criminal offence or in the exercise of public authority

or if in other cases there are especially serious grounds for the awarding of damages?

6. (a) If compensation is awarded under national law because of a breach of requirements or omission concerning the free movement of goods, does EC law require that the compensation to be awarded is an effective and deterrent sanction, and is it incompatible with the requirements of EC law concerning liability that under national law an official who has committed an infringement or omission is liable for reasonable but not necessarily full compensation and is not liable at all for compensation if he is culpable of only slight negligence, or that an official and the State which is liable for the official's fault or omission may be ordered to pay compensation for economic damage other than damage to persons or things only if the damage has been caused by a criminal offence or in the exercise of public authority or if in other cases there are especially serious grounds for the awarding of compensation?
   (b) If any of the limitations of liability mentioned in Question 6(a) is incompatible with EC law, is the limitation of compensation under national law to be disapplied with respect to the official in question even though the official's liability would be more severe or more extensive than under national law?

The CJEU looked at the questions in sub-groups:

8.3.3.1 Free movement of goods (Questions 1,[89] 3 and 4)

The CJEU found that statements which, by reason of their form and circumstances, give the persons to whom they are addressed the impression that they are official positions taken by the State, not personal opinions of the official, are attributable to the State. The decisive factor for the statements of an official to be attributed to the State is whether the persons to whom those statements are addressed can reasonably suppose, in the given context, that they are positions taken by the official with the authority of his office. To the extent that they are attributable to the State, statements by an official describing machinery certified as conforming to the Machinery Directive[90] as contrary to the relevant harmonised standard and dangerous thus constitute a breach of Article 4(1) of then machinery Directive.

8.3.3.2 Justification (Questions 3 and 4)

In view of the fact that the safety rules for the placing of machinery on the market which affect the free movement of goods have been harmonised exhaustively, a Member State cannot rely on a justification on the ground of the

89. The CJEU didn't find it necessary to answer question 2.
90. 98/37/EC.

protection of health outside the framework created by Article 7 of the Directive.[91]

Under Article 10(1) ECHR, everyone within the jurisdiction of the Member States is guaranteed the right to freedom of expression. That freedom is an essential foundation of any democratic society. Member States, however, cannot rely on their officials' freedom of expression to justify an obstacle and thereby evade their own liability under EU law.

8.3.3.3 Liability of the Finnish State and of officials (Questions 5 and 6)

The CJEU held on the question of liability:

3. Article 4(1) of Directive 98/37 must be interpreted as meaning that, first, it confers rights on individuals and, second, it leaves the Member States no discretion in this case as regards machinery that complies with the directive or is presumed to do so. A failure to

91. Article 7 of the directive provides 1. Where a Member State ascertains that: – machinery bearing the CE marking, or – safety components accompanied by the EC declaration of conformity, used in accordance with their intended purpose are liable to endanger the safety of persons, and, where appropriate, domestic animals or property, it shall take all appropriate measures to withdraw such machinery or safety components from the market, to prohibit the placing on the market, putting into service or use thereof, or to restrict free movement thereof. Member States shall immediately inform the Commission of any such measure, indicating the reason for its decision and, in particular, whether non-conformity is due to: (a) failure to satisfy the essential requirements referred to in Article 3; (b) incorrect application of the standards referred to in Article 5(2); (c) shortcomings in the standards themselves referred to in Article 5(2).
2. The Commission shall enter into consultation with the parties concerned without delay. Where the Commission considers, after this consultation, that the measure is justified, it shall immediately so inform the Member State which took the initiative and the other Member States. Where the Commission considers, after this consultation, that the action is unjustified, it shall immediately so inform the Member State which took the initiative and the manufacturer or his authorized representative established within the Community. Where the decision referred to in paragraph 1 is based on a shortcoming in the standards, and where the Member State at the origin of the decision maintains its position, the Commission shall immediately inform the committee in order to initiate the procedures referred to in Article 6(1).
3. Where: – machinery which does not comply bears the CE marking, – a safety component which does not comply is accompanied by an EC declaration of conformity, the competent Member State shall take appropriate action against whom so ever has affixed the marking or drawn up the declaration and shall so inform the Commission and other Member States.
4. The Commission shall ensure that Member States are kept informed of the progress and outcome of this procedure.

comply with that provision as a result of statements made by an official, assuming that they are attributable to the Member State, constitutes a sufficiently serious breach of Community law for the Member State to incur liability.

4. Community law does not preclude specific conditions from being laid down by the domestic law of a Member State with reference to compensation for damage other than damage to persons or property, provided that those conditions are not framed in such a way as to make it impossible or excessively difficult in practice to obtain compensation for loss or damage resulting from a breach of Community law.

5. In the event of a breach of Community law, Community law does not preclude an official from being held liable in addition to the Member State, but does not require this.

CHAPTER TEN

Conclusion

1 Underlying rationales

In brief schematic form the main differences between the Internal Market and the Fundamental rights/EMU perspective on EU labour law can be outlined as follows:

	Internal Market perspective	Fundamental rights/ EMU perspective
Historical period	Rome 1957 ⇨	Maastricht 1992 ⇨
Scope of application of EU-labour law	Only cross border situations	Both cross-border situations and purely internal situations in a Member State of the EU if they take place in an EU context
Economic and market perspective	*Micro-economic*, based on a liberal market economy with free movement on the *internal market* and high and equal competition	*Macro-economic*, based on an open market economy with free competition and coordination of economic and employment policies, flexibility of labour law and increased adaptability of businesses to structural and cyclical changes on the *global market*

Role of workers/ labour	Labour is a commodity[1]	Workers constitute the majority of the union citizens who have both individual and collective fundamental rights. Member States should encourage framework conditions for wage bargaining systems and labour cost developments consistent with the need to reduce macroeconomic imbalances
Role of the social partners	Marginal	Important
Main legal actors and sources of law	Treaty provisions on free movement (in particular Articles 34, 45, 49 and 56 TFEU) and competition law CJEU case law on the Internal Market	Primary law on fundamental rights (Article 6 TEU and CFREU), TFEU Title VIII on Economic and Monetary policy (Articles 119-144 TFEU) and TFEU Title IX on Employment Policy (Articles 145-150 TFEU), Soft law related to the OMC
Judicially enforceable	The free movement and competition law provisions are judicially enforceable, the commodity value of labour is not	Fundamental rights are judicially enforceable, coordination provisions are not
Legal system(s)	Separate legal systems (national-, EU- and international labour law)	'the one big system model', in particular as regards fundamental rights

1. As mentioned in the previous chapters this is the opposite view of that expressed in the Constitution of ILO, see Chapter Two and O'Higgins, Paul: Labour is not a Commodity' – an Irish Contribution to International Labour Law, Industrial Law Journal1997, Vol. 26 Issue 3, p. 225.

1.1 Historical period

The internal market perspective constitutes the old, original layer of EU law, economics and policies. It is still relevant – the Eastern enlargement of the EU in 2004 renewed the focus on the internal market perspective, see e.g. *Laval*[2] discussed above in Chapter Three – but has after the establishment of the EU by adoption of the Maastricht Treaty 1992 been complemented by the fundamental rights/EMU perspective which is more concerned with preventing or reducing macro-economic imbalances and – partly as a means to that end – ensure fundamental rights for union citizens.

The subjects dealt with in this book are to varying degrees affected by the internal market perspective and the fundamental rights/EMU perspective respectively and it varies from subject to subject to which extent there is a shift in focus from the internal market perspective to the fundamental rights/EMU perspective.

1.2 Scope of application of EU labour law

The fundamental rights/EMU approach has a wider scope of application than the internal market context. Free movement rules and EU competition law only apply to cases with cross-border aspects. Many employment or labour conflicts in a Member States take place in situations that are purely internal to that Member State. In such situations EU free movement law and competition law is not applicable. There are, however, a number of labour law cases which are of a cross-border nature, for example trans-national posting of workers cases. Since the Eastern enlargement of the EU in 2004, the potential 'clash' between EU free movement law and national collective labour law has acquired renewed actuality, see on the *Laval*[3] and *Viking*[4] cases above in Chapter Three.

1.3 Economic and internal and global market perspective

In the internal market perspective the main economic problem law is used to help solving is to remove or reduce barriers to *access to the internal market* for economic actors who want to take advantage of the free movement on that market. In the fundamental rights/EMU perspective the main economic problem law is used to help solving seems rather to be the need to reduce *macroeconomic imbalances*. This aim plays a prominent role in the EU's efforts to coordinate economic and employment policies, see e.g. the Council Recom-

2. Case C-341/05 *Laval* [2007] ECR I-11767.
3. Case C-341/05 *Laval* [2007] ECR I-11767.
4. Case C-438/05 *Viking* [2007] ECR I-10779.

mendations on broad guidelines for the economic policies of the Member States and of the Union.

1.4 Role of workers/labour

The sentence 'Labour is not a commodity' has been used by ILO since 1944 to signal its view on the proper role of workers in labour law, see above in Chapter Two. In both the internal market perspective and the macroeconomic perspective used in connection with the EMU labour/workers are primarily seen as a commodity. In the fundamental rights/EMU perspective workers constitute the majority of the union citizens who have both individual and collective fundamental rights. At the same time Member States of the EU are in this context obligated to encourage framework conditions for wage bargaining systems and labour cost developments consistent with the need to ensure competitiveness and reduce macroeconomic imbalances.

1.5 Role of the social partners

The role of the social partners – the trade unions and the employers' organizations – varies considerably from country to country at national level. In the early layer of EU labour law adapted to an internal market perspective, the social partners played only a marginal role. In the fundamental rights/EMU perspective, on the other hand, the social partners are key collaborators with the Member States and EU institutions in coordinating economic and employment policies with a view to reduce macroeconomic imbalances, see above in Chapter Three on the report 'A new Strategy for the Single Market'[5] by Mario Monti. According to Monti, the case law of the CJEU in *Laval*[6] and *Viking*[7] has the potential to alienate from the Single Market and the EU a segment of public opinion, workers' movements and trade unions, which has been over time a key supporter of economic integration.

1.6 Main legal actors and sources of law

The internal market perspective has primarily been developed by the Member States as Treaty-makers and the CJEU through its case law. The fundamental rights/EMU perspective has primarily been developed by the Member States through primary law on fundamental rights (Article 6 TEU and CFREU). The

5. Monti, Mario: A New Strategy for the Single Market at the Service of Europe's Economy and Society: Report to the President of the European Commission José Manuel Barroso, Bruxelles 2010.
6. Case C-341/05 *Laval* [2007] ECR I-11767.
7. Case C-438/05 *Viking* [2007] ECR I-10779.

legal regulation on coordination of economic and employment policies are found in TFEU Title VIII on Economic and Monetary policy (Articles 119 - 144 TFEU) and TFEU Title IX on Employment Policy (Articles 145 -150 TFEU) and in soft law related to the OMC.

1.7 Judicially enforceable

The free movement and competition law provisions are judicially enforceable, the commodity value of labour is not. Fundamental rights are judicially enforceable, coordination provisions are not.

1.8 Legal system(s)

In the internal market perspective national labour law, EU-labour law and public international labour law are primarily seen as separate legal systems, see *Costa/ENEL*[8] and above in Chapter One. In the fundamental rights/EMU perspective national labour law, EU labour law and European human rights law is increasingly developing towards 'the one big system model', in particular as regards European fundamental rights.

2 Purpose of the book

The purpose of the book is set out in Chapter One. The book gives a systematic account of valid EU labour law as it stands in 2013 and of its development over the years from 1958 to 2013. The book describes and analyses the general development of EU labour law, with particular emphasis on two important shifts in contexts and perspectives:

- A shift in focus from an older layer where EU labour law was seen primarily in an Internal Market perspective to a newer layer where EU labour law is seen as part of the legal regulation of both the Internal Market and the fundamental rights the EU guarantees union citizens in the context of Economic and Monetary Union (EMU)
- A shift in focus from seeing labour law as part of many different, separate legal systems (national law, EU law and international law) to a 'one big system model' comprising the mutually interlocked labout law systems at national level in the Member States, at EU-level and in the European part of international labour law.

8. Case 6/64 *Costa* v *ENEL* [1964] ECR 614.

The basic rules on free movement on the internal market and competition law are usually regarded as the first – micro-economic – layer of EU's economic constitution. Since the establishment of the European Union by the Maastricht Treaty 1992 which contains rules on economic and monetary union a second more macro-economic phase of the economic constitution is – as mentioned in Chapter One – developing. The Maastricht Treaty also created union citizenship and strengthened the role of fundamental rights. Workers make up the majority of union citizens and are no longer seen by EU legal actors as solely or primarily a commodity on the internal market. In order for the EU to be able to develop a coordinated economic and employment policy with a view to enable businesses and work-places in the EU to be competitive on the global market it is necessary for EU law and policy to be perceived as legitimate by the people of the EU (the union citizens). In parallel with the development of the EMU, the EU has therefore developed strong fundamental rights for the union citizens. Discrimination and equality law is not only seen as a fundamental right but also increasingly being designed to promote inclusion of groups at risk of discrimination and the collaboration of the social partners (trade unions and employers' organizations) in developing coordinated employment and economic policies is actively sought by different EU actors.

3 The sources of EU labor law

In Chapter Two it was shown that there has been a multiplication of the sources of law. The sources of EU labour law is described under the following headings: Primary law (Treaty provisions and general principles and fundamental rights), Secondary law, Soft law, Case law, Scholarly Legal writing, Public international law and National law of the EU Member States. The adoption of the Maastricht Treaty 1992 marks a turning point in the development of EU labour law. It elevated both the establishment of an economic, monetary and financial union (the second layer of the EU economic constitution) and fundamental rights in the EU to primary EU law.

There was no provision on the values of the EU in the Treaties before the Lisbon Treaty. Today (2013), the EU is founded on the values of respect for human dignity, freedom, democracy, equality, the rule of law (Rechtsstaatlichkeit) and respect for human rights.

Fundamental rights in EU law appeared first in the case law of the CJEU. It was originally introduced by the CJEU mainly as a means to ensure acceptance by national supreme courts in particular in Germany and Italy of its case law on supremacy and direct effect. With regard to the labour market the case law of the CJEU on fundamental rights mainly covers equality and non-discrimination. The background to the provisions on Solidarity in the CFREU are mainly found in soft loft law, in particular the the Community Charter of Fundamental Rights of Workers from 1989 and in international labour law, in particular the Council of Europe Social Charter 1961 and the revised European Social Charter 1996.

CFREU and other fundamental rights are, if they are sufficiently precise, according to the case law of the CJREU binding in the Member States both vertically and horizontally but only when the Member States act in the scope of EU law. The expression 'Situations that happen in the scope of EU law' covers at least: 1. situations with cross-border elements where the free movement rules apply and 2. situations where a Member State is implementing a directive, including situations where they go further than the requirements laid down in a minimum directive and including national enforcement measures.

Soft law has played a decisive role in the development of fundamental rights in EU labour law and non-binding recommendations are the major legal instruments used to coordinate economic and employment policies in the Economic and Monetary Union (EMU).

4 Collective labour law

Chapter Three described the rules on classic collective labour law issues like freedom of association, the positive and negative right to organize, collective bargaining and industrial action, i.e. the workers' right to strike, make blockades and use sympathetic actions (secondary actions) in support of strikes or blockades and the employers' right to impose lockouts or boycotts on workers.

The EC/EU didn't address core collective labour law issues like the right to organize, collective bargaining and the right to strike until the 1980's. By Article 118 b EEC which was inserted in the EEC Treaty by the Single European Act 1986, the Commission was put under a duty to endeavor to develop the dialogue between management and labour at European level which could, if the two sides considered it desirable, lead to relations based on agreement. The Community Charter of the Fundamental Social Rights of Workers 1989 goes rather far in providing for collective labour law rights as part of EU law.

The EU is – and has for the last 25 years or thereabouts been – in the process of integrating the social partners into its decisions-making processes in regard to a wide spectrum of issues in connection with development of the fundamental rights/EMU perspective on labour law.

In Chapter Four it was shown that the general understanding in EU is that information, consultation and participation of workers in relation to their employers' decision making processes are useful means to increase the ability of businesses to adapt to structural and cyclical changes. Completion of the internal market in which national economies are closely associated, while strengthening the competitiveness of the undertakings, is expected to accelerate mutations and restructurations of a large number of European industries. Timely information and consultation are seen as key to meeting the globalisation challenge through the development of new forms of work organisation. Social dialogue is expected to improve risk anticipation and make work organisation more flexible.

5 Migrant workers and union citizens

In Chapter Five it was shown that the basic rules on free movement for workers date back to the Rome Treaty 1957. In the early internal market perspective workers/Labour were primarily seen as a commodity.[9] With the adoption of the Maastricht Treaty in 1992 the Internal Market goal was complemented by the second layer of the EU's macro-economic constitution focusing on establishing an economic and monetary union (EMU). The Maastricht Treaty also inserted a provision on fundamental rights in Article 6 TEU and created union citizenship. Since then, workers constitute the majority of the union citizens. They have both individual and collective fundamental rights, e.g. the right to strike. Workers' status as union citizens has been used by the CJEU to put an expansive interpretation on the principle of free movement of workers.

6 Discrimination and equality

In Chapter Six it was shown that equality and non-discrimination law is a substantive area where the change in context from an internal market per-

9. As mentioned in the previous chapters this is the opposite view of that expressed in the Constitution of ILO, see Chapter Two and O'Higgins, Paul: Labour is not a Commodity' – an Irish Contribution to International Labour Law, Industrial Law Journal1997, Vol. 26 Issue 3, p. 225.

spective to a fundamental rights/EMU perspective is very visible and recognized in legal practice both by the EU legislator, judiciary and legal scholars. Originally – when the EC was founded in the 1950's – EC anti-discrimination law was mainly seen as an appendix to the internal market. The EU only later developed into a more legal, political and macroeconomic union. In the proposal for the directive on Equal treatment between women and men in the access to and supply of goods and services the Commission thus stated (emphasis added):[10]

> Equal treatment between women and men and non-discrimination on grounds of sex are fundamental principles of Community law. The European Union's approach to equality has developed considerably over time, so that the original emphasis on equal pay and on avoiding distortions of competition between Member States has been replaced by *a concern for equality as a fundamental right.*

In the Council Recommendation on broad guidelines for the economic policies of the Member States and of the Union[11] the aim of promoting Inclusive growth in connection with the development of the EMU is underlined. It is stated:

> (10) The policies of the Union, and Member States' reform programmes should finally also aim at *'inclusive growth'*. Inclusive growth means building a cohesive society in which people are empowered to anticipate and manage change, thus to actively participate in society and the economy. Member States' reforms should therefore ensure access and opportunities for all throughout the lifecycle, thus *reducing poverty and social exclusion, through removing barriers to labour market participation especially for women, older workers, young people, the disabled and legal migrants.*

Equality and non-discrimination is an issue both in national law, EU law and public international law and has served as an area where – in particular national law and EU law – is increasingly being locked together. It can therefore also be seen as an exemplification of the change towards 'the one big system model'.

10. COM(2003)657 p. 2.
11. Recommendation 2010/410/EU.

7 Employment contracts and employment relations

Chapter Seven describes the EU regulation of employment contracts and employment relationships, in particular posting of workers, the employer's obligation to inform employees of the conditions applicable to the contract or employment relationship, part-time work, fixed term contracts and temporary agency work. Employment contracts of indefinite duration are the general form of employment relationship. Since the 1990's, the EU has, however, focused on regulating various forms of atypical employment contracts or employment relationships with a view to promoting the fundamental rights/EMU perspective on law and – as stated e.g. in the Preamble to the Temporary Works Agency directive – flexicurity, which strikes a balance between *flexibility* and *security* in the labour market and helps both workers and employers to seize the opportunities offered by globalisation.

8 Restructuring of Business

In Chapter Eight restructuring of businesses refer to collective redundancies, transfer of undertakings and insolvency of the employer. The basic rules on these subject date back to the 1970's, i.e. the early period of EU labour law dominated by the internal market perspective on employment law. In *Nolan*,[12] the CJEU explicitly stated that the collective redundancies directive forms part of the legislation concerning the internal market and used that as an argument for interpreting the directive as not covering public sector employees. The rules described in this Chapter has been codified or recast in the years after the adoption of the Maastricht Treaty 1992 and the ensuing development of the fundamental rights/EMU perspective on EU labour law.

9 Working Environment

Before the adoption of the Single European Act 1986 there was no specific provision on the protection of the safety and health of workers. The Framework Directive on the Working Environment[13] with its wide scope of application as well as individual working environment directives focusing on specif-

12. Case C-583/10 *Nolan* [2012] ECR nyr.
13. 89/391/EEC.

ic aspects of safety and health at work constitutes the fundamentals of EU working environment legislation. These directives set out *minimum requirements* and *fundamental principles*, such as the principle of prevention and risk assessment, as well as the responsibilities of employers and employees.

Free movement on the internal market for dangerous machinery or chemical substances may cause harm to workers' health and safety when they use the machinery or are exposed to the chemicals in their working environment. It is the purpose of working environment provisions to protect workers against physical and psychological risks at work.

Article 31(2) CFREU provides that 'Every worker has the right to limitation of maximum working hours, to daily and weekly rest periods and to an annual period of paid leave'. The CJEU has developed a considerable case law on paid annual leave as a fundamental right.

10 The 'one big system model'

10.1 Legal Pluralism

There has been much debate in recent years on pluralism and diversity in EU law.[14] It is now common to argue that Europe's intermingling legal systems demand a pluralist interpretation. It seems obvious that the development of the EU has led to a multiplication of the sources of law.[15] Often the same fact is covered by rules of national, EU and international origin. The increased expansion of the EU has led to increased diversity (from 4 to 23 languages, from 6 countries belonging to the civil law legal tradition to 27 countries that between them have legal orders comprising both the civil law and common law traditions, *etc.*). There has been much debate in recent years on pluralism, diversity fragmentation and inconsistencies in EU law.

The development of the EU legal order has also given rise to much debate about constitutional pluralism.[16] In regard to the economic constitution there

14. There is abundant literature; see for example Modéer, Kjell-Åke: The Historical Roots of European Legal Culture, JFT (Tidskrift utgiven av Juridiska Föreningen i Finland) 2010, p. 493.
15. See Petersen, Hanne and Henrik Zahle (eds): Legal Polycentricity. Consequences of Pluralism in Law, Dartmouth 1995.
16. See Walker, Neil: The Idea of Constitutional Pluralism, Modern Law Review 2002, p. 317.

is a distinction[17] between the first – micro-economic – layer of the economic constitution which focuses on the Internal Market and which has been provided for in the goal provision of the basic treaties since the Rome Treaty 1957 and the second – macro-economic – layer of the economic constitution which focuses on the Economic and Monetary Union (EMU) with a financial union based (in the long term) on the euro as its currency. The second layer of the economic constitution was first formulated as a goal for the EU in the Maastricht Treaty 1992. The establishment and development of the internal market is still a goal for the EU whose economic constitution thus now has two layers – the establishment of the Internal Market and of the Economic and Monetary Union (EMU).

In the internal market perspective, the main economic problem law is used to help solving is to remove or reduce barriers to *access to the internal market* for economic actors who want to take advantage of the free movement on that market. In the fundamental rights/EMU perspective the main economic problem law is used to help solving is the need to *coordinate economic and employment policies and to reduce macroeconomic imbalances*, see the Council Recommendation on broad guidelines for the economic policies of the Member States and of the Union.[18]

Many legal scholars have commented on the relationship between the economic constitution of the EU and the social constitution. Most of them see the social constitution as subordinate to the economic constitution.[19] Dagmar Schiek argues, however, that the CJEU has developed a socially embedded judicial constitution.[20]

The two shifts in perspective I highlight in this book 1) from an internal market perspective on labour law to a fundamental rights perspective and 2) from many separate legal systems to a 'one big system model' are related to a

17. See further Tuori, Kaarlo: The European Financial Crisis – Constitutional Aspects and Implications, EUI Working Paper LAW 2012/28.
18. Recommendation 2010/410/EU, OJ 2010 L 191.
19. See for example Bruun, Niklas, Klaus Lörcher and Isabelle Schömann (eds): The Lisbon Treaty and Social Europe, Oxford 2012, Giubboni, Stefano: Social Rights and Market Freedom in the European Constitution: A Labour Law Perspective. Cambridge 2006 and Hervey, Tamara and Jeff Kenner (eds): Economic and Social Rights Under the EU Charter of Fundamental Rights: A Legal Perspective, Oxford 2003.
20. See Schiek, Dagmar: Economic and Social integration. The challenge for EU constitutional law, Cheltenham 2012 and Schiek, Dagmar: Is there a social ideal of the European Court of Justice? In Neergaard, Ulla, Ruth Nielsen and Lynn Roseberry (eds): The Role of Courts in Developing a European Social Model – Theoretical and Methodological Perspectives, Copenhagen 2010.

shift from adapting the view on EU labour law mainly or solely to the first layer of the economic constitution (the Internal Market) to also include the second layer of the economic constitution (the EMU and the concern for macroeconomic balance). In the Preamble to the TEU, the Member States confirm their attachment to fundamental social rights as defined *inter alia* in the 1989 Community Charter of the Fundamental Social Rights of Workers and their resolve to achieve the strengthening and the convergence of their economies and to establish an economic and monetary union. The internal market is not mentioned in the Preamble to the TEU but it is still mentioned as one of the economic goals of the EU in Article 3 TEU, see further above in Chapter Two.

10.2 Interlockedness between national law, EU law and international law

EU law contributes greatly to linking/locking national law, EU law and public international law, in particular European human rights law together. The CJEU has often used labour law cases to introduce new rules or interpretation principles into EU law. Many labour law conflicts arise between individual employees and private employers or between collective actors in the private sector. It is therefore not surprising that labour law cases have been among the first where the CJEU has held that Treaty provisions have direct horizontal effect as binding for private individuals (typically employers), see *Angonese*.[21] Directives do not have horizontal direct effect, see *Marshall I*.[22] The principle of consistent interpretation, i.e. the duty for national authorities to interpret national law in conformity with EU law was launched by CJEU in 1984 in *von Colson and Kamann*.[23] Today, the ECHR is regarded as an integral part of EU law and an important source of EU fundamental rights, see *ERT*.[24] EU Discrimination law started as gender discrimination law in employment in the 1970´s. After the adoption of the Amsterdam Treaty which came into force 1 May 1999, the principle of non-discrimination and the way it was tackled in gender discrimination law in relation to the labour market has been generalized to other discrimination grounds (ethnicity, religion, age, disability, sexual orientation, etc.) and other fields of society than the labour market. Balancing economic and social rights has become a general issue since the Lisbon Treaty according to which it is one of the Union's goals to

21. Case C-281/98 *Angonese* [2000] ECR I-4139.
22. Case 152/84 *Marshall I* [1986] ECR p. 723.
23. Case 14/83 *von Colson* [1984] ECR p. 1891, Para. 26.
24. Case C-260/89, *ERT* [1991] ECR I-2925.

develop a highly competitive social market economy, see Article 3(3)TEU. At least since the 1970's the CJEU has held that the EC/EU has this double aim, both economic and social, in labour law cases, see *Defrenne II*.[25] EU Labour law is a major example of an area of law where the Member States by and large only have conferred power to the EU legislator to adopt minimum harmonisation by secondary legislation, see Article 153 TFEU which is the typical legal basis for secondary legislation in EU labour law and above in section 3. There is no specific EU labour law enforcement system. In EU law, it is settled case-law that, in the absence of EU rules governing the matter, it is for the domestic legal system of each Member State to designate the courts and tribunals having jurisdiction and to lay down the procedural rules and sanctions, provided, however, that such rules are not less favourable than those governing similar domestic actions and do not render virtually impossible or excessively difficult the exercise of rights conferred by EU law. Enforcement of the rules adopted at EU level thus takes place in the national legal systems of the Member States in accordance with their normal rules on sanctions and procedures. They must observe the EU fundamental rights and general principles when enforcing EU law, see *Cavallero*.[26]

National legal orders within the EU have traditionally differed greatly as to the identification and relative primacy/weight of different sources of law. The continental tradition emphasizes the text of the statute as an expression of the will of the sovereign legislature and the same tradition may restrict the use of other, potentially competing sources, such as judicial decisions. In common law traditions, the role of the judiciary is acknowledged as 'finding' the law, judge-made case law therefore becoming an important source of law, often coupled with the legally binding nature of judicial precedents by higher courts. In some EU Member States, notably the Nordic countries, collective agreements have traditionally played a very important role as source of national labour law before entry into the EC/EU.[27] The traditional preference for collective agreements in the Nordic countries has partly changed. In connection with implementation of directives EU law requires Member States to

25. Case 43/75 *Defrenne II* [1976] ECR 455.
26. Case C-442/00 *Cavallero* [2002] ECR I-11915.
27. See further Fahlbeck, Rheinhold: Industrial Relations and Collective Labour Law: Characteristics, Principles and Basic Features', and Hasselbalch, Ole: The Roots – the History of Nordic Labour Law', both in *Scandinavian Studies in Law*, Stockholm, Vol. 43, Stability and Change in Nordic Labour Law, 2002, pp. 87 and 11 respectively.

use some sources of law rather than others,[28] in particular legislation. Collective agreements as implementing measures are only partly accepted, see further above in Chapter Three.

In its pure form, the monist approach to the relationship between international and national law considers the rules of international law to be part of the domestic legal system and requires the domestic courts to apply them directly. Conflicts between international law and rules of domestic origin may in a monist system be solved in various ways, for example by giving priority to international law, to the domestic rules, to the domestic rules of a certain rank, etc. Under EU law, international treaties entered into by the EU form part of EU law without any incorporation being necessary. EU law is thus in principle based on the monist approach.

The Scandinavian countries, on the other hand, have traditionally followed the dualist approach according to which international law is a separate legal system, not directly applicable in national courts.[29] This means that conflicts between international and domestic law can in principle not arise before national courts, which are not allowed to apply international law directly but have a duty to interpret national law in accordance with international law if that is possible. In order for treaties ratified by 'dualist' states to become part of national law, they must be incorporated by national legislation of some kind. In most cases the Scandinavian courts will be able to interpret domestic law so as to comply with the country's international obligations, but on a few occasions the principled dualist approach has been upheld by the courts.

Due to a preference for collective bargaining over statutory regulation,[30] the Nordic (parliamentary) legislators have been somewhat reluctant to fulfil international obligations fully in the field of labour law. Until 1996, it was for example still arguable that Danish private employers under domestic Danish law were legally free to take racist employment decisions, though Denmark ratified the United Nations Convention on the Elimination of All Forms of Racial Discrimination in 1971.

Membership of the EU places the Nordic EU-countries in a new context. The Nordic Member States are now under a duty to follow those parts of in-

28. See further Nielsen, Ruth: Implementation of EC Directives in Denmark, The International Journal of Comparative Labour Law and Industrial Relations, Volume 18 2002. Issue 4, p. 459.
29. See further Scheinin, Martin: International Law and Human Rights – Good or Bad for European Union Law? In Neergaard, Ulla and Ruth Nielsen (eds): European Legal Method – in a Multi-Level EU Legal Order, Copenhagen 2012.
30. Bruun et al.: The Nordic Labour Relations Model, Dartmouth 1992.

ternational law which the EU has incorporated into EU law in the same way as they must observe other EU law and at the same time 'dualist' as individual nation-states in their individual relation to public international law. It follows from *Kamberaj*,[31] that EU Member States retain their free choice in regard to whether they want to follow the monist or the dualist approach to international law. *Kamberaj* is an Albanian national who has resided and been employed in Italy since 1994. He is the holder of a residence permit for an indefinite period. He complained that he as a third country national with status as long term resident was treated less favourably than EU citizens in regard to housing benefit. The referring Italian court asked *inter alia*:

> (2) When there is a conflict between a provision of domestic law and the ECHR, does the reference to the ECHR in Article 6 TEU oblige the national court to apply Articles 14 ECHR and Article 1 of [Protocol No 12] directly, disapplying the incompatible source of domestic law, without having first to raise the issue of constitutionality before the national constitutional court?

The CJEU stated that Article 6(3) TEU does not govern the relationship between the ECHR and the legal systems of the Member States and nor does it lay down the consequences to be drawn by a national court in case of conflict between the rights guaranteed by that convention and a provision of national law. The EU Member States can thus still choose at their own discretion whether they want to follow the monist or dualist approach in relation to their interntional law commitments.

10.3 Law and (nation) states

Older versions of legal positivism and legal realism defined – both in relation to public international law and national law – law and states as different aspects of the same totality. Today, the reality is that both modern public international law[32] and EU law to a considerable extent have to function without direct support – coercive or otherwise – from a nation state.

The question therefore arises whether the EU can do without state(s) to underpin its legal system or whether state support can be found in other ways than those used in the relationship between national law and the nation state. A possible answer is that EU law can obtain state support through reliance on 'The One Big System Model'. Most EU Member States probably enforce rules of EU origin in much the same way as rules of national origin.

31. Case C-571/10 *Kamberaj* [2012] ECR nyr.
32. See Teubner, Günther: Global Law without a State, Dartmouth 1997.

Literature

Aaron, Benjamin and K.W. Wedderburn: Industrial Conflict. A comparative legal survey, London 1972

Ahlberg, Kerstin (ed.): EU&Arbetsrätt, newsletter (in Swedish), http://arbetsratt.juridicum.su.se/euarb/tidigare_nummer.asp

Alston, Philip (ed.): Labour Rights as Human Rights, Oxford 2005

Arnardóttir, Oddny Mjöll: Equality and Non-discrimination under the European Convention on Human Rights, The Hague, London, New York, 2003.

Arnull, Anthony: The Americanization of EU Law Scholarship in Arnull, Anthony, Piet Eeckhout, and Takis Tridimas (eds): Continuity and Change in EU Law: Essays in Honour of Sir Francis Jacobs, Oxford 2008

Asscher-Vonk, Irene: Instruction to Discriminate, EGELR (European Gender Equality Law Review) 2012/1

Barnard, Catherine: A proportionate response to proportionality in the field of collective action, European law Review 2012 p. 117

Barnard, Catherine: EU Employment Law, Oxford 2012

Barnard, Catherine: The Substantive Law of the EU: The Four Freedoms, Oxford 2010

Barnard, Catherine: The Social Partners and the Governance Agenda', European Law Journal, 2002, Vol. 8, p. 80

Barnard, Catherine and Simon Deakin: 'Negative' and 'Positive' Harmonization of Labor Law in the European Union, Columbia Journal of European Law 2002 p. 389

Bercusson, Brian: The Collective Labour Law of the European Union, European Law Journal. 1995, Vol. 1 Issue 2, p. 157

Bercusson, Brian: European Labour Law in Context: A Review of the Literature, European Law Journal 1999, Vol. 5 Issue 2, p. 87

Besson, Samantha: Gender Discrimination under EU and ECHR Law: Never Shall the TwainMeet?, Human Rights Law Review 2008 p. 647

Biagi, Marco: From Conflict to Participation in Safety: Industrial Relations and the Working Environment in Europe 1992 in The International Journal of Comparative Labour Law and Industrial Relations 1990 p. 67

Blanpain, Roger and Andrzej M. Swiatkowski (eds): The Laval and Viking Cases. Freedom of Services and Establishment v. Industrial Conflict in the European Union, Bulletin of Comparative Labour Relations – 69

Von Bogdandy, Armin: Founding Principles of EU Law: A Theoretical and Doctrinal Sketch, European Law Journal, 2010 p. 95.

Bruun, Niklas, Klaus Lörcher and Isabelle Schömann (eds): The Lisbon Treaty and Social Europe, Oxford 2012

de Búrca, Gráinne, Bruno de Witte and Larissa Ogertschnig (eds): Social Rights in Europe, Oxford 2005

CJEU: The Court of Justice and the Construction of Europe: Analyses and Perspectives on Sixty Years of Case-law – La Cour de Justice et la Construction de l'Europe: Analyses et Perspectives de Soixante Ans de Jurisprudence, The Hague 2013
Commission: Industrial Relations in Europe, 2000
Commission: Industrial Relations in Europe, 2001
Commission: Industrial Relations in Europe, 2002
Commission: Industrial Relations in Europe, 2004
Commission: Industrial Relations in Europe, 2004
Commission: Industrial Relations in Europe, 2006
Commission: Industrial Relations in Europe, 2007
Commission: Industrial Relations in Europe, 2008
Commission: Industrial Relations in Europe, 2010
Council of Europe: European Social Charter, Collected texts (6th edition), (updated to 30 June 2008), http://www.coe.int/t/dghl/monitoring/socialcharter/presentation /ESCCollectedTexts_en.pdf
Docksey, Christopher: Information and Consultation of Employees: The United Kingdom and
The Vredeling Directive, The Modern Law Review 1986 p. 281
Dorsemont, Philip: Values and Objectives, in Bruun, Niklas, Klaus Lörcher and Isabelle Schömann (eds): The Lisbon Treaty and Social Europe, Oxford 2012
Dougan, Michael and Eleanor Spaventa (eds): Social Welfare and EU Law, Oxford, 2005
Dougan, Michael: The Spatial Restructuring of National Welfare States within the European Union: the Contribution of Union Citizenship and the Relevance of the Treaty of Lisbon in Ulla Neergaard, Ruth Nielsen and Lynn Roseberry (eds): Integrating Welfare Functions into EU Law – From Rome to Lisbon, Copenhagen 2009.
Edlund, Steen (ed.): Labour Law Research in Twelve Countries, Stockholm 1986
Eklund, Ronnie: A Swedish Perspective on Laval, Comparative Labor Law and Policy Journal 2008 p. 551
European Foundation for the Improvement of Living and Working Conditions: Employee involvement in companies under the European Company Statute, Luxembourg 2011
Europe in figures – Eurostat yearbook, http://epp.eurostat.ec.europa.eu/statistics_explained /index.php/Europe_in_figures_-_Eurostat_yearbook
Evju, Stein: Collective Agreements and Competition Law. The Albany Puzzle, and van der Woude, International Journal of Comparative Labour Law and Industrial Relations, Volume 17, Issue 2, Summer 2001
Ewing, K. D. and John Hendy: The Dramatic Implications of Demir and Baykara, Industrial Law Journal 2010 p. 2
Fahlbeck, Rheinhold: Industrial Relations and Collective Labour Law: Characteristics, Principles and Basic Features', in Scandinavian Studies in Law, Stockholm, Vol. 43, Stability and Change in Nordic Labour Law, 2002, p. 87, available from http://www.scandinavianlaw.se/index.php?page=index-database
Fahlbeck, Reinhold: Flexibility. Potentials and Pitfalls for Labour Law. An International Analysis, Lund 1998
Gernigon, Bernard, Alberto Odero and Horacio Guido: ILO Principles Concerning The Right To Strike, ILO 1998, International Labour Review, Vol. 137 (1998) No. 4, http://www.ilo.org/wcmsp5/groups/public/@ed_norm/@normes/documents/publicatio n/wcms_087987.pdf

Gestel, Rob van and Hans-Wolfgang Micklitz: Revitalizing Doctrinal Legal Research in Europe: What About Methodology? in Neergaard, Ulla, Nielsen, Ruth & Roseberry, Lynn (eds): European Legal Method – Paradoxes and Revitalisation, Copenhagen 2011

Gestel, Rob van Hans-W. Micklitz & Miguel Poiares Maduro: Methodology in the New Legal World, EUI Working Papers, LAW 2012/13

Giubboni, Stefano: Social Rights and Market Freedom in the European Constitution: A Labour Law Perspective. Cambridge 2006

Hart, H.L.A: The Concept of Law, Oxford, 1994

Hart, H.L.A.: Scandinavian Realism, The Cambridge Law Journal 1959 p. 233 (review of Alf Ross: On Law and Justice)

Hasselbalch, Ole: The Roots – the History of Nordic Labour Law', in Scandinavian Studies in Law, Stockholm, Vol. 43, Stability and Change in Nordic Labour Law, 2002, p. 11, available from http://www.scandinavianlaw.se/index.php?page=index-database

Hepple, Bob and Bruno Veneziani (eds): The Transformation of Labour Law in Europe, A Comparative Study of 15 Countries 1945-2004, Oxford 2009

Hepple, Bob (ed.): The Making of Labour Law in Europe: A Comparative Study of Nine Countries up to 1945, London 1986

Hepple, Bob: The Crisis in EEC Labour Law, Industrial Law Journal 1987 p. 129

Hervey, T amara and Jeff Kenner (eds): Economic and Social Rights Under the EU Charter of Fundamental Rights: A Legal Perspective, Oxford 2003

Hesselink, Martijn: The New European Legal Culture, Kluwer 2001

Hesselink, Martijn: A European Legal Method? On European Private Law and Scientific Method, European Law Journal 2009 p. 20

Joerges, Christian: A Renaissance of the European Economic Constitution? In Ulla Neergaard, Ruth Nielsen and Lynn Roseberry (eds): Integrating Welfare Functions into EU Law – From Rome to Lisbon, Copenhagen 2009

Kahn-Freund, Otto (ed.): Labour Relations and the Law. A Comparative Study, London 1965

Kahn-Freund, Otto: Labour and the Law. London 1977

Kahn-Freund, Otto: Selected Writings, London 1978

Kelemen, R.D.: Eurolegalism: The Transformation of Law and Regulation in the European *Union,* Cambridge, MA (Harvard University Press), 2011

Kelemen, R. Daniel: Eurolegalism and Democracy, Journal of Common Market Studies 2012 p. 55

Kelsen, Hans: Reine Rechtslehre, 2. Neudruck der 1. Auflage Leipzig und Wien 1934, Aalen, 1994

Kelsen, Hans: Introduction to the Problems of Legal Theory (A Translation of the First edition of Reine Rechtslehre 1934), Oxford, 1992

Kilpatrick, Claire: The ECJ and Labour Law: A 2008 Retrospective, Industrial Law Journal (2009) 38(2): 180-208

Kilpatrick, Claire: The European Court of Justice and Labour Law in 2009, Industrial Law Journal (2010) 39(3): 287-299

Kilpatrick, Claire: The Court of Justice and Labour Law in 2010: A New EU Discrimination Law Architecture, Industrial Law Journal (2011) 40(3): 280-301

Laulom Sylvaine: Transfers of Undertakings. Part I. The European Court of Justice in the dialogue on transfers of undertakings: A fallible interlocutor? in Sciarra, Silvana (ed.): Labour Law in the Courts, Oxford 2001

Lenaerts, Koen and Eddy de Smijter: A 'Bill of Rights' for the European Union, Common Market Law Review 2001 p. 273

Lenaerts, Koen and Tinne Heremans: Contours of a European Social Union in the Case-Law of the European Court of Justice, European Constitutional Law Review 2006 p. 101

Liisberg, Maria Ventegodt: Disability and Employment – A Contemporary Disability Human Rights Approach Applied to Danish, Swedish and EU Law and Policy, Intersentia, 2011

Lu, Haina: The Right to Work in China – Chinese Labor Legislation in the Light of the International Covenant on Economic, Social and Cultural rights, Intersentia 2011

MacCormick, N.: Questioning Sovereignty, Oxford 1999

MacCormick, Neil (ed.): Constructing Legal Systems. 'European Union' in Legal Theory, Dordrecht 1997

MacCormick, Neil and Ota Weinberger: An Institutional Theory of Law. New Approaches to Legal Positivism, Dordrecht, 1986

Maduro, Miguel Poiares: We the Court: The European Court of Justice and the European Economic Constitution: a Critical Reading of Article 30 of the EC Treaty, London 1998

Malmberg, Jonas and Caroline Johansson: The Commission's Posting Package, European Policy Analysis, July Issue 2012

Malmberg, Jonas (ed.): Effective Enforcement of EC Labour Law, Uppsala 2003

Menéndez, Agustín José: The Sinews of Peace: Rights to Solidarity in the Charter of Fundamental Rights of the European Union, Ratio Juris 2003 p. 374

Monti, Mario: A New Strategy for the Single Market at the Service of Europe's Economy and Society: Report to the President of the European Commission José Manuel Barroso, Bruxelles 2010

Moreau, Marie-Ange (ed.): Before and After the Economic Crisis. What Implications for the 'European Social Model'?, London 2011

Murray, Jill: Transnational Labour Regulation: The ILO and EC Compared, The Hague, London, Boston 2001

Neergaard, Ulla and Ruth Nielsen: Blurring Boundaries: From the Danish Welfare State to the European Social Model? in European Labour Law Journal, Vol. 1, No. 4, 2010 p. 434, a longer version is published as Working Paper at SSRN http://papers.ssrn.com/sol3/papers.cfm?abstract_id=1618758

Neergaard, Ulla, Ruth Nielsen and Lynn Roseberry (eds): The Services Directive – Consequences for the Welfare State and the European Social Model, Copenhagen 2008

Neergaard, Ulla. Ruth Nielsen and Lynn Roseberry (eds): Integrating Welfare Functions into EU Law – From Rome to Lisbon, Copenhagen 2009

Neergaard, Ulla, Ruth Nielsen and Lynn Roseberry (eds): The Role of Courts in Developing a European Social Model – Theoretical and Methodological Perspectives, Copenhagen 2010

Neergaard, Ulla and Ruth Nielsen (eds): European Legal Method – Paradoxes and Revitalisation, Copenhagen 2011

Neergaard, Ulla and Ruth Nielsen (eds): European Legal Method – in a Multi-Level EU Legal Order, Copenhagen 2012

Neergaard, Ulla and Ruth Nielsen: European Legal method – towards a new European Legal Realism?, Copenhagen 2013 (forthcoming)

Nielsen, Ruth: New European Legal Realism – New Problems, New Solutions? in Neergaard, Ulla and Ruth Nielsen: European Legal method – towards a new European Legal Realism?, Copenhagen 2013 (forthcoming)

Nielsen, Ruth: Free Movement and Fundamental Rights, European Labour Law Journal, Vol. 1, No. 1, 2010 p. 17

Nielsen, Ruth: Europeanization of Nordic Labour Law', Scandinavian Studies in Law, Stockholm, 2002, Vol. 43, Stability and Change in Nordic Labour Law, p. 37, available from http://www.scandinavianlaw.se/index.php?page=index-database

Nielsen, Ruth: Implementation of EC Directives in Denmark, The International Journal of Comparative Labour Law and Industrial Relations, Volume 18 2002.Issue 4, p. 459

Nielsen, Ruth: European Labour Law, Copenhagen 2000

Nyström, Birgitta: The future of European Labour Law – the Nordic Perspective, European Labour Law Journal 2010

O'Higgins, Paul: Labour is not a Commodity' – an Irish Contribution to International Labour Law, Industrial Law Journal1997, Vol. 26 Issue 3, p. 225

O'Leary, Siofra: Employment Law at the European Court of Justice, Judicial Structures, Policies and Processes, Oxford 2002

Olsson, Petra Herzfeldt: The ILO Acquis and EU Labour Law, in Rönnmar, Mia (ed.): Labour Law. Fundamental Rights and Social Europe, Oxford 2011

Pernice, Ingolf: Integrating the Charter of Fundamental Rights into the Constitution of the European Union: Practical and Theoretical Propositions, Columbia Journal of European Law 2003 p. 5

Preisler, Marie: EU directive on temporary agency work could reduce social dumping, Nordic Labour Journal April 07, 2011

Reich, Norbert: Free Movement v. Social Rights in an Enlarged Union – the Laval and Viking Cases before the CJEU, German Law Journal 2008 p. 125, http://germanlawjournal.com/pdfs/Vol09No02/PDF_Vol_09_No_02_125-160_Developments_Reich.pdf

Riesenhuber, Karl: European Employment Law, Intersentia 2012

Robin-Olivier, Sophie European Legal Method from a French Perspective. The magic of combination: uses and abuses of the globalization of sources by European Courts in Neergaard, Ulla and Ruth Nielsen (eds): European Legal Method – Paradoxes and Revitalisation, Copenhagen 2011

Rodière, Pierre: Droit Social de l'Union Européenne, Paris 1998

Roseberry, Lynn: The Integration of Welfare Functions into EU Law through the Principle of Non-discrimination and the Consequences for Third Country Nationals in Ulla Neergaard, Ruth Nielsen and Lynn M. Roseberry (eds): Integrating Welfare Functions into EU Law, Copenhagen 2009

Ross, Alf: TÛ-TÛ, first published in Danish in Festskrift til Henry Ussing, Copenhagen 1951 p. 468. In 1957, an English translation was published in two identical versions first in Scandinavian Studies in Law, Stockholm 1957 p. 137, http://www.scandinavianlaw.se/pdf/1-5.pdf and then in Harvard Law Review 1957 p. 812

Ross, Alf: Ret og Retfærdighed, Copenhagen1953

Ross, Alf: On Law and Justice, London 1958 (English translation of Alf Ross: Ret og Retfærdighed, København 1953)

Rönnmar, Mia (ed.): Labour Law. Fundamental Rights and Social Europe, oxford 2011

Rönnmar, Mia: Labour Law in the Courts. The Role of European Case Law on Fundamental Trade Union Rights in an Evolving EU Industrial Relations System in Ulla

Neergaard, Ruth Nielsen and Lynn Roseberry (eds): The Role of Courts in Developing a European Social Model – Theoretical and Methodological Perspectives, Copenhagen 2010

Samuel, Lenia: Fundamental Social Rights. Case Law of the European Social Charter, Strassbourg 1997

Scharpf, Fritz W.: The asymmetry of European integration, or why the EU cannot be a 'social market economy', Socio-Econ Review 2010 p. 211

Scheinin, Martin: International Law and Human Rights – Good or Bad for European Union Law? In Neergaard, Ulla and Ruth Nielsen (eds): European Legal Method – in a Multi-Level EU Legal Order, Copenhagen 2012

Schiek, Dagmar: Economic and Social integration. The challenge for EU constitutional law, Cheltenham 2012

Schiek, Dagmar: Is there a social ideal of the European Court of Justice? In Neergaard, Ulla, Ruth Nielsen and Lynn Roseberry (eds): The Role of Courts in Developing a European Social Model – Theoretical and Methodological Perspectives, Copenhagen 2010

Schiek, Dagmar: Europäisches Arbeitsrecht, Baden-Baden 2005

Schiek, Dagmar: Positive Action before the European Court of Justice – New Conceptions of Equality in Community Law? From Kalanke and Marschall to Badeck, The International Journal of Comparative Labour Law and Industrial Relations 2000 p. 251

Schmidt, Folke: Industrial action: the role of trade unions and employers' associations in Aaron, Benjamin and K.W. Wedderburn: Industrial Conflict. A comparative legal survey, London 1972 p 2

Sciarra, Silvana (ed.): Labour Law in the Courts, Oxford 2001

Senden, Linda: Changes in the relative importance of sources of law – The case of EU soft law in Neergaard, Ulla and Ruth Nielsen (eds): European Legal Method – Paradoxes and Revitalisation, Copenhagen 2011

Spaventa, Eleanor: The Constitutional Impact of Union Citizenship in Ulla Neergaard, Ruth Nielsen and Lynn Roseberry (eds): The Role of Courts in Developing a European Social Model – Theoretical and Methodological Perspectives, Copenhagen 2010

Syrpis, Phil: The Treaty of Lisbon: Much Ado ... But About What?, Industrial Law Journal 2008 p. 219

Szyszczak, Erika: EC labour Law, Harlow 2000

Tuori, Kaarlo: The Relationality of European Constitution(S) – Justifying a new research programme for European constitutional scholarship in Neergaard, Ulla and Ruth Nielsen: European Legal method – towards a new European Legal Realism?, Copenhagen 2013 (forthcoming)

Tuori, Kaarlo: The European Financial Crisis – Constitutional Aspects and Implications, EUI Working Paper LAW 2012/28

Tuori, Kaarlo: Ratio and Voluntas: The Tension between Reason and Will in Law. Aldershot: Ashgate 2011

Tuori, Kaarlo and Suvi Sankari: The Many Constitutions of Europe, 2010

Tuori, Kaarlo: Critical Legal Positivism, 2002

Vigneau, Christophe, Kerstin Ahlberg, Brian Bercusson and Niklas Bruun: Fixed-Term Work in the EU, Stockholm 1999

Weiler, J.H.H. Transformation of Europe. Yale Law Journal, 1991 p. 2403

List of Abbreviations

CFREU:	Charter of Fundamental Rights of the European Union
CJEU:	Court of Justice of the European Union
EC:	European Community
ECHR:	European Convention on Human Rights
ECtHR:	European Court of Human Rights
EC Treaty:	Treaty on the European Community (from Maastricht to Lisbon)
EEC:	European Economic Community
EEC Treaty:	Treaty on the European Economic Community (from Rome to Maastricht)
EEIG:	The European Economic Interest Grouping
EMU:	Economic and Monetary Union
ETUC:	European Trade Union Confederation
EU:	European Union
EWC:	European Works Council
ILO:	International Labour Organisation
OMC:	Open Method of Coordination
SCE:	European Cooperative Society
SE-company:	European Company
SNB:	Special Negotiating Body
TEU:	Treaty on the European Union
TFEU:	Treaty on the Functioning of the European Union
UNICE:	Since 2007 Business Europe,

Article in the TEU and TFEU are referred to as Article 1 TEU, etc. and Article 1 TFEU, etc.

Table of Cases

Index